Mergers & Acquisitions
A Valuation Handbook

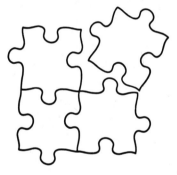

Mergers & Acquisitions
Acquisitions
A Valuation Handbook

Joseph H. Marren

IRWIN
Professional Publishing®
Chicago • London • Singapore

Project editor: Rebecca Dodson
Production manager: Ann Cassady
Jacket designer: Sam Concialdi
Designer: Teresa Offinger
Art coordinator: Mark Malloy
Compositor: TCSystems, Inc.
Typeface: 10/12 Palatino
Printer: Book Press, Inc.

Library of Congress Cataloging-in-Publication Data

Marren, Joseph H.
    Mergers & acquisitions : a valuation handbook / Joseph H. Marren.
      p.   cm.
    Includes index.
    ISBN 1–55623–676–X
    1. Consolidation and merger of corporations. 2. Corporations-
-Valuation. I. Title. II. Title: Mergers and acquisitions.
HG4028.M4M37   1993
658.15—dc20   92–13662

Printed in the United States of America

5 6 7 8 9 0 BP 9 8 7 6 5

Preface

The most difficult decision an executive faces in negotiating an acquisition is the price to be paid. The decision is difficult because there are so many factors to consider—the process by which the target company is being sold, the expected competition, the future profitability of the target, expected synergies, complex tax rules, alternate legal forms of effecting a transaction and accounting considerations.

This book attempts to integrate all the key legal, accounting, financial and tax considerations into a unified approach for analyzing transactions. This approach will provide the information chief executives require to make an informed decision with respect to the price issue.

This book is written principally for managers, professionals (lawyers, accountants, bankers, consultants and intermediaries) and others involved in the acquisition process. However, it should prove worthwhile reading for individuals concerned with valuing companies in the stock market including investors, security analysts and arbitrageurs.

Joseph H. Marren

To my wife, Joan

Acknowledgments

I have received a great deal of assistance in writing this book and would like to thank those who contributed significantly. My brother, Bernard D. Marren, Jr., an accomplished tax attorney who is currently Vice President, Taxes, The Sequor Group, a subsidiary of Security Pacific Corporation, provided many valuable insights. Other key contributors were Mark Kenyon, Vice President—Finance and Administration, The Blackstone Group; Charles Philippin, National Director of Mergers & Acquisitions in the Stamford office of Coopers & Lybrand; and Ray Beier, a partner in the New York office of Deloitte & Touche. Additional helpful comments were received from Jun Okazaki, Director, The Bridgeford Group; and Gregg Garville, Vice President—Corporate Development, Mickelberry Corporation.

There are several people and organizations that I would like to thank for the information that they provided, including Joseph O'Sullivan formerly President of James Crean Inc.; Edward I. Altman, Max L. Heine Professor of Finance at New York University's Leonard N. Stern School of Business; the numerous leveraged investment firms that participated in an informal survey of analytical techniques described in Chapter 15, Securities Data Company, Texaco, Inc., and Pennzoil Company.

In particular, Jonathan Underhill of Securities Data Company was very helpful in providing data on the M&A market in the U.S. This wealth of data should be useful for most readers.

Texaco, Inc., and Pennzoil Company provided a substantial amount of information which was used in the chapter describing the *Texaco v. Pennzoil* litigation. In addition, Texaco and Pennzoil officials reviewed drafts of the chapter describing the litigation and provided significant comments. Thank you, Wilbur L. Gay, Vice President, Pennzoil—Investor Relations; Elizabeth P. Smith, Vice President, Texaco—Investor Relations and Shareholder Services; and an attorney for Texaco, David Luttinger. Although both organizations provided valuable assistance, I am quite sure that neither organization will be completely happy with the outcome.

This book would have been impossible to complete without the endorsement and encouragement of John A. Herrmann, Jr., President and Chief Executive Officer of The Bridgeford Group. Others at my firm that provided assistance include Nicholas Amos, Associate; Edward Vazquez, Information Specialist; and my secretary, Heidi Seroy.

At Irwin I am indebted to Ralph Rieves, Editor; Katie McGowan, Marketing Specialist; and Becky Dodson, Project Editor, for their efforts in bringing this book to market.

Finally, I would like to thank my wife, Joan, and my children—Anne, Kathleen, Elizabeth, and Patricia for their many sacrifices and loving support.

J. H. M.

Contents in Brief

Appendixes   **427**

Contents

Section Six: **Investment Returns and Risk**   **409**

Section One

Introduction

Section One

Introduction

Section One introduces the reader to the broad range of topics covered in the book. Chapter 1 portrays a typical acquisition situation and asks the reader to make a preliminary judgment regarding the value of a target company. Chapter 2 provides an overview of the U.S. merger and acquisition marketplace, including volume and pricing trends and key economic influences. Chapter 3 outlines the key factors that will determine whether an acquisition in the 1990s is successful. Chapter 4 discusses the key issue in the Getty Oil litigation—when do you have a binding agreement? This case resulted in the largest judgment in the history of American jurisprudence. Finally, Chapter 5 outlines how the book is organized to address the key valuation questions.

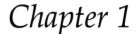

Chapter 1

Value Is in the Eye
of the Beholder!

1.0 INTRODUCTION

You have dreamed about this moment all your life. You were recently appointed CEO by the board of directors of the company and thus have the capability to execute a sizable acquisition transaction you believe is attractive.

1.1 THE TARGET

The acquisition target that catches your fancy is a food products company called Northeast Gourmet Frozen Foods ("Northeast" or the "Company"). Northeast produces and distributes a line of branded frozen foods to the retail trade east of the Mississippi. It has the number one or two market position in its product lines in the majority of its markets. Generally, products are sold under the "Northeast" brand, which is well-known to both the trade and consumers.

1.11 The Situation

The corporation that owns 100 percent of the stock of Northeast, Amalgamated Frozen Foods of Tulsa (Amalgamated), is having financial difficulties and has announced publicly that it is "exploring alternatives with respect to its investment in Northeast." Amalgamated's board of directors has not retained an investment banker, but it has decided to have Amalgamated's planning department attempt to sell the Company very quickly. Northeast's management is attempting a buyout of the Company and has put in a preliminary bid that Amalgamated is actively considering.

Amalgamated's corporate planning department has had a very limited amount of time to put together materials on Northeast, and therefore, the "selling memorandum" you received, after signing a confidentiality letter, is quite sketchy. The planning department has informed you that additional information will not be provided, and access to Northeast's management will be restricted until Amalgamated receives a preliminary price indication based on the information provided thus far.

Amalgamated's planning department has acknowledged the limitations of the information provided. It recognizes that any "bid" you submit is no more than an indication of interest subject to extensive due diligence as well as the negotiation and execution of a definitive purchase agreement. It is in this context that you are actively re-reading the information below to arrive at your price. You have decided to submit a preliminary bid. The only issue remaining is price.

1.12 History of the Company

The Company was founded in the late 1950s by an entrepreneur who started the business in his kitchen. The business grew slowly in the 1960s until a competing frozen foods company of similar size was acquired. This acquisition, coupled with the construction of a state-of-the-art facility in Altoona, Pennsylvania in 1980, allowed the Company to prosper. In the early 1980s the Company was doing so well that a major U.S. food company, Sara Quaker Corporation acquired it.

The Company floundered under the auspices of a multibillion dollar organization, with sales dropping dramatically. By the mid-1980s the Company was losing a significant amount of money. The amount of the losses was never fully determined because of the large number of inter-company charges that Sara Quaker imposed on Northeast. In this environment, management was changed several times. Finally, in December 1989, Northeast was sold to Amalgamated for approximately $7 million.

After Amalgamated purchased Northeast it brought in new management to effect a number of changes, including increasing co-pack revenues (revenues from producing private label goods), and reducing manufacturing and selling, general and administrative costs.

1.13   Marketing

Management changed Northeast's marketing strategy to strengthen the Company's "Northeast" brand name. Sales were expanded geographically. Higher margin product lines were added. All product packaging was redesigned and product quality was improved. The sales force was expanded and upgraded, as well as the network of approximately 50 food brokers.

According to available market data, Northeast currently has a 25 percent market share for the "A" product line and approximately an 18 percent share for the "B" product line. In both product lines it has the second largest market share.

To capitalize on the growth in the single-serve category, Northeast developed and introduced a single-serve product line in fiscal 1991.

The Company has not spent meaningful amounts on advertising in recent years. Total advertising for the year ending December 1992 is expected to amount to approximately $125,000.

The programs described above resulted in the unit volumes and gross revenues appearing in Exhibit 1–1.

EXHIBIT 1–1
Northeast's Unit Volumes and Gross Revenues

	Year Ended December 31,			
	1989	1990	1991	1992F
Unit Volumes (in millions of pounds)				
A product line	26.0	27.7	30.6	32.8
B product line	6.9	7.7	8.2	8.4
Single-serve product line			0.5	2.8
Co-pack volume	4.1	4.6	14.5	15.2
Total unit volume	37.0	40.0	53.8	59.2
Percent increase		8.1%	34.4%	10.1%
Gross Revenues (in millions of dollars)				
A product line	$19.5	$21.8	$25.3	$26.4
B product line	7.7	8.7	9.4	10.8
Single-serve product line			0.8	4.9
Co-pack and other	4.4	5.0	5.1	4.8
Total gross revenues	$31.6	$35.5	$40.6	$46.9
Percent increase		12.2%	14.5%	15.3%

1.14 Production

Management has implemented programs to reduce operating costs and use excess plant capacity. The Company's technical and manufacturing expertise and responsiveness to co-packing customers' needs have enabled the Company to obtain increased co-pack volume and it is currently discussing new co-pack projects with several national food companies. Currently, the bulk of co-pack volume is generated by a few customers.

The Company's headquarters and only facility are located in Altoona, Pennsylvania. The facility is 300,000 square feet on six floors and is located on a 20-acre site which is owned. The facility is in compliance with all applicable governmental federal and state regulations.

The Company has spent a minimal amount of money (well under $1 million) since 1989 in capital improvements to achieve cost savings. The prior owner had spent substantial amounts of money to maintain a state-of-the-art facility. The Company estimates that output can be increased by 50 percent before any significant capital expenditures would be required.

Amalgamated's planning department has provided an appraisal that indicates that the replacement value of the property, plant and equipment is approximately $22 million and the insurable value of the property, plant and equipment is approximately $16 million.

1.15 Management and Employees

Northeast is run by capable and experienced management that has been together since Amalgamated acquired the Company. The top seven officers have an average of 15 years' experience in the food business.

The Company has approximately 375 employees. All plant hourly employees are represented by unions. Relations with employees have been good since Amalgamated purchased Northeast. The current union contract expires in 1995.

1.16 Relationship with Amalgamated

Northeast operates as a stand-alone operation except that cash management, tax and legal services are provided by Amalgamated and charged to the Company.

1.17   Outlook for Northeast

The Company has not completed its budget for the year ending December 1993. However, the planning department has indicated that Northeast management expects to have another outstanding year. Progress will be made in expanding geographic distribution and in the single-serve product line.

1.18   Financial Results

EXHIBIT 1–2
Income Statements (in Millions of Dollars)

	Year Ended December 31,			
	1989	1990	1991	1992F
Gross revenues	$31.6	$35.5	$40.6	$46.9
Allowances	7.3	7.7	8.7	10.4
Net revenue	24.4	27.7	31.9	36.5
Cost of goods sold	19.9	21.1	22.6	25.5
Gross profit	4.5	6.7	9.3	11.0
Gross margin %	18.4%	24.0%	29.1%	30.0%
Selling, general & administrative*	3.1	3.8	4.1	4.3
Depreciation	0.0	0.1	0.1	0.1
Earnings before interest, taxes, depreciation and amortization (EBITDA)	$1.4	$2.8	$5.1	$6.5
EBITDA %	5.6%	10.0%	16.0%	17.9%

* Excludes corporate charges for cash management, legal and tax services.
‡ Rounded numbers are used for calculations in this table and throughout this book.

EXHIBIT 1–3
Net Capital Employed (in Millions of Dollars)

	Year Ended December 31,			
	1989	1990	1991	1992F
Total current assets	$8.8	$8.4	$6.3	$6.3
Total current liabilities	2.4	2.8	2.7	3.2
Net working capital	6.4	5.6	3.6	3.1
Net property, plant & equipment	0.3	0.7	0.8	0.9
Other assets	0.1	0.1	0.1	0.1
Net capital employed	$6.8	$6.4	$4.5	$4.1

1.2   DECISION ON PRICE

Well, that is all the information you have to make your decision. Please write down your decision on price before continuing.

Purchase price to offer   _____

Most people believe that the vast majority of people presented with the case study will come out with roughly the same valuation they have estimated for Northeast. In addition, if told that the people evaluating the case are corporate development professionals, most people believe the dispersion of expected valuation estimates would be less. Let's find out.

1.3   THE FACTS

The case study has been presented numerous times to both students and professionals over the last several years, and their responses have been catalogued. Exhibit 1–4 represents the responses received from a group of 110 corporate development professionals just prior to the stock market crash in 1987.

EXHIBIT 1–4
Number of Offers at Various Prices

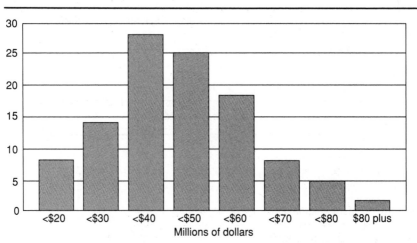

1.4   GUT FEEL IMPACTS VALUATION!

How can people's valuation of the same company differ so widely? The answer lies within each of us. Our comfort level with a given transaction depends on two key factors: (a) our knowledge of the industry that the target company operates in—the technology involved, the expected growth in its markets, the people we can get involved etc., and (b) our personal interest in the particular industry and type of business.

Whenever one's comfort level is low, a business's value is significantly discounted. Conversely, a high comfort level with a particular company may lead one to place a higher valuation on a business than is warranted.

Let us look at the supply/demand curve of the potential deal involving Northeast, using data from the author's 1987 lecture.

EXHIBIT 1–5
Percent Willing to Purchase at a Given Price

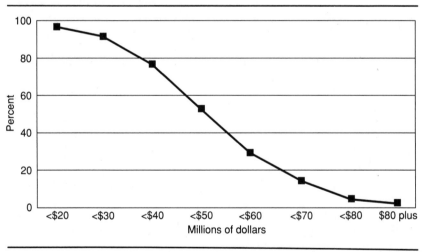

The graph in Exhibit 1–5 indicates that all 110 corporate development professionals would be interested in purchasing Northeast at a price under $20 million. However, only 2 would pay more than $80 million and a total of 7 would consider paying more than $70 million. The high end of the purchase price spectrum is the only relevant portion of the graph because there is a supply of one company.

It is fair to assume that the people who bid at the high end of the range had a high comfort level with investing in the frozen food business and/or believed that they could add significant value to Northeast by combining it with their existing operations or bringing some particular expertise or resource to the business.

All the financial, legal, accounting and tax topics in the mergers and acquisitions field discussed in this book are relevant in helping to analyze an acquisition target only if the prospective purchaser has, or expects to develop, a fairly high degree of comfort with the acquisition candidate.

Chapter 2

The United States M&A Marketplace

2.0 MERGER AND ACQUISITION ACTIVITY

The level of M&A activity has varied widely in the United States (U.S.), as Exhibits 2–1 and 2–2 indicate. What activity level can be expected in the 1990s? The following factors would indicate that the activity level in the 1990s will be similar to that in the 1980s.

- U.S. companies will continue to restructure to become "world class" competitors.
- Foreign companies will continue to invest in the U.S. to globalize their operations.
- American executives have been schooled in the trading of assets to achieve strategic objectives.
- Market shares held by the leading firms in most industries did not increase in the 1980s.
- A large number of companies currently controlled by LBO firms will be sold in the 1990s.
- Substantial equity was raised in the late 1980s by LBO sponsors that remains available for transactions in the 1990s. In addition, LBO firms are actively searching for add-on acquisitions for their portfolio companies.

The following factors support the argument that activity levels will be lower than the 1980s:

- Companies will be focusing more heavily on the Pacific Rim and Europe for acquisitions in the 1990s.

EXHIBIT 2–1
Total Dollar Value Paid in Completed Deals

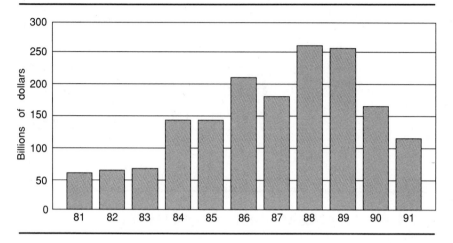

Source: Securities Data Company's "Mergers and Corporate Transactions Database," copyright 1992. Reprinted with permission of Securities Data Company, Inc.

EXHIBIT 2–2
Total Number of Completed Deals

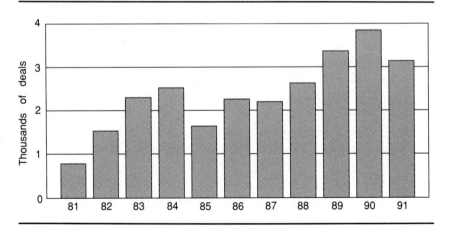

Source: Securities Data Company's "Mergers and Corporate Transactions Database," copyright 1992. Reprinted with permission of Securities Data Company, Inc.

- There are a limited number of public conglomerates to break apart.
- The lack of availability of acquisition financing has significantly reduced activity by financial buyers.
- The repeal of the General Utilities doctrine has increased the cost of acquisitions permanently.
- It is likely that antitrust regulations will be more stringently enforced in the 1990s than they were in the 1980s.

2.1 DEAL PRICING IN THE 1980s

Exhibit 2–3 describes the median *price-to-earnings multiples (P/E multiples)* paid for going private transactions (LBOs) and all other transactions involving publicly held companies since 1981. The median transactions are depicted rather than the averages to more clearly reflect the price paid in the typical transaction each year. Exhibit 2–4 describes the median acquisition price paid as a percentage of book value for the same two categories and time frame.

Exhibits 2–3 and 2–4 clearly indicate the heights that were reached in pricing in 1987, prior to the stock market crash. They also indicate that pricing for companies taken private in LBOs was substantially better than pricing for all other transactions up until 1986.

It should be clear that in the early 1980s, LBO firms were buying assets cheaply relative to their book values. Although the prices paid looked high relative to the targets' earnings, LBO firms sold off selected assets to pay down debt or utilized assets more productively to justify paying the high P/E multiples.

EXHIBIT 2–3
Median P/E Prices

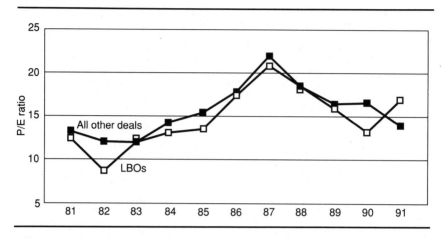

Source: Securities Data Company's "Mergers and Corporate Transactions Database," copyright 1992. Reprinted with permission of Securities Data Company, Inc.

EXHIBIT 2–4
Median Multiple of Book Value Prices

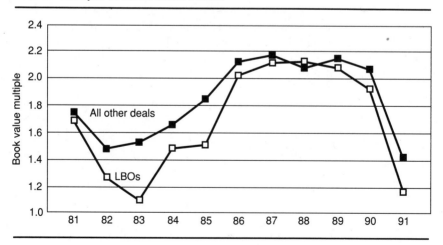

Source: Securities Data Company's "Mergers and Corporate Transactions Database," copyright 1992. Reprinted with permission of Securities Data Company, Inc.

2.2   THE BUYING UNIVERSE

The buying universe for businesses can be grouped into three categories: corporate buyers, financial buyers ("LBO" firms) and foreign buyers. See Exhibit 2–5.

Domestic corporate buyers have always represented the largest buying segment (see Exhibits 2–6 and 2–7). However, LBO firms played an increasingly important role in the 1980s (see Exhibits 2–8 and 2–9). Finally, foreign investment has varied over the decade largely as a result of the health of the world economy and exchange rates (see Exhibits 2–10 and 2–11).

Exhibit 2–12 depicts the percent of total dollar volume of transactions involving foreign buyers in the U.S. by country from 1989 to 1991. This exhibit indicates that the bulk (63 percent) of acquisitions during this period were accomplished by companies based in Great Britain, Japan and France.

EXHIBIT 2–5
Percent of Dollar Volume by Type of Buyer

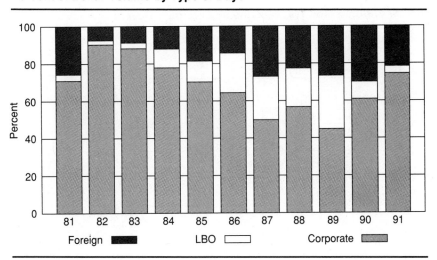

Source: Securities Data Company's "Mergers and Corporate Transactions Database," copyright 1992. Reprinted with permission of Securities Data Company, Inc.

EXHIBIT 2–6
Total Dollar Value Paid by Corporate Buyers

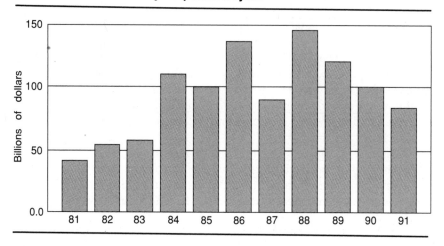

Source: Securities Data Company's "Mergers and Corporate Transactions Database," copyright 1992. Reprinted with permission of Securities Data Company, Inc.

EXHIBIT 2–7
Number of Completed Transactions by Corporate Buyers

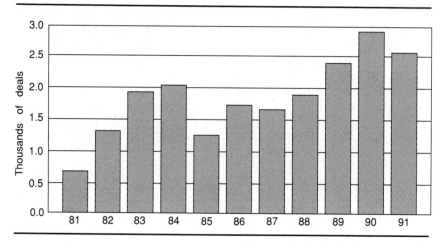

Source: Securities Data Company's "Mergers and Corporate Transactions Database," copyright 1992. Reprinted with permission of Securities Data Company, Inc.

EXHIBIT 2–8
Total Dollar Value Paid in LBOs

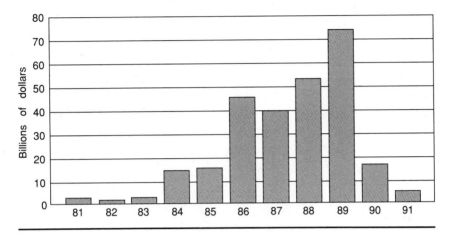

Source: Securities Data Company's "Mergers and Corporate Transactions Database," copyright 1992. Reprinted with permission of Securities Data Company, Inc.

EXHIBIT 2–9
Number of Completed LBOs

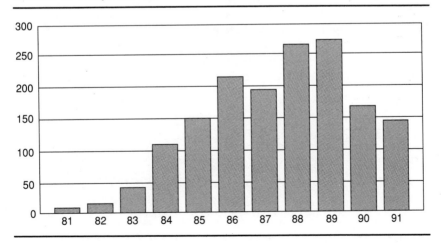

Source: Securities Data Company's "Mergers and Corporate Transactions Database," copyright 1992. Reprinted with permission of Securities Data Company, Inc.

EXHIBIT 2–10

Total Dollar Value Paid by Foreign Buyers

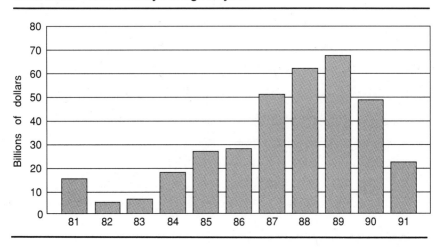

EXHIBIT 2–11

Number of Completed Deals by Foreign Buyers

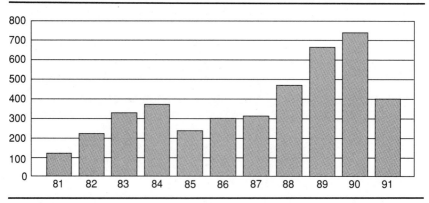

EXHIBIT 2–12
Dollar Volume by Foreign Buyers (by Country for Period January 1989 to December 1991)

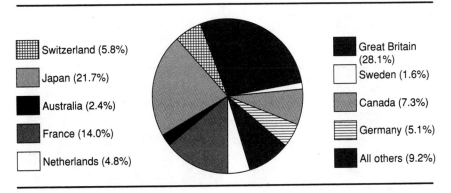

Switzerland (5.8%)	Great Britain (28.1%)
Japan (21.7%)	Sweden (1.6%)
Australia (2.4%)	Canada (7.3%)
France (14.0%)	Germany (5.1%)
Netherlands (4.8%)	All others (9.2%)

Source: Securities Data Company's "Mergers and Corporate Transactions Database," copyright 1992. Reprinted with permission of Securities Data Company, Inc.

2.3   THE SELLING UNIVERSE

The selling universe is segmented into four types of sellers: public companies, divestitures, private companies and foreign sellers. Exhibit 2–13 indicates that the percent of total dollar volume for the four segments was relatively constant during the late 1980s.

2.4   M&A ACTIVITY BY INDUSTRY

M&A activity by industry fluctuates widely on an annual basis. Therefore, Exhibit 2–14 depicts M&A activity by industry over the last three years.

EXHIBIT 2–13
Percent of Dollar Volume by Type of Seller

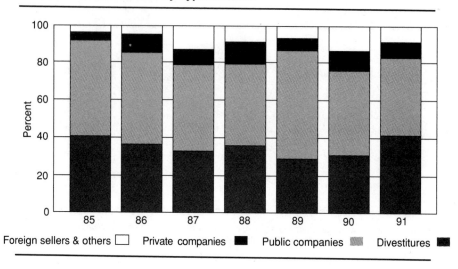

Foreign sellers & others ☐   Private companies ■   Public companies ▨   Divestitures ■

Source: Securities Data Company's "Mergers and Corporate Transactions Database," copyright 1992. Reprinted with permission of Securities Data Company, Inc.

EXHIBIT 2–14
M&A Activity by Industry (Percent of Dollar Volume—January 1989 to December 1991)

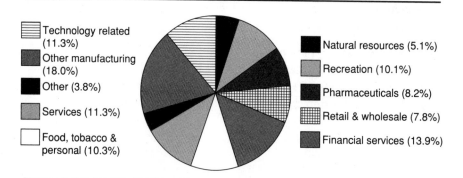

Technology related (11.3%)
Other manufacturing (18.0%)
Other (3.8%)
Services (11.3%)
Food, tobacco & personal (10.3%)

Natural resources (5.1%)
Recreation (10.1%)
Pharmaceuticals (8.2%)
Retail & wholesale (7.8%)
Financial services (13.9%)

Source: Securities Data Company's "Mergers and Corporate Transactions Database," copyright 1992. Reprinted with permission of Securities Data Company, Inc.

2.5 KEY ECONOMIC INFLUENCES

Broad economic factors that affect the pricing level of transactions in the U.S. include:

- Availability of financing.
- Interest rates.
- Health of the economy.
- Stock prices for public companies.
- Foreign exchange rates.

2.51 Availability of Financing

Exhibit 2–15 indicates the amount of high yield debt issued during the 1981–1991 period. It is interesting to review this exhibit in conjunction with Exhibits 2–1, 2–3 and 2–4. It is clear from these exhibits that the run up in acquisition pricing and dollar volume in the late 1980s was largely a result of the availability of high yield acquisition financing.

EXHIBIT 2–15
Public and Private High Yield New Issue Volume

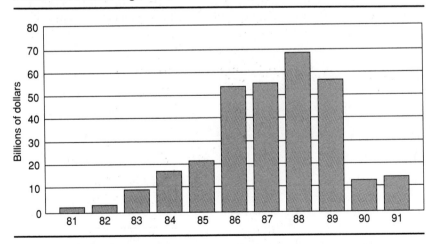

Source: Securities Data Company's "Mergers and Corporate Transactions Database," copyright 1992. Reprinted with permission of Securities Data Company, Inc.

Given the collapse of the high yield new issue marketplace late in 1989, it is unlikely that the deal pricing levels achieved in 1987 will be reached in the early 1990s.

Generally, bank financing during the 1980s was easily obtained. However, in the early 1990s banks are under tremendous pressure to reduce their exposure to LBOs and improve their capitalization ratios. One of the most significant ways the Federal Reserve applied pressure on banks to reduce this exposure was through the issuance of *Highly Leveraged Transaction (HLT)* regulations. The HLT rules require banks to report separately all loans to highly leveraged transactions. These regulations went into effect in 1990. However, they were phased out as of June 30, 1992.

The combined pressures of the recession and the regulators in the early 1990s are forcing banks to be extremely selective in financing transactions.

2.52 Interest Rates

Interest rates fluctuated widely during the 1980s as indicated in Exhibit 2–16. However, interest rate spreads for high yield securities were fairly close to investment grade debt securities until recently (see Exhibit 2–17).

Interest rate movements during the early 1980s were generally very favorable for leveraged acquirers. Interest rates declined from 1981 to 1986. In this environment most buyers who acquired operating assets on a leveraged basis did extremely well in creating value for themselves.

EXHIBIT 2–16
Interest Rate Trends

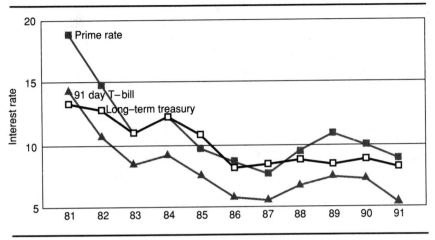

Source: Federal Reserve.

EXHIBIT 2–17
High Yield Bond/10-Year Treasury Spread (Promised Yield Percent)

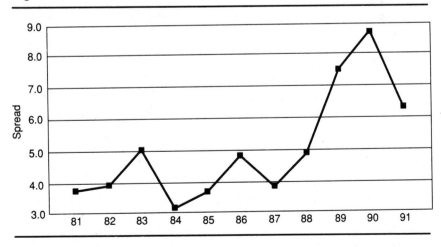

Source: Edward I. Altman, "Defaults and Returns on High Yield Bonds," *Merrill Lynch High Yield Securities Research*, March 6, 1992, p. 17.

Interest rate movements since 1986 have not been as kind for leveraged acquirers. The combination of a harsh economic and interest rate environment coupled with higher acquisition multiples has caused default rates on high yield debt to soar. This fact is depicted in Exhibit 2–18.

EXHIBIT 2–18
Dollar Volume of Junk Bond Defaults (Straight Debt Only)

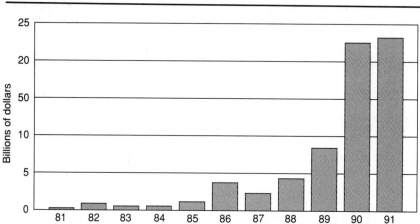

Note: 1987 data excludes defaults by Texaco, Inc., Texaco Capital, and Texaco N.V.; defaults at par value.

Source: Edward I. Altman, "Defaults and Returns on HighYield Bonds," *Merrill Lynch High Yield Securities Research*, March 6, 1992, p. 7.

2.53   Health of the Economy

The 1980s were a period of prolonged expansion. Other than the recession in the early 1980s the economy expanded throughout the decade (see Exhibit 2–19). This economic environment proved very friendly to acquirers, especially those that were financing transactions with a significant amount of debt.

EXHIBIT 2–19
Percent Change in Gross Domestic Product (Constant 1987 Dollars)

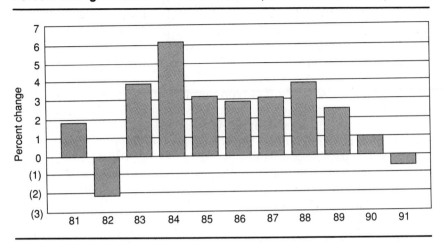

Source: Federal Reserve.

The prolonged favorable economic environment led lenders to go too far in extending credit. Just prior to the stock market crash in 1987, it was not uncommon to see deals being done with approximately a 1 to 1 interest expense to cash flow coverage ratio projected in the first year. For such deals to work out for all parties, there had to be no downturn in the economy for a minimum of several years. The bankruptcies that occurred in the late 1980s and early 1990s are testaments to lenders agreeing to overly aggressive financial acquisitions.

The recession in the early 1990s is having a negative impact on acquisition activity for a variety of reasons. First, the near-term outlook for most businesses is not favorable, and therefore, the price that sellers can obtain has been reduced. It is not surprising that sellers are not looking to sell at this time. Second, acquisition financing is difficult to obtain because lenders have become more cautious. This has negatively impacted both acquiring companies' appetites and their ability to pay high prices. Third, the downturn has reduced the absolute number of potential buyers in the marketplace by causing acquirers to spend more time and effort on their existing portfolio of businesses in an attempt to improve performance.

2.54   Stock Prices for Public Companies

It is typical in transactions involving publicly traded companies for an acquirer to pay a premium over the current stock price. Exhibit 2–20 depicts the average percent premium paid over the stock price of the target company 30 days prior to any announcement that the target was being purchased.

Stock prices are a result of economic conditions, not a cause. Therefore, one might argue that they do not affect deal pricing. However, stock prices significantly influence many decision makers, especially owners of privately owned companies. These individuals typically follow a select group of comparable companies that they use as a benchmark to judge the value of their own company. Therefore, the fluctuations of the stock market have an indirect bearing on pricing for a significant part of the M&A marketplace.

EXHIBIT 2–20

Average Premium Paid over Stock Price (One Month Prior to Announcement of Deal)

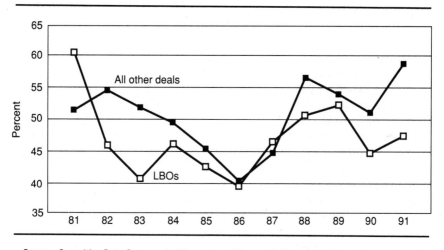

Source: Securities Data Company's "Mergers and Corporate Transactions Database," copyright 1992. Reprinted with permission of Securities Data Company, Inc.

2.55   Foreign Exchange Rates

Exhibit 2–21 depicts the U.S. Dollar Exchange Rate Index movement over the last decade. This index compares the U.S. dollar against a market basket of 10 major currencies including Germany, Japan, France, United Kingdom, Canada, Italy, Netherlands, Belgium, Sweden and Switzerland. This exhibit indicates that the dollar strengthened significantly in the 1982–85 time frame. When we compare this exhibit to Exhibits 2–10 and 2–11, it is easy to understand why foreign investment in the U.S. slackened considerably during this time frame. The resurgence of foreign investment in the U.S. in the late 1980s and early 1990s is also more

EXHIBIT 2–21
U.S. Dollar Exchange Rate Index

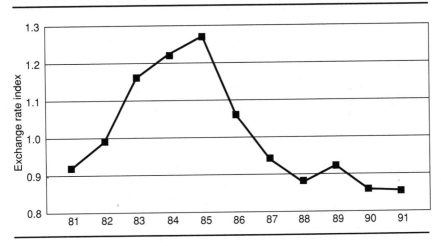

Source: Federal Reserve of Dallas; trade weighted value of the dollar index; 1973 = 1.0.

understandable when viewed in light of Exhibit 2–21. Exhibit 2–22 shows the exchange rate movements of some of the world's major currencies against the dollar over the last decade.

EXHIBIT 2–22
Major Foreign Exchange Rates

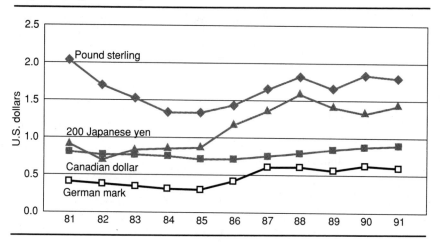

Source: Average spot rates based on London close.

Chapter 3

Successful Deals in the 1990s

3.0 ACQUISITIONS GENERALLY DON'T WORK OUT

Acquisitions, on average, have not worked out well for corporate acquirers. However, there are measurable differences between various types of deals. Academic studies have shown that the likelihood of a successful acquisition is less if the acquirer makes a diversifying acquisition and greater if the acquirer "sticks to the knitting" and focuses on targets in related industries. The academic analyses are fully supported by the financial dailies, which have described in great detail the triumphs and missteps of investing in acquisitions. One is not hard pressed to remember some of the major stories in each category:

Type of Acquisition	Triumphs	Disasters
Related	UAL/Pan Am Pacific Routes Wells Fargo/Crocker National GE/RCA	Blue Arrow/Manpower GE/Kidder Peabody Continental/Eastern
Unrelated	Hanson Trust/Kidde	Exxon/Reliance Electric
LBOs	Gibson Greeting Cards Safeway Avis	Allied/Federated Macy's Revco

In making a diversifying acquisition, an acquirer must be particularly careful to obtain sound business and financial advice and conduct a thorough due diligence. All too often acquirers of unrelated companies find out shortly after completing the transaction that no competing company in the target's industry was interested in acquiring the company because of significant "obvious" flaws.

3.1 THE LBO—STAR OF THE 1980s

The transaction structure that defined the 1980s was the *leveraged buyout (LBO)*. The LBO, or bootstrap acquisition as it was known until the late 1970s, has been around since the 1960s, but it did not have a material effect on the M&A marketplace until the 1980s.

In the late 1970s and early 1980s, LBOs were put together by a handful of sophisticated financial boutiques such as Kohlberg Kravis Roberts & Co. (KKR) and Wesray Capital Corp. (Wesray) that correctly identified the value gap between the acquisition cost of unwanted corporate assets and their financial value. The rates of return that these firms achieved were astounding. For example, since Wesray put little, if any, net investment into a transaction, a successful deal would have an infinite return. LBO firms that put significant net equity dollars into transactions typically achieved internal rates of return on their equity investments of 50 to 125 percent.

One of the reasons value gaps existed is that many corporations at that time were anxious to unload nonstrategic assets acquired in the conglomerate craze of the late 1960s and early 1970s. However, the universe of buyers for these assets was very limited. Unless a corporate acquirer had a strategic reason to purchase a division or subsidiary, it had to be sold at a low price to attract a buyer. It was often the case that no strategic buyer could be located because the operation's sales growth prospects were poor. Enter the LBO boutiques. As private firms they were not concerned with reporting *earnings per share (EPS)* increases. Their only goal was to achieve an acceptable return on their money over a relatively short time horizon.

Generally, LBOs done before 1987 were successful because of the interest rate and economic environment, while LBOs done after this period have had a much higher probability of failure. One reason for the poor performance of recent LBOs is that the LBO business became more of a fund raising business than an investment management business. In the mid-1980s a great amount of equity capital was raised for LBOs. To raise their next fund, equity sponsors had to put money raised to work, despite the fact that M&A prices were at all-time highs. This led to numerous poorly conceived LBOs consummated at prices that could not provide any significant investment returns.

3.2   ADVICE FOR THE 1990s

Corporate America would do well in the 1990s if it followed some of the basic tenets that made LBO firms successful in the 1980s. These include:

- Pay the right price.
- Invest other people's money.
- Invest with an edge—management.
- Understand the risks.
- Understand the acquisition process.
- Focus on cash flows and market values.
- Buy wholesale.
- Undertake commonsense strategies.

3.21   Pay the Right Price

The right price for an LBO firm is one that will generate a huge return on its investment. Up until 1988–89 most LBO firms were looking for returns of 40 percent or more on their leveraged investment. The primary reason that LBO firms set a high hurdle rate for investment is that they understood the risks associated with acquisitions. There are too many variables that can go wrong in an acquisition to set a low investment hurdle rate.

Another way to state this rule is, Don't overpay! There are many things that can be changed in a deal after it is done, including management, the product line, and facilities. However, once the purchase price has been paid, you have to live with it. If you significantly overpaid because you got too emotional over the opportunity, you have dug a very deep hole to climb out of.

There are many ways to make the numbers work in acquisition analysis. Tweaking the forecast growth rate, the operating margin, the capital expenditure requirements or any number of key variables a little bit may be enough to get the acquisition model to spit out the required returns. However, remember "garbage in, garbage out" when it comes to acquisition models. If your financial forecast is not founded on a realistic set of operating assumptions, you are only kidding yourself. One way to check yourself in this regard is to compare the operating assumptions in your latest acquisition model with your initial operating assumptions. If your current forecast looks like your beginning Best Case scenario, you should reexamine your due diligence data to confirm that the better forecast is really a reasonable Base Case scenario. Ask yourself whether your initial conservative assumptions were wrong. Another commonsense test is to ask if you are making your investment decision based on a scenario where everything must go perfectly for the acquisition to reach the required rate of return. If this is the case, the high probability of a poor economic outcome should deter you from completing the deal.

3.22 Invest Other People's Money

LBO firms have generated huge returns for the investors in their funds (their shareholders or partners) by significantly leveraging their equity. In the mid 1980s 9 to 1 leverage ratios were the norm. In today's environment, where senior bank lending is being severely restricted, leverage ratios of 3 to 1 are more prevalent.

The suggestion that an acquiring corporation leverage its equity investment is not meant to imply that the corporation should employ an imprudent amount of leverage. However, an appropriate amount of leverage may well exceed that employed by the acquiring corporation as a whole.

Acquisitions in which the acquiring corporation is planning to operate the target as a stand-alone entity provide an opportunity to be creative in structuring the acquirer's equity investment. There are various off balance sheet structures, including partnership arrangements with financial institutions, that permit a corporate acquirer to gain effective control of an operation in the future. Such structures can often enhance the acquirer's return on its equity investment. Moreover, they afford the opportunity for the acquirer to reduce the initial dilution associated with high priced acquisitions.

The concept of significantly leveraging an acquisition where the acquiring corporation intends to immediately assimilate the acquired assets into its present operations affords the same possibilities. Once the acquirer has completed the acquisition and linked the target's operations with its own, it can put the combined operations off balance sheet in a leveraged structure. This can be accomplished for either a limited or indefinite period. The length of time the acquirer wants the structure leveraged and off balance sheet, as well as governance considerations, will determine the type of equity partner that the corporation will want.

The concept of investing other people's money includes attempting to negotiate a transaction that involves some amount of seller financing. Corporate America has a reluctance to negotiate seller paper when it has cash available to complete a transaction. This reluctance is ill-founded. In situations where seller financing is available, there is no cheaper source of financing that the acquiring company can tap.

3.23   Invest with an Edge—Management

Probably the most important factor in the success of LBO firms investing in the 1980s was their involving management of the target in their investment decision making. In the ideal situation, LBO firms would co-opt management of the target to work with them on analyzing every aspect of the target company. Having management on its side enabled the LBO firm to learn of risks and opportunities in the target's business that would not otherwise have become known until after a transaction. This knowledge significantly reduced the risk associated with an acquisition and thus permitted the buyout firm to know, with a higher degree of certainty, the value of the target.

In addition, involving management in its investment decision making process allows the LBO firm to better assess the quality of the management as well as forge their commitment to deliver the projected results. Management's interest level in attaining the financial projections goes up dramatically after the deal is closed for both "carrot and stick" reasons. Management's equity stake is their incentive, and the loans that they took out to purchase their equity stakes (most collateralized by their net worth, including their house) are the stick. Suddenly, 9-to-5 five day workweeks give way to seven days a week, 24 hours a day.

Management of the target is willing to be co-opted in the sale process because they are looking out for their personal interests. Generally, LBO firms offer the management team an equity stake of approximately 5–15 percent in the company. Very often this equity stake is granted at a very low cost or no cost to the management team. With this kind of economic inducement to cooperate with the LBO firm, it is very difficult for the selling company to maintain control over its employees.

The fact that management of the target often switches sides before the transaction is completed raises a host of ethical and legal issues regarding the duty of loyalty owed by management to the company and its selling shareholder(s) and breaches the standard confidentiality agreement that most prospective buyers sign. Buyers often disregard these issues because they feel that the worst that can happen to them is that they can get thrown out of the process, an outcome they are willing to risk if they do not achieve the "inside track." The management of the target is in the toughest spot, for they must fulfill their duty of loyalty.

The ethical answer for management is to clear discussions with their parent or the target company's board of directors.

3.24 Understand the Risks

The principal method that LBO firms use to evaluate the risks associated with a transaction is to maximize their knowledge base about the business and its markets. Since most LBO firms are composed of individuals with financial backgrounds, they are ordinarily not hesitant to admit that they know little about a particular industry and its participants. Therefore, they are always looking for high quality information sources that can help them evaluate a particular opportunity.

Another approach that LBO firms employ to improve their understanding of the risk profile of a business in a particular industry is to hire a partner into the LBO firm that has operating experience. These individuals (a) provide insight into the workings of a particular industry, (b) bring management contacts that can be brought to bear on the situation, and (c) often are the management talent that the LBO firm injects into a company to exploit the opportunity to its maximum extent.

LBO firms' due diligence process also works to their advantage. All acquirers perform a due diligence review designed to surface the important risk factors in the business of the target. However, LBO firms spend more time and effort building them into their financial models of the target. This allows them to evaluate the impact of changes in risk assumptions more completely.

The fact that LBO firms put a great deal of financial leverage on a target makes them extremely sensitive to understanding the operating leverage in the business. Generally, LBO firms are more interested in acquiring businesses that have low fixed costs because such businesses have a lower risk profile in a leveraged environment than high fixed cost businesses. Volume downturns in a high fixed cost "commodity" business are usually devastating if a business is leveraged.

3.25 Understand the Acquisition Process

One of the chief reasons many corporate executives get emotionally involved in a deal and end up overpaying for a target company is that the standard Two Stage Auction Process is purposely designed to elicit this type of behavior. Investment bankers create an atmosphere of uncertainty where the buyer does not know where his bid stands. However, a good selling agent is careful not to create so much uncertainty that a good prospective buyer is lost. Real bidders are kept in the hunt, with each one knowing that the thrill of victory can be had for just a few more dollars. The seller's investment banker creates this atmosphere by constantly telling prospective buyers that they are just a little short on price and that competitive bidders are out there ready to scoop up the target.

The auction process often has the desired effect on a prospective purchaser's CEO. This competitive individual has watched his staff spend months of effort analyzing and arranging financing for this transaction. In addition, his company has expended substantial sums for legal, accounting, financing and consulting services which will have to be written off immediately if the acquisition is not completed. With these factors weighing on his mind and the thrill of victory within his grasp, many CEOs will stretch that extra mile to get a deal done. The investment banker has really done a terrific job for his client if he gets a buyer to go that extra mile when the "winning" bidder was the only bidder.

To maximize the chance of winning any sale at a reasonable price, a buyer must have a clear understanding of the process that the seller and his agent have devised. Understanding this process and how it can be exploited is fundamental to winning. For example, in a situation where the target company is a "hot property" that will attract many bidders, what is the best strategy for a company that is one of several most likely strategic buyers? Generally, it is in this prospective buyer's best interest to attempt to preempt the process by putting a fully priced all-cash indication of interest on the table before the seller has distributed a selling memorandum. The reason that this makes more sense for the buyer, rather than proceeding along in an auction, is that (1) it increases the probability that the prospective buyer will actually buy the target at a price that makes economic sense; (2) it gives the buyer a chance to negotiate terms and conditions; (3) at the point when the buyer makes a preemptive indication, the seller is faced with as much uncertainty as the buyer about the target's fair market value. The longer the auction process progresses, the greater the amount of information that the seller will obtain as to the marketability and expected value to be realized from the property. This knowledge will always work to the seller's advantage.

3.26   Focus on Cash Flows and Market Values

Whether an acquisition makes sense economically depends on the expected cash flows of the target. The fact that there may be EPS dilution to the acquiring company is totally irrelevant. However, many publicly held U.S. companies have policies that steer them away from any acquisition that would dilute earnings or would create goodwill on their books.

These policies exemplify corporate America's often criticized focus on quarterly earnings instead of long-term value creation.

Cash flows do not just depend on earnings levels. Capital expenditures and changes in working capital investment are equally important cash flow variables that must be scrutinized. Successful LBO firms have always spent an extensive amount of time reviewing capital expenditure plans, pruning gold-plated corporate budgets down to essential economic projects.

The market values of all the target's assets, especially unwanted or unneeded assets, is critical information to properly analyze a deal. Book value and replacement value are irrelevant in analyzing such assets.

3.27 Buy Wholesale

Most corporations are unwilling to acquire a company if that company has significant assets unrelated to the acquiring corporation's strategic objectives. The reason cited most often for such a policy is that the corporation is not in the business of buying and selling assets—its business is producing a specific type of good or service. This policy has the effect of insuring that corporate America will pay top dollar for acquisitions. Why? The prospective list of buyers for a collection of operations is relatively small. In the 1980s this list generally was limited to LBO firms and a few conglomerates, such as Hanson Trust. However, once a group of assets is broken down and individual operations are auctioned off, the prospective buyers that line up to get an opportunity to purchase each operation include all its logical strategic bidders. This results in the purchaser of the collection of assets "buying wholesale" and "selling retail" to corporate America.

The obvious solution for corporate acquirers is to take a higher risk profile in their acquisitions and take on nonstrategic assets they know they will immediately divest. In order to execute such a strategy and minimize the associated risks, the corporation should have substantial in-house talent and/or competent outside advisors. The advantages of this approach to the corporate acquirer are not limited to the lower net purchase price that the acquirer will pay for the desired operation. It is often the case that the acquirer would have no chance to purchase the desired operation if it did not take this aggressive approach, because in an auction of the desired operation there might be other bidders who would be willing to pay a higher premium. Another advantage to this strategy is that as the corporation gets a reputation as an aggressive acquirer of assets, the probability increases that it will be shown acquisition opportunities by investment banks before they are shown to the general marketplace.

An example of the strategy advocated here was the 1986 acquisition of Anderson Clayton by Quaker Oats (Quaker). Quaker was primarily interested in acquiring Anderson Clayton's Gaines Pet Food operations. Initially, Quaker was willing to pay $250 million for Gaines in a straight-forward acquisition of this operation. However, as Quaker was negotiating, Ralston-Purina, a pet food competitor, indicated that it was willing to purchase all of Anderson Clayton. If Ralston had purchased Anderson Clayton, Quaker's existing pet food operations would have been put in a poor strategic position. Thus, Quaker elected to step up and buy the entire company for over $600 million. Quaker sold off five of the six non-pet food operations within six months of the acquisition. These included Anderson Clayton Foods, Igloo, Acco Feeds, Western Cotton and Long Reach Hydraulics. Paymaster Oil, the sixth operation, was sold within one year of the acquisition. Quaker's purchase price for Gaines after all these transactions was approximately $225 million, net of all transaction costs.

3.28 Undertake Commonsense Strategies

A large number of transactions in the 1980s were successful because new investors executed an operating strategy that should have been patently obvious to the target's management. In some cases the problems were obvious to the current owner, but for some reason, typically related to personnel issues, the owner could not fix these problems. Bloated selling, general and administrative costs were slashed; unprofitable product lines or plants were closed or sold off; high margin product lines with growth potential were funded, and excess investment in working capital or fixed assets was reduced. These strategies were the basis for the success of the bulk of the leveraged transactions involving underperforming assets completed in the 1980s.

Another area in which LBO firms have excelled is their ability to identify the entire range of financial alternatives available to them so as to maximize their return on investment. For example, LBO firms have been very adept at completing *Initial Public Offerings (IPOs)* of high growth subsidiaries and financings such as sale/leasebacks. LBO firms' success reflects an aggressiveness in exploring all financial alternatives and an alertness to changing economic conditions in the financial markets.

3.3   ADDITIONAL COMMENTS FOR CORPORATE ACQUISITIONS

In addition to the tenets described above, corporate acquirers reviewing the acquisition of a business related to one of its existing businesses should:

- Make sure cultures are compatible.
- Have a viable integration plan.
- Plan to integrate quickly.

3.31   Make Sure Cultures Are Compatible

Corporate cultures must be somewhat compatible if a corporate acquirer expects to successfully integrate a related acquisition into its organization. Otherwise, the target company's personnel will work very hard to make sure that the integration fails. There are countless examples where corporate cultures were so different that they almost guaranteed the deal would have problems:

General Motors/EDS: Ross Perot's battles with GM's management were front-page news for years after this 1984 deal.

Westinghouse/Unimation: Westinghouse's rigid adherence to its corporate decision making processes and compensation plans did not sit well with Unimation's free wheeling robotic software specialists. Ultimately this group of employees was allowed to set up its own company to supply services to Unimation.

3.32   Have a Viable Integration Plan

It is not enough that a corporate acquirer has analyzed the value of the target correctly and has paid the right price. If the acquirer's analysis assumes the integration of the target with its business, the acquirer must have a viable integration plan. This planning is absolutely essential for correctly valuing the target. Failure to adequately plan how the integration of the target would proceed dooms a company to some unpleasant surprises. For example, Pan Am acquired National Airlines for $400 million in 1980. Pan Am was attracted to National because Pan Am had few domestic routes while National had few foreign routes. A merger of the two operations would presumably enable Pan Am to use National's routes to feed Pan Am's overseas routes. Sounds very logical. However, there turned out to be tremendous integration problems, most of which could have been identified before the deal was completed. The two companies' fleets had to be significantly changed to properly service the combined route structure. In addition, a power struggle between the two companies' unions should have been foreseen.

3.33   Plan to Integrate Quickly

Most successful corporate acquirers integrate related acquisitions as quickly as possible to maximize the "savings" and opportunities that they included in the analysis to justify the acquisition price paid. Good examples of acquirers that were successful because of their rapid integration of the target's business include:

> *Tyson/Holly Farms:* After paying what many commentators believed to be a very high price, Tyson moved rapidly to consolidate Holly Farms' chicken operations into its own, while simultaneously selling off Holly Farms' unrelated operations. Tyson's stock price soared as a result.

> *Wells Fargo/Crocker National:* Within a year of the acquisition, Wells assimilated Crocker's operations by consolidating branch locations and corporate functions. This acquisition significantly enhanced Wells' strategic position in California, as well as its profitability.

Chapter 4

A Deal Is a Deal! Or the Texas Sting!

4.0 PENNZOIL v. TEXACO

Every businessperson with an interest in mergers and acquisitions should be familiar with the circumstances that produced the largest judgment ever rendered in an American courtroom! This chapter outlines the fight between Pennzoil and Texaco over the acquisition of Getty Oil.

The *Pennzoil v. Texaco* litigation over Getty Oil primarily involves the issue of when negotiations ripen into a binding agreement to buy or sell a business. In addition, the case highlights the actions that an unsuccessful suitor may take if he believes that he has been wronged in the sale process, the concept of tortious interference, the pressures that members of the board of directors of a target company experience in a takeover and the uncertainties of litigation.

Although the case is useful in reviewing the issues outlined above, some believe that the propriety of the outcome is suspect because of a variety of disturbing events involving the Texas judges who presided over the case. However, Texaco could not persuade any court in any jurisdiction that it could not or did not receive a fair hearing.

4.01 The Getty Oil Company

The Getty Oil Company was built by J. Paul Getty into one of the foremost energy companies in the world. The company's most valuable asset was its domestic oil and gas reserves, estimated at 2.35 billion barrels.

At the time of the transaction, 40.2 percent of the company's common stock was held by the Sarah C. Getty Trust (the "Trust") and 11.8 percent of the stock was held by the J. Paul Getty Museum (the "Museum"), a charitable trust established to collect and exhibit art. The descendents of J. Paul Getty were beneficiaries of the Trust. The remaining 48 percent of Getty Oil stock was publicly owned.

4.02 Dispute Puts the Company "In Play"

Gordon Getty, the son of J. Paul Getty, was the sole trustee of the Trust. Management of Getty Oil viewed Gordon Getty as an unsophisticated businessman and potentially a threat to their continued control of the company. Throughout 1983, management, the Board of Directors of Getty (the "Board") and the two majority shareholders were involved in a number of highly publicized disputes that had the effect of putting the company "in play." These disputes caused Gordon Getty to be at odds with the entire Board, with the exception of those directors he had chosen to be on the Board.

On December 27, 1983 Pennzoil Company (Pennzoil) announced an offer to purchase at least 20 percent of the outstanding common stock of Getty Oil for $100 cash per share. Hugh Liedtke, Pennzoil's chairman, launched the offer because he believed that Pennzoil could create significant value for itself if it could gain control of Getty and undertake a restructuring.

4.03 Pennzoil, the Trust and the Museum Reach Agreement

After launching his offer, Liedtke met with Gordon Getty and agreed on a plan to jointly own Getty Oil. Gordon Getty wanted to be Chairman and Pennzoil wanted to control the restructuring. Each side achieved its objective by agreeing to a 4 to 3 ownership ratio for the Trust and Pennzoil, with Liedtke to be named CEO and Getty to be named Chairman. Their agreement provided a mechanism for breaking apart the company should the two parties complete the transaction and find that they had differences over how to run the company. As part of the deal Pennzoil would raise its offer to $110 cash per share and buy enough shares to give it three sevenths ownership, once the company completed a cash merger for all shares other than those held by the Trust or Pennzoil. The Trust would not tender its shares and thereby it would own four sevenths of Getty Oil's stock. Pennzoil reached agreement with the Museum shortly thereafter at the $110 cash per share price. As part of the deal, the Museum negotiated a provision that allowed it to get the benefit of any higher price paid for any other large block of stock. On January 2, 1984, Gordon Getty as Trustee, the President of the Museum and Liedtke for Pennzoil executed a Memorandum of Agreement which memorialized their intentions. Both Gordon Getty and the President of the Museum were members of the Board.

Also on January 2, 1984, Gordon Getty, in his capacity as Trustee, executed a written statement in which he indicated that, subject only to his fiduciary obligations, it was his intention to support the plan outlined in the Memorandum of Agreement and oppose any alternative proposal that did not provide for Pennzoil's participation in Getty on the basis outlined in the plan.

4.04   The Getty Board Meeting

The agreement among Pennzoil, the Trust and the Museum was expressly conditioned on acceptance by the Board at its meeting to begin January 2, 1984. This meeting began at 6 P.M. The meeting was a hectic one because the directors felt that the Pennzoil tender offer, followed by the proposal of the Trustee, the Museum and Pennzoil, was unfairly putting the squeeze on the Getty board.

According to directors who attended the meeting and later testified at the trial, at about 10 P.M. the Board, by a vote of 9 to 6, rejected the Memorandum of Agreement and, after rejecting it, never again considered it. This Board meeting lasted until 2:30 A.M., when the Board decided to convey a counteroffer of $110 cash plus a $10 note per share.

Pennzoil rejected this counteroffer and proposed a choice between $110 in cash or $90 in cash plus a proportionate interest in Employers Reinsurance Corporation (ERC), an insurance subsidiary that Getty's investment banker had indicated might have a value of $30 per share. After discussing this proposal with the Museum's lawyer, Pennzoil increased its offer to $110 plus a guaranteed $3-per-share deferred compensation stub based on the sale of ERC.

The Getty Board reconvened in the afternoon of January 3 to consider Pennzoil's new proposal. At this meeting the Board voted 14 to 1 to accept the Pennzoil proposal provided that (a) the amount being paid relating to ERC be $5 per share, and (b) that Pennzoil accept certain golden parachute and indemnification agreements which the Board had approved in the afternoon's meeting. This proposal was immediately conveyed to Liedtke, who accepted for Pennzoil. The Board reconvened at 6:55 P.M on January 3 and was advised that Pennzoil had indicated to the Museum's investment banker that it would accept the counterproposal presented by the Board.

The sworn testimony of Getty directors who voted was that the Getty board had reached an agreement with Pennzoil on the price element alone, and they considered that a contract embodying all relevant items of the proposed transaction would be drafted and submitted to the Getty board for approval before a binding agreement could be reached. However, on cross examination at the trial one Getty director testified that the Board had voted on and approved both the price and the structure of the Pennzoil proposal, as the subsequent Getty press release indicated. Another Getty director testified ("It was a bird-in-the-handish situation. We approved the deal but we did not favor it."). The Board minutes reflect that ("Williams [the President of the Museum] then moved that the Board accept the Pennzoil proposal [with a $5 ERC stub]. . . . The vote was . . . all directors voting "For" other than Mr. Medberry"). No member of the Board, other than Gordon Getty and the President of the Museum, or management of Getty Oil signed the Memorandum of Agreement. It is at this point that Pennzoil claimed and the Texas jury ultimately agreed that a binding contract between Pennzoil and the Getty entities came into being.

After the Board meeting adjourned, Mr. and Mrs. Getty invited Mr. Liedtke to their hotel suite for a champagne celebration. Mr. Liedtke declined.

4.05   Public Announcement of the Deal

On the morning of January 4, 1984, Getty Oil, the Trust and the Museum issued a joint press release on Getty Oil letterhead announcing that they had an "agreement in principle" with Pennzoil with respect to a merger of Getty Oil and a newly formed entity owned by Pennzoil and the Trust. The agreement in principle corresponded with the structure outlined in the plan between Pennzoil, the Trustee and the Museum, as reflected in the Memorandum of Agreement, with the exception that the press release included Pennzoil's supplemental proposal that the shares of Getty held by the public would be acquired through a merger whereby the shareholders would receive $110 per share plus deferred cash in a formula amount for their interests in the reinsurance subsidiary—in any event, at least $5 per share within five years—and that upon the execution of such a merger agreement the tender offer would be withdrawn. The release also stated that the transaction was subject to the execution of a definitive merger agreement, shareholder and regulatory approval. Pennzoil issued the same press release on its letterhead.

The press release had originally been drafted to indicate that the parties had reached an agreement. However, the Museum and Getty Oil lawyers found this to be totally misleading and inaccurate, and they redrafted the language.

On January 5, *The Wall Street Journal* ran a feature article describing the transaction.

On January 4, Getty Oil's investment banker presented it a bill for $6 million, which is the minimum amount it was owed under its retainer agreement. The presentation of a bill by an investment banker is usually not done unless a deal has been agreed to.

4.06   The Merger Drafts

Attorneys for Pennzoil and the Trust worked on the formal document implementing the transaction. One draft was produced on January 4 and a second on January 5. These drafting sessions were particularly difficult because a number of terms of the proposed merger remained unresolved, including: (1) who was to purchase the Museum's shares in order to alleviate the risk of a $2 billion tax penalty; (2) whether the proposed acquisition was to be a tender offer and second step merger, or simply a merger transaction; (3) when and how the proceeds from the sale of ERC would be distributed; (4) who, if anyone, would pay Getty Oil's first quarter dividend and to whom it would be paid. It is also important to note that these draft documents provided that the parties' obligations would come into effect only after execution and delivery of the definitive purchase agreement.

4.07   The California Litigation

On January 4, a beneficiary of the Trust brought suit in a California probate court to obtain more information about the transaction and obtained a temporary restraining order prohibiting Gordon Getty from signing any formal merger papers. At a hearing the following day, Getty's financial and legal advisors stated, "There is presently a transaction agreed upon among [Getty, the Museum, the Trustee, and Pennzoil]. This is the first time there has been agreement among the four of these parties. . . . This is an agreement which has been entered into after extremely careful consideration."

4.08   Texaco Enters the Picture

Texaco Inc. (Texaco) had done a nominal amount of work up until the press release on January 4 announcing the agreement with Pennzoil. Once the deal was announced, Texaco's president called Getty Oil's investment banker and determined that the formal merger papers had not yet been signed but that they were being worked on. That night Texaco hired an investment bank and legal advisors. After the deal was successfully concluded, Texaco's investment bank was paid $10 million.

According to Pennzoil's interpretation of the facts, the strategy that Texaco and its advisors came up with to stop the signing of the formal merger papers was to approach the Museum with an offer it couldn't refuse. If Texaco could lock up the Museum's shares, it would be in a position to successfully tender for the public's shares, thus making the Trust the sole minority shareholder in Getty Oil, assuming it did not tender its shares. According to the terms of the Trust, Gordon Getty could not sell the Getty Oil shares the Trust controlled except to save the trust estate from a substantial loss. The prospect of the Trust changing its position from being the largest, most influential, shareholder of Getty Oil to merely a locked-out minority shareholder would probably be sufficient pressure for Gordon Getty to abandon the Trust's deal with Pennzoil.

Once a deal had been struck with the Museum and the Trust, Texaco would cut a deal with Getty's Board for the public shares.

On January 5, Texaco's board of directors authorized management to offer up to $125 per share to acquire the shares held by the Museum, the Trust, Getty Oil (treasury shares), and the public. A preference was expressed that 100 percent of the shares be purchased, but it was left to management to determine if a lesser number of shares should be purchased. There is no record of any discussion at the board meeting of the announced transaction.

4.09 Texaco Acquires the Museum's Shares

When Texaco and its representatives met with the Museum's lawyer on January 5, he indicated that a requirement of the transaction would be that Texaco would have to indemnify the Museum and its employees, officers and members of its board of trustees fully for any liability under the Pennzoil agreement should the Museum enter into an agreement with Texaco and that Texaco guarantee that the Museum receive $112.50 for each of its shares, whether or not Texaco purchased them. However, Texaco did not reveal the price it was willing to pay until the meeting with Gordon Getty later that night. At that meeting Texaco indicated to both the Trustee and the Museum that Texaco was willing to pay $125 per share. The Museum's lawyer immediately presented the above terms to the Museum's trustees, and they were accepted. The Texaco/Museum stock purchase agreement was hammered out that night and executed. A final requirement included in this document was that Texaco accept the

Museum stock without any warranty that the sale by the Museum did not breach the Pennzoil agreement.

Upon the execution of the agreement, Texaco issued a press release announcing its success in locking up the Museum's stock.

4.10 Texaco Acquires the Trust's Shares

After reaching an understanding concerning the Museum's shares, the Texaco contingent moved on to a meeting with Gordon Getty at 9 P.M. on January 5. Getty had been advised by his investment banker that he should be a buyer of Getty at $110 per share and a seller at $120 or greater. After a number of conferences with various people, Getty agreed to sell the Trust's shares for $125 per share to Texaco. The Trust was also indemnified fully for any liability for breaching the Pennzoil agreement. However, no agreement could be signed immediately because of the California restraining order prohibiting Gordon Getty from signing formal merger documents.

On the morning of January 6, Getty's investment banker called Pennzoil's attorney to explain that Texaco had wrapped up the Museum's stock before they came to see Getty and that he had no choice but to go along.

4.11 Texaco Obtains the Approval of the Getty Oil Board

The Getty Oil board met at noon on January 6 to consider Texaco's offer. The directors were told that the Texaco/Museum stock purchase agreement had been signed and that Gordon Getty had agreed to the Texaco offer. The Texaco offer included full indemnities for Getty Oil's directors and officers, and Texaco agreed to honor all golden parachute contracts for the top nine senior executives.

The Board approved the Texaco offer at $125 per share. Getty Oil soon after issued a press release announcing the definitive merger agreement.

While in negotiations with the Museum, the Trust, and Getty Oil management between January 5 and January 8, Texaco read the Memorandum of Agreement signed by Pennzoil, the Trust, and the Museum. In addition, Texaco read the Getty press release.

4.12 California Litigation Revisited

On January 6, one of Gordon Getty's lawyers filed a corrected affidavit with the court indicating that a deal with Pennzoil had not in fact been agreed on.

The California injunction was lifted on January 8 and soon thereafter Getty executed the Texaco/Trustee stock exchange agreement.

4.13 The Litigation Begins

Shortly after signing the merger agreement Getty Oil began a suit in Delaware Chancery Court for a declaration that it had no agreement with Pennzoil.

On January 10, Pennzoil brought suit in Delaware Chancery Court against the various Getty parties seeking a decree of specific performance requiring the defendants to cause Pennzoil to receive its three sevenths interest. In the alternative, Pennzoil sought a judgment for compensatory damages of no less than $7 billion. A tortious interference with contract claim against Texaco was added 10 days later.

To succeed in its case, Pennzoil had the burden of demonstrating a number of points, including:

1. The reasonable probability that, upon a final hearing, it would be able to establish under New York law that a binding agreement had been actually entered into between it, the Trustee, the Museum and Getty.
2. That Texaco, with knowledge of Pennzoil's preexisting contractual rights, induced Getty, the Trustee and the Museum to renounce their contractual commitments.

The court reviewed applicable New York law concerning the formation of contracts in its decision. (All citations and references to citations omitted here.)

Indeed, it is well established that where parties reach an agreement they are bound by it, whatever its form and however it is manifested.

What is looked to in determining whether an agreement has been reached is not the parties' after-the-fact professed subjective intent, but their objective intent as manifested by their expressed words and deeds at the time. If the parties' expressions and conduct would lead a reasonable man to determine that they intended to reach a binding agreement, their agreement will be enforced. In determining whether the parties entered into a contractual agreement and what were its terms, disproportionate emphasis is not to be put on any single act, but, instead, on the totality of all of these, given the attendant circumstances, the situation of the parties, and the objectives they were striving to attain.

Moreover, while there is no enforceable agreement if the parties have not agreed on the essential terms, in New York and across the country a binding contract can be formed despite "material open issues." As the New York Court of Appeals held . . . "Under the Uniform Commercial Code [2–204(3)], if the parties have intended to contract, and if an appropriate remedy may be fashioned, a contract for sale does not fail for indefiniteness if terms, even important terms, are left open. . . . It is no longer true that dispute over material terms inevitably prevents formation of a binding contract. What is true . . . is that when a dispute over material terms manifests a lack of intention to contract, no contract results.

Thus, when there is basic agreement, however manifested and whether or not the precise moment of agreement may be determined, failure to articulate that agreement in the precise language of a lawyer, with every difficulty and contingency considered and resolved, will not prevent formation of a contract. . . .

It is recognized that if the parties intend not to be bound until they have executed a formal document embodying their agreement, they will not be bound until then. On the other hand the mere fact that the parties contemplate memorializing their agreement in a formal document does not prevent their less formal agreement from taking effect prior to that event.

As to the Statute of Frauds issue, it appears that New York has adopted the Uniform Commercial Code and at paragraph 8–319 it is provided that a contract for the sale of securities is not enforceable unless there is some writing signed by the party against whom the enforcement is sought which is sufficient to indicate that a contract has been made for the sale of a stated quantity of described securities at a defined or stated price.

At the same time, New York decisions hold that compliance with the Statute may be found if an agreement can be "pieced together out of separate writings," not all of which need be signed, provided that they clearly refer to the same transaction, include all the terms of the contract, and at least one of them bears the signature of the party to be charged "with the intent to authenticate the information contained therein and that such information does evidence the terms of the contract." In the latter case decision, one such writing that was considered in "piecing together" the evidence of an agreement was a press release concerning the acquisition of one company by another.[1]

The court also reviewed New York law concerning Pennzoil's tortious interference claim against Texaco. The court found that under New York law, Pennzoil was required to prove that:

1. It had a valid contract.
2. Texaco had "actual knowledge" of that contract.
3. Texaco intentionally induced a breach.
4. Pennzoil suffered damages.

On February 6, the Delaware Chancery Court denied Pennzoil's request for preliminary equitable relief. The court stated that Pennzoil had succeeded in showing the likelihood of a contract with the Getty parties but had failed to show the likelihood of proving a tortious interference by Texaco.

The court cited the following evidence in determining that Pennzoil would be able to establish at a full hearing that it had a contract:

1. The Getty board vote on the "Pennzoil proposal" coupled with Pennzoil's acceptance of that proposal.
2. Contemporaneous notes of the board meeting.
3. The press release.
4. The Memorandum of Agreement.
5. Other objective factors, including the statements in the California litigation, and the specific refusal of Getty, the Trustee and the Museum to warrant to Texaco that they had no contractual impediment with Pennzoil that would inhibit their ability to sell Getty shares to Texaco.

However, the court was not convinced that Pennzoil would be able to prove that the contract on which Pennzoil relied was enforceable. The agreement depended from the outset on fulfillment by the Trustee of his initial commitment. However, the Trustee refused to do so, claiming that his agreement with Pennzoil was subject to his fiduciary obligations, and the price offered by Texaco was sufficiently high that he deemed it his fiduciary duty to the Trust beneficiaries to sell the Trust's shares. If Pennzoil could not enforce the contract against its coventurer, how could it have a right against Getty, the Museum or the Trustee to become a three sevenths owner?

With respect to the tortious interference claim, the court could not conclude that Pennzoil would be likely to prove at a trial that Texaco knew of the existence of a contract or that Texaco intentionally set out to cause a breach of that contract. The court based its ruling on three factors:

1. Getty, the Museum and the Trustee repeatedly assured Texaco that they were free to deal.
2. Getty's investment banker first contacted Texaco and encouraged an offer for Getty, even after the press release.
3. The press release did describe an "agreement in principle" that was "subject to" the execution of a written merger agreement and other conditions, a representation that might well have indicated to one not privy to those negotiations that a final agreement had not been reached.

The court did note, however, that the evidence was such that its determination was a close call. In denying preliminary injunctive relief, the Delaware Chancellor relegated Pennzoil to a claim for money damages.

On February 8 Pennzoil dismissed its tortious interference action against Texaco in Delaware and brought suit in Texas, seeking actual and punitive damages. Some possible motives for this change of venue include:

1. Punitive damages are unavailable in Delaware.
2. The Delaware court's ruling indicated that it was unlikely that Pennzoil would prevail in Delaware.
3. Pennzoil might have believed that it would have a greater chance of success in the Texas courts.

On a number of occasions, Texaco and/or its indemnitees (the Trust, the Museum and the Board) asked the Delaware Chancery Court to delay or prohibit the prosecution of the Texas litigation. These efforts were denied. Texaco's indemnitees also sought summary judgment from the Chancery Court, which was denied.

4.14   The Texas Jury Trial

On July 9, 1985, a jury trial on Pennzoil's claims commenced in a state district court in Houston, Texas. Pennzoil's legal argument was based on the premise that this was a straightforward tortious interference with contract case. Overwhelming evidence existed to support a jury finding that the agreement between Pennzoil and the Getty entities was binding, that Texaco knowingly interfered with that agreement, and that actual and punitive damages could be awarded.

Pennzoil argued that the governing principles of New York law, which were to be applied in the case, were substantially the same as those of Texas: the controlling factual inquiry necessary to determine the existence of a contract is whether the parties intended to be bound. Intent to be bound is shown by:

1. The Memorandum of Agreement signed by Pennzoil and the majority shareholders of Getty Oil and allegedly approved by the Getty Board with a price sweetener.
2. The sequence of offer, counteroffer and acceptance reflected by documentary evidence and testimony.
3. Getty Oil's record of the critical January 2–3 board meeting.
4. The January 4 press release announcing the agreement to the world.

Pennzoil also argued that the agreement was sufficiently definite to be enforceable and that Texaco's knowledge of the Pennzoil agreement was demonstrated by:

1. Texaco's admitted knowledge of the Memorandum of Agreement and the January 4 press release.
2. Texaco's knowledge that the indemnities it gave to the Museum, the Trust and the Board were essential to its acquisition of Getty Oil.
3. The express refusal of the Museum and the Trust to warrant that the sale of their stock to Texaco was free of any obligation arising from the Pennzoil agreement.
4. Texaco's guarantee to the Museum of the agreed Pennzoil price, should Texaco fail for any reason to complete its acquisition.
5. Texaco's awareness of, or willful, intentional or bad faith refusal to ascertain, additional facts, including public confirmations of the Pennzoil agreement by the Trustee's representatives to a California court and the Getty Oil board notes, which reflect the board's approval of the Memorandum of Agreement with a price sweetener.

Texaco interfered with the Pennzoil agreement by:

1. Inducing the Museum with a higher price and a complete indemnity against Pennzoil.
2. Threatening to leave the Trust in the position of a locked-out minority shareholder if Gordon Getty did not renege on his obligation to Pennzoil by agreeing to the Texaco takeover.
3. Coupling the threat against the Trust with a complete indemnity to the Trust against Pennzoil; inducing the Getty Oil board with a higher price and a complete indemnity for any liability for breach of the Pennzoil agreement.

Texaco decided not to present evidence to rebut Pennzoil's damages claims. This approach proved disastrous.

The trial judge's charge to the jury was to become the cornerstone of the appeals that followed the verdict. Texaco would argue vehemently that the judge substantially misstated the applicable New York case law.

On November 19, 1985, the jury decided a $10.53 billion verdict in Pennzoil's favor against Texaco, finding unanimously that in January 1984 Pennzoil had a binding agreement with the board of directors and majority shareholders of Getty Oil Company to acquire three sevenths of Getty Oil at a fair price, that Texaco knowingly interfered with that agreement, that the interference caused Pennzoil actual damages of $7.53 billion, and that Pennzoil was entitled to receive an additional $3 billion in punitive damages because Texaco's conduct was intentional, willful and in wanton disregard of Pennzoil's rights.

On December 10, 1985, the trial judge entered judgment for Pennzoil based on the jury's verdict.

4.15   The Federal Court Appeals

Shortly before the judgment was entered by the trial court, Texaco filed suit against Pennzoil in U.S. District Court in White Plains, New York, asking the court to enjoin Pennzoil from attempting to attach liens on Texaco's property or otherwise begin execution of the judgment until Texaco had exhausted its appeal of the judgment through the Texas appellate courts and any appeal to the U.S. Supreme Court, and until the federal suit had been finally resolved.

The District Court issued the requested injunction, prompting Pennzoil to appeal to the U.S. Court of Appeals for the Second Circuit. The Second Circuit for the most part upheld the District Court's order, as Pennzoil continued to be enjoined from securing its judgment. Pennzoil appealed this decision to the U.S. Supreme Court, which agreed to consider the appeal.

In April 1987 the U.S. Supreme Court unanimously vacated as improper the District Court's order barring Pennzoil from securing the judgment, holding that the action of the District Court was an unwarranted and unprecedented intrusion into the Texas judicial system, contrary to governing principles of federalism and comity between state and federal courts; that the State of Texas has an important interest in enforcing the judgments of its courts; and that Texaco's claim that it could obtain no relief from the Texas courts, even though it never requested such relief, was plainly insufficient and incorrect.

4.16   The Court of Appeals in Houston

Meanwhile back in Texas, Texaco appealed the judgment to the Court of Appeals for the First Supreme Judicial District of Texas in Houston. Texaco's appeal sought to overturn the verdict principally on the basis of errors by the trial judge in applying New York law. Texaco's arguments are summarized below:

1. There was no contract. An agreement in principle, subject to the execution of a definitive agreement, is not a contract under New

York law. All the essential terms of an agreement had not been agreed on as of the end of the January 3 board meeting. The three directors who testified about the January 2–3 meetings indicated that there was no intent to be bound. Finally, the agreement alleged by Pennzoil would have been void under federal securities laws (SEC Rule 10b–13) and thus void under New York law.

2. Texaco did not have "actual knowledge" of the contract. New York law requires that a defendant actually know there was a valid contract. Getty Oil, the Museum and the Trust, who knew the facts at the time, told Texaco that there was no binding agreement. Had Pennzoil reached a binding contract, it would have been required under federal law to disclose that fact. The press release only indicated an agreement in principle, subject to the execution of a definitive agreement.

3. Texaco did not intentionally induce a breach. Under New York law a defendant who makes a bid after having been solicited cannot be held to have induced a breach.

4. Under New York law a plaintiff's damage claim for the lost opportunity to acquire stock is the difference between the contract price and the market price. This difference would result in maximum compensatory damages of about $500 million.

The Attorney General of the State of New York filed a friend-of-the-court brief with the Court of Appeals for the First Supreme Judicial District of Texas wherein the Attorney General argued as follows:

The tort of intentional interference with contractual relations is neither well established nor familiar to the general public. Therefore, given the extraordinary nature of this case, the trial judge should have expended special care in imparting what to the jury were unfamiliar waters: the purpose of the tort, the interests it seeks to protect, and its legal elements—all under the law of a distant state. . . .

More specifically, in view of all the circumstances—especially the disputed evidence regarding the existence, validity, and enforceability of Pennzoil's alleged interests—the jury should have been instructed that an agreement to agree or an oral contract for the sale of securities is only entitled to minimal protection from interference by competitors. Likewise, the trial judge should have instructed the jury that even if it found that Pennzoil possessed an enforceable contract with the Getty related entities, it could nonetheless find that Texaco's interference was not improper and did not subject it to liability. Because the jury charge failed to include these instructions and misstated numerous principles of New York law, the judgment of the trial court should be reversed.[2]

In February 1987 the Court of Appeals unanimously upheld the judgment in its entirety, on the condition that Pennzoil agree to remit $2 billion of the jury's punitive damages award.

4.17   Texaco Files Bankruptcy

On April 19, 1987, less than a week after the U.S. Supreme Court's decision vacating the District Court's order, Texaco and two of its wholly owned subsidiaries filed under Chapter 11 of the Bankruptcy Code.

4.18   The SEC and the Texas Supreme Court

Texaco applied to the Texas Supreme Court in June 1987 for a writ of error to appeal the action of the Court of Appeals.

On July 22, 1987, the Securities and Exchange Commission filed a friend-of-the-court brief with the Texas Supreme Court stating that the "contract" Pennzoil claims it had to purchase Getty Oil Company shares from the Getty entities violated federal securities law. It urged the Texas Supreme Court to review the case on the grounds that the alleged contract between Pennzoil and the Getty entities plainly violated Rule 10b–13, which is intended to protect shareholders by prohibiting those who have made public tender offers from negotiating more favorable private agreements with selected shareholders of a target company.

The Texas Supreme Court denied Texaco's application, finding that Texaco did not show error in the opinion of the Court of Appeals sufficient to require reversal.

4.19   The Texas Litigation: An Alternate View

There are a series of events, principally concerning the two judges that handled the trial, that some believe should lead to the conclusion that Texaco received less than a fair trial. To understand the relevance of these events, some background about Texas court procedure is necessary.

4.19a   Texas Court Procedure

Harris County, Texas, court procedures in effect when the case began required that a judge be assigned to preside at pretrial proceedings only (that is, up to the point when an action was determined to be "ready for trial"). Once a case was ready for trial it was transferred to a central calendar, where it became part of a list of cases awaiting assignment to one of the 25 district judges for Harris County for trial.

4.19b *Campaign Contributions*

A few months before Judge Anthony J. P. Farris, a Republican, was assigned to the case, Joseph Jamail, Pennzoil's counsel, contributed $100 to his reelection campaign. In March 1984, a few days after Judge Farris was assigned jurisdiction over all pretrial legal matters in the case, Jamail contributed $10,000 to his reelection campaign. At the time of this contribution Farris was running unopposed in the upcoming primary and no Democratic opponent had yet emerged. This campaign contribution was significantly larger than any contribution the judge had ever reported receiving.

Upon learning of the contribution, Texaco filed a motion to have Judge Farris removed from the case. The Honorable E. E. Jordan of Amarillo was assigned as a visiting judge to hear Texaco's motion. Judge Jordan decided that even though the Judicial Code of Ethics could be construed to suggest that Judge Farris should have been removed from the case, the Texas Constitution was controlling and it provided that a judge could be removed only if he had a direct financial interest in the outcome or if he were related to the litigants. "Mere bias," under Texas case law, is insufficient grounds to disqualify a judge. Judge Jordan found no evidence to remove the judge and so ordered.

Judge Farris's view of the contribution is contained in a letter to a Houston lawyer in December 1984, in which he indicated ". . . if Mr. Miller [Texaco's counsel] had come to me and told me how concerned he was about the Jamail contribution and the fact that I was presiding over the pretrial matters in the subject case, I would have recused myself . . . . Instead, Mr. Miller chose to go the other route. He found out about the Jamail contribution in August. He drew up his motion and attached the exhibits and *then* waited until five weeks before election day, filed the motion and provided copies to both the *Post* and the *Chronicle* simultaneously."[3]

It should be noted that Judge Farris's suggestion that Miller approach him privately would have been improper. After this incident, it is unlikely that Judge Farris could ever have been unbiased in his handling of the case.

Jamail also contributed $10,000 in early March 1984 to the campaign of Judge Peter Solito, the administrative judge for Harris County, Texas. This judge appears to have been in a position to influence the selection of (1) Judge Jordan, who heard Texaco's motion to disqualify Judge Farris, (2) Judge Farris to be the trial judge and (3) Judge Casseb, the judge who replaced Judge Farris in the final days of the trial.

4.19c   Change in Procedure Permits Farris to Be Trial Judge

Once the case was declared ready for trial, the calendar judge at that time set the case for trial on May 29, 1985, and made the reasonable suggestion that each side should identify those Harris County judges with whom they would feel comfortable, and if any names on the lists matched, he would try to have one of them available on May 29.

Before any such selection process could be implemented, Judge Solito convened a weekend meeting in mid-January to consider a proposal that the Harris County judges adopt the practice of assigning cases to a single judge who would preside over all stages of the case from the beginning. By a vote of 13 to 12, the judges approved the practice in principle, and set April 1 as the effective date for this yet-to-be-articulated case assignment procedure.

Many lawyers in Houston assumed that the new practice would be applicable to cases filed on or after April 1 and that pending cases would be assigned under existing procedures. However, Judge Farris reappeared in the case. It appears that Judge Solito was in a position to affect this decision.

4.19d   Under Texas Law Judge Casseb Was Not Permitted to Be Trial Judge

The trial began on July 1, 1985, with Judge Farris presiding. Fifteen weeks into the trial Judge Farris had to withdraw because of failing health. On October 28, 1985, Judge Solomon Casseb, Jr., replaced Judge Farris. The new judge's first action was to deny Texaco's motion for a mistrial based on the change in judges.

In May 1985, at the age of 69 years, 11 months, after more than 15 years had elapsed since serving as a judge in the Texas courts, Solomon Casseb volunteered to serve as a judge. On the form Judge Casseb completed in May 1985, he indicated that he was a "former judge." This document was subsequently altered to read "and am now a retired judge."

Texas law prescribed that there are no age restrictions on appointing "retired judges" to serve on the bench. However, "former judges" may not serve after their 70th birthday. To qualify as a retired judge, a judge had to be credited with 12 years of judicial and/or military service. An ex-judge with less service held the status of "former judge." Judge Casseb was assigned to the case after his 70th birthday.

Texaco attempted to have the verdict overturned on the basis that Casseb was ineligible to serve. However, no Texas court would even grant a hearing.

4.19e Judge Casseb Was Unfamiliar with New York Law

Judge Casseb, by his own admission, was unfamiliar with New York law. In a speech in Los Angeles in 1986, Judge Casseb admitted that he might have read the cases wrong and not applied New York law correctly, since it was his first attempt at trying to apply New York law.

4.19f Every Non-Texas Court Rejected Lack of Fairness Claim

Despite repeated attempts to have courts in other jurisdictions intervene, Texaco's claims of "judicial corruption" in the Texas courts were rejected by both Delaware and federal courts.

4.20 Holmes à Court Buys 13 Percent of Texaco

In the months following the bankruptcy filing, Robert Holmes à Court bought up approximately 13 percent of Texaco's stock. However, the stock market crash in October forced Holmes à Court to unload his shares.

4.21 Icahn Buys Holmes à Court's Stock

The buyer of Holmes à Court's shares was Carl Icahn. Icahn, in conjunction with another large Texaco shareholder, Robert Norris, worked with the creditors' committee in forcing through a settlement.

4.22 The Settlement and Payment

On December 19, 1987, Pennzoil and Texaco announced a proposed $3 billion settlement of the litigation, subject to approval of two thirds of Texaco's shareholders and confirmation by the bankruptcy court. The plan of reorganization was confirmed by the bankruptcy court on March 13, 1988, after being approved by Texaco's shareholders.

Texaco paid Pennzoil $3 billion on April 7, 1988.

Chapter 5

The Four Basic Questions

5.0 INTRODUCTION

There are four principal questions to address in reaching an informed judgment about a target operation's value:

- *Cost:* What will the acquisition cost?
- *Market Value:* What is the fair market value of the target?
- *Return:* What is the target worth to the prospective buyer? Another way to express this notion is, What is the maximum price the acquirer can pay and still achieve the desired rate of return on its investment?
- *Risk:* What is the probability of achieving the expected return?

This chapter sets forth how the book is organized to address these four basic questions and deals with various issues associated with each question.

5.1 BUYING A BUSINESS IS DIFFERENT!

How many times have you made purchases of products for either personal or business use? The obvious answer is thousands. Generally, for personal and some business purchases you physically examine the merchandise or interview the prospective service providers to form an opinion as to value. For more important business purchases you collect information about available alternatives, including their costs and benefits, both financial and nonfinancial. The information you collect takes many forms, including comparative bids, internal studies, research reports or capital budgeting analyses.

In all of these situations a person can achieve a high level of comfort concerning the value of the good or service being purchased. Why? The cost of the good or service and the expected returns and risks can be identified. In addition, what other individuals or companies think about the value of a particular product or service does not directly affect your decision making process. The seller of the good or service sets the price based on overall market conditions.

However, if you are contemplating an acquisition of a business, you should understand that the cost, market value, return, and risk questions are much more complex than in this "standard purchase situation."

5.2   THE COST QUESTION

In evaluating an acquisition there are alternative ways of effecting an acquisition, each having tax ramifications that are beyond comprehension for most CEOs in any reasonable time frame. The worst thing that a CEO can do in this instance is to force the acquisition decision into the standard purchase mold of "we will pay you $X for your company" and think that $X represents the true cost of acquiring the target.

For example, let us assume that a company is purchasing two production lines, one from the manufacturer and the other by purchasing the stock of a competitor that has comparable equipment. In the first case, the company will be able to take full depreciation deductions for U.S. tax purposes over the appropriate economic life of the equipment. However, in the second case, the company may be unable to take full depreciation deductions for U.S. tax purposes. Thus, even though the CEO paid the same absolute dollar amount in both cases, the after-tax costs of acquiring the production lines are very different.

The standard purchase situation applies only if the acquiring company is making one particular type of acquisition—an Asset Acquisition. However, there are six other methods of consummating a deal. A brief description of each of the seven methods appears below. Detailed descriptions of each method and their variations appear in Chapter 7.

- *Asset Acquisition:* In an Asset Acquisition, the acquiring company purchases part or all of the assets of the target company for cash, stock, securities, or other consideration. Payment is made to the target company, which continues in existence after the transaction. Generally, the transaction is a taxable sale by the target company of its assets. In addition, as a general rule, if the target company liquidates, the company's shareholders will pay a second tax on any gain associated with the assets distributed to them.

- *338 Transaction:* The acquiring company purchases the stock of the target from the target's shareholders for cash, stock, securities, or other consideration and elects pursuant to Section 338 of the *Internal Revenue Code of 1986, as amended (IRC)* by the 15th day of the ninth month after the month of acquisition to treat the transaction as if the target company sold its assets for a price equal to their fair market value. This transaction is a taxable sale by the target company of its assets, as well as a taxable sale by the target's shareholders of their stock.

- *338(h)(10) Transaction:* This transaction is a variation of the 338 Transaction that can be used when the target company is a member of an affiliated group that files a consolidated federal tax return. In this transaction, the tax burden associated with the target's asset sale is shifted from the target company to the selling group. This shift is advantageous in certain limited circumstances.

- *Stock Acquisition:* The acquiring company purchases the stock of the target for cash, stock, securities, or other consideration. This transaction is a taxable sale of their stock by the target's shareholders.

- *Type A Reorganization:* In a Type A Reorganization, the acquiring company purchases the target through merger or consolidation. The acquiring company pays for the acquisition by exchanging various consideration—voting or nonvoting common or preferred stock, cash, securities, or other consideration. Any combination of these kinds of consideration is acceptable as long as greater than 50 percent of the total consideration paid is some form of equity security. The transaction is nontaxable to all parties if only equity securities are used by the acquiring company. If cash, securities, or other consideration are exchanged, the target's shareholders will be taxed to some extent. (Note: For tax purposes, this cash, securities, or other consideration received by the seller is called "boot.")

- *Type B Reorganization:* In a Type B Reorganization, the acquiring company uses its own voting stock to purchase the stock of the target. The transaction is nontaxable to all parties involved.

- *Type C Reorganization:* In a Type C Reorganization, the acquiring company purchases substantially all of the target company's assets with its own voting stock. In certain instances, the acquiring company can give as part of the consideration a minor amount of cash, nonvoting stock, securities, or other consideration. Generally, this transaction is nontaxable to all parties, except if boot is received by the seller.

As mentioned above, each of these acquisition methods can produce a different economic cost. This causes problems when, as all too often happens in acquisitions, the CEO reaches an agreement in principle with the seller as to the purchase price and the method of acquisition before having the company's tax counsel review the transaction. This situation is typical because (a) the buyer is looking to cut a deal and (b) the seller knows its tax situation extremely well and starts all discussions stating that it wants the transaction effected using a particular acquisition method, which just happens to minimize taxes for the seller.

Section Two of the book is devoted to exploring the issues described above that are associated with the "cost" question in acquisitions. The Cost Analysis section describes a methodology for producing information on the real cost of effecting a transaction at various purchase prices using different acquisition methods. Failure to wait for the completion of this analysis will often result in the decision maker having to backtrack in negotiations as he learns of the economic burden of consummating the deal in a certain manner. Cost Analysis starts with the acquisition method that is easiest to understand—the Asset Acquisition. All other transactions are then related to it.

5.3   AN EXAMPLE

Section Three is devoted to analyzing in detail a realistic example using the Cost Analysis described in Section Two. In addition, this example is used extensively in Sections Four and Five.

5.4   THE MARKET VALUE QUESTION

Fair market value is defined by the IRS as "the price at which a property would change hands between a willing buyer and willing seller, neither being under any compulsion to buy or to sell, and both having reasonable knowledge of the facts." In the majority of purchase decisions the fair market value of the good or service being sold has been determined over numerous transactions. This is also true, in a macroeconomic sense, with regard to pricing acquisition transactions. However, in a transaction involving a business, the market value of the target is often not well defined, principally because the market can be very thin, with only a handful of potential buyers.

It is difficult to determine the market value of a company for several other reasons. Chapter 1 illustrated that value is in the eye of the beholder. Value depends on who a prospective buyer is and what knowledge the buyer possesses. Furthermore, value also depends on the process that will be used to realize value. Finally, valuation is difficult because each company is one of a kind. Valuing a company is a little like valuing a piece of art; no other property is exactly like it.

Despite the difficulties, a prospective buyer must undertake an analysis to determine the proper valuation range for the target. How does one go about undertaking such an analysis? No single approach will yield the desired answer. However, a variety of valuation techniques, used in tandem, will provide a reasonable estimate of the target's fair market value range. Brief descriptions of these valuation techniques appear below:

- *Analysis of Stock Price and Volume History:* This valuation technique involves analyzing the stock trading range of the target over various time frames. The stock price performance of the target is analyzed against (a) broad market indices such as the Dow Jones Industrial Average, the S&P 400 and selected composite indices, and (b) comparable companies' stock price performances.
- *Comparable Company Analysis:* Comparable Company Analysis involves evaluating the target against all comparable public companies. *Comparable companies* are those that operate in the same or similar industries. The analysis compares all vital financial statistics for the target and comparable companies both in absolute dollars and indexed amounts. These statistics would include (a) the market value of each company's stock as a multiple of the book value of common stockholders' equity, (b) the total market value of each company's capitalization as a multiple of its last 12-months' sales, (c) the total market value of each company's capitalization as a multiple of total assets, and (d) each company's price/earnings multiple.

  Comparable Company Analysis can be used to determine the feasibility of selling all or part of the company to the public, as well as the likely public valuation of an operation, assuming it were spun off to the company's shareholders. It can also be used in connection with valuing a company that is for sale. If Comparable Company Analysis is used in this manner, a Change of Control

Premium must be added to the public market values to arrive at an estimated valuation range for the company. A *Change of Control Premium* is the premium over a target company's current stock market value required to entice a sufficient number of target company shareholders to sell enough equity securities at the same time to a purchaser that the purchaser obtains control of the target company. See Exhibit 2–18.

- *Comparable Transactions Analysis:* Comparable Transactions Analysis involves analyzing all transactions involving companies in the target company's industry or similar industries over the last several years. Acquisition multiples are calculated for all such transactions, to the extent that data is available. These multiples are then applied to the target company's financial results to estimate a value range for the target. This valuation approach requires a great deal of judgment in choosing comparable transactions and analyzing the results.

   Acquisition multiples calculated and analyzed include (a) the market value of the company's stock as a multiple of the book value of common stockholders' equity, (b) the total market value of the company's capitalization as a multiple of its last 12-months' sales, (c) the total market value of the company's capitalization as a multiple of total assets, and (d) the company's price/earnings multiple.

- *Analysis of M&A Market Multiples:* This valuation technique involves analyzing the current broad M&A market acquisition multiples and Change of Control Premiums being paid. The analysis should also include a longer-term trend analysis in acquisition multiples and Change of Control Premiums. This valuation technique is relied on only if there are no worthwhile comparable transactions or comparable companies.

- *Discounted Cash Flow (DCF) Analysis:* DCF Analysis is an important valuation technique for determining the market value of the target company. However, it is the most important valuation technique for estimating the value of a company to an individual acquirer.

   There are two DCF approaches, *Net Present Value (NPV) Analysis* and *Internal Rate of Return (IRR) Analysis:* NPV Analysis involves estimating the value of a business by forecasting the future cash flows the business is expected to produce and discounting those cash flows back to the present using a rate that reflects the risk associated with the cash flows. IRR Analysis involves determining the discount rate that results in the present value of the future cash flows being equal to the acquisition cost of the target.

- *Strategic Buyer DCF Analysis:* This valuation technique is used if there is a readily identified strategic buyer for the target company. In many cases, this strategic buyer has publicly expressed an interest in acquiring the target company because it would fit well with the buyer's existing operations. The valuation technique involves estimating the most likely cash flow forecast for this strategic buyer, including any expected synergies. This cash flow forecast is used to calculate the range of values the strategic buyer could pay.

- *Leveraged Buyout (LBO) Analysis:* LBO Analysis is completed whenever a target is a potential candidate for an LBO. The goal of this valuation technique is to determine the highest likely value that a management led LBO group could pay for the company, using estimated financial projections for the target that management would prepare for an LBO of the company. The value that can be achieved in an LBO often sets the floor price for the target company. In addition, it may also set the upper value for the target company if a corporate buyer cannot be located or does not exist.

    The primary distinction between LBO Analysis and DCF Analysis is that LBO Analysis incorporates financing for the LBO.

- *Leveraged ESOP (LESOP) Analysis:* An *employee stock ownership plan (ESOP)* is a defined benefit plan designed to invest primarily in employer stock. An ESOP can be structured to purchase a controlling interest in a company. Generally, the funds required to effect the purchase of a controlling interest come from two sources: (1) equity provided by the company's employees, and (2) debt financing raised by leveraging the equity provided by the company's employees. This type of transaction is called a *Leveraged ESOP (LESOP)* or alternatively, an *ESOP LBO.*

    The easiest way to think about a LESOP is as a tax-advantaged LBO. Hence, LESOP Analysis is a variation of LBO Analysis that requires the substitution of lower cost ESOP related debt financing for some of the traditional financing in an LBO.

- *Leveraged Recapitalization (Recap) Analysis:* Recap Analysis is a valuation technique aimed at determining the maximum value that a public company can deliver to its shareholders today. Generally, Recap Analysis is undertaken in the context of a probable or pending hostile offer for the target. The value delivered in a Recap sets the minimum value the target company's shareholders will realize in this context.

In Recap Analysis an assumption is made that the target company wants to maintain its independence at all costs and will stretch to the maximum extent possible to recapitalize the company. Value in a Recap is typically delivered in two ways: (1) a massive stock buy-back or dividend of cash and/or securities, and (2) a continuing equity interest (*Stub Equity*) in a highly leveraged company.

If a target company operates in a number of businesses, an effective Recap Analysis can only be done after a complete valuation analysis of each of the target's business units.

- *Breakup Analysis:* Breakup Analysis is a valuation technique that must be employed if a target company operates in a number of different businesses. It involves estimating the market value of each of the target's constituent businesses (using the other techniques described herein) and totaling these individual values to arrive at a value for the entire company.

  It is typical in Breakup Analysis for the total value of the target to be compared to one of two values: (1) the estimated acquisition cost of the company, or (2) the current total market capitalization of the company (assuming the target is a public company). Which yardstick to measure the total breakup value of the company against depends on whether (1) the entity performing the analysis is a potential acquirer or the target company, and (2) the target is currently the subject of a takeover bid or speculation.

- *Other Valuation Techniques:* Other techniques for valuing companies include: Dividend Discount Analysis, Capitalization of Earnings, Capitalization of Excess Earnings, Book Value Analysis, Unit-of-Capacity Analysis, Liquidation Analysis, Replacement Cost Analysis and Greenfield Plant Analysis.

Importance of Changes in Business Strategies   In all of the valuation techniques described above it is *essential* to understand the alternate operating strategies that *can be* or *should be* used for the target company's businesses. Reviewing these alternate strategies must be an integral part of the evaluation of the target's overall business.

5.5   VALUE TO THE ACQUIRER ISSUE

One of the traps that managers fall into when pricing transactions is to focus on the market value of the target as the key determinant in their pricing decision. The valuation techniques described above are effective in determining the value range for a target company. However, they should not be determinative with respect to what you should bid. Each prospective bidder should be guided by the technique that mirrors its goals.

Generally, if the acquirer is a hostile acquirer, Breakup Analysis will provide the required guidance. Alternatively, if the acquirer is an LBO firm, LBO Analysis will be determinative. Finally, corporate acquirers should generally be guided by DCF Analysis.

5.6   DCF AND LBO MODELS

The risk and return questions are best addressed in the context of a detailed acquisition model that incorporates all of the key business variables. Section Five contains chapters that describe detailed DCF and LBO models that incorporate the tax considerations described in Section Two.

5.7   INVESTMENT RETURN AND RISK QUESTIONS

Section Six brings together the results of the valuation techniques described in Sections Four and Five. These results are depicted in summary market valuation and value to the acquirer schedules.

The topic of risk is also covered in Section Six. An important part of analyzing the risk of any proposed transaction is reviewing the sensitivity of the investment returns to changes in (1) operating scenarios, and (2) key individual operating or financing variables. Section Five outlines how to undertake these analyses.

In addition, the impact of the acquisition on the acquiring company's liquidity and overall financial strength must be reviewed. Although the acquiring company may be financially able to consummate the transaction today, what will the acquirer's balance sheet look like a year or two from now, within the context of the acquiring company's and target company's respective financial forecasts? Two acquisitions that had disastrous results because of management's failure to adequately analyze the impact of the acquiring company's liquidity and overall financial strength were Wickes Cos.' acquisition of Gamble-Skogmo and Baldwin United Corporation's purchase of Mortgage Guaranty Insurance Corporation. These companies were forced into bankruptcy proceedings as a direct result of the acquisitions.

The book concludes with a chapter that discusses the importance of the seller's motivation to sell, due diligence and timing. The final chapter also offers some advice on pitfalls to avoid in analyzing acquisitions.

Section One

Conclusion

Section One introduced a variety of merger and acquisition topics including the subjective nature of valuation, a description of the overall merger and acquisition marketplace including volume and pricing trends, the key factors that will affect successful investing in the 1990s, the issue of contract formation, and the concept of tortious interference with a contract. Section One closed with a chapter that outlined how the book is organized to address the four basic valuation questions: (1) What will an acquisition cost? (2) What is the fair market value of the target? (3) What is the value of the target to the acquirer? (4) What is the risk associated with the acquisition?

Section Two

Cost Analysis

Section Two

Introduction

Section Two is devoted to answering the question, "What will an acquisition cost?" The section consists of Chapters 6 through 9. In Chapter 6 we explore some basic concepts of acquisition cost, including the importance of the tax basis of assets and the categorization of the various acquisition methods. Chapter 7 describes those acquisition methods and their tax treatment. Chapter 8 lays out a theoretical framework for calculating the real economic cost and proceeds in a transaction and contains a review of the nontax factors that influence the buyer and seller. Finally, Chapter 9 proposes an analytical approach for comparing the costs and proceeds under different acquisition methods and purchase prices.

Chapter 6

Fundamental M&A
Tax Concepts

6.0 INTRODUCTION

The purpose of this chapter is to highlight the economic importance of
the tax basis of the target business's assets and categorize the seven
acquisition methods according to how they handle this issue. Furthermore, this chapter explores the difference between taxable and nontaxable acquisition methods and the distinctions between stock and asset
deals.

6.1 ECONOMICS OF THE TAX BASIS OF ASSETS

The importance of the tax basis of the target business's assets can be
understood by discussing some examples. However, before turning to
these examples, it is worthwhile to review some basic tax concepts.
Generally, a corporation's or individual's *tax basis* in any property is equal
to its original cost, while the *adjusted tax basis* of property is equal to its
original cost adjusted for certain items. An example of a common adjustment for fixed assets is depreciation, and a common adjustment for
stock is dividends paid.

> ***Example 6A*** *ABC Corporation commenced manufacturing operations
> in 1983 and over several years purchased land, buildings, and machines A and B.*

On December 31, 1992, the company owned property, land and equipment recorded for tax purposes as indicated below.

Tax Basis and Fair Market Values of Selected Assets

	Cost	Accumulated Depreciation	Adjusted Tax Basis	Assumed Fair Market Value	Difference
Land	$ 50.0	$ 0.0	$ 50.0	$110.0	$ 60.0
Buildings and improvements	150.0	30.0	120.0	180.0	60.0
Machine A	100.0	80.0	20.0	10.0	(10.0)
Machine B	200.0	150.0	50.0	300.0	250.0
	$500.0	$260.0	$240.0	$600.0	$360.0

XYZ Corporation is considering purchasing ABC. If the tax basis of the assets is unchanged in the acquisition of ABC, the acquiring company must continue to depreciate the adjusted tax basis of the buildings and improvements and the machines. Furthermore, these assets must be depreciated using the depreciation methods and useful lives in effect when the assets were placed in service. However, if the tax basis of the assets is changed to reflect their fair market values, the acquiring company can take MACRS depreciation deductions based on these fair market values. (See Appendix paragraph B.71 for a description of MACRS depreciation.)

Let us see what this means over the initial five-year period. We will assume that the buildings and improvements are currently being depreciated for tax purposes using straight-line depreciation and will be fully depreciated in 12 more years, and the machinery will be fully depreciated over the next 2 years. We will disregard for this example the effects of depreciation recapture or any loss limitations. (See paragraph B.126 for a discussion of Built-in Losses.)

Depreciation Deductions Assuming No Change in Basis

	1993	1994	1995	1996	1997
Buildings and improvements	$10.0	$10.0	$10.0	$10.0	$10.0
Machine A	10.0	10.0			
Machine B	25.0	25.0			
Total deductions	$45.0	$45.0	$10.0	$10.0	$10.0

MACRS Depreciation Deductions Assuming New Basis[*]

	Fair Market Value	MACRS Class of Property	1993	1994	1995	1996	1997
Buildings and improvements	$180.0	31.5 yr.	$ 5.5	$ 5.7	$ 5.7	$ 5.7	$ 5.7
Machine A	10.0	5 yr.	2.0	3.2	1.9	1.2	1.2
Machine B	300.0	5 yr.	60.0	96.0	57.6	34.6	34.6
Total deductions	$490.0		$67.5	$104.9	$65.2	$41.4	$41.4

[*] Depreciation deductions calculated using depreciation rates in Exhibits B–6 and B–8.

Comparative Analysis of Difference in Depreciation Deductions

	1993	1994	1995	1996	1997
No change in basis	$45.0	$ 45.0	$10.0	$10.0	$10.0
New basis	67.5	104.9	65.2	41.4	41.4
Difference	(22.5)	(59.9)	(55.2)	(31.4)	(31.4)
Assumed tax rate	38%	38%	38%	38%	38%
After-tax difference	($8.5)	($22.8)	($21.0)	($11.9)	($11.9)
Net present value at 10%	($57.9)				

If we assume a 10 percent discount rate, the present value of the difference in after-tax cost for the two alternative approaches is $58. Given that the assumed total market value of the assets is $600, this figure represents approximately 10 percent of the fair market value of the assets.

It should be noted that because of significant inflation in the U.S. during the 1970s and 1980s, a large difference between the fair market value of assets and their adjusted tax basis is the norm rather than the exception.

Example 6B   *Same facts as Example 6A except the company's assets are valued at below their adjusted tax basis. We will also continue to disregard depreciation recapture and any loss limitations issues.*

Tax Basis and Fair Market Values of Selected Assets

	Cost	Accumulated Depreciation	Adjusted Tax Basis	Assumed Fair Market Value	Difference
Land	$ 50.0	$ 0.0	$ 50.0	$ 40.0	($10.0)
Buildings and improvements	150.0	30.0	120.0	90.0	(30.0)
Machine A	100.0	80.0	20.0	15.0	(5.0)
Machine B	200.0	150.0	50.0	40.0	(10.0)
	$500.0	$260.0	$240.0	$185.0	($55.0)

In this example it is fairly obvious that the acquiring company will get larger depreciation deductions if it uses an acquisition method that does not change the tax basis of the assets of the acquired business. The calculations that substantiate this notion are as follows:

MACRS Depreciation Deductions Assuming New Basis[*]

	Fair Market Value	MACRS Class of Property	1993	1994	1995	1996	1997
Buildings and improvements	$ 90.0	31.5 yr.	$ 2.7	$ 5.7	$ 5.7	$ 5.7	$ 5.7
Machine A	15.0	5 yr.	3.0	4.8	2.9	1.7	1.7
Machine B	40.0	5 yr.	8.0	12.8	7.7	4.6	4.0
Total deductions	$145.0		$13.7	$23.3	$16.3	$12.1	$12.1

[*] Depreciation deductions calculated using depreciation rates in Exhibits B–6 and B–8.

Comparative Analysis of Difference in Depreciation Deductions

	1993	1994	1995	1996	1997
No change in basis	$45.0	$45.0	$10.0	$10.0	$10.0
New basis	13.7	23.3	16.3	12.1	12.1
Difference	31.3	21.7	(6.3)	(2.1)	(2.1)
Assumed tax rate	38%	38%	38%	38%	38%
After-tax difference	$11.9	$8.2	($2.4)	($0.8)	($0.8)
Net present value at 10%	$14.8				

If we assume a 10 percent discount rate, the present value of the difference in after-tax cost for the two alternative categories of acquisition methods is $15. Given that the total value of the assets purchased is $185, the difference in the after-tax cost of the two alternate approaches represents a significant 8 percent.

The message that the two examples is trying to convey should be clear. There is real economic significance in the choice between an acquisition method that results in a new tax basis for the target's assets and one that does not.

6.2   TWO CATEGORIES OF ACQUISITION METHODS

Generally, the tax basis of the acquired business's assets is the tax consideration with the most significant economic consequences for an acquiring corporation in the U.S. Therefore, the various acquisition methods are categorized as to how they handle this consideration. The seven acquisition methods are divided into two categories: (1) New Cost Basis Acquisition Methods, and (2) No Change in Basis Acquisition Methods. Chapter 7 explores these acquisition methods in detail.

	Paragraph
New Cost Basis Acquisition Methods:	7.1
Asset Acquisition	7.11
338 Transaction	7.12
338(h)(10) Transaction	7.13
No Change in Basis Acquisition Methods:	7.2
Stock Acquisition	7.21
Type A Reorganization	7.22
Type B Reorganization	7.23
Type C Reorganization	7.24

6.3 LEGAL AND TAX FRAMEWORK

Even though we have identified the tax basis of the target's assets as the consideration that will drive our economic analysis, we must be cognizant of the legal and tax classifications of the various acquisition methods. The matrix below indicates that acquisitions fall into three broad legal categories that represent alternative legal forms for effecting a transaction, and can be characterized as either taxable or nontaxable transactions. The characterization of a transaction as taxable or nontaxable relates solely to the taxability of the transaction to the selling corporation in the case of an asset deal or to the selling shareholders in a stock transaction.

EXHIBIT 6–1
U.S. Acquisition Methods within Legal and Tax Framework

		Tax	
		Taxable Acquisition	Nontaxable Acquisition
	Acquisition of Assets	Asset Acquisition	Type C Reorganization
Legal	Statutory Merger or Consolidation	Asset Acquisition Stock Acquisition	Type A Reorganization
	Acquisition of Stock	Stock Acquisition 338 Transaction 338(h)(10) Transaction	Type B Reorganization

6.31 Legal Forms for Effecting a Transaction

Shareholders who are looking to sell their company can effect a transaction in three ways. They can (1) arrange for the company to sell its assets to the acquiring company, (2) effect a statutory merger or consolidation, or (3) sell their stock.

In an *Asset Acquisition* the acquiring company purchases a part or all of the assets of the target company. An Asset Acquisition requires that each asset and liability acquired be separately conveyed. For example, if a company sold all its assets, which consisted primarily of land and buildings, separate legal documents would have to be prepared transferring each parcel of property. This requirement makes an Asset Acquisition more complicated than a Stock Acquisition, which merely requires the transfer of stock.

Negotiations in an Asset Acquisition are conducted between the managements of the acquiring and target companies. Payment for the assets acquired is made to the target company. The target company remains in existence after the transaction, and stock ownership of the target company is unaffected. However, often the target company is liquidated after such a sale to place the proceeds of the sale in the hands of the target's shareholders.

If an Asset Acquisition involves the sale of all or substantially all of the assets of the target many states require that the target company's board of directors and shareholders approve the transaction.

A *Statutory Merger* occurs when two or more corporations combine in such a way that one of the combining corporations remains in existence while the other participating corporation(s) disappear. Statutory mergers are effected pursuant to state merger statutes. All states have enacted such statutes into their general corporation laws.

Example 6C   *ABC Corporation is merged into XYZ Corporation. ABC Corporation disappears, and XYZ Corporation is the surviving corporation.*

A *Consolidation* is effected when two or more corporations are combined into a new corporation. The new corporation sometimes comes into existence by operation of law and sometimes it must be formed. Applicable state law determines which rule is operative.

Example 6D   *ABC Corporation and XYZ Corporation are combined in a statutory consolidation. Both ABC and XYZ disappear, and an entirely new corporation results (assuming that it is formed by operation of law).*

In a *Stock Acquisition* the acquiring company buys the stock of the target company from the individual shareholders of the target company. When the target company is a wholly owned subsidiary, the sole stockholder is the parent company. However, in cases where the target is a public company, the acquiring company must deal with a large group of shareholders. Typically, the acquiring company addresses these stockholders by making a tender offer. The Securities and Exchange Commission promulgates rules and regulations governing such tender offers. See Appendix E.

Although a Stock Acquisition occurs between the acquiring company and the target company's shareholders, the target company's board of directors is directly involved in negotiating the form and terms of the transaction.

6.32 Taxable versus Nontaxable Deals

Whether a deal is taxable or nontaxable in the U.S. depends on various IRC provisions. Certain basic concepts must be understood before one can address these complex provisions. The amount that a taxpayer realizes on the sale of any property is equal to the fair market value of all property received. The amount of gain or loss that a taxpayer "realizes" on the sale of property is computed by deducting the adjusted basis of the property sold from the amount realized. As mentioned previously, a taxpayer's original tax basis in any property is equal to its cost, while the adjusted basis of the property is equal to its original cost adjusted for certain items.

The fact that a gain or loss is realized on a sale does not necessarily mean that a gain or loss will have current tax consequences. The gain or loss must be "recognized" to have current tax effects. The general rule under the present tax code is that all realized gains or losses will be recognized. Acquisition transactions effected under this general rule are labeled *Taxable Transactions.* The tax code also contains special provisions that defer the recognition of gain or loss until some future act triggers tax recognition of the gain or loss. Transactions effected under these provisions are characterized as *Nontaxable Transactions.*

The theory behind deferring the recognition of gain or loss in tax-free transactions is that the shareholder is merely changing the form of his investment or exchanging stock in one company for stock in another. Both before and after the transaction, the stockholder has retained his investment in the business, so the stockholder should not be taxed. This is why the tax-free acquisition provisions are called *Reorganization Provisions.* Philosophically, they involve reorganizations, not acquisitions.

For a transaction to be a nontaxable reorganization, it must fit within one of the types of reorganizations described in the tax code. Each of these types of reorganizations has detailed requirements that are outlined in the next chapter. However, all reorganizations have certain general requirements that must also be met for a transaction to qualify as a tax-free reorganization. These general requirements have been created judicially to deny tax-free status to transactions that do not comply with the spirit of the reorganization provisions, although they satisfy the requirements of one of the tax-free provisions. They include (a) the Continuity of Interest Doctrine, (b) the Continuity of Business Enterprise

Doctrine, (c) the Business Purpose Doctrine, and (d) the Step Transaction Doctrine.[1]

6.32a   Continuity of Interest Doctrine

The *Continuity of Interest Doctrine* requires that the shareholders of the target company obtain a continuing equity interest in the acquiring corporation. This has been interpreted to mean that a substantial portion of the consideration moving from the acquiring corporation must be in the form of an equity interest in the acquiring corporation.

Although the doctrine applies to all types of reorganizations, the Continuity of Interest Doctrine has the most meaning in the context of a Type A Reorganization because specific statutory requirements cover the types of permissible consideration in the other types of reorganizations. Based on case precedent, it appears that if the equity consideration paid by the acquiring corporation in a Type A Reorganization is less than 20 percent of the total consideration paid, tax-free treatment will probably be disallowed. Conversely, if the equity consideration is greater than 50 percent, there should not be any problem with the Continuity of Interest Doctrine. Between 20 and 50 percent is a gray area where it is unclear how a particular case might be decided if it were fully litigated.

The Continuity of Interest Doctrine must be applied within the framework of any pre-reorganization and post-reorganization transactions. If stock is sold by the target company's shareholders to the acquiring company or the target company redeems some of its stock prior to the tax-free reorganization, these transactions will generally be considered in determining whether the Continuity of Interest test has been met. If stockholders of the target dispose of the entire equity interest received from the acquiring corporation promptly after the tax-free reorganization, this would normally disqualify the tax-free nature of the transaction. A difficult question is how long the target company's shareholders must hold onto the equity interest received to preserve the tax-free nature of the transaction. The IRS considers a five-year holding period sufficient for continuity of interest purposes, although a shorter time should be adequate, especially if there is a substantial change in the taxpayer's position.

6.32b   Continuity of Business Enterprise Doctrine

The *Continuity of Business Enterprise Doctrine* requires that the acquiring company must either continue the target company's historic business or at least one significant line of business, or use a significant portion of the target company's assets in its ongoing business. The target company's *historic business* is defined as the business it conducted immediately preceding the plan of reorganization. Basically, if the acquiring company sells the target company's assets and discontinues all of its lines of business, the Continuity of Business Enterprise test will not be met and the transaction will be a taxable event to the target company's shareholders.

6.32c   Business Purpose Doctrine

The *Business Purpose Doctrine* requires that every reorganization must have a legitimate business purpose. This doctrine does not present problems for transactions between unrelated parties.

6.32d   Step Transaction Doctrine

The *Step Transaction Doctrine* requires that the tax treatment of a transaction carried out in a series of steps follow the economic substance of the transaction, rather than its form. For example, if a series of transactions entered into includes a tax-free reorganization, the transactions may be viewed as one taxable transaction. A number of factors come into play in determining whether a series of steps should be integrated, including the time between transactions, the intent of the parties, and the extent to which the transactions are linked.

Chapter 7

Alternate
Acquisition Methods

7.0 INTRODUCTION

The seven basic acquisition methods are introduced in this chapter. These methods are grouped into two categories—*New Cost Basis Acquisition Methods* and *No Change in Basis Acquisition Methods*. If a transaction is completed using a New Cost Basis Acquisition Method, the acquiring company generally obtains a tax basis in the target's operating assets equal to their fair market values. In contrast, if a deal is consummated using a No Change in Basis Acquisition Method, the acquiring company's tax basis in the underlying operating assets is unchanged. For tax purposes this treatment is called *carryover basis*.

The discussion of each acquisition method includes a general introduction that describes the method followed by subsections analyzing (1) the treatment of the acquirer, in which the various tax consequences of the acquisition to the acquiring corporation are discussed; and (2) the treatment of the target, in which the tax consequences of the acquisition to the selling corporation or the selling shareholders are reviewed.

7.1 NEW COST BASIS ACQUISITION METHODS

There are three basic acquisition methods that result in a new cost basis for the acquiring company. These three methods are (1) an *Asset Acquisition*, (2) a stock transaction treated as an Asset Acquisition (hereafter called a *338 Transaction*) and (3) a *338(h)(10) Transaction*, a variation of a 338 Transaction.

Each New Cost Basis Acquisition Method requires that values be allocated to specific assets and liabilities in the same manner.

7.11   Asset Acquisition

There are three types of Asset Acquisition: (1) a straightforward *Asset Acquisition*, (2) a *Forward Merger*, and (3) a *Forward Subsidiary Merger* (also called a *Forward Triangular Merger*).

7.11a   In General

1. *Asset Acquisition:* In a straightforward Asset Acquisition the acquiring company purchases part or all of the target company's assets. The acquiring company pays cash or other consideration such as stock, bonds or other assets to the target company. After the acquisition the target company remains in existence. However, the target company often liquidates to place the proceeds of the sale in the hands of its shareholders.

Example 7A   *XYZ Corporation purchases all of the assets of ABC Corporation in an Asset Acquisition for $1,000. The target intends to take the proceeds from the sale and enter a new business.*

Asset Acquisition

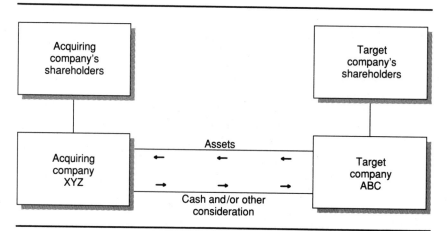

2. *Forward Merger:* A Forward Merger occurs when the target corporation merges into the acquiring company. For tax purposes, the target (merged) corporation is considered to have exchanged its assets for consideration received (i.e., cash, notes, stock). The target is deemed liquidated and distributes the consideration received to its shareholders in exchange for their target corporation stock.

Example 7B *Target ABC Corporation is merged into XYZ Corporation. ABC Corporation disappears by operation of law and XYZ Corporation survives. For tax purposes, ABC is considered to have exchanged its assets for the consideration received (i.e., cash, notes, etc.) and distributed such consideration to its shareholders in exchange for their ABC stock.*

Forward Merger

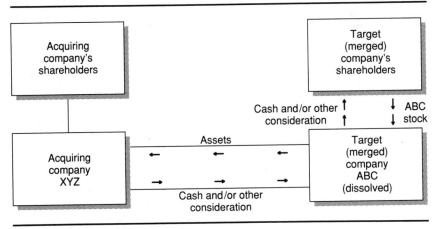

3. *Forward Subsidiary Merger:* In a Forward Subsidiary Merger the target company merges into a controlled subsidiary of the acquiring company in exchange for consideration (i.e., cash, notes, or stock). For tax purposes, the target (merged) corporation is considered to have exchanged its assets for the consideration received. The target corporation is deemed liquidated and distributes the consideration received to its shareholders in exchange for target corporation stock.

Example 7C *Target ABC is merged into Sub Corporation, a wholly owned subsidiary of acquirer XYZ Corporation. ABC Corporation disappears by operation of law, and its shareholders receive consideration such as cash, notes, and stock. ABC is considered, for tax purposes, to have exchanged its assets for* *such consideration. ABC then distributes this consideration to its shareholders in exchange for their ABC stock.*

Forward Subsidiary Merger

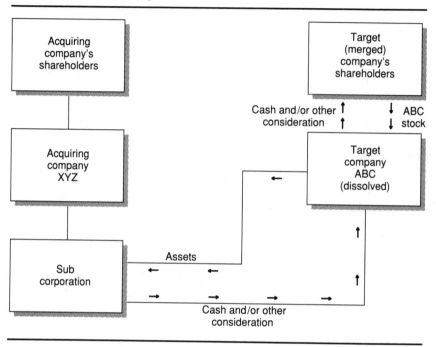

7.11b Treatment of Acquirer

In any Asset Acquisition there are three important areas for the acquiring corporation. These are (1) the tax basis of the assets acquired, (2) allocation of the purchase price, and (3) the lack of carryover of tax attributes.

1. *Tax Basis of Assets Acquired:* In an Asset Acquisition the acquiring corporation purchases part or all of the assets of the target company for a price. This price is generally allocated among the assets acquired based on their fair market values. These acquired assets may include intangible assets that were not previously recorded on the target company's books. The result is that each asset purchased ends up with a tax basis equal to its acquisition cost.

2. *Allocation of the Purchase Price:* How the total purchase price is allocated to the various assets in an Asset Acquisition can be extremely important to the acquiring corporation and the target because it has direct economic consequences for both.

Generally, the acquiring corporation is interested in assigning higher fair market values to *ordinary income* items such as receivables, inventory, depreciable assets and intangibles (e.g. covenant not to compete). Moreover, within the depreciable asset categories an acquirer will want to assign greater values to assets that are in the 3-, 5- or 7-year classes rather than the 20-, 27.5- or 31.5-year classes. Higher valuations assigned to ordinary income items will flow through the acquirer's tax books in a relatively short time frame and reduce taxable income. Higher values assigned to depreciable assets, especially assets with relatively short MACRS recovery periods, will also act to reduce the tax burden on the acquiring company. (See paragraph B.7 for a complete description of tax depreciation methods, including MACRS.) Finally, the acquiring company is extremely interested in keeping goodwill at a minimum because goodwill amortization is not deductible for tax purposes. The concept of goodwill is defined below.

The target corporation often takes a position diametrically opposed to that of the acquirer. The target generally wants lower allocations of value to receivables and inventory because any gain associated with the sale of these assets will be ordinary taxable income. In addition, the target also does not want high cost allocations to depreciable assets because the target would incur depreciation recapture (see paragraph B.8). Finally, the target favors allocating significant value to goodwill because it is a capital asset and any gain on the sale will be capital gain. However, the elimination of the difference between capital gains and ordinary income tax rates has had a significant dampening effect on the seller's economic incentive to negotiate strenuously for higher valuations for *capital assets* and lower values for ordinary income items.

If acquired assets constitute a trade or business, consideration paid for these assets must be allocated by both the buyer and seller in accordance with the Residual Method of Allocation. The Residual Method of Allocation rules apply for all New Cost Basis Acquisition Methods.

Under the *Residual Method of Allocation (Residual Method)* the *adjusted grossed-up basis (AGB)*, which is equal to the purchase price of the assets acquired plus liabilities assumed, is allocated to various classes of assets. IRC regulations provide for four asset classifications:

Class I : Cash, demand deposits and similar accounts in banks.

Class II : Certificates of deposit, U.S. government securities, readily marketable securities and foreign currency.

Class III: All other assets, other than Class I, II and IV assets, including both tangible and intangible assets without regard to whether they are depreciable, depletable or amortizable.

Class IV: Intangible assets in the nature of goodwill and going concern value.

The Residual Method requires AGB to be allocated first to Class I assets, next to Class II assets in proportion to their fair market values, then to Class III assets in proportion to their fair market values; finally, if there is any AGB remaining after the allocations to Classes I, II and III, it is allocated to Class IV assets in proportion to their fair market values.

The Residual Method requires that the amount allocated to Classes I, II or III assets cannot exceed the fair market value of the assets in each class as of the day after the acquisition date.

Example 7D   *XYZ Corporation purchases all of the net assets of ABC Corporation in an Asset Acquisition for $1,000. The net assets have a tax basis on ABC's books and a fair market value as indicated.*

Under the Residual Method, XYZ Corporation has an AGB of $1,500 ($1,000 plus $500 in liabilities assumed) to allocate to the various assets and liabilities. The fair market values of the Class I, II and III assets total only $1,300. Therefore, XYZ must record $200 as goodwill.

Fair Market Values and Old and New Tax Basis of Selected Assets

Asset/Liability	Asset Class	ABC's Tax Basis	Fair Market Value	XYZ's New Tax Basis
Cash	I	$100	$100	$100
Marketable securities	II	200	300	300
Land	III	300	500	500
Buildings and improvements	III	200	400	400
Goodwill	IV	0	200	200
Total assets		800	1,500	1,500
Total liabilities		(500)	(500)	(500)
Net assets acquired		$300	$1,000	$1,000

Example 7E   *Same as Example 7D except that XYZ Corporation pays only $700. In this case XYZ's AGB is $1,200 ($700 plus $500 liabilities assumed) to allocate to the various assets. After allocating value to Class I and Class II assets XYZ must allocate the remaining AGB to the Class III assets in proportion to their fair market values. Thus, land is allocated $444 ($800 remaining AGB times ($500/$900)) and buildings and improvements are allocated $356 ($800 remaining AGB times ($400/$900)).*

Fair Market Values and Old and New Tax Basis of Selected Assets

Asset/Liability	Asset Class	ABC's Tax Basis	Fair Market Value	XYZ's New Tax Basis
Cash	I	$100	$100	$100
Marketable securities	II	200	300	300
Land	III	300	500	444
Buildings and improvements	III	200	400	356
Goodwill	IV	0	0	0
Total assets		800	1,300	1,200
Total liabilities		(500)	(500)	(500)
Net assets acquired		$300	$800	$700

Tax regulations require that both the buyer and the seller in an Asset Acquisition report the allocation of value among the assets involved in the transaction on IRS *Form 8594*. These reporting requirements do not mandate that the buyer and seller agree on the purchase price allocation. However, the regulations do require that the buyer and seller indicate if the amounts being reported were agreed to in a purchase contract. Where there was such agreement, this allocation will generally be respected by the IRS.

3. *Lack of Carryover of Tax Attributes:* In an Asset Acquisition there are no carryovers of any tax attributes such as accounting method, earnings and profits account, capital loss carryovers, inventory methods, depreciation methods, and so forth. Thus, the acquiring company is not locked into any tax methods or characteristics of the target company. *Net operating losses (NOLs)*, another tax attribute of the target, are not available to the acquiring company.

7.11c Treatment of Target

The target corporation in a straightforward Asset Acquisition often remains in existence after the sale and is responsible for the tax due on any gain associated with the transaction. Basically, the target corporation is treated as if it had sold each asset individually. Thus, the target must deal with the rules governing capital gains and losses, ordinary income, depreciation recapture, and Section 1231 assets. See Appendix B for a review of these rules.

The target corporation is responsible for the tax due on any gain associated with the transaction even if it liquidates simultaneously with the transaction. Corporations liquidate in order to place the proceeds of the transaction in the hands of its shareholders. In addition to the tax paid by the target corporation on any gain associated with the asset sale, the shareholders of the target corporation must recognize capital gain on any assets distributed to them in liquidation.

Example 7F *XYZ Corporation purchases all of the assets of ABC Corporation in an Asset Acquisition for $1,000. The target is owned 20 percent each by individual shareholders A, B, C, D and E. ABC Corporation's assets have a fair market value of $1,000 and a tax basis of $500. A, B, C, D and E all purchased their ABC Corporation stock at the same time several years ago and each has a basis of $100. After the asset sale ABC Corporation liquidates to place the proceeds of the transaction in the hands of its shareholders.*

In this example, a double tax is paid. The target pays a corporate level tax of $190 ($1,000 proceeds less $500 basis times 38 percent combined federal and state effective tax rate). On liquidation, the shareholders will each receive $162 or a total of $810 ($1,000 less $190). Each individual shareholder pays an additional $23.56 ($162 proceeds less $100 basis × 38 percent effective U.S. personal income tax rate). In total, the asset sale and subsequent liquidation caused the target corporation and its shareholders to pay taxes of $307.80.

The principal exception to the double taxation rule is where the target corporation is owned 80 percent or more by a parent company from and after the date a plan of liquidation is adopted. Generally, the parent will recognize no gain on the liquidation in this situation.

Example 7G *Same as Example 7D except that ABC Corporation is owned 100 percent by Parent Corporation. In this instance, Parent Corporation does not recognize gain on the subsidiary liquidation. Therefore, only ABC Corporation's tax of $190 is paid.*

The practical result of the double taxation rules is that sellers want to structure most transactions as Stock Acquisitions rather than Asset Acquisitions. When a seller expects to sell assets at a profit there are only limited circumstances in which the seller will want to structure the transaction as an Asset Acquisition:

1. Where the target company has a sufficiently large NOL to offset the gain (see paragraph B.12 for a discussion of NOLs).

2. Where the targt is a subsidiary in a consolidated group that has a large NOL.

3. Where the target company is a consolidated subsidiary owned 80 percent or more by a large parent corporation and the target company's gain on the sale of assets is approximately the same as the gain that the parent company would realize on the sale of its target company stock. In this instance, if the target company sells its assets, the parent company will not incur a double tax when it liquidates the target.

7.12   338 Transaction

7.12a   In General

A *338 Transaction* is effected when an acquiring corporation purchases, within a 12-month period, at least 80 percent of the voting shares, and at least 80 percent of all other stock, of the target and elects, within approximately nine months after it has purchased the stock, to treat the transaction as if the target company sold its assets on the acquisition date to a new corporation for a price equal to the stock acquisition price. In this transaction, the target company is considered to have sold its assets at their fair market value. This sale price is called the *deemed sale price* for tax purposes. The acquiring company is deemed to have purchased the assets of the target for an amount equal to the price paid for the target's stock plus, if a proper election is made, the target's liabilities. This is called, for tax purposes, the *deemed purchase price*.

A 338 Transaction results in the target corporation recognizing and being taxed on the full gain associated with its deemed asset sale. In addition, the target company's shareholders are taxed on the sale of their stock. Generally, the cost of an acquirer *stepping-up* the tax basis of the target company's assets to their fair market value is prohibitive due to this double taxation. Therefore, transactions are not structured as 338 Transactions where the target company would recognize a gain, unless the target company has a sufficiently large NOL to offset the gain.

Example 7H   *XYZ Corporation purchases all of the outstanding stock of ABC Corporation in a 338 Transaction. XYZ Corporation makes the necessary tax election.*

338 Transaction

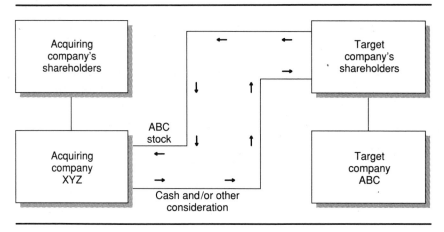

7.12b   Treatment of Acquirer

The discussion of how a 338 Transaction affects the acquiring corporation is broken down into nine segments: (1) the target company's deemed selling price, (2) the target company's gain or loss on the sale, (3) who pays the target company's tax, (4) the lack of carryover of tax attributes, (5) the effect of the subsequent liquidation of the target, (6) the acquiring company's "deemed purchase price," (7) the tax basis of the assets acquired, (8) the allocation of the purchase price and (9) liability for the selling group's tax liability.

 1. *Target company's deemed selling price:* The target company is considered to have sold its assets to a new corporation at their fair market value.

 2. *Target company's gain or loss:* The calculation of the target company's gain or loss is extremely complex. The gain or loss on the deemed sale is calculated as if the target sold each of its assets at their fair market value. This calculation normally excludes the target's liabilities. However, temporary regulations under Section 338 permit a special election that enables a taxpayer to calculate the gain or loss on the sale by a formula that includes the target company's liabilities. This special election is called the elective ADSP formula. The elective ADSP formula is self-referencing (i.e., recapture gain both increases the ADSP [by creating a tax liability] and is computed by reference to the ADSP). The *Aggregate Deemed Sale Price (ADSP)* is the sum of (a) the grossed-up basis of the purchased stock, (b) the liabilities of the target, and (c) other relevant items. The "allowable ADSP amount" is the portion of the ADSP that is allocable to each particular asset of the target. Recapture gain on each

asset is computed by reference to its allowable ADSP amount. See Section 338 Temporary Regulations for detailed examples illustrating how to properly calculate a company's gain or loss.

3. *Who pays the target company's tax?* The target pays the tax liability arising from the deemed sale, but the acquiring company actually bears the economic burden. How? When the target's results are included in its selling parent company consolidated tax return up until the acquisition date, the target must file a separate final tax return (one-day tax return) to report the tax liability arising from the deemed sale of assets. This tax return (*deemed sale return*) includes only the deemed sale, except for certain miscellaneous carryover items from the consolidated return of the selling group. The tax liability from the deemed sale cannot be included in the selling corporation's consolidated return because the target is presumed disaffiliated from the selling group immediately before the deemed sale. Furthermore, the deemed sale cannot be reported in the consolidated return of the acquiring corporation. The net effect of these rules is to place responsibility for payment of any tax liability on the target. Since this liability must be paid out of the target's assets, it diminishes the net assets available to the acquiring corporation.

If the target is not a part of a consolidated group prior to the transaction, the target still files a final tax return that includes the deemed sale. The acquiring company bears the economic burden in this situation because the transaction has the effect of reducing the net assets of the target that are available to the acquiring company.

4. *Lack of carryover of tax attributes:* In a 338 Transaction there is no carryover of any tax attributes of the target company.

5. *Liquidation of the target:* The liquidation of the target company has no tax effects.

6. *Acquiring company's deemed purchase price:* Generally, the new corporation is deemed to have purchased the assets of the target for an amount equal to the *adjusted grossed-up basis (AGB)*. AGB is equal to the purchase price of the stock plus the target's liabilities. The target's liabilities include any tax liability resulting from the deemed sale. See Section 338 Temporary Regulations for examples concerning these calculations. Special rules exist if the acquiring company did not purchase all the target's stock within the 12-month acquisition period.

7. *Tax basis of the assets acquired:* The new corporation takes a basis in the assets acquired equal to the AGB.

8. *Allocation of the purchase price:* The AGB is allocated to individual assets in the same manner that value is allocated in Asset Acquisitions.

9. *Liability for selling group's taxes:* If an acquiring corporation purchases the stock of a target that is a member of a consolidated group, IRS regulations require that the target remains liable for any federal income taxes, interest or penalties imposed on the consolidated group for years when the target corporation was a member of the consolidated group. The fact that the acquiring corporation makes an election to treat the transaction as an Asset Acquisition has no effect on this potential liability. Therefore, the acquisition agreement should make some provision for this issue.

7.12c   Treatment of Target

Generally, the tax considerations for the target's shareholders in a 338 Transaction are straightforward. The stock that is sold is generally a capital asset in the hands of the stockholders and, when sold, the stockholders recognize a capital gain or loss equal to the difference between the amount realized and the stockholder's basis in the stock. However, if part of the consideration received by the target's shareholders is for an employment or consulting contract or a covenant not to compete, some portion of the purchase price should be allocated to that item, in which case the shareholder would recognize ordinary income.

7.13   338(h)(10) Transaction

7.13a   In General

A 338(h)(10) Transaction is a variation of a 338 Transaction. In a *338(h)(10) Transaction* the target corporation is treated as if it sold all of its assets to the acquiring corporation and then liquidated. In this transaction the target corporation is treated as a member of the selling group for tax purposes with regard to the *deemed asset sale*.

A 338(h)(10) Transaction can be used only in situations where (a) the target company is currently a member of an affiliated group that files a consolidated tax return, (b) the acquiring corporation elects to treat the transaction as a 338 Transaction, and (c) the acquiring company and the seller jointly agree to make the 338(h)(10) election.

Since a 338(h)(10) election merely shifts the tax burden associated with the sale from the target company to the selling group, transactions will not be structured as 338(h)(10) Transactions unless the selling group has a sufficiently large NOL to offset the gain, or the selling group is relatively indifferent to a stock or asset sale because the gain is about the same for either transaction.

Example 7I *XYZ Corporation purchases all of the outstanding stock of ABC Corporation from Parent Company. XYZ and Parent Company make the necessary 338(h)(10) tax election.*

338(h)(10) Transaction

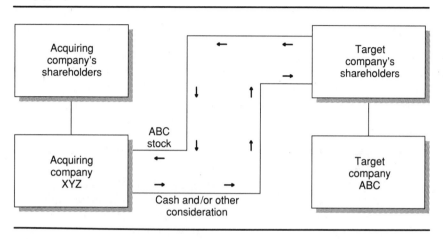

7.13b Treatment of Acquirer

The discussion of how a 338(h)(10) Transaction affects the acquiring corporation is broken down into nine segments: (1) the target company's selling price, (2) the selling group's gain or loss on the sale, (3) who pays the target company's tax, (4) carryover of tax attributes, (5) the effect of the deemed liquidation of the target, (6) the acquiring company's "deemed purchase price," (7) the tax basis of the assets acquired, (8) the allocation of the purchase price, and (9) liability for the selling group's tax liability.

1. *Target company's selling price:* The target company is considered to have sold its assets to a new corporation at their fair market value.

2. *Selling group's gain or loss:* The target corporation is treated as if, while a member of the selling consolidated group, it sold all of its assets in a single transaction. Thus, the target corporation must deal with the rules governing capital gains and losses, ordinary income, depreciation recapture, and Section 1231 assets. Any gain or loss associated with the sale of stock is ignored. Temporary regulations under Section 338(h)(10) provide an elective *modified aggregate deemed sale price (MADSP)* formula for calculating recapture on the deemed asset sale. The MADSP is the sum of (a) the grossed-up basis of the purchased stock, (b) the liabilities of the target as of the day after the acquisition, and (c) other relevant items. Section 338 Temporary Regulations provide detailed examples.

3. *Who pays the target company's tax?* The selling group pays the tax liability arising from the deemed sale.

4. *Carryover of tax attributes:* In a 338(h)(10) Transaction the tax attributes of the target (i.e. loss carryovers), adjusted for the deemed sale, are preserved for the parent corporation into which the target is deemed liquidated.

5. *Liquidation of the target:* In a 338(h)(10) Transaction the target is deemed liquidated at the end of the acquisition date, after the deemed asset sale. No gain or loss is recognized on this liquidation.

6. *Acquiring company's deemed purchase price:* Generally, the new corporation is deemed to have purchased the assets of the target for an amount equal to AGB. Special rules exist if the acquiring company did not purchase all the target's stock within the 12-month acquisition period. See Section 338 Temporary Regulations for examples.

7. *Tax basis of the assets acquired:* The new corporation takes a basis in the assets acquired equal to the AGB. Remember that since the selling group is responsible for the tax on the deemed asset sale the acquiring company does not get a step-up in the target's assets for this liability.

8. *Allocation of the purchase price:* The AGB is allocated to individual assets pursuant to the same regulations that govern Asset Acquisitions.

9. *Liability for selling group's taxes:* If an acquiring corporation purchases the stock of a target that is a member of a consolidated group, IRS regulations require that the target remains liable for any federal income taxes, interest or penalties imposed on the consolidated group for years when the target corporation was a member of the consolidated group. The fact that a 338(h)(10) election is made has no effect on this potential liability.

7.13c   Treatment of Target

The tax considerations for the target's shareholder in a 338(h)(10) Transaction have been outlined above. No gain or loss is recognized by the selling group on the sale of the target's stock. However, the target is deemed to have sold its assets in a single transaction at the close of the acquisition date while the target was still a member of the selling group. Thus, the selling group is liable for the tax liability on the target's deemed asset sale. The target is deemed liquidated after the deemed asset sale. This liquidation does not give rise to a tax liability. In the liquidation the target corporation transfers its tax attributes, after giving effect to the deemed asset sale, to the corporation it is liquidated into.

7.2   NO CHANGE IN BASIS ACQUISITION METHODS

7.21   Stock Acquisition

7.21a   In General

There are three types of Stock Acquisitions: (1) a straightforward *Stock Acquisition,* (2) a *Reverse Merger,* and (3) a *Reverse Subsidiary Merger* (also called a *Reverse Triangular Merger*).

   1. *Stock Acquisition:* A straightforward Stock Acquisition occurs when the acquiring corporation purchases the stock of the target company from its shareholders and does nothing else.

   Example 7J   *XYZ Corporation acquires all of the stock of ABC Corporation in a Stock Acquisition.*

Stock Acquisition

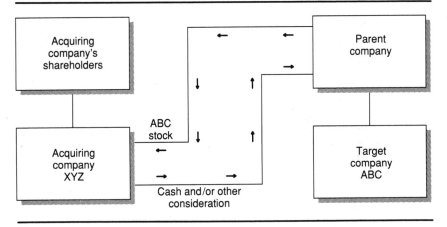

   2. *Reverse Merger:* A Reverse Merger is merely a statutory merger accomplished by merging the acquiring company into the target company. For tax purposes, the transaction is treated as a sale and purchase of stock, with the acquiring company merged downstream into the target.

   Example 7K   *Acquiring corporation XYZ merges into target ABC Corporation. XYZ Corporation disappears by operation of law, and ABC Corporation survives. For tax purposes, XYZ Corporation is considered to have purchased the stock of ABC Corporation.*

Reverse Merger

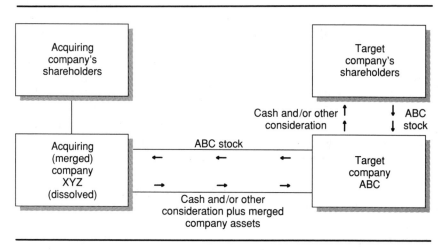

3. *Reverse Subsidiary Merger:* In a Reverse Subsidiary Merger a controlled subsidiary of the acquiring corporation merges into the target company. The primary reason for this type of transaction is the legal need to maintain the target corporation's existence. The target company's shareholders receive cash, notes, stock, or other consideration, and the acquiring company receives the stock of the target company. For tax purposes, the transaction is viewed as a sale of stock by the target company's shareholders.

Example 7L   *Sub Corporation, a wholly owned subsidiary of XYZ Corporation, merges into ABC Corporation, the target company. Sub Corporation disappears by operation of law. The target company's shareholders receive cash, notes, stock, or other consideration in exchange for their target company stock.*

Reverse Subsidiary Merger

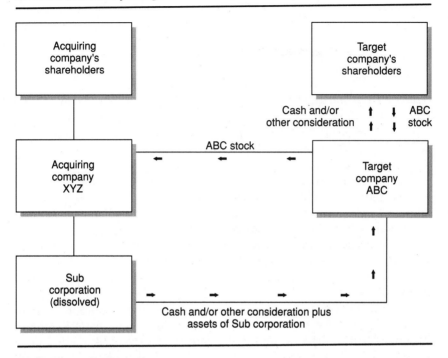

7.21b   *Treatment of Acquirer*

The tax treatment of the acquiring company in a Stock Acquisition is fairly simple. The acquiring company takes a basis in the stock of the target company equal to its acquisition cost, and the tax attributes of the target company (e.g., accounting methods, tax basis of its assets, net operating losses, etc.) are generally unaffected by the change in ownership. However, see paragraph B.12 for a review of the rules concerning net operating loss carryovers and built-in losses.

7.21c   *Treatment of Target*

Generally, the tax considerations for the target's shareholders in a Stock Acquisition are straightforward. Stock, in most instances, is a capital asset, and when it is sold, stockholders recognize a capital gain or loss equal to the difference between the amount realized and their basis in the stock. However, if part of the consideration received by the target's shareholders is for an employment or consulting contract or a covenant not to compete, some portion of the purchase price should be allocated to that item, in which case the shareholder would recognize ordinary income.

7.22   Type A Reorganization

7.22a   In General

Transactions that are effected as a Type A Reorganization come in four different forms: (1) *Type A Forward Merger*, (2) *Type A Statutory Consolidation*, (3) *Type A Forward Subsidiary Merger*, and (4) *Type A Reverse Subsidiary Merger* (also called a *Type A Reverse Triangular Merger*).

As a general rule, the acquiring company can use voting or nonvoting common stock, voting or nonvoting preferred stock, or a combination thereof to effect a nontaxable merger. However, in a Type A Reverse Subsidiary Merger the stockholders of the target corporation must receive only voting stock of the acquiring corporation in exchange for control of the target. "Control" is defined to be stock possessing 80 percent of the target's voting power and 80 percent of the total number of shares of each of the other outstanding classes of stock of the target.

The acquiring company can also use a substantial amount of boot (e.g., cash, debt instruments, warrants, or options) in a Type A Reorganization subject to the Continuity of Interest Doctrine. The ability to use boot in a Type A Reorganization makes this acquisition method extremely popular. The name given to a Type A Reorganization where cash is used as boot is a Cash Option Merger. In a *Cash Option Merger* the acquiring company gives an option to the target company's shareholders of accepting either cash or stock in exchange for their target company stock. The purpose in granting such an option is to afford tax-free results to those shareholders who desire it and cash to those shareholders not concerned with a taxable transaction. In fulfilling the Continuity of Interest requirement in this context, it is important to note that only one or more shareholders of the target need receive the requisite proprietary interest in the acquiring company. Pro rata receipt of the acquiring company's stock is not required.

Typically, Cash Option Mergers are used if the target is owned primarily by one person or family (say, 40 to 60 percent) with the rest of the common stock owned by the public. The principal stockholders may want an ownership interest in the acquiring company as well as tax-free treatment. The acquiring company would offer a package of cash and stock to the target's shareholders, with the public taking the cash and the controlling shareholders the stock.

1. *Type A Forward Merger:* A Type A Forward Merger occurs when the target corporation merges into the acquiring corporation. For tax purposes, the target (merged) corporation is considered to have exchanged its assets for the stock of the acquiring (surviving) corporation. The target corporation distributes the stock of the acquiring corporation to its shareholders in exchange for their target corporation stock.

Example 7M   *ABC Corporation is merged into XYZ Corporation. ABC Corporation disappears, and XYZ Corporation is the surviving corporation. For tax purposes, ABC is considered to have exchanged its assets for XYZ stock and distributed the XYZ stock to its shareholders in exchange for their ABC stock.*

Type A Forward Merger

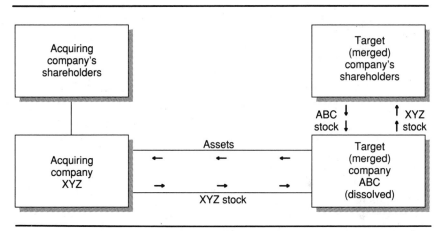

2. *Type A Statutory Consolidation:* Type A Statutory Consolidations are effected when two or more corporations are combined into a new corporation. For tax purposes, the combined corporations are considered to have exchanged their assets for the stock of the new corporation. Upon receiving the stock of the new corporation, the combined corporations distribute it to their shareholders in exchange for their stock in the combined corporation.

Example 7N   *ABC Corporation and XYZ Corporation are combined in a statutory consolidation. Both ABC and XYZ disappear, and an entirely new corporation results (assuming that it is formed by operation of law). For tax purposes, ABC Corporation and XYZ Corporation are considered to have exchanged their assets for the stock of the new corporation. ABC and XYZ distribute this stock to their shareholders in exchange for their stock.*

Type A Statutory Consolidation

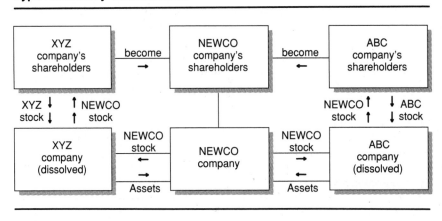

3. *Type A Forward Subsidiary Merger:* A Type A Forward Subsidiary Merger occurs when the target company merges into a controlled subsidiary of the acquiring corporation in exchange for the stock of the acquiring corporation. The acquiring company must acquire substantially all of the assets of the target company, and no stock of the subsidiary can be given as consideration to the shareholders of the target company. However, boot may be used in this type of transaction subject to the Continuity of Interest Doctrine limitations. To receive an advance ruling from the IRS indicating the transaction will qualify as a reorganization, the acquiring corporation must meet the IRS definition of "substantially all," which is at least 90 percent of the fair market value of the target's net assets and at least 70 percent of the fair market value of the target's gross assets immediately preceding the transaction.

The target (merged) corporation is considered, for tax purposes, to have exchanged its assets for stock. The target corporation distributes the stock received to its shareholders in exchange for their company stock.

Example 70   *Target ABC is merged into Sub Corporation, a wholly owned subsidiary of XYZ Corporation. ABC disappears by operation of law, and its shareholders receive stock of XYZ Corporation. ABC is considered, for tax purposes, to have exchanged its assets for XYZ stock. ABC then distributes the XYZ stock to its shareholders in exchange for their ABC stock.*

4. *Type A Reverse Subsidiary Merger:* In a Type A Reverse Subsidiary Merger a controlled subsidiary of the acquiring corporation merges into the target company. The primary reason for this type of transaction is a

Type A Forward Subsidiary Merger

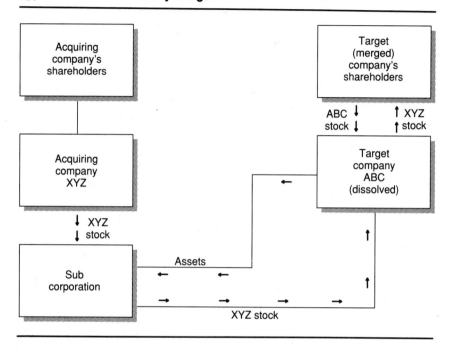

legal need to maintain the target corporation's existence. The target company's shareholders receive stock of the acquiring corporation (not subsidiary stock) and the acquiring company receives the stock of the target company. The merger agreement usually provides that when the merger takes place, the shares of the subsidiary automatically become shares of the target company. The net effect is that the target company survives the transaction and becomes a subsidiary of the acquiring company. After the transaction the target company must hold substantially all (as previously defined) of the assets it held before the transaction, as well as substantially all the assets of the subsidiary (excluding stock or cash dropped down from the acquiring corporation to effect the transaction) that merged with it.

Example 7P   *Sub Corporation, a wholly owned subsidiary of XYZ Corporation, merges into ABC Corporation, the target company. Sub Corporation disappears by operation of law. The target company's shareholders receive stock of XYZ in exchange for their stock in ABC.*

Type A Reverse Subsidiary Merger

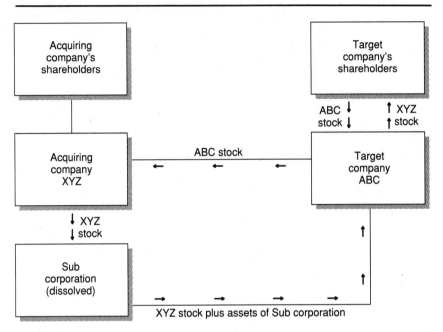

Post Transaction

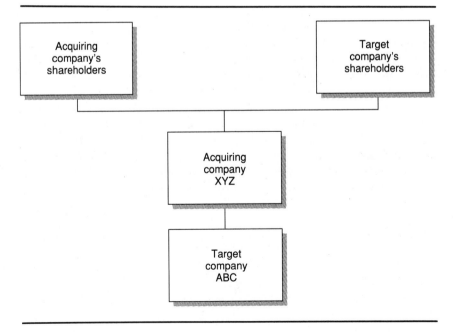

7.22b   Treatment of Acquirer

Neither the acquiring company nor its subsidiary recognizes any gain or loss in any Type A Reorganization and both take a carryover basis in the assets of the target company. It is the rule, rather than the exception, that boot is paid in this method of acquisition. Yet the use of boot and any recognition of gain by the shareholders of the target does not effect the basis of the target company's assets in the hands of the acquiring company or its subsidiary.

Proposed regulations indicate that, generally, the acquiring company's basis in its subsidiary corporation stock after a Type A Subsidiary Merger is equal to the sum of: (1) the acquiring company's basis in its subsidiary corporation stock immediately before the transaction, (2) the net basis of the property acquired by subsidiary corporation from its parent company that is not transferred to the target corporation or the target corporation's shareholders, and (3) the target's basis in its assets.

Proposed regulations indicate that, generally, the acquiring company's basis in its target corporation stock after a Type A Reverse Subsidiary Merger is equal to the sum of: (1) the acquiring company's basis in its subsidiary corporation stock immediately before the transaction, (2) the net basis of the property transferred by the acquiring company to subsidiary corporation that is not transferred to the target corporation's shareholders, and (3) the target's basis in its assets after the transaction.

7.22c   Treatment of Target

In general, a Type A Reorganization is tax-free to both the target company and its shareholders. The shareholders who receive only stock do not recognize any gain or loss and take a basis in the stock received that is the same as the basis in the stock they surrendered. The shareholders that receive only boot are taxed as if they had sold their stock in a Stock Acquisition. A stockholder who receives both stock and boot is taxed as follows: The stock is received tax-free, but the boot is taxed as either capital gain or ordinary income. If the receipt of boot has the effect of a distribution of a dividend, it will be taxed as ordinary income. If not, the boot will be treated as gain on the sale of a capital asset. Assuming the stock exchanged was held for the requisite holding period, any gain or loss will be taxed as gain or loss on the sale of a capital asset. In any event, where there is boot, the stockholder's basis in any stock received will be decreased for the amount of the boot and increased for the amount of the gain recognized.

A Type A Reorganization can be a viable estate planning technique for a target company shareholder, because generally, heirs will receive a step-up in the tax basis of the stock received at the date of the shareholder's death.

7.23 Type B Reorganization

7.23a In General

Generally, a Type B Reorganization is effected in two forms: (1) a *Type B Stock Exchange* between the acquiring corporation and the target's shareholders, and (2) a *Type B Subsidiary Stock Exchange* between a subsidiary of the acquiring company and the target's shareholders.

In either transaction the only consideration that can be used by the acquiring company is voting stock. *Voting stock* is defined as any class of stock that has a right to vote for directors and includes voting preferred stock. Any consideration, no matter how small, other than voting stock will destroy the transaction's status as a Type B Reorganization. However, the target company can make ordinary dividend distributions or redeem shares prior to the reorganization without affecting its tax-free status. In any redemption, care must be taken not to run afoul of the Continuity of Interest Doctrine.

1. *Type B Stock Exchange:* In this transaction the acquiring company exchanges its voting stock for stock of the target company. After the transaction the acquiring company must have control of the target. "Control" is defined as ownership of stock possessing at least 80 percent of the total combined voting power of all classes of stock entitled to vote and at least 80 percent of the total number of shares of all other classes of stock of the target. The effect of the transaction is that the target company becomes a subsidiary of the acquiring company.

Example 7Q *XYZ Corporation agrees to buy ABC Corporation in a Type B Stock Exchange. XYZ issues its stock to ABC's shareholders in exchange for their ABC stock.*

Type B Stock Exchange

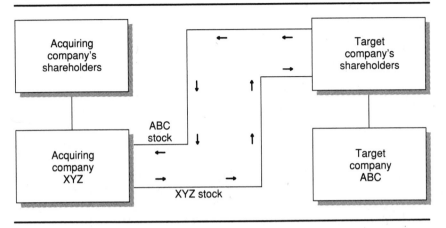

2. *Type B Subsidiary Stock Exchange:* In a Type B Subsidiary Stock Exchange the acquiring company uses only its own stock or that of its subsidiary as consideration. A combination of the two is not allowed. The mechanics work the same as a Type B Stock Exchange, except that the acquiring company contributes its stock down to the subsidiary (assuming the acquiring company's stock is the consideration to be used), which then exchanges this stock for the stock of the target. The subsidiary must have control of the target after the transaction. The use of a subsidiary to effect the transaction makes the target a subsidiary of the acquiring corporation's subsidiary.

Example 7R   *XYZ Corporation agrees to buy ABC Corporation in a Type B Subsidiary Stock Exchange. XYZ contributes its stock down to its wholly owned subsidiary, Sub Corporation, which then exchanges this stock for the target company's stock.*

Type B Subsidiary Stock Exchange

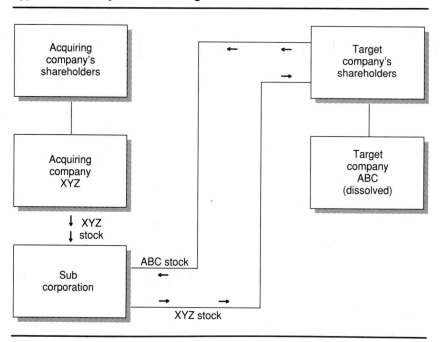

7.23b Treatment of Acquirer

Neither the acquiring company nor its subsidiary recognizes any gain or loss in a Type B Reorganization, and both take a carryover basis in the assets of the target company. In a Type B Subsidiary Stock Exchange the acquiring company takes a basis in the stock of its original subsidiary ("Sub Corporation") equal to the basis of the stock of the target's shareholders. The target shareholder's basis is often very difficult to determine.

7.23c Treatment of Target

The transaction has no effect on the target company and the target company's shareholders do not recognize any gain or loss in the transaction. In addition, the target's shareholders take a basis in the stock received equal to their basis in the stock of the target company.

A Type B Reorganization can be a viable estate planning technique for a target company shareholder. Generally, heirs will receive a step-up in the tax basis of the stock received at the date of the shareholder's death.

7.24   Type C Reorganization

7.24a   In General

Generally, a Type C Reorganization is effected in two forms: (1) a *Type C Stock for Assets Exchange* between the acquiring company and the target company, and (2) a *Type C Subsidiary Stock for Assets Exchange* between a subsidiary of the acquiring company and the target company. In these transactions the acquiring company or its subsidiary purchases substantially all of the assets of the target (subject to all or part of its liabilities) in exchange for voting stock (common or preferred) of either (but not both) the acquiring company or its subsidiary.

Generally, "substantially all" of the assets of the target means 90 percent of the net assets of the target company. However, a lower percentage can be adequate in certain circumstances based on the nature of the properties retained, the reason for retaining them, and their amount. The key seems to be that the operating assets of the target company must be conveyed.

In certain limited instances the acquiring company can give as consideration boot rather than voting stock. Boot may be given to the extent that the liabilities assumed by the acquiring company or its subsidiary are less than 20 percent of the gross value of the assets conveyed.

The assumption by the acquiring company or its subsidiary of the target's liabilities does not affect the tax-free nature of the transaction unless the liabilities constitute a disproportionately large percentage of the fair market value of the target's assets. In such event the transaction may be treated as a taxable sale.

The target must distribute the stock, securities, and other consideration received in the reorganization, as well as its other assets, for the transaction to qualify as a Type C Reorganization.

1. *Type C Stock for Assets Exchange:* This transaction consists of the acquiring company exchanging its voting stock for substantially all of the assets of the target company.

Example 7S   *XYZ Corporation agrees to purchase all of ABC Corporation's assets and liabilities in a Type C Stock for Assets Exchange. XYZ Corporation exchanges its voting stock for substantially all of the assets of ABC Corpora-*

tion. ABC Corporation distributes all of its assets including the XYZ stock to its shareholders.

Type C Stock for Assets Exchange

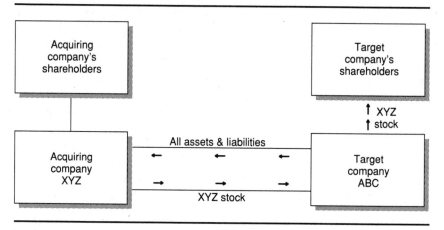

2. *Type C Subsidiary Stock for Assets Exchange:* This transaction consists of the subsidiary of the acquiring company exchanging either its voting stock or the voting stock of the acquiring company for substantially all of the assets of the target company.

Example 7T   *XYZ Corporation agrees to purchase all ABC Corporation's assets and liabilities in a Type C Subsidiary Stock for Assets Exchange. Sub Corporation, a wholly owned subsidiary of XYZ Corporation, exchanges the voting stock of XYZ Corporation for all of the assets of ABC Corporation. ABC Corporation distributes the XYZ stock to its shareholders.*

Type C Subsidiary Stock for Assets Exchange

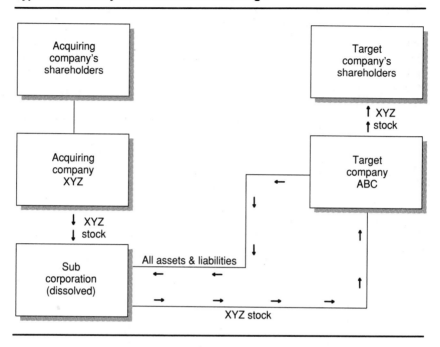

7.24b   *Treatment of Acquirer*

Generally, neither the acquiring company nor its subsidiary recognizes any gain or loss in a Type C Reorganization and both take a carryover basis in the assets acquired. If boot is given to the target company and distributed to its shareholders, their recognition of gain will not affect the basis of the target company's assets in the hands of the acquiring company.

Proposed regulations provide that the acquiring company's basis in its subsidiary corporation stock after a Type C Subsidiary Stock for Assets Exchange is equal to the sum of: (1) the acquiring company's basis in its Sub Corporation stock immediately before the transaction, (2) the net basis of the property acquired by Sub Corporation from its parent company that is not transferred to the target corporation or the target corporation's shareholders, and (3) the target's net basis in its assets.

7.24c   Treatment of Target

The target company and its shareholders do not recognize any gain or loss if only voting stock of the acquiring company or its subsidiary is received by the target company for its assets and distributed to its shareholders. When the target company is liquidated, the shareholders will take a basis in the acquiring company's stock equal to the basis in their target company stock. Any boot used in the transaction and distributed to the target's shareholders is taxable to the shareholders.

A Type C Reorganization can be a viable estate planning technique for a target company shareholder. Generally, heirs will receive a step-up in the tax basis of the stock received at the date of the shareholder's death.

Chapter 8

Theoretical Framework

8.0 INTRODUCTION

The buyer and seller in any transaction have diametrically opposed economic interests. Simply put, the buyer is looking to negotiate a deal at the lowest cost, whereas the seller wants to maximize the sale proceeds. These basic economic principles are difficult to apply in the context of acquiring a business because of tax law complications. The purpose of this chapter is to outline a theoretical framework for calculating the real economic cost and proceeds in a transaction, as well as to review the nontax factors that influence the buyer and seller.

8.1 BUYER'S PERSPECTIVE

8.11 Net Present Tax Cost

The discounted cash flow techniques used to analyze acquisitions are reviewed in Chapter 15 and Appendix A. One of the techniques involves finding the net present value of a project. This concept will be modified slightly to allow us to determine the true economic cost of an acquisition. Remember, we are only discussing cost in this section, and accordingly, operating cash flows do not yet enter our analysis.

Generally, for any given price the buyer should opt for the acquisition method that yields the lowest *Net Present Tax Cost (NPTC)*. NPTC is defined as the present cash outflow for an acquisition less the present value of the future tax benefits associated with the target's tax basis in its assets and liabilities immediately after the transaction. In calculating the NPTC, a buyer should take into account any anticipated exit strategy for the investment. For illustration purposes, we will only discuss the target company's tax basis in assets that are depreciated or amortized for tax purposes. Let us take a look at a few examples to flesh out the concept.

Example 8A   *XYZ Corporation buys all the assets and assumes all of the liabilities of ABC Corporation for their fair market value ($1,000) in an Asset Acquisition. The assumed fair market values are as follows:*

	Fair Market Values
Accounts receivable	$100
Inventory	400
Land	200
Machinery and equipment	500
Accounts payable	(200)
	$1,000

We will assume that the machinery and equipment is 5-year MACRS property. The depreciation deductions (calculated using the depreciation percentages in Exhibit B–6) and tax savings, assuming that the acquiring company has sufficient income against which to offset these deductions, are as follows:

	Year 1	Year 2	Year 3	Year 4	Year 5
Original tax basis	$500	$500	$500	$500	$500
MACRS depreciation %	20.00%	32.00%	19.20%	11.52%	11.52%
Depreciation deductions	100	160	96	58	58
Tax rate	38%	38%	38%	38%	38%
Tax benefit	$38	$61	$36	$22	$22

To determine the NPTC we must discount the tax savings back to the date of acquisition and subtract them from the initial cost. But what rate should we use to discount the tax savings? One could argue for a number of rates, including the acquiring company's or target company's weighted average cost of capital. A firm's weighted average cost of capital (WACC) *is defined as the weighted average of the costs of debt, preferred stock and common stock. The WACC reflects the current cost of raising an additional dollar of the various components and not the historical cost of the various components. However, if there is little risk that the tax savings will be realized, it is reasonable to use a Treasury bond ("risk free") rate adjusted upward slightly to reflect some risk. For purposes of this example, we will assume a 10 percent discount rate for the savings.*

	Tax Savings	10 Percent Discount Factor	Present Value
Year 1	$38	0.9091	$35
Year 2	61	0.8264	50
Year 3	36	0.7513	27
Year 4	22	0.6830	15
Year 5	22	0.6209	14
Present value of tax benefit			$141

Calculation of NPTC

Purchase price	$1,000
Less: present value of tax benefit	(141)
NPTC	$859

Example 8B   *XYZ Corporation buys all of the stock of ABC Corporation for $1,000 in a Stock Acquisition. The acquiring company in this instance will only be able to continue to depreciate the adjusted basis of the assets purchased. The basis of each of the target's assets is listed below.*

	Adjusted Tax Basis
Accounts receivable	$100
Inventory	200
Land	50
Machinery and equipment	144
Accounts payable	(200)
	$294

We will assume that the machinery and equipment was all purchased three years ago at a cost of $500 and is being depreciated over six years using MACRS recovery percentages for 5-year property. The depreciation deductions and associated tax savings are developed below:

	Year 1	Year 2	Year 3
Original tax basis	$500	$500	$500
MACRS depreciation %	11.52%	11.52%	5.76%
Depreciation deductions	58	58	29
Tax rate	38%	38%	38%
Tax benefit	$22	$22	$11

	Tax Savings	10 Percent Discount Factor	Present Value
Year 1	$22	0.9091	$20
Year 2	22	0.8264	18
Year 3	11	0.7513	8
Present value of tax benefit			$46
Calculation of NPTC			
Purchase price			$1,000
Less: present value of tax benefit			(46)
NPTC			$954

The examples provide some guidance as to how the NPTC concept works. However, there are a number of practical problems to address in performing the calculations. For instance, how did we come up with the fair market value of the machinery and equipment in the first example, especially if we are early in the sale process?

Most buyers will initially assume that the fair market value of the target's depreciable or amortizable assets is equal to those assets' net book value. Hence, any expected premium to be paid over the target's book value of stockholders' equity will be assigned to goodwill. This is a reasonable approach early in the process. However, the acquirer should refine this estimate as additional information becomes available. Focusing attention on the fair market value of these assets provides two substantial benefits to the acquirer: (1) it enables management to take a posture in negotiations regarding the method of consummating the acquisition and (2) it sensitizes the buyer to the impact that a change in their opinion as to the value of these assets will have on the NPTC of the acquisition. In all cases, the acquirer should obtain a reasonable estimate of the market value of the depreciable and amortizable assets before finalizing a transaction.

8.12   Nontax Factors Affecting Buyers

The buyer must also consider certain nontax factors in deciding how to effect a transaction. In some cases these factors will dictate that a particular method be employed, even if that method results in a greater NPTC to the buyer. For example, a buyer may have to acquire the stock of the target in order to effectively gain control of certain leases that run to the target company or to execute a planned initial public offering for the target company.

Generally, nontax factors involve legal requirements that must be met in effecting a transaction as a stock deal, asset deal or merger/consolidation. The discussion below focuses on the advantages and disadvantages of each type of transaction.

8.12a   Stock Deal

Advantages

- This type of deal is the least complex in terms of the documents that must be prepared. Basically, all that is involved is a transfer of stock certificates in exchange for immediate (or sometimes deferred) payment.
- Due to the simplicity of the deal, it can be accomplished very quickly.
- A Stock Deal can be executed over the objections of the target's management through a tender offer.
- The fact that the controlling shareholders have sold their stock does not automatically give minority shareholders appraisal rights. See paragraph E.12 for a discussion of appraisal rights.
- Generally, shareholder votes authorizing the purchase or the sale are not required.

Disadvantages

- The acquiring company purchasing the stock of the target purchases the target subject to all of its liabilities, whether disclosed or undisclosed, contingent or otherwise.
- A tender offer may be opposed by the target's board of directors and management.
- Although the minority shareholders do not ordinarily have appraisal rights, the acquiring company must still deal with them.
- If the acquiring company plans to liquidate the target company subsequent to the acquisition, a substantial amount of work will be involved in conveying all of the target company's assets as part of the liquidation.
- State and local transfer taxes can be imposed.

8.12b   Asset Deal

Advantages

- In an asset deal the acquiring company has complete control over the assets it will purchase and the liabilities it will assume.
- Generally, a shareholder vote by the acquiring company is not required.

Disadvantages

- An asset deal is the most complex transaction to effect because every asset must be separately conveyed.
- The transaction must comply with the applicable state's Bulk Sales laws.
- In an asset deal one must be careful not to violate creditors' rights. Furthermore, certain consents and assignments may be needed in an asset deal.
- This type of transaction requires a substantial favorable vote of shareholders of the target company.
- State and local transfer and gains taxes are imposed.
- This type of deal carries a greater possibility of disrupting suppliers and customers because of the complexities associated with changing ownership in all the target operation's assets.

8.12c   Merger or Consolidation

Advantages

- Straightforward procedures.
- Assets are transferred by operation of law.
- No minority interest in the target company remains.

Disadvantages

- The acquiring company assumes all of the liabilities of the target, whether disclosed or undisclosed, contingent or otherwise.
- Any representations or warranties made on behalf of the target company do not survive the transaction.
- Dissenting minority shareholders of both the acquiring and target companies have appraisal rights.
- Generally, shareholders of both the acquiring and target companies must vote to approve the transaction.
- The target company loses its identity.

8.2   SELLER'S PERSPECTIVE

Although this paragraph deals with the seller's perspective in a transaction, it is must reading for the buyer because the buyer must understand the consequences the seller is faced with in a transaction. This knowledge always works to the buyer's advantage in negotiations.

8.21   Net Present Proceeds

In general, the seller wants the transaction effected using a method that will maximize its *Net Present Proceeds (NPP)*. NPP is defined as the value of all cash and cash equivalents, plus the present value of all other forms of consideration, less the present value of the tax burden that the seller will bear as a result of the transaction. The examples below illustrate this concept.

Example 8C   *XYZ Corporation purchases all of the assets and liabilities of ABC Corporation for $1,000 in an Asset Acquisition. The target company plans to liquidate after the transaction. The target is owned by a single stockholder, who has a tax basis of $700 in his stock. He has held the stock for several years. The parties agree on the fair market values of the assets as listed below. ABC's tax basis for each asset also appears.*

	Fair Market Value	Adjusted Tax Basis	Taxable Gain
Accounts receivable	$100	$100	
Inventory	400	200	$200
Land	200	50	150
Machinery and equipment	500	144	356
Accounts payable	(200)	(200)	
	$1,000	$294	$706

We will assume that the machinery and equipment was all purchased three years ago at a cost of $500 and is being depreciated over six years using MACRS recovery percentages. ABC's depreciation recapture and Section 1231 gain are detailed below.

	Original Tax Basis	Accumulated Depreciation	Adjusted Tax Basis	Sale Price	Taxable Gain	Depreciation Recapture	Section 1231 Gain
Land	$50		$50	$200	$150		$150
Inventory	200		200	400	200		200
Machinery and equipment	500	$356	144	500	356	356	
					$706	$356	$350

Calculation of ABC's Tax Burden

Depreciation recapture	$356
Section 1231 gain	350
Total taxable income	706
Effective corporate tax rate	38%
Tax burden	$268

Calculation of NPP to ABC Corporation

Sale price	$1,000
Less: tax burden	(268)
NPP	$732

Calculation of Stockholder's Tax Burden

Proceeds from distribution	$732
Tax basis of stock	700
Taxable gain	32
Effective capital gains tax rate for individuals	32%
Tax burden on shareholder	$10

Calculation of NPP to Stockholder

Liquidation proceeds	$732
Less: tax burden	(10)
NPP	$722

Example 8D   *Same facts as EXAMPLE 8C except the transaction is a Stock Acquisition.*

Calculation of Stockholder's Tax Burden

Sale price	$1,000
Tax basis of stock	700
Taxable gain	300
Effective capital gains tax rate for individuals	32%
Tax burden on shareholder	$96

Calculation of NPP to Stockholder

Liquidation proceeds	$1,000
Less: tax burden	(96)
NPP	$904

The examples illustrate the concept of NPP. The calculations in the examples are easily done by the seller but a real struggle for the buyer. Why? In many cases it is unlikely that the buyer will know the seller's tax basis for his stock. In addition, if the target company is willing to sell assets in an Asset Acquisition, it is unlikely that the buyer will learn of the seller's tax basis in its assets. However, in most cases the buyer can request the target company's tax returns and determine the tax basis information.

Let us look at one final example concerning a nontaxable transaction:

Example 8E   XYZ Corporation, a publicly owned company, purchases all of the stock of ABC Corporation in a Type B Reorganization. The sole stockholder, who is 68 years old, receives voting common stock of XYZ Corporation valued at $25 million in exchange for his ABC Corporation stock, a company he started 40 years ago with $5,000. The stockholder's basis in his stock is estimated to be less than $2 million.

If the stockholder holds the stock of XYZ Corporation until death, his heirs will receive a basis in the XYZ stock equal to its fair market value at the date of death. Assuming they sold the XYZ stock immediately thereafter, they would not have any income tax liability because there would be no gain or loss on the sale. However, this type of transaction is not without real economic risk. The seller has exchanged his shares for stock in a company whose value may fluctuate widely.

A nontaxable transaction such as this is an excellent estate planning technique because it converts a nonliquid asset into a publicly traded stock, as well as eliminating a large potential income tax liability. However, the executor of an estate is often faced with a liquidity issue related to the payment of estate taxes. The topic of estate tax planning is beyond the scope of this book.

8.22   Nontax Factors Affecting Sellers

The seller is affected by certain nontax factors in deciding on an acquisition method. Generally, these nontax factors involve legal requirements associated with completing a transaction. The discussion below deals with the advantages and disadvantages of a stock deal, asset deal or merger/consolidation.

8.22a Stock Deal

Advantages

- Relatively simple deal. The seller exchanges stock for consideration.
- Deal can be executed quickly.
- Management's opinion does not stop shareholders from selling stock.
- Minority shareholders cannot prevent a controlling shareholder from selling his stock.
- A shareholder vote is not required.
- This transaction gives the acquiring company responsibility for all liabilities.

Disadvantages

- The transaction may require SEC filings.
- A seller of a control position may owe a fiduciary duty to minority shareholders in certain limited circumstances.

8.22b Asset Deal

Advantages

- A straightforward sale.
- In most cases the seller does not receive stock of the acquiring company.

Disadvantages

- An asset deal is the most complex transaction to effect because every asset must be separately conveyed.
- The transaction must comply with the applicable state's Bulk Sales laws. One must be careful not to violate creditors' rights. Furthermore, certain consents and assignments may be needed in an asset deal.
- This type of transaction requires a substantial (generally, majority) favorable vote of shareholders of the target company.
- State and local transfer taxes are imposed.
- In most cases seller does not receive stock of the acquiring company.

8.22c   Merger or Consolidation

Advantages

- Relatively straightforward procedures.
- Assets are transferred by operation of law.
- Wide range of consideration can be received.
- Participation in future growth through interest in merged entity.

Disadvantages

- The acquiring company assumes all of the liabilities of the target, whether disclosed or undisclosed, contingent or otherwise.
- Any representations or warranties made on behalf of the target company do not survive the transaction.
- Dissenting minority shareholders of both the acquiring and target companies have appraisal rights.
- Shareholders of both the acquiring and target companies must generally vote to approve the transaction.
- Participation in future growth through interest in merged entity.

Chapter 9

Comparing
Acquisition Methods

9.0 INTRODUCTION

The previous chapter laid the foundation for calculating the real economic cost and proceeds of an acquisition. This chapter describes how to complete an analysis that compares the real cost and proceeds under different acquisition methods and purchase prices.

In most cases the parties interested in completing a transaction do not wish to consider all seven alternate forms of effecting a transaction. The three nontaxable transaction methods, as well as the 338 Transaction and 338(h)(10) Transaction are of interest only in limited circumstances. Furthermore, the transaction may have to be effected using a particular acquisition method because of an overriding nontax consideration. Therefore, financial analysis is usually limited to a comparative analysis of two or three acquisition methods.

For illustration purposes, this chapter will touch on all seven acquisition methods using a common example.

9.1 COMPARATIVE ANALYSIS

Comparative analysis starts with an Asset Acquisition because this is the acquisition method the decision maker understands best. Once this benchmark method is analyzed, all other methods are compared to it.

Typically, comparative analysis is not required where an acquisition is contemplated to be an Asset Acquisition from the start of negotiations. In this instance, an analysis of the NPTC and NPP at various purchase prices should suffice.

9.11   Common Example

XYZ Corporation enters into negotiations with ABC Corporation to purchase its business. XYZ Corporation is a Fortune 500 company with a good track record in acquisitions. ABC Corporation is a public corporation with 40 percent of its stock owned by one family. The family consists of parents in their mid-50s, who started the business 26 years ago, and three young children. Both parents are in good health. However, they are tiring of the day to day wear and tear on their lives from managing the business. Also, neither believes that any of their children will be interested in the business. Therefore, they are looking to sell. The business has been very profitable over the years. Its balance sheet appears in Exhibit 9–1.

The family has a tax basis of $2.5 million in their stock. The remaining shareholders' estimated tax basis in their stock is approximately $27.5 million. The prospective deal would close on January 1, 1993, the first day of both companies' fiscal year.

EXHIBIT 9–1
ABC Corporation

Interim Balance Sheet as of September 30, 1992
(in Millions of Dollars)

Assets		Liabilities	
Cash & marketable securities	$2.5	Accounts payable & accrued	
Accounts receivable	7.5	expenses	$20.0
Inventory	20.0		
Land	5.0	Stockholders' equity	
Buildings & improvements	10.0	Common stock	5.0
Machinery & equipment	25.0	Retained earnings	45.0
		Total liabilities & stockholders'	
Total Assets	$70.0	equity	$70.0

9.2   ASSET ACQUISITION

Initially, we will analyze the transaction as an Asset Acquisition. The first step in the analysis is to estimate a purchase price range. Based on a number of valuation techniques described in Section 4, XYZ estimates that a deal for all the assets and liabilities would cost between $80 and $120 million. Having chosen the purchase price range, the specific purchase prices to be analyzed must be determined. Furthermore, an allocation of value to the various asset categories must be completed based on available information. After consulting with various members of XYZ's organization, the financial staff was able to come up with prelimi-

EXHIBIT 9–2
Allocation of Purchase Price to Asset Categories (in Millions of Dollars)

	Purchase Price		
	$80.0	$100.0	$120.0
Cash & marketable securities	$2.5	$2.5	$2.5
Accounts receivable	7.5	7.5	7.5
Inventory	20.0	20.0	20.0
Land	20.0	20.0	20.0
Buildings & improvements	20.0	22.5	25.0
Machinery & equipment	30.0	45.0	50.0
Goodwill	0.0	2.5	15.0
Accounts payable & accrued expenses	(20.0)	(20.0)	(20.0)
	$80.0	$100.0	$120.0

nary estimates of the fair market values for all assets and liabilities for the selected purchase prices it would analyze. For simplicity, no allocation of value was made to a covenant not to compete.

Due to the preliminary nature of these estimates, it is reasonable to assume that the fair market values of certain assets (e.g., buildings and improvements, machinery and equipment, and goodwill) will be greater given a higher purchase price. Why? If a buyer is willing to pay a higher price, this indicates that he has higher profit expectations. Given this higher profit expectancy, the underlying business assets are more valuable to him. One might argue that any increase in value over the figures for the lowest purchase price is all attributable to goodwill, but this probably does not reflect reality. Remember, these are preliminary estimates. Once hard information (appraisals) are available, such information should be used in estimating purchase price allocations. Typically, by the time such information is available, the purchase price or the range of purchase prices being considered has narrowed considerably.

We have assumed, for simplicity, that the allocations of value for both book and tax purposes are the same. See paragraphs 7.11b and C.11 for a discussion of the proper book and tax allocation methods.

9.21 NPTC

The next step is to compute the NPTC to the buyer given a range of purchase prices. We will assume that the buyer has adequate taxable income to offset any deductions associated with ABC's operation. We

EXHIBIT 9–3
Net Present Value of the Tax Benefit from Depreciation Deductions (in Millions of Dollars)

	Purchase Price					
	$80.0		$100.0		$120.0	
Year	Bldgs & Improv.	Mach & Equip.	Bldgs & Improv.	Mach & Equip.	Bldgs & Improv.	Mach & Equip.
Estimated fair market value	$20.0	$30.0	$22.5	$45.0	$25.0	$50.0
MACRS depreciation %						
1	3.042%	14.290%	3.042%	14.290%	3.042%	14.290%
2	3.175	24.490	3.175	24.490	3.175	24.490
3	3.175	17.490	3.175	17.490	3.175	17.490
4	3.175	12.490	3.175	12.490	3.175	12.490
5	3.175	8.930	3.175	8.930	3.175	8.930
6	3.175	8.920	3.175	8.920	3.175	8.920
7	3.175	8.930	3.175	8.930	3.175	8.930
8	3.175	4.460	3.175	4.460	3.175	4.460
9	3.174		3.174		3.174	
10	3.175		3.175		3.175	
Depreciation deductions						
1	$0.6	$4.3	$0.7	$6.4	$0.8	$7.1
2	0.6	7.3	0.7	11.0	0.8	12.2
3	0.6	5.2	0.7	7.9	0.8	8.7
4	0.6	3.7	0.7	5.6	0.8	6.2
5	0.6	2.7	0.7	4.0	0.8	4.5
6	0.6	2.7	0.7	4.0	0.8	4.5
7	0.6	2.7	0.7	4.0	0.8	4.5
8	0.6	1.3	0.7	2.0	0.8	2.2
9	0.6		0.7		0.8	
10	0.6		0.7		0.8	

Tax benefit at 38%

1	$0.2	$1.6	$0.3	$2.4	$0.3	$2.7
2	0.2	2.8	0.3	4.2	0.3	4.7
3	0.2	2.0	0.3	3.0	0.3	3.3
4	0.2	1.4	0.3	2.1	0.3	2.4
5	0.2	1.0	0.3	1.5	0.3	1.7
6	0.2	1.0	0.3	1.5	0.3	1.7
7	0.2	1.0	0.3	1.5	0.3	1.7
8	0.2	0.5	0.3	0.8	0.3	0.8
9	0.2		0.3		0.3	
10	0.2		0.3		0.3	
	$1.5	$8.2	$1.7	$12.3	$1.8	$13.7

10% present value factors

1	0.9091	0.9091	0.9091	0.9091	0.9091	0.9091
2	0.8264	0.8264	0.8264	0.8264	0.8264	0.8264
3	0.7513	0.7513	0.7513	0.7513	0.7513	0.7513
4	0.6830	0.6830	0.6830	0.6830	0.6830	0.6830
5	0.6209	0.6209	0.6209	0.6209	0.6209	0.6209
6	0.5645	0.5645	0.5645	0.5645	0.5645	0.5645
7	0.5132	0.5132	0.5132	0.5132	0.5132	0.5132
8	0.4665	0.4665	0.4665	0.4665	0.4665	0.4665
9	0.4241	0.4241	0.4241	0.4241	0.4241	0.4241
10	0.3855	0.3855	0.3855	0.3855	0.3855	0.3855

Present value of tax benefit

1	$0.2	$1.5	$0.2	$2.2	$0.3	$2.5
2	0.2	2.3	0.2	3.5	0.2	3.8
3	0.2	1.5	0.2	2.2	0.2	2.5
4	0.2	1.0	0.2	1.5	0.2	1.6
5	0.1	0.6	0.2	0.9	0.2	1.1
6	0.1	0.6	0.2	0.9	0.2	1.0
7	0.1	0.5	0.1	0.8	0.2	0.9
8	0.1	0.2	0.1	0.4	0.2	0.4
9	0.1		0.1		0.1	
10	0.1		0.1		0.1	
	$1.5	$8.2	$1.7	$12.3	$1.8	$13.7

will also assume that XYZ should discount the tax savings associated with the acquisition at 10 percent. Finally, the analysis will go forward 10 years because of the certainty of the tax deductions involved.

To determine the NPTC we must calculate the depreciation deductions and related tax savings for the buildings and improvements and machinery and equipment. These calculations appear in Exhibit 9–3.

Now that we have computed the present value of the future tax benefit associated with depreciation deductions, we can calculate the NPTC for the buyer under the various purchase prices (Exhibit 9–4).

EXHIBIT 9–4
Calculation of NPTC (in Millions of Dollars)

Purchase price	$80.0	$100.0	$120.0
Less: Present value of tax savings for			
Machinery & equipment	(8.2)	(12.3)	(13.7)
Buildings & improvements	(1.5)	(1.7)	(1.8)
NPTC	$70.3	$86.0	$104.5

9.22   NPP

The NPP analysis is difficult because the buyer does not know (1) the tax basis of the seller's assets, (2) whether or not the target's stockholders intend to liquidate the target after the asset transaction, or (3) the target shareholders' tax basis in their stock. However, based on a review of ABC's financials and discussions with ABC officials, XYZ was able to make certain estimates (Exhibit 9–5).

EXHIBIT 9–5
Estimated Book and Tax Values at January 1, 1993 (in Millions of Dollars)

	Book Values	Tax Basis
Buildings & improvements (gross)	$35.0	$35.0
Accumulated depreciation	(25.0)	(30.0)
Buildings & improvements (net)	$10.0	$5.0
Machinery & equipment (gross)	$45.0	$45.0
Accumulated depreciation	(20.0)	(35.0)
Machinery & equipment (net)	$25.0	$10.0

XYZ does not know if the seller intends to liquidate ABC Corporation. Therefore, two analyses must be done: (1) assuming no liquidation, and (2) assuming liquidation. The calculations common to both analyses are given in Exhibits 9–6 and 9–7. These include calculations of depreciation recapture for ABC Corporation, the character of ABC's gain on the sale and the tax burden to ABC associated with the sale.

ABC depreciated its buildings and improvements using the straight-line depreciation method. Accordingly, there is no depreciation recapture for this asset category. See paragraph B.8 for a complete description of depreciation recapture and paragraph B.64 for a discussion of the interplay between Section 1231 and the depreciation recapture provisions.

The Gain on Net Assets Sold schedule (Exhibit 9–6) calculates the taxable gain at various prices and the character of any gain. Let us review the calculations for the $120 million purchase price. Cash, accounts receivable and inventory are purchased at a price equal to their adjusted basis, so no gain or loss is associated with these items. The depreciation recapture and Section 1231 income amounts associated with machinery and equipment have been calculated. Land and buildings and improvements are both Section 1231 assets. The gain associated with either is Section 1231 income. Goodwill is a capital asset, not a Section 1231 asset, in the hands of the target. The gain associated with goodwill is capital gain. Finally, no taxable gain or loss is associated with XYZ's assumption of ABC's liabilities.

ABC Corporation's NPP are calculated in Exhibit 9–7. The tax burden has three components: (1) the tax due on the Section 1245 recapture income; (2) the tax on the Section 1231 gain; and (3) the tax on the capital gain. Regardless of whether ABC Corporation liquidates, ABC will incur a tax burden of between $19.0 and $34.2 million. The NPP to ABC Corporation will be between $61.0 and $85.8 million.

Assuming that ABC Corporation is liquidated, the shareholders will be taxed on the proceeds distributed. In most instances the stock is a capital asset for the stockholders, and assuming that it has been held for the required holding period, the gain that the shareholders realize will be treated as capital gain. The net result is that the shareholders will realize NPP of between $51.1 and $67.9 million (Exhibit 9–8).

EXHIBIT 9–6
Gain on Net Assets Sold (in Millions of Dollars)

	Original Tax Basis (A)	Accumulated Depreciation (B)	Adjusted Basis (A − B) (C)	Fair Market Value (D)	Taxable Gain (D − C) (E)	Character of Gain		
						Section 1245 Income (Lesser of (B) or (E)) (F)	Section 1231 Income (G)	Capital Gain (H)
$80.0 Million Price								
Cash & mkt. securities	$2.5		$2.5	$2.5				
Accounts receivable	7.5		7.5	7.5				
Inventory	20.0		20.0	20.0				
Land	5.0		5.0	20.0	$15.0		$15.0	
Buildings & improvements	35.0	$30.0	5.0	20.0	15.0		$15.0	
Machinery & equipment	45.0	35.0	10.0	30.0	20.0	$20.0		
Goodwill	0.0		0.0	0.0				
Accounts payable & accrued expenses	(20.0)		(20.0)	(20.0)				
Totals	$95.0	$65.0	$30.0	$80.0	$50.0	$20.0	$30.0	

134

$100.0 Million Price

Cash & mkt. securities	$2.5		$2.5	$2.5				
Accounts receivable	7.5		7.5	7.5				
Inventory	20.0		20.0	20.0				
Land	5.0		5.0	20.0	$15.0		$15.0	
Buildings & improvements	35.0	30.0	5.0	22.5	17.5		17.5	
Machinery & equipment	45.0	35.0	10.0	45.0	35.0	$35.0		
Goodwill	0.0		0.0	2.5	2.5			$2.5
Accounts payable & accrued expenses	(20.0)		(20.0)	(20.0)				
Totals	$95.0	$65.0	$30.0	$100.0	$70.0	$35.0	$32.5	$2.5

$120.0 Million Price

Cash & mkt. securities	$2.5		$2.5	$2.5				
Accounts receivable	7.5		7.5	7.5				
Inventory	20.0		20.0	20.0				
Land	5.0		5.0	20.0	$15.0		$15.0	
Buildings & improvements	35.0	30.0	5.0	25.0	20.0		20.0	
Machinery & equipment	45.0	35.0	10.0	50.0	40.0	$35.0	5.0	
Goodwill	0.0		0.0	15.0	15.0			$15.0
Accounts payable & accrued expenses	(20.0)		(20.0)	(20.0)				
Totals	$95.0	$65.0	$30.0	$120.0	$90.0	$35.0	$40.0	$15.0

EXHIBIT 9–7
Calculation of NPP to ABC Corporation (in Millions of Dollars)

Purchase price	$80.0	$100.0	$120.0
Taxable gain			
Section 1245 income	$20.0	$35.0	$35.0
Section 1231 income	30.0	32.5	40.0
Capital gain	0.0	2.5	15.0
Total taxable gain	50.0	70.0	90.0
Tax rate	38%	38%	38%
Tax burden	19.0	26.6	34.2
NPP to ABC Corporation	$61.0	$73.4	$85.8

EXHIBIT 9–8
Calculation of NPP to ABC's Shareholders Assuming Liquidation
(in Millions of Dollars)

Purchase price	$80.0	$100.0	$120.0
Proceeds available for distribution	$61.0	$73.4	$85.8
Tax basis of stock	30.0	30.0	30.0
Capital gain	31.0	43.4	55.8
Effective capital gains tax rate for individuals	32%	32%	32%
Tax burden	9.9	13.9	17.9
NPP to ABC's shareholders	$51.1	$59.5	$67.9

9.23 Presentation of Results

Exhibit 9–9 conveys the results. XYZ's NPTC will be between $70.3 and $104.5 million if an Asset Acquisition is consummated within the range of purchase prices analyzed. ABC's NPP from such a transaction would be between $61.0 and $85.8 million, and ABC's stockholders' NPP would be between $51.1 and $67.9 million.

EXHIBIT 9-9
Asset Acquisition—Comparison of NPTC and NPP

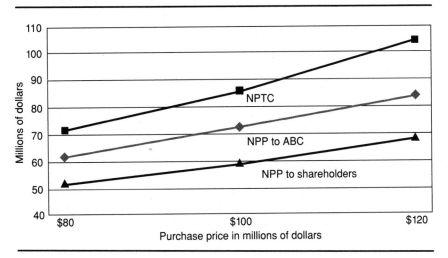

9.3 338 TRANSACTION

It is not productive to analyze a 338 Transaction because ABC Corporation does not have a substantial NOL. The cost of stepping up the basis of the target's assets is prohibitive. As indicated earlier, this will be true in the vast majority of acquisition situations.

9.4 338(h)(10) TRANSACTION

A 338(h)(10) Transaction is not a viable alternative because ABC is not a member of an affiliated group that files a consolidated tax return.

9.5 STOCK ACQUISITION

In analyzing this acquisition method we will assume that XYZ Corporation purchases all of the outstanding stock of ABC Corporation and that the same price range, $80 to $120 million, is to be analyzed.

9.51   NPTC

The NPTC in this type of deal is equal to the price paid for the stock less the present value of the tax savings from future depreciation deductions, calculated using the target company's existing adjusted tax basis and depreciation methods. Since there will not be a disposition of assets of the target, there will be no depreciation recapture. The adjusted basis of the depreciable assets is assumed to be (in millions of dollars):

Machinery and equipment	$10
Buildings and improvements	5

   If this type of deal is contemplated, these figures should be known with certainty because the target company should provide the target company's latest tax returns to the acquirer. We will assume, for simplicity, that the above assets would be depreciated as shown in Exhibit 9–10.

EXHIBIT 9–10
Net Present Value of the Tax Benefit from Depreciation Deductions
(in Millions of Dollars)

	Depreciation Deductions					
Year	Machinery and Equipment	Buildings and Improvments	Total	Tax Savings at 38%	10 Percent Present Value Factor	Present Value of Tax Benefit
1	$2.0	$0.8	$2.8	$1.1	0.9091	$1.0
2	2.0	0.7	2.7	1.0	0.8264	0.8
3	2.0	0.7	2.7	1.0	0.7513	0.8
4	2.0	0.7	2.7	1.0	0.6830	0.7
5	2.0	0.7	2.7	1.0	0.6209	0.6
6		0.7	0.7	0.3	0.5645	0.2
7		0.7	0.7	0.3	0.5132	0.1
	$10.0	$5.0	$15.0	$5.7		$4.2

   The NPTC for the buyer will range between $75.8 and $115.8 if a Stock Acquisition is consummated (Exhibit 9–11).

EXHIBIT 9–11
Calculation of NPTC (in Millions of Dollars)

Purchase price	$80.0	$100.0	$120.0
Less: Present value of tax savings for depreciable assets	(4.2)	(4.2)	(4.2)
NPTC	$75.8	$95.8	$115.8

9.52 NPP

The NPP calculations appear in Exhibit 9–12. XYZ has estimated that the stockholders' basis in their stock is $30 million.

EXHIBIT 9–12
Calculation of NPP to ABC's Shareholders (in Millions of Dollars)

Selling price	$80.0	$100.0	$120.0
Tax basis of stock	30.0	30.0	30.0
Capital gain	50.0	70.0	90.0
Effective capital gains tax rate for individuals	32%	32%	32%
Tax burden to shareholders	16.0	22.4	28.8
NPP	$64.0	$77.6	$91.2

Deducting the tax burden from the selling price, the stockholders will net between $64.0 and $91.2 million.

9.53 Presentation of Results

The NPTC and NPP are displayed in the same format used for an Asset Acquisition. XYZ's NPTC will be between $75.8 and $115.8 million, whereas ABC's shareholders' NPP will range between $64.0 and $91.2 million (Exhibit 9–13).

EXHIBIT 9–13
Stock Acquisition—Comparison of NPTC and NPP

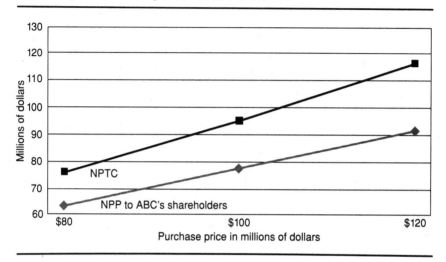

9.6   TYPE A REORGANIZATION

There are four different types of Type A Reorganizations. However, for illustrative purposes, we will assume that XYZ wishes to merge the target company into a controlled subsidiary in exchange for stock of XYZ Corporation and cash. At the time of the merger, cash will represent one half of the total purchase price. This transaction is a Cash Option Merger executed as a Type A Forward Subsidiary Merger.

9.61   NPTC

The NPTC in a Type A Reorganization is equal to the market value of securities exchanged, plus the fair market value of all other consideration paid, less the present value of the tax savings associated with future depreciation deductions, calculated using the target company's existing adjusted tax basis and depreciation methods. A Type A Reorganization does not give rise to a disposition of assets that would cause depreciation recapture.

The present value of tax savings associated with future depreciation deductions is calculated the same as under a Stock Acquisition. The calculations are not repeated here (see Exhibit 9–10). The NPTC to XYZ Corporation ranges from $75.8 to $115.8 million (Exhibit 9–14).

EXHIBIT 9–14
Calculation of NPTC (in Millions of Dollars)

Purchase price	$80.0	$100.0	$120.0
Less: Present value of tax savings for depreciable assets	(4.2)	(4.2)	(4.2)
NPTC	$75.8	$95.8	$115.8

9.62 NPP

Since the stockholders of ABC receive boot in the contemplated transaction, they must recognize gain to the extent of the lesser of boot received or the gain realized. We will assume that the cash does not constitute a dividend. Therefore, the entire gain will be capital gain.

The NPPs that ABC's shareholders can expect to receive if a Type A Reorganization is completed is approximately $67.2 to $100.8 million. In performing the calculations in Exhibit 9–15, we have assumed that the stockholders of ABC intend to hold onto the stock of XYZ indefinitely. If this were not the case, it would be necessary to calculate the present value of the estimated sale price of the stock, as well as the associated tax burden. It should be noted that certain of the target company's shareholders are taking the risk associated with holding the acquiring company's stock. How these shareholders feel about the stability of this investment will heavily influence whether or not they would be interested in this type of transaction.

EXHIBIT 9–15
Calculation of NPP to ABC's Shareholders (in Millions of Dollars)

Selling price	$80.0	$100.0	$120.0
Tax basis of stock	30.0	30.0	30.0
Realized gain	$50.0	$70.0	$90.0
Boot received	$40.0	$50.0	$60.0
Taxable capital gain	$40.0	$50.0	$60.0
Effective capital gains tax rate for individuals	32%	32%	32%
Tax burden to stockholders	$12.8	$16.0	$19.2
NPP	$67.2	$84.0	$100.8

9.63   Presentation of Results

XYZ's NPTC will be between $75.8 and $115.8 million, whereas ABC's shareholders' NPP will range between $67.2 and $100.8 million (Exhibit 9–16).

EXHIBIT 9–16
Type A Reorganization—Comparison of NPTC and NPP

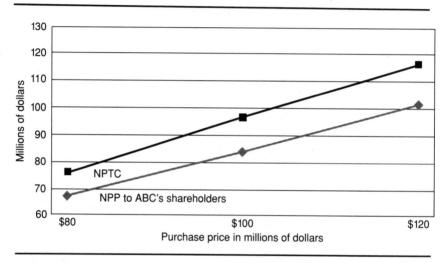

9.7   TYPE B REORGANIZATION

Analyzing a Type B Reorganization is very straightforward. In this transaction we will assume XYZ will be able to purchase all the outstanding stock of ABC in a Type B Stock Exchange.

9.71   NPTC

The NPTC for the acquiring company is equal to the market value of the voting stock exchanged less the present value of the tax benefit from future depreciation deductions calculated using the target company's existing adjusted tax basis and depreciation methods. The present values of the tax benefit are the same as those calculated under a Stock Acquisition. XYZ's NPTC in a Type B Reorganization will range from $75.8 to $115.8 million (Exhibit 9–17).

EXHIBIT 9–17
Calculation of NPTC (in Millions of Dollars)

Purchase price	$80.0	$100.0	$120.0
Less: Present value of tax savings for depreciable assets	(4.2)	(4.2)	(4.2)
NPTC	$75.8	$95.8	$115.8

9.72   NPP

The stockholders of the target company will not have any tax burden with this type of transaction unless they liquidate their stock holdings of XYZ at some point. If this is the case, then a calculation should be performed estimating the present value of the proceeds to be received and the associated tax burden. Otherwise the selling price represents the stockholders' NPP. Thus ABC's stockholders' NPP will be between $80 and $120 million. In this transaction the target company's shareholders are assuming the risk associated with holding the acquiring company's stock. How they view such an investment will determine whether or not they are interested in this type of transaction.

9.73   Presentation of Results

XYZ's NPTC will be between $75.8 and $115.8 million, whereas ABC's shareholders' NPP will range between $80 and $120 million (Exhibit 9–18).

EXHIBIT 9–18
Type B Reorganization—Comparison of NPTC and NPP

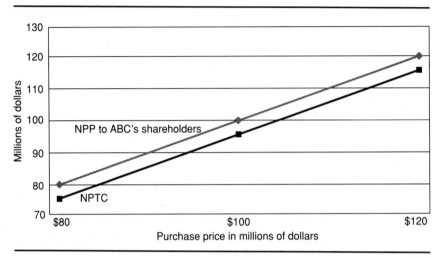

Purchase price in millions of dollars

9.8   TYPE C REORGANIZATION

In analyzing a Type C Reorganization we will assume that XYZ Corporation will purchase in a Type C Subsidiary Stock for Assets Exchange all the assets and assume all the stated liabilities of ABC in exchange solely for voting stock of XYZ. ABC Corporation will distribute all of the XYZ stock received to its shareholders as part of the transaction.

9.81   NPTC

The NPTC will mirror the cost in a Type B Reorganization. XYZ's NPTC will range between $75.8 and $115.8 million (Exhibit 9–19).

EXHIBIT 9–19
Calculation of NPTC (in Millions of Dollars)

Purchase price	$80.0	$100.0	$120.0
Less: Present value of tax savings for depreciable assets	(4.2)	(4.2)	(4.2)
NPTC	$75.8	$95.8	$115.8

9.82 NPP

The NPP is the same as under a Type B Reorganization, given that ABC exchanges its assets and liabilities solely for XYZ's stock. The NPP would change if the target's shareholders received any boot in the transaction or if they intend to liquidate their stockholdings of XYZ in the future. As with the other reorganization transactions, the target company's shareholders are assuming the risk associated with holding the acquiring company's stock.

9.83 Presentation of Results

XYZ's NPTC will be between $75.8 and $115.8 million, whereas ABC's shareholders' NPP will range between $80 and $120 million (Exhibit 9–20).

EXHIBIT 9–20
Type C Reorganization—Comparison of NPTC and NPP

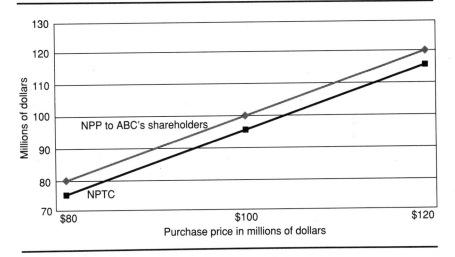

9.9 RESULTS OF COMPARATIVE ANALYSIS

The goal of the comparative approach described in this chapter is to provide useful information to the decision maker concerning the real cost of effecting a transaction under different acquisition methods. The graphs appearing at the end of each analysis of the sample problem assist the decision maker somewhat toward this goal. However, what the decision maker really needs to see is (1) a comparative analysis of the NPTC to XYZ under the various methods and (2) a comparative analysis of the NPP to ABC's stockholders under the various methods. These graphs appear below.

Exhibits 9–21 and 9–22 are useful for several reasons. First, the comparative analysis of NPTC identifies the type of acquisition method that would be the least costly for each of the purchase prices being considered. Second, it permits the decision maker to easily compare costs assuming different purchase prices and acquisition methods. For example, the NPTC comparative analysis graph indicates that the NPTC for an Asset Acquisition, assuming a $100 million purchase price, is approximately $86 million. The real cost of a Stock Acquisition or an A, B or C Reorganization would be approximately $10 million higher at the same nominal purchase price of $100 million. Third, the comparative analysis of NPP highlights the type of acquisition method the target company's shareholders should prefer under any purchase price being considered, all other things being equal. Fourth, the comparative analysis of NPP allows the acquirer's decision maker to understand the trade-offs that the

EXHIBIT 9–21
Comparative Analysis of NPTC

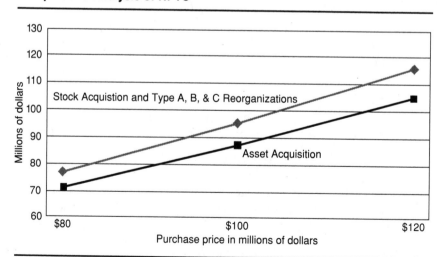

EXHIBIT 9–22
Comparative Analysis of NPP

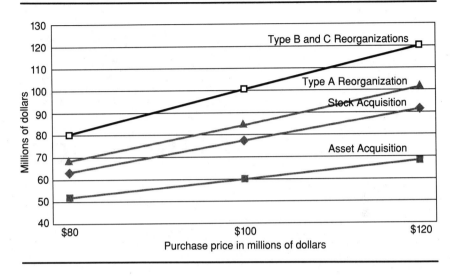

target's shareholders are facing. Assuming the selling shareholders do not want a nontaxable transaction, they will generally attempt to negotiate the transaction as a Stock Acquisition because the NPP under this method clearly exceeds the NPP in an Asset Acquisition. How much is a Stock Acquisition worth versus an Asset Acquisition? At a price of $80 million the seller would receive approximately $12.9 million more if the deal is executed as a Stock Acquisition. The figure rises to $18.1 million at the $100 million price level and to $23.3 million at a price of $120 million. The importance of a Stock Acquisition increases as the price rises because of the double tax (corporate and personal income tax) being paid by the seller in an Asset Acquisition.

Section Two

Conclusion

The objective of the Cost Analysis Section was to answer the question, "What will an acquisition cost?" It should be clear by now that the cost of an acquisition depends heavily on the acquisition method used to effect the transaction. Therefore, the best answer we can give the decision maker is an analysis of acquisition costs assuming different methods and purchase prices.

In laying the foundation for this analysis, we reviewed some fundamental concepts of acquisition cost, the alternate acquisition methods that can be used to effect a transaction, and the nontax factors that influence the buyer and seller. Finally, Chapter 9 outlined the analytical approach for comparing the costs and proceeds under different acquisition methods and purchase prices.

Section Three

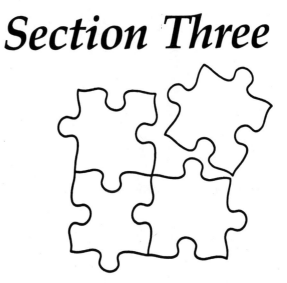

An Example

Chapter 10

Case of Mareight Corporation

10.0 INTRODUCTION

This chapter presents a case study of an acquisition and analyzes the target using the cost analysis described in Section Two. This example will also be used extensively in Sections Three and Four to illustrate various valuation techniques.

A target company that is attractive to a number of prospective buyers is *Mareight Corporation ("Mareight"* or the *"Company")*. Mareight is a wholly owned subsidiary of *United Industries, Inc. (United)*, a Fortune 500 conglomerate. Interested parties include *Harrison Corporation (Harrison)*, a large diversified conglomerate, and *New World Associates (New World)*, a leveraged buyout firm that has recently raised $175 million in equity and subordinated debt capital for investment in LBOs. In addition, *General Grocery Products, Inc. (General)*, a billion dollar multinational consumer products company, has expressed interest. General's chief executive officer has publicly stated that his company would take a hard look at acquiring Mareight if it became available. General is searching for profitable U.S. businesses that have products General can market through its existing sales force. The transaction will be analyzed from Harrison's perspective.

United announced in June 1992 that it had hired *Wall Street Investment Bank (Wall Street)* to explore options with respect to its investment in Mareight. The conglomerate is interested in divesting the subsidiary to help fund its growth plans for another operating division. United is interested in an all-cash transaction.

Shortly after United's announcement, Wall Street contacted numerous prospective purchasers, including General, Harrison, and New World and forwarded descriptive selling memorandums once officers of each entity executed a confidentiality agreement. All three submitted indications of interest in July 1992. Harrison's and General's indications of interest were sufficiently high to warrant an invitation into the second phase of the auction. However, as expected, Wall Street informed both companies that their indications of interest were at the low end of the range that the seller had received.

In August 1992, Wall Street distributed a draft contract of sale, which confirmed that United was proposing to sell the stock of Mareight Corporation. Wall Street also informed all bidders that final bids, including a copy of the draft contract, marked for any proposed changes, were due on November 15, 1992. The expected closing date for the transaction was December 31, 1992, the last day of United's and Mareight's fiscal years.

10.1 DESCRIPTION OF MAREIGHT CORPORATION

The Company, founded in 1903, manufactures and distributes a line of food flavorings. It has the number two market position in its market segment. There are two major competitors and several smaller competitors in the food flavoring market. The largest competitor is only slightly larger than Mareight. However, this competitor was recently acquired by a large multinational food company. The other major competitor is a company similar in size to General. Smaller competitors are all privately owned mom and pop operators.

Industry unit volumes in the flavoring market have been increasing at a rate of 3 percent per year over the last five years, and Mareight's unit sales in both its product lines have followed this industry trend. In addition, the company has raised prices as costs have risen to maintain its operating profit margin.

Exhibit 10–1 contains information regarding Mareight's shipments in millions of units and average unit prices for its two brands. Mareight's income statements, net capital employed and selected other data appear in Exhibits 10–2, 10–3 and 10–4. Prospective bidders received an abbreviated balance sheet in the selling memorandum. Detailed balance sheets were provided during due diligence.

EXHIBIT 10–1
Shipments and Pricing Data

	Year Ended December 31,			
	1989	*1990*	*1991*	*1992E*
Sales volume (millions of units)				
Product A	296	305	312	328
Product B	296	308	324	333
	592	613	636	661
Selling prices per unit (in dollars)				
Product A	$0.123	$0.126	$0.130	$0.134
Product B	$0.243	$0.248	$0.258	$0.272
Gross sales (millions of dollars)				
Product A	$36,408	$38,430	$40,560	$43,952
Product B	$71,965	$76,384	$83,592	$90,576
	$108,373	$114,814	$124,152	$134,528

EXHIBIT 10–2
Income Statements (in Thousands of Dollars)

	Year Ended December 31,			
	1989	*1990*	*1991*	*1992E*
Gross sales	$108,373	$114,814	$124,152	$134,528
Freight & returns	956	1,158	1,212	1,226
Net sales	107,417	113,656	122,940	133,302
Cost of goods sold	69,714	74,445	80,895	87,046
Gross profit	37,704	39,211	42,045	46,256
Gross margin	35.1%	34.5%	34.2%	34.7%
SG&A expenses*	20,409	21,595	23,359	25,327
Depreciation & amortization	5,435	6,297	6,777	7,022
Total expenses	25,844	27,892	30,136	32,349
Operating profit	$ 11,859	$ 11,320	$ 11,910	$ 13,906

* Figures exclude any allocation of corporate overhead.

EXHIBIT 10–3
Net Capital Employed (in Thousands of Dollars)

	Year Ended December 31,			
	1989	1990	1991	1992E
Cash & marketable securities	$3,313	$3,288	$1,111	$2,856
Accounts receivable	14,123	15,083	13,677	14,732
Inventory	24,344	23,357	27,075	25,903
Prepaid expenses	5,211	5,421	4,369	5,109
Total current assets	46,991	47,149	46,232	48,600
Accounts payable	9,973	9,555	8,993	7,475
Accrued expenses	4,939	5,627	5,133	5,421
Income taxes payable	826	1,436	3,034	1,333
Total current liabilities	15,738	16,618	17,160	14,229
Net working capital	31,253	30,531	29,072	34,371
Net property, plant & equipment	43,378	45,001	45,965	44,965
Other assets	3,141	3,289	2,704	3,616
Net assets	$77,772	$78,821	$77,741	$82,952
Financed by:				
Intercompany payable	$48,777	$50,241	$46,772	$49,388
Common stock	1,000	1,000	1,000	1,000
Common stockholders' equity	27,995	27,580	29,969	32,564
Total capitalization	$77,772	$78,821	$77,741	$82,952

Note: Shaded figures were not in selling memo but were provided during due diligence.

EXHIBIT 10–4
Selected Additional Data (in Thousands of Dollars)

	1989	1990	1991	1992E
Average accounts receivable	$13,064	$13,841	$13,946	$16,586
Number of days sales	44	44	41	45
Average inventory	$23,238	$24,815	$27,895	$29,015
Turnover based on cost of goods sold	3.0	3.0	2.9	3.0
Capital expenditures	$5,658	$7,402	$6,285	$6,022

Note: Shaded figures were not in selling memo but were provided during due diligence.

The selling memorandum provided by Wall Street included three years of forecast income and cash flow statements. This forecast was extended by Harrison to six years for analytical purposes. For convenience, these forecasts are shown together in Exhibits 10–5 and 10–6. The forecast assumes that demand for the industry's products will increase at a compound rate of 4 percent as baby boomers come of age.

The financial forecast for Mareight was supplemented by Best and Worst Case scenarios developed by Harrison. Harrison's Worst Case estimates provided for flat volume while its Best Case forecast was for unit volumes to rise 10 percent annually.

The Company owns and operates five manufacturing facilities with approximately 1,400,000 square feet of manufacturing and warehouse space. In addition, the Company operates two 500,000 square foot warehouses, one of which houses corporate headquarters.

The Company expects to spend approximately $7,700,000 on capital expenditures in the coming year and similar amounts in each year in the future. The Company has traditionally depreciated property, plant and equipment quickly for accounting purposes.

Harrison's chief economist has forecast a 3 percent inflation rate for all costs related to Mareight's operations over the next few years.

10.11   General's Expected Synergies

Mareight currently uses a direct sales force of 162 people to market its products nationally. General expects to eliminate approximately 50 of these people. The annual cost of a salesperson for the year ended December 31, 1992, is estimated to be $48,000. Accordingly, the expected annual savings from reducing the sales force will be $2,400,000. Moreover, General expects to reap about $500,000 in cost savings annually because Mareight's packaging requirments can be produced at one of General's existing plants. Finally, General anticipates eliminating a substantial amount of Mareight's duplicative administrative expenses. General has quantified these administrative expenses as outlined below. These figures are in thousands of dollars.

	1989	1990	1991	1992E
Duplicative administration expenses	$1,350	$1,400	$1,450	$1,500

General does not anticipate any cost savings from synergies in the first year after a transaction due to severence costs.

EXHIBIT 10–5
Forecast Income Statements (in Thousands of Dollars)

Year Ended December 31,

	1993	1994	1995	1996	1997	1998
Net sales	$143,300	$154,047	$165,601	$178,021	$191,372	$205,725
Cost of goods sold	93,861	100,901	108,468	116,604	125,349	134,750
Gross profit	49,438	53,146	57,132	61,417	66,023	70,975
Gross margin	34.5%	34.5%	34.5%	34.5%	34.5%	34.5%
SG&A expenses	27,227	29,269	31,464	33,824	36,361	39,088
Depreciation & amortization	7,595	8,164	8,777	9,435	10,143	10,903
Total expenses	34,822	37,433	40,241	43,259	46,503	49,991
Operating profit	14,617	15,713	16,891	18,158	19,520	20,984
Tax provision—38%	5,554	5,971	6,419	6,900	7,418	7,974
Net income	$ 9,062	$ 9,742	$ 10,473	$ 11,258	$ 12,102	$ 13,010
Capital Requirements:						
Capital expenditures	$7,738	$8,319	$8,942	$9,613	$10,334	$11,109
Increase in working capital	1,444	2,472	2,657	2,857	3,071	3,301

Note: Shaded areas represent extended forecast by Harrison Corporation.

EXHIBIT 10–6

Cash Flow Forecast (in Thousands of Dollars)

	Year Ended December 31,					
	1993	1994	1995	1996	1997	1998
Sources						
Net income	$9,062	$9,742	$10,473	$11,258	$12,102	$13,010
Depreciation & amortization	7,595	8,164	8,777	9,435	10,143	10,903
Deferred taxes	526	668	731	841	1,036	1,048
Total sources	17,183	18,574	19,980	21,534	23,281	24,961
Uses						
Capital expenditures	7,738	8,319	8,942	9,613	10,334	11,109
Increase in working capital	1,444	2,472	2,657	2,857	3,071	3,301
Total uses	9,182	10,790	11,600	12,470	13,405	14,410
After-tax net cash flows	$8,001	$7,784	$8,381	$9,064	$9,876	$10,551

Note: Shaded areas represent extended forecast by Harrison Corporation.

10.2   COST ANALYSIS

Three alternate methods of consummating the transaction must be analyzed to understand the cost of acquiring Mareight: (1) an Asset Acquisition, (2) a 338(h)(10) Transaction, and (3) a Stock Acquisition. However, for illustration purposes, we will only analyze the Asset Acquisition and Stock Acquisition methods. The cost analysis was completed by Harrison only after it was invited into the second round of the auction.

10.3   ASSET ACQUISITION

The first step in the analysis is to estimate a purchase price range. Based on a number of valuation techniques described in Section Four, Harrison and its financial advisors estimate that the appropriate purchase price range to analyze was between $100 and $220 million. Five specific purchase prices were analyzed. However, only three ($100, $160 and $220 million) are shown in the exhibits that follow.

Harrison and its advisors came up with the preliminary estimates in Exhibit 10–7 of the fair market values for all assets and liabilities for the selected purchase prices it would analyze. In performing an analysis for the first round, Harrison assumed that the fair market values of the target's assets and liabilities were equal to their net book values. Hence, the entire premium paid over book value represented goodwill, except that transaction costs were approximately $2.5 million.

Harrison assumed, for simplicity, that the allocations of value for both book and tax purposes would be the same. However, see paragraphs 7.11b and C.11 for a discussion of the proper book and tax allocation methods.

EXHIBIT 10–7
Allocation of Purchase Price (in Millions of Dollars)

	Purchase Price		
	$100.0	$160.0	$220.0
Cash & marketable securities[1]	$1.5	$1.5	$1.5
Accounts receivable	14.7	14.7	14.7
Inventory[2]	25.9	25.9	25.9
Prepaid expenses	5.1	5.1	5.1
Land	6.0	8.0	10.0
Buildings & improvements	12.0	18.0	24.0
Machinery & equipment	38.8	58.8	78.8
Goodwill	2.7	34.7	66.7
Other assets[3]	6.1	6.1	6.1
Accounts payable & accrued expenses	(12.9)	(12.9)	(12.9)
	$100.0	$160.0	$220.0

[1] Assumes payment of $1.3 million in income taxes and $2.5 million in transaction expenses.
[2] A simplifying assumption was made that inventory values were constant.
[3] Includes $2.5 million in capitalized transaction expenses.

10.31   NPTC

Harrison expects to have adequate taxable income to offset any tax deductions associated with Mareight's operation. Therefore, Harrison has decided to discount the tax benefits associated with the acquisition at 10 percent, which is a few percentage points over the current risk-free rate. The calculations for the depreciation deductions and related tax benefits for buildings and improvements and machinery and equipment for a 10-year period appear in Exhibit 10–8.

EXHIBIT 10–8

Net Present Value of the Tax Benefit from Depreciation Deductions (in Millions of Dollars)

		Purchase Price				
		$100.0		$160.0		$220.0	
	Year	Bldgs & Improv.	Mach & Equip.	Bldgs & Improv.	Mach & Equip.	Bldgs & Improv.	Mach & Equip.
Estimated fair market value		$12.0	$38.8	$18.0	$58.8	$24.0	$78.8
MACRS depreciation %	1	3.042%	14.290%	3.042%	14.290%	3.042%	14.290%
	2	3.175	24.490	3.175	24.490	3.175	24.490
	3	3.175	17.490	3.175	17.490	3.175	17.490
	4	3.175	12.490	3.175	12.490	3.175	12.490
	5	3.175	8.930	3.175	8.930	3.175	8.930
	6	3.175	8.920	3.175	8.920	3.175	8.920
	7	3.175	8.930	3.175	8.930	3.175	8.930
	8	3.175	4.460	3.175	4.460	3.175	4.460
	9	3.174		3.174		3.174	
	10	3.175		3.175		3.175	
Depreciation deductions	1	$0.4	$5.5	$0.5	$8.4	$0.7	$11.3
	2	0.4	9.5	0.6	14.4	0.8	19.3
	3	0.4	6.8	0.6	10.3	0.8	13.8
	4	0.4	4.8	0.6	7.3	0.8	9.8
	5	0.4	3.5	0.6	5.2	0.8	7.0
	6	0.4	3.5	0.6	5.2	0.8	7.0
	7	0.4	3.5	0.6	5.2	0.8	7.0
	8	0.4	1.7	0.6	2.6	0.8	3.5
	9	0.4		0.6		0.8	
	10	0.4		0.6		0.8	
Tax benefit at 38%	1	$0.1	$2.1	$0.2	$3.2	$0.3	$4.3
	2	0.1	3.6	0.2	5.5	0.3	7.3

Year						
3	0.1	2.6	0.2	3.9	0.3	5.2
4	0.1	1.8	0.2	2.8	0.3	3.7
5	0.1	1.3	0.2	2.0	0.3	2.7
6	0.1	1.3	0.2	2.0	0.3	2.7
7	0.1	1.3	0.2	2.0	0.3	2.7
8	0.1	0.7	0.2	1.0	0.3	1.3
9	0.1		0.2		0.3	
10	0.1					

10% present value factors

Year						
1	0.9091	0.9091	0.9091	0.9091	0.9091	0.9091
2	0.8264	0.8264	0.8264	0.8264	0.8264	0.8264
3	0.7513	0.7513	0.7513	0.7513	0.7513	0.7513
4	0.6830	0.6830	0.6830	0.6830	0.6830	0.6830
5	0.6209	0.6209	0.6209	0.6209	0.6209	0.6209
6	0.5645	0.5645	0.5645	0.5645	0.5645	0.5645
7	0.5132	0.5132	0.5132	0.5132	0.5132	0.5132
8	0.4665	0.4665	0.4665	0.4665	0.4665	0.4665
9	0.4241	0.4241	0.4241	0.4241	0.4241	0.4241
10	0.3855	0.3855	0.3855	0.3855	0.3855	0.3855

Present value of tax benefit

Year						
1	$0.1	$1.9	$0.2	$2.9	$0.3	$3.9
2	0.1	3.0	0.2	4.5	0.2	6.1
3	0.1	1.9	0.2	2.9	0.2	3.9
4	0.1	1.3	0.1	1.9	0.2	2.6
5	0.1	0.8	0.1	1.2	0.2	1.7
6	0.1	0.7	0.1	1.1	0.2	1.5
7	0.1	0.7	0.1	1.0	0.1	1.4
8	0.1	0.3	0.1	0.5	0.1	0.6
9	0.1		0.1		0.1	
10	0.1		0.1		0.1	
	$0.9	$10.6	$1.3	$16.1	$1.8	$21.6

Rounded numbers are used for calculations throughout this book.

EXHIBIT 10–9
Calculation of NPTC for Harrison Assuming an Asset Acquisition
(in Millions of Dollars)

Purchase price	$100.0	$160.0	$220.0
Less: Present value of tax benefit for			
Machinery & equipment	(10.6)	(16.1)	(21.6)
Buildings & improvements	(0.9)	(1.3)	(1.8)
NPTC for Harrison	$88.5	$142.5	$196.6

10.32 NPP

The NPP analysis is difficult because the buyer does not know United's tax basis in Mareight's stock. However, during due diligence United provided information concerning the regular tax basis of Mareight's assets and liabilities. United did not provide information concerning the tax basis of its assets and liabilities for Alternative Minimum Tax or Adjusted Current Earnings purposes.

EXHIBIT 10–10
Estimated Book and Tax Values at December 31, 1992
(in Millions of Dollars)

	Book Values	Tax Basis
Land	$3.0	$3.0
Buildings & improvements (gross)	$26.9	$26.9
Accumulated depreciation	(19.2)	(22.6)
Buildings & improvements (net)	$7.7	$4.3
Machinery & equipment (gross)	$53.7	$53.7
Accumulated depreciation	(19.4)	(31.0)
Machinery & equipment (net)	$34.3	$22.7
Total net PP&E	$45.0	$30.0

Harrison performed the NPP Analysis assuming that United would liquidate Mareight Corporation after the transaction was completed. The depreciation recapture calculations, the character of Mareight's gain on the sale and the tax burden to Mareight associated with the sale appear in Exhibits 10–11 and 10–12.

Harrison assumed that Mareight depreciated its buildings and improvements for tax purposes using the straight-line depreciation method. Therefore, there was no depreciation recapture for this asset category.

The Mareight's Gain (Loss) on Net Assets Sold schedule (Exhibit 10–11) calculates the taxable gain or loss at various prices and the character of any gain or loss. Let us review the calculations for the $220 million purchase price. Cash, accounts receivable and inventory are purchased at a price equal to their adjusted basis so no gain or loss is associated with these items. The depreciation recapture and Section 1231 income amounts for machinery and equipment have been calculated. Land and buildings and improvements are both Section 1231 assets. Therefore, the gain associated with either is Section 1231 income. Goodwill is a capital asset, not a Section 1231 asset, in the hands of the target. Therefore, the gain associated with its sale is capital gain. Finally, there is no taxable gain or loss on the assumption of Mareight's liabilities.

Mareight Corporation's NPP are calculated in Exhibit 10–12. The tax burden has three components: (1) the tax due on the Section 1245 recapture income, (2) the tax on the Section 1231 gain and (3) the tax on the capital gain. Mareight will incur a tax burden of between $11.2 and $56.8 million, and therefore, the NPP to Mareight will be between $88.8 and $163.2 million.

United will not be taxed on the liquidation of Mareight Corporation since it owns 100 percent of its stock. Therefore, United's NPP will be equal to Mareight's NPP.

EXHIBIT 10–11

Mareight's Gain (Loss) on Net Assets Sold (in Millions of Dollars)

	Original Tax Basis (A)	Accumulated Depreciation (B)	Adjusted Basis (A − B) (C)	Fair Market Value (D)	Taxable Gain (D − C) (E)	Character of Gain		
						Section 1245 Income (Lesser of (B) or (E)) (F)	Section 1231 Income (G)	Capital Gain (H)
$100.0 Million Price								
Net working capital (excluding income taxes)	$34.4		$34.4	$34.4				
Land	3.0		3.0	6.0	$3.0		$3.0	
Buildings & improvements	26.9	$22.6	4.3	12.0	7.7		7.7	
Machinery & equipment	53.7	31.0	22.7	38.8	16.1	$16.1		
Goodwill	0.0		0.0	2.7	2.7			$2.7
Other assets*	6.1		6.1	6.1				
Totals	$124.1	$53.6	$70.5	$100.0	$29.5	$16.1	$10.7	$2.7

$160.0 Million Price

Net working capital (excluding income taxes)	$34.4		$34.4	$34.4				
Land	3.0		3.0	8.0	$5.0	$5.0		
Buildings & improvements	26.9	22.6	4.3	18.0	13.7	13.7		
Machinery & equipment	53.7	31.0	22.7	58.8	36.1	5.1	$31.0	
Goodwill	0.0		0.0	34.7	34.7			$34.7
Other assets*	6.1		6.1	6.1				
Totals	$124.1	$53.6	$70.5	$160.0	$89.5	$23.8	$31.0	$34.7

$220.0 Million Price

Net working capital (excluding income taxes)	$34.4		$34.4	$34.4				
Land	3.0		3.0	10.0	$7.0	$7.0		
Buildings & improvements	26.9	22.6	4.3	24.0	19.7	19.7		
Machinery & equipment	53.7	31.0	22.7	78.8	56.1	25.1	$31.0	
Goodwill	0.0		0.0	66.7	66.7			$66.7
Other assets*	6.1		6.1	6.1				
Totals	$124.1	$53.6	$70.5	$220.0	$149.5	$51.8	$31.0	$66.7

* Includes $2.5 million in capitalized transaction expenses.

EXHIBIT 10-12
Calculation of NPP to Mareight Corporation Assuming an Asset Acquisition (in Millions of Dollars)

Purchase price	$100.0	$160.0	$220.0
Taxable gain			
Section 1245 income	$16.1	$31.0	$31.0
Section 1231 income	10.7	23.8	51.8
Capital gain	2.7	34.7	66.7
Total taxable gain	29.5	89.5	149.5
Tax rate	38%	38%	38%
Tax burden	11.2	34.0	56.8
NPP to Mareight Corporation	$88.8	$126.0	$163.2

10.4 STOCK ACQUISITION

In analyzing this acquisition method, Harrison assumed that it would purchase all of the outstanding stock of Mareight Corporation and that the same price range, $100 to $220 million, and specific purchase prices should be analyzed.

10.41 NPTC

United provided Harrison with estimates of tax depreciation charges over the next several years for existing assets. These estimates appear in Exhibit 10-13.

EXHIBIT 10–13
Net Present Value of the Tax Benefit from Depreciation Deductions
(in Millions of Dollars)

Year	Depreciation Deductions Machinery and Equipment	Buildings and Improvements	Total	Tax Benefit at 38%	10 Percent Present Value Factor	Present Value of Tax Benefit
1	$3.4	$0.2	$3.6	$1.4	0.9091	$1.3
2	3.4	0.2	3.6	1.4	0.8264	1.1
3	2.7	0.2	2.9	1.1	0.7513	0.8
4	2.3	0.2	2.5	0.9	0.6830	0.6
5	2.3	0.2	2.5	0.9	0.6209	0.6
6	2.3	0.2	2.5	0.9	0.5645	0.5
7	2.3	0.2	2.5	0.9	0.5132	0.5
8	2.3	0.2	2.5	0.9	0.4665	0.4
9	1.8	0.2	2.0	0.8	0.4241	0.3
10		0.2	0.2	0.1	0.3855	0.0
	$22.7	$2.1	$24.9	$9.4		$6.3

Rounded numbers are used for calculations in this table.

The NPTC for the buyer will range between $93.7 and $213.7 if a Stock Acquisition is consummated (Exhibit 10–14).

EXHIBIT 10–14
Calculation of NPTC for Harrison Assuming a Stock Acquisition
(in Millions of Dollars)

Purchase price	$100.0	$160.0	$220.0
Less: Present value of tax savings for depreciable assets	(6.3)	(6.3)	(6.3)
NPTC for Harrison	$93.7	$153.7	$213.7

10.42   NPP

The NPP calculations appear in Exhibit 10–15. Harrison has estimated that United's tax basis in Mareight Corporation stock is approximately $65 million, assuming the conversion of the intercompany debt to equity.

EXHIBIT 10–15
Calculation of NPP to United Corporation Assuming a Stock Acquisition
(in Millions of Dollars)

Selling price	$100.0	$160.0	$220.0
Less: Tax basis of stock	65.0	65.0	65.0
Capital gain	35.0	95.0	155.0
Effective capital gains tax rate	38%	38%	38%
Tax burden to United	13.3	36.1	58.9
NPP to United Corporation	$86.7	$123.9	$161.1

Deducting the tax burden from the selling price, United will net between $86.7 and $161.1 million.

10.5 COMPARATIVE ANALYSIS OF ALTERNATIVES

The comparative analysis of NPTC (Exhibit 10–16) indicates to the decision maker which acquisition method would be the least costly for each of the purchase prices being considered. Also, it permits the decision maker

EXHIBIT 10–16
Comparative Analysis of NPTC—Stock versus Asset Acquisition

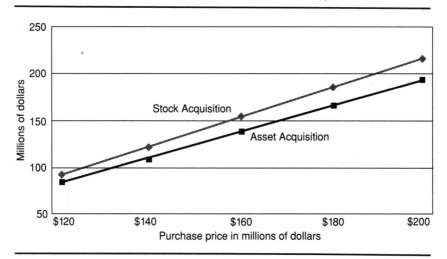

to easily compare the after-tax acquisition costs for the two acquisition methods assuming different purchase prices. For example, the NPTC comparative analysis graph indicates that the NPTC for an Asset Acquisition, assuming a $160 million purchase price, is approximately $142.5 million. The cost of a Stock Acquisition would be approximately $11.2 million higher at the same nominal purchase price of $160 million.

The comparative analysis of NPP (Exhibit 10–17) indicates that a Stock Acquisition is preferable to United under any purchase price being considered. At all prices, a Stock Acquisition is worth approximately $2,090,000 more to United than a transaction structured as an Asset Acquisition. This minor differential is due to the relatively small difference between Mareight's tax basis in its assets (approximately $70.5 million) and United's basis in Mareight's stock (estimated to be $65 million).

EXHIBIT 10–17
Comparative Analysis of NPP—Stock versus Asset Acquisition

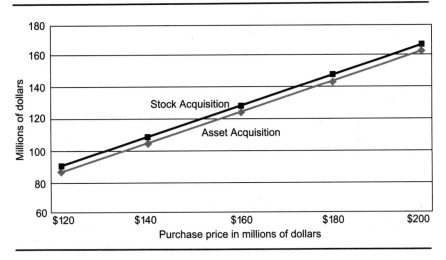

Section Four

Valuation
Techniques

Section Four

Introduction

The purpose of Section Four is to describe the various valuation approaches used to estimate the value of a company. These include reviewing the historic trading pattern of a company's outstanding securities (Chapter 11), comparing a target company's financial statistics with other comparable public companies (Chapter 12), analyzing transactions in the target company's industry over the last several years (Chapter 13), and analyzing trends in the overall M&A marketplace (Chapter 14). Additional techniques that look specifically at the cash flows of the target include Discounted Cash Flow Analysis (Chapter 15) and Strategic Buyer DCF Analysis (Chapter 16). Techniques that focus on the value of the company in a leveraged environment include Leveraged Buyout Analysis (Chapter 17), Leveraged ESOP Analysis (Chapter 18) and Leveraged Recapitalization Analysis (Chapter 19). A technique designed to value a company with many lines of business is Breakup Analysis (Chapter 20). Finally, Chapter 21 discusses additional valuation techniques.

Chapter 11

Analysis of Stock Price and Volume History

11.0 INTRODUCTION

This valuation technique involves analyzing (a) the target company's stock price and volume, (b) the percent of volume traded at specified prices, and (c) the target company's stock price performance relative to various indices. All of these analyses are performed over various time frames.

11.1 ANALYSIS OF STOCK PRICE AND VOLUME

The trading ranges and sales volumes of the target company's stock are analyzed graphically over a variety of time frames. The time frames analyzed usually include (a) a very short time frame (30–60 days) to show how the stock price and volume reacted to either public announcements or recent speculation concerning the possibility of a transaction; (b) a one-year time frame; and (c) several longer time frames (usually 3 years and 5 years). See Exhibits 11–1 and 11–2 for sample short time frame price and volume graphs.

11.2 ANALYSIS OF VOLUME PURCHASED AT SPECIFIED PRICE LEVELS

A second type of graph depicts the percent of total volume traded at specific prices during the time frames selected. The purpose of this graph

EXHIBIT 11–1
ABC Corporation

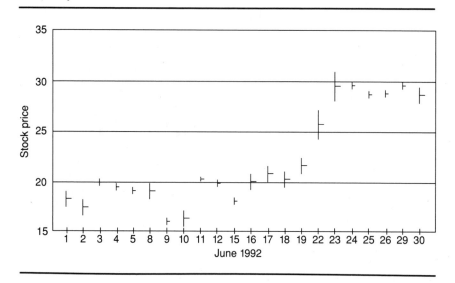

EXHIBIT 11–2
ABC Corporation Stock Volume

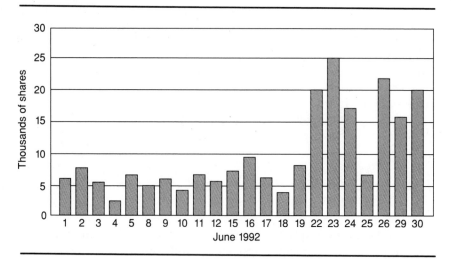

is to give the directors of the target company a better understanding of what the current owners of the company's equity securities actually paid for their stock. See Exhibit 11–3.

EXHIBIT 11–3
Percent of Volume Traded at Specified Ranges
(between July 1, 1991 and June 30, 1992)

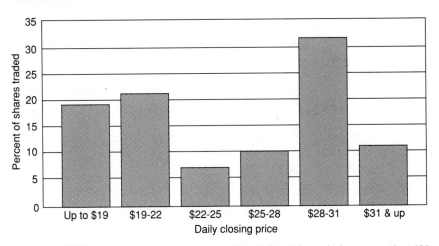

Note: 8,755,000 cumulative shares were traded during this period representing 108 percent of shares outstanding at June 30, 1992.

11.3   COMPARISON OF PERFORMANCE AGAINST VARIOUS INDICES

To gain some perspective on a stock's performance over selected time frames, graphs are created that compare a stock's performance to (a) one or more broad market indices such as the *Dow Jones Industrial Average* or the *Standard & Poor 400 (S&P 400)*, and (b) a selected composite index of comparable public companies. See Exhibit 11–4 for an example.

EXHIBIT 11–4
ABC Indexed Stock Price History vs. the S&P 400

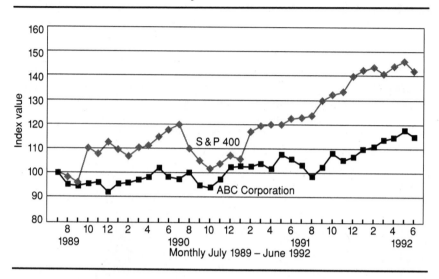

11.4 STRENGTHS AND WEAKNESSES

This valuation technique does not provide a good indication of the value of the target company's equity in a change of control situation because the analysis fails to take into account the future prospects of the company, and the price at which the company's stock has historically traded does not include a change of control premium. Nevertheless, the analysis does provide board members with concise historical information that many find useful in framing their valuation thoughts.

Chapter 12

Comparable
Company Analysis

12.0 INTRODUCTION

Comparable Company Analysis compares the target's financial statistics
with the financial statistics of all relevant comparable public companies.
This analytical approach estimates the value of the target company by
analogy.

12.1 CHOOSING COMPARABLE COMPANIES

Generally, comparable companies are all companies that operate in the
same or similar industries. However, for valuation purposes, comparable
companies need to be chosen with great care. It is important to include in
the valuation analysis only those companies that have operating characteristics similar to the target company.

12.2 COMPARABLE COMPANY ANALYSIS

An example of a Comparable Company Analysis appears in Exhibit 12–1.
This example illustrates the difficulties in choosing comparable companies. The building material retailing industry initially appears to the
uninformed to be a prosaic industry. After all, how much different can
one home center or building center be from another? However, the truth
is that they can be profoundly different, as a discussion of selected
industry competitors will reveal.

EXHIBIT 12–1
Analysis of Selected Building Material Retailers (Figures in Millions Except Per Share Data and Ratios)

	Grossmans	Lowes	Home Depot	Averages[6][7]
Exchange/Ticker	OTC/GROS	OTC/LOW	NYSE/HD	
Closing price (11/16/90)	$2.125	$20.500	$35.000	
Common shares outstanding	25.9	37.5	116.8	
Market value of common stock	$55.1	$769.3	$4,087.8	
Current dividend yield	0.0%	2.5%	0.4%	
LTM earnings per share	$0.26	$2.20	$1.65	
Current price/LTM earnings	8.2×	9.3×	21.2×	10.9×
Total market capitalization/LTM sales[1]	0.16×	0.34×	1.31×	0.42×
Total market capitalization/LTM OCF[1]	3.9×	6.2×	14.1×	7.5×
Total market capitalization/LTM EBIT[1]	11.5×	7.3×	18.9×	10.2×
Market value/book value	0.4×	1.1×	6.9×	1.5×
Latest fiscal year ended	12/31/89	1/31/90	1/28/90	
Latest 12 months ended	9/30/90	7/31/90	7/29/90	

Earnings/Share Data:[2][3]

	EPS	Index	EPS	Index	EPS	Index
LTM	$0.26	30%	$2.20	156%	$1.65	220%
1989	0.67	77	2.01	143	1.42	189
1988	0.50	57	1.83	130	1.00	133
1987	0.87	100	1.41	100	0.75	100

Dividend Payout Ratio Data:

	Dividend/Share	Payout Ratio	Dividend/Share	Payout Ratio	Dividend/Share	Payout Ratio	Payout Ratio
LTM	$0.00	0.0%	$0.51	23.2%	$0.13	7.9%	9.1%
1989	0.00	0.0	0.49	24.4	0.11	7.7	9.3
1988	0.00	0.0	0.46	25.1	0.07	7.0	8.2
1987	0.00	0.0	0.43	30.5	0.04	5.3	9.0

Book Value Per Share:

	Book Value	Index	Book Value	Index	Book Value	Index	Averages[6][7] Index
LTM	$4.73	140%	$18.49	125%	$5.04	116%	118%
1989	4.48	133	17.33	117	6.67	154	122
1988	3.88	115	15.80	107	5.08	117	112
1987	3.37	100	14.75	100	4.33	100	100

Income Statement Analysis[3]

	Grossmans		Lowes		Home Depot		Averages[6][7]
Revenue Data:	Sales	Index	Sales	Index	Sales	Index	Index
LTM	$811.3	75%	$2,841.1	116%	$3,284.2	226%	135%
1989	1,052.1	98	2,650.5	109	2,758.5	190	133
1988	1,141.6	106	2,516.9	103	1,999.5	138	122
1987	1,077.3	100	2,442.2	100	1,453.7	100	100

	Grossmans		Lowes		Home Depot		Averages[6][7]
Gross Income Data:	Gross Income	Gross Margin	Gross Income	Gross Margin	Gross Income	Gross Margin	Gross Margin
LTM	$228.8	28.2%	$689.9	24.3%	$909.1	27.7%	26.8%
1989	296.4	28.2	646.4	24.4	766.8	27.8	26.8
1988	331.8	29.1	600.4	23.9	539.7	27.0	27.2
1987	315.7	29.3	583.9	23.9	403.7	27.8	27.8

(continued)

EXHIBIT 12–1 *(concluded)*
Analysis of Selected Building Material Retailers (Figures in Millions Except Per Share Data and Ratios)

Operating Income Data:[4]

	Operating		Operating		Operating		
	Income	Margin	Income	Margin	Income	Margin	Operating Margin
LTM	$11.2	1.4%	$133.5	4.7%	$228.8	7.0%	4.6%
1989	24.0	2.3	128.0	4.8	184.6	6.7	4.0
1988	28.5	2.5	126.6	5.0	126.8	6.3	4.9
1987	40.1	3.7	120.0	4.9	98.2	6.8	6.4

Net Income Data:

	Net		Net		Net		
	Income	Margin	Income	Margin	Income	Margin	Net Margin
LTM	$6.9	0.9%	$82.3	2.9%	$141.1	4.3%	2.9%
1989	17.6	1.7	74.9	2.8	112.0	4.1	3.0
1988	13.2	1.2	69.2	2.7	76.8	3.8	2.8
1987	19.8	1.8	56.0	2.3	54.1	3.7	3.7

Balance Sheet Analysis

Balance Sheet Data:

	Common Equity	Total Assets	Common Equity	Total Assets	Common Equity	Total Assets
LTM	$122.7	$319.2	$693.8	$1,288.4	$588.9	$1,514.8
1989	117.1	323.7	645.6	1,147.4	512.1	1,117.5
1988	101.3	396.0	586.9	1,085.8	382.9	699.2
1987	88.2	378.8	582.4	1,027.3	320.6	528.3

Operating Working Capital:[5]

	Grossmans Working Capital	% of Sales	Lowes Working Capital	% of Sales	Home Depot Working Capital	% of Sales
LTM	$80.7	9.9%	$347.2	12.2%	$136.0	4.1%
1989	71.2	6.8	245.1	9.2	139.9	5.1
1988	104.3	9.1	244.2	9.7	127.2	6.4
1987	94.5	8.8	288.5	11.8	85.3	5.9

Returns Analysis

Rate of Return:

	Grossmans ROE	ROA	Lowes ROE	ROA	Home Depot ROE	ROA	Averages[6][7] ROE/ROA
LTM	5.6%	2.2%	11.9%	6.4%	24.0%	9.3%	13.3%/6.3%
1989	15.0	5.4	11.6	6.5	21.9	10.0	14.8/7.2
1988	13.0	3.3	11.8	6.4	20.1	11.0	13.3/6.4
1987	22.4	5.2	9.6	5.5	16.9	10.2	16.6/8.4

Capitalization (Latest 10-Q):

	Grossmans	Lowes	Home Depot
Cash & equivalents	$13.3	$54.9	$302.9
Short-term debt	32.0	92.4	1.9
Long-term debt & capitalized leases	54.6	163.8	531.7
Deferred liabilities & other	0.0	27.4	8.4
Common equity	122.7	693.8	588.9
Total equity	122.7	693.8	588.9
Total capitalization	177.3	857.6	1,120.6

[1] Total market capitalization equals market value of equity plus debt less cash.

[2] Primary earnings per share.

[3] All income statement items are from continuing operations before all extraordinary charges and unusual items.

[4] EBIT or operating income equals earnings before interest and taxes.

[5] Operating working capital equals (current assets less cash) less (current liabilities less current debt).

[6] OCF equals earnings before interest and taxes, depreciation and amortization.

[7] Extreme data point values are excluded from comparable average calculations.

Home Depot, a Georgia based company, operates one of the fastest growing retailing concepts in America today. Its building material stores are actually "warehouses" that average over 100,000 square feet. Grossmans, on the other hand, is an old-line New England lumberyard operator with relatively small stores, but large lumberyards. Lowes, a North Carolina based firm, has operations that conceptually fall somewhere between Home Depot and Grossmans. It is currently building warehouse style facilities in larger markets, yet operates a significant number of smaller facilities in smaller markets.

Someone preparing a Comparable Company Analysis to value a building material retailer would have to understand the nature of the target company's operation. Depending on the answer, a person would eliminate one or more of the comparables in the exhibit. Why? A careful analysis of the values that the public market places on the different operations indicates that there are material differences. It would not be prudent to value the target using noncomparable entities or industry averages that include noncomparable operations.

In preparing a Comparable Company Analysis, one must be careful to highlight any significant differences in accounting policies between the target and the comparable companies.

There is no standard format for preparing a comparative analysis. Alternative approaches range from preparing an analysis that focuses on a few key variables to preparing a comprehensive speadsheet analysis. Typically, a comprehensive spreadsheet analysis is prepared first, and then select ratios are applied to the target company's financial results. See Exhibits 12–1 and 12–2 for abbreviated examples.

In addition to an analysis of financial statistics, the Comparable Company Analysis typically includes graphic stock price comparisons of comparable public companies over various time frames. These are similar to the graphs prepared in the previous chapter.

12.3 STRENGTHS AND WEAKNESSES

This technique is useful for determining the likely public market value for a business. The public market value is a good starting point for determining the value of the target in a change of control situation. However, a change of control premium must be added to the public market value estimate to arrive at a valid estimate of the market value of the company in a sale. See paragraph 2.54.

One of the weaknesses of this technique is that it works well only when there are good comparables for the target. If the companies chosen

EXHIBIT 12–2
Comparable Company Valuation Analysis
(Figures in Millions Except Per Share Data and Ratios)

	Public Company Comparable Multiples		Target Company LTM[3] Results	Valuation Range	
	Mean	Median		Mean	Median
Total market capitalization[1]/ sales	0.42×	0.32×	$1,050.0	$441	$336
Total market capitalization[1]/ operating cash flow[2]	7.5×	5.3×	55.0	413	292
Total market capitalization[1]/ EBIT	10.2×	7.7×	35.0	357	270
			Range	$270 –	$441

[1] Total market capitalization equals market value of equity plus total debt less cash.
[2] Operating cash flow equals EBIT plus depreciation and amortization.
[3] LTM means last 12 months.

are not directly comparable, one must use a great deal of judgment in analyzing the results of this analysis. For example, the "Public Company Comparable Multiples" in Exhibit 12–2 reflect the mean and median for all the public companies in the building material retailing industry. The mean numbers are high because of the inclusion of Home Depot in the average. As discussed, the nature of the target company's operations should determine which building material retailing companies are included in the analysis. A refinement of the list of comparable companies usually results in a tighter range of estimated values for the target company.

Another significant weakness of Comparable Company Analysis is that accounting policies can differ substantially from one company to the next. These differences often result in material differences in reported earnings or balance sheet amounts among otherwise comparable companies.

Chapter 13

Comparable Transactions Analysis

13.0 INTRODUCTION

Comparable Transactions Analysis examines all transactions over the last several years involving companies in the target's industry or similar industries. Acquisition multiples are calculated for each transaction, and mean and median acquisition multiples are calculated for the universe of comparable transactions. These multiples are then applied to the target company's financial results to estimate the value at which the target would likely trade.

This technique is limited by the amount of data that is publicly available concerning transactions.

13.1 CHOOSING COMPARABLE TRANSACTIONS

Identifying comparable transactions is a relatively straightforward exercise that involves accessing transaction databases, reviewing industry literature and discussing the industry with available experts. However, judgment is required with respect to which transactions are used to value the target. The similarity of the business characteristics of the target and the companies that were the subject of prior transactions is key to determining whether a prior transaction is comparable. In many cases it is not enough that the target and an acquired company are in the same industry. They may operate in completely different segments of that industry and, therefore, have entirely different growth and profitability prospects.

13.2   COMPARABLE TRANSACTIONS ANALYSIS

A Comparable Transactions Analysis includes several schedules. A summary spreadsheet analyzes all comparable transactions in detail. This spreadsheet is often supplemented by summary analysis of individual transactions that outline, in further detail, the businesses that were involved in a transaction. Finally, a schedule is prepared that applies the acquisition multiples deemed relevant to the target company's financial results. See Exhibits 13–1 and 13–2.

EXHIBIT 13–1
Comparable Transactions Valuation Analysis (Figures in Millions except Ratios)

	Comparable Transaction Multiples		Target Company LTM[3] Results	Valuation Range	
	Mean	Median		Mean	Median
Aggregate consideration[1]/ sales	0.64	0.64	$1,050	$668	$677
Aggregate consideration[1]/ operating cash flow[2]	9.44	9.38	55	519	516
Aggregate consideration[1]/ EBIT	14.53	15.15	35	509	530
			Range	$509 –	$677

[1] Aggregate consideration equals purchase price of equity plus total debt less cash.
[2] Operating cash flow equals EBIT plus depreciation and amortization.
[3] LTM means last 12 months.

13.3   STRENGTHS AND WEAKNESSES

This technique is often the most effective for determining the value range for the target. Assuming there are recent, truly comparable, transactions in the target company's industry, one can estimate the value of the target company with a high degree of certainty.

However, one of the obvious weaknesses of this approach is that it works well only when comparable recent transactions exist. If the comparable transactions are not directly comparable, one must use a great deal of judgment in analyzing the results. For example, the "Comparable Transaction Multiples" in Exhibit 13–2 reflect the mean and median for

EXHIBIT 13–2
Analysis of Selected Transactions Involving Building Material Retailers (Figures in Millions except Ratios)

Date Final	Target/Acquirer	AC PP	Sales AC/Sales	OCF AC/OCF	EBIT AC/EBIT	Net Income PP/Net Income	TBV PP/TBV
7/89	Scotty's/ GB Inno BM SA	$303.8 243.9	$574.4 0.53×	$32.4 9.4×	$19.4 15.7×	$11.9 20.5×	$174.6 1.40×
10/88	Payless Cashways/ PCI Acquisition Corp.	1,189.3 911.9	$1,844.9 0.64×	$131.0 9.1×	$93.0 12.8×	$52.4 17.4×	$397.5 2.29×
3/88	Pay 'N Pak Stores/ PNP Prime Corp.	292.3 212.6	$398.1 0.73×	$29.6 9.9×	$19.3 15.1×	$5.7 37.3×	$100.1 2.12×
				Statistical Summary			
	Low:		0.53	9.08	12.79	17.40	1.40
	High:		0.73	9.87	15.66	37.30	2.29
	Mean:		0.64	9.44	14.53	25.07	1.94
	Median:		0.64	9.38	15.15	20.50	2.12
	Sample:		3	3	3	3	3

PP = Purchase price for all equity securities including options and convertible debt.

AC = Aggregate consideration (PP plus total debt less cash).

EBIT = Earnings before interest and taxes.

OCF = Operating cash flow (EBIT plus depreciation and amortization).

TBV = Tangible book value (total book value less intangibles).

all the transactions in the building material retailing industry. These transactions are not recent and may involve companies that are operating in different segments of the industry than the target. As discussed previously, the nature of the target company's operations should determine which building material retailing companies are included in an analysis. A refinement of the list of comparable transactions usually results in a tighter range of estimated values for the target company.

Chapter 14

Analysis of M&A Market Multiples

14.0 INTRODUCTION

The Analysis of M&A Market Multiples technique involves analyzing broad M&A market transaction multiples and trends to help identify a value range for the target. This technique is used only when there are no acceptable comparable transactions.

14.1 SELECTING APPROPRIATE M&A MARKET TRANSACTIONS

Generally, an acquirer will limit the broad market transactions analyzed in some way, usually by size of transaction or broad industry category. For example, the transactions analyzed could be limited to all transactions in the last six months involving a target company in the food industry where the deal size, as defined by aggregate consideration, was less than $150 million but greater than $50 million.

Broad M&A market averages are available from a number of databases. Selected historical M&A market multiple prices appear in paragraph 2.1.

14.2 M&A MARKET TRANSACTIONS ANALYSIS

An M&A Market Transactions Analysis usually includes two types of schedules. First, a summary spreadsheet lists relevant transactions in detail. The second schedule applies the mean and median acquisition

multiples for these transactions to the target company's financial results.
See Exhibits 14–1 and 14–2.

EXHIBIT 14–1

M&A Market Transactions Valuation Analysis (Figures in Millions except Ratios)

	Comparable Transaction Multiples		Target Company LTM Results	Valuation Range	
	Mean	Median		Mean	Median
Aggregate consideration[1]/ sales	0.54	0.45	$185	$100	$82
Aggregate consideration[1]/ operating cash flow[2]	10.67	9.79	14	149	137
Aggregate consideration[1]/ EBIT	12.76	10.57	12	153	127
			Range	$82 –	$153

[1] Aggregate consideration equals purchase price of equity plus total debt less cash.
[2] Operating cash flow equals EBIT plus depreciation and amortization.

14.3 STRENGTHS AND WEAKNESSES

This technique does not create a high level of comfort as to the value of
the target company. By definition, it is based on broad market averages
that may be totally inapplicable to a single transaction. However, in the
absence of comparable transactions or comparable public companies, this
technique provides some guidance with respect to the value of the target.

EXHIBIT 14–2

Analysis of Selected Transactions Involving Food Companies (Figures in Millions except Ratios)

Date Final	Target/Acquirer	AC PP	Sales AC/Sales	OCF AC/OCF	EBIT AC/EBIT	Net Income PP/Net Income	TBV PP/TBV
5/92	Target A/ Acquirer 1	$123.0 88.0	$276.0 0.45×	$14.0 8.8×	$12.0 10.3×	$7.0 12.6×	$56.0 1.57×
5/92	Target B/ Acquirer 2	$77.0 44.0	$266.0 0.29×	$12.0 6.4×	$9.0 8.6×	$4.7 9.4×	$46.0 0.96×
4/92	Target C/ Acquirer 3	$148.0 98.0	$120.0 1.23×	$15.0 9.9×	$14.2 10.4×	$8.0 12.3×	$26.0 3.77×
3/92	Target D/ Acquirer 4	$56.0 15.0	$208.0 0.27×	$6.0 9.3×	$4.5 12.4×	$2.4 6.3×	$4.0 3.75×
3/92	Target E/ Acquirer 5	$122.0 49.0	$389.0 0.31×	$8.0 15.3×	$6.6 18.5×	$2.9 16.9×	$23.0 2.13×
2/92	Target F/ Acquirer 6	$93.0 77.0	$398.1 0.23×	$9.5 9.8×	$8.8 10.6×	$2.1 36.7×	$55.0 1.40×
2/92	Target G/ Acquirer 7	$104.0 99.0	$110.0 0.95×	$11.0 9.5×	$10.3 10.1×	$6.6 15.0×	$44.0 2.25×
1/92	Target H/ Acquirer 8	$66.0 66.0	$111.0 0.59×	$4.0 16.5×	$3.1 21.3×	$1.8 36.7×	$45.0 1.47×

Statistical Summary	Sales	OCF	EBIT	Net Income	TBV
Low:	0.23	6.42	8.56	6.25	0.96
High:	1.23	16.50	21.29	36.67	3.77
Mean:	0.54	10.67	12.76	18.21	2.16
Median:	0.45	9.79	10.57	15.00	2.13
Sample:	8	8	8	8	8

PP = Purchase price for all equity securities including options and convertible debt.

AC = Aggregate consideration (PP plus total debt less cash).

EBIT = Earnings before interest and taxes.

OCF = Operating cash flow (EBIT plus depreciation and amortization).

TBV = Tangible book value (total book value less intangibles).

Chapter 15

Discounted Cash
Flow Analysis

15.0   INTRODUCTION

Discounted Cash Flow (DCF) Analysis is a significant valuation technique for purposes of determining the market value of the target company. However, it is the most important valuation technique for estimating the worth of a business to an individual bidder.

There are two DCF approaches: *Net Present Value (NPV) Analysis* and *Internal Rate of Return (IRR) Analysis.* NPV Analysis estimates the value of a business by forecasting the future cash flows the business is expected to produce and discounting those cash flows back to the present using a discount rate that reflects the related risk. IRR Analysis determines the discount rate that results in the present value of the future cash flows associated with the target being equal to the acquisition cost of the target. A basic description of each of these methods is included in Appendix A.

This chapter is devoted to exploring the key issues associated with performing a DCF Analysis of a target company. These issues include determining a proper methodology for estimating the target company's residual value; defining the target's cash flow over the forecast period; and identifying the appropriate discount rate to use to discount both the cash flows over the forecast period and the residual value. Descriptions of an initial DCF model and a final detailed DCF model are provided in Chapter 22.

15.1 AN EXAMPLE

Before tackling the complex issues let us review a simple example based on the case study originally presented in Chapter 10. It will put the discussion that follows into perspective.

> *Example 15A* *Harrison, a diversified conglomerate, would like to purchase Mareight from United Corporation. Initially, Harrison received an offering memorandum that contained a three-year earnings and cash flow forecast. Harrison supplemented this forecast with three additional years of forecast data for analytical purposes. These figures appear in Exhibits 10–5 and 10–6 and are repeated here for convenience.*

> *For purposes of this example, we will assume that the residual value of the business at the end of December 1998 is $225 million and that the appropriate discount rate for all cash flows is 12 percent. We will also assume, for purposes of the IRR analysis, that the acquisition cost is $160 million, which includes $2.5 million of transaction expenses.*

Mareight Corporation Forecast Income Statements (in Millions of Dollars)

	Year Ended December 31,					
	1993	*1994*	*1995*	*1996*	*1997*	*1998*
Net sales	$143.3	$154.0	$165.6	$178.0	$191.4	$205.7
Cost of goods sold	93.9	100.9	108.5	116.6	125.3	134.7
Gross profit	49.4	53.1	57.1	61.4	66.0	71.0
Gross margin	34.5%	34.5%	34.5%	34.5%	34.5%	34.5%
SG&A expenses	27.2	29.3	31.5	33.8	36.4	39.1
Depreciation & amortization	7.6	8.2	8.8	9.4	10.1	10.9
Total operating expenses	34.8	37.4	40.2	43.3	46.5	50.0
EBIT	14.6	15.7	16.9	18.2	19.5	21.0
Tax provision—38%	5.6	6.0	6.4	6.9	7.4	8.0
Net income	$9.1	$9.7	$10.5	$11.3	$12.1	$13.0
Capital Requirements						
Capital expenditures	$7.7	$8.3	$8.9	$9.6	$10.3	$11.1
Increase in working capital	1.4	2.5	2.7	2.9	3.1	3.3

Mareight Corporation Cash Flow Forecast (in Millions of Dollars)

	1993	*1994*	*1995*	*1996*	*1997*	*1998*
			Year Ended December 31,			
Sources						
Net income	$9.1	$9.7	$10.5	$11.3	$12.1	$13.0
Depreciation & amortization	7.6	8.2	8.8	9.4	10.1	10.9
Deferred taxes	0.5	0.7	0.7	0.8	1.0	1.0
Total sources	17.2	18.6	20.0	21.5	23.3	25.0
Uses						
Capital expenditures	(7.7)	(8.3)	(8.9)	(9.6)	(10.3)	(11.1)
Increase in working capital	(1.4)	(2.5)	(2.7)	(2.9)	(3.1)	(3.3)
Total uses	(9.2)	(10.8)	(11.6)	(12.5)	(13.4)	(14.4)
After-tax net cash flows	$8.0	$7.8	$8.4	$9.1	$9.9	$10.6

Rounded numbers are used for the calculations in this table.

The analysis indicates that the NPV of the acquisition is $150.0 and the IRR for the acquisition is 10.7 percent. Therefore, according to the NPV Analysis, the acquisition should be completed only if the acquisition cost is less than $150. The IRR Analysis indicates that the expected rate of return is approximately 10.7 percent. If this rate of return exceeds an appropriate hurdle rate, the acquisition should be completed.

NPV Analysis (in Millions of Dollars)

	*Cash Flow**	*12% Discount Rate*	*Present Value*
1993	$8.0	0.8929	$7.1
1994	7.8	0.7972	6.2
1995	8.4	0.7118	6.0
1996	9.1	0.6355	5.8
1997	9.9	0.5674	5.6
1998	235.6	0.5066	119.3
		Net present value	$150.0

* 1998 cash flow includes both after-tax annual cash flow and residual value.

IRR Analysis (in Millions of Dollars)

	Cash Flow	10.7% Discount Rate	Present Value
1993	($160.0)	1.0000	($160.0)
1993	8.0	0.9036	7.2
1994	7.8	0.8165	6.4
1995	8.4	0.7378	6.2
1996	9.1	0.6667	6.0
1997	9.9	0.6025	6.0
1998	235.6	0.5444	128.2
	Present value		$0.0

15.2 RESIDUAL VALUE—THE MOST SIGNIFICANT ISSUE

There are two components to discount in DCF Analysis: (1) cash flow over a period that can be forecast, and (2) a residual value for the continuing value of the business after the forecast period. The value of a company is equal to the sum of the present values of these two components.

The most significant factor associated with estimating the overall value of a target company is its residual value. Let us review the example above to understand why. The present value of the $225 residual value in 1998 is $114. The NPV of the acquisition is only $150. Therefore, the residual value of the business represents 76 percent of the value of the company. This example is typical of most transactions.

One of the principal ways to reduce the importance of the residual value is to lengthen the time horizon of the explicit cash flow forecast. An increase in the forecast period from 6 to 10 years will materially reduce the significance of the residual value. However, the residual value will still remain an important component of the overall value of the company.

In an academic setting it is easy to say, let us reduce the significance of the residual value by extending the length of the forecast. However, in most businesses, managers are comfortable and experienced with providing budgets for the coming year, as well as a long-range financial forecast for the annual business plan, typically three to five years in length. It is unusual to find managers preparing financial forecasts on a very extended basis. Given their reluctance to create extended forecasts of the target company's cash flows, most acquiring companies will analyze the cash flow forecast provided (assuming that it is a minimum of five years) and deal with the residual value issue by getting as comfortable as they can with the methodology used to estimate that value.

15.21   Alternative Residual Value Approaches

A wide variety of approaches for estimating residual value have been advocated over the years. However, five approaches are either widely accepted in the marketplace or enjoy the backing of the academic community. A DCF Analysis of a target company should include several of these approaches. These alternate approaches include:

- Price-to-Earnings Ratio Method (P/E Multiple Method).
- Multiple of Earnings before Depreciation, Interest and Amortization but after Taxes (EBDIAT Multiple Method).
- Growing Perpetuity Method.
- Multiple of Earnings before Interest, Taxes, Depreciation and Amortization (EBITDA Multiple Method).
- Multiple of Earnings before Interest, Taxes and Amortization (EBITA Multiple Method).

A recent survey of current practice at leading LBO firms indicates that the last two approaches are the principal residual value methodologies used in LBO Analysis. This survey indicated that all firms surveyed used either the EBITDA Multiple Method or the EBITA Multiple Method. However, a number of firms indicated that they also look closely at Net Cash Flow (defined as EBITDA less normalized capital expenditures) entrance and exit multiples. A small percentage of firms also relied on the P/E Multiple Method. LBO Analysis is discussed in Chapters 17 and 23.

An acquirer must answer a very basic question about the residual value issue: Does the acquirer presently intend to dispose of the target or keep the target forever? The answer to this question has profound implications as to how the residual value of the target is calculated. If the acquirer intends to dispose of the business, as most LBO firms do, then the estimate of the residual value of the business should include a calculation of the tax effects of a sale of the business. However, if the acquirer intends to keep the target indefinitely, then such tax calculations are unnecessary.

Many LBO firms ignore the tax effects of a probable sale because the funds they manage are investment partnerships where all taxable gains and losses are passed through to the partners. Since partners have significantly different tax positions, any "average" tax calculations are inappropriate.

15.21a   The P/E Multiple Method

The P/E Multiple Method is based on the assumption that the equity of the target company will be worth some multiple of its net income at the end of the forecast period. The method multiplies the forecast net income in the last year of the cash flow forecast by an estimated P/E multiple that an acquirer would pay for the company. If the acquirer expects to dispose of the target, the tax effect of the sale would be calculated. Otherwise, the gross residual value of the equity is included in the cash flow analysis at the end of the forecast period.

One of the principal criticisms of this technique is that it is very difficult to predict the appropriate P/E multiples for either the target company or its industry. Another criticism is directed at the relevance that an estimated P/E multiple has for the continuing value of the business to the acquirer. Critics believe that an approach that discounts the future cash flows of the business would be much more relevant. Finally, the projected residual value for the target will change if different purchase prices are assumed because earnings are affected (i.e., goodwill amortization).

There are a number of practical answers to these questions. First, the P/E multiple method is a concept with which key decision makers are very familiar. The decision maker usually understands or can be made to understand the difficulties associated with using P/E multiples when the quality of the income streams at the time of the transaction and at the end of the forecast period can be very different. In addition, the decision maker in many cases has a good perspective with respect to the long-term industry P/E multiple trends. The importance of this familiarity with the P/E concept cannot be overstated. The decision maker's comfort level with how the value of the company is derived can have a significant effect on his overall perception of the value of the target. Second, the analysis never is limited to showing a value based on a single P/E multiple. Generally, three to five P/E terminal multiples are included in the analysis. Third, using the P/E Method to calculate residual value may be more relevant than other methods if the purpose of the residual value calculation is to determine the expected sale price of the company. The acquirer's estimate of the value that the market will place on the company, assuming the target company's principal markets develop as he expects, can be one of the most important estimates in the analysis. Employing another residual value approach may significantly distort how the acquirer views the acquisition and why the acquirer is looking to buy the target company.

Example 15B *Same facts as Example 15A. The schedule below calculates the residual value of the target assuming that the appropriate P/E multiples to analyze are 18, 20, and 22. NPV and IRR calculations using the 20 × P/E multiple value are shown for both continuing value and sale assumptions.*

Gross Residual Value—P/E Method
(in Millions of Dollars)

	P/E Multiple		
	18×	*20×*	*22×*
1998 net income	$13.0	$13.0	$13.0
Applicable P/E multiple	18×	20×	22×
Gross residual value	$234.2	$260.2	$286.2

Tax Effected Residual Value—P/E Method
(in Millions of Dollars)

	P/E Multiple		
	18×	*20×*	*22×*
Sale price	$234.2	$260.2	$286.2
Less: Tax basis	(160.0)	(160.0)	(160.0)
Taxable gain	74.2	100.2	126.2
Tax rate	38%	38%	38%
Tax on sale	$28.2	$38.1	$48.0
Sale proceeds	$234.2	$260.2	$286.2
Less: Tax on sale	(28.2)	(38.1)	(48.0)
Net residual value	$206.0	$222.1	$238.3

Rounded numbers are used for calculations in this table.

NPV Analysis—P/E Method: Assumes P/E Multiple of 20× (in Millions of Dollars)

	Continuing Value Assumption			Sale Assumption		
	Cash Flow	12% Discount Rate	Present Value	Cash Flow	12% Discount Rate	Present Value
1993	$8.0	0.8929	$7	$8.0	0.8929	$7
1994	7.8	0.7972	6	7.8	0.7972	6
1995	8.4	0.7118	6	8.4	0.7118	6
1996	9.1	0.6355	6	9.1	0.6355	6
1997	9.9	0.5674	6	9.9	0.5674	6
1998	270.8	0.5066	137	232.7	0.5066	118
	Net present value		$168	Net present value		$149

IRR Analysis—P/E Method: Assumes P/E Multiple of 20× (in Millions of Dollars)

	Continuing Value Assumption			Sale Assumption		
	Cash Flow	13.0% Discount Rate	Present Value	Cash Flow	10.5% Discount Rate	Present Value
1993	($160.0)	1.0000	($160)	($160.0)	1.0000	($160)
1993	8.0	0.8850	$7	8.0	0.9053	$7
1994	7.8	0.7832	6	7.8	0.8195	6
1995	8.4	0.6932	6	8.4	0.7419	6
1996	9.1	0.6135	6	9.1	0.6716	6
1997	9.9	0.5429	5	9.9	0.6080	6
1998	270.8	0.4805	130	232.7	0.5504	128
	Net present value		$0	Net present value		$0

If we assume (1) that the target company's stock is sold at the end of 1998 for the residual value amount; (2) the tax basis of the target company's stock is $160; and (3) the tax rate is 38 percent, the tax effected residual value is as indicated. Note: This calculation is presented only to illustrate the significant effect that taxes can have on residual value.

The example clearly indicates the importance of the assumption as to whether the company will be held indefinitely or resold. It is also important to note that the residual value in both cases was calculated as of the end of 1998. An alternative approach that is acceptable if the continuing value assumption is made would be to estimate net income in 1999, capitalize that amount, and include the resulting gross residual value amount in the cash flow calculations as of the end of 1999.

15.21b   The EBDIAT Multiple Method

The EBDIAT Multiple Method is based on the assumption that the target company will be worth some multiple of its after-tax cash flow at the end of the forecast period. The method involves taking the forecast after-tax cash flow in the last year of the cash flow forecast and multiplying it by an estimated after-tax cash flow multiple. If the acquirer expects to dispose of the target, the tax effect of the sale would then be calculated. Otherwise, the gross residual value would be included in the cash flow analysis at the end of the forecast period.

The criticisms and associated responses are virtually identical for both the P/E Method and the EBDIAT Method, with the exception that key decision makers are generally less familiar with EBDIAT multiples than with P/E multiples.

Example 15C   Same facts as Example 15A. The schedule below calculates the residual value of the target assuming that the appropriate EBDIAT multiples to analyze are 11, 13 and 15. NPV and IRR calculations using the 13 × EBDIAT multiple value are shown for both continuing value and sale assumptions.

Gross Residual Value—EBDIAT Method
(in Millions of Dollars)

	EBDIAT Multiple		
	11×	*13×*	*15×*
1998 net income	$13.0	$13.0	$13.0
1998 depreciation & amortization	10.9	10.9	10.9
1998 EBDIAT	23.9	23.9	23.9
Applicable EBDIAT multiple	11×	13×	15×
Gross residual value	$263.0	$310.9	$358.7

Tax Effected Residual Value—EBDIAT Method
(in Millions of Dollars)

	EBDIAT Multiple		
	11×	13×	15×
Sale price	$263.0	$310.9	$358.7
Less: Tax basis	(160.0)	(160.0)	(160.0)
Taxable gain	103.0	150.9	198.7
Tax rate	38%	38%	38%
Tax on sale	$39.2	$57.3	$75.5
Sale proceeds	$263.0	$310.9	$358.7
Less: Tax on sale	(39.2)	(57.3)	(75.5)
Net residual value	$223.9	$253.5	$283.2

Rounded numbers are used for calculations in this table.

NPV Analysis—EBDIAT Method: Assumes EBDIAT Multiple of 13 ×
(in Millions of Dollars)

	Continuing Value Assumption			Sale Assumption		
	Cash Flow	12% Discount Rate	Present Value	Cash Flow	12% Discount Rate	Present Value
1993	$8.0	0.8929	$7	$8.0	0.8929	$7
1994	7.8	0.7972	6	7.8	0.7972	6
1995	8.4	0.7118	6	8.4	0.7118	6
1996	9.1	0.6355	6	9.1	0.6355	6
1997	9.9	0.5674	6	9.9	0.5674	6
1998	321.4	0.5066	163	264.1	0.5066	134
	Net present value		$194	Net present value		$164

IRR Analysis—EBDIAT Method: Assumes EBDIAT Multiple of 13 ×
(in Millions of Dollars)

	Continuing Value Assumption			Sale Assumption		
	Cash Flow	16.0% Discount Rate	Present Value	Cash Flow	12.6% Discount Rate	Present Value
1993	($160.0)	1.0000	($160)	($160.0)	1.0000	($160)
1993	8.0	0.8624	$7	8.0	0.8883	$7
1994	7.8	0.7437	6	7.8	0.7891	6
1995	8.4	0.6413	5	8.4	0.7010	6
1996	9.1	0.5531	5	9.1	0.6227	6
1997	9.9	0.4770	5	9.9	0.5531	5
1998	321.4	0.4113	132	264.1	0.4914	130
	Net present value		$0	Net present value		$0

If we assume (1) that the target company's stock is sold at the end of 1998 for the residual value amount; (2) the tax basis of the target company's stock is $160; and (3) the tax rate is 38 percent, the tax effected residual value is as indicated.

15.21c   The Growing Perpetuity Method

The Growing Perpetuity Method is based on the assumption that the target company's cash flow is expected to continue to grow after the end of the forecast period. This assumption is the most reasonable one that can be made beyond the forecast period in the majority of acquisition situations. The method involves estimating the target's cash flow in the year after the forecast period ends and capitalizing this cash flow by a rate equal to the target's *weighted average cost of capital (WACC)* less the assumed perpetuity growth rate. This method will yield spurious results if the expected growth rate in perpetuity exceeds the target's WACC. The formula appears below:

$$\text{Present value of a growing perpetuity} = \frac{\text{Cash flow in year after forecast period}}{\text{WACC} - \text{Growth rate in perpetuity}}$$

If the acquirer expects to dispose of the target, the tax effect of the sale should be calculated.

There are a number of possible criticisms of this technique. The history of business has shown that businesses do not grow in perpetuity. Furthermore, the key decision maker may not be comfortable with the Growing Perpetuity Method's underlying concept for a variety of reasons: (a) the residual value accounts for a majority of the value of the target in the DCF Analysis; (b) the market risk associated with the target's cash flows after the forecast period is greater than cash flows during the forecast period; and (c) the Growing Perpetuity Method of calculating residual value does not take into account market conditions at the end of the forecast period. These reasons tend to drive executives to rely on the other methods outlined above that they are more familiar with and which relate residual value more closely to the executives' perceptions of what market conditions will be.

Example 15D   Same facts as Example 15A. The schedule below calculates the residual value of the target assuming the Growing Perpetuity Method is used. The assumed WACC is 12 percent and the growth rate in perpetuity is 5–7 percent.

Gross Residual Value—Growing Perpetuity Method
(in Millions of Dollars)

| | Perpetuity Growth Rate | | |
	5%	6%	7%
1999 Estimated cash flow	$12.2	$11.8	$11.5
WACC less growth rate	7%	6%	5%
Gross residual value	$174.0	$197.4	$230.2

If we assume (1) that the target company's stock is sold at the end of 1998 for the residual value amount; (2) the tax basis of the target company's stock is $160; and (3) the tax rate is 38 percent, the tax effected residual value is as indicated below.

Tax Effected Residual Value—Growing Perpetuity Method (in Millions of Dollars)

	Perpetuity Growth Rate		
	5%	6%	7%
Sale price	$174.0	$197.4	$230.2
Less: Tax basis	(160.0)	(160.0)	(160.0)
Taxable gain	14.0	37.4	70.2
Tax rate	38%	38%	38%
Tax on sale	$5.3	$14.2	$26.7
Sale proceeds	$174.0	$197.4	$230.2
Less: Tax on sale	(5.3)	(14.2)	(26.7)
Net residual value	$168.7	$183.2	$203.5

NPV Analysis—Growing Perpetuity Method: Assumes Perpetuity Growth Rate of 6% (in Millions of Dollars)

	Continuing Value Assumption			Sale Assumption		
	Cash Flow	12% Discount Rate	Present Value	Cash Flow	12% Discount Rate	Present Value
1993	$8.0	0.8929	$7	$8.0	0.8929	$7
1994	7.8	0.7972	6	7.8	0.7972	6
1995	8.4	0.7118	6	8.4	0.7118	6
1996	9.1	0.6355	6	9.1	0.6355	6
1997	9.9	0.5674	6	9.9	0.5674	6
1998	10.6	0.5066	5	10.6	0.5066	5
	197.4	0.5066	100	183.2	0.5066	93
	Net present value		$136	Net present value		$129

IRR Analysis—Growing Perpetuity Method: Assumes Perpetuity Growth Rate of 6% (in Millions of Dollars)

	Continuing Value Assumption			Sale Assumption		
	Cash Flow	8.6% Discount Rate	Present Value	Cash Flow	7.5% Discount Rate	Present Value
1993	($160.0)	1.0000	($160)	($160.0)	1.0000	($160)
1993	8.0	0.9205	7	8.0	0.9312	7
1994	7.8	0.8472	7	7.8	0.8671	7
1995	8.4	0.7798	7	8.4	0.8075	7
1996	9.1	0.7178	7	9.1	0.7519	7
1997	9.9	0.6607	7	9.9	0.7002	7
1998	10.6	0.6082	7	10.6	0.6520	7
	197.4	0.6082	126	183.2	0.6072	119
	Net present value		$0	Net present value		$0

15.21d   The EBITDA Multiple Method

The EBITDA Multiple Method is primarily used by LBO firms in evaluating potential leveraged investments. It is based on the assumption that the target company will be worth some multiple of its pretax cash flow at the end of the forecast period. LBO firms use this residual value method because it is consistent with their approach in searching out leveraged investment opportunities.

The method involves taking the forecast pretax cash flow, defined as earnings before interest, taxes, depreciation and amortization, in the last year of the forecast period and multiplying it by an estimated pretax cash flow (EBITDA) multiple.

If the acquirer expects to dispose of the target, the tax effect of the sale should be calculated. Otherwise, the gross residual value is included in the cash flow analysis at the end of the forecast period.

A residual value calculated using the EBITDA Multiple Method can be criticized for its lack of relevance to the ongoing value of the business. However, LBO firms that use this technique would counter that it provides a valid estimate of the sale price for the target.

Example 15E *Same facts as Example 15A. The schedule below calculates the residual value of the target assuming the appropriate EBITDA multiples to analyze are 8, 9, and 10. NPV and IRR calculations using the 9× EBITDA multiple value are also shown for both continuing value and sale assumptions.*

Gross Residual Value—EBITDA Method
(in Millions of Dollars)

	EBITDA Multiple		
	8×	9×	10×
1998 EBIT	$21.0	$21.0	$21.0
1998 depreciation & amortization	10.9	10.9	10.9
1998 EBITDA	31.9	31.9	31.9
Applicable EBITDA multiple	8×	9×	10×
Gross residual value	$255.1	$287.0	$318.9

If we assume (1) that the target company's stock is sold at the end of 1998 for the residual value amount; (2) the tax basis of the target company's stock is $160; and (3) the tax rate is 38 percent, the tax effected residual value is as indicated.

Tax Effected Residual Value—EBITDA Method
(in Millions of Dollars)

	EBITDA Multiple		
	8×	9×	10×
Sale price	$255.1	$287.0	$318.9
Less: Tax basis	(160.0)	(160.0)	(160.0)
Taxable gain	95.1	127.0	158.9
Tax rate	38%	38%	38%
Tax on sale	$36.1	$48.3	$60.4
Sale proceeds	$255.1	$287.0	$318.9
Less: Tax on sale	(36.1)	(48.3)	(60.4)
Net residual value	$219.0	$238.7	$258.5

NPV Analysis—EBITDA Method: Assumes EBITDA Multiple of 9×
(in Millions of Dollars)

	Continuing Value Assumption			Sale Assumption		
	Cash Flow	12% Discount Rate	Present Value	Cash Flow	12% Discount Rate	Present Value
1993	$8.0	0.8929	$7	$8.0	0.8929	$7
1994	7.8	0.7972	6	7.8	0.7972	6
1995	8.4	0.7118	6	8.4	0.7118	6
1996	9.1	0.6355	6	9.1	0.6355	6
1997	9.9	0.5674	6	9.9	0.5674	6
1998	297.5	0.5066	151	249.3	0.5066	126
	Net present value		$181	Net present value		$157

IRR Analysis—EBITDA Method: Assumes EBITDA Multiple of 9×
(in Millions of Dollars)

	Continuing Value Assumption			Sale Assumption		
	Cash Flow	14.6% Discount Rate	Present Value	Cash Flow	11.6% Discount Rate	Present Value
1993	($160.0)	1.0000	($160)	($160.0)	1.0000	($160)
1993	8.0	0.8725	$7	8.0	0.8960	$7
1994	7.8	0.7613	$6	7.8	0.8029	6
1995	8.4	0.6642	$6	8.4	0.7194	6
1996	9.1	0.5796	$5	9.1	0.6446	6
1997	9.9	0.5057	$5	9.9	0.5776	6
1998	297.5	0.4412	$131	249.3	0.5175	129
	Net present value		$0	Net present value		$0

15.21e   The EBITA Multiple Method

The EBITA Multiple Method is another method primarily used by LBO firms. It is based on the assumption that the target company will be worth some multiple of its pretax cash flow at the end of the forecast period. The difference between this method and the EBITDA Multiple Method is the exclusion of depreciation from the multiple. Firms that use the EBITA methodology believe that an accurate estimate of a company's pretax cash flow should include depreciation because for most companies the annual amount of "maintenance" capital expenditures equals the depreciation charge.

The method involves taking the forecast pretax cash flow, defined as earnings before interest, taxes, and amortization, in the last year of the forecast period and multiplying it times an estimated pretax cash flow (EBITA) multiple.

If the acquirer expects to dispose of the target, the tax effect of the sale should be calculated. Otherwise, the gross residual value is included in the cash flow analysis at the end of the forecast period.

Example 15F Same facts as Example 15A. However, we will assume that Mareight's amortization amount in 1998 is $1.5 million. The schedule below calculates the residual value of the target assuming that the appropriate EBITA multiples to analyze are 10, 11 and 12. NPV and IRR calculations using the 11× EBITA multiple value are also shown for continuing value and sale assumptions.

Gross Residual Value—EBITA Method
(in Millions of Dollars)

	EBITA Multiple		
	10×	11×	12×
1998 EBIT	$21.0	$21.0	$21.0
1998 amortization	1.5	1.5	1.5
1998 EBITA	22.5	22.5	22.5
Applicable EBITA multiple	10×	11×	12×
Gross residual value	$224.8	$247.3	$269.8

If we assume (1) that the target company's stock is sold at the end of 1998 for the residual value amount; (2) the tax basis of the target company's stock is $160; and (3) the tax rate is 38 percent, the tax effected residual value is as indicated below.

Tax Effected Residual Value—EBITA Method
(in Millions of Dollars)

	EBITA Multiple		
	10×	*11×*	*12×*
Sale price	$224.8	$247.3	$269.8
Less: Tax basis	(160.0)	(160.0)	(160.0)
Taxable gain	64.8	87.3	109.8
Tax rate	38%	38%	38%
Tax on sale	$24.6	$33.2	$41.7
Sale proceeds	$224.8	$247.3	$269.8
Less: Tax on sale	(24.6)	(33.2)	(41.7)
Net residual value	$200.2	$214.1	$228.1

NPV Analysis—EBITA Method: Assumes EBITA Multiple of 11 ×
(in Millions of Dollars)

	Continuing Value Assumption			Sale Assumption		
	Cash Flow	*12% Discount Rate*	*Present Value*	*Cash Flow*	*12% Discount Rate*	*Present Value*
1993	$8.0	0.8929	$7	$8.0	0.8929	$7
1994	7.8	0.7972	6	7.8	0.7972	6
1995	8.4	0.7118	6	8.4	0.7118	6
1996	9.1	0.6355	6	9.1	0.6355	6
1997	9.9	0.5674	6	9.9	0.5674	6
1998	257.9	0.5066	131	224.7	0.5066	114
	Net present value		$161	Net present value		$145

IRR Analysis—EBITA Method: Assumes EBITA Multiple of 11 ×
(in Millions of Dollars)

	Continuing Value Assumption			Sale Assumption		
	Cash Flow	12.2% Discount Rate	Present Value	Cash Flow	9.9% Discount Rate	Present Value
1993	($160.0)	1.0000	($160)	($160.0)	1.0000	($160)
1993	8.0	0.8915	7	8.0	0.9100	7
1994	7.8	0.7948	6	7.8	0.8281	6
1995	8.4	0.7085	6	8.4	0.7535	6
1996	9.1	0.6316	6	9.1	0.6857	6
1997	9.9	0.5631	6	9.9	0.6240	6
1998	257.9	0.5020	129	224.7	0.5678	128
	Net present value		$0	Net present value		$0

15.3   KEY COMPONENTS OF THE CASH FLOW FORECAST

The key components of any cash flow forecast include: the target's after-tax earnings from operations, depreciation and amortization, deferred taxes, changes in working capital and capital expenditures. The key components and how they fit into an acquisition cash flow model are discussed in detail in Chapter 22.

There are several key issues related to any cash flow acquisition analysis, the two most important of which are: (1) the cash flow analysis must incorporate an assumption regarding how the target company is being acquired (e.g., Asset Acquisition, Stock Acquisition, etc.) and (2) the tax aspects of the transaction must be incorporated into the analysis. Chapter 6 describes the importance of the tax aspects of any transaction.

15.4   ALTERNATIVE SCENARIOS AND SENSITIVITY ANALYSIS

Typically, alternative operating scenarios are developed in DCF Analysis to quantify the risks associated with the target's business. These alternative operating scenarios are usually labeled (Best Case, Worst Case and Most Likely Case). In addition, sensitivity analyses are performed on selected variables to quantify the impact on the overall financials that a change in any one variable would have on the acquisition's returns. Both of these topics are discussed in Chapter 24.

15.5   APPROPRIATE DISCOUNT RATE IN NPV ANALYSIS

The appropriate discount rate to use in NPV analysis is the WACC of the target, assuming a given capital structure for the target company. The WACC of the target company will change substantially depending on the assumption regarding the target's capital structure. See Exhibits 15–1 and 15–2.

Most basic financial texts contain detailed discussions regarding the calculation of a company's WACC, as well as its underlying theory. Therefore, we will only focus on a few significant issues in applying the WACC to DCF analysis in acquisitions.

EXHIBIT 15–1
Calculation of WACC for Sample Company

	Debt & Equity as a Percent of Total Capitalization					
Equity	100%	80%	60%	40%	20%	5%
Senior debt		20%	40%	60%	50%	50%
Subordinated debt		0	0	0	30	45
Total debt	0%	20%	40%	60%	80%	95%
	Cost of Debt and Equity Assuming Above Capital Structure					
Cost of equity	15.0%	15.0%	16.0%	18.5%	30.0%	50.0%
Cost of debt						
Senior debt		8.5%	9.0%	10.0%	10.0%	12.5%
Subordinated debt					25.0	30.0
	Weighted Average Cost of Capital*					
Cost of equity	15.0%	12.0%	9.6%	7.4%	6.0%	2.5%
After-tax cost of debt						
Senior debt	0.0%	1.1%	2.2%	3.7%	3.1%	3.9%
Subordinated debt	0.0	0.0	0.0	0.0	4.7	8.4
WACC	15.0%	13.1%	11.8%	11.1%	13.8%	14.7%

* Assumes tax rate of 38 percent.

EXHIBIT 15–2
Weighted Average Cost of Capital (Sample Company)

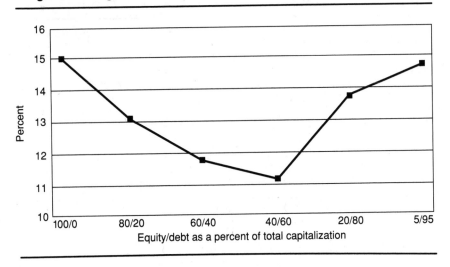

Equity/debt as a percent of total capitalization

15.51   Estimating the Cost of Equity Capital

The two principal models for calculating the cost of equity capital are the *Capital Asset Pricing Model (CAPM)* and the *Arbitrage Pricing Theory (APT)*. These models generally yield similar estimates. However, there can be meaningful differences.

One can have a high confidence level when estimating the cost of equity capital under these two methods if the target company being analyzed is a large publicly traded entity. However, as the target company moves farther away from this description, the confidence level in the estimates tends to drop. If there is uncertainty regarding the cost of equity capital, a range of discount rates is typically used in an analysis. When this range is coupled with a range of residual value multiples (e.g., P/E or EBDIAT multiples), the most meaningful summary analysis is a matrix of NPVs. See Exhibit 15–3.

EXHIBIT 15-3

Summary NPV Analysis—EBDIAT Multiple Method: Residual Value Not Tax Effected (in Millions of Dollars)

Discount Rate	EBDIAT Multiple					Residual Value as a % of Net Present Value	
	11×	12×	13×	14×	15×	Minimum	Maximum
10%	$187	$200	$214	$227	$241	79.5%	84.1%
11%	178	191	203	216	229	79.1	83.8
12%	169	181	194	206	218	78.7	83.5
13%	161	173	184	196	207	78.3	83.1
14%	154	165	176	186	197	77.9	82.8

Note: The above matrix is appropriate for all residual value methods.

15.51a   Capital Asset Pricing Model

The cost of equity capital according to the CAPM is equal to the sum of the risk-free rate of return plus an amount equal to the market risk premium (the expected return on the market in excess of the risk-free rate) multiplied by the beta of the target company. The beta of the target represents the level of systematic risk associated with the target company's stock:

Cost of equity capital = Risk-free rate + (the Market risk
premium × the Target company's beta)

As discussed, if the target company is a public company, it should be relatively easy to calculate the cost of equity capital. However, if the target company is privately owned or a small division of a large public company, the calculations become more difficult because a beta must be estimated for the target company. In ideal circumstances there will be publicly traded comparable companies that can be analyzed to develop an industry beta. However, in many cases a beta must be estimated without good comparable company data. Needless to say, in these circumstances the confidence level in the estimated beta will not be very high, and a matrix of net present values using different discount rates, reflecting different WACCs, is required.

Once the target company's beta is determined, the formula for levering and unlevering betas can be used to adjust the beta of the target company to the new expected capital structure for the target company:

$$\text{Levered beta} = \text{Unlevered beta} / (\text{Market value of debt/Market value of equity})$$

15.51b   Arbitrage Pricing Theory

APT assumes that a stock's rate of return depends on a variety of macro-economic factors, as well as events that are unique to each company. The macroeconomic factors are not defined in the theory. However, research on appropriate macroeconomic factors is focused on several including the level of industrial activity, the rate of inflation, the spread between long- and short-term interest rates and a few others.

The use of APT does not reduce the problems associated with esti-mating the cost of capital when the target is not a public entity. It requires the estimation of a beta for the target that represents its sensitivity to each macroeconomic factor included in the overall formula. There generally are four or five macroeconomic factors, each requiring a separate beta.

15.6   CALCULATING THE NPV OF THE TARGET'S EQUITY

After the NPV of a target has been estimated, the calculation of the target's equity is easy. The present value of all the target's liabilities is deducted from the target's NPV to arrive at the value of the target's equity. In performing this calculation it is important to convert all con-vertible securities into common equity to arrive at the proper equity value per share.

15.7   STRENGTHS AND WEAKNESSES

DCF Analysis is an important technique for valuing a company. The strength of the DCF approach is that it provides a rational economic framework for valuing acquisitions that the marketplace generally follows. However, it does not always reflect what transpires in the marketplace. This is why the other valuation techniques discussed in this section are also important. In addition, significant differences in expectations as to what can be done with the target company's assets will lead to material differences in valuation under this method.

One of the complexities with using the NPV method is that a target company's future cash flows depend on the method of acquisition and the purchase price. How? A target company's future cash flows are directly impacted by the taxes it will pay. The taxes it will pay depend on its taxable income. The target's taxable income will depend, in part, on the company's taxable deductions for depreciation and the amortization of intangible assets. Such deductions depend on the target's tax basis for its assets, which in turn often depend directly on the purchase price paid for the business.

Another weakness of DCF Analysis is that it explicitly does not take into account the effects of leverage. This presents real problems in certain situations. For example, in many cases the target company has existing debt obligations that either cannot be paid off without incurring a significant prepayment penalty, or should not be paid off because they are economically attractive to stay in place (e.g., very low interest loans associated with job development programs). How should these items be handled in the analysis? Should one ignore the penalties and assume that all loans are repaid in keeping with the DCF approach that the entire purchase price is funded with equity? The best approach is to assume that all existing debts are refinanced without penalty. However, the acquirer should use the LBO Model described in Chapter 23 to analyze the company's projected results given the anticipated capitalization of the target. A DCF Model is not designed to provide this analysis.

Chapter 16

Strategic Buyer
DCF Analysis

16.0 INTRODUCTION

A *Strategic Buyer DCF Analysis* is a valuation technique that should be performed if a readily identifiable strategic buyer is believed to be bidding for the target company. A Strategic Buyer DCF Analysis is undertaken from this prospective bidder's point of view. Generally, the analysis proves useful in defining the high end of the value range for the target.

A Strategic Buyer DCF Analysis takes into account the expected economic synergies that will result from a combination of the target's operations with those of the strategic buyer. Expected synergies can come from a variety of areas, including additional sales volume from the sale of product through the strategic buyer's existing distribution channels, savings from the consolidation of manufacturing facilities or better utilization of manufacturing facilities, the elimination of duplicate sales forces and the reduction of general and administrative expenses.

16.1 AN EXAMPLE

The example used to illustrate Strategic Buyer DCF Analysis is the case study first described in Chapter 10. However, several additional facts will be considered.

Harrison Corporation, a diversified conglomerate, is considering its initial bid for Mareight Corporation. Harrison is aware that General Corporation has indicated publicly its interest in acquiring Mareight.

Therefore, Harrison has decided to undertake a DCF analysis from General's perspective. This analysis appears in Exhibits 16–1 through 16–13.

Harrison estimates that if General were to acquire Mareight, it would realize significant operating synergies related to a reduction in the sales force (approximately $2 million) and a reduction in general and administrative expenses (approximately $1 million). Harrison estimates that severance costs will eliminate any cost savings related to the sales force reduction in the first year after the transaction is completed.

In performing the Strategic Buyer DCF Analysis, Harrison assumed that the relevant residual value multiples and growth rates were the same as for its own DCF Analysis. See Chapter 15. In addition, Harrison believed that General did not intend to dispose of Mareight. Therefore, the tax effect of a sale was not calculated. Harrison also assumed for purposes of the IRR Analysis, that the purchase price General would be willing to pay would be approximately $200 million. Finally, Harrison estimated that the WACC General would use for discounting the target's cash flows was 12 percent.

The reader should note that this example is not intended to be technically correct with respect to taxes. It is intended to illustrate the approach that should be taken. See Chapter 22 for a complete description of the acquisition models that would be completed.

16.11   Results of Analysis

The Strategic Buyer DCF Analysis indicates that at a discount rate of 12 percent and using a residual P/E multiple of 20× or an EBDIAT multiple of 13×, General Corporation can afford to pay approximately $199–$216 million. This purchase price exceeds the values calculated using the same assumptions in Harrison's own DCF analysis by a margin of $22–$48 million.

EXHIBIT 16–1
Mareight Corporation Estimated Synergies (in Millions of Dollars)

	Year Ended December 31,					
	1993	1994	1995	1996	1997	1998
Forecast SG&A expenses	$27.2	$29.3	$31.5	$33.8	$36.4	$39.1
Cost Savings						
Reduction in sales force	(2.0)	(2.1)	(2.2)	(2.2)	(2.3)	(2.4)
Severance benefits	2.0					
General & admin savings	(1.0)	(1.0)	(1.1)	(1.1)	(1.2)	(1.2)
Total estimated cost savings	(1.0)	(3.1)	(3.2)	(3.4)	(3.5)	(3.6)
Revised SG&A forecast	$26.2	$26.1	$28.2	$30.4	$32.9	$35.4

EXHIBIT 16–2
Mareight Corporation Forecast Income Statements: Assuming Buyer Synergies
(in Millions of Dollars)

	Year Ended December 31,					
	1993	1994	1995	1996	1997	1998
Sales	$143.3	$154.0	$165.6	$178.0	$191.4	$205.7
Cost of goods sold	93.9	100.9	108.5	116.6	125.3	134.7
Gross profit	49.4	53.1	57.1	61.4	66.0	71.0
Gross margin	34.5%	34.5%	34.5%	34.5%	34.5%	34.5%
SG&A expenses	26.2	26.1	28.2	30.4	32.9	35.4
Depreciation & amortization	7.6	8.2	8.8	9.4	10.1	10.9
Operating profit	15.6	18.8	20.1	21.5	23.0	24.6
Tax provision—38%	5.9	7.2	7.7	8.2	8.8	9.4
Net income	$9.7	$11.7	$12.5	$13.4	$14.3	$15.3
Capital Requirements						
Capital expenditures	$7.7	$8.3	$8.9	$9.6	$10.3	$11.1
Increase in working capital	0.4	2.5	2.7	2.9	3.1	3.3

EXHIBIT 16–3

Mareight Corporation Cash Flow Forecast: Assuming Buyer Synergies
(in Millions of Dollars)

	Year Ended December 31,					
	1993	1994	1995	1996	1997	1998
Sources						
Net income	$9.7	$11.7	$12.5	$13.4	$14.3	$15.3
Depreciation & amortization	7.6	8.2	8.8	9.4	10.1	10.9
Deferred taxes	0.5	0.6	0.7	0.8	1.0	1.0
Total sources	17.8	20.4	22.0	23.6	25.4	27.2
Uses						
Capital expenditures	(7.7)	(8.3)	(8.9)	(9.6)	(10.3)	(11.1)
Increase in working capital	(0.4)	(2.5)	(2.7)	(2.9)	(3.1)	(3.3)
Total uses	(8.1)	(10.8)	(11.6)	(12.5)	(13.4)	(14.4)
After-tax net cash flows	$9.6	$9.7	$10.4	$11.1	$12.0	$12.8

EXHIBIT 16–4

Gross Residual Value—P/E Method
(in Millions of Dollars)

	P/E Multiple		
	18×	20×	22×
1998 Net income	$15.3	$15.3	$15.3
Applicable P/E multiple	18×	20×	22×
Gross residual value	$274.9	$305.5	$336.0

EXHIBIT 16–5
NPV Analysis—P/E Method: Assuming
P/E Multiple of 20×
(in Millions of Dollars)

		Continuing Value Assumption	
	Cash Flow	12% Discount Rate	Present Value
1993	$9.6	0.8929	$9
1994	9.7	0.7972	8
1995	10.4	0.7118	7
1996	11.1	0.6355	7
1997	12.0	0.5674	7
1998	318.2	0.5066	161
Net present value			$199

EXHIBIT 16–6
IRR Analysis—P/E Method: Assuming
P/E Multiple of 20×
(in Millions of Dollars)

		Continuing Value Assumption	
	Cash Flow	11.9% Discount Rate	Present Value
1993	($200.0)	1.0000	($200)
1993	9.6	0.8939	9
1994	9.7	0.7990	8
1995	10.4	0.7142	7
1996	11.1	0.6384	7
1997	12.0	0.5707	7
1998	318.2	0.5101	162
Net present value			$0

EXHIBIT 16–7
Gross Residual Value—EBDIAT Multiple Method
(in Millions of Dollars)

	EBDIAT Multiple		
	11×	13×	15×
1998 Net income	$15.3	$15.3	$15.3
1998 Depreciation & amortization	10.9	10.9	10.9
1998 EBDIAT	26.2	26.2	26.2
Applicable EBDIAT multiple	11×	13×	15×
Gross residual value	$287.9	$340.3	$392.6

EXHIBIT 16–8
NPV Analysis—EBDIAT Multiple Method:
Assuming EBDIAT Multiple of 13×
(in Millions of Dollars)

	Continuing Value Assumption		
	Cash Flow	12% Discount Rate	Present Value
1993	$9.6	0.8929	$9
1994	9.7	0.7972	8
1995	10.4	0.7118	7
1996	11.1	0.6355	7
1997	12.0	0.5674	7
1998	353.1	0.5066	179
Net present value			$216

EXHIBIT 16-9
IRR Analysis—EBDIAT Multiple Method:
Assuming EBDIAT Multiple of 13×
(in Millions of Dollars)

		Continuing Value Assumption	
	Cash Flow	13.6% Discount Rate	Present Value
1993	($200.0)	1.0000	($200)
1993	9.6	0.8800	$8
1994	9.7	0.7744	7
1995	10.4	0.6815	7
1996	11.1	0.5997	7
1997	12.0	0.5278	6
1998	353.1	0.4645	164
	Net present value		$0

EXHIBIT 16-10
Gross Residual Value—Growing Perpetuity Method
(in Millions of Dollars)

	Perpetuity Growth Rate		
	5%	6%	7%
1999 Estimated cash flow	$14.8	$15.0	$15.0
WACC less growth rate	7%	6%	5%
Gross residual value	$211.2	$249.4	$300.8

EXHIBIT 16–11
NPV Analysis—Growing Perpetuity
Method: Assuming Perpetuity Growth
Rate of 6% (in Millions of Dollars)

		Continuing Value Assumption	
	Cash Flow	12% Discount Rate	Present Value
1993	$9.6	0.8929	$9
1994	9.7	0.7972	8
1995	10.4	0.7118	7
1996	11.1	0.6355	7
1997	12.0	0.5674	7
1998	12.8	0.5066	6
	249.4	0.5066	126
Net present value			$170

EXHIBIT 16–12
IRR Analysis—Growing Perpetuity
Method: Assuming Perpetuity Growth
Rate of 6% (in Millions of Dollars)

		Continuing Value Assumption	
	Cash Flow	8.7% Discount Rate	Present Value
1993	($200.0)	1.0000	($200)
1993	9.6	0.9201	$9
1994	9.7	0.8465	8
1995	10.4	0.7788	8
1996	11.1	0.7166	8
1997	12.0	0.6593	8
1998	12.8	0.6066	8
	249.4	0.6066	151
Net present value			$0

EXHIBIT 16–13
Summary NPV Analysis—EBDIAT Multiple Method: Residual Value Not Tax Effected (in Millions of Dollars)

Discount Rate	EBDIAT Multiple					Residual Value as a % of Net Present Value	
	11×	12×	13×	14×	15×	Minimum	Maximum
10.0%	$209	$224	$239	$254	$268	77.7%	82.6%
11.0	199	213	227	241	255	77.2	82.2
12.0	190	203	216	230	243	76.8	81.9
13.0	181	194	206	219	231	76.4	81.5
14.0	173	185	197	208	220	76.0	81.2

Note: This schedule would be prepared for all residual value methods.

16.2   STRENGTHS AND WEAKNESSES

In certain circumstances, the Strategic Buyer DCF Analysis can be the most important valuation technique to undertake. Generally, however, it is not feasible to identify the most likely strategic bidder for a target company and complete a DCF analysis that is reasonably accurate with respect to how that particular bidder is going to look at the acquisition of the target company.

Another criticism of this valuation technique is that it is speculative with respect to how another company will look at a prospective acquisition. Therefore, the results of the analysis have to be viewed with some degree of skepticism.

Chapter 17

Leveraged Buyout Analysis

17.0 INTRODUCTION

A *Leveraged Buyout (LBO) Analysis* should be completed whenever the target company is a good LBO candidate. Why? Even in the 1990s difficult economic environment, the value that can be achieved in an LBO often sets the lower limit of the valuation range for the target company. It may also set the upper limit, if a corporate buyer cannot be located or does not exist.

LBO Analysis is similar in approach to DCF Analysis. However, DCF Analysis must be modified to incorporate the various layers of financing that will be used. LBO Analysis should (1) include an analysis of the cash flows associated with each individual layer of capital, (2) properly calculate the rates of return that the various capital providers will earn on their invested funds, (3) adequately disclose the financial ratios (e.g., cash flow interest coverage ratio) that financing sources will review closely to determine the amount and type of financing they will provide, (4) take into account the tax effects associated with all the various layers of financing and their associated transaction costs.

This chapter will discuss some of the critical concerns in performing an LBO Analysis. Discussion of LBO models is reserved for Chapter 23.

17.1 LBO ANALYSIS VERSUS DCF ANALYSIS

Traditional NPV and IRR analyses are largely ignored in an LBO. The fact that the acquisition has an attractive IRR or the NPV significantly exceeds the asking price for the company does not matter. The key in LBO

Analysis is to determine the maximum amount of financing likely to be available for the transaction, assuming an equity financing source that is willing to be aggressive and accept a marginal rate of return on its invested equity capital. The availability of financing in these situations is highly dependent on the timing of cash flows, particularly in the first 18–24 months after the transaction is completed.

17.2   WHAT COMPANIES ARE GOOD LBO CANDIDATES?

Generally, a target company is considered a good LBO candidate if it (1) is not engaged in high technology or some other industry where rapid product obsolescence occurs, (2) is not engaged in a highly cyclical industry where cash flows can vary significantly from year to year depending on economic factors outside the control of management, (3) is not engaged in an industry that must make regular significant capital expenditures, (4) produces or is expected to produce a stable cash flow stream over the next several years, (5) has a competent management team in place, and (6) does not have any significant contingent liabilities.

If the target company is a marginal LBO candidate, an LBO Analysis should be performed. However, careful judgment should be exercised with respect to the likely purchase price that could be financed in such a situation. If the target is a poor LBO candidate, an LBO Analysis would be meaningless.

17.3   KNOWLEDGE OF THE FINANCING MARKETS IS KEY!

The key to completing an LBO Analysis is knowledge of the financing markets for LBO transactions. LBO structures continue to evolve as economic changes, as well as government policy and regulatory changes, affect capital providers.

Today, senior lenders for LBO transactions are few. Lenders have scaled back their appetite for loans to LBO transactions for a variety of reasons.

The discussion below highlights several areas of concern to LBO lenders in the 1990s.

17.31   Fraudulent Conveyance Issue

The fraudulent conveyance and avoidable preference provisions of the federal *Bankruptcy Reform Act of 1978 (Bankruptcy Act)* and state fraudulent conveyance statutes (either the *Uniform Fraudulent Transfer Act*, the *Uniform Fraudulent Conveyence Act*, or the state's debtor-creditor provisions) are designed to protect existing creditors of the target company.

The fraudulent conveyance issue is important because the creditors of the target at the time of the acquisition may be able to (1) recover proceeds of the sale received by the selling shareholders, and (2) invalidate claims or liens by the lenders to the transaction.

A transfer or conveyance made or an obligation incurred by the target company is constructively fraudulent if (a) it is accomplished without the target company receiving "fair consideration," and (b) any of the following is true: (i) the target company becomes insolvent on the date of the transfer or as a result of the transfer; (ii) the target company is left with an unreasonably small amount of capital; or (iii) the target company expects to incur debts that will be beyond its ability to repay. The statutes discussed above also have provisions that invalidate transfers where actual intent to defraud existing creditors exists.

The fair consideration issue is heavily impacted by the structure of the transaction (Stock Acquisition, Forward Subsidiary Merger, etc.). The key is to identify the fair consideration received by the target company—not the target company's shareholders.

The solvency issue is determined by analyzing whether the present *fair saleable value* of the target company's assets exceeds its liabilities (including contingent liabilities). The question of whether or not the target was solvent is generally determined in a bankruptcy or insolvency proceeding. Therefore, it is not surprising that the length of time between the transaction and the proceeding will impact the court's view as to whether the transaction rendered the target insolvent. Most acquirers seek to protect themselves by obtaining independent appraisals to support their position that the transaction did not render the company insolvent.

The issues of small capitalization and lack of capital to meet its obligations are generally reviewed in light of the acquirer's projections for the target company.

17.32   Accounting Issues

Accounting for LBO transactions where the acquiring entity has shareholders who are completely different from the existing shareholders of the target company is very straightforward. However, if the shareholders of the company formed to acquire the target company (NEWCO) include some of the existing shareholders of the target company, the proper accounting becomes quite complex.

Proper accounting for NEWCO's investment in the target company now requires part fair value and part predecessor basis. *Predecessor Basis* is the shareholders' basis of the target company prior to the LBO transaction.

A detailed discussion of the proper accounting treatment for these types of LBO transactions appears in paragraph C.2.

17.33 Margin Rules

The *Federal Reserve Board (FRB)* has issued regulations regarding the extension of credit in connection with the purchase of margin stock. These regulations impact the structuring and negotiation of leveraged buyouts.

FRB Regulation G limits the extension of credit for the purpose of directly or indirectly purchasing or holding publicly traded margin securities where the credit is secured, either directly or indirectly, by the margin stock. Regulation G currently limits the amount of credit that can be extended to 50 percent of the value of the margin stock.

Generally, in an LBO of a publicly held company, the target is bought by a shell company that is capitalized with a relatively small amount of equity and a large amount of debt. Several years ago the FRB issued an interpretation that indicated it will treat debt securities issued by a shell corporation as indirectly secured by the margin stock of the public target unless there is a merger agreement between the parties or the acquiring company can effect a short-form merger prior to the advance of funds. See paragraph E.12 for a description of a short-form merger.

17.4 RESIDUAL VALUE

Since an LBO acquirer, in most cases contemplates holding its investment for a relatively limited period of time (generally, three to ten years) calculating the tax effect of the expected sale is appropriate.

In addition, as noted in Chapter 15, most LBO firms find the EBITDA or EBITA methods of calculating residual value more useful than other methods.

17.5   REQUIRED DISCLOSURE IN A GOING-PRIVATE TRANSACTION

Going-Private Transactions are governed by special disclosure rules designed to provide additional safeguards for the target company's shareholders. See paragraph E.3 for a discussion of these rules.

17.6 STRENGTHS AND WEAKNESSES

LBO Analysis is important because in many cases it establishes the minimum price that a seller should agree to. Also, LBO Analysis is more appropriate than DCF Analysis for analyzing leveraged acquisitions because the impact of leverage is the key to the transaction. Conducting an acquisition analysis without including the impact of this leverage is ludicrous.

The value derived by LBO Analysis depends highly on the state of the financing markets at a particular time. These conditions can affect the valuation for a target company as much as changes in its operating results. Hence, one of the weaknesses of LBO Analysis as a valuation technique is that it can be significantly affected by temporary changes in financing conditions.

Chapter 18

Leveraged ESOP Analysis

18.0 INTRODUCTION

An *Employee Stock Ownership Plan (ESOP)* is a defined benefit plan designed to invest primarily in employer stock. Employers set up ESOPs for a variety of reasons, totally unrelated to mergers and acquisitions, including creating a stock-based incentive compensation program and providing stock ownership by employees. However, ESOPs can also be used for M&A purposes in two ways: (1) an ESOP can be structured to purchase a controlling interest in a company, and (2) an ESOP can be used to help defend a public corporation from attack by a hostile acquirer.

The best way to think of an ESOP as a potential acquirer for a company is as a tax-advantaged LBO. However, instead of the sponsor equity for the transaction coming from a third party, the equity is provided by the target's employees. This type of transaction is called a *Leveraged ESOP ("LESOP" or alternatively, an "ESOP LBO")*. Please note that many LESOPs are established for reasons totally unrelated to M&A. This chapter provides an overview of LESOPs and LESOP Analysis.

LESOP Analysis is similar to LBO Analysis. However, LBO Analysis must be modified to take into account the special tax incentives and accounting associated with LESOPs.

LESOP Analysis is only appropriate in selected situations where the target company is a good candidate for a leveraged transaction. The chapter will not focus on the substantial technical requirements related to setting up and maintaining an ESOP as set forth in the Employee Retirement Income Security Act of 1974 (ERISA), or the use of an ESOP as a defensive technique in the hostile takeover context.

18.1   WHAT COMPANIES ARE GOOD LESOP CANDIDATES?

As a general rule, it is appropriate to consider a LESOP transaction if the target company has operating characteristics that can support a substantial amount of leverage.

In addition, in most cases the process of entering into a LESOP transaction will be more complicated if the target company is a unionized operation because the union contract will have to be modified substantially to replace existing benefit plans. This contract must be reviewed, negotiated and ratified by the union. These steps add delays and uncertainties.

18.2   LESOP TRANSACTIONS DEFINED

In a LESOP, an ESOP is set up and borrows funds (either from the target company or from a third-party lender with the target company's guarantee) and purchases stock of the target company, either from the target itself or from its existing shareholders. The interest and principal payments associated with the ESOP's debt are funded through the target company's annual ESOP contributions and any dividends paid on the target company stock held by the ESOP. ESOP contributions typically replace payments for other preexisting employee benefit programs (e.g., pension or profit sharing plans) that are terminated when the ESOP is set up.

There are a variety of structures for completing a LESOP. A typical structure for a LESOP of a subsidiary of a public company appears in Exhibit 18–1.

EXHIBIT 18–1
LESOP of a Subsidiary

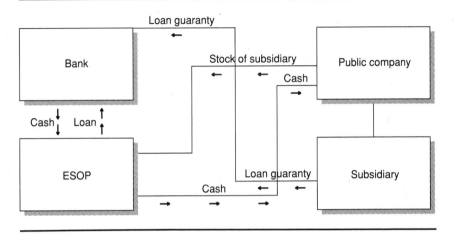

In this structure the ESOP uses existing funds (in many cases these funds would come from the conversion of a 401(k) plan), as well as borrowed funds from a financial institution, to acquire over 50 percent of the stock of the subsidiary from the public company. The loan is guaranteed by the subsidiary. The ESOP funds the repayment of the loan and related interest through annual contributions made by the subsidiary to the ESOP.

18.3 TAX BENEFITS TO THE BUYER

A LESOP transaction has numerous tax benefits. The principal tax benefit is that the target company can deduct 100 percent of the company's annual contributions to the ESOP. This has the effect of making principal repayments tax deductible.

A second substantial tax benefit is that the ESOP may be able to obtain financing at a lower tax-advantaged rate because financial institutions that lend to an ESOP are able to exclude 50 percent of the interest income on such loans from their taxable income pursuant to IRC Section 133. However, to obtain this exclusion, the ESOP must own more than 50 percent of each class of outstanding stock and more than 50 percent of the total value of all outstanding stock, excluding certain straight preferred stock.

A final tax advantage is that a corporation is permitted to deduct the amount of cash dividends paid (a) on a stock held by an ESOP when the dividends are used to make payments of principal or interest on an ESOP loan, and (b) to ESOP participants, either directly or indirectly through the ESOP.

18.4 TAX BENEFITS TO THE SELLER

A sale to a LESOP is extremely advantageous for stockholders of a closely held corporation. Generally, whenever the target company is such an entity, a LESOP Analysis should be undertaken.

IRC Section 1042 allows shareholders of closely held corporations to defer the taxation of long-term capital gain on the sale of stock to an ESOP to the extent that such shareholders reinvest the proceeds of the sale in certain qualified securities. Two key requirements for tax deferral are: (1) after the transaction, the ESOP must own at least 30 percent of the fully diluted equity of the corporation, and (2) the seller must have held the stock sold for at least three years. Given these requirements, the use of a LESOP can be appealing if shareholders want to sell only a portion of their equity.

Qualified replacement securities must be debt or equity securities of a domestic operating company that must not have a substantial amount (more than 25 percent) of passive income (e.g., interest or dividends from securities it holds). In addition, all replacement securities must be purchased within a period of 15 months (from 3 months prior to the sale to the ESOP to 12 months after). Under no conditions will any type of government securities constitute qualified replacement securities.

The tax deferral is effected by deducting from the tax basis of the replacement securities purchased the amount of the nonrecognized gain on the sale of stock to the ESOP.

18.41 Estate Planning Opportunity

The option of selling stock to an ESOP and purchasing replacement securities can be an attractive estate planning technique. If these steps are completed before death, the decedent's beneficiaries will receive a date of death fair value basis in the replacement securities. In most cases, this is preferable for the beneficiaries.

18.5   VALUATION

A sale to a LESOP can be accomplished within the fair value range for the target company. However, in establishing the value to be paid it is very important that proper procedure be followed. This means an independent trustee must be appointed for the ESOP and this trustee must hire an independent financial advisor to report on valuation issues.

Some of the valuation methodologies used to determine the value of the target company include the current market value of the target company's stock, Comparable Transactions Analysis, Comparable Company Analysis and DCF Analysis. In valuing the target company using the DCF approach, the analysis cannot take into account the various tax benefits associated with the potential transaction.

18.6   ACCOUNTING

Generally, accounting for an LBO that has an ESOP as a shareholder is the same as accounting for any other LBO. However, there are a few important distinctions. First, the ESOP loan must be recorded on the books of the target company as a liability if, as is always the case, the target company either guarantees the debt or commits to make future contributions to the ESOP sufficient to meet the ESOP's debt service requirements. Second, a contra equity account must be established to reflect the obligation recorded in the target company's liability accounts. The contra equity account is reduced as debt is retired. Third, interest expense is accrued and recorded for the ESOP debt. Contributions to the ESOP for repayment of principal are recorded as compensation expense. Once the contributions to the ESOP have been made to cover debt service requirements, the ESOP debt and contra equity accounts are adjusted by the reduction in principal. Other distinctions exist for companies that have ESOPs, but such distinctions are beyond the scope of this book.

18.7   ESOPs IN A MULTI-INVESTOR LBO

At the present time, the *Department of Labor (DOL)* has taken a position with respect to a trustee's fiduciary duties under ERISA that make it all but impossible for an LBO firm to treat an ESOP as a financing source for a transaction. The DOL's position is that the only way an ESOP can be treated fairly in a multi-investor LBO is as an equal to any other investor.

If the ESOP puts up a disproportionate amount of the financing, it is then entitled to that same proportion of the equity.

18.8 STRENGTHS AND WEAKNESSES

LESOP Analysis is not appropriate in all situations. However, in those situations where a LESOP is a reasonable alternative, this analysis should be completed.

LESOP Analysis is effective at identifying the values that could be obtained in what might be appropriately described as an in-house LBO. However, LESOP transactions have other nonquantifiable positive characteristics, including: (1) the fact that the target company does not have to be "shopped" to any buyers, and, therefore, there is minimal disruption in the day to day activity of the target's business; and (2) LESOPs improve employee morale and motivation, which often leads to improved employee productivity.

The biggest negative associated with LESOP Analysis is its complexity. LESOP transactions are very difficult to analyze and require specialized knowledge of ERISA laws and regulations. They require a great deal more information about the target company's operations than any other valuation technique. This valuation approach is nearly impossible to complete with a high degree of certainty if one does not have direct access to the company.

Chapter 19

Leveraged Recapitalization Analysis

19.0 INTRODUCTION

Leveraged Recapitalization Analysis (Recap Analysis) is a valuation technique that seeks to determine the maximum value that a public company can deliver to its shareholders immediately. Generally, Recap Analysis is undertaken in the context of a probable or pending hostile offer for the target company. It is unusual for a company to perform a Recap Analysis outside of this context, although such an analysis may prove useful.

Value in a *Recapitalization (Recap)* is typically delivered in two ways: (1) a massive stock buy-back or dividend of cash and/or securities, and (2) a continuing equity interest *(Stub Equity)* in a highly leveraged company. The value delivered in a Recap is extremely important in the context of a hostile takeover because it sets the minimum value that the target company's shareholders will realize.

Recap Analysis, in a narrow sense, focuses on the parent company's capital structure. However, the financing for a Recap usually depends on a variety of corporate actions related to the company's operations (e.g., sale of a key subsidiary—sometimes called a *Crown Jewel* sale). Therefore, it is not surprising that an effective Recap Analysis can only be completed after a complete valuation analysis of each of the target company's business units is completed. This *Breakup Analysis* is discussed in Chapter 20.

19.1 RECAPITALIZATION STRUCTURES

All Recaps have the following basic similarities: (1) the target company's shareholders receive a large sum of cash, (2) the target is significantly leveraged after the shareholders receive their cash, (3) generally, management and employee benefit plans do not receive any upfront cash but significantly increase their ownership of the target company, and (4) the recap is usually submitted to the shareholders for their approval because "shark repellents" are being added to the company's charter and/or bylaws. See paragraph E.13b for a discussion of shark repellents.

There are five principal Recap structures:

- Merger.
- Reclassification.
- Dividend.
- Self-Tender.
- Exchange Offer.

19.11 Merger Recap

In a Merger Recap a shell corporation is merged with and into the target company. In this merger, shares of common stock of the target company are converted into cash and/or securities plus common shares of the new surviving corporation. The merger must be approved by the target's shareholders and proxy materials must be prepared for the shareholders to vote on the proposed merger. The law of the state of the company's incorporation and the company's charter determine the shareholder approval requirements.

To improve the target's defenses, the surviving corporation may be incorporated in a state different than the one in which the target is currently incorporated.

Example 19A   On August 6, 1986, Wickes Cos. launched an unsolicited tender offer at $70 per share for Owens-Corning Fiberglas (OCF). This offer was subsequently increased to $74 per share. On August 28, when OCF's stock was trading at approximately $81, OCF announced a recapitalization plan that provided that public shareholders would receive a package consisting of $52 in cash, $35 face amount of junior subordinated debt due 2006 valued at $15.40, and one new common share valued at $12.125. The plan also provided that management and certain employee benefit plans would exchange each current OCF common share for 5.6 new common shares. The plan was approved by share-

holders on November 6, 1986. The OCF Stub Equity stock price performance relative to the S&P 400 for the two years subsequent to November 6 is depicted below.

OCF Stock Performance vs. S&P400 (November 1986–October 1988)

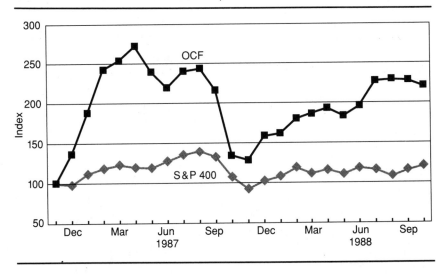

19.12   Reclassification Recap

In a Reclassification Recap a company's existing stock is reclassified by charter amendment. Each share of common stock held by public share-holders is reclassified into preferred stock and a share of common stock in a new company (NEWCO). The preferred stock is immediately redeemed for cash and/or other consideration (e.g., subordinated debt securities). Common stock held by management and employee benefit plans is converted only into NEWCO common stock equal in value to the consid-eration received by public shareholders.

Reclassification Recaps do not generally give rise to appraisal rights for dissenting shareholders. See paragraph E.1 for a discussion of ap-praisal rights.

Example 19B   *On February 21, 1986,* FMC Corporation (FMC) *an-nounced a recapitalization plan. At the time, the company was the subject of takeover rumors, its stock having run up from the high $60s to the mid $80s. The consideration given to public shareholders consisted of preferred stock that was* *immediately redeemed for $80 in cash and one new share of FMC valued at $19.25. FMC's Thift Plan received preferred stock that was redeemed for $25 plus 4.209 shares of NEWCO. Management and other employee benefit plans received 5.667 new shares for each share of common stock. The plan was confirmed by shareholders on May 29, 1986. The performance of FMC's Stub Equity is shown below.*

FMC Stock Performance vs. S&P400 (May 1986–April 1988)

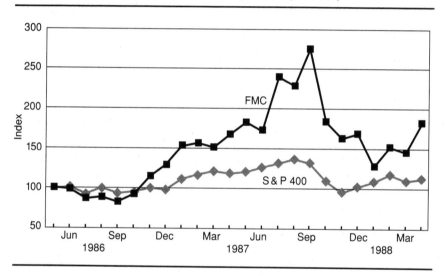

19.13   Dividend Recap

In a Dividend Recap the company is unchanged. However, all share-holders receive a large dividend consisting of cash and/or other consider-ation, such as debt securities or preferred stock of the company. Manage-ment and employee benefit plans increase their stakes by reinvesting their cash dividends and receiving additional shares through new stock plans.

One of the attractive features of a Dividend Recap is that shareholder approval is generally not required. In addition, appraisal rights are not available for dissenting shareholders.

State law will determine the extent to which a dividend can be paid. If the state in which the target company is incorporated does not permit the desired dividend a reincorporation merger may be required.

Example 19C   *On May 18, 1987,* British Printing and Communication Corporation *announced a $44 per share tender offer for* Harcourt Brace Jovanovich (HBJ). *One month earlier the stock had been trading in the low $30s. On May 26th HBJ announced a Dividend Recap plan in which each public shareholder received $40 in cash plus a share of 12 percent preferred stock with no voting rights, valued at $13.50. The plan did not include any special benefits for management. The dividend was paid July 27. The graph depicts the stock price performance of the HBJ Stub Equity over the ensuing two years.*

HBJ Stock Performance vs. S&P400 (July 1987–June 1989)

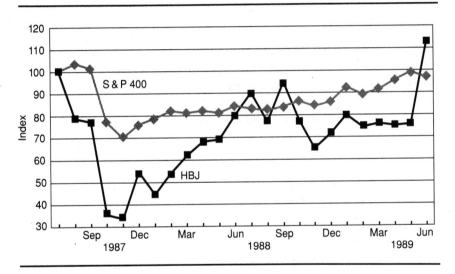

19.14   Self-Tender

In a Self-Tender Recap the company repurchases a significant percentage of its stock for cash. Shareholder approval is not required to effect a Self-Tender in most circumstances. In addition, appraisal rights are not applicable.

As with any tender offer, SEC rules require that the tender offer remain open for at least 20 business days. Generally, management and the company's employee benefit plans do not tender their shares.

19.15 Exchange Offer

In an Exchange Offer Recap the company repurchases a significant per-centage of its stock for consideration. Generally, the consideration share-holders receive includes a significant amount of cash as well as securities (subordinated debt or preferred stock). In most circumstances, share-holder approval is not required to effect an Exchange Offer Recap. In addition, appraisal rights are not applicable.

As with any exchange offer, SEC rules require that the offer remain open for at least 20 business days. Generally, management and the company's employee benefit plans do not tender their shares.

Example 19D   *Asher Edelman launched a tender offer for Lucky Stores Inc. (Lucky) at $35 per share on September 25, 1986. The bid was subsequently increased to $37 per share. In response, Lucky announced a recapitalization plan on November 7, 1986. In this Self-Tender Recap Lucky offered to buy back approximately 27 percent of its outstanding common shares in exchange for $40 in cash and one third of a share of Hancock Fabrics, Inc. (a subsidiary of Lucky), valued at $6.42. The value of the total package was $46.42 per share.*

Lucky Stock Performance vs. S&P400 (December 1986–November 1988)

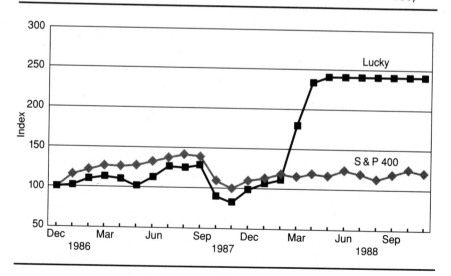

19.2   FINANCING IS KEY!

Generally, shareholders will equate value with the amount of cash they receive in the Recap. Therefore, the amount of cash that the company can raise and deliver to its shareholders is critical. Securities are considered interesting, but many investors will question their value in a recapitalization.

It is important to remember that recaps are usually attempted in the context of a hostile tender offer for the company. Hence, shareholders have a substantial cash offer to compare to the consideration the company is offering in the Recap.

19.3   TAX CONSEQUENCES

There is no gain or loss to the corporation upon the issuance of its stock securities, or a distribution of cash. Shareholders do not recognize gain or loss on the receipt of new stock exchanged for their old stock. However, shareholders will recognize income on the receipt of cash in a recapitalization. The only issue is whether the income will be a capital gain or loss or, alternatively, dividend income.

In a Dividend Recap, the cash received is generally treated as a dividend. Under the other recap methods, if a shareholder's interest in NEWCO is reduced significantly and the requirements for a redemption are thereby met, the shareholder can treat the cash received as a distribution in exchange for the shareholder's stock. The shareholder will be entitled to capital gains treatment in this instance.

19.4   STRENGTHS AND WEAKNESSES

Recap Analysis is extremely important in the limited circumstance where the target company is a public entity and is experiencing external pressure such that it needs to deliver significant value to shareholders immediately. In many respects, a Recap is an internal LBO that allows the company's existing shareholders to continue to participate in its ownership. One advantage that Recaps have over the LBO alternative is that they do not have the same conflict-of-interest issues that arise when management of the company attempts to take a company private.

The two critical elements in a Recap Analysis are: (1) the company's ability to service the debt taken on to finance the cash payment to shareholders, and (2) the forecast market price for the Stub Equity. Generally, the company will assume that it can achieve significant cost reductions or asset sales that will help it meet its debt service requirement.

To adequately analyze the company's ability to service the anticipated debt, it is necessary to review the terms of all the company's outstanding securities to determine the feasibility of the proposed financing. It is typical that existing debt will have to be refinanced and existing equity security agreements will provide antidilution protection for security holders.

The forecast market price of the company's stock will generally be estimated through Comparable Company Analysis. However, the significant differences in leverage between the target and the "comparable companies" will make the analysis very difficult. As a result, the market judgment of knowledgeable advisors is relied on with respect to the price of the Stub Equity.

The weakness of Recap Analysis as a valuation technique is that the value that can be delivered to shareholders is largely determined by the availability of debt financing at a particular time (usually a fairly short period of time after a hostile tender offer has been launched). This obviously restricts the company's ability to achieve maximum value for its shareholders. Furthermore, the leverage placed on the company may have a significant detrimental effect on the company's ability to deliver value to its shareholders over the long term.

Chapter 20

Breakup Analysis

20.0 INTRODUCTION

Breakup Analysis is an appropriate valuation technique for all multi-business entities, regardless of whether they are public or private. Breakup Analysis involves analyzing the value of each of a company's discrete assets (usually business units, but can be individual assets) and summing these individual values to arrive at a value for the entire company.

It is typical in Breakup Analysis for the total value of the target to be compared to one of two values: (1) the estimated acquisition cost of the company, or (2) the current market capitalization of the company (assuming the target is a public company). Which value is used depends on whether the entity performing the analysis is a potential acquirer *(raider)* or the target company and whether the target is currently the subject of a takeover bid or speculation.

Breakup Analysis is best conducted from the perspective of a raider. A raider does not care about long-term plans, employee welfare, or the welfare of the company's communities. A raider is concerned with one thing—maximizing value for himself today.

The raider goes about analyzing the target in the following fashion: First the raider determines the value of the target in his hands. Second, the raider estimates the cost to acquire the target. The cost includes the acquisition cost of the target's outstanding equity securities and the debt that the acquirer will assume. Third, assuming that there is a positive "value gap" between the value of the target to him and the acquisition cost of the company, the raider computes the rate of return he can expect on his invested equity over a relatively short period of time (see Exhibit 20–1).

EXHIBIT 20–1
Raider's Breakup Analysis
(in Millions of Dollars)

Value of Target's Operations		
Business unit A	$100	
Business unit B	50	
Business unit C	75	
Corporate overhead	(35)	
Total estimated value		$190
Cost to Acquire		
Equity	$77	
Debt	63	
Total cost		140
Value gap		$50

Generally, raiders identify good breakup candidates by analyzing companies (1) whose stock has underperformed the market for some period of time but which have significant operating assets, and (2) that have mediocre rates of return.

20.1   THE RAIDER'S ESTIMATE OF THE VALUE OF THE TARGET

A raider will value the assets of the target company by using every analytical technique described in Section Four to identify the highest value for each of the target's business units or assets. These analytical techniques include Comparable Company Analysis, Comparable Transactions Analysis, Analysis of M&A Market Multiples, Discounted Cash Flow Analysis, Strategic Buyer DCF Analysis, Leveraged Buyout Analysis, Leveraged ESOP Analysis, Liquidation Analysis, Unit of Production Analysis and other applicable analytical techniques. The raider will develop a matrix that depicts the value ranges for each of the target's assets.

In completing the various analyses, the raider will develop cash flow forecasts for each of the target's business units (as defined by the raider). In most cases the target will not have granted the raider access to its business plans and forecasts. Lacking inside information, the raider's forecasts will usually extrapolate the target's actual or estimated historical performance. However, the raider often has good reason to deviate from this approach with regard to certain of the target's businesses because he has detailed industry knowledge.

20.11   Focus on Asset Values

The fact that a business unit has poor historical cash flow characteristics is irrelevant to the raider. The raider is interested in the value that the target's assets would bring in the marketplace. Examples of assets that may be worthless in the target company's hands yet be extremely valuable include: store leases in prime retail areas for an operation that needs to be liquidated because the retailing concept is no longer viable; a shutdown plant; a brand name that the target cannot effectively use because it does not have the necessary distribution system for the product; a sales force for an operation that is losing money but provides unparalled access to the marketplace.

20.12   Analysis of Corporate Overhead

Raiders spend a great deal of time analyzing a target's corporate overhead. In preparing a cash flow forecast for the restructured company the raider will size the required corporate staff to the organization that will exist after all the targeted sales are completed. Generally, this means significant staff reductions.

20.13   Liability Analysis

The raider will also spend an appropriate amount of time determining if there is any way that the target's existing liabilities, whether contractual or contingent, can be reduced. In certain cases a raider's estimate as to what may be accomplished on the liability side of the target's balance sheet can be extremely important. A good example is Carl Icahn's purchase of a significant amount of Texaco stock while it was in financial difficulty. Icahn played a major role in the settlement of the Pennzoil litigation (see Chapter 4).

20.14   All Analysis Is After-Tax

The valuation techniques that analyze the sale of any business unit are done on a "net after-tax proceeds" basis. This is important because the raider wants to compare whether it is better to sell or keep a given operation on an after-tax basis.

20.15   Definition of Business Units Is Key!

In performing Breakup Analysis, the raider will typically disregard the target company's present groupings of business. The raider will make assumptions as to what the proper business unit organization should be to maximize the value of the target.

20.16   Valuation Example

Exhibit 20–2 depicts the raider's summary valuation analysis of a target's various business units. It indicates that the raider believes that the target is worth between $225 and $265 million. To achieve this valuation the raider will have to break apart the company's Automotive Segment, which is presently being operated as a single business. The Automotive Electronics business is worth substantially more to a competitor than it is to the target company. In addition the raider expects to sell both businesses in the company's Machinery Segment.

EXHIBIT 20–2
Summary Valuation Analysis (in Millions of Dollars)

	Machinery Segment		Automotive Segment		
Valuation Technique	Robotics	Industrial Machinery	Ball Bearings	Ignition Parts	Auto Electronics
Comparable company	$32–36	$12–15	$22–25	$45–54	$32–60
Comparable transactions	35–44	15–18	14–33	35–52	66–83
M&A market multiples	N.A.	14–18	N.A.	22–68	45–64
Discounted cash flow	25–30	12–14	33–39	65–81	39–46
Strategic buyer DCF	41–47	15–18	31–36	51–57	71–79
LBO analysis	N.A.	14–18	16–20	45–53	35–38
Leveraged ESOP	N.A.	15–19	N.A.	N.A.	N.A.
Unit-of-production	N.A.	12–14	N.A.	N.A.	N.A.
Liquidation analysis	N.A.	9–10	N.A.	N.A.	N.A.
Value range	$25–47	$9–19	$14–39	$22–81	$32–83

Business Unit	Highest Value Range	Strategy to Achieve Highest Value
Robotics	$41–47	Sell to strategic buyer
Industrial Machinery	15–19	Sell—probably to ESOP
Ball Bearings	33–39	Keep
Ignition Parts	65–81	Keep
Auto Electronics	71–79	Sell to strategic buyer
Range of highest values	$225–265	

20.17 Importance of Changes in Business Strategies

In applying the various valuation techniques, the raider will make assumptions regarding business strategies that impact the valuation of the target. Examples of strategic assumptions the raider might make include closing down underutilized manufacturing facilities or discontinuing a speculative research and development project that is requiring significant capital expenditures. If the raider is a strategic industrial company, the raider will make detailed assumptions concerning the integration of the target's operations.

20.2 THE RAIDER'S SOURCES AND USES OF FUNDS

The raider's cost analysis is very straightforward. Generally, a raider acquires control of a target through a tender offer for the target's stock. After acquiring the controlling interest, the raider effects a merger to squeeze out minority shareholders.

The raider's estimate of the acquisition cost of the target and his preliminary financing plans are contained in an analysis of Sources (Sources of Funds for the acquisition) and Uses (acquisition cost). Exhibit 20–3, the Raider's Sources and Uses Analysis, indicates that the cost to acquire the target is approximately $187 million and that the raider intends to put up only $37 million of his money to complete the transaction.

EXHIBIT 20–3
The Raider's Sources and Uses Analysis (in Millions of Dollars)

		% of Capitalization
Sources of Funds		
Excess cash & marketable securities	$13.3	7%
Bank revolver	43.3	23
Senior term loan	37.0	20
Senior subordinated debt	56.1	30
Common equity	37.4	20
Total sources of funds	$187.1	100%
Uses of Funds		
Purchase price per share	$9.875	
Estimated premium	51%	
	$14.875	per share
Common shares outstanding (in millions)	8.25	
	$122.7	million
Options outstanding (in millions)	1.275	
Average exercise price	$9.000	
Net cost of options	$7.5	
Cost of common equity	$130.2	million
Purchase of preferred stock	12.5	
Liabilities to be refinanced	35.5	
Transaction expenses	8.9	
Total uses of funds	$187.1	

20.3   THE RAIDER'S VALUE GAP

At this juncture the raider has determined the target's value and its estimated cost. The one-year and two-year rates of return for achieving the targeted values appear in Exhibit 20–4.

A significant value gap will increase the likelihood that the raider will proceed with the hostile tender offer. It should be noted that a raider must expect high returns to go forward with a hostile tender offer, as this type of acquisition has the greatest amount of risk.

EXHIBIT 20–4
Value Gap Analysis

Estimated value range	$225–265
Estimated acquisition cost	$187
Value gap	$38–78
Raider's investment	$37.4
Rates of return	
One-year	102–209%
Two-year	42–76%

20.4   FEASIBILITY OF A HOSTILE TAKEOVER

In addition to the economic analysis described above, a raider and his legal and financial advisors will undertake a detailed review to determine the feasibility of successfully completing a hostile tender offer. This feasibility analysis will generally include an analysis of the target's shareholder base, charter and bylaws, and the expected reactions of both the target company and other potential bidders.

20.5   BREAKUP ANALYSIS FROM THE COMPANY'S STANDPOINT

Conducting a Breakup Analysis from the company's standpoint is easy because information about the company's operations is readily available. However, it is often more difficult for a company to complete a realistic Breakup Analysis because senior executives are wedded to their viewpoints as to how the company should be run and are unwilling to look at alternatives. This is why many corporations opt to have a Breakup Analysis completed by their independent financial advisor. Conceptually, a Breakup Analysis conducted by the company or its advisors should be as rigorous as that done by a raider. All options for maximizing shareholder value should be considered.

20.51   Breakup Analysis as a Strategic Planning Tool

Breakup Analysis should be a regular feature of a company's strategic planning effort, for it can be a valuable tool for reviewing the company's current business strategies.

20.52 Background and Value Gap Analysis

The starting point for an internal Breakup Analysis is to analyze the company's stock performance over the last several years and compare it to the performance of the overall market and similarly situated industrial competitors (Comparable Company Analysis). In addition, the company should analyze its shareholders' rate of return on their investment in the company's stock over the same period. The goal of these analyses is to realistically assess the company's recent performance and how the market viewed that performance.

The next step is to compare the value of a company's assets with the company's current market value. The value of a company's assets is computed by discounting the cash flows projected in each business unit's long-term business plans and adding the market value of other assets. A significant value gap between the company's computed value and its market value indicates that the company should seriously review its business strategies, as well as the disclosure of those strategies to the investing public. In some cases, a company can improve its valuation through better communication of its business strategies and results of operations. In other cases, it will be appropriate for the company to complete a Breakup Analysis that outlines all the company's alternatives for each of its business units.

20.53 Identify the Key Value Drivers for Each Business

In calculating the value of each of the company's business units, it is extremely important to identify the key factors that significantly affect the value of each of these businesses. Generally, the key value drivers are operating margin, sales growth rate, level of capital expenditures and working capital requirements.

20.54 Identify Impact of Operational and Restructuring Alternatives

The company's Breakup Analysis should identify each operational and restructuring value enhancement opportunity separately. This is done so that management can clearly understand which actions will provide the most value for shareholders.

20.6   STRENGTHS AND WEAKNESSES

Breakup Analysis is an essential analytical approach when the target company operates in a number of businesses. Its strength is that it incorporates a variety of analytical techniques to identify the highest and best use for each of the target's assets. In addition, it includes an analysis of the target's liabilities to determine if any value enhancement opportunities exist there.

The greatest shortcoming of Breakup Analysis is that it is short-term oriented. However, this accurately reflects the raider's mentality. Breakup Analysis often dictates that longer-term risky projects be dropped, especially if the market does not currently appreciate their potential value.

Chapter 21

Other Valuation Techniques

21.0 INTRODUCTION

A number of other valuation techniques are used in practice and are appropriate in certain circumstances. These include:

- Dividend Discount Analysis.
- Capitalization of Earnings.
- Capitalization of Excess Earnings.
- Book Value Analyses (includes Book Value, Tangible Book Value and Net Adjusted Book Value).
- Unit-of-Capacity Analysis.
- Liquidation Analysis.
- Replacement Cost Analysis.
- Greenfield Plant Analysis.

21.1 DIVIDEND DISCOUNT ANALYSIS

Dividend Discount Analysis involves valuing the target company by analyzing the dividends an investor expects to receive from the target company. It is generally applied in two ways: (1) a simple analysis that uses the growing perpetuity formula (described in paragraph 15.21c) to value the company based on future years' expected cash flows, and (2) a more complex analysis that involves discounting expected dividends for a limited period of time and adding this discounted value to the discounted residual value of the company. Typically, the residual value is estimated using the P/E Method or EBDIAT Method described in Chapter 15.

The two methods outlined above mirror the approach taken in the DCF Analysis valuation technique. However, they only focus on cash flows to the equity holder. Although conceptually the same, DCF Analysis is a more useful technique for analyzing transactions than Dividend Discount Analysis.

21.2 CAPITALIZATION OF EARNINGS

This analytical approach involves estimating a value for the operating assets of the target company by taking either a historical average (3- or 5-year) or current year earnings, usually *Earnings before Interest and Taxes (EBIT)* and capitalizing the selected earnings amount by a capitalization rate. In most instances the capitalization rate is subjectively determined by adding to the current risk-free rate of return a risk premium appropriate for the target.

The chief benefit of this approach is that it is very simple.

21.3 CAPITALIZATION OF EXCESS EARNINGS

This is a valuation technique used by the Internal Revenue Service to value intangible assets. The technique is based on the theory that the value of intangible assets (goodwill) is equal to a business's excess earnings on net assets over some appropriate industry average return on net assets. The excess earnings are capitalized at a rate that reflects the risk inherent in the target company's business.

This technique should not be used for valuation purposes.

21.4 BOOK VALUE ANALYSIS

There are a variety of book value multiple calculations that most buyers want to be aware of in an acquisition. These include: (1) purchase price of common equity as a multiple of common stockholders' equity; (2) purchase price of common equity as a multiple of tangible book value (common stockholders' equity reduced by the net book value of any intangible assets on the target's balance sheet); and (3) purchase price as a multiple of the target's fair market value of its tangible assets (usually, this means the book value of working capital adjusted for any LIFO inventory reserve plus the fair market value of the target's fixed assets).

Most buyers find book value multiples helpful in deciding whether a particular purchase price is appropriate. See Exhibit 2–4 for an illustration of historical price to book ratios.

21.5   UNIT-OF-CAPACITY ANALYSIS

In many industries it is common for decision makers to discuss purchase prices in unit measures (e.g., cost per bushel of grind capacity in the corn wet milling industry; cost per POP in the cable TV or telecommunications industries; or cost per barrel of reserves in the oil industry). These analyses are often very helpful. They provide a useful benchmark for an acquisition.

This analysis does not indicate whether a particular acquisition candidate is attractive or not. It merely provides a way to compare the cost of this acquisition with other transactions in the past.

21.6   LIQUIDATION ANALYSIS

Liquidation Analysis attempts to determine the expected net proceeds from liquidating an operation. In most instances, a Liquidation Analysis is undertaken when a business is not operating profitably. The liquidation value of a business always sets the absolute minimum that a seller should accept in a transaction. In performing Liquidation Analysis it is important to set forth the time period for the liquidation, that is, whether it is an orderly liquidation or a forced sale *(Fire Sale)*.

It is typical that a significant portion of the company's net working capital is recovered. The extent of the recovery of receivables and inventory usually depends on the nature of the company and its industry. The amount recovered through the liquidation of the target company's long-term assets depends entirely on the nature of those assets. Amounts recovered can vary tremendously.

In a Liquidation Analysis, the costs to close down the business should always be taken into account.

21.7   REPLACEMENT COST ANALYSIS

In certain acquisition situations, a buyer wants to know what it would cost the target to replace its assets. A buyer might want to know this when viewing the acquisition in the context of a "buy or build" decision.

21.8   GREENFIELD PLANT ANALYSIS

A buyer wants to know what it would cost to build assets comparable to the target's if he is seriously considering the acquisition in the context of a "buy or build" decision.

Section Four

Conclusion

Section Four outlined the various valuation techniques that can be used to estimate the value of the target company. These techniques include examining the historical trading pattern of the target company's stock (Chapter 11), comparing the target company's financial statistics with other comparable public companies (Chapter 12), and analyzing transactions that have occurred in the target company's industry and transactions in the overall M&A market (Chapters 13 and 14).

The most important valuation techniques for an acquirer are the discounted cash flow analysis described in Chapters 15 and 16. Chapters 17–19 examine the value of the target company in a leveraged setting (Chapter 17, LBO Analysis; Chapter 18, Leveraged ESOP Analysis; and Chapter 19, Leveraged Recap Analysis).

Breakup Analysis (Chapter 20) is the key valuation technique for multibusiness entities. Finally, Chapter 21 discussed some other valuation techniques.

Section Five

DCF and LBO Models

Section Five

Introduction

Chapters 22 and 23 describe preliminary DCF and LBO acquisition models (*Initial DCF* or *LBO Models*) that enable an acquirer to determine if further analysis is warranted and detailed acquisition models (*Final DCF* or *LBO Models*) that include all the tax considerations identified in Section Two. The LBO Models require numerous assumptions regarding financing, including amount and type of debt, financing fees, interest rates, and repayment schedules. The LBO Model provides an analysis of the debt servicing capability of the target company.

Chapter 22

Discounted Cash Flow Models

22.0 INTRODUCTION

Chapter 22 is devoted to describing acquisition models that can be used for completing an initial DCF Analysis when information is often limited, as well as a later stage DCF Analysis when due diligence has been completed. Chapter 15 describes the theoretical underpinnings for the models.

22.1 WHY AN INITIAL DCF MODEL?

An acquisition professional's most important skill is time management, for it is easy to get mired in details surrounding acquisitions. The key to managing time efficiently is to understand the acquisition process and put in the right amount of effort at each stage in the process. Thus, when information concerning an acquisition opportunity is received, a senior executive should make an initial determination whether the opportunity is appealing from a strategic or financial standpoint, and assuming the answer is positive, have an initial number crunching analysis (hereafter, the *Initial DCF Model*) performed. An Initial DCF Model is completed to achieve a preliminary understanding of the net present values and returns associated with different price levels. This understanding is required in order to submit a well thought out indication of interest to the seller.

Typically, selling memorandums produced by Wall Street investment banks contain projections for the target for the next several years.

These projections are incorporated in the Initial DCF Model along with any modifications that the acquiring company believes are reasonable.

22.2   THE INITIAL DCF MODEL

The Initial DCF Model consists of the schedules listed below. The figures used in the model are those associated with the example discussed in Chapter 10. See Chapters 10 and 15 for a discussion of the case study and the rationale for various assumptions.

- Executive Summary (Exhibit 22–1).
- Tax, Transaction Cost, Acquisition Method and Cash Balance Assumptions (Exhibit 22–2).
- Economic and Operating Assumptions (Exhibit 22–3).
- Income Statements (Exhibit 22–4).
- Statements of Net Assets (Exhibit 22–5).
- Statements of Changes in Financial Position (Exhibit 22–6).
- Calculation of Residual Values (Exhibit 22–7).
- NPV Calculations—EBDIAT Multiple Method (Exhibit 22–8).
- NPV Calculations—P/E Multiple Method (Exhibit 22–9).
- NPV Calculations—Growing Perpetuity Method (Exhibit 22–10).
- NPV Calculations—EBITDA Multiple Method (Exhibit 22–11).
- IRR Calculations (Exhibit 22–12).
- Summary Amortization Schedule (Exhibit 22–13).
- Financial Statement Tax Provision (Exhibit 22–14).

22.21   Executive Summary

The Executive Summary describes the key assumptions used in the Initial DCF Model and the results of the analysis. The information contained in the Executive Summary is broken down into eight sections, as Exhibit 22–1 indicates.

- *Sources and Uses of Funds:* The Sources and Uses of Funds section depicts the purchase price for the target operation ($160 million) and the required equity funding. The acquisition cost includes the cost to acquire (1) the common stock, (2) any common stock options, and (3) preferred stock. The acquisition cost also includes the value of liabilities (excluding trade payables, accrued expenses and any deferred taxes) assumed by the acquirer and transaction expenses.

In DCF Analysis the entire purchase price is assumed to be funded with equity.

- *Goodwill Calculation:* This section discloses the amount of goodwill that is created as a result of the transaction at the assumed purchase price. Note that, in this example, the entire amount of any excess purchase price over the existing book value of the target is allocated to goodwill. In an Initial DCF Model this assumption is proper, unless the acquirer has substantive information concerning the value of the target's assets.

- *Transaction Costs:* This section displays the estimated transaction costs in absolute dollars ($2.5 million) and as a percent of the value of the transaction (1.6 percent). Detailed transaction cost assumptions are input in a later schedule.

- *Amortization Periods:* This section displays the amortization periods chosen for selected assets.

- *Miscellaneous:* This section contains a number of critical assumptions for the DCF Analysis, including the fiscal year that will be used, the beginning years for historical and projected results, the accounting method, and the Acquisition Method used to effect the transaction (e.g., New Tax Basis Method or a No Change in Tax Basis Method). The choice of acquisition method does not matter in an Initial DCF Model.

- *Net Present Value:* This section contains the results of the Net Present Value Analysis computed using four Residual Value Methods and the five discount rates chosen to be analyzed. The residual values are computed under both continuing value and sale assumptions as described in Chapter 15. Generally, the middle residual value and discount rate assumptions represent the most likely assumptions. This section also displays the percent of the target's estimated value attributable to the net present value of the residual value.

- *Internal Rates of Return:* This section depicts the results of the Internal Rate of Return Analysis computed using the four Residual Value Methods under both the continuing value and sale assumptions.

- *Purchase and Residual Multiples:* this section contains calculations of the purchase price and residual value as a multiple of sales, EBITDA, EBITA, EBIT, and net income.

22.22   Tax, Transaction Cost, Acquisition Method and Cash Balance Assumptions

Exhibit 22–2 depicts (1) the tax assumptions used in the model, (2) transaction cost assumptions, (3) the two categories of alternative acquisition methods that can be used to effect a transaction, and (4) the minimum cash balance requirement for the operation.

Tax assumptions for the Initial DCF Model include federal, state and local ordinary income tax and capital gains tax rates.

Typically, transaction costs include investment banking fees, accounting, legal, appraisal, printing and miscellaneous other expenses. These expenses are broken out so that a realistic overall estimate of transaction costs can be made. In an Initial DCF Model, transaction costs should be amortized for accounting purposes over the goodwill amortization period. Generally, these expenses are not currently deductible for tax purposes. They are only deductible for tax purposes to the extent that they relate to financing a transaction. In this instance, they are capitalized and amortized over the life of the financing.

The Acquisition Method Assumption section merely recites the alternative structures to choose from. The decision as to which method (New Tax Basis or No Change in Tax Basis Method) to use is not relevant in an Initial DCF Model because a simplifying assumption is made that book and tax depreciation are equal. Alternatively, if the seller has clearly indicated the acquisition method to use and comprehensive captial expenditure and depreciation information is available, the acquirer should consider using the Final DCF Model, even at an early stage.

22.23   Economic and Operating Assumptions

Exhibit 22–3 includes four sections: (1) an Economic Assumptions section, (2) a Sales and Margin Assumptions section, (3) a Capital Expenditures, Book and Tax Depreciation, and Deferred Taxes section, and (4) a Net Working Capital Assumption section.

The Economic Assumption section depicts the key economic factors that impact the results of the target company. These factors might include the ones listed in Exhibit 22–3 or other relevant factors.

The Sales and Margin section includes the historical results of the target and assumptions for the projection period.

Capital expenditures in the Initial DCF Model are not broken down among asset categories and are related to sales. Alternatively, capital expenditure levels can be set to specified dollar limits if that is more appropriate.

A simplifying assumption made in the Initial DCF Model is that book and tax depreciation are equal. In addition, book depreciation is projected to be equal to a percentage of the target's sales. This relationship between sales and depreciation can be changed in each period to reflect anticipated changes in capital expenditure levels.

Deferred taxes are estimated as a percentage of the total tax provision. Generally, this methodology assures that the cash flow forecast for the target will reflect some benefit for the tax deferral associated with depreciation and other deductions that give rise to temporary differences between book and taxable income. This assumption has the effect of mitigating the impact of the assumption that book and tax depreciation are the same.

The Net Working Capital section displays historical and projected net working capital as a percent of sales. If the acquirer has more detailed information about the various working capital components, the acquirer should modify the model to include the individual components method for estimating working capital. If the acquirer does not have detailed working capital information, a complete balance sheet cannot be prepared. Therefore, the Initial DCF Model includes a Statement of Net Assets.

22.24   Income Statements

The Income Statements include several years of historical information, an estimate for the current year, and a projection for a minimum of five years going forward. The Income Statements schedule in Exhibit 22–4 is fairly simple. However, they can and should be expanded to reflect additional supporting assumptions if information is available to do so.

22.25   Statements of Net Assets

The Statements of Net Assets in Exhibit 22–5 displays an abbreviated balance sheet that reflects the limited available data concerning net working capital.

22.26   Statements of Changes in Financial Position

The Statements of Changes in Financial Position in Exhibit 22–6 displays the cash flow results of the assumptions in the model.

22.27 Calculation of Residual Values

Exhibit 22–7 depicts the calculation of residual values under four different methods—the P/E Multiple Method, the EBDIAT Multiple Method, the Growing Perpetuity Method and the EBITDA Multiple Method. The calculations are performed using two underlying assumptions—continuing value and sale assumptions.

22.28 NPV Calculations

The detailed NPV calculations for all four residual value methods are calculated in Exhibits 22–8 through 22–11. Each page contains the 50 calculations of net present value for each residual value method. For example, the NPV calculations for the EBDIAT Multiple Method include five different EBDIAT Multiples, five different discount rate assumptions, and two underlying sale assumptions—continuing value and sale.

22.29 IRR Calculations

The detailed IRR calculations for all four residual value methods are calculated in Exhibit 22–12.

22.30 Summary Amortization Schedule

The Amortization Schedule appearing in Exhibit 22–13 displays the calculations for the amortization of goodwill, intangible assets and leased property under capital leases. The schedule also contains a summary of amortization expenses by appropriate tax category (deductible versus nondeductible).

22.31 Financial Statement Tax Provision

The Financial Statement Tax Provision schedule in Exhibit 22–14 adjusts the target's earnings before taxes by the amount of any goodwill amortization and any net operating loss before calculating the tax provision for accounting purposes. The tax provision calculated consists of both current and deferred tax amounts. The assumptions for deferred taxes are input in Exhibit 22–3.

MARRIOTT CORPORATION
Discounted Cash Flow Analysis
Executive Summary

Sources and Uses of Funds

Uses

	Amount	Percent
Common Shares Outstanding	1,000	
Options Outstanding	0	
Average Exercise Price	$0.00	
Purchase Price per Share	$108,112.00	
% of Shares Purchased	100.00%	

Purchase Common Equity	$108,112	67.6%
Purchase Preferred Stock	0	0.0%
Existing Liabilities	49,388	30.9%
Transaction Expenses	2,500	1.6%
Obligations under Capitalized Leases	0	0.0%
Pre-Payment Penalty (Tax Basis)	0	0.0%
Tax on Sale of Assets (Tax Basis)	0	0.0%
Additional Working Capital Cash	0	0.0%
Total Uses	$160,000	100.0%

Sources

Common Equity	$160,000	100.0%

Goodwill Calculation

Total Equity Purchase Price		$108,112
Adjustments to Book Value		
Existing Shareholders' Equity	$33,364	
Plus: Deferred Income Taxes	0	
Less: Existing Goodwill	0	
Less: Existing Organizational Costs	0	
Less: Value Allocated to PP&E	39,300	
Less: Value Allocated to Intangibles	0	
Net Book Value		73,364
Total Goodwill Created		$34,748

Transaction Costs

Total Transaction Costs		$2,500
% of Total Consideration		1.6%

Amortization Periods

	Years
Goodwill Amortization	40
Intangible Asset Amortization	5
Amortization of Leased Property under Capital Leases	25

Miscellaneous

	Years Ended December 31
Fiscal Year	
First Historical Year	1989
Estimated Financial Statements Beginning	1993

	Purchase Accting (1)
Accounting Method ("Purchase" or "Recap")	"Purchase"
Initial "Stub" Period ("No Change in")	New Tax Basis(2)
Initial "Stub" Period Length	12 months
% of Annual Sales Occuring in Stub Period	100.0%
"Initial" or "Final" model	Initial

FOOTNOTES:
(1) Model not applicable for a transaction involving Pooling of
    Interests Accounting.
(2) Choice of method not applicable in Initial model.
(3) Net Cash Flow equals EBITDA less Cash Taxes less Capital
    Expenditures.

Net Present Value - Continuing Value Assumption

EBDIAT Multiple

Dis-count	11.0	12.0	13.0	14.0	15.0
10.0%	$180,061	$201,564	$215,067	$228,570	$242,074
10.0%	179,043	191,832	204,622	217,412	230,201
11.0%	170,558	182,678	194,797	206,917	219,037
13.0%	162,571	174,061	185,551	197,041	198,531
14.0%	155,047	165,946	176,844	197,743	198,641

P/E Multiple

	18.0	19.0	20.0	21.0	22.0
10.0%	162,337	169,140	175,983	182,806	189,629
11.0%	156,079	161,161	167,604	174,046	180,508
11.0%	147,471	153,162	159,759	165,841	171,966
13.0%	140,493	146,489	152,394	158,100	163,806
14.0%	134,286	139,793	145,300	150,807	156,313

Growing Perpetuity Method - Growth Rate

	5.5%	6.0%	6.5%	7.0%
10.0%	129,000	136,570	144,928	154,943	167,081
11.0%	123,040	129,099	134,496	147,676	159,172
12.0%	117,490	124,074	131,756	140,835	151,729
13.0%	112,259	118,501	125,784	134,391	144,713
14.0%	107,326	113,247	120,155	128,318	138,315

Net Present Value - Sale Assumption

EBDIAT Multiple

Dis-count	11.0	12.0	13.0	14.0	15.0
10.0%	189,521	192,521	201,521	210,521	219,521
10.0%	174,743	183,268	191,793	200,318	208,843
11.0%	166,488	174,582	182,677	190,771	198,866
13.0%	150,608	158,367	166,367	174,367	181,683
14.0%	151,384	158,647	165,911	173,175	180,439

P/E Multiple

	18.0	19.0	20.0	21.0	22.0
10.0%	165,937	174,309	182,681	191,053	199,425
11.0%	156,688	166,218	173,947	181,877	189,807
11.0%	146,388	154,390	162,393	170,395	178,398
13.0%	136,382	143,775	151,793	163,117	173,241
14.0%	137,191	143,948	150,705	157,462	164,220

Growing Perpetuity Method - Growth Rate

	5.5%	6.0%	6.5%	7.0%
10.0%	129,278	133,826	139,133	145,404	152,920
11.0%	123,367	127,675	132,701	138,661	145,768
12.0%	117,789	131,693	126,664	132,233	139,527
13.0%	111,553	119,429	120,192	126,678	132,678
14.0%	107,664	113,275	113,558	120,619	126,693

Residual Value as a Percent of NPV

Continuing Value Assumption

	Minimum	Maximum
	79.0%	80.7%
	78.6%	83.3%
	78.2%	82.3%
	77.9%	82.1%
	77.3%	82.0%

	75.7%	78.2%
	75.0%	78.0%
	74.7%	78.3%
	74.3%	77.8%
	73.8%	77.0%

	69.3%	76.0%
	68.6%	75.0%
	68.3%	75.3%
	67.6%	75.0%
	67.2%	74.5%

Sale Assumption

	Minimum	Maximum
	78.9%	82.0%
	77.6%	81.3%
	77.4%	81.0%
	77.2%	80.9%
	76.8%	80.0%

	76.5%	78.8%
	75.8%	79.0%
	75.3%	79.0%
	74.4%	78.4%

	75.0%	74.2%
	73.6%	74.2%
	73.2%	73.7%
	72.7%	73.9%
	73.9%	77.2%

Internal Rates of Return - Continuing Value Assumption

EBDIAT Multiple Method

	11.0	12.0	13.0	14.0	15.0
Terminal EBDIAT Multiple	13.5%	14.6%	16.1%	17.4%	18.6%

P/E Multiple Method

	18.0	19.0	20.0	21.0	22.0
Terminal P/E Multiple					
Common Equity	10.3%	11.3%	12.7%	13.5%

Growing Perpetuity Method

	5.0%	5.5%	6.0%	6.5%	7.0%
Growth Rate	5.0%	5.8%	6.7%	7.3%	8.9%

EBITDA Multiple Method

	8.0	8.5	9.0	9.5	10.0
Terminal EBITDA Multiple	13.4%	14.6%	15.7%	16.5%

Internal Rates of Return - Sale Assumption

EBDIAT Multiple Method

	11.0	12.0	13.0	14.0	15.0
Terminal EBDIAT Multiple	10.4%	11.3%	12.7%	13.7%	14.6%

P/E Multiple Method

	18.0	19.0	20.0	21.0	22.0
Terminal P/E Multiple					
Common Equity	7.4%	9.2%	9.4%	10.9%

Growing Perpetuity Method

	5.0%	5.5%	6.0%	6.5%	7.0%
Growth Rate	5.4%	6.3%	7.1%	8.0%	9.1%

EBITDA Multiple Method

	8.0	8.5	9.0	9.5	10.0
Terminal EBITDA Multiple	10.4%	11.1%	11.8%		
Common Equity		13.7%			

Purchase and Exit Multiple EBDIAT Multiple Method Midpoint

	1992	1993	1994	Terminal
Sales	1.16	1.0	4.5	1.31
EBDIAT		1.0	4.8	9.8
EBITDA	11.1	10.6		14.6
EBIT	11.1	11.3	10.5	15.5
Net Cash Flow (3)	16.1	14.1	13.1	22.4
Net Income	17.3	13.2	17.5	23.1

275

MAREIGHT CORPORATION
Discounted Cash Flow Analysis
Tax, Transaction Cost, Acquisition Method and Cash Balance Assumptions

EXHIBIT 22.2
05/21/92
09:31 AM

Tax Assumptions

Federal Tax Rate	34.00%
State and Local Tax Rate	6.00%
Capital Gains Tax Rate	38.00%
Alternative Minimum Tax Rate	20.00%
Long-Term Federal Tax-Exempt Bond Rate	8.75%
Built-In Gains (Losses) Qualifier	25.00%
Book Income Adjustment Rate (Post-1989)	75.00%
AMT NOL Use Limitation	90.00%
Acquired Book NOL	$0
Acquired Tax NOL	$0
Acquired AMT NOL	$0
Acquired MTC Credit	$0

Transaction Cost Assumptions

Advisory & Underwriting Fees

Transaction Fees	1.25%
Accounting/Legal & Printing/Miscellaneous	567
	1.62%
	$1,933
Total Fees and Expenses	$2,500

Amortization of Transaction Costs

Transaction	40	years
% related to financing	0%	
Accounting & Legal	40	year
% related to financing	0%	
Prepayment penalty	7	year

Acquisition Methods

Method Used: New Tax Basis Acquisition Method

New Tax Basis Acquisition Methods

1) Asset Acquisition
   A) Asset Acquisition
   B) Forward Merger
   C) Forward subsidiary Merger
2) 338 Transaction
3) 338 (h)(10) Transaction

No Change in Tax Basis Acquisition Methods

1) Stock Acquisition
   A) Stock Acquisition
   B) Reverse Merger
   C) Reverse Subsidiary Merger
2) Type A Reorganization
   A) Type A Forward Merger
   B) Type A Statutory Consolidation
   C) Type A Forward Subsidiary Merger
   D) Type A Reverse Subsidiary Merger
3) Type B Reorganization
   A) Type B Stock Exchange
   B) Tyoe B Subsidiary Stock Exchange
4) Type C Reorganization
   A) Type C Stock for Assets Exchange
   B) Type C Subsidiary Stock for Assets Exchange

Cash Balance Requirements

Minimum Cash Balance Requirements	$0

MANFREIGHT CORPORATION
Discounted Cash Flow Analysis
Economic and Operating Assumptions

Economic Assumptions

Year	Historical 1989	1990	1991	1992	Average 1989-92	Projected 1993	1994	1995	1996	1997	1998	Average 1993-98
GNP Growth Rate	3.5%	1.7%	0.0%	1.0%	1.5%	2.0%	2.5%	3.0%	3.0%	3.0%	3.0%	2.8%
Inflation Rate	4.6%	4.7%	5.5%	3.9%	4.7%	3.0%	3.0%	3.0%	3.0%	3.0%	3.0%	3.0%
Prime Interest Rate	9.6%	10.3%	9.5%	8.0%	9.3%	7.5%	7.5%	7.5%	7.5%	7.5%	7.5%	7.5%
Long-Term Treasury Bond Interest Rate	9.1%	8.4%	8.6%	7.9%	8.5%	6.8%	6.8%	6.8%	6.8%	6.8%	6.8%	6.8%

Sales and Margin Assumptions

Years Ended December 31,

	Historical 1989	1990	1991	1992	Average 1989-92	Projected 1993	1994	1995	1996	1997	1998	Average 1993-98
Total Sales	$107,417	$113,656	$122,940	$133,302		$143,300	$154,047	$165,601	$178,021	$191,372	$205,725	
Growth Rate		5.8%	8.2%	8.4%	7.5%	7.5%	7.5%	7.5%	7.5%	7.5%	7.5%	7.5%
Gross Margin %	35.1%	34.5%	34.2%	34.7%	34.6%	34.5%	34.5%	34.5%	34.5%	34.5%	34.5%	34.5%
SG&A %	19.0%	19.0%	19.0%	19.0%	19.0%	19.0%	19.0%	19.0%	19.0%	19.0%	19.0%	19.0%
EBITDA Margin %	16.1%	15.5%	15.2%	15.7%	15.6%	15.5%	15.5%	15.5%	15.5%	15.5%	15.5%	15.5%

Capital Expenditure, Book and Tax Depreciation, and Deferred Tax Assumptions

Years Ended December 31,

	Historical 1989	1990	1991	1992	Average 1989-92	Projected 1993	1994	1995	1996	1997	1998	Average 1993-98
Net Sales	$107,417	$113,656	$122,940	$133,302		$143,300	$154,047	$165,601	$178,021	$191,372	$205,725	
Cost of Goods Sold	$69,714	$74,445	$80,895	$87,046		$93,861	$100,901	$108,468	$116,604	$125,349	$134,750	
Selling, General & Admin Expense	$20,409	$21,595	$23,359	$25,327		$27,227	$29,269	$31,464	$33,824	$36,361	$39,088	
Book and Tax Depreciation	$5,435	$6,297	$6,777	$7,022		$7,595	$8,164	$8,777	$9,435	$10,143	$10,903	
Book and Tax Depreciation as a % of Sales	5.1%	5.5%	5.5%	5.3%	5.3%	5.3%	5.3%	5.3%	5.3%	5.3%	5.3%	5.3%
Deferred Taxes	$0	$0	$0	$0		$526	$668	$731	$841	$1,036	$1,048	
Deferred Taxes as a % of Tax Provision				0.0%		9.5%	11.2%	11.4%	12.2%	14.0%	13.2%	
Capital Expenditures	$5,658	$7,402	$6,285	$6,022		$7,738	$8,319	$8,942	$9,613	$10,334	$11,109	
Capital Expenditures as a % of Sales	5.3%	6.5%	5.1%	4.5%	5.4%	5.4%	5.4%	5.4%	5.4%	5.4%	5.4%	5.4%

Net Working Capital Assumptions

	Historical 1989	1990	1991	1992	Average 1989-92	Projected 1993	1994	1995	1996	1997	1998	Average 1993-98
Net Working Capital	$27,940	$27,243	$27,961	$31,515		$32,959	$35,431	$38,088	$40,945	$44,016	$47,317	
Net Working Capital as a % of Sales	26.0%	24.0%	22.7%	23.6%	24.1%	23.0%	23.0%	23.0%	23.0%	23.0%	23.0%	23.0%

MAREIGHT CORPORATION
Discounted Cash Flow Analysis
Income Statements

Years Ended December 31,	Historical				Average 1989-92	Projected						Average 1993-98
	1989	1990	1991	1992		1993	1994	1995	1996	1997	1998	
Net Sales	$107,417	$113,656	$122,940	$133,302		$143,300	$154,047	$165,601	$178,021	$191,372	$205,725	
Sales Growth %		*5.8%*	*8.2%*	*8.4%*	*7.5%*	*7.5%*	*7.5%*	*7.5%*	*7.5%*	*7.5%*	*7.5%*	*7.5%*
Cost of Goods Sold	$69,714	$74,445	$80,895	$87,046		$93,861	$100,901	$108,468	$116,604	$125,349	$134,750	
Gross Profit	37,703	39,211	42,045	46,256		49,438	53,146	57,132	61,417	66,023	70,975	
Gross Margin %	*35.1%*	*34.5%*	*34.2%*	*34.7%*	*34.6%*	*34.5%*	*34.5%*	*34.5%*	*34.5%*	*34.5%*	*34.5%*	*34.5%*
Selling, General & Admin. Expenses	$20,409	$21,595	$23,359	$25,327		$27,227	$29,269	$31,464	$33,824	$36,361	$39,088	
ESOP contribution	0	0	0	0		0	0	0	0	0	0	
EBITDA	17,294	17,616	18,686	20,929		22,211	23,877	25,668	27,593	29,663	31,887	
EBITDA Margin %	*16.1%*	*15.5%*	*15.2%*	*15.7%*	*15.6%*	*15.5%*	*15.5%*	*15.5%*	*15.5%*	*15.5%*	*15.5%*	*15.5%*
Depreciation	5,435	6,297	6,777	7,022		7,595	8,164	8,777	9,435	10,143	10,903	
Amortization of Goodwill	0	0	0	0		869	869	869	869	869	869	
Amortization of Transaction Costs	0	0	0	0		63	63	63	63	63	63	
Amortization of Intangibles	0	0	0	0		0	0	0	0	0	0	
Total Depreciation & Amortization	5,435	6,297	6,777	7,022		8,526	9,096	9,708	10,366	11,074	11,835	
EBIT	11,859	11,319	11,909	13,907		13,685	14,782	15,960	17,227	18,589	20,053	
EBIT Margin %	*11.0%*	*10.0%*	*9.7%*	*10.4%*	*10.3%*	*9.6%*	*9.6%*	*9.6%*	*9.7%*	*9.7%*	*9.7%*	*9.7%*
Other Expenses (Income)				0		0	0	0	0	0	0	
Earnings Before Taxes				13,907		13,685	14,782	15,960	17,227	18,589	20,053	
Provision for Taxes												
Current				5,285		5,022	5,297	5,681	6,052	6,374	6,918	
Deferred				0		526	668	731	841	1,036	1,048	
Total Tax Provision				5,285		5,548	5,965	6,412	6,893	7,410	7,966	
Net Income Before Extraordinary Item & Minority Interest				8,622		8,137	8,817	9,548	10,334	11,179	12,087	
Minority Interest				0		0	0	0	0	0	0	
Extraordinary Item (After-Tax)				0		0	0	0	0	0	0	
Net Income to Common				$8,622		$8,137	$8,817	$9,548	$10,334	$11,179	$12,087	

EXHIBIT 22.5
05/21/92
09:31 AM

MAREIGHT CORPORATION
Discounted Cash Flow Analysis
Statements of Net Assets

Years Ended December 31,	Historical				Closing Date Bal. Sheet	Adjustments		Beginning Bal. Sheet	Projected					
	1989	1990	1991	1992	1992	DEBITS	CREDITS		1993	1994	1995	1996	1997	1998
Cash and Cash Equivalents	$3,313	$3,288	$1,111	$2,856	$2,856	$0	$1,333	$1,523	$10,863	$18,653	$27,041	$36,112	$45,996	$56,556
Net Working Capital	27,940	27,243	27,961	31,515	31,515	1,333	0	32,848	32,959	35,431	38,088	40,945	44,016	47,317
Gross Property, Plant & Equipment	43,378	45,001	45,965	44,965	44,965	39,800	0	84,765	92,503	100,822	109,764	119,377	129,711	140,821
Less: Accumulated Depreciation	0	0	0	0	0	0	0	0	(7,595)	(15,759)	(24,536)	(33,971)	(44,114)	(55,017)
Net Property, Plant & Equipment	43,378	45,001	45,965	44,965	44,965	39,800	0	84,765	84,908	85,062	85,228	85,406	85,597	85,803
Leased Property Under Capital Leases	0	0	0	0	0	0	0	0	0	0	0	0	0	0
Goodwill	0	0	0	0	0	34,748	0	34,748	33,879	33,011	32,142	31,273	30,405	29,536
Other Intangibles	0	0	0	0	0	0	0	0	0	0	0	0	0	0
Other Assets	3,141	3,289	2,704	3,616	3,616	0	0	3,616	3,616	3,616	3,616	3,616	3,616	3,616
Organizational Costs	0	0	0	0	0	2,500	0	2,500	2,438	2,375	2,313	2,250	2,188	2,125
Net Assets	$77,772	$78,821	$77,741	$82,952	$82,952	$78,381	$1,333	$160,000	$168,663	$178,148	$188,427	$199,602	$211,817	$224,952
Financed By:														
Long-Term Liabilities	48,777	50,241	46,772	49,388	49,388	49,388	0	0	0	0	0	0	0	0
Unearned Profit on Capital Leases	0	0	0	0	0	0	0	0	0	0	0	0	0	0
Deferred Income Taxes	0	0	0	0	0	0	0	0	526	1,194	1,925	2,766	3,802	4,850
Minority Interest	0	0	0	0	0	0	0	0	0	0	0	0	0	0
Common Stock	1,000	1,000	1,000	1,000	1,000	1,000	160,000	160,000	160,000	160,000	160,000	160,000	160,000	160,000
Retained Earnings	27,995	27,580	29,969	32,564	32,564	32,564	0	0	8,137	16,954	26,502	36,836	48,015	60,102
Common Shareholders' Equity	28,995	28,580	30,969	33,564	33,564	33,564	160,000	160,000	168,137	176,954	186,502	196,836	208,015	220,102
Total Liabilities & Equity	$93,510	$95,439	$94,901	$97,181	$97,181	$161,333	$161,333	$160,000	$168,663	$178,148	$188,427	$199,602	$211,817	$224,952

EXHIBIT 22.6

MAREIGHT CORPORATION
Discounted Cash Flow Analysis
Statements of Changes in Financial Position

Years Ended December 31,	1993	1994	1995	1996	1997	1998
Sources of Cash						
Net Income to Common	$8,137	$8,817	$9,548	$10,334	$11,179	$12,087
Book Depreciation	7,595	8,164	8,777	9,435	10,143	10,903
Amortization of Intangibles	0	0	0	0	0	0
Deferred Tax	526	668	731	841	1,036	1,048
Amort. of Leased Prop. under Capitalized Leases	0	0	0	0	0	0
Amortization of Goodwill & Fees	931	931	931	931	931	931
Total Sources	17,189	$18,581	$19,987	$21,541	$23,289	$24,970
Uses of Cash						
Increase (Decrease) in Working Capital	111	$2,472	$2,657	$2,857	$3,071	$3,301
Capital Expenditures	7,738	8,319	8,942	9,613	10,334	11,109
Total Uses	7,849	$10,790	$11,600	$12,470	$13,405	$14,410
Net Cash Flow	$9,340	$7,790	$8,387	$9,072	$9,884	$10,560

EXHIBIT 22.7
05/21/92
09:31 AM

Page 7   FILE: SHT_I1

MAREIGHT CORPORATION
Discounted Cash Flow Analysis
Calculation of Residual Values

Residual Value Calculations – EBDIAT Multiple Method

	11.0	12.0	13.0	14.0	15.0
EBDIAT Multiple	11.0	12.0	13.0	14.0	15.0
1998 EBDIAT	$23,922	$23,922	$23,922	$23,922	$23,922
Residual Value (Continuing Value)	263,141	287,063	310,985	334,906	358,828
Gross Residual Value	263,141	287,063	310,985	334,906	358,828
Tax Basis	160,000	160,000	160,000	160,000	160,000
Gain (Loss) on Sale	103,141	127,063	150,985	174,906	198,828
Capital Gains Tax Rate	38.0%	38.0%	38.0%	38.0%	38.0%
Tax on Sale	39,193	48,284	57,374	66,464	75,555
Gross Residual Value	263,141	287,063	310,985	334,906	358,828
Taxes on Sale	39,193	48,284	57,374	66,464	75,555
Residual Value (Sale Assumption)	$223,947	$238,779	$253,610	$268,442	$283,274

Residual Value Calculations – P/E Multiple Method

	18.0	19.0	20.0	21.0	22.0
P/E Multiple	18.0	19.0	20.0	21.0	22.0
1998 Net Income	$12,087	$12,087	$12,087	$12,087	$12,087
Residual Value (Continuing Value)	217,571	229,658	241,745	253,832	265,920
Gross Residual Value	217,571	229,658	241,745	253,832	265,920
Tax Basis	160,000	160,000	160,000	160,000	160,000
Gain (Loss) on Sale	57,570	69,658	81,745	93,832	105,920
Capital Gains Tax Rate	38.0%	38.0%	38.0%	38.0%	38.0%
Tax on Sale	21,877	26,470	31,063	35,656	40,249
Gross Residual Value	217,571	229,658	241,745	253,832	265,920
Taxes on Sale	21,877	26,470	31,063	35,656	40,249
Residual Value (Sale Assumption)	$195,694	$203,188	$210,682	$218,176	$225,670

Residual Value Calculations – Growing Perpetuity Method

	7.0%	6.5%	6.0%	5.5%	5.0%
1999 Estimated After-tax Cash Flow	$11,088	$11,140	$11,193	$11,246	$11,299
WACC less Growth Rate	7.0%	6.5%	6.0%	5.5%	5.0%
Residual Value (Continuing Value)	158,393	171,390	186,552	204,471	225,975
Gross Residual Value	158,393	171,390	186,552	204,471	225,975
Tax Basis	160,000	160,000	160,000	160,000	160,000
Gain (Loss) on Sale	(1,607)	11,390	26,552	44,471	65,974
Capital Gains Tax Rate	38.0%	38.0%	38.0%	38.0%	38.0%
Tax on Sale	(611)	4,328	10,090	16,899	25,070
Gross Residual Value	158,393	171,390	186,552	204,471	225,975
Taxes on Sale	(611)	4,328	10,090	16,899	25,070
Residual Value (Sale Assumption)	$159,004	$167,062	$176,462	$187,572	$200,904

Value Calculations – EBITDA Multiple Method

	8.0	8.5	9.0	9.5	10.0
EBITDA Multiple	8.0	8.5	9.0	9.5	10.0
1998 EBITDA	$31,887	$31,887	$31,887	$31,887	$31,887
Residual Value (Continuing Value)	255,099	271,043	286,987	302,930	318,874
Gross Residual Value	255,099	271,043	286,987	302,930	318,874
Tax Basis	160,000	160,000	160,000	160,000	160,000
Gain (Loss) on Sale	95,099	111,043	126,987	142,930	158,874
Capital Gains Tax Rate	38.0%	38.0%	38.0%	38.0%	38.0%
Tax on Sale	36,138	42,196	48,255	54,314	60,372
Gross Residual Value	255,099	271,043	286,987	302,930	318,874
Taxes on Sale	36,138	42,196	48,255	54,314	60,372
Residual Value (Sale Assumption)	$218,962	$228,847	$238,732	$248,617	$258,502

Discounted Cash Flow Analysis
NPV Calculations - EBDIAT Multiple Method

NPV Calculations - Continuing Value Assumption

EBDIAT Multiple Method	1993	1994	1995	1996	1997	1998	1999	NPV	Residual Value as % of NPV
After-tax Cash Flow	$9,340	$7,790	$8,387	$9,072	$9,884	$10,560			
Residual Value									
11.0 x EBDIAT Multiple						263,141			
12.0 x EBDIAT Multiple						287,063			
13.0 x EBDIAT Multiple						310,985			
14.0 x EBDIAT Multiple						334,906			
15.0 x EBDIAT Multiple						358,828			
10.0% Discount Rate	0.9091	0.8264	0.7513	0.6830	0.6209	0.5645	0.5132		
11.0 x EBDIAT Multiple	8,491	6,438	6,302	6,196	6,137	154,497		188,061	79.0%
12.0 x EBDIAT Multiple	8,491	6,438	6,302	6,196	6,137	168,000		201,564	80.4%
13.0 x EBDIAT Multiple	8,491	6,438	6,302	6,196	6,137	181,503		215,067	81.6%
14.0 x EBDIAT Multiple	8,491	6,438	6,302	6,196	6,137	195,007		228,570	82.7%
15.0 x EBDIAT Multiple	8,491	6,438	6,302	6,196	6,137	208,510		242,074	83.7%
11.0% Discount Rate	0.9009	0.8116	0.7312	0.6587	0.5935	0.5346	0.4817		
11.0 x EBDIAT Multiple	8,414	6,323	6,133	5,976	5,866	146,331		179,043	78.6%
12.0 x EBDIAT Multiple	8,414	6,323	6,133	5,976	5,866	159,121		191,832	80.0%
13.0 x EBDIAT Multiple	8,414	6,323	6,133	5,976	5,866	171,911		204,622	81.3%
14.0 x EBDIAT Multiple	8,414	6,323	6,133	5,976	5,866	184,700		217,412	82.4%
15.0 x EBDIAT Multiple	8,414	6,323	6,133	5,976	5,866	197,490		230,201	83.3%
12.0% Discount Rate	0.8929	0.7972	0.7118	0.6355	0.5674	0.5066	0.4523		
11.0 x EBDIAT Multiple	8,339	6,210	5,970	5,765	5,608	138,665		170,558	78.2%
12.0 x EBDIAT Multiple	8,339	6,210	5,970	5,765	5,608	150,785		182,678	79.6%
13.0 x EBDIAT Multiple	8,339	6,210	5,970	5,765	5,608	162,904		194,797	80.5%
14.0 x EBDIAT Multiple	8,339	6,210	5,970	5,765	5,608	175,024		206,917	82.0%
15.0 x EBDIAT Multiple	8,339	6,210	5,970	5,765	5,608	187,143		219,037	83.0%
13.0% Discount Rate	0.8850	0.7831	0.6931	0.6133	0.5428	0.4803	0.4251		
11.0 x EBDIAT Multiple	8,265	6,101	5,813	5,564	5,365	131,463		162,571	77.8%
12.0 x EBDIAT Multiple	8,265	6,101	5,813	5,564	5,365	142,953		174,061	79.2%
13.0 x EBDIAT Multiple	8,265	6,101	5,813	5,564	5,365	154,444		185,551	80.5%
14.0 x EBDIAT Multiple	8,265	6,101	5,813	5,564	5,365	165,934		197,041	81.6%
15.0 x EBDIAT Multiple	8,265	6,101	5,813	5,564	5,365	177,424		208,532	82.7%
14.0% Discount Rate	0.8772	0.7695	0.6750	0.5921	0.5194	0.4556	0.3996		
11.0 x EBDIAT Multiple	8,193	5,994	5,661	5,371	5,133	124,694		155,047	77.3%
12.0 x EBDIAT Multiple	8,193	5,994	5,661	5,371	5,133	135,593		165,946	78.8%
13.0 x EBDIAT Multiple	8,193	5,994	5,661	5,371	5,133	146,491		176,844	80.1%
14.0 x EBDIAT Multiple	8,193	5,994	5,661	5,371	5,133	157,390		187,743	81.6%
15.0 x EBDIAT Multiple	8,193	5,994	5,661	5,371	5,133	168,288		198,641	82.3%

NPV Calculations - Sale Assumption

EBDIAT Multiple Method	1993	1994	1995	1996	1997	1998	1999	NPV	Residual Value as % of NPV
After-tax Cash Flow	$9,340	$7,790	$8,387	$9,072	$9,884	$10,560			
Residual Value									
11.0 x EBDIAT Multiple						223,947			
12.0 x EBDIAT Multiple						238,779			
13.0 x EBDIAT Multiple						253,610			
14.0 x EBDIAT Multiple						268,442			
15.0 x EBDIAT Multiple						283,274			
10.0% Discount Rate	0.9091	0.8264	0.7513	0.6830	0.6209	0.5645	0.5132		
11.0 x EBDIAT Multiple	8,491	6,438	6,302	6,196	6,137	132,373		165,937	76.2%
12.0 x EBDIAT Multiple	8,491	6,438	6,302	6,196	6,137	140,745		174,309	77.3%
13.0 x EBDIAT Multiple	8,491	6,438	6,302	6,196	6,137	149,117		182,681	78.4%
14.0 x EBDIAT Multiple	8,491	6,438	6,302	6,196	6,137	157,489		191,053	79.3%
15.0 x EBDIAT Multiple	8,491	6,438	6,302	6,196	6,137	165,861		199,425	80.2%
11.0% Discount Rate	0.9009	0.8116	0.7312	0.6587	0.5935	0.5346	0.4817		
11.0 x EBDIAT Multiple	8,414	6,323	6,133	5,976	5,866	125,377		158,088	75.7%
12.0 x EBDIAT Multiple	8,414	6,323	6,133	5,976	5,866	133,307		166,018	76.9%
13.0 x EBDIAT Multiple	8,414	6,323	6,133	5,976	5,866	141,236		173,947	77.9%
14.0 x EBDIAT Multiple	8,414	6,323	6,133	5,976	5,866	149,166		181,877	78.9%
15.0 x EBDIAT Multiple	8,414	6,323	6,133	5,976	5,866	157,095		189,807	79.8%
12.0% Discount Rate	0.8929	0.7972	0.7118	0.6355	0.5674	0.5066	0.4523		
11.0 x EBDIAT Multiple	8,339	6,210	5,970	5,765	5,608	118,808		150,702	75.3%
12.0 x EBDIAT Multiple	8,339	6,210	5,970	5,765	5,608	126,323		158,216	76.5%
13.0 x EBDIAT Multiple	8,339	6,210	5,970	5,765	5,608	133,837		165,730	77.5%
14.0 x EBDIAT Multiple	8,339	6,210	5,970	5,765	5,608	141,351		173,244	78.5%
15.0 x EBDIAT Multiple	8,339	6,210	5,970	5,765	5,608	148,865		180,758	79.4%
13.0% Discount Rate	0.8850	0.7831	0.6931	0.6133	0.5428	0.4803	0.4251		
11.0 x EBDIAT Multiple	8,265	6,101	5,813	5,564	5,365	112,638		143,746	74.8%
12.0 x EBDIAT Multiple	8,265	6,101	5,813	5,564	5,365	119,762		150,870	76.0%
13.0 x EBDIAT Multiple	8,265	6,101	5,813	5,564	5,365	126,886		157,993	77.1%
14.0 x EBDIAT Multiple	8,265	6,101	5,813	5,564	5,365	134,010		165,117	78.1%
15.0 x EBDIAT Multiple	8,265	6,101	5,813	5,564	5,365	141,134		172,241	79.0%
14.0% Discount Rate	0.8772	0.7695	0.6750	0.5921	0.5194	0.4556	0.3996		
11.0 x EBDIAT Multiple	8,193	5,994	5,661	5,371	5,133	106,838		137,191	74.4%
12.0 x EBDIAT Multiple	8,193	5,994	5,661	5,371	5,133	113,595		143,948	75.6%
13.0 x EBDIAT Multiple	8,193	5,994	5,661	5,371	5,133	120,352		150,705	76.7%
14.0 x EBDIAT Multiple	8,193	5,994	5,661	5,371	5,133	127,109		157,462	77.7%
15.0 x EBDIAT Multiple	8,193	5,994	5,661	5,371	5,133	133,866		164,220	78.6%

EXHIBIT 22.9
05/21/92
09:31 AM

MAREIGHT CORPORATION
Discounted Cash Flow Analysis
NPV Calculations - P/E Multiple Method

NPV Calculations - Continuing Value Assumption

NPV Multiple Method	1993	1994	1995	1996	1997	1998	1999	NPV	Residual Value as % of NPV
After-tax Cash Flow	$9,340	$7,790	$8,387	$9,072	$9,884	$10,560			
Residual Value									
18.0 x P/E Multiple						217,571			
19.0 x P/E Multiple						229,658			
20.0 x P/E Multiple						241,745			
21.0 x P/E Multiple						253,832			
22.0 x P/E Multiple						265,920			
10.0% Discount Rate	0.9091	0.8264	0.7513	0.6830	0.6209	0.5645	0.5132		
18.0 x P/E Multiple	8,491	6,438	6,302	6,196	6,137	128,773		162,337	75.7%
19.0 x P/E Multiple	8,491	6,438	6,302	6,196	6,137	135,596		169,160	76.6%
20.0 x P/E Multiple	8,491	6,438	6,302	6,196	6,137	142,419		175,983	77.5%
21.0 x P/E Multiple	8,491	6,438	6,302	6,196	6,137	149,242		182,806	78.4%
22.0 x P/E Multiple	8,491	6,438	6,302	6,196	6,137	156,065		189,629	79.2%
11.0% Discount Rate	0.9009	0.8116	0.7312	0.6587	0.5935	0.5346	0.4817		
18.0 x P/E Multiple	8,414	6,323	6,133	5,976	5,866	121,968		154,679	75.2%
19.0 x P/E Multiple	8,414	6,323	6,133	5,976	5,866	128,430		161,141	76.2%
20.0 x P/E Multiple	8,414	6,323	6,133	5,976	5,866	134,892		167,604	77.1%
21.0 x P/E Multiple	8,414	6,323	6,133	5,976	5,866	141,355		174,066	78.0%
22.0 x P/E Multiple	8,414	6,323	6,133	5,976	5,866	147,817		180,528	78.8%
12.0% Discount Rate	0.8929	0.7972	0.7118	0.6355	0.5674	0.5066	0.4523		
18.0 x P/E Multiple	8,339	6,210	5,970	5,765	5,608	115,578		147,471	74.7%
19.0 x P/E Multiple	8,339	6,210	5,970	5,765	5,608	121,702		153,595	75.8%
20.0 x P/E Multiple	8,339	6,210	5,970	5,765	5,608	127,825		159,719	76.7%
21.0 x P/E Multiple	8,339	6,210	5,970	5,765	5,608	133,949		165,842	77.5%
22.0 x P/E Multiple	8,339	6,210	5,970	5,765	5,608	140,073		171,966	78.3%
13.0% Discount Rate	0.8850	0.7831	0.6931	0.6133	0.5428	0.4803	0.4251		
18.0 x P/E Multiple	8,265	6,101	5,813	5,564	5,365	109,575		140,683	74.3%
19.0 x P/E Multiple	8,265	6,101	5,813	5,564	5,365	115,381		146,489	75.3%
20.0 x P/E Multiple	8,265	6,101	5,813	5,564	5,365	121,187		152,294	76.2%
21.0 x P/E Multiple	8,265	6,101	5,813	5,564	5,365	126,992		158,100	77.1%
22.0 x P/E Multiple	8,265	6,101	5,813	5,564	5,365	132,798		163,906	77.9%
14.0% Discount Rate	0.8772	0.7695	0.6750	0.5921	0.5194	0.4556	0.3996		
18.0 x P/E Multiple	8,193	5,994	5,661	5,371	5,133	103,933		134,286	73.8%
19.0 x P/E Multiple	8,193	5,994	5,661	5,371	5,133	109,440		139,793	74.8%
20.0 x P/E Multiple	8,193	5,994	5,661	5,371	5,133	114,947		145,300	75.8%
21.0 x P/E Multiple	8,193	5,994	5,661	5,371	5,133	120,453		150,806	76.7%
22.0 x P/E Multiple	8,193	5,994	5,661	5,371	5,133	125,960		156,313	77.5%

NPV Calculations - Sale Assumption

P/E Multiple Method	1993	1994	1995	1996	1997	1998	1999	NPV	Residual Value as % of NPV
After-tax Cash Flow	$9,340	$7,790	$8,387	$9,072	$9,884	$10,560			
Residual Value									
18.0 x P/E Multiple						195,694			
19.0 x P/E Multiple						203,188			
20.0 x P/E Multiple						210,682			
21.0 x P/E Multiple						218,176			
22.0 x P/E Multiple						225,670			
10.0% Discount Rate	0.9091	0.8264	0.7513	0.6830	0.6209	0.5645	0.5132		
18.0 x P/E Multiple	8,491	6,438	6,302	6,196	6,137	116,425		149,988	73.6%
19.0 x P/E Multiple	8,491	6,438	6,302	6,196	6,137	120,655		154,219	74.4%
20.0 x P/E Multiple	8,491	6,438	6,302	6,196	6,137	124,885		158,449	75.1%
21.0 x P/E Multiple	8,491	6,438	6,302	6,196	6,137	129,115		162,679	75.7%
22.0 x P/E Multiple	8,491	6,438	6,302	6,196	6,137	133,346		166,909	76.3%
11.0% Discount Rate	0.9009	0.8116	0.7312	0.6587	0.5935	0.5346	0.4817		
18.0 x P/E Multiple	8,414	6,323	6,133	5,976	5,866	110,271		142,983	73.2%
19.0 x P/E Multiple	8,414	6,323	6,133	5,976	5,866	114,278		146,989	73.9%
20.0 x P/E Multiple	8,414	6,323	6,133	5,976	5,866	118,285		150,996	74.6%
21.0 x P/E Multiple	8,414	6,323	6,133	5,976	5,866	122,291		155,003	75.3%
22.0 x P/E Multiple	8,414	6,323	6,133	5,976	5,866	126,298		159,009	75.9%
12.0% Discount Rate	0.8929	0.7972	0.7118	0.6355	0.5674	0.5066	0.4523		
18.0 x P/E Multiple	8,339	6,210	5,970	5,765	5,608	104,494		136,388	72.7%
19.0 x P/E Multiple	8,339	6,210	5,970	5,765	5,608	108,291		140,184	73.4%
20.0 x P/E Multiple	8,339	6,210	5,970	5,765	5,608	112,088		143,981	74.1%
21.0 x P/E Multiple	8,339	6,210	5,970	5,765	5,608	115,885		147,778	74.8%
22.0 x P/E Multiple	8,339	6,210	5,970	5,765	5,608	119,681		151,574	75.4%
13.0% Discount Rate	0.8850	0.7831	0.6931	0.6133	0.5428	0.4803	0.4251		
18.0 x P/E Multiple	8,265	6,101	5,813	5,564	5,365	99,067		130,175	72.2%
19.0 x P/E Multiple	8,265	6,101	5,813	5,564	5,365	102,667		133,775	73.0%
20.0 x P/E Multiple	8,265	6,101	5,813	5,564	5,365	106,266		137,374	73.7%
21.0 x P/E Multiple	8,265	6,101	5,813	5,564	5,365	109,866		140,974	74.3%
22.0 x P/E Multiple	8,265	6,101	5,813	5,564	5,365	113,466		144,573	75.0%
14.0% Discount Rate	0.8772	0.7695	0.6750	0.5921	0.5194	0.4556	0.3996		
18.0 x P/E Multiple	8,193	5,994	5,661	5,371	5,133	93,966		124,319	71.7%
19.0 x P/E Multiple	8,193	5,994	5,661	5,371	5,133	97,380		127,734	72.5%
20.0 x P/E Multiple	8,193	5,994	5,661	5,371	5,133	100,795		131,148	73.2%
21.0 x P/E Multiple	8,193	5,994	5,661	5,371	5,133	104,209		134,562	73.9%
22.0 x P/E Multiple	8,193	5,994	5,661	5,371	5,133	107,623		137,976	74.5%

MAREIGHT CORPORATION
Discounted Cash Flow Analysis
NPV Calculations - Growing Perpetuity Method

EXHIBIT 22.10
08/28/92
05:26 PM

NPV Calculations - Continuing Value Assumption

Growing Perpetuity Method	1993	1994	1995	1996	1997	1998		NPV	Residual Value as % of NPV
After-tax Cash Flow	$9,340	$7,790	$8,387	$9,072	$9,884	$10,560			
Residual Value							158,393		
5.0% Growth Rate							171,390		
5.5% Growth Rate							186,552		
6.0% Growth Rate							204,471		
6.5% Growth Rate							225,975		
7.0% Growth Rate									
10.0% Discount Rate	0.9091	0.8264	0.7513	0.6830	0.6209	0.5645			69.3%
5.0% Growth Rate	8,491	6,438	6,302	6,196	6,137	5,961	89,409	128,933	69.3%
5.5% Growth Rate	8,491	6,438	6,302	6,196	6,137	5,961	96,745	136,270	71.0%
6.0% Growth Rate	8,491	6,438	6,302	6,196	6,137	5,961	105,304	144,828	72.7%
6.5% Growth Rate	8,491	6,438	6,302	6,196	6,137	5,961	115,419	154,943	74.5%
7.0% Growth Rate	8,491	6,438	6,302	6,196	6,137	5,961	127,557	167,081	76.3%
11.0% Discount Rate	0.9009	0.8116	0.7312	0.6587	0.5935	0.5346			68.8%
5.0% Growth Rate	8,414	6,323	6,133	5,976	5,866	5,646	84,684	123,040	68.8%
5.5% Growth Rate	8,414	6,323	6,133	5,976	5,866	5,646	91,632	129,989	70.5%
6.0% Growth Rate	8,414	6,323	6,133	5,976	5,866	5,646	99,738	138,095	72.2%
6.5% Growth Rate	8,414	6,323	6,133	5,976	5,866	5,646	109,319	147,676	74.0%
7.0% Growth Rate	8,414	6,323	6,133	5,976	5,866	5,646	120,815	159,172	75.9%
12.0% Discount Rate	0.8929	0.7972	0.7118	0.6355	0.5674	0.5066			68.3%
5.0% Growth Rate	8,339	6,210	5,970	5,765	5,608	5,350	80,247	117,490	68.3%
5.5% Growth Rate	8,339	6,210	5,970	5,765	5,608	5,350	86,831	124,074	70.0%
6.0% Growth Rate	8,339	6,210	5,970	5,765	5,608	5,350	94,513	131,756	71.7%
6.5% Growth Rate	8,339	6,210	5,970	5,765	5,608	5,350	103,592	140,835	73.6%
7.0% Growth Rate	8,339	6,210	5,970	5,765	5,608	5,350	114,486	151,729	75.5%
13.0% Discount Rate	0.8850	0.7831	0.6931	0.6133	0.5428	0.4803			67.8%
5.0% Growth Rate	8,265	6,101	5,813	5,564	5,365	5,072	76,079	112,259	67.8%
5.5% Growth Rate	8,265	6,101	5,813	5,564	5,365	5,072	82,322	118,501	69.5%
6.0% Growth Rate	8,265	6,101	5,813	5,564	5,365	5,072	89,604	125,784	71.2%
6.5% Growth Rate	8,265	6,101	5,813	5,564	5,365	5,072	98,211	134,391	73.1%
7.0% Growth Rate	8,265	6,101	5,813	5,564	5,365	5,072	108,540	144,719	75.0%
14.0% Discount Rate	0.8772	0.7695	0.6750	0.5921	0.5194	0.4556			67.2%
5.0% Growth Rate	8,193	5,994	5,661	5,371	5,133	4,811	72,162	107,326	67.2%
5.5% Growth Rate	8,193	5,994	5,661	5,371	5,133	4,811	78,083	113,247	68.9%
6.0% Growth Rate	8,193	5,994	5,661	5,371	5,133	4,811	84,991	120,155	70.7%
6.5% Growth Rate	8,193	5,994	5,661	5,371	5,133	4,811	93,154	128,318	72.6%
7.0% Growth Rate	8,193	5,994	5,661	5,371	5,133	4,811	102,951	138,115	74.5%

NPV Calculations - Sale Assumption

Growing Perpetuity Method	1993	1994	1995	1996	1997	1998		NPV	Residual Value as % of NPV
After-tax Cash Flow	$9,340	$7,790	$8,387	$9,072	$9,884	$10,560			
Residual Value							159,004		
5.0% Growth Rate							167,062		
5.5% Growth Rate							176,462		
6.0% Growth Rate							187,572		
6.5% Growth Rate							200,904		
7.0% Growth Rate									
10.0% Discount Rate	0.9091	0.8264	0.7513	0.6830	0.6209	0.5645			69.4%
5.0% Growth Rate	8,491	6,438	6,302	6,196	6,137	5,961	89,754	129,278	69.4%
5.5% Growth Rate	8,491	6,438	6,302	6,196	6,137	5,961	94,302	133,826	70.5%
6.0% Growth Rate	8,491	6,438	6,302	6,196	6,137	5,961	99,608	139,133	71.6%
6.5% Growth Rate	8,491	6,438	6,302	6,196	6,137	5,961	105,880	145,404	72.8%
7.0% Growth Rate	8,491	6,438	6,302	6,196	6,137	5,961	113,405	152,930	74.2%
11.0% Discount Rate	0.9009	0.8116	0.7312	0.6587	0.5935	0.5346			68.9%
5.0% Growth Rate	8,414	6,323	6,133	5,976	5,866	5,646	85,010	123,367	68.9%
5.5% Growth Rate	8,414	6,323	6,133	5,976	5,866	5,646	89,318	127,675	70.0%
6.0% Growth Rate	8,414	6,323	6,133	5,976	5,866	5,646	94,344	132,701	71.1%
6.5% Growth Rate	8,414	6,323	6,133	5,976	5,866	5,646	100,284	138,641	72.3%
7.0% Growth Rate	8,414	6,323	6,133	5,976	5,866	5,646	107,412	145,768	73.7%
12.0% Discount Rate	0.8929	0.7972	0.7118	0.6355	0.5674	0.5066			68.4%
5.0% Growth Rate	8,339	6,210	5,970	5,765	5,608	5,350	80,556	117,799	68.4%
5.5% Growth Rate	8,339	6,210	5,970	5,765	5,608	5,350	84,639	121,882	69.4%
6.0% Growth Rate	8,339	6,210	5,970	5,765	5,608	5,350	89,401	126,644	70.6%
6.5% Growth Rate	8,339	6,210	5,970	5,765	5,608	5,350	95,030	132,273	71.8%
7.0% Growth Rate	8,339	6,210	5,970	5,765	5,608	5,350	101,784	139,027	73.2%
13.0% Discount Rate	0.8850	0.7831	0.6931	0.6133	0.5428	0.4803			67.9%
5.0% Growth Rate	8,265	6,101	5,813	5,564	5,365	5,072	76,373	112,552	67.9%
5.5% Growth Rate	8,265	6,101	5,813	5,564	5,365	5,072	80,243	116,422	68.9%
6.0% Growth Rate	8,265	6,101	5,813	5,564	5,365	5,072	84,758	120,938	70.1%
6.5% Growth Rate	8,265	6,101	5,813	5,564	5,365	5,072	90,094	126,274	71.3%
7.0% Growth Rate	8,265	6,101	5,813	5,564	5,365	5,072	96,498	132,678	72.7%
14.0% Discount Rate	0.8772	0.7695	0.6750	0.5921	0.5194	0.4556			67.3%
5.0% Growth Rate	8,193	5,994	5,661	5,371	5,133	4,811	72,440	107,604	67.3%
5.5% Growth Rate	8,193	5,994	5,661	5,371	5,133	4,811	76,111	111,275	68.4%
6.0% Growth Rate	8,193	5,994	5,661	5,371	5,133	4,811	80,394	115,558	69.6%
6.5% Growth Rate	8,193	5,994	5,661	5,371	5,133	4,811	85,455	120,619	70.8%
7.0% Growth Rate	8,193	5,994	5,661	5,371	5,133	4,811	91,529	126,693	72.2%

MAREIGHT CORPORATION
Discounted Cash Flow Analysis
NPV Calculations - EBITDA Multiple Method

EXHIBIT 22.11
05/21/92
09:31 AM

NPV Calculations - Continuing Value Assumption

EBITDA Multiple Method	1993	1994	1995	1996	1997	1998	1999	NPV	Residual Value as % of NPV
After-tax Cash Flow	$9,340	$7,790	$8,387	$9,072	$9,884	$10,560			
Residual Value									
8.0 x EBITDA Multiple						255,099			
8.5 x EBITDA Multiple						271,043			
9.0 x EBITDA Multiple						286,987			
9.5 x EBITDA Multiple						302,930			
10.0 x EBITDA Multiple						318,874			
10.0% Discount Rate	0.9091	0.8264	0.7513	0.6830	0.6209	0.5645	0.5132		
8.0 x EBITDA Multiple	8,491	6,438	6,302	6,196	6,137	149,957		183,521	78.5%
8.5 x EBITDA Multiple	8,491	6,438	6,302	6,196	6,137	158,957		192,521	79.5%
9.0 x EBITDA Multiple	8,491	6,438	6,302	6,196	6,137	167,957		201,521	80.4%
9.5 x EBITDA Multiple	8,491	6,438	6,302	6,196	6,137	176,957		210,521	81.2%
10.0 x EBITDA Multiple	8,491	6,438	6,302	6,196	6,137	185,957		219,521	82.0%
11.0% Discount Rate	0.9009	0.8116	0.7312	0.6587	0.5935	0.5346	0.4817		
8.0 x EBITDA Multiple	8,414	6,323	6,133	5,976	5,866	142,032		174,743	78.0%
8.5 x EBITDA Multiple	8,414	6,323	6,133	5,976	5,866	150,556		183,268	79.1%
9.0 x EBITDA Multiple	8,414	6,323	6,133	5,976	5,866	159,080		191,792	80.0%
9.5 x EBITDA Multiple	8,414	6,323	6,133	5,976	5,866	167,604		200,316	80.9%
10.0 x EBITDA Multiple	8,414	6,323	6,133	5,976	5,866	176,129		208,840	81.6%
12.0% Discount Rate	0.8929	0.7972	0.7118	0.6355	0.5674	0.5066	0.4523		
8.0 x EBITDA Multiple	8,339	6,210	5,970	5,765	5,608	134,591		166,484	77.6%
8.5 x EBITDA Multiple	8,339	6,210	5,970	5,765	5,608	142,669		174,562	78.7%
9.0 x EBITDA Multiple	8,339	6,210	5,970	5,765	5,608	150,746		182,639	79.6%
9.5 x EBITDA Multiple	8,339	6,210	5,970	5,765	5,608	158,824		190,717	80.5%
10.0 x EBITDA Multiple	8,339	6,210	5,970	5,765	5,608	166,901		198,794	81.3%
13.0% Discount Rate	0.8850	0.7831	0.6931	0.6133	0.5428	0.4803	0.4251		
8.0 x EBITDA Multiple	8,265	6,101	5,813	5,564	5,365	127,601		158,708	77.2%
8.5 x EBITDA Multiple	8,265	6,101	5,813	5,564	5,365	135,259		166,367	78.3%
9.0 x EBITDA Multiple	8,265	6,101	5,813	5,564	5,365	142,917		174,025	79.2%
9.5 x EBITDA Multiple	8,265	6,101	5,813	5,564	5,365	150,575		181,683	80.1%
10.0 x EBITDA Multiple	8,265	6,101	5,813	5,564	5,365	158,233		189,341	80.8%
14.0% Discount Rate	0.8772	0.7695	0.6750	0.5921	0.5194	0.4556	0.3996		
8.0 x EBITDA Multiple	8,193	5,994	5,661	5,371	5,133	121,031		151,384	76.8%
8.5 x EBITDA Multiple	8,193	5,994	5,661	5,371	5,133	128,294		158,647	77.8%
9.0 x EBITDA Multiple	8,193	5,994	5,661	5,371	5,133	135,558		165,911	78.8%
9.5 x EBITDA Multiple	8,193	5,994	5,661	5,371	5,133	142,822		173,175	79.6%
10.0 x EBITDA Multiple	8,193	5,994	5,661	5,371	5,133	150,086		180,439	80.5%

NPV Calculations - Sale Assumption

EBITDA Multiple Method	1993	1994	1995	1996	1997	1998	1999	NPV	Residual Value as % of NPV
After-tax Cash Flow	$9,340	$7,790	$8,387	$9,072	$9,884	$10,560			
Residual Value									
8.0 x EBITDA Multiple						218,962			
8.5 x EBITDA Multiple						228,847			
9.0 x EBITDA Multiple						238,732			
9.5 x EBITDA Multiple						248,617			
10.0 x EBITDA Multiple						258,502			
10.0% Discount Rate	0.9091	0.8264	0.7513	0.6830	0.6209	0.5645	0.5132		
8.0 x EBITDA Multiple	8,491	6,438	6,302	6,196	6,137	129,559		163,123	75.8%
8.5 x EBITDA Multiple	8,491	6,438	6,302	6,196	6,137	135,139		168,702	76.6%
9.0 x EBITDA Multiple	8,491	6,438	6,302	6,196	6,137	140,718		174,282	77.3%
9.5 x EBITDA Multiple	8,491	6,438	6,302	6,196	6,137	146,298		179,862	78.0%
10.0 x EBITDA Multiple	8,491	6,438	6,302	6,196	6,137	151,878		185,442	78.7%
11.0% Discount Rate	0.9009	0.8116	0.7312	0.6587	0.5935	0.5346	0.4817		
8.0 x EBITDA Multiple	8,414	6,323	6,133	5,976	5,866	122,711		155,423	75.3%
8.5 x EBITDA Multiple	8,414	6,323	6,133	5,976	5,866	127,996		160,708	76.1%
9.0 x EBITDA Multiple	8,414	6,323	6,133	5,976	5,866	133,281		165,993	76.9%
9.5 x EBITDA Multiple	8,414	6,323	6,133	5,976	5,866	138,566		171,278	77.6%
10.0 x EBITDA Multiple	8,414	6,323	6,133	5,976	5,866	143,851		176,563	78.3%
12.0% Discount Rate	0.8929	0.7972	0.7118	0.6355	0.5674	0.5066	0.4523		
8.0 x EBITDA Multiple	8,339	6,210	5,970	5,765	5,608	116,283		148,176	74.9%
8.5 x EBITDA Multiple	8,339	6,210	5,970	5,765	5,608	121,291		153,184	75.7%
9.0 x EBITDA Multiple	8,339	6,210	5,970	5,765	5,608	126,299		158,192	76.5%
9.5 x EBITDA Multiple	8,339	6,210	5,970	5,765	5,608	131,307		163,200	77.2%
10.0 x EBITDA Multiple	8,339	6,210	5,970	5,765	5,608	136,315		168,208	77.9%
13.0% Discount Rate	0.8850	0.7831	0.6931	0.6133	0.5428	0.4803	0.4251		
8.0 x EBITDA Multiple	8,265	6,101	5,813	5,564	5,365	110,243		141,351	74.4%
8.5 x EBITDA Multiple	8,265	6,101	5,813	5,564	5,365	114,991		146,099	75.2%
9.0 x EBITDA Multiple	8,265	6,101	5,813	5,564	5,365	119,739		150,847	76.0%
9.5 x EBITDA Multiple	8,265	6,101	5,813	5,564	5,365	124,487		155,595	76.7%
10.0 x EBITDA Multiple	8,265	6,101	5,813	5,564	5,365	129,235		160,343	77.4%
14.0% Discount Rate	0.8772	0.7695	0.6750	0.5921	0.5194	0.4556	0.3996		
8.0 x EBITDA Multiple	8,193	5,994	5,661	5,371	5,133	104,567		134,920	73.9%
8.5 x EBITDA Multiple	8,193	5,994	5,661	5,371	5,133	109,070		139,423	74.8%
9.0 x EBITDA Multiple	8,193	5,994	5,661	5,371	5,133	113,574		143,927	75.6%
9.5 x EBITDA Multiple	8,193	5,994	5,661	5,371	5,133	118,077		148,430	76.3%
10.0 x EBITDA Multiple	8,193	5,994	5,661	5,371	5,133	122,581		152,934	77.0%

Page 12   FILE: SHT_J

MAREIGHT CORPORATION
Discounted Cash Flow Analysis
IRR Calculations

EXHIBIT 22.12
08/28/92
05:26 PM

IRR Calculations - Continuing Value Assumption

	Investment	1993	1994	1995	1996	1997	1998	IRR
EBDIAT Multiple Method								
11.0 x EBDIAT Multiple	(160,000)	9,340	7,790	8,387	9,072	9,884	273,700	13.3%
12.0 x EBDIAT Multiple	(160,000)	9,340	7,790	8,387	9,072	9,884	297,622	14.8%
13.0 x EBDIAT Multiple	(160,000)	9,340	7,790	8,387	9,072	9,884	321,544	16.1%
14.0 x EBDIAT Multiple	(160,000)	9,340	7,790	8,387	9,072	9,884	345,466	17.4%
15.0 x EBDIAT Multiple	(160,000)	9,340	7,790	8,387	9,072	9,884	369,388	18.6%
P/E Multiple Method								
18.0 x P/E Multiple	(160,000)	9,340	7,790	8,387	9,072	9,884	228,130	10.3%
19.0 x P/E Multiple	(160,000)	9,340	7,790	8,387	9,072	9,884	240,217	11.1%
20.0 x P/E Multiple	(160,000)	9,340	7,790	8,387	9,072	9,884	252,305	12.0%
21.0 x P/E Multiple	(160,000)	9,340	7,790	8,387	9,072	9,884	264,392	12.7%
22.0 x P/E Multiple	(160,000)	9,340	7,790	8,387	9,072	9,884	276,479	13.5%
Growing Perpetuity Method								
5.0% Growth Rate	(160,000)	9,340	7,790	8,387	9,072	9,884	168,953	5.6%
5.5% Growth Rate	(160,000)	9,340	7,790	8,387	9,072	9,884	181,949	6.7%
6.0% Growth Rate	(160,000)	9,340	7,790	8,387	9,072	9,884	197,112	7.9%
6.5% Growth Rate	(160,000)	9,340	7,790	8,387	9,072	9,884	215,031	9.3%
7.0% Growth Rate	(160,000)	9,340	7,790	8,387	9,072	9,884	236,534	10.9%
EBITDA Multiple Method								
8.0 x EBITDA Multiple	(160,000)	9,340	7,790	8,387	9,072	9,884	265,659	12.8%
8.5 x EBITDA Multiple	(160,000)	9,340	7,790	8,387	9,072	9,884	281,602	13.8%
9.0 x EBITDA Multiple	(160,000)	9,340	7,790	8,387	9,072	9,884	297,546	14.8%
9.5 x EBITDA Multiple	(160,000)	9,340	7,790	8,387	9,072	9,884	313,490	15.7%
10.0 x EBITDA Multiple	(160,000)	9,340	7,790	8,387	9,072	9,884	329,434	16.5%

IRR Calculations - Sale Assumption

	Investment	1993	1994	1995	1996	1997	1998	IRR
EBDIAT Multiple Method								
11.0 x EBDIAT Multiple	(160,000)	9,340	7,790	8,387	9,072	9,884	234,507	10.8%
12.0 x EBDIAT Multiple	(160,000)	9,340	7,790	8,387	9,072	9,884	249,338	11.8%
13.0 x EBDIAT Multiple	(160,000)	9,340	7,790	8,387	9,072	9,884	264,170	12.7%
14.0 x EBDIAT Multiple	(160,000)	9,340	7,790	8,387	9,072	9,884	279,002	13.7%
15.0 x EBDIAT Multiple	(160,000)	9,340	7,790	8,387	9,072	9,884	293,833	14.6%
P/E Multiple Method								
18.0 x P/E Multiple	(160,000)	9,340	7,790	8,387	9,072	9,884	195,694	7.8%
19.0 x P/E Multiple	(160,000)	9,340	7,790	8,387	9,072	9,884	213,747	9.2%
20.0 x P/E Multiple	(160,000)	9,340	7,790	8,387	9,072	9,884	221,242	9.8%
21.0 x P/E Multiple	(160,000)	9,340	7,790	8,387	9,072	9,884	228,736	10.3%
22.0 x P/E Multiple	(160,000)	9,340	7,790	8,387	9,072	9,884	236,230	10.9%
Growing Perpetuity Method								
5.0% Growth Rate	(160,000)	9,340	7,790	8,387	9,072	9,884	169,563	5.6%
5.5% Growth Rate	(160,000)	9,340	7,790	8,387	9,072	9,884	177,621	6.3%
6.0% Growth Rate	(160,000)	9,340	7,790	8,387	9,072	9,884	187,022	7.1%
6.5% Growth Rate	(160,000)	9,340	7,790	8,387	9,072	9,884	198,132	8.0%
7.0% Growth Rate	(160,000)	9,340	7,790	8,387	9,072	9,884	211,464	9.1%
EBITDA Multiple Method								
8.0 x EBITDA Multiple	(160,000)	9,340	7,790	8,387	9,072	9,884	229,521	10.4%
8.5 x EBITDA Multiple	(160,000)	9,340	7,790	8,387	9,072	9,884	239,406	11.1%
9.0 x EBITDA Multiple	(160,000)	9,340	7,790	8,387	9,072	9,884	249,291	11.8%
9.5 x EBITDA Multiple	(160,000)	9,340	7,790	8,387	9,072	9,884	259,176	12.4%
10.0 x EBITDA Multiple	(160,000)	9,340	7,790	8,387	9,072	9,884	269,061	13.0%

MAREIGHT CORPORATION
Discounted Cash Flow Analysis
Summary Amortization Schedule

Years Ended December 31,			Opening Bal. sheet	1993	1994	1995	1996	1997	1998
Transaction Fees									
Beginning Balance				$2,500	$2,438	$2,375	$2,313	$2,250	$2,188
Amortization:		Years							
Transaction		40	$1,933	48	48	48	48	48	48
Accounting & Legal		40	567	14	14	14	14	14	14
Pre-Payment Penalty		7	0	0	0	0	0	0	0
Ending Balance			$2,500	$2,438	$2,375	$2,313	$2,250	$2,188	$2,125

NOTE: Transaction costs not directly related to the financing are not deductible.

		Initial	1993	1994	1995	1996	1997	1998
Goodwill								
Beginning Balance	40 Years		$34,748	$33,879	$33,011	$32,142	$31,273	$30,405
Amortization			869	869	869	869	869	869
Ending Goodwill		$34,748	$33,879	$33,011	$32,142	$31,273	$30,405	$29,536

		Initial	1993	1994	1995	1996	1997	1998
Intangible Assets								
Beginning Balance			$0	$0	$0	$0	$0	$0
Plus: Additions			0	0	0	0	0	0
Amortization	5 Years		0	0	0	0	0	0
Ending Intangible Assets		$0	$0	$0	$0	$0	$0	$0

		Initial	1993	1994	1995	1996	1997	1998
Leased Property Under Capital Leases								
Beginning Balance			$0	$0	$0	$0	$0	$0
Plus: Additions			0	0	0	0	0	0
Amortization	25 Years		0	0	0	0	0	0
Ending Intangible Assets		$0	$0	$0	$0	$0	$0	$0

	1993	1994	1995	1996	1997	1998
Deductible Amortization	$0	$0	$0	$0	$0	$0
Non-Deductible Amortization	931	931	931	931	931	931
Total Amortization	$931	$931	$931	$931	$931	$931

MAREIGHT CORPORATION
LBO Analysis
Financial Statement Tax Provision

Years Ended December 31,	1993	1994	1995	1996	1997	1998
Earnings Before Taxes	$13,685	$14,782	$15,960	$17,227	$18,589	$20,053
Permanent Differences						
Goodwill Amortization	869	869	869	869	869	869
Other Non-Deductible Amortization	63	63	63	63	63	63
Total Permanent Differences	931	931	931	931	931	931
Taxable Income Before NOL	14,617	15,713	16,891	18,158	19,520	20,984
NOL						
Available	0	0	0	0	0	0
Current	0	0	0	0	0	0
Utilized	0	0	0	0	0	0
Taxable Income After NOL	14,617	15,713	16,891	18,158	19,520	20,984
State Taxes 6.00%	877	943	1,013	1,089	1,171	1,259
Taxable Income After NOL and State Taxes	13,740	14,770	15,878	17,069	18,349	19,725
Federal Tax 34.00%	4,671	5,022	5,398	5,803	6,239	6,706
Credits	0	0	0	0	0	0
Net Federal Taxes	4,671	5,022	5,398	5,803	6,239	6,706
State Taxes	877	943	1,013	1,089	1,171	1,259
Foreign Taxes	0	0	0	0	0	0
Total Book Tax Provision	$5,548	$5,965	$6,412	$6,893	$7,410	$7,966
Effective Tax Rate	40.5%	40.4%	40.2%	40.0%	39.9%	39.7%

22.4 DIFFERENCES BETWEEN THE INITIAL AND FINAL DCF MODELS

There are four principal differences between the Initial DCF Model and the Final DCF Model.

- In the Initial DCF Model, net working capital requirements are estimated in the aggregate as a percent of sales. In the Final DCF Model, each component of working capital is estimated separately.
- In the Initial DCF Model, tax and book depreciation are assumed to be the same and are estimated as a percent of the target operation's sales. This assumption reduces the complexity of the Initial DCF Model significantly. In the Final DCF Model, a large number of schedules are devoted to determining projected book and tax depreciation.
- Third, because of its simplifying tax depreciation assumptions, the Initial DCF Model deals with the distinction between current and deferred taxes in a very simplistic manner. Furthermore, it does not provide at all for the Alternative Minimum Tax. The Final Model provides for more complex tax calculations.
- Finally, the Initial DCF Model's income statement schedule is generated from fairly simple assumptions regarding sales, gross margins and operating expenses. Typically, in a Final DCF Model these assumptions are replaced by detailed supporting schedules that depict product volumes and prices, and operating expense assumptions.

22.5 THE FINAL DCF MODEL

The Final DCF Model consists of the schedules listed below. Schedules that are not boldface are the same as in the Initial DCF Model. As with the Initial DCF Model the figures used in the Final DCF Analysis are associated with the example first described in Chapter 10.

- **Executive Summary (Exhibit 22–15).**
- **Tax, Transaction Cost, Acquisition Method and Cash Balance Assumptions (Exhibit 22–16).**
- **Economic and Operating Assumptions (Exhibit 22–17).**
- **Capital Expenditure Assumptions (Exhibit 22–18).**
- **Book and Tax Depreciation Rate Assumptions (Exhibit 22–19).**

- Book and Tax Depreciation Rate Assumptions(Continued) (Exhibit 22–20).
- Book and Tax Depreciation Rate Assumptions(Continued) (Exhibit 22–21).
- Income Statements (Exhibit 22–22).
- Balance Sheets (Exhibit 22–23).
- Statements of Changes in Financial Position (Exhibit 22–24).
- Calculation of Residual Values (Exhibit 22–25).
- NPV Calculations—EBDIAT Multiple Method (Exhibit 22–26).
- NPV Calculations—P/E Multiple Method (Exhibit 22–27).
- NPV Calculations—Growing Perpetuity Method (Exhibit 22–28).
- NPV Calculations—EBITDA Multiple Method (Exhibit 22–29).
- IRR Calculations (Exhibit 22–30).
- Summary Amortization Schedule (Exhibit 22–31).
- Financial Statement Tax Provision (Exhibit 22–32).
- Current and Deferred Taxes (Exhibit 22–33).
- Alternative Minimum Tax (Exhibit 22–34).
- Comparison of Calculated and Actual Values of Net Property, Plant and Equipment (Exhibit 22–35).
- Historical Capital Expenditures (Exhibit 22–36).
- Summary Historical Book Depreciation Schedule (Exhibit 22–37).
- Summary Projected Book Depreciation Schedule (Exhibit 22–38).
- Summary Regular Tax Depreciation Schedule (Exhibit 22–39).
- Summary AMT Depreciation Schedule (Exhibit 22–40).
- Summary ACE Depreciation Schedule (Exhibit 22–41).
- Historical and Projected Book, Regular Tax, AMTI and ACE Depreciation—3-Year (Exhibits 22–42 and 22–43).
- Historical and Projected Book, Regular Tax, AMTI and ACE Depreciation—5-Year (Exhibits 22–44 and 22–45).
- Historical and Projected Book, Regular Tax, AMTI and ACE Depreciation—7-Year (Exhibits 22–46 and 22–47).
- Historical and Projected Book, Regular Tax, AMTI and ACE Depreciation—10-Year (Exhibits 22–48 and 22–49).
- Historical and Projected Book, Regular Tax, AMTI and ACE Depreciation—15-Year (Exhibits 22–50 and 22–51).
- Historical and Projected Book, Regular Tax, AMTI and ACE Depreciation—20-Year (Exhibits 22–52 and 22–53).

- Historical and Projected Book, Regular Tax, AMTI and ACE Depreciation—Real Estate (Exhibits 22–54 and 22–55).

22.51   Executive Summary

The Miscellaneous section contains the switch that changes the model from an Initial Model to a Final Model. Although the way the results are calculated changes in the Final Model, the Executive Summary format remains the same.

22.52   Tax, Transaction Cost, Acquisition Method and Cash Balance Assumptions

The items on this schedule that pertain to the Final DCF Model involve certain tax assumptions, including the alternative minimum tax rate, the book income adjustment rate for AMT purposes, the AMT NOL use limitation percentage, the amount of any acquired book, tax, or AMT net operating loss and the acquired MTC Credit.

22.53   Economic and Operating Assumptions

In the Final Model, the sections Capital Expenditures, Book and Tax Depreciation, and Deferred Taxes are eliminated from this schedule. Detailed assumptions regarding these items are developed on other schedules. In addition, the section devoted to working capital assumptions is changed substantially. The component method of estimating working capital is used. Accounts receivable are determined by estimating a figure for days' sales outstanding; inventory is determined by estimating inventory turnover; other current assets are estimated as a percent of sales; accounts payable are determined by estimating days' payables outstanding, and accrued liabilities are estimated as a percent of selling, general and administrative expenses.

The most difficult working capital component to estimate is current taxes payable. The Final DCF Model estimates current taxes payable as 20 percent of the amount of the target's current tax liability. The current tax liability is calculated through a number of schedules, including the Financial Statement Tax Provision, Current and Deferred Taxes and Alternative Minimum Tax schedules.

22.54   Capital Expenditures and Depreciation

The Final DCF Model is designed to deal with both acquisition methods (New Cost Basis and No Change in Basis Acquisition Methods). If a New Cost Basis acquisition is to be modeled, the Final DCF Model allows the acquirer to allocate value among all the acquired depreciable assets and have the model compute appropriate book and tax depreciation. Alternatively, in a No Change in Basis acquisition, the Final DCF Model permits the acquirer to input estimated depreciation expenses for existing assets by asset category. All capital expenditures expected postclosing are input by asset category under both methods.

Exhibit 22–18 is the schedule for inputting recent historical and projected capital expenditures by asset category. The book life of each asset category can be defined on this schedule.

Exhibits 22–19, 22–20 and 22–21 contain book and tax depreciation rate assumptions for all asset categories. The rates appearing on these schedules should be adjusted as required to reflect the actual class lives of asset categories of the target company.

Chapter 6 describes the importance of depreciation as a deduction. To properly calculate depreciation deductions, a substantial number of support schedules are required. Depreciation calculations for book, regular tax, Alternative Minimum Tax and Adjusted Current Earnings purposes for all asset categories are calculated in Exhibits 22–41 through 22–55. The calculations on these pages are summarized in Exhibits 22–38 through 22–41.

In an effort to convey how the various depreciation related schedules work together, we will examine an example under the New Cost Basis and No Change in Basis assumptions. First, we will review the situation where a buyer is acquiring a company in an Asset Acquisition. In this instance, the acquirer allocates the total value of the acquired depreciable assets to various asset categories in the Capital Expenditure Assumptions schedule (Exhibit 22–18) in the column, in the middle of the page, labeled "Acquired Assets." In addition, the acquirer allocates the estimated capital expenditures during the projection period to the various asset categories. Exhibit 22–18 indicates that the acquirer has purchased a company that has 5-year production equipment valued at $25 million and expects to continue spending approximately $2 million a year on production equipment. The model incorporates the following assumptions: (1) for book purposes the production equipment will be written off over eight years, (2) for regular tax purposes it is 5-year MACRS property, (3) for *Alternative Minimum Taxable Income (AMTI)* and *Adjusted Current Earnings (ACE)* purposes the asset has a 9.5-year class life and the half-year convention applies. In the example, all detailed depreciation calculations are completed in Exhibits 22–44 and 22–45—Historical and Projected Book, Regular Tax, AMTI and ACE Depreciation—5-Year Property. These depreciation calculations are driven by the Book and Tax Depreciation Rate Assumptions appearing in Exhibit 22–19. The results of each depreciation calculation (e.g., book, regular tax, AMTI and ACE) are carried up to its applicable summary schedule (Exhibits 22–38, 22–39, 22–40 and 22–41). The depreciation totals on these schedules are used in applicable financial and tax schedules.

The other example involves a transaction structured as a No Change in Basis Acquisition (e.g., Stock Acquisition) where the target would have a carryover basis in its assets. In this instance, the fair market values of the assets at the date of acquisition would be input in Exhibit 22–18, Capital Expenditures Assumptions, in exactly the same way. In addition, the book depreciation calculations would work the same as in the prior example. However, because the Miscellaneous box on the Executive Summary page would have been changed to "No Change in Tax Basis," the tax calculations would be changed.

In a No Change in Basis Acquisition the best alternative for the acquirer is to obtain projections of regular tax, AMTI and ACE depreciation charges by asset category from the seller. The seller, in many cases, should be willing and able to provide these projections. Assuming these projections are obtained, the projections should be input in Exhibits 22–39, 22–40 and 22–41. Inputting these projections would override the calculations that would be completed if these projections were not available.

22.54a Estimating Forward Tax Depreciation in the Absence of Any Seller Forecast

If the seller is unable or unwilling to provide estimates of tax depreciation or if it is too early in the process to pursuade the seller to provide these estimates, in a situation where a No Change in Basis Acquisition is planned, the acquirer must estimate the projected depreciation charges for assets that the target owns as of the expected closing date. The Final DCF Model provides a mechanism for making these estimates.

The exhibits that permit the calculation of these projections include Exhibits 22–35 and 22–36. The acquirer inputs the target's historical capital expenditures by asset category back as far as the acquirer can obtain data, preferably back to 1981. Once these capital expenditures have been input, the model will automatically calculate the book, regular tax, AMTI and ACE depreciation amounts for these capital expenditures (see Exhibits 22–42 through 22–55). Whether the tax projections are reasonable depends on the outcome of comparing the calculated book value of net property, plant and equipment to the target's actual current net property, plant and equipment. This comparison appears in Exhibit 22–35. If the calculated amount approximates the actual amount, it is reasonable to use the projected tax depreciation figures that the model calculates. If the calculated net book value estimate differs widely from the actual value, then the acquirer needs to devise another method of estimating tax depreciation charges.

22.55   Current and Deferred Taxes

This schedule calculates the breakdown of the current tax provision between current taxes payable and deferred taxes. It accomplishes this by adjusting book earnings before taxes for both permanent and timing differences between book and taxable income. The resulting sum, reduced by any tax loss carryforward, is then subject to federal and state income taxes. The Alternative Minimum Tax, discussed in the following paragraph, is compared to the regular tax liability, and the target's net federal tax liability is calculated. The target's MTC Credit is also calculated.

The target's deferred tax amount is equal to the difference between the company's book tax provision and its current tax liability.

22.56   Alternative Minimum Tax

The Alternative Minimum Tax rules are discussed at length in paragraph B.10. This schedule puts the AMT rules into effect in the model. Note that the largest AMT adjustments tend to be the AMT depreciation adjustment and the ACE income adjustment.

EXHIBIT 22.13
08/28/92
05:48 PM

MARRIOTT CORPORATION
Discounted Cash Flow Analysis
Executive Summary

Page 1   FILE: GET_A

Sources and Uses of Funds

Uses

	Amount	Percent
Common Shares Outstanding	1,000	
Options Outstanding	0.00	
Average Exercise Price	$0.00	
Purchase Price per Share	$108,112.00	
# of Shares Purchased	100.00%	
Purchase Common Equity	$108,112	67.6%
Purchase Preferred Stock	0	0.0%
Existing Liabilities	49,388	30.9%
Transaction Expenses	2,500	1.6%
Obligations under Capitalized Leases	0	0.0%
Pre-Payment Penalty	0	0.0%
Tax on Sale of Asset (Tax Basis)	0	0.0%
Additional Working Capital Cash	0	0.0%
Total Uses	**$160,000**	**100.0%**

Sources

	Amount	Percent
Common Equity	$160,000	100.0%

Goodwill Calculation

Total Equity Purchase Price		$108,112
Adjustments to Book Value		
Plus: Non-Shareholder Equity	$33,564	
Plus: Deferred Income Taxes	0	
Less: Existing Goodwill	0	
Less: Existing Organizational Costs	0	
Less: Value Allocated to PP&E	39,900	
Less: Value Allocated to Intangibles	0	
Net Book Value		73,364
Total Goodwill Created		**$34,748**

Transaction Costs

Total Transaction Costs	$2,500
% of Total Consideration	1.6%

Amortization Periods

	Years
Goodwill Amortization	40
Intangible Asset Amortization	5
Amortization of Leased Property under Capital Leases	25

Miscellaneous

Fiscal Year	Years Ended December 31
First Historical Year	1989
Estimated Financial Statements Beginning	1993
Accounting Method ('Purchase' or 'Recap')	Purchase Acctng (1)
Acquire. Method ('New' or 'No Change in')	New Tax Basis(2)
Initial 'Stub' Period Length	12 months
% of Annual Sales Occurring in Stub Period	100.0%
'Initial' or 'Final' model	Final

FOOTNOTES:
(1) Model not applicable for a transaction involving pooling of Interests Accounting.
(2) Choice of method not applicable in Initial model.
(3) Net Cash Flow equals EBITDA less Cash Taxes less Capital Expenditures.

Net Present Value - Continuing Value Assumption

EBDIAT Multiple

Discount Rate	11.0	12.0	13.0	14.0	15.0	Residual Value as a Percent of NPV Maximum
10.0%	$189,519	$202,779	$216,040	$229,300	$242,560	77.0% 82.0%
11.0%	186,580	199,139	205,699	207,870	230,817	76.5% 81.6%
12.0%	172,146	184,668	195,969	208,293	219,772	76.0% 81.2%
13.0%	164,243	175,526	186,810	198,093	209,376	75.0% 80.6%
14.0%	136,377	147,479	178,132	189,182	199,386	74.0% 80.0%

P/E Multiple

	18.0	19.0	20.0	21.0	22.0	
10.0%	173,621	180,865	188,665	195,285	202,506	74.0% 78.0%
11.0%	165,323	172,364	179,202	186,661	193,860	74.5% 77.8%
12.0%	157,989	164,931	172,901	177,870	183,772	73.5% 77.1%
13.0%	150,718	156,862	164,862	167,150	175,294	72.5% 77.1%
14.0%	143,548	149,776	155,603	161,431	167,259	72.9% 76.7%

Growing Perpetuity Method - Growth Rate

	5.5%	6.0%	6.5%	7.0%	7.5%	
10.0%	124,777	131,432	139,191	145,669	159,289	65.0% 72.6%
11.0%	119,288	125,562	132,917	141,469	152,099	44.4% 72.1%
12.0%	114,057	120,031	127,001	135,237	145,131	65.2% 71.6%
13.0%	109,152	114,816	121,433	139,232	138,403	63.2% 71.5%
14.0%	104,323	109,995	116,102	123,569	132,457	63.0% 70.5%

Net Present Value - Sale Assumption

EBDIAT Multiple

Discount Rate	11.0	12.0	13.0	14.0	15.0	Residual Value as a Percent of NPV Minimum Maximum
10.0%	168,412	176,633	184,855	193,076	201,297	76.0% 80.0%
11.0%	160,488	168,375	176,162	183,949	191,737	75.5% 79.5%
12.0%	153,332	160,689	178,046	175,390	182,760	75.1% 79.3%
13.0%	146,528	153,778	160,984	167,229	175,245	74.7% 79.0%
14.0%	139,742	146,377	153,012	159,648	166,289	74.3% 78.0%

P/E Multiple

	18.0	19.0	20.0	21.0	22.0	
10.0%	152,384	159,404	166,424	173,444	180,464	74.1% 78.0%
11.0%	145,377	151,935	159,734	165,451	169,449	75.3% 78.7%
12.0%	137,897	145,315	152,413	156,431	159,331	72.9% 78.0%
13.0%	131,788	138,262	145,516	149,325	159,186	72.5% 78.0%
14.0%	131,766	139,401	139,001	144,627	149,646	72.0% 78.1%

Growing Perpetuity Method - Growth Rate

	5.5%	6.0%	6.5%	7.0%	7.5%	
10.0%	128,371	132,398	137,212	142,982	149,739	66.0% 79.0%
11.0%	122,569	126,477	131,937	135,426	142,899	65.6% 74.3%
12.0%	117,194	120,896	125,319	130,326	136,456	64.9% 74.6%
13.0%	112,162	115,938	119,971	129,355	131,483	64.3% 73.5%
14.0%	107,344	110,471	114,346	119,133	124,663	63.6% 73.1%

Internal Rates of Return - Continuing Value Assumption

EBDIAT Multiple Method

	11.0	12.0	13.0	14.0	15.0
Terminal EBDIAT Multiple	11.0	12.0	13.0	14.0	15.0
Common Equity	13.6%	15.0%	16.3%	17.6%	18.8%

P/E Multiple Method

	18.0	19.0	20.0	21.0	22.0
Terminal P/E Multiple	18.0	19.0	20.0	21.0	22.0
Common Equity	11.7%	12.6%	13.6%	14.6%	15.6%

Growing Perpetuity Method

	5.5%	6.0%	6.5%	7.0%	7.5%
Growth Rate	5.5%	6.0%	6.5%	7.0%	7.5%
Common Equity	4.7%	5.4%	6.3%	7.1%	8.1%

EBITDA Multiple Method

	13.0	14.0	15.0	16.0	17.0
Terminal EBITDA Multiple	13.0%	14.0%	15.3%	16.2%	17.1%
Common Equity					

Internal Rates of Return - Sale Assumption

EBDIAT Multiple Method

	11.0	12.0	13.0	14.0	15.0
Terminal EBDIAT Multiple	11.0	12.0	13.0	14.0	15.0
Common Equity	11.1%	12.0%	13.0%	14.0%	14.9%

P/E Multiple Method

	18.0	19.0	20.0	21.0	22.0
Terminal P/E Multiple	18.0	19.0	20.0	21.0	22.0
Common Equity	9.1%	10.0%	11.0%	11.9%	12.1%

EBITDA Multiple Method

	8.0	8.5	9.0	9.5	10.0
Terminal EBITDA Multiple	8.0	8.5	9.0	9.5	10.0
Common Equity	10.9%	11.9%	12.9%	13.9%	14.9%

Growing Perpetuity Method

	5.5%	6.0%	6.5%	7.0%	7.5%
Growth Rate	5.5%	6.0%	6.5%	7.0%	7.5%
Common Equity	5.9%	6.4%	6.4%	7.4%	8.4%

Purchase and Exit Multiples

EBDIAT Multiple Method Midpoint

	1992	1993	1994	Terminal
Sales	1.14	1.00		1.40
EBITDA	7.6	7.0	6.7	9.6
EBDIAT	12.1	11.2	10.2	14.4
EBIT	14.1	13.1	12.4	24.1
Net Cash Flow (3)	17.9	18.5	12.2	22.5
Net Income				

Page 2   FILE: SHT_D

MAREIGHT CORPORATION
Discounted Cash Flow Analysis
Tax, Transaction Cost, Acquisition Method and Cash Balance Assumptions

EXHIBIT 22-16
05/20/92
03:26 PM

Tax Assumptions

Federal Tax Rate	34.00%
State and Local Tax Rate	6.00%
Capital Gains Tax Rate	38.00%
Alternative Minimum Tax Rate	20.00%
Long-Term Federal Tax-Exempt Bond Rate	8.75%
Built-In Gains (Losses) Qualifier	25.00%
Book Income Adjustment Rate (Post-1989)	75.00%
AMT NOL Use Limitation	90.00%
Acquired Book NOL	$0
Acquired Tax NOL	$0
Acquired AMT NOL	$0
Acquired MTC Credit	$0

Transaction Cost Assumptions

Advisory & Underwriting Fees

Transaction Fees	$1,933	1.25%
Accounting/Legal & Printing/Miscellaneous	567	
Total Fees and Expenses	$2,500	1.62%

Amortization of Transaction Costs

Transaction	40	years
% related to financing	0%	
Accounting & Legal	40	year
% related to financing	0%	
Prepayment penalty	7	year

Acquisition Methods

Method Used: New Tax Basis Acquisition Method

New Tax Basis Acquisition Methods

1) Asset Acquisition
   A) Asset Acquisition
   B) Forward Merger
   C) Forward Subsidiary Merger
2) 338 Transaction
3) 338 (h)(10) Transaction

No Change in Tax Basis Acquisition Methods

1) Stock Acquisition
   A) Stock Acquisition
   B) Reverse Merger
   C) Reverse Subsidiary Merger
2) Type A Reorganization
   A) Type A Forward Merger
   B) Type A Statutory Consolidation
   C) Type A Forward Subsidiary Merger
   D) Type A Reverse Subsidiary Merger
3) Type B Reorganization
   A) Type B Stock Exchange
   B) Type B Subsidiary Stock Exchange
4) Type C Reorganization
   A) Type C Stock for Assets Exchange
   B) Type C Subsidiary Stock for Assets Exchange

Cash Balance Requirements

Minimum Cash Balance Requirements	$0

EXHIBIT 22.17

05/20/92
03:26 PM

HAREIGHT CORPORATION
Discounted Cash Flow Analysis
Economic and Operating Assumptions

Economic Assumptions

Year	Historical				Average	Projected						Average
	1989	1990	1991	1992	1989-92	1993	1994	1995	1996	1997	1998	1993-98
GNP Growth Rate	3.5%	1.7%	0.0%	1.0%	1.5%	2.0%	2.5%	3.0%	3.0%	3.0%	3.0%	2.8%
Inflation Rate	4.6%	4.7%	5.5%	3.9%	4.7%	3.0%	3.0%	3.0%	3.0%	3.0%	3.0%	3.0%
Prime Interest Rate	9.6%	10.3%	9.5%	8.0%	9.3%	7.5%	7.5%	7.5%	7.5%	7.5%	7.5%	7.5%
Long-Term Treasury Bond Interest Rate	9.1%	8.4%	8.6%	7.9%	8.5%	6.8%	6.8%	6.8%	6.8%	6.8%	6.8%	6.8%

Sales and Margin Assumptions
Years Ended December 31,

	Historical				Average	Projected						Average
	1989	1990	1991	1992	1989-92	1993	1994	1995	1996	1997	1998	1993-98
Total Sales	$107,417	$113,656	$122,940	$133,302		$143,300	$154,047	$165,601	$178,021	$191,372	$205,725	
Growth Rate		5.8%	8.2%	8.4%	7.5%	7.5%	7.5%	7.5%	7.5%	7.5%	7.5%	7.5%
Gross Margin %	35.1%	34.5%	34.2%	34.7%	34.6%	34.5%	34.5%	34.5%	34.5%	34.5%	34.5%	34.5%
SG&A %	19.0%	19.0%	19.0%	19.0%	19.0%	19.0%	19.0%	19.0%	19.0%	19.0%	19.0%	19.0%
EBITDA Margin %	16.1%	15.5%	15.2%	15.7%	15.6%	15.5%	15.5%	15.5%	15.5%	15.5%	15.5%	15.5%

Calculation of Components of Net Working Capital

	1989	1990	1991	1992	Average 1989-92	1993	1994	1995	1996	1997	1998	Average 1993-98
Accounts Receivable	$14,123	$15,083	$13,677	$14,732		$15,704	$16,882	$18,148	$19,509	$20,972	$22,545	
Days Sales Outstanding (365 days/yr)	48.0	48.4	40.6	40.3	40.5	40.0	40.0	40.0	40.0	40.0	40.0	40.0
Inventory	$24,344	$23,357	$27,075	$25,903		$28,443	$30,576	$32,869	$35,334	$37,984	$40,833	
Inventory Turnover	2.9	3.2	3.0	3.4	3.2	3.3	3.3	3.3	3.3	3.3	3.3	3.3
Other Current Assets	$5,211	$5,421	$4,369	$5,109		$5,015	$5,392	$5,796	$6,231	$6,698	$7,200	
% of Sales	4.9%	4.8%	3.6%	3.8%	3.7%	3.5%	3.5%	3.5%	3.5%	3.5%	3.5%	3.5%
Accounts Payable	$9,973	$9,555	$8,993	$7,475		$9,952	$10,699	$11,501	$12,364	$13,291	$14,288	
Days Payables Outstanding (365 days/yr)	40.4	36.3	31.5	24.3	27.9	30.0	30.0	30.0	30.0	30.0	30.0	30.0
Accrued Liabilities	$4,939	$5,627	$5,133	$5,421		$5,933	$6,378	$6,857	$7,371	$7,924	$8,518	
% of COGS and SG&A	5.5%	5.9%	4.9%	4.8%	4.9%	4.9%	4.9%	4.9%	4.9%	4.9%	4.9%	4.9%
Current Taxes Payable	$826	$1,436	$3,034	$1,333		$816	$665	$791	$1,051	$1,397	$1,617	
% of Current Taxes Payable	0.0%	0.0%	0.0%	25.2%	12.6%	20.0%	20.0%	20.0%	20.0%	20.0%	20.0%	20.0%
Net Working Capital	$27,940	$27,243	$27,961	$31,515		$32,461	$35,107	$37,664	$40,289	$43,043	$46,156	
% of Sales	26.0%	24.0%	22.7%	23.6%	23.2%	22.7%	22.8%	22.7%	22.6%	22.5%	22.4%	22.6%
Increase (Decrease)		($697)	$718	$3,554		($387)	$2,647	$2,557	$2,624	$2,754	$3,113	

MAREIGHT CORPORATION
Discounted Cash Flow Analysis
Capital Expenditure Assumptions

EXHIBIT 22.18
05/20/92
03:26 PM

Capital Expenditures and Acquired Property, Plant and Equipment by Category

Accounting Category	Book Class Life	Tax Life Category	Historical				Average 1988-91	Acquired PP&E	Projected					
			1989	1990	1991	1992			1993	1994	1995	1996	1997	1998
Land	NA	Land	$0	$0	$0	$0	$0	$8,000	$0	$0	$0	$0	$0	$0
Autos	5	3-Year (1)	0	0	0	0	0	6,765	650	675	700	725	750	775
Prod Eqp	8	5-Year (2)	0	0	0	0	0	25,000	2,000	1,800	2,100	2,500	2,250	2,400
Prod Eqp	12	7-Year (3)	0	0	0	0	0	15,000	1,888	2,444	2,842	2,838	3,784	4,084
Barges	15	10-Year (4)	0	0	0	0	0	0	0	0	0	0	0	0
Waste Facil.	20	15-Year (5)	0	0	0	0	0	12,000	500	500	550	550	550	600
Sewers	30	20-Year (6)	0	0	0	0	0	0	0	0	0	0	0	0
Real Estate	30	Real Est. (7)	0	0	0	0	0	18,000	2,700	2,900	2,750	3,000	3,000	3,250
Total Capital Expenditures			$0	$0	$0	$0		$84,765	$7,738	$8,319	$8,942	$9,613	$10,334	$11,109

Property, Plant and Equipment Acquired $84,765 (8)

(1) Includes autos.
(2) Includes trucks, computers, office equipment.
(3) Includes office furniture.
(4) Includes vessels, single purpose agricultural facilities.
(5) Includes telephone distribution facilities.
(6) Includes municipal sewers.
(7) Includes non-residential real property; does not include land.
(8) Must allocate acquired gross property, plant and equipment to various asset categories.

EXHIBIT 22.12
05/20/92
03:26 PM

MARRIOTT CORPORATION
Discounted Cash Flow Analysis
Book and Tax Depreciation Rate Assumptions

Autos

Accounting Description	Book Class Life	Tax Category	Year	Book Depr. %	Acq'd Assets Book Depr. %	ACRS Depr. %	MACRS Depr. % (1)	AMTI Depr. % (2)	ACE Depr. % (3)
Autos	5	3-Year	1	10.00%	20.00%	25.00%	33.33%	41.43%	14.29%
			2	20.00%	20.00%	38.00%	44.45%	33.57%	28.57%
			3	20.00%	20.00%	37.00%	14.81%	22.45%	28.57%
			4	20.00%	20.00%		7.41%	22.45%	28.57%
			5	20.00%	20.00%				
			6	10.00%					

(1) MACRS Depreciation Percentages - Half-Year Convention
(2) 150% Declining Balance with Switch to Straight Line - Assumes 3.5-yr class life and half-year convention.
(3) Straight Line Depreciation - Assumes 3.5-year class life and half-year convention

Prod Eqp (5-Year)

Accounting Description	Book Class Life	Tax Category	Year	Book Depr. %	Acq'd Assets Book Depr. %	ACRS Depr. %	MACRS Depr. % (1)	AMTI Depr. % (2)	ACE Depr. % (3)
Prod Eqp	8	5-Year	1	6.25%	12.50%	15.00%	20.00%	15.00%	5.26%
			2	12.50%	12.50%	22.00%	32.00%	25.50%	10.53%
			3	12.50%	12.50%	21.00%	19.20%	17.85%	10.53%
			4	12.50%	12.50%	21.00%	11.52%	16.66%	10.53%
			5	12.50%	12.50%	21.00%	11.52%	16.66%	10.53%
			6	12.50%	12.50%		5.76%	9.17%	10.53%
			7	12.50%	12.50%			9.17%	10.53%
			8	12.50%	12.50%			9.17%	10.53%
			9	6.25%				9.17%	10.53%
			10						10.53%

(1) MACRS Depreciation Percentages - Half-Year Convention
(2) 150% Declining Balance with Switch to Straight Line - Assumes 9.5-year class life and half-year convention.
(3) Straight Line Depreciation - Assumes 9.5-year class life and half-year convention

Prod Eqp (7-Year)

Accounting Description	Book Class Life	Tax Category	Year	Book Depr. %	Acq'd Assets Book Depr. %	ACRS Depr. %	MACRS Depr. % (1)	AMTI Depr. % (2)	ACE Depr. % (3)
Prod Eqp	12	7-Year	1	4.17%	8.33%	Not	14.29%	6.25%	4.17%
			2	8.33%	8.33%	Applic.	24.49%	11.72%	8.33%
			3	8.33%	8.33%		17.49%	10.94%	8.33%
			4	8.33%	8.33%		12.49%	8.97%	8.33%
			5	8.33%	8.33%		8.93%	7.65%	8.33%
			6	8.33%	8.33%		8.92%	7.33%	8.33%
			7	8.33%	8.33%		8.93%	7.33%	8.33%
			8	8.33%	8.33%		4.46%	7.33%	8.33%
			9	8.33%	8.33%			7.33%	8.33%
			10	8.33%				7.33%	8.33%
			11	8.33%				7.33%	8.33%
			12	8.33%				3.66%	8.33%
			13	4.17%					4.17%

(1) MACRS Depreciation Percentages - Half-Year Convention
(2) 150% Declining Balance with Switch to Straight Line - Assumes 12-yr class life and half-year convention.
(3) Straight Line Depreciation - Assumes 12-year class life and half-year convention

Barges

Accounting Description	Book Class Life	Tax Category	Year	Book Depr. %	Acq'd Assets Book Depr. %	ACRS Depr. %	MACRS Depr. % (1)	AMTI Depr. % (2)	ACE Depr. % (3)
Barges	15	10-Year	1	3.33%	6.67%	6.00%	10.00%	4.29%	2.86%
			2	6.67%	6.67%	10.00%	18.00%	7.50%	5.71%
			3	6.67%	6.67%	12.00%	14.40%	6.83%	5.71%
			4	6.67%	6.67%	10.00%	11.52%	6.23%	5.71%
			5	6.67%	6.67%	10.00%	9.22%	6.27%	5.71%
			6	6.67%	6.67%	10.00%	7.37%	5.71%	5.71%
			7	6.67%	6.67%	9.00%	6.55%	5.71%	5.71%
			8	6.67%	6.67%	9.00%	6.55%	5.71%	5.71%
			9	6.67%	6.67%	9.00%	6.56%	5.71%	5.71%
			10	6.67%			6.55%	5.71%	5.71%
			11	6.67%			3.28%	5.71%	5.71%
			12	6.67%				5.71%	5.71%
			13	6.67%				5.71%	5.71%
			14	6.67%				5.71%	5.71%
			15	6.67%				5.71%	5.71%
			16	3.33%					5.71%

(1) MACRS Depreciation Percentages - Half-Year Convention
(2) 150% Declining Balance with Switch to Straight Line - Assumes 17.5-yr class life and half-year convention.
(3) Straight Line Depreciation - Assumes 17.5-year class life and half-year convention

Waste Fac

Accounting Description	Book Class Life	Tax Category	Year	Book Depr. %	Acq'd Assets Book Depr. %	ACRS Depr. %	MACRS Depr. % (1)	AMTI Depr. % (2)	ACE Depr. % (3)
Waste Fac	20	15-Year	1	2.50%	5.00%	5.00%	5.00%	3.57%	2.38%
			2	5.00%	5.00%	10.00%	9.50%	6.88%	4.76%
			3	5.00%	5.00%	9.00%	8.55%	6.39%	4.76%
			4	5.00%	5.00%	8.00%	7.70%	5.93%	4.76%
			5	5.00%	5.00%	7.00%	6.93%	5.52%	4.76%
			6	5.00%	5.00%	7.00%	6.23%	5.13%	4.76%
			7	5.00%	5.00%	6.00%	5.90%	4.75%	4.76%
			8	5.00%	5.00%	6.00%	5.90%	4.75%	4.76%
			9	5.00%	5.00%	6.00%	5.91%	4.75%	4.76%
			10	5.00%		6.00%	5.90%	4.75%	4.76%
			11	5.00%		6.00%	5.91%	4.75%	4.76%
			12	5.00%			5.90%	4.75%	4.76%
			13	5.00%			5.91%	4.75%	4.76%
			14	5.00%			5.90%	4.75%	4.76%
			15	5.00%			5.91%	4.75%	4.76%
			16	5.00%			2.95%	4.75%	4.76%
			17	5.00%				4.75%	4.76%
			18	5.00%				4.75%	4.76%
			19	5.00%				4.75%	4.76%
			20	5.00%				4.75%	4.76%
			21	2.50%				4.75%	4.76%
			22					2.38%	2.38%

(1) MACRS Depreciation Percentages - Half-Year Convention
(2) 150% Declining Balance with Switch to Straight Line - Assumes 21-yr class life and half-year convention.
(3) Straight Line Depreciation - Assumes 21-year class life and half-year convention

NOTE: Review IRS Publication 534 on Depreciation to determine if class life assumptions are correct.
Change from half-year convention to mid-quarter convention if more than 40% of property is placed in service during the last 3 months of the year.

299

MARRIOTT CORPORATION
Discounted Cash Flow Analysis
Book and Tax Depreciation Rate Assumptions (continued)

EXHIBIT 22.20
05/20/92
03:26 PM

Account-ing Descrip-tion	Book Class Life	Tax Category	Year	Book Depr. %	Acq'd Assets Book Depr. %	Regular Tax ACRS Depr. %	MACRS Depr. % (1)	AMTI Depr. % (2)	ACE Depr. % (3)
Sewers	30	20-Year	1	1.67%	3.33%	Not Applic.	3.750%	2.113%	1.408%
			2	3.33%	3.33%		7.219%	4.136%	2.817%
			3	3.33%	3.33%		6.677%	3.961%	2.817%
			4	3.33%	3.33%		6.177%	3.794%	2.817%
			5	3.33%	3.33%		5.713%	3.634%	2.817%
			6	3.33%	3.33%		5.285%	3.480%	2.817%
			7	3.33%	3.33%		4.888%	3.333%	2.817%
			8	3.33%	3.33%		4.522%	3.192%	2.817%
			9	3.33%	3.33%		4.462%	3.057%	2.817%
			10	3.33%	3.33%		4.461%	2.928%	2.817%
			11	3.33%	3.33%		4.462%	2.804%	2.817%
			12	3.33%	3.33%		4.461%	2.686%	2.817%
			13	3.33%	3.33%		4.462%	2.572%	2.817%
			14	3.33%	3.33%		4.461%	2.535%	2.817%
			15	3.33%	3.33%		4.462%	2.535%	2.817%
			16	3.33%	3.33%		4.461%	2.535%	2.817%
			17	3.33%	3.33%		4.462%	2.535%	2.817%
			18	3.33%	3.33%		4.461%	2.535%	2.817%
			19	3.33%	3.33%		4.462%	2.535%	2.817%
			20	3.33%	3.33%		4.461%	2.535%	2.817%
			21	3.33%	3.33%		2.231%	2.535%	2.817%
			22	3.33%	3.33%			2.535%	2.817%
			23	3.33%	3.33%			2.535%	2.817%
			24	3.33%	3.33%			2.535%	2.817%
			25	3.33%	3.33%			2.535%	2.817%
			26	3.33%	3.33%			2.535%	2.817%
			27	3.33%	3.33%			2.536%	2.817%
			28	3.33%	3.33%			2.535%	2.817%
			29	3.33%	3.33%			2.536%	2.817%
			30	3.33%	3.33%			2.535%	2.817%
			31	1.67%	---			2.536%	2.817%
			32		---			2.535%	2.817%
			33		---			2.536%	2.817%
			34		---			2.535%	2.817%
			35		---			2.536%	2.817%
			36		---			2.535%	2.817%

(1) MACRS Depreciation Percentages - Half-Year Convention
(2) 150% Declining Balance with Switch to Straight Line - Assumes 35.5-yr class life and half-year convention.
(3) Straight Line Depreciation - Assumes 35.5-year class life and half-year convention.

NOTES: Review IRS Publication 534 on Depreciation to determine if class life assumptions are change from half-year convention to mid-quarter convention if more than 40% of proper during the last 3 months of the year.

MARRIOTT CORPORATION
Discounted Cash Flow Analysis
Book and Tax Depreciation Rate Assumptions (continued)

EXHIBIT 11.11
05/20/92
03:26 PM

Account-ing Descrip-tion	Book Class Life	Tax Category	Year	Actual Applicable Dates Acq'd Assets Book Depr. %	Assumed Applicable Years — Regular Tax			Acquired Assets			New Capital Expenditures		
					1/1/81– 3/15/84 15-Yr ACRS Depr. % (1)	3/15/84– 5/8/85 18-Yr ACRS Depr. % (1)	5/8/85–12/31/86 1984 / 1985-86 19-Yr ACRS Depr. % (1)	MACRS Depr. % (2)	AMTI Depr. % (3)	ACE Depr. % (3)	MACRS Depr. % (2)(4)	AMTI Depr. % (5)	ACE Depr. % (5)
Real Estate	30	15-Year ACRS	1	1.67%	12.00%	10.00%	8.80%	3.042%	2.39%	2.39%	1.720%	1.25%	1.25%
		18-Year ACRS	2	3.33%	10.00%	9.00%	8.40%	3.175%	2.50%	2.50%	3.175%	2.50%	2.50%
		19-Year ACRS	3	3.33%	9.00%	8.00%	7.60%	3.175%	2.50%	2.50%	3.175%	2.50%	2.50%
		ACRS	4	3.33%	8.00%	7.00%	6.90%	3.175%	2.50%	2.50%	3.175%	2.50%	2.50%
			5	3.33%	7.00%	6.00%	6.30%	3.175%	2.50%	2.50%	3.175%	2.50%	2.50%
		31.5-Year MACRS	6	3.33%	6.00%	5.70%	5.70%	3.175%	2.50%	2.50%	3.175%	2.50%	2.50%
			7	3.33%	6.00%	5.20%	5.20%	3.175%	2.50%	2.50%	3.174%	2.50%	2.50%
			8	3.33%	6.00%	4.70%	4.70%	3.174%	2.50%	2.50%	3.175%	2.50%	2.50%
			9	3.33%	6.00%	4.20%	4.20%	3.175%	2.50%	2.50%	3.174%	2.50%	2.50%
			10	3.33%	5.00%	4.20%	4.20%	3.174%	2.50%	2.50%	3.175%	2.50%	2.50%
			11	3.33%	5.00%	4.20%	4.20%	3.175%	2.50%	2.50%	3.174%	2.50%	2.50%
			12	3.33%	5.00%	4.00%	4.20%	3.174%	2.50%	2.50%	3.175%	2.50%	2.50%
			13	3.33%	5.00%	4.00%	4.20%	3.175%	2.50%	2.50%	3.174%	2.50%	2.50%
			14	3.33%	5.00%	4.00%	4.20%	3.174%	2.50%	2.50%	3.175%	2.50%	2.50%
			15	3.33%	5.00%	4.00%	4.20%	3.175%	2.50%	2.50%	3.174%	2.50%	2.50%
			16	3.33%		4.00%	4.20%	3.174%	2.50%	2.50%	3.175%	2.50%	2.50%
			17	3.33%		4.00%	4.20%	3.175%	2.50%	2.50%	3.174%	2.50%	2.50%
			18	3.33%		4.00%	4.20%	3.174%	2.50%	2.50%	3.175%	2.50%	2.50%
			19	3.33%			4.20%	3.175%	2.50%	2.50%	3.174%	2.50%	2.50%
			20	3.33%			4.20%	3.174%	2.50%	2.50%	3.175%	2.50%	2.50%
			21	3.33%			0.20%	3.175%	2.50%	2.50%	3.174%	2.50%	2.50%
			22	3.33%				3.174%	2.50%	2.50%	3.175%	2.50%	2.50%
			23	3.33%				3.175%	2.50%	2.50%	3.174%	2.50%	2.50%
			24	3.33%				3.174%	2.50%	2.50%	3.175%	2.50%	2.50%
			25	3.33%				3.175%	2.50%	2.50%	3.174%	2.50%	2.50%
			26	3.33%				3.174%	2.50%	2.50%	3.175%	2.50%	2.50%
			27	3.33%				3.175%	2.50%	2.50%	3.174%	2.50%	2.50%
			28	3.33%				3.174%	2.50%	2.50%	3.175%	2.50%	2.50%
			29	3.33%				3.175%	2.50%	2.50%	3.174%	2.50%	2.50%
			30	3.33%				3.174%	2.50%	2.50%	3.175%	2.50%	2.50%
			31	1.67%				1.720%	2.50%	2.50%	3.042%	2.50%	2.50%
			32						2.50%	2.50%		2.50%	2.50%
			33						2.50%	2.50%		2.50%	2.50%
			34						2.50%	2.50%		2.50%	2.50%
			35						2.50%	2.50%		2.50%	2.50%
			36						2.50%	2.50%		2.50%	2.50%
			37						2.50%	2.50%		2.50%	2.50%
			38						2.50%	2.50%		2.50%	2.50%
			39						2.50%	2.50%		2.50%	2.50%
			40						2.50%	2.50%		2.50%	2.50%
			41						0.11%	0.11%		1.25%	1.25%

(1) ACRS Depreciation Percentages – Assumes property placed in service in the first month of the year.
(2) MACRS Depreciation Percentages – Assumes property placed in service in middle of first month of the year.
(3) Straight Line Depreciation – Assumes 40-year class life and property placed in service in middle of first month of the year.
(4) MACRS Depreciation Percentages – Assumes property placed in service in middle of 6th month of the year.
(5) Straight Line Depreciation – Assumes 40-year class life and half-year convention.

NOTES: Review IRS Publication 534 on Depreciation to determine if class life assumptions are correct.
Change from half-year convention to mid-quarter convention if more than 40% of property is placed in service during the l...

EXHIBIT 22.22

05/20/92
03:26 PM

MAREIGHT CORPORATION
Discounted Cash Flow Analysis
Income Statements

Years Ended December 31,	Historical				Average	Projected						Average
	1989	1990	1991	1992	1989-92	1993	1994	1995	1996	1997	1998	1993-98
Net Sales	$107,417	$113,656	$122,940	$133,302		$143,300	$154,047	$165,601	$178,021	$191,372	$205,725	
Sales Growth %		5.8%	8.2%	8.4%	7.5%	7.5%	7.5%	7.5%	7.5%	7.5%	7.5%	7.5%
Cost of Goods Sold	$69,714	$74,445	$80,895	$87,046		$93,861	$100,901	$108,468	$116,604	$125,349	$134,750	
Gross Profit	37,703	39,211	42,045	46,256		49,438	53,146	57,132	61,417	66,023	70,975	
Gross Margin %	35.1%	34.5%	34.2%	34.7%	34.6%	34.5%	34.5%	34.5%	34.5%	34.5%	34.5%	34.5%
Selling, General & Admin. Expenses	$20,409	$21,595	$23,359	$25,327		$27,227	$29,269	$31,464	$33,824	$36,361	$39,088	
ESOP Contribution	0	0	0	0		0	0	0	0	0	0	
EBITDA	17,294	17,616	18,686	20,929		22,211	23,877	25,668	27,593	29,663	31,887	
EBITDA Margin %	16.1%	15.5%	15.2%	15.7%	15.6%	15.5%	15.5%	15.5%	15.5%	15.5%	15.5%	15.5%
Depreciation	5,435	6,297	6,777	7,022		7,254	7,923	8,645	9,435	10,283	9,769	
Amortization of Goodwill	0	0	0	0		869	869	869	869	869	869	
Amortization of Transaction Costs	0	0	0	0		63	63	63	63	63	63	
Amortization of Intangibles	0	0	0	0		0	0	0	0	0	0	
Total Depreciation & Amortization	5,435	6,297	6,777	7,022		8,185	8,854	9,576	10,366	11,214	10,700	
EBIT	11,859	11,319	11,909	13,907		14,026	15,023	16,092	17,227	18,449	21,188	
EBIT Margin %	11.0%	10.0%	9.7%	10.4%	10.3%	9.8%	9.8%	9.7%	9.7%	9.6%	10.3%	9.8%
Other Expenses (Income)				0		0	0	0	0	0	0	
Earnings Before Taxes				13,907		14,026	15,023	16,092	17,227	18,449	21,188	
Provision for Taxes												
Current				5,285		4,080	3,326	3,954	5,254	6,986	8,085	
Deferred				0		1,597	2,730	2,508	1,639	370	312	
Total Tax Provision				5,285		5,678	6,056	6,462	6,893	7,357	8,396	
Net Income Before Extraordinary Item & Minority Interest				8,622		8,348	8,967	9,630	10,334	11,092	12,791	
Minority Interest				0		0	0	0	0	0	0	
Extraordinary Item (After-Tax)				0		0	0	0	0	0	0	
Net Income to Common				$8,622		$8,348	$8,967	$9,630	$10,334	$11,092	$12,791	

EXHIBIT 22-23

05/20/92
03:26 PM

Page 9   FILE: SHT_G

MARRIGHT CORPORATION
Discounted Cash Flow Analysis
Balance Sheets

Years Ended December 31,	Historical 1989	1990	1991	1992	Closing Date Bal. Sheet	Adjustments DEBITS	Adjustments CREDITS	Beginning Bal. Sheet	1993	1994	1995	1996	1997	1998
Current Assets														
Cash & Cash Equivalents	$3,313	$3,288	$1,111	$2,856	$2,856	$0	$1,333	$1,523	$12,303	$21,890	$32,104	$42,206	$51,794	$61,374
Accounts Receivable (Net)	14,123	15,083	13,677	14,732	14,732	0	0	$14,732	15,704	16,882	18,148	19,509	20,972	22,545
Inventory	24,344	23,357	27,075	25,903	25,903	0	0	$25,903	28,443	30,576	32,869	35,334	37,984	40,833
Other Current Assets	5,211	5,421	4,369	5,109	5,109	0	0	$5,109	5,015	5,392	5,796	6,231	6,698	7,200
Total Current Assets	46,991	47,149	46,232	48,600	48,600	0	1,333	47,267	61,466	74,739	88,917	103,280	117,449	131,953
Gross Property, Plant & Equipment	43,378	45,001	45,965	44,965	44,965	39,800	0	$84,765	92,503	100,822	109,764	119,377	129,711	140,821
Less: Accumulated Depreciation	0	0	0	0	0	0	0	$0	(7,254)	(15,177)	(23,822)	(33,257)	(43,540)	(53,308)
Net Property, Plant & Equipment	43,378	45,001	45,965	44,965	44,965	39,800	0	84,765	85,249	85,645	85,942	86,120	86,172	87,512
Leased Property Under Capital Leases	0	0	0	0	0	0	0	0	0	0	0	0	0	0
Goodwill	0	0	0	0	0	34,748	0	34,748	33,879	33,011	32,142	31,273	30,405	29,536
Other Intangible Assets	0	0	0	0	0	0	0	0	0	0	0	0	0	0
Other Assets	3,141	3,289	2,704	3,616	3,616	0	0	3,616	3,616	3,616	3,616	3,616	3,616	3,616
Organizational Costs	0	0	0	0	0	2,500	0	2,500	2,438	2,375	2,313	2,250	2,188	2,125
Total Assets	$93,510	$95,439	$94,901	$97,181	$97,181	$77,048	$1,333	$172,896	$186,648	$199,385	$212,930	$226,539	$239,828	$254,742
Current Liabilities														
Current Portion of LT Debt	$0	$0	$0	$0	$0	$0	$0	$0	9,952	10,699	11,501	12,364	13,291	14,288
Accounts Payable	9,973	9,555	8,993	7,475	$7,475	0	0	7,475	5,933	6,378	6,857	7,371	7,924	8,518
Accrued Liabilities	4,939	5,627	5,133	5,421	$5,421	0	0	5,421	816	665	791	1,051	1,397	1,617
Current Taxes Payable	826	1,436	3,034	1,333	$1,333	1,333	0	0						
Total Current Liabilities	15,738	16,618	17,160	14,229	14,229	1,333	0	12,896	16,702	17,742	19,149	20,786	22,612	24,423
Long-Term Liabilities	48,777	50,241	46,772	49,388	49,388	49,388	0	0	0	0	0	0	0	0
Obligations under Capitalized Leases	0	0	0	0	0	0	0	0	0	0	0	0	0	0
Deferred Income Taxes	0	0	0	0	0	0	0	0	1,597	4,328	6,836	8,474	8,845	9,156
Minority Interest	0	0	0	0	0	0	0	0	0	0	0	0	0	0
Preferred Stock	0	0	0	0	0	0	0	0	0	0	0	0	0	0
Common Stock	1,000	1,000	1,000	1,000	1,000	1,000	160,000	160,000	160,000	160,000	160,000	160,000	160,000	160,000
Retained Earnings	27,995	27,580	29,969	32,564	32,564	32,564	0	8,348	17,315	26,945	37,279	48,371	61,163
Common shareholders' Equity	28,995	28,580	30,969	33,564	33,564	33,564	160,000	160,000	168,348	177,315	186,945	197,279	208,372	221,163
Total Liabilities & Equity	$93,510	$95,439	$94,901	$97,181	$97,181	$161,333	$161,333	$172,896	$186,648	$199,385	$212,930	$226,539	$239,828	$254,742

EXHIBIT 22.24

05/20/92
03:26 PM

MAREIGHT CORPORATION
Discounted Cash Flow Analysis
Statements of Changes in Financial Position

Years Ended December 31,	1993	1994	1995	1996	1997	1998
Sources of Cash						
Net Income to Common	$8,348	$8,967	$9,630	$10,334	$11,092	$12,791
Book Depreciation	7,254	7,923	8,645	9,435	10,283	9,769
Amortization of Intangibles	0	0	0	0	0	0
Deferred Tax	1,597	2,730	2,508	1,639	370	312
Amort. of Leased Prop. under Capitalized Leases	0	0	0	0	0	0
Amortization of Goodwill & Fees	931	931	931	931	931	931
Total Sources	18,131	$20,551	$21,714	$22,339	$22,676	$23,803
Uses of Cash						
Increase (Decrease) in Working Capital	(387)	$2,647	$2,557	$2,624	$2,754	$3,113
Capital Expenditures	7,738	8,319	8,942	9,613	10,334	11,109
Total Uses	7,351	$10,965	$11,500	$12,237	$13,088	$14,223
Net Cash Flow	$10,780	$9,586	$10,214	$10,102	$9,588	$9,580

MAREIGHT CORPORATION
Discounted Cash Flow Analysis
Calculation of Residual Values

EXHIBIT 22.25
05/20/92
03:26 PM

Residual Value Calculations - EBDIAT Multiple Method

EBDIAT Multiple	11.0	12.0	13.0	14.0	15.0
1998 EBDIAT	$23,491	$23,491	$23,491	$23,491	$23,491
Residual Value (Continuing Value)	258,402	281,893	305,384	328,876	352,367
Gross Residual Value	258,402	281,893	305,384	328,876	352,367
Tax Basis	160,000	160,000	160,000	160,000	160,000
Gain (Loss) on Sale	98,402	121,893	145,384	168,876	192,367
Capital Gains Tax Rate	38.0%	38.0%	38.0%	38.0%	38.0%
Tax on Sale	37,393	46,319	55,246	64,173	73,099
Gross Residual Value	258,402	281,893	305,384	328,876	352,367
Taxes on Sale	37,393	46,319	55,246	64,173	73,099
Residual Value (Sale Assumption)	$221,009	$235,574	$250,138	$264,703	$279,267

Residual Value Calculations - Growing Perpetuity Method

1999 Estimated After-tax Cash Flow	$10,059	$10,107	$10,155	$10,203	$10,251
WACC less Growth Rate	7.0%	6.5%	6.0%	5.5%	5.0%
Residual Value (Continuing Value)	143,705	155,496	169,253	185,510	205,019
Gross Residual Value	143,705	155,496	169,253	185,510	205,019
Tax Basis	160,000	160,000	160,000	160,000	160,000
Gain (Loss) on Sale	(16,295)	(4,504)	9,253	25,510	45,019
Capital Gains Tax Rate	38.0%	38.0%	38.0%	38.0%	38.0%
Tax on Sale	(6,192)	(1,711)	3,516	9,694	17,107
Gross Residual Value	143,705	155,496	169,253	185,510	205,019
Taxes on Sale	(6,192)	(1,711)	3,516	9,694	17,107
Residual Value (Sale Assumption)	$149,897	$157,208	$165,737	$175,816	$187,912

Residual Value Calculations - P/E Multiple Method

P/E Multiple	18.0	19.0	20.0	21.0	22.0
1998 Net Income	$12,791	$12,791	$12,791	$12,791	$12,791
Residual Value (Continuing Value)	230,243	243,035	255,826	268,617	281,408
Gross Residual Value	230,243	243,035	255,826	268,617	281,408
Tax Basis	160,000	160,000	160,000	160,000	160,000
Gain (Loss) on Sale	70,243	83,034	95,826	108,617	121,408
Capital Gains Tax Rate	38.0%	38.0%	38.0%	38.0%	38.0%
Tax on Sale	26,692	31,553	36,414	41,274	46,135
Gross Residual Value	230,243	243,035	255,826	268,617	281,408
Taxes on Sale	26,692	31,553	36,414	41,274	46,135
Residual Value (Sale Assumption)	$203,551	$211,481	$219,412	$227,343	$235,273

Value Calculations - EBITDA Multiple Method

EBITDA Multiple	8.0	8.5	9.0	9.5	10.0
1998 EBITDA	$31,887	$31,887	$31,887	$31,887	$31,887
Residual Value (Continuing Value)	255,099	271,043	286,987	302,930	318,874
Gross Residual Value	255,099	271,043	286,987	302,930	318,874
Tax Basis	160,000	160,000	160,000	160,000	160,000
Gain (Loss) on Sale	95,099	111,043	126,987	142,930	158,874
Capital Gains Tax Rate	38.0%	38.0%	38.0%	38.0%	38.0%
Tax on Sale	36,138	42,196	48,255	54,314	60,372
Gross Residual Value	255,099	271,043	286,987	302,930	318,874
Taxes on Sale	36,138	42,196	48,255	54,314	60,372
Residual Value (Sale Assumption)	$218,962	$228,847	$238,732	$248,617	$258,502

Page 12   FILE: NPV1

MAREIGHT CORPORATION
Discounted Cash Flow Analysis
NPV Calculations - EBDIAT Multiple Method

EXHIBIT 22.26
05/20/92
03:26 PM

NPV Calculations - Continuing Value Assumption

EBDIAT Multiple Method	1993	1994	1995	1996	1997	1998	1999	NPV	Residual Value as % of NPV
After-tax Cash Flow	$10,780	$9,586	$10,214	$10,102	$9,588	$9,580			
Residual Value									
11.0 x EBDIAT Multiple							258,402		
12.0 x EBDIAT Multiple							281,893		
13.0 x EBDIAT Multiple							305,384		
14.0 x EBDIAT Multiple							328,876		
15.0 x EBDIAT Multiple							352,367		
10.0% Discount Rate	0.9091	0.8264	0.7513	0.6830	0.6209	0.5645	0.5132		
11.0 x EBDIAT Multiple	9,800	7,922	7,674	6,900	5,954			189,519	77.0%
12.0 x EBDIAT Multiple	9,800	7,922	7,674	6,900	5,954			202,779	78.5%
13.0 x EBDIAT Multiple	9,800	7,922	7,674	6,900	5,954			216,040	79.8%
14.0 x EBDIAT Multiple	9,800	7,922	7,674	6,900	5,954			229,300	81.0%
15.0 x EBDIAT Multiple	9,800	7,922	7,674	6,900	5,954			242,560	82.0%
11.0% Discount Rate	0.9009	0.8116	0.7312	0.6587	0.5935	0.5346	0.4817		
11.0 x EBDIAT Multiple	9,712	7,780	7,469	6,654	5,690			180,580	76.5%
12.0 x EBDIAT Multiple	9,712	7,780	7,469	6,654	5,690			193,139	78.0%
13.0 x EBDIAT Multiple	9,712	7,780	7,469	6,654	5,690			205,699	79.4%
14.0 x EBDIAT Multiple	9,712	7,780	7,469	6,654	5,690			218,258	80.6%
15.0 x EBDIAT Multiple	9,712	7,780	7,469	6,654	5,690			230,817	81.6%
12.0% Discount Rate	0.8929	0.7972	0.7118	0.6355	0.5674	0.5066	0.4523		
11.0 x EBDIAT Multiple	9,625	7,642	7,270	6,420	5,441			172,166	76.0%
12.0 x EBDIAT Multiple	9,625	7,642	7,270	6,420	5,441			184,068	77.6%
13.0 x EBDIAT Multiple	9,625	7,642	7,270	6,420	5,441			195,969	78.9%
14.0 x EBDIAT Multiple	9,625	7,642	7,270	6,420	5,441			207,870	80.2%
15.0 x EBDIAT Multiple	9,625	7,642	7,270	6,420	5,441			219,772	81.2%
13.0% Discount Rate	0.8850	0.7831	0.6931	0.6133	0.5428	0.4803	0.4251		
11.0 x EBDIAT Multiple	9,540	7,507	7,079	6,196	5,204			164,243	75.6%
12.0 x EBDIAT Multiple	9,540	7,507	7,079	6,196	5,204			175,526	77.1%
13.0 x EBDIAT Multiple	9,540	7,507	7,079	6,196	5,204			186,810	78.5%
14.0 x EBDIAT Multiple	9,540	7,507	7,079	6,196	5,204			198,093	79.7%
15.0 x EBDIAT Multiple	9,540	7,507	7,079	6,196	5,204			209,376	80.8%
14.0% Discount Rate	0.8772	0.7695	0.6750	0.5921	0.5194	0.4556	0.3996		
11.0 x EBDIAT Multiple	9,457	7,376	6,894	5,981	4,980			156,777	75.1%
12.0 x EBDIAT Multiple	9,457	7,376	6,894	5,981	4,980			167,479	76.7%
13.0 x EBDIAT Multiple	9,457	7,376	6,894	5,981	4,980			178,182	78.1%
14.0 x EBDIAT Multiple	9,457	7,376	6,894	5,981	4,980			188,884	79.3%
15.0 x EBDIAT Multiple	9,457	7,376	6,894	5,981	4,980			199,586	80.4%

NPV Calculations - Sale Assumption

EBDIAT Multiple Method	1993	1994	1995	1996	1997	1998	1999	NPV	Residual Value as % of NPV
After-tax Cash Flow	$10,780	$9,586	$10,214	$10,102	$9,588	$9,580			
Residual Value									
11.0 x EBDIAT Multiple							221,009		
12.0 x EBDIAT Multiple							235,574		
13.0 x EBDIAT Multiple							250,138		
14.0 x EBDIAT Multiple							264,703		
15.0 x EBDIAT Multiple							279,267		
10.0% Discount Rate	0.9091	0.8264	0.7513	0.6830	0.6209	0.5645	0.5132		
11.0 x EBDIAT Multiple	9,800	7,922	7,674	6,900	5,954			168,412	74.1%
12.0 x EBDIAT Multiple	9,800	7,922	7,674	6,900	5,954			176,633	75.3%
13.0 x EBDIAT Multiple	9,800	7,922	7,674	6,900	5,954			184,855	76.4%
14.0 x EBDIAT Multiple	9,800	7,922	7,674	6,900	5,954			193,076	77.4%
15.0 x EBDIAT Multiple	9,800	7,922	7,674	6,900	5,954			201,297	78.3%
11.0% Discount Rate	0.9009	0.8116	0.7312	0.6587	0.5935	0.5346	0.4817		
11.0 x EBDIAT Multiple	9,712	7,780	7,469	6,654	5,690			160,588	73.6%
12.0 x EBDIAT Multiple	9,712	7,780	7,469	6,654	5,690			168,375	74.8%
13.0 x EBDIAT Multiple	9,712	7,780	7,469	6,654	5,690			176,162	75.9%
14.0 x EBDIAT Multiple	9,712	7,780	7,469	6,654	5,690			183,949	76.9%
15.0 x EBDIAT Multiple	9,712	7,780	7,469	6,654	5,690			191,735	77.9%
12.0% Discount Rate	0.8929	0.7972	0.7118	0.6355	0.5674	0.5066	0.4523		
11.0 x EBDIAT Multiple	9,625	7,642	7,270	6,420	5,441			153,222	73.1%
12.0 x EBDIAT Multiple	9,625	7,642	7,270	6,420	5,441			160,601	74.3%
13.0 x EBDIAT Multiple	9,625	7,642	7,270	6,420	5,441			167,980	75.4%
14.0 x EBDIAT Multiple	9,625	7,642	7,270	6,420	5,441			175,359	76.5%
15.0 x EBDIAT Multiple	9,625	7,642	7,270	6,420	5,441			182,737	77.4%
13.0% Discount Rate	0.8850	0.7831	0.6931	0.6133	0.5428	0.4803	0.4251		
11.0 x EBDIAT Multiple	9,540	7,507	7,079	6,196	5,204			146,283	72.6%
12.0 x EBDIAT Multiple	9,540	7,507	7,079	6,196	5,204			153,298	73.8%
13.0 x EBDIAT Multiple	9,540	7,507	7,079	6,196	5,204			160,274	75.0%
14.0 x EBDIAT Multiple	9,540	7,507	7,079	6,196	5,204			167,270	76.0%
15.0 x EBDIAT Multiple	9,540	7,507	7,079	6,196	5,204			174,265	77.0%
14.0% Discount Rate	0.8772	0.7695	0.6750	0.5921	0.5194	0.4556	0.3996		
11.0 x EBDIAT Multiple	9,457	7,376	6,894	5,981	4,980			139,742	72.1%
12.0 x EBDIAT Multiple	9,457	7,376	6,894	5,981	4,980			146,377	73.3%
13.0 x EBDIAT Multiple	9,457	7,376	6,894	5,981	4,980			153,012	74.5%
14.0 x EBDIAT Multiple	9,457	7,376	6,894	5,981	4,980			159,648	75.5%
15.0 x EBDIAT Multiple	9,457	7,376	6,894	5,981	4,980			166,283	76.5%

MAREIGHT CORPORATION
Discounted Cash Flow Analysis
NPV Calculations - P/E Multiple Method

EXHIBIT 22.27
05/20/92
03:26 PM

NPV Calculations - Continuing Value Assumption

P/E Multiple Method	1993	1994	1995	1996	1997	1998	1999	NPV	Residual Value as % of NPV
After-tax Cash Flow	$10,780	$9,586	$10,214	$10,102	$9,588	$9,580			
Residual Value						$9,580			
18.0 x P/E Multiple						230,243			
19.0 x P/E Multiple						243,035			
20.0 x P/E Multiple						255,826			
21.0 x P/E Multiple						268,617			
22.0 x P/E Multiple						281,408			
10.0% Discount Rate	0.9091	0.8264	0.7513	0.6830	0.6209	0.5645	0.5132		
18.0 x P/E Multiple	9,800	7,922	7,674	6,900	5,954	135,374		173,624	74.9%
19.0 x P/E Multiple	9,800	7,922	7,674	6,900	5,954	142,595		180,845	75.9%
20.0 x P/E Multiple	9,800	7,922	7,674	6,900	5,954	149,815		188,065	76.8%
21.0 x P/E Multiple	9,800	7,922	7,674	6,900	5,954	157,035		195,285	77.6%
22.0 x P/E Multiple	9,800	7,922	7,674	6,900	5,954	164,256		202,506	78.4%
11.0% Discount Rate	0.9009	0.8116	0.7312	0.6587	0.5935	0.5346	0.4817		
18.0 x P/E Multiple	9,712	7,780	7,469	6,654	5,690	128,219		165,525	74.4%
19.0 x P/E Multiple	9,712	7,780	7,469	6,654	5,690	135,058		172,364	75.4%
20.0 x P/E Multiple	9,712	7,780	7,469	6,654	5,690	141,897		179,202	76.3%
21.0 x P/E Multiple	9,712	7,780	7,469	6,654	5,690	148,736		186,041	77.2%
22.0 x P/E Multiple	9,712	7,780	7,469	6,654	5,690	155,574		192,880	78.0%
12.0% Discount Rate	0.8929	0.7972	0.7118	0.6355	0.5674	0.5066	0.4523		
18.0 x P/E Multiple	9,625	7,642	7,270	6,420	5,441	121,502		157,900	73.9%
19.0 x P/E Multiple	9,625	7,642	7,270	6,420	5,441	127,983		164,381	74.9%
20.0 x P/E Multiple	9,625	7,642	7,270	6,420	5,441	134,463		170,861	75.9%
21.0 x P/E Multiple	9,625	7,642	7,270	6,420	5,441	140,943		177,342	76.7%
22.0 x P/E Multiple	9,625	7,642	7,270	6,420	5,441	147,424		183,822	77.6%
13.0% Discount Rate	0.8850	0.7831	0.6931	0.6133	0.5428	0.4803	0.4251		
18.0 x P/E Multiple	9,540	7,507	7,079	6,196	5,204	115,192		150,718	73.4%
19.0 x P/E Multiple	9,540	7,507	7,079	6,196	5,204	121,336		156,862	74.4%
20.0 x P/E Multiple	9,540	7,507	7,079	6,196	5,204	127,479		163,006	75.4%
21.0 x P/E Multiple	9,540	7,507	7,079	6,196	5,204	133,623		169,150	76.3%
22.0 x P/E Multiple	9,540	7,507	7,079	6,196	5,204	139,767		175,294	77.1%
14.0% Discount Rate	0.8772	0.7695	0.6750	0.5921	0.5194	0.4556	0.3996		
18.0 x P/E Multiple	9,457	7,376	6,894	5,981	4,980	109,260		143,948	72.9%
19.0 x P/E Multiple	9,457	7,376	6,894	5,981	4,980	115,088		149,776	73.9%
20.0 x P/E Multiple	9,457	7,376	6,894	5,981	4,980	120,915		155,603	74.9%
21.0 x P/E Multiple	9,457	7,376	6,894	5,981	4,980	126,743		161,431	75.8%
22.0 x P/E Multiple	9,457	7,376	6,894	5,981	4,980	132,571		167,259	76.7%

NPV Calculations - Sale Assumption

P/E Multiple Method	1993	1994	1995	1996	1997	1998	1999	NPV	Residual Value as % of NPV
After-tax Cash Flow	$10,780	$9,586	$10,214	$10,102	$9,588	$9,580			
Residual Value						$9,580			
18.0 x P/E Multiple						203,551			
19.0 x P/E Multiple						211,481			
20.0 x P/E Multiple						219,412			
21.0 x P/E Multiple						227,343			
22.0 x P/E Multiple						235,273			
10.0% Discount Rate	0.9091	0.8264	0.7513	0.6830	0.6209	0.5645	0.5132		
18.0 x P/E Multiple	9,800	7,922	7,674	6,900	5,954	120,307		158,557	72.5%
19.0 x P/E Multiple	9,800	7,922	7,674	6,900	5,954	124,784		163,034	73.2%
20.0 x P/E Multiple	9,800	7,922	7,674	6,900	5,954	129,260		167,510	73.9%
21.0 x P/E Multiple	9,800	7,922	7,674	6,900	5,954	133,737		171,987	74.6%
22.0 x P/E Multiple	9,800	7,922	7,674	6,900	5,954	138,213		176,464	75.3%
11.0% Discount Rate	0.9009	0.8116	0.7312	0.6587	0.5935	0.5346	0.4817		
18.0 x P/E Multiple	9,712	7,780	7,469	6,654	5,690	113,949		151,254	71.9%
19.0 x P/E Multiple	9,712	7,780	7,469	6,654	5,690	118,189		155,494	72.7%
20.0 x P/E Multiple	9,712	7,780	7,469	6,654	5,690	122,429		159,734	73.4%
21.0 x P/E Multiple	9,712	7,780	7,469	6,654	5,690	126,669		163,974	74.1%
22.0 x P/E Multiple	9,712	7,780	7,469	6,654	5,690	130,909		168,214	74.8%
12.0% Discount Rate	0.8929	0.7972	0.7118	0.6355	0.5674	0.5066	0.4523		
18.0 x P/E Multiple	9,625	7,642	7,270	6,420	5,441	107,979		144,377	71.4%
19.0 x P/E Multiple	9,625	7,642	7,270	6,420	5,441	111,997		148,395	72.2%
20.0 x P/E Multiple	9,625	7,642	7,270	6,420	5,441	116,015		152,413	72.9%
21.0 x P/E Multiple	9,625	7,642	7,270	6,420	5,441	120,033		156,431	73.6%
22.0 x P/E Multiple	9,625	7,642	7,270	6,420	5,441	124,050		160,449	74.3%
13.0% Discount Rate	0.8850	0.7831	0.6931	0.6133	0.5428	0.4803	0.4251		
18.0 x P/E Multiple	9,540	7,507	7,079	6,196	5,204	102,371		137,897	70.9%
19.0 x P/E Multiple	9,540	7,507	7,079	6,196	5,204	106,180		141,706	71.7%
20.0 x P/E Multiple	9,540	7,507	7,079	6,196	5,204	109,989		145,516	72.4%
21.0 x P/E Multiple	9,540	7,507	7,079	6,196	5,204	113,798		149,325	73.1%
22.0 x P/E Multiple	9,540	7,507	7,079	6,196	5,204	117,608		153,134	73.8%
14.0% Discount Rate	0.8772	0.7695	0.6750	0.5921	0.5194	0.4556	0.3996		
18.0 x P/E Multiple	9,457	7,376	6,894	5,981	4,980	97,100		131,788	70.4%
19.0 x P/E Multiple	9,457	7,376	6,894	5,981	4,980	100,713		135,401	71.2%
20.0 x P/E Multiple	9,457	7,376	6,894	5,981	4,980	104,326		139,014	71.9%
21.0 x P/E Multiple	9,457	7,376	6,894	5,981	4,980	107,939		142,627	72.6%
22.0 x P/E Multiple	9,457	7,376	6,894	5,981	4,980	111,552		146,240	73.3%

MAREIGHT CORPORATION
Discounted Cash Flow Analysis
NPV Calculations – Growing Perpetuity Method

NPV Calculations – Continuing Value Assumption

Growing Perpetuity Method

	1993	1994	1995	1996	1997	1998	Residual Value	NPV	Residual Value as % of NPV
After-tax Cash Flow	$10,780	$9,586	$10,214	$10,102	$9,588	$9,580			
Residual Value						$9,580		143,705	
								155,496	
								169,253	
								185,510	
								205,019	
10.0% Discount Rate	0.9091	0.8264	0.7513	0.6830	0.6209	0.5645			
5.0% Growth Rate	9,800	7,922	7,674	6,900	5,954	5,408	81,118	124,776	65.0%
5.5% Growth Rate	9,800	7,922	7,674	6,900	5,954	5,408	87,774	131,432	66.6%
6.0% Growth Rate	9,800	7,922	7,674	6,900	5,954	5,408	95,539	139,197	68.6%
6.5% Growth Rate	9,800	7,922	7,674	6,900	5,954	5,408	104,716	148,374	70.6%
7.0% Growth Rate	9,800	7,922	7,674	6,900	5,954	5,408	115,728	159,386	72.6%
11.0% Discount Rate	0.9009	0.8116	0.7312	0.6587	0.5935	0.5346			
5.0% Growth Rate	9,712	7,780	7,469	6,654	5,690	5,122	76,831	119,258	64.4%
5.5% Growth Rate	9,712	7,780	7,469	6,654	5,690	5,122	83,135	125,562	66.2%
6.0% Growth Rate	9,712	7,780	7,469	6,654	5,690	5,122	90,489	132,917	68.1%
6.5% Growth Rate	9,712	7,780	7,469	6,654	5,690	5,122	99,181	141,609	70.0%
7.0% Growth Rate	9,712	7,780	7,469	6,654	5,690	5,122	109,612	152,039	72.1%
12.0% Discount Rate	0.8929	0.7972	0.7118	0.6355	0.5674	0.5066			
5.0% Growth Rate	9,625	7,642	7,270	6,420	5,441	4,854	72,805	114,057	63.8%
5.5% Growth Rate	9,625	7,642	7,270	6,420	5,441	4,854	78,779	120,031	65.6%
6.0% Growth Rate	9,625	7,642	7,270	6,420	5,441	4,854	85,749	127,001	67.5%
6.5% Growth Rate	9,625	7,642	7,270	6,420	5,441	4,854	93,985	135,237	69.5%
7.0% Growth Rate	9,625	7,642	7,270	6,420	5,441	4,854	103,869	145,121	71.6%
13.0% Discount Rate	0.8850	0.7831	0.6931	0.6133	0.5428	0.4803			
5.0% Growth Rate	9,540	7,507	7,079	6,196	5,204	4,602	69,024	109,152	63.2%
5.5% Growth Rate	9,540	7,507	7,079	6,196	5,204	4,602	74,688	114,816	65.1%
6.0% Growth Rate	9,540	7,507	7,079	6,196	5,204	4,602	81,295	121,423	67.0%
6.5% Growth Rate	9,540	7,507	7,079	6,196	5,204	4,602	89,104	129,232	68.9%
7.0% Growth Rate	9,540	7,507	7,079	6,196	5,204	4,602	98,475	138,602	71.0%
14.0% Discount Rate	0.8772	0.7695	0.6750	0.5921	0.5194	0.4556			
5.0% Growth Rate	9,457	7,376	6,894	5,981	4,980	4,365	65,470	104,523	62.6%
5.5% Growth Rate	9,457	7,376	6,894	5,981	4,980	4,365	70,842	109,895	64.5%
6.0% Growth Rate	9,457	7,376	6,894	5,981	4,980	4,365	77,109	116,162	66.4%
6.5% Growth Rate	9,457	7,376	6,894	5,981	4,980	4,365	84,516	123,569	68.4%
7.0% Growth Rate	9,457	7,376	6,894	5,981	4,980	4,365	93,404	132,457	70.5%

NPV Calculations – Sale Assumption

Growing Perpetuity Method

	1993	1994	1995	1996	1997	1998	Residual Value	NPV	Residual Value as % of NPV
After-tax Cash Flow	$10,780	$9,586	$10,214	$10,102	$9,588	$9,580			
Residual Value						$9,580		149,897	
								157,208	
								165,737	
								175,816	
								187,912	
10.0% Discount Rate	0.9091	0.8264	0.7513	0.6830	0.6209	0.5645			
5.0% Growth Rate	9,800	7,922	7,674	6,900	5,954	5,408	84,613	128,271	66.0%
5.5% Growth Rate	9,800	7,922	7,674	6,900	5,954	5,408	88,740	132,398	67.0%
6.0% Growth Rate	9,800	7,922	7,674	6,900	5,954	5,408	93,554	137,212	68.2%
6.5% Growth Rate	9,800	7,922	7,674	6,900	5,954	5,408	99,244	142,902	69.4%
7.0% Growth Rate	9,800	7,922	7,674	6,900	5,954	5,408	106,071	149,729	70.8%
11.0% Discount Rate	0.9009	0.8116	0.7312	0.6587	0.5935	0.5346			
5.0% Growth Rate	9,712	7,780	7,469	6,654	5,690	5,122	80,141	122,569	65.4%
5.5% Growth Rate	9,712	7,780	7,469	6,654	5,690	5,122	84,050	126,477	66.5%
6.0% Growth Rate	9,712	7,780	7,469	6,654	5,690	5,122	88,610	131,037	67.6%
6.5% Growth Rate	9,712	7,780	7,469	6,654	5,690	5,122	93,999	136,426	68.9%
7.0% Growth Rate	9,712	7,780	7,469	6,654	5,690	5,122	100,465	142,893	70.3%
12.0% Discount Rate	0.8929	0.7972	0.7118	0.6355	0.5674	0.5066			
5.0% Growth Rate	9,625	7,642	7,270	6,420	5,441	4,854	75,943	117,194	64.8%
5.5% Growth Rate	9,625	7,642	7,270	6,420	5,441	4,854	79,646	120,898	65.9%
6.0% Growth Rate	9,625	7,642	7,270	6,420	5,441	4,854	83,967	125,219	67.1%
6.5% Growth Rate	9,625	7,642	7,270	6,420	5,441	4,854	89,074	130,326	68.3%
7.0% Growth Rate	9,625	7,642	7,270	6,420	5,441	4,854	95,202	136,454	69.8%
13.0% Discount Rate	0.8850	0.7831	0.6931	0.6133	0.5428	0.4803			
5.0% Growth Rate	9,540	7,507	7,079	6,196	5,204	4,602	71,998	112,126	64.2%
5.5% Growth Rate	9,540	7,507	7,079	6,196	5,204	4,602	75,510	115,638	65.3%
6.0% Growth Rate	9,540	7,507	7,079	6,196	5,204	4,602	79,606	119,734	66.5%
6.5% Growth Rate	9,540	7,507	7,079	6,196	5,204	4,602	84,448	124,576	67.8%
7.0% Growth Rate	9,540	7,507	7,079	6,196	5,204	4,602	90,258	130,385	69.2%
14.0% Discount Rate	0.8772	0.7695	0.6750	0.5921	0.5194	0.4556			
5.0% Growth Rate	9,457	7,376	6,894	5,981	4,980	4,365	68,291	107,344	63.6%
5.5% Growth Rate	9,457	7,376	6,894	5,981	4,980	4,365	71,622	110,674	64.7%
6.0% Growth Rate	9,457	7,376	6,894	5,981	4,980	4,365	75,507	114,560	65.9%
6.5% Growth Rate	9,457	7,376	6,894	5,981	4,980	4,365	80,100	119,152	67.2%
7.0% Growth Rate	9,457	7,376	6,894	5,981	4,980	4,365	85,610	124,663	68.7%

EXHIBIT 22-22
05/20/92
03:26 PM

Page 15   FILE: NPV4

MARRIOTT CORPORATION
Discounted Cash Flow Analysis
NPV Calculations - EBITDA Multiple Method

NPV Calculations - Continuing Value Assumption

EBITDA Multiple Method	1993	1994	1995	1996	1997	1998	1999	NPV	Residual Value % of NPV
After-tax Cash Flow	$10,780	$9,586	$10,214	$10,102	$9,588	$9,580			
Residual Value									
8.0 x EBITDA Multiple						255,099			
8.5 x EBITDA Multiple						271,043			
9.0 x EBITDA Multiple						286,987			
9.5 x EBITDA Multiple						302,930			
10.0 x EBITDA Multiple						318,874			
10.0% Discount Rate	0.9091	0.8264	0.7513	0.6830	0.6209	0.5645	0.5132		
8.0 x EBITDA Multiple	9,800	7,922	7,674	6,900	5,954	149,405		187,655	76.7%
8.5 x EBITDA Multiple	9,800	7,922	7,674	6,900	5,954	158,405		196,655	77.7%
9.0 x EBITDA Multiple	9,800	7,922	7,674	6,900	5,954	167,404		205,654	78.8%
9.5 x EBITDA Multiple	9,800	7,922	7,674	6,900	5,954	176,404		214,654	79.7%
10.0 x EBITDA Multiple	9,800	7,922	7,674	6,900	5,954	185,404		223,654	80.5%
11.0% Discount Rate	0.9009	0.8116	0.7312	0.6587	0.5935	0.5346	0.4817		
8.0 x EBITDA Multiple	9,712	7,780	7,469	6,654	5,690	141,509		178,814	76.3%
8.5 x EBITDA Multiple	9,712	7,780	7,469	6,654	5,690	150,033		187,338	77.4%
9.0 x EBITDA Multiple	9,712	7,780	7,469	6,654	5,690	158,557		195,862	78.3%
9.5 x EBITDA Multiple	9,712	7,780	7,469	6,654	5,690	167,081		204,386	79.2%
10.0 x EBITDA Multiple	9,712	7,780	7,469	6,654	5,690	175,605		212,911	80.1%
12.0% Discount Rate	0.8929	0.7972	0.7118	0.6355	0.5674	0.5066	0.4523		
8.0 x EBITDA Multiple	9,625	7,642	7,270	6,420	5,441	134,095		170,493	75.8%
8.5 x EBITDA Multiple	9,625	7,642	7,270	6,420	5,441	142,172		178,571	76.9%
9.0 x EBITDA Multiple	9,625	7,642	7,270	6,420	5,441	150,250		186,648	77.8%
9.5 x EBITDA Multiple	9,625	7,642	7,270	6,420	5,441	158,328		194,726	78.8%
10.0 x EBITDA Multiple	9,625	7,642	7,270	6,420	5,441	166,405		202,803	79.7%
13.0% Discount Rate	0.8850	0.7831	0.6931	0.6133	0.5428	0.4803	0.4251		
8.0 x EBITDA Multiple	9,540	7,507	7,079	6,196	5,204	127,130		162,657	75.3%
8.5 x EBITDA Multiple	9,540	7,507	7,079	6,196	5,204	134,789		170,315	76.4%
9.0 x EBITDA Multiple	9,540	7,507	7,079	6,196	5,204	142,447		177,973	77.5%
9.5 x EBITDA Multiple	9,540	7,507	7,079	6,196	5,204	150,105		185,631	78.4%
10.0 x EBITDA Multiple	9,540	7,507	7,079	6,196	5,204	157,763		193,289	79.2%
14.0% Discount Rate	0.8772	0.7695	0.6750	0.5921	0.5194	0.4556	0.3996		
8.0 x EBITDA Multiple	9,457	7,376	6,894	5,981	4,980	120,584		155,272	74.8%
8.5 x EBITDA Multiple	9,457	7,376	6,894	5,981	4,980	127,848		162,536	76.0%
9.0 x EBITDA Multiple	9,457	7,376	6,894	5,981	4,980	135,112		169,800	77.0%
9.5 x EBITDA Multiple	9,457	7,376	6,894	5,981	4,980	142,376		177,064	77.9%
10.0 x EBITDA Multiple	9,457	7,376	6,894	5,981	4,980	149,639		184,327	78.8%

NPV Calculations - Sale Assumption

EBITDA Multiple Method	1993	1994	1995	1996	1997	1998	1999	NPV	Residual Value % of NPV
After-tax Cash Flow	$10,780	$9,586	$10,214	$10,102	$9,588	$9,580			
Residual Value									
8.0 x EBITDA Multiple						218,962			
8.5 x EBITDA Multiple						228,847			
9.0 x EBITDA Multiple						238,732			
9.5 x EBITDA Multiple						248,617			
10.0 x EBITDA Multiple						258,502			
10.0% Discount Rate	0.9091	0.8264	0.7513	0.6830	0.6209	0.5645	0.5132		
8.0 x EBITDA Multiple	9,800	7,922	7,674	6,900	5,954	129,006		167,256	73.9%
8.5 x EBITDA Multiple	9,800	7,922	7,674	6,900	5,954	134,586		172,836	74.7%
9.0 x EBITDA Multiple	9,800	7,922	7,674	6,900	5,954	140,166		178,416	75.5%
9.5 x EBITDA Multiple	9,800	7,922	7,674	6,900	5,954	145,746		183,996	76.3%
10.0 x EBITDA Multiple	9,800	7,922	7,674	6,900	5,954	151,325		189,576	77.0%
11.0% Discount Rate	0.9009	0.8116	0.7312	0.6587	0.5935	0.5346	0.4817		
8.0 x EBITDA Multiple	9,712	7,780	7,469	6,654	5,690	122,188		159,493	73.4%
8.5 x EBITDA Multiple	9,712	7,780	7,469	6,654	5,690	127,473		164,778	74.3%
9.0 x EBITDA Multiple	9,712	7,780	7,469	6,654	5,690	132,758		170,063	75.1%
9.5 x EBITDA Multiple	9,712	7,780	7,469	6,654	5,690	138,043		175,348	75.8%
10.0 x EBITDA Multiple	9,712	7,780	7,469	6,654	5,690	143,328		180,633	76.5%
12.0% Discount Rate	0.8929	0.7972	0.7118	0.6355	0.5674	0.5066	0.4523		
8.0 x EBITDA Multiple	9,625	7,642	7,270	6,420	5,441	115,786		152,185	72.9%
8.5 x EBITDA Multiple	9,625	7,642	7,270	6,420	5,441	120,795		157,193	73.8%
9.0 x EBITDA Multiple	9,625	7,642	7,270	6,420	5,441	125,803		162,201	74.6%
9.5 x EBITDA Multiple	9,625	7,642	7,270	6,420	5,441	130,811		167,209	75.3%
10.0 x EBITDA Multiple	9,625	7,642	7,270	6,420	5,441	135,819		172,217	76.0%
13.0% Discount Rate	0.8850	0.7831	0.6931	0.6133	0.5428	0.4803	0.4251		
8.0 x EBITDA Multiple	9,540	7,507	7,079	6,196	5,204	109,773		145,299	72.4%
8.5 x EBITDA Multiple	9,540	7,507	7,079	6,196	5,204	114,521		150,047	73.3%
9.0 x EBITDA Multiple	9,540	7,507	7,079	6,196	5,204	119,269		154,795	74.1%
9.5 x EBITDA Multiple	9,540	7,507	7,079	6,196	5,204	124,017		159,543	74.8%
10.0 x EBITDA Multiple	9,540	7,507	7,079	6,196	5,204	128,765		164,291	75.6%
14.0% Discount Rate	0.8772	0.7695	0.6750	0.5921	0.5194	0.4556	0.3996		
8.0 x EBITDA Multiple	9,457	7,376	6,894	5,981	4,980	104,121		138,809	71.9%
8.5 x EBITDA Multiple	9,457	7,376	6,894	5,981	4,980	108,624		143,312	72.7%
9.0 x EBITDA Multiple	9,457	7,376	6,894	5,981	4,980	113,128		147,816	73.6%
9.5 x EBITDA Multiple	9,457	7,376	6,894	5,981	4,980	117,631		152,319	74.4%
10.0 x EBITDA Multiple	9,457	7,376	6,894	5,981	4,980	122,135		156,823	75.1%

MAREIGHT CORPORATION
Discounted Cash Flow Analysis
IRR Calculations

EXHIBIT 22-30
08/28/92
05:48 PM

IRR Calculations – Continuing Value Assumption

	Investment	1993	1994	1995	1996	1997	1998	IRR
EBDIAT Multiple Method								
11.0 x EBDIAT Multiple	(160,000)	10,780	9,586	10,214	10,102	9,588	267,983	13.6%
12.0 x EBDIAT Multiple	(160,000)	10,780	9,586	10,214	10,102	9,588	291,474	15.0%
13.0 x EBDIAT Multiple	(160,000)	10,780	9,586	10,214	10,102	9,588	314,965	16.3%
14.0 x EBDIAT Multiple	(160,000)	10,780	9,586	10,214	10,102	9,588	338,456	17.6%
15.0 x EBDIAT Multiple	(160,000)	10,780	9,586	10,214	10,102	9,588	361,947	18.8%
P/E Multiple Method								
18.0 x P/E Multiple	(160,000)	10,780	9,586	10,214	10,102	9,588	239,824	11.7%
19.0 x P/E Multiple	(160,000)	10,780	9,586	10,214	10,102	9,588	252,615	12.6%
20.0 x P/E Multiple	(160,000)	10,780	9,586	10,214	10,102	9,588	265,406	13.4%
21.0 x P/E Multiple	(160,000)	10,780	9,586	10,214	10,102	9,588	278,197	14.2%
22.0 x P/E Multiple	(160,000)	10,780	9,586	10,214	10,102	9,588	290,989	15.0%
Growing Perpetuity Method								
5.0% Growth Rate	(160,000)	10,780	9,586	10,214	10,102	9,588	153,285	4.7%
5.5% Growth Rate	(160,000)	10,780	9,586	10,214	10,102	9,588	165,077	5.8%
6.0% Growth Rate	(160,000)	10,780	9,586	10,214	10,102	9,588	178,833	7.1%
6.5% Growth Rate	(160,000)	10,780	9,586	10,214	10,102	9,588	195,090	8.4%
7.0% Growth Rate	(160,000)	10,780	9,586	10,214	10,102	9,588	214,599	9.9%
EBITDA Multiple Method								
8.0 x EBITDA Multiple	(160,000)	10,780	9,586	10,214	10,102	9,588	264,680	13.4%
8.5 x EBITDA Multiple	(160,000)	10,780	9,586	10,214	10,102	9,588	280,623	14.3%
9.0 x EBITDA Multiple	(160,000)	10,780	9,586	10,214	10,102	9,588	296,567	15.3%
9.5 x EBITDA Multiple	(160,000)	10,780	9,586	10,214	10,102	9,588	312,511	16.2%
10.0 x EBITDA Multiple	(160,000)	10,780	9,586	10,214	10,102	9,588	328,454	17.1%

IRR Calculations – Sale Assumption

	Investment	1993	1994	1995	1996	1997	1998	IRR
EBDIAT Multiple Method								
11.0 x EBDIAT Multiple	(160,000)	10,780	9,586	10,214	10,102	9,588	230,590	11.1%
12.0 x EBDIAT Multiple	(160,000)	10,780	9,586	10,214	10,102	9,588	245,154	12.1%
13.0 x EBDIAT Multiple	(160,000)	10,780	9,586	10,214	10,102	9,588	259,719	13.0%
14.0 x EBDIAT Multiple	(160,000)	10,780	9,586	10,214	10,102	9,588	274,283	14.0%
15.0 x EBDIAT Multiple	(160,000)	10,780	9,586	10,214	10,102	9,588	288,848	14.8%
P/E Multiple Method								
18.0 x P/E Multiple	(160,000)	10,780	9,586	10,214	10,102	9,588	203,551	9.1%
19.0 x P/E Multiple	(160,000)	10,780	9,586	10,214	10,102	9,588	221,062	10.4%
20.0 x P/E Multiple	(160,000)	10,780	9,586	10,214	10,102	9,588	228,992	11.0%
21.0 x P/E Multiple	(160,000)	10,780	9,586	10,214	10,102	9,588	236,923	11.5%
22.0 x P/E Multiple	(160,000)	10,780	9,586	10,214	10,102	9,588	244,854	12.1%
Growing Perpetuity Method								
5.0% Growth Rate	(160,000)	10,780	9,586	10,214	10,102	9,588	159,477	5.3%
5.5% Growth Rate	(160,000)	10,780	9,586	10,214	10,102	9,588	166,788	6.0%
6.0% Growth Rate	(160,000)	10,780	9,586	10,214	10,102	9,588	175,317	6.8%
6.5% Growth Rate	(160,000)	10,780	9,586	10,214	10,102	9,588	185,397	7.6%
7.0% Growth Rate	(160,000)	10,780	9,586	10,214	10,102	9,588	197,492	8.6%
EBITDA Multiple Method								
8.0 x EBITDA Multiple	(160,000)	10,780	9,586	10,214	10,102	9,588	228,542	10.9%
8.5 x EBITDA Multiple	(160,000)	10,780	9,586	10,214	10,102	9,588	238,427	11.6%
9.0 x EBITDA Multiple	(160,000)	10,780	9,586	10,214	10,102	9,588	248,312	12.3%
9.5 x EBITDA Multiple	(160,000)	10,780	9,586	10,214	10,102	9,588	258,197	12.9%
10.0 x EBITDA Multiple	(160,000)	10,780	9,586	10,214	10,102	9,588	268,082	13.6%

MAREIGHT CORPORATION
Discounted Cash Flow Analysis
Summary Amortization Schedule

EXHIBIT 22.31

05/20/92
03:26 PM

Years Ended December 31,		Opening Bal. Sheet	1993	1994	1995	1996	1997	1998
Transaction Fees								
Beginning Balance			$2,500	$2,438	$2,375	$2,313	$2,250	$2,188
Amortization:	Years							
Transaction	40	$1,933	48	48	48	48	48	48
Accounting & Legal	40	567	14	14	14	14	14	14
Pre-Payment Penalty	7	0	0	0	0	0	0	0
Ending Balance		$2,500	$2,438	$2,375	$2,313	$2,250	$2,188	$2,125

NOTE: Transaction costs not directly related to the financing are not deductible.

Goodwill	Initial	1993	1994	1995	1996	1997	1998
Beginning Balance		$34,748	$33,879	$33,011	$32,142	$31,273	$30,405
Amortization 40 Years		869	869	869	869	869	869
Ending Goodwill	$34,748	$33,879	$33,011	$32,142	$31,273	$30,405	$29,536

Intangible Assets	Initial	1993	1994	1995	1996	1997	1998
Beginning Balance		$0	$0	$0	$0	$0	$0
Plus: Additions		0	0	0	0	0	0
Amortization 5 Years		0	0	0	0	0	0
Ending Intangible Assets	$0	$0	$0	$0	$0	$0	$0

Leased Property Under Capital Leases	Initial	1993	1994	1995	1996	1997	1998
Beginning Balance		$0	$0	$0	$0	$0	$0
Plus: Additions		0	0	0	0	0	0
Amortization 25 Years		0	0	0	0	0	0
Ending Intangible Assets	$0	$0	$0	$0	$0	$0	$0

		1993	1994	1995	1996	1997	1998
Deductible Amortization		$0	$0	$0	$0	$0	$0
Non-Deductible Amortization		931	931	931	931	931	931
Total Amortization		$931	$931	$931	$931	$931	$931

MAREIGHT CORPORATION
LBO Analysis
Financial Statement Tax Provision

EXHIBIT 22.32

05/20/92
03:26 PM

Years Ended December 31,	1993	1994	1995	1996	1997	1998
Earnings Before Taxes	$14,026	$15,023	$16,092	$17,227	$18,449	$21,188
Permanent Differences						
Goodwill Amortization	869	869	869	869	869	869
Other Non-Deductible Amortization	63	63	63	63	63	63
Total Permanent Differences	931	931	931	931	931	931
Taxable Income Before NOL	14,957	15,954	17,023	18,158	19,380	22,119
NOL						
Available	0	0	0	0	0	0
Current	0	0	0	0	0	0
Utilized	0	0	0	0	0	0
Taxable Income After NOL	14,957	15,954	17,023	18,158	19,380	22,119
State Taxes 6.00%	897	957	1,021	1,089	1,163	1,327
Taxable Income After NOL and State Taxes	14,060	14,997	16,002	17,069	18,217	20,792
Federal Tax 34.00%	4,780	5,099	5,441	5,803	6,194	7,069
Credits	0	0	0	0	0	0
Net Federal Taxes	4,780	5,099	5,441	5,803	6,194	7,069
State Taxes	897	957	1,021	1,089	1,163	1,327
Foreign Taxes	0	0	0	0	0	0
Total Book Tax Provision	$5,678	$6,056	$6,462	$6,893	$7,357	$8,396
Effective Tax Rate	40.5%	40.3%	40.2%	40.0%	39.9%	39.6%

FILE: SHT_P

MAREIGHT CORPORATION
Discounted Cash Flow Analysis
Current and Deferred Taxes

EXHIBIT 22.33

05/20/92
03:26 PM

Years Ended December 31,	1993	1994	1995	Projected 1996	1997	1998
Earnings Before Taxes	$14,026	$15,023	$16,092	$17,227	$18,449	$21,188
Permanent Differences						
Goodwill Amortization	869	869	869	869	869	869
Other Non-Deductible Amortization	63	63	63	63	63	63
Total Permanent Differences	931	931	931	931	931	931
Timing Differences						
Depreciation - Regular Tax/Book Diff.	4,250	11,003	5,065	2,007	975	821
Other	0	0	0	0	0	0
Total Timing Differences	4,250	11,003	5,065	2,007	975	821
Regular Taxable Income Before NOL	10,708	4,952	11,958	16,151	18,405	21,298
NOL						
Available	0	0	0	0	0	0
Current	0	0	0	0	0	0
Utilized	0	0	0	0	0	0
Regular Taxable Income After NOL	10,708	4,952	11,958	16,151	18,405	21,298
State Taxes	642	297	717	969	1,104	1,278
Regular Taxable Income After NOL and State	10,065	4,655	11,240	15,182	17,300	20,020
Federal Tax	3,422	1,583	3,822	5,162	5,882	6,807
Tentative Minimum Tax	3,438	3,029	3,237	3,451	4,098	4,374
Indicated Alternative Minimum Tax	16	1,446	0	0	0	0
MTC Credit						
Available	0	16	1,462	877	0	0
Current	16	1,446	0	0	0	0
Utilized	0	0	585	877	0	0
Net Federal Taxes	3,438	3,029	3,237	4,285	5,882	6,807
State Taxes	642	297	717	969	1,104	1,278
Foreign Taxes	0	0	0	0	0	0
Total Current Taxes	4,080	3,326	3,954	5,254	6,986	8,085
Total Book Tax Provision	5,678	6,056	6,462	6,893	7,357	8,396
Deferred Taxes	$1,597	$2,730	$2,508	$1,639	$370	$312

MAREIGHT CORPORATION
LBO Analysis
Alternative Minimum Tax

EXHIBIT 22-34

05/20/92
03:26 PM

Years Ended December 31,	1993	1994	1995	1996	1997	1998
Regular Taxable Income	$10,708	$4,952	$11,958	$16,151	$18,405	$21,298
State Taxes	642	297	717	969	1,104	1,278
Regular Taxable Income After State Taxes	10,065	4,655	11,240	15,182	17,300	20,020
AMT Adjustments						
Depreciation - AMTI/Regular Tax Diff.	5,819	8,652	4,260	1,924	3,096	1,853
Long-Term Contracts post 2/28/86	0	0	0	0	0	0
Installment Sales of Certain Property	0	0	0	0	0	0
Total AMT Adjustments	5,819	8,652	4,260	1,924	3,096	1,853
Regular Tax NOL Deduction	0	0	0	0	0	0
AMT Corporate Tax Preference Items						
Depletion	0	0	0	0	0	0
Intangible Drilling Costs	0	0	0	0	0	0
Accelerated Depreciation of Real Property Placed into Service Before 1987	0	0	0	0	0	0
Total Tax Preferences	0	0	0	0	0	0
Pre-Adjustment AMT Income	15,884	13,306	15,501	17,106	20,397	21,872
ACE Income Adjustment						
Pre-Adjustment AMT Income	15,884	13,306	15,501	17,106	20,397	21,872
Depreciation - ACE/AMTI Difference	1,740	2,451	909	197	124	(6
Other	0	0	0	0	0	0
ACE Income	17,624	15,757	16,410	17,303	20,521	21,866
Less: Pre-Adjustment AMT Income	(15,884)	(13,306)	(15,501)	(17,106)	(20,397)	(21,872)
subtotal	1,740	2,451	909	197	124	(6
	x 75.0%	x 75.0%	x 75.0%	x 75.0%	x 75.0%	x 75.0%
ACE Adjustment	1,305	1,838	682	148	93	(4
AMT Income Before NOL	17,189	15,145	16,183	17,254	20,490	21,868
AMT NOL Deduction (90% limitation)						
Available	0	0	0	0	0	0
Current	0	0	0	0	0	0
Utilized	0	0	0	0	0	0
AMT Income	17,189	15,145	16,183	17,254	20,490	21,868
Tentative Minimum Tax	3,438	3,029	3,237	3,451	4,098	4,374
AMT Credits	0	0	0	0	0	0
Regular Tax Liability	3,422	1,583	3,822	5,162	5,882	6,807
Alternative Minimum Tax	$16	$1,446	$0	$0	$0	$0

Page 21   FILE: SHT_T

MAREIGHT CORPORATION
Discounted Cash Flow Analysis
Comparison of Calculated and Actual Values of
Net Property, Plant and Equipment

EXHIBIT 22.35

05/20/92
03:26 PM

Comparison of Calculated and Actual Values

	Net Property, Plant and Equipment
Calculated Value	$0
Actual Value	44,965
Difference	($44,965)
	=========
Percent of Actual Value	-100.00%
	=========

Calculated Value of Net Property, Plant and Equipment

Book Description	Book Life	Tax Category	1981-1992 Capital Expenditures	1981-1992 Accumulated Depreciation	Net Property, Plant and Equipment
Land	NA	Land	$0	-	$0
Autos	5	3-Year	0	0	0
Prod Eqp	8	5-Year	0	0	0
Prod Eqp	12	7-Year	0	0	0
Barges	15	10-Year	0	0	0
Waste Facil.	20	15-Year	0	0	0
Sewers	30	20-Year	0	0	0
Real Estate	30	Real Estate (1)	0	0	0
		Total Calculated Value			$0
					=========

(1) Real Estate excludes all land.
Note: If the calculated and actual property, plant and equipment book value numbers are roughly the same then it is appropriate to use the
calculated tax depreciation figures in the projections. However, the best alternative is to get tax depreciation forecasts from the target

315

MAREIGHT CORPORATION
Discounted Cash Flow Analysis
Historical Capital Expenditures
1981 - 1988

EXHIBIT 22.36

05/20/92
03:26 PM

Book Description	Book Life	Tax Category	1981	1982	1983	1984	1985	1986	1987	1988
Land	NA	Land	$0	$0	$0	$0	$0	$0	$0	$0
Autos	5	3-Year	0	0	0	0	0	0	0	0
Prod Eqp	8	5-Year	0	0	0	0	0	0	0	0
Prod Eqp	12	7-Year								0
Barges	15	10-Year	0	0	0	0	0	0	0	0
Waste Facil.	20	15-Year						0		0
Sewers	30	20-Year							0	0
Real Estate	30	Real Estate (1)	0	0	0	0	0	0	0	0
Total Capital Expenditures			$0	$0	$0	$0	$0	$0	$0	$0

(1) Excluding land.

MAREIGHT CORPORATION
LBO Analysis
Summary Historical Book Depreciation schedule
For Purposes of Calculating Current Net Property, Plant and Equipment

EXHIBIT 22.37
05/20/92
03:26 PM

Book Description	Book Life	Tax Category	1981	1982	1983	1984	1985	1986	1987	1988	1989	1990	1991	1992	1981-1992 Total
Autos	5	3-Year	$0	$0	$0	$0	$0	$0	$0	$0	$0	$0	$0	$0	$0
Prod Eqp	8	5-Year	0	0	0	0	0	0	0	0	0	0	0	0	0
Prod Eqp	12	7-Year	0	0	0	0	0	0	0	0	0	0	0	0	0
Barges	15	10-Year	0	0	0	0	0	0	0	0	0	0	0	0	0
Waste Facil.	20	15-Year	0	0	0	0	0	0	0	0	0	0	0	0	0
Sewers	30	20-Year	0	0	0	0	0	0	0	0	0	0	0	0	0
Real Estate	30	Real Estate (1)	0	0	0	0	0	0	0	0	0	0	0	0	0
		Total Depreciation	$0	$0	$0	$0	$0	$0	$0	$0	$0	$0	$0	$0	$0

(1) Excluding land.

EXHIBIT 22.38

05/20/92
03:26 PM

MAREIGHT CORPORATION
Discounted Cash Flow Analysis
Summary Projected Book Depreciation Schedule

Book Description	Book Life	Acquired Assets	1993	1994	1995	1996	1997	1998
Autos	5	3-Year	$1,353	$1,353	$1,353	$1,353	$1,353	$0
Prod Eqp	8	5-Year	3,125	3,125	3,125	3,125	3,125	3,125
Prod Eqp	12	7-Year	1,250	1,250	1,250	1,250	1,250	1,250
Barges	15	10-Year	0	0	0	0	0	0
Waste Facil.	20	15-Year	600	600	600	600	600	600
Sewers	30	20-Year	0	0	0	0	0	0
Real Estate	30	Real Estate (1)	600	600	600	600	600	600
		New Capital Expenditures						
Autos	5	3-Year	$65	$198	$335	$478	$625	$713
Prod Eqp	8	5-Year	125	363	606	894	1,191	1,481
Prod Eqp	12	7-Year	79	259	479	716	992	1,320
Barges	15	10-Year	0	0	0	0	0	0
Waste Facil.	20	15-Year	13	38	64	91	119	148
Sewers	30	20-Year	0	0	0	0	0	0
Real Estate	30	Real Estate (1)	45	138	232	328	428	533
			$7,254	$7,923	$8,645	$9,435	$10,283	$9,769

EXHIBIT 22-39
05/20/92
03:26 PM

MAREIGHT CORPORATION
LBO Analysis
Summary Regular Tax Depreciation Schedule

Book Description	Book Life		1981	1982	1983	1984	1985	1986	1987	1988	1989	1990	1991	1992	1981-1992 Total	1993	1994	1995	1996	1997	1998
Carryover Basis Assets																					
Autos	5	3-Year	$0	$0	$0	$0	$0	$0	$0	$0	$0	$0	$0	$0	$0	$0	$0	$0	$0	$0	$0
Prod Eqp	8	5-Year	0	0	0	0	0	0	0	0	0	0	0	0	0	0	0	0	0	0	0
Prod Eqp	12	7-Year	0	0	0	0	0	0	0	0	0	0	0	0	0	0	0	0	0	0	0
Barges	15	10-Year	0	0	0	0	0	0	0	0	0	0	0	0	0	0	0	0	0	0	0
Waste Facil.	20	15-Year	0	0	0	0	0	0	0	0	0	0	0	0	0	0	0	0	0	0	0
Sewers	30	20-Year	0	0	0	0	0	0	0	0	0	0	0	0	0	0	0	0	0	0	0
Real Estate	30	Real Estate	0	0	0	0	0	0	0	0	0	0	0	0	0	0	0	0	0	0	0
Acquired Assets																					
Autos	5	3-Year														$2,255	$3,007	$1,002	$501		
Prod Eqp	8	5-Year														5,000	8,000	4,800	2,880	2,880	1,440
Prod Eqp	12	7-Year														2,144	3,674	2,624	1,874	1,340	1,338
Barges	15	10-Year														0	0	0	0	0	0
Waste Facil.	20	15-Year														600	1,140	1,026	924	832	748
Sewers	30	20-Year														0	0	0	0	0	0
Real Estate	30	Real Estate														548	572	572	572	572	572
New Capital Expenditures																					
Autos	5	3-Year														$217	$514	$630	$701	$726	$751
Prod Eqp	8	5-Year														400	1,000	1,380	1,748	2,091	2,244
Prod Eqp	12	7-Year														270	812	1,335	1,765	2,207	2,748
Barges	15	10-Year														0	0	0	0	0	0
Waste Facil.	20	15-Year														25	73	118	161	200	237
Sewers	30	20-Year														0	0	0	0	0	0
Real Estate	30	Real Estate														46	136	225	317	412	512
			$0	$0	$0	$0	$0	$0	$0	$0	$0	$0	$0	$0	$0	$11,504	$18,926	$13,710	$11,442	$11,258	$10,590

Note: If possible, obtain projected regular tax depreciation figures from target company and input on this schedule.

EXHIBIT 22.40
05/20/92
03:26 PM

MAREIGHT CORPORATION
Discounted Cash Flow Analysis
Summary Alternative Minimum Tax Depreciation Schedule

Book Description	Book Life	Carryover Basis Assets	1981	1982	1983	1984	1985	1986	1987	1988	1989	1990	1991	1992	1981-1992 Total	1993	1994	1995	1996	1997	1998
Autos	5	3-Year	$0	$0	$0	$0	$0	$0	$0	$0	$0	$0	$0	$0	$0	$0	$0	$0	$0	$0	$0
Prod Eqp	8	5-Year	0	0	0	0	0	0	0	0	0	0	0	0	0	0	0	0	0	0	0
Prod Eqp	12	7-Year	0	0	0	0	0	0	0	0	0	0	0	0	0	0	0	0	0	0	0
Barges	15	10-Year	0	0	0	0	0	0	0	0	0	0	0	0	0	0	0	0	0	0	0
Waste Facil.	20	15-Year	0	0	0	0	0	0	0	0	0	0	0	0	0	0	0	0	0	0	0
Sewers	30	20-Year	0	0	0	0	0	0	0	0	0	0	0	0	0	0	0	0	0	0	0
Real Estate	30	Real Estate	0	0	0	0	0	0	0	0	0	0	0	0	0	0	0	0	0	0	0
Acquired Assets																					
Autos	5	3-Year														$1,450	$2,278	$1,519	$1,519		
Prod Eqp	8	5-Year														1,973	3,635	3,063	2,578	2,293	2,293
Prod Eqp	12	7-Year														938	1,758	1,538	1,346	1,178	1,100
Barges	15	10-Year														0	0	0	0	0	0
Waste Facil.	20	15-Year														429	827	768	713	662	615
Sewers	30	20-Year														0	0	0	0	0	0
Real Estate	30	Real Estate														430	450	450	450	450	450
New Capital Expenditures																					
Autos	5	3-Year														$139	$364	$523	$689	$714	$739
Prod Eqp	8	5-Year														158	433	672	929	1,167	1,388
Prod Eqp	12	7-Year														118	374	658	930	1,228	1,575
Barges	15	10-Year														0	0	0	0	0	0
Waste Facil.	20	15-Year														18	52	86	119	150	180
Sewers	30	20-Year														0	0	0	0	0	0
Real Estate	30	Real Estate														0	0	0	0	0	0
			$0	$0	$0	$0	$0	$0	$0	$0	$0	$0	$0	$0	$0	$5,685	$10,274	$9,450	$9,518	$8,162	$8,737

Note: If possible, obtain projected alternative minimum tax depreciation figures from target company and input on this schedule.

MAREIGHT CORPORATION
Discounted Cash Flow Analysis
Summary ACE Depreciation Schedule

EXHIBIT 22.41
05/20/92
03:26 PM

Book Description	Book Life	1981	1982	1983	1984	1985	1986	1987	1988	1989	1990	1991	1992	1981-1992 Total	1993	1994	1995	1996	1997	1998
Carryover Basis Assets																				
Autos	5	3-Year	$0	$0	$0	$0	$0	$0	$0	$0	$0	$0	$0	$0	$0	$0	$0	$0	$0	$0
Prod Eqp	8	5-Year	0	0	0	0	0	0	0	0	0	0	0	0	0	0	0	0	0
Prod Eqp	12	7-Year	0	0	0	0	0	0	0	0	0	0	0	0	0	0	0	0	0
Barges	15	10-Year	0	0	0	0	0	0	0	0	0	0	0	0	0	0	0	0	0
Waste Facil.	20	15-Year	0	0	0	0	0	0	0	0	0	0	0	0	0	0	0	0	0
Sewers	30	20-Year	0	0	0	0	0	0	0	0	0	0	0	0	0	0	0	0	0
Real Estate	30	30-Year	0	0	0	0	0	0	0	0	0	0	0	0	0	0	0	0	0
Real Estate	30	Real Estate	0	0	0	0	0	0	0	0	0	0	0	0	0	0	0	0	0
Acquired Assets																				
Autos	5	3-Year													$966	$1,933	$1,933	$1,933		
Prod Eqp	8	5-Year													1,315	2,633	2,633	2,633	2,630	2,633
Prod Eqp	12	7-Year													625	1,250	1,250	1,250	1,250	1,250
Barges	15	10-Year													0	0	0	0	0	0
Waste Facil.	20	15-Year													286	571	571	571	571	571
Sewers	30	20-Year													0	0	0	0	0	0
Real Estate	30	30-Year													430	450	450	450	450	450
Real Estate	30	Real Estate																		
New Capital Expenditures																				
Autos	5	3-Year													$93	$282	$479	$682	$707	$732
Prod Eqp	8	5-Year													105	305	511	753	1,003	1,248
Prod Eqp	12	7-Year													79	259	479	716	992	1,320
Barges	15	10-Year													0	0	0	0	0	0
Waste Facil.	20	15-Year													12	36	61	87	113	140
Sewers	30	20-Year													0	0	0	0	0	0
Real Estate	30	30-Year													34	104	174	246	321	399
Real Estate	30	Real Estate																		
			$0	$0	$0	$0	$0	$0	$0	$0	$0	$0	$0	$0	$0	$3,945	$7,823	$8,540	$9,321	$8,038	$8,743

Note: If possible, obtain projected ACE tax depreciation figures from target company and input on this schedule.

EXHIBIT 22.42
05/20/92
03:26 PM

DEPRECIATION CALCULATIONS:
Page D-1   FILE: DEPR_3   3-YEAR PROPERTY

Acct. Desc.	Book Life	Tax Category	Year	Acquired Assets	Capital Expend.	1981	1982	1983	1984	1985	1986	1987	1988	1989	1990	1991	1992	sub-totals 1981-1992	1993	1994	1995	1996	1997	1998
Autos	5																							

Historical Book Depreciation

		Tax Category	Year	Acquired Assets	Capital Expend.	1981	1982	1983	1984	1985	1986	1987	1988	1989	1990	1991	1992		1993	1994	1995	1996	1997	1998
		ACRS - 3	1981		0	0																		
		ACRS - 3	1982		0		0	0																
		ACRS - 3	1983		0			0	0	0														
		ACRS - 3	1984		0				0	0	0													
		ACRS - 3	1985		0					0	0	0												
		ACRS - 3	1986		0						0	0	0											
		MACRS - 3	1987		0							0	0	0	0									
		MACRS - 3	1988		0								0	0	0	0								
		MACRS - 3	1989		0									0	0	0	0							
		MACRS - 3	1990		0										0	0	0	0						
		MACRS - 3	1991		0											0	0	0						
		MACRS - 3	1992		0												0	0						

Projected Book Depreciation for Acquired Assets —>

		Tax Category	Year	Acquired Assets	Capital Expend.														1993	1994	1995	1996	1997	1998
		MACRS - 3	1993	6,765	650														1,353	1,353	1,353	1,353	1,353	
		MACRS - 3	1993		675														65	130	130	130	130	65
		MACRS - 3	1994		700															68	135	135	135	135
		MACRS - 3	1995		725																70	140	140	140
		MACRS - 3	1996		750																	73	145	145
		MACRS - 3	1997		750																		75	150
		MACRS - 3	1998		775																			78
SUBTOTALS:				6,765		0	0	0	0	0	0	0	0	0	0	0	0	1,418	1,551	1,688	1,831	1,978	713

Subtotal: Projected Book Depreciation —> 65 198 335 478 625 713

Regular Tax Depreciation

REGULAR TAX:

		Tax Category	Year	Acquired Assets	Capital Expend.	1981	1982	1983	1984	1985	1986	1987	1988	1989	1990	1991	1992		1993	1994	1995	1996	1997	1998
		ACRS - 3	1981		0	0																		
		ACRS - 3	1982		0		0	0																
		ACRS - 3	1983		0			0	0	0														
		ACRS - 3	1984		0				0	0	0													
		ACRS - 3	1985		0					0	0	0												
		ACRS - 3	1986		0						0	0	0											
		MACRS - 3	1987		0							0	0	0	0									
		MACRS - 3	1988		0								0	0	0	0								
		MACRS - 3	1989		0									0	0	0	0							
		MACRS - 3	1990		0										0	0	0	0						
		MACRS - 3	1991		0											0	0	0						
		MACRS - 3	1992		0												0	0						

Subtotal: Projected Regular Tax Depreciation for No Change in Basis Assets —> 0 0 0 0 0 0

Projected Regular Tax Depreciation for Acquired Assets with New Basis

Proj. Regular Tax Depr. on Acq. Assets/New Capex

		Tax Category	Year	Acquired Assets	Capital Expend.														1993	1994	1995	1996	1997	1998
		MACRS - 3	1993	6,765	650														2,255	3,007	1,002	501		
		MACRS - 3	1993		675														217	289	96	48		
		MACRS - 3	1994		700															225	300	100	50	
		MACRS - 3	1995		725																233	311	104	52
		MACRS - 3	1996		750																	242	322	107
		MACRS - 3	1997		750																		250	333
		MACRS - 3	1998		775																			258
SUBTOTALS:				6,765		0	0	0	0	0	0	0	0	0	0	0	0	2,471	3,521	1,632	1,202	726	751

Subtotal: Projected Regular Tax Depreciation for New Capital Expenditures —> 217 514 630 701 726 751

EXHIBIT 22.43
05/20/92
03:26 PM

DEPRECIATION CALCULATIONS:
Page D-2 FILE: DEPR_3A **3-YEAR PROPERTY**

AMTI TAX:

AMTI Depreciation

Projected AMTI Depr. on Historical Capex

Acct. Desc.	Book Tax Category	Life	Year	Acquired Assets	Capital Expend.	1981	1982	1983	1984	1985	1986	1987	1988	1989	1990	1991	1992	sub-totals 1981–1992	1993	1994	1995	1996	1997	1998
	ACRS – 3		1981		0													0						
	ACRS – 3		1982		0													0						
	ACRS – 3		1983		0													0						
	ACRS – 3		1984		0													0						
	ACRS – 3		1985		0													0						
	ACRS – 3		1986		0							0						0						
	MACRS – 3		1987		0								0					0						
	MACRS – 3		1988		0									0				0						
	MACRS – 3		1989		0										0			0						
	MACRS – 3		1990		0											0		0						
	MACRS – 3		1991		0												0	0						
	MACRS – 3		1992		0													0						
			SUBTOTALS:	6,765		0	0	0	0	0								0						

Subtotal: Projected AMTI Depreciation for No Change in Basis Assets →
| | | | | | | | | | | | | | | | | | | 0 | 1,450 | 2,278 | 1,519 | 1,519 | 0 | 0 |

Projected AMTI Depreciation for Acquired Assets with New Basis →

Book Tax Category	Life	Year	Capital Expend.	1993	1994	1995	1996	1997	1998
MACRS – 3		1993	650	139	219	146	146		
MACRS – 3		1994	675		145	227	152	152	
MACRS – 3		1995	700			150	236	157	157
MACRS – 3		1996	725				155	244	163
MACRS – 3		1997	750					161	253
MACRS – 3		1998	775						166

Subtotal: Projected AMTI Depreciation for New Capital Expenditures →
| 139 | 364 | 523 | 689 | 714 | 739 |

| **TOTAL** | 1,589 | 2,641 | 2,042 | 2,207 | 714 | 739 |

ACE TAX:

ACE Depreciation

Projected ACE Depr. on Historical Capex

Acct. Desc.	Book Tax Category	Life	Year	Acquired Assets	Capital Expend.	1981	1982	1983	1984	1985	1986	1987	1988	1989	1990	1991	1992	sub-totals 1981–1992	1993	1994	1995	1996	1997	1998
	ACRS – 3		1981		0													0						
	ACRS – 3		1982		0													0						
	ACRS – 3		1983		0													0						
	ACRS – 3		1984		0													0						
	ACRS – 3		1985		0													0						
	ACRS – 3		1986		0							0						0						
	MACRS – 3		1987		0								0					0						
	MACRS – 3		1988		0									0				0						
	MACRS – 3		1989		0										0			0						
	MACRS – 3		1990		0											0		0						
	MACRS – 3		1991		0												0	0						
	MACRS – 3		1992		0													0						
			SUBTOTALS:	6,765		0	0	0	0	0								0						

Subtotal: Projected ACE Depreciation for No Change in Basis Assets →
| | | | | | | | | | | | | | | | | | | 0 | 966 | 1,933 | 1,933 | 1,933 | 0 | 0 |

Projected ACE Depreciation for Acquired Assets with New Basis →

Book Tax Category	Life	Year	Capital Expend.	1993	1994	1995	1996	1997	1998
MACRS – 3		1993	650	93	186	186	185		
MACRS – 3		1994	675		96	193	193	193	
MACRS – 3		1995	700			100	200	200	200
MACRS – 3		1996	725				104	207	207
MACRS – 3		1997	750					107	214
MACRS – 3		1998	775						111

Subtotal: Projected ACE Depreciation for New Capital Expenditures →
| 93 | 282 | 479 | 682 | 707 | 732 |

| **TOTAL** | 1,059 | 2,215 | 2,411 | 2,615 | 707 | 732 |

EXHIBIT 22.44
05/20/92
03:26 PM

DEPRECIATION CALCULATIONS:
Page D-3   FILE: DEPR_5

5-YEAR PROPERTY

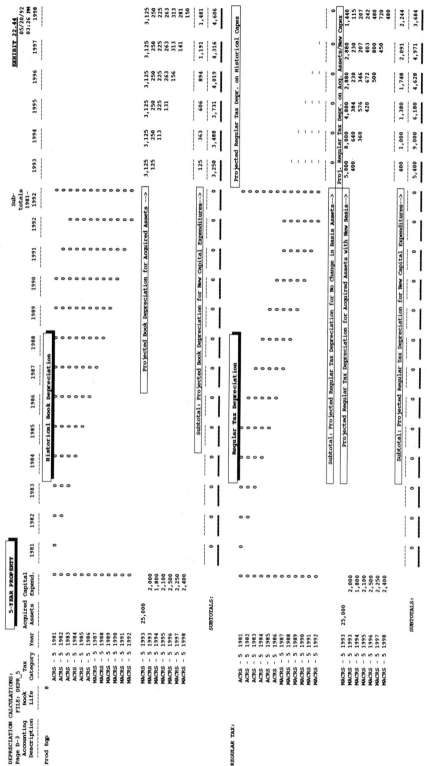

Accounting Description	Book Life	Tax Category	Year	Acquired Assets	Capital Expend.	1981	1982	1983	1984	1985	1986	1987	1988	1989	1990	1991	1992	sub-totals 1981-1992	1993	1994	1995	1996	1997	1998
Prod Exp	8																							

Historical Book Depreciation

		Tax Category	Year	Acquired Assets	Capital Expend.	1981	1982	1983	1984	1985	1986	1987	1988	1989	1990	1991	1992	subtotals 1981-1992	1993	1994	1995	1996	1997	1998
		ACRS - 5	1981	0	0	0																		
		ACRS - 5	1982	0	0		0	0																
		ACRS - 5	1983	0	0			0	0	0														
		ACRS - 5	1984	0	0				0	0	0													
		ACRS - 5	1985	0	0					0	0	0												
		ACRS - 5	1986	0	0						0	0	0											
		ACRS - 5	1987	0	0							0	0	0										
		MACRS - 5	1988	0	0								0	0	0	0								
		MACRS - 5	1989	0	0									0	0	0	0							
		MACRS - 5	1990	0	0										0	0	0	0						
		MACRS - 5	1991	0	0											0	0	0						
		MACRS - 5	1992	0	0												0	0						

Projected Book Depreciation for Acquired Assets -->

		Tax Category	Year	Acquired Assets	Capital Expend.	subtotals 1981-1992	1993	1994	1995	1996	1997	1998
		MACRS - 5	1993	25,000		0	3,125	3,125	3,125	3,125	3,125	3,125
		MACRS - 5	1993		2,000	0	125	250	250	250	250	250
		MACRS - 5	1994		1,800	0		113	225	225	225	225
		MACRS - 5	1995		2,100	0			131	263	263	263
		MACRS - 5	1996		2,500	0				156	263	313
		MACRS - 5	1997		2,250	0					141	313
		MACRS - 5	1998		2,400	0						150

Subtotal: Projected Book Depreciation for New Capital Expenditures -->

	1993	1994	1995	1996	1997	1998
Subtotal	125	363	606	894	1,191	1,481
SUBTOTALS: 25,000	3,250	3,488	3,731	4,019	4,316	4,606

REGULAR TAX:

Regular Tax Depreciation

Projected Regular Tax Depr. on Historical Capex

		Tax Category	Year	Acquired Assets	Capital Expend.	1981	1982	1983	1984	1985	1986	1987	1988	1989	1990	1991	1992	subtotals 1981-1992
		ACRS - 5	1981	0	0	0												0
		ACRS - 5	1982	0	0		0	0										0
		ACRS - 5	1983	0	0			0	0	0								0
		ACRS - 5	1984	0	0				0	0	0							0
		ACRS - 5	1985	0	0					0	0	0						0
		ACRS - 5	1986	0	0						0	0	0					0
		MACRS - 5	1987	0	0							0	0	0				0
		MACRS - 5	1988	0	0								0	0	0	0		0
		MACRS - 5	1989	0	0									0	0	0	0	0
		MACRS - 5	1990	0	0										0	0	0	0
		MACRS - 5	1991	0	0											0	0	0
		MACRS - 5	1992	0	0												0	0

Subtotal: Projected Regular Tax Depreciation for No Change in Basis Assets -->

Projected Regular Tax Depreciation for Acquired Assets with New Basis -->

Proj. Regular Tax Depr. on Acq. Assets/New Capex

		Tax Category	Year	Acquired Assets	Capital Expend.	1993	1994	1995	1996	1997	1998
		MACRS - 5	1993	25,000		5,000	8,000	4,800	2,880	2,880	1,440
		MACRS - 5	1993		2,000	400	640	576	346	230	115
		MACRS - 5	1994		1,800		360	420	672	384	207
		MACRS - 5	1995		2,100				500	403	242
		MACRS - 5	1996		2,500					800	480
		MACRS - 5	1997		2,250					450	720
		MACRS - 5	1998		2,400						480

Subtotal: Projected Regular Tax Depreciation for New Capital Expenditures -->

	1993	1994	1995	1996	1997	1998
Subtotal	400	1,000	1,380	1,748	2,091	2,244
SUBTOTALS: 25,000	5,400	9,000	6,180	4,628	4,971	3,684

DEPRECIATION CALCULATIONS:
Page D-4 FILE: DEPR_5A

5-YEAR PROPERTY

EXHIBIT 22.45
05/20/92
03:26 PM

AMTI TAX:

AMTI Depreciation

Accounting Description	Book Life	Tax Category	Year	Acquired Assets	Capital Expend.	1981	1982	1983	1984	1985	1986	1987	1988	1989	1990	1991	1992	subtotals 1981-1992	1993	1994	1995	1996	1997	1998
		ACRS - 5	1981	0														0						
		ACRS - 5	1982	0														0						
		ACRS - 5	1983	0														0						
		ACRS - 5	1984	0														0						
		ACRS - 5	1985	0														0						
		ACRS - 5	1986	0														0						
		ACRS - 5	1987	0														0						
		ACRS - 5	1988	0														0						
		ACRS - 5	1989	0														0						
		ACRS - 5	1990	0														0						
		ACRS - 5	1991	0														0						
		ACRS - 5	1992	0														0						
Subtotal: Projected AMTI Depreciation for No Change in Basis Assets--->						0	0	0	0	0	0	0	0	0	0	0	0	0	0	0	0	0	0	0
Projected AMTI Depreciation for Acquired Assets with New Basis--->																								
Projected AMTI Depr. on Acq. Assets/New Capex		MACRS - 5	1993	25,000															1,973	3,635	3,063	2,578	2,293	2,293
		MACRS - 5	1993		2,000														158	142	245	206	206	183
		MACRS - 5	1994		1,800															291	262	221	186	165
		MACRS - 5	1995		2,100																166	305	257	217
		MACRS - 5	1996		2,500																	197	364	306
		MACRS - 5	1997		2,250																		178	327
		MACRS - 5	1998		2,400																			189
Subtotal: Projected AMTI Depreciation for New Capital Expenditures--->						0	0	0	0	0	0	0	0	0	0	0	0	0	158	433	672	929	1,167	1,388
SUBTOTALS:						0	0	0	0	0	0	0	0	0	0	0	0	0	2,130	4,068	3,735	3,507	3,460	3,680

ACE TAX:

ACE Depreciation

Accounting Description	Book Life	Tax Category	Year	Acquired Assets	Capital Expend.	1981	1982	1983	1984	1985	1986	1987	1988	1989	1990	1991	1992	subtotals 1981-1992	1993	1994	1995	1996	1997	1998
		ACRS - 5	1981	0														0						
		ACRS - 5	1982	0														0						
		ACRS - 5	1983	0														0						
		ACRS - 5	1984	0														0						
		ACRS - 5	1985	0														0						
		ACRS - 5	1986	0														0						
		ACRS - 5	1987	0														0						
		ACRS - 5	1988	0														0						
		ACRS - 5	1989	0														0						
		ACRS - 5	1990	0														0						
		ACRS - 5	1991	0														0						
		ACRS - 5	1992	0														0						
Subtotal: Projected ACE Depreciation for No Change in Basis Assets--->						0	0	0	0	0	0	0	0	0	0	0	0	0	0	0	0	0	0	0
Projected ACE Depreciation for Acquired Assets with New Basis--->																								
Projected ACE Depr. on Acq. Assets/New Capex		MACRS - 5	1993	25,000															1,315	2,633	2,633	2,633	2,630	2,633
		MACRS - 5	1993		2,000														105	211	211	211	211	211
		MACRS - 5	1994		1,800															95	190	190	190	189
		MACRS - 5	1995		2,100																110	221	221	221
		MACRS - 5	1996		2,500																	132	263	263
		MACRS - 5	1997		2,250																		118	237
		MACRS - 5	1998		2,400																			126
Subtotal: Projected ACE Depreciation for New Capital Expenditures--->						0	0	0	0	0	0	0	0	0	0	0	0	0	105	305	511	753	1,003	1,248
SUBTOTALS:						0	0	0	0	0	0	0	0	0	0	0	0	0	1,420	2,938	3,143	3,385	3,633	3,880

EXHIBIT 22.46
05/20/92
03:26 PM

DEPRECIATION CALCULATIONS:
Page D-5
FILE: DEPR_7

7-YEAR PROPERTY

Prod Exp (Book Life: 12)

Historical Book Depreciation

Accounting Description	Tax Category	Year	Acquired Assets	Capital Expend.	1987	1988	1989	1990	1991	1992	Sub-totals 1981-1992	1993	1994	1995	1996	1997	1998
	MACRS - 7	1987	0			0	0	0	0	0	0						
	MACRS - 7	1988	0				0	0	0	0	0						
	MACRS - 7	1989	0					0	0	0	0						
	MACRS - 7	1990	0						0	0	0						
	MACRS - 7	1991	0							0	0						
	MACRS - 7	1992	0								0						

Projected Book Depreciation for Acquired Assets -->

Tax Category	Year	Acquired Assets	Capital Expend.	1993	1994	1995	1996	1997	1998
MACRS - 7	1993	15,000		1,250	1,250	1,250	1,250	1,250	1,250
MACRS - 7	1993		1,888	79	157	157	157	157	157
MACRS - 7	1994		2,444		102	204	204	204	204
MACRS - 7	1995		2,842			118	237	237	237
MACRS - 7	1996		2,838				118	237	237
MACRS - 7	1997		3,784					158	315
MACRS - 7	1998		4,084						170

Subtotal: Projected Book Depreciation for New Capital Expenditures -->

	1993	1994	1995	1996	1997	1998
	79	259	479	716	992	1,320

SUBTOTALS:

1981	1982	1983	1984	1985	1986	1987	1988	1989	1990	1991	1992	Sub-totals 1981-1992	1993	1994	1995	1996	1997	1998
0	0	0	0	0	0	0	0	0	0	0	0	0	1,329	1,509	1,729	1,966	2,242	2,570

REGULAR TAX:

Regular Tax Depreciation

Tax Category	Year	Acquired Assets	Capital Expend.	1987	1988	1989	1990	1991	1992	Sub-totals 1981-1992
MACRS - 7	1987	0			0	0	0	0	0	0
MACRS - 7	1988	0				0	0	0	0	0
MACRS - 7	1989	0					0	0	0	0
MACRS - 7	1990	0						0	0	0
MACRS - 7	1991	0							0	0
MACRS - 7	1992	0								0

Subtotal: Projected Regular Tax Depreciation for No Change in Basis Assets -->

Projected Regular Tax Depr. on Historical Capex / Projected Regular Tax Depr. on Acq. Assets/New Capex

Projected Regular Tax Depreciation for Acquired Assets with New Basis -->

Tax Category	Year	Acquired Assets	Capital Expend.	1993	1994	1995	1996	1997	1998
MACRS - 7	1993	15,000		2,144	3,674	2,624	1,874	1,340	1,338
MACRS - 7	1993		1,888	270	462	330	236	169	168
MACRS - 7	1994		2,444		349	599	427	305	218
MACRS - 7	1995		2,842			406	596	497	355
MACRS - 7	1996		2,838				406	695	496
MACRS - 7	1997		3,784					541	927
MACRS - 7	1998		4,084						584

Subtotal: Projected Regular Tax Depreciation for New Capital Expenditures -->

	1993	1994	1995	1996	1997	1998
	270	812	1,335	1,765	2,207	2,748

SUBTOTALS:

1981	1982	1983	1984	1985	1986	1987	1988	1989	1990	1991	1992	Sub-totals 1981-1992	1993	1994	1995	1996	1997	1998
0	0	0	0	0	0	0	0	0	0	0	0	0	2,413	4,485	3,958	3,638	3,546	4,086

EXHIBIT 22.4I
05/20/92
03:26 PM

DEPRECIATION CALCULATIONS:
Page D-6   FILE: DEPR.7A

7-YEAR PROPERTY

AMTI TAX:

AMTI Depreciation

Projected AMTI Depr. on Historical Capex

Accounting Description	Book Life	Tax Category	Year	Acquired Assets	Capital Expend.	1981	1982	1983	1984	1985	1986	1987	1988	1989	1990	1991	1992	Subtotals 1981-1992	1993	1994	1995	1996	1997	1998
		MACRS – 7	1987		0							0	0	0	0	0	0	0	—	—	—	—	—	—
		MACRS – 7	1988		0								0	0	0	0	0	0	—	—	—	—	—	—
		MACRS – 7	1989		0									0	0	0	0	0	—	—	—	—	—	—
		MACRS – 7	1990		0										0	0	0	0	—	—	—	—	—	—
		MACRS – 7	1991		0											0	0	0	—	—	—	—	—	—
		MACRS – 7	1992		0												0	0	—	—	—	—	—	—
Subtotal: Projected AMTI Depreciation for No Change in Basis Assets-->																		0	0	0	0	0	0	0

Projected AMTI Depr. on Acq. Assets/New Capex

Projected AMTI Depreciation for Acquired Assets with New Basis-->

Accounting Description	Tax Category	Year	Acquired Assets	Capital Expend.	1993	1994	1995	1996	1997	1998
	MACRS – 7	1993	15,000		938	1,758	1,538	1,346	1,178	1,100

Projected AMTI Depreciation for New Capital Expenditures-->

Accounting Description	Tax Category	Year	Capital Expend.	1993	1994	1995	1996	1997	1998
	MACRS – 7	1993	1,888	118	221	194	169	148	138
	MACRS – 7	1994	2,444		153	286	251	219	192
	MACRS – 7	1995	2,842			178	333	291	255
	MACRS – 7	1996	2,838				177	333	291
	MACRS – 7	1997	3,784					237	444
	MACRS – 7	1998	4,084						255
Subtotal: Projected AMTI Depreciation for New Capital Expenditures-->				118	374	658	930	1,228	1,575
SUBTOTALS:				1,056	2,132	2,195	2,276	2,405	2,674

ACE TAX:

ACE Depreciation

Projected ACE Depr. on Historical Capex

Accounting Description	Book Life	Tax Category	Year	Acquired Assets	Capital Expend.	1981	1982	1983	1984	1985	1986	1987	1988	1989	1990	1991	1992	Subtotals 1981-1992	1993	1994	1995	1996	1997	1998
		MACRS – 7	1987		0							0	0	0	0	0	0	0	—	—	—	—	—	—
		MACRS – 7	1988		0								0	0	0	0	0	0	—	—	—	—	—	—
		MACRS – 7	1989		0									0	0	0	0	0	—	—	—	—	—	—
		MACRS – 7	1990		0										0	0	0	0	—	—	—	—	—	—
		MACRS – 7	1991		0											0	0	0	—	—	—	—	—	—
		MACRS – 7	1992		0												0	0	—	—	—	—	—	—
Subtotal: Projected ACE Depreciation for No Change in Basis Assets-->																		0	0	0	0	0	0	0

Projected ACE Depr. on Acq. Assets/New Capex

Projected ACE Depreciation for Acquired Assets with New Basis-->

Accounting Description	Tax Category	Year	Acquired Assets	Capital Expend.	1993	1994	1995	1996	1997	1998
	MACRS – 7	1993	15,000		625	1,250	1,250	1,250	1,250	1,250

Projected ACE Depreciation for New Capital Expenditures-->

Accounting Description	Tax Category	Year	Capital Expend.	1993	1994	1995	1996	1997	1998
	MACRS – 7	1993	1,888	79	157	157	157	157	157
	MACRS – 7	1994	2,444		102	204	204	204	204
	MACRS – 7	1995	2,842			118	237	237	237
	MACRS – 7	1996	2,838				118	237	237
	MACRS – 7	1997	3,784					158	315
	MACRS – 7	1998	4,084						170
Subtotal: Projected ACE Depreciation for New Capital Expenditures-->				79	259	479	716	992	1,320
SUBTOTALS:				704	1,509	1,729	1,966	2,242	2,570

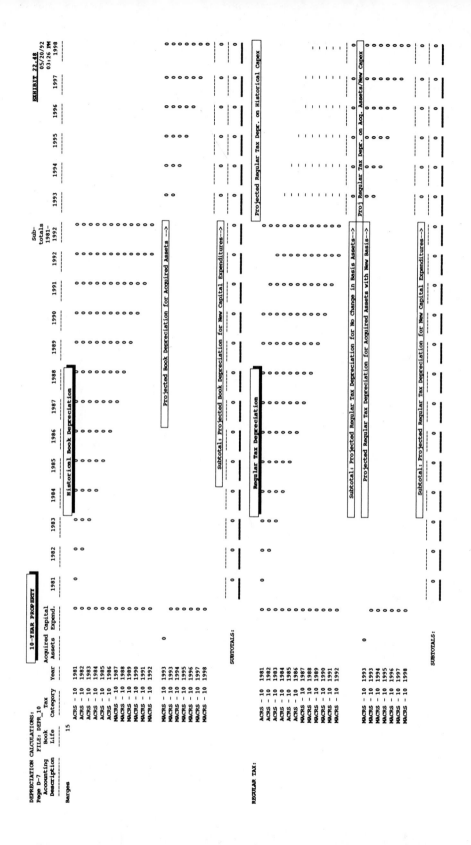

DEPRECIATION CALCULATIONS:
Page D-8
FILE: DEPR_10A

EXHIBIT 22.42
05/20/92
03:26 PM

10-YEAR PROPERTY

Accounting Description	Book Tax Category	Tax Life	Year	Acquired Assets	Capital Expend.	1981	1982	1983	1984	1985	1986	1987	1988	1989	1990	1991	1992	sub-totals 1981-1992	1993	1994	1995	1996	1997	1998

AMTI TAX:

AMTI Depreciation

	ACRS	- 10	1981		0													0						
	ACRS	- 10	1982		0													0						
	ACRS	- 10	1983		0													0						
	ACRS	- 10	1984		0													0						
	ACRS	- 10	1985		0													0						
	ACRS	- 10	1986		0													0						
	MACRS	- 10	1987		0							0						0	-	-	-	-	-	-
	MACRS	- 10	1988		0								0					0	-	-	-	-	-	-
	MACRS	- 10	1989		0									0				0	-	-	-	-	-	-
	MACRS	- 10	1990		0									0				0	-	-	-	-	-	-
	MACRS	- 10	1991		0											0		0	-	-	-	-	-	-
	MACRS	- 10	1992		0												0	0	-	-	-	-	-	-

Subtotal: Projected AMTI Depreciation for No Change in Basis Assets--> 0 0 0 0 0 0 0 0 0 0 0 0 0 0 0 0 0 0 0

Projected AMTI Depreciation for Acquired Assets with New Basis-->

	MACRS	- 10	1993	0	0														0	0	0	0	0	0
	MACRS	- 10	1993		0														0	0	0	0	0	0
	MACRS	- 10	1994		0														0	0	0	0	0	0
	MACRS	- 10	1995		0															0	0	0	0	0
	MACRS	- 10	1996		0																0	0	0	0
	MACRS	- 10	1997		0																	0	0	0
	MACRS	- 10	1998		0																		0	0

Subtotal: Projected AMTI Depreciation for New Capital Expenditures--> 0 0 0 0 0 0 0 0 0 0 0 0 0 0 0 0 0 0 0

SUBTOTALS: 0 0 0 0 0 0 0 0 0 0 0 0 0 0 0 0 0 0 0

ACE TAX:

ACE Depreciation

	ACRS	- 10	1981		0													0						
	ACRS	- 10	1982		0													0						
	ACRS	- 10	1983		0													0						
	ACRS	- 10	1984		0													0						
	ACRS	- 10	1985		0													0						
	ACRS	- 10	1986		0													0						
	MACRS	- 10	1987		0							0						0	-	-	-	-	-	-
	MACRS	- 10	1988		0								0					0	-	-	-	-	-	-
	MACRS	- 10	1989		0									0				0	-	-	-	-	-	-
	MACRS	- 10	1990		0									0				0	-	-	-	-	-	-
	MACRS	- 10	1991		0											0		0	-	-	-	-	-	-
	MACRS	- 10	1992		0												0	0	-	-	-	-	-	-

Subtotal: Projected ACE Depreciation for No Change in Basis Assets--> 0 0 0 0 0 0 0 0 0 0 0 0 0 0 0 0 0 0 0

Projected ACE Depreciation for Acquired Assets with New Basis-->

	MACRS	- 10	1993	0	0														0	0	0	0	0	0
	MACRS	- 10	1993		0														0	0	0	0	0	0
	MACRS	- 10	1994		0														0	0	0	0	0	0
	MACRS	- 10	1995		0															0	0	0	0	0
	MACRS	- 10	1996		0																0	0	0	0
	MACRS	- 10	1997		0																	0	0	0
	MACRS	- 10	1998		0																		0	0

Subtotal: Projected ACE Depreciation for New Capital Expenditures--> 0 0 0 0 0 0 0 0 0 0 0 0 0 0 0 0 0 0 0

SUBTOTALS: 0 0 0 0 0 0 0 0 0 0 0 0 0 0 0 0 0 0 0

Projected AMTI Depr. on Historical Capex

Projected AMTI Depr. on Acq. Assets/New Capex

Projected ACE Depr. on Historical Capex

Projected ACE Depr. on Acq. Assets/New Capex

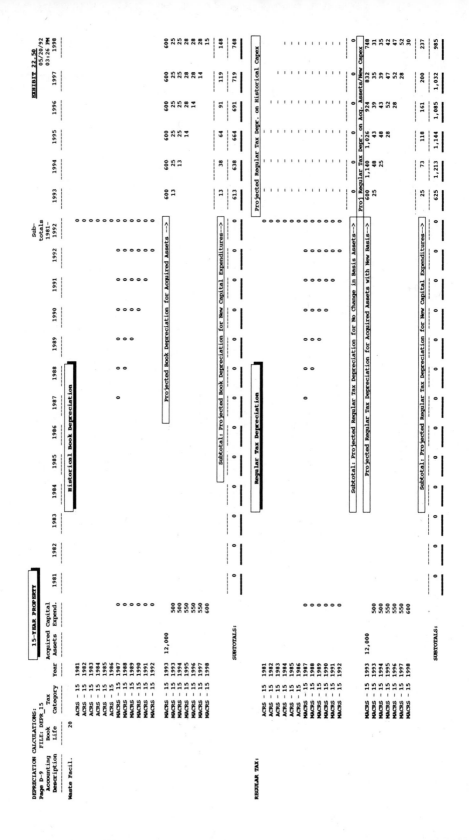

DEPRECIATION CALCULATIONS:
Page D-9   FILE: DEPR_15

15-YEAR PROPERTY

EXHIBIT 22.50
05/20/92
03:26 PM

Accounting Description	Book Life	Tax Category	Year	Acquired Assets	Capital Expend.	1981	1982	1983	1984	1985	1986	1987	1988	1989	1990	1991	1992	sub-totals 1981-1992	1993	1994	1995	1996	1997	1998
Waste Facil.	20																							

Historical Book Depreciation

	Book Life	Tax Category	Year	Acquired Assets	Capital Expend.	1981	1982	1983	1984	1985	1986	1987	1988	1989	1990	1991	1992	subtotals 1981-1992	1993	1994	1995	1996	1997	1998
	ACRS - 15		1981			0	0	0	0	0	0	0	0	0	0	0	0	0						
	ACRS - 15		1982				0	0	0	0	0	0	0	0	0	0	0	0						
	ACRS - 15		1983					0	0	0	0	0	0	0	0	0	0	0						
	ACRS - 15		1984						0	0	0	0	0	0	0	0	0	0						
	ACRS - 15		1985							0	0	0	0	0	0	0	0	0						
	ACRS - 15		1986								0	0	0	0	0	0	0	0						
	ACRS - 15		1987									0	0	0	0	0	0	0						
	MACRS - 15		1988										0	0	0	0	0	0						
	MACRS - 15		1989											0	0	0	0	0						
	MACRS - 15		1990												0	0	0	0						
	MACRS - 15		1991													0	0	0						
	MACRS - 15		1992														0	0						

Projected Book Depreciation for Acquired Assets --->

	MACRS - 15		1993	12,000															600	600	600	600	600	600
	MACRS - 15		1993		500														13	25	25	25	25	25
	MACRS - 15		1994		500															13	25	25	25	25
	MACRS - 15		1995		550																14	28	28	28
	MACRS - 15		1996		550																	14	28	28
	MACRS - 15		1997		550																		14	28
	MACRS - 15		1998		600																			15

Subtotal: Projected Book Depreciation for New Capital Expenditures --->

| | | | | | | | | | | | | | | | | | | | 13 | 38 | 64 | 91 | 119 | 148 |

| SUBTOTALS: | | | | | | 0 | 0 | 0 | 0 | 0 | 0 | 0 | 0 | 0 | 0 | 0 | 0 | 0 | 613 | 638 | 664 | 691 | 719 | 748 |

Regular Tax Depreciation

	Book Life	Tax Category	Year	Acquired Assets	Capital Expend.	1981	1982	1983	1984	1985	1986	1987	1988	1989	1990	1991	1992	subtotals 1981-1992	1993	1994	1995	1996	1997	1998
	ACRS - 15		1981			0	0	0	0	0	0	0	0	0	0	0	0	0						
	ACRS - 15		1982				0	0	0	0	0	0	0	0	0	0	0	0						
	ACRS - 15		1983					0	0	0	0	0	0	0	0	0	0	0						
	ACRS - 15		1984						0	0	0	0	0	0	0	0	0	0						
	ACRS - 15		1985							0	0	0	0	0	0	0	0	0						
	ACRS - 15		1986								0	0	0	0	0	0	0	0						
	ACRS - 15		1987									0	0	0	0	0	0	0						
	MACRS - 15		1988										0	0	0	0	0	0						
	MACRS - 15		1989											0	0	0	0	0						
	MACRS - 15		1990												0	0	0	0						
	MACRS - 15		1991													0	0	0						
	MACRS - 15		1992														0	0						

Subtotal: Projected Regular Tax Depreciation for No Change in Basis Assets --->
Projected Regular Tax Depreciation for Acquired Assets with New Basis --->

| | | | | | | | | | | | | | | | | | | | 0 | 0 | 0 | 0 | 0 | 0 |

Proj Regular Tax Depr. on Acq. Assets/New Capex

	MACRS - 15		1993	12,000															600	1,140	1,026	924	832	748
	MACRS - 15		1993		500														25	25	48	43	39	35
	MACRS - 15		1994		500															48	43	39	35	31
	MACRS - 15		1995		550																28	52	47	42
	MACRS - 15		1996		550																	28	52	47
	MACRS - 15		1997		550																		28	52
	MACRS - 15		1998		600																			30

Subtotal: Projected Regular Tax Depreciation for New Capital Expenditures --->

| | | | | | | | | | | | | | | | | | | | 25 | 73 | 118 | 161 | 200 | 237 |

| SUBTOTALS: | | | | | | 0 | 0 | 0 | 0 | 0 | 0 | 0 | 0 | 0 | 0 | 0 | 0 | 0 | 625 | 1,213 | 1,144 | 1,085 | 1,032 | 985 |

Projected Regular Tax Depr. on Historical Capex

EXHIBIT 22-51
05/20/92
03:26 PM

DEPRECIATION CALCULATIONS:
Page D-10
FILE: DEPR_15A

15-YEAR PROPERTY

AMTI TAX:

AMTI Depreciation

Projected AMTI Depr. on Historical Capex

Accounting Description	Book Life	Tax Category	Year	Acquired Assets	Capital Expend.	1981	1982	1983	1984	1985	1986	1987	1988	1989	1990	1991	1992	Sub-totals 1981-1992	1993	1994	1995	1996	1997	1998
		ACRS - 15	1981																					
		ACRS - 15	1982																					
		ACRS - 15	1983																					
		ACRS - 15	1984																					
		ACRS - 15	1985																					
		ACRS - 15	1986									0												
		MACRS - 15	1987		0								0											
		MACRS - 15	1988		0								0	0										
		MACRS - 15	1989		0									0	0									
		MACRS - 15	1990		0									0	0	0								
		MACRS - 15	1991		0										0	0								
		MACRS - 15	1992		0										0	0								

Subtotal: Projected AMTI Depreciation for No Change in Basis Assets--> 0 0 0 0 0 0 0 0 0 0 0 0 | 0 | 0 0 0 0 0 0

Projected AMTI Depreciation for Acquired Assets with New Basis-->

Tax Category	Year	Acquired Assets	Capital Expend.	Sub-totals 1981-1992	1993	1994	1995	1996	1997	1998
MACRS - 15	1993	12,000		0	429	827	768	713	662	615
MACRS - 15	1993		500	0	18	34	32	30	28	26
MACRS - 15	1994		500	0		18	34	32	30	28
MACRS - 15	1995		550	0			20	38	35	33
MACRS - 15	1996		550	0				20	38	35
MACRS - 15	1997		550	0					20	38
MACRS - 15	1998		600	0						21

Subtotal: Projected AMTI Depreciation for New Capital Expenditures--> 0 (1981-1992) | 18 52 86 119 150 180

SUBTOTALS: 0 (1981-1992) | 446 879 854 832 812 795

ACE TAX:

ACE Depreciation

Projected ACE Depr. on Historical Capex

Accounting Description	Book Life	Tax Category	Year	Acquired Assets	Capital Expend.	1981-1992	1993	1994	1995	1996	1997	1998
		ACRS - 15	1981									
		ACRS - 15	1982									
		ACRS - 15	1983									
		ACRS - 15	1984									
		ACRS - 15	1985									
		ACRS - 15	1986									
		MACRS - 15	1987		0							
		MACRS - 15	1988		0							
		MACRS - 15	1989		0							
		MACRS - 15	1990		0							
		MACRS - 15	1991		0							
		MACRS - 15	1992		0							

Subtotal: Projected ACE Depreciation for No Change in Basis Assets--> 0 | 0 0 0 0 0 0

Projected ACE Depreciation for Acquired Assets with New Basis-->

Tax Category	Year	Acquired Assets	Capital Expend.	Sub-totals 1981-1992	1993	1994	1995	1996	1997	1998
MACRS - 15	1993	12,000		0	286	571	571	571	571	571
MACRS - 15	1993		500	0	12	24	24	24	24	24
MACRS - 15	1994		500	0		12	24	24	24	24
MACRS - 15	1995		550	0			13	26	26	26
MACRS - 15	1996		550	0				13	26	26
MACRS - 15	1997		550	0					13	26
MACRS - 15	1998		600	0						14

Subtotal: Projected ACE Depreciation for New Capital Expenditures--> 0 (1981-1992) | 12 36 61 87 113 140

SUBTOTALS: 0 (1981-1992) | 298 607 632 658 685 712

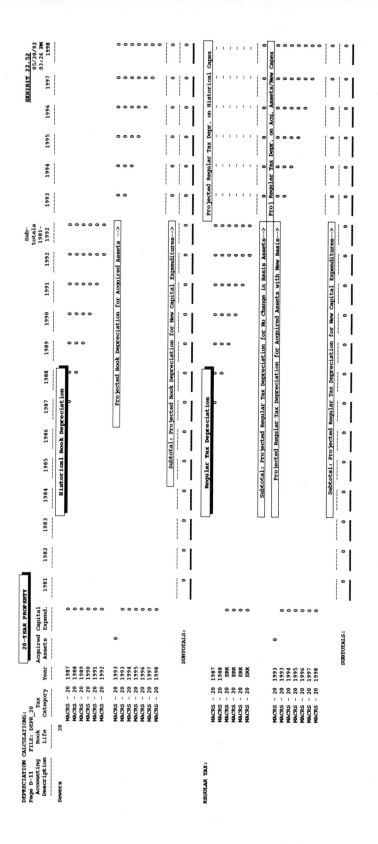

EXHIBIT 22.52
05/20/92
03:26 PM

DEPRECIATION CALCULATIONS:
Page D-11   FILE: DEPR_20

20-YEAR PROPERTY

Accounting Description	Book Life	Tax Category	Year	Acquired Assets	Capital Expend.	1981	1982	1983	1984	1985	1986	1987	1988	1989	1990	1991	1992	Subtotals 1981-1992	1993	1994	1995	1996	1997	1998

Sewers   30

Historical Book Depreciation

MACRS – 20	1987		0								0												
MACRS – 20	1988		0								0	0											
MACRS – 20	1989		0									0	0	0									
MACRS – 20	1990		0										0	0	0								
MACRS – 20	1991		0											0	0	0							
MACRS – 20	1992		0												0	0	0						

Projected Book Depreciation for Acquired Assets --->

MACRS – 20	1993		0														0	0				
MACRS – 20	1994		0															0	0			
MACRS – 20	1995		0																0	0		
MACRS – 20	1996		0																	0	0	
MACRS – 20	1997		0																		0	0
MACRS – 20	1998		0																			0

Subtotal: Projected Book Depreciation for New Capital Expenditures --->

SUBTOTALS: 0   0   0   0   0   0   0   0   0   0   0   0   0   0   0   0   0   0

REGULAR TAX:

Regular Tax Depreciation

Projected Regular Tax Depr. on Historical Capex

MACRS – 20	1987			0								-	-	-	-	-	-	-	-	-	-	-	-
MACRS – 20	1988			0								0	-	-	-	-	-	-	-	-	-	-	-
MACRS – 20	ERR			0									-	-	-	-	-	-	-	-	-	-	-
MACRS – 20	ERR			0										-	-	-	-	-	-	-	-	-	-
MACRS – 20	ERR			0											-	-	-	-	-	-	-	-	-
MACRS – 20	ERR			0												-	-	-	-	-	-	-	-

Subtotal: Projected Regular Tax Depreciation for No Change in Basis Assets --->

Proj Regular Tax Depr. on Acq. Assets/New Capex

Projected Regular Tax Depreciation for Acquired Assets with New Basis --->

MACRS – 20	1993			0													0	0				
MACRS – 20	1993			0													0	0				
MACRS – 20	1994			0														0	0			
MACRS – 20	1995			0															0	0		
MACRS – 20	1996			0																0	0	
MACRS – 20	1997			0																	0	0
MACRS – 20	1998			0																		0

Subtotal: Projected Regular Tax Depreciation for New Capital Expenditures --->

SUBTOTALS: 0   0   0   0   0   0   0   0   0   0   0   0   0   0   0   0   0   0

EXHIBIT 22.53
05/20/92
03:26 PM

DEPRECIATION CALCULATIONS:
Page D-12
FILE: DEPR_20A

20-YEAR PROPERTY

Accounting Description	Book Life	Tax Category	Year	Acquired Assets	Capital Expend.	1981	1982	1983	1984	1985	1986	1987	1988	1989	1990	1991	1992	subtotals 1981-1992	1993	1994	1995	1996	1997	1998

AMTI TAX:

AMTI Depreciation

Projected AMTI Depr. on Historical Capex

	MACRS - 20	1987	0									0						0						
	MACRS - 20	1988	0										0	0				0						
	MACRS - 20	1989	0											0	0			0						
	MACRS - 20	1990	0												0	0		0						
	MACRS - 20	1991	0													0	0	0						
	MACRS - 20	1992	0														0	0						

Subtotal: Projected AMTI Depreciation for No Change in Basis Assets —> 0 0 0 0 0 0 0 0 0 0 0 0 0 0 0 0 0 0 0 0

Projected AMTI Depr. on Acq. Assets/New Capex

Projected AMTI Depreciation for Acquired Assets with New Basis

	MACRS - 20	1993	0																0					
	MACRS - 20	1994		0															0	0				
	MACRS - 20	1995		0															0	0	0			
	MACRS - 20	1996		0															0	0	0	0		
	MACRS - 20	1997		0															0	0	0	0	0	
	MACRS - 20	1998		0															0	0	0	0	0	0

Subtotal: Projected AMTI Depreciation for New Capital Expenditures —> 0 0 0 0 0 0 0 0 0 0 0 0 0 0 0 0 0 0 0 0

SUBTOTALS: 0 0 0 0 0 0 0 0 0 0 0 0 0 0 0 0 0 0 0 0

ACE TAX:

ACE Depreciation

Projected ACE Depr. on Historical Capex

	MACRS - 20	1987	0									0						0						
	MACRS - 20	1988	0										0	0				0						
	MACRS - 20	1989	0											0	0			0						
	MACRS - 20	1990	0												0	0		0						
	MACRS - 20	1991	0													0	0	0						
	MACRS - 20	1992	0														0	0						

Subtotal: Projected ACE Depreciation for No Change in Basis Assets —> 0 0 0 0 0 0 0 0 0 0 0 0 0 0 0 0 0 0 0 0

Projected ACE Depr. on Acq. Assets/New Capex

Projected ACE Depreciation for Acquired Assets with New Basis

	MACRS - 20	1993	0																0					
	MACRS - 20	1994		0															0	0				
	MACRS - 20	1995		0															0	0	0			
	MACRS - 20	1996		0															0	0	0	0		
	MACRS - 20	1997		0															0	0	0	0	0	
	MACRS - 20	1998		0															0	0	0	0	0	0

Subtotal: Projected ACE Depreciation for New Capital Expenditures —> 0 0 0 0 0 0 0 0 0 0 0 0 0 0 0 0 0 0 0 0

SUBTOTALS: 0 0 0 0 0 0 0 0 0 0 0 0 0 0 0 0 0 0 0 0

333

EXHIBIT 22-54
05/20/92
03:26 PM

DEPRECIATION CALCULATIONS:
Page D-13   FILE: DEPR_REAL

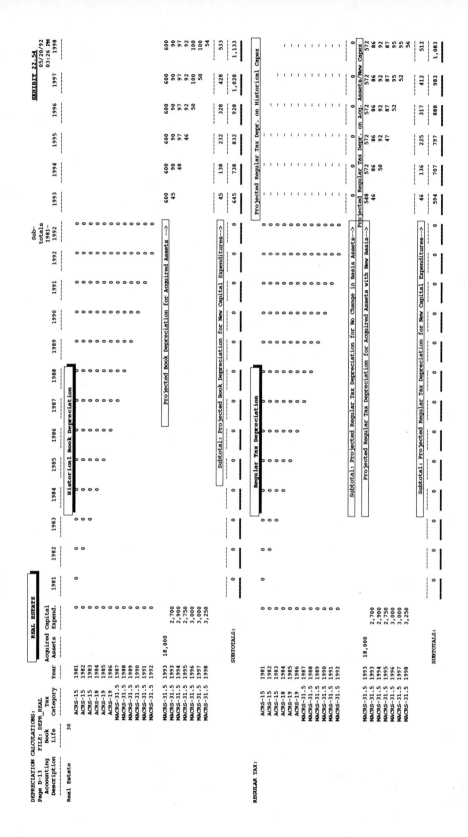

Real Estate   Book Life: 30

Historical Book Depreciation

Accounting Description	Book Life	Tax Category	Year	Acquired Assets	Capital Expend.	1981	1982	1983	1984	1985	1986	1987	1988	1989	1990	1991	1992	1993	1994	1995	1996	1997	1998
Real Estate	30	ACRS-15	1981			0	0	0	0	0	0	0	0	0	0	0	0						
		ACRS-15	1982				0	0	0	0	0	0	0	0	0	0	0						
		ACRS-15	1983					0	0	0	0	0	0	0	0	0	0						
		ACRS-18	1984						0	0	0	0	0	0	0	0	0						
		ACRS-19	1985							0	0	0	0	0	0	0	0						
		ACRS-19	1986								0	0	0	0	0	0	0						
		MACRS-31.5	1987									0	0	0	0	0	0						
		MACRS-31.5	1988										0	0	0	0	0						
		MACRS-31.5	1989											0	0	0	0						
		MACRS-31.5	1990												0	0	0						
		MACRS-31.5	1991													0	0						
		MACRS-31.5	1992														0						

Projected Book Depreciation for Acquired Assets -->

		MACRS-31.5	1993	18,000															600	600	600	600	600	600
		MACRS-31.5	1993		2,700														45	90	90	90	90	90
		MACRS-31.5	1994		2,900															48	97	97	97	97
		MACRS-31.5	1995		2,750																46	92	92	92
		MACRS-31.5	1996		3,000																	50	100	100
		MACRS-31.5	1997		3,000																		50	100
		MACRS-31.5	1998		3,250																			54

Subtotal: Projected Book Depreciation for New Capital Expenditures-->

| | | | | | | 0 | 0 | 0 | 0 | 0 | 0 | 0 | 0 | 0 | 0 | 0 | 0 | 45 | 138 | 232 | 328 | 428 | 533 |

| SUBTOTALS: | | | | 18,000 | | 0 | 0 | 0 | 0 | 0 | 0 | 0 | 0 | 0 | 0 | 0 | 0 | 645 | 738 | 832 | 928 | 1,028 | 1,133 |

REGULAR TAX:

Regular Tax Depreciation

		ACRS-15	1981			0	0	0	0	0	0	0	0	0	0	0	0						
		ACRS-15	1982				0	0	0	0	0	0	0	0	0	0	0						
		ACRS-15	1983					0	0	0	0	0	0	0	0	0	0						
		ACRS-18	1984						0	0	0	0	0	0	0	0	0						
		ACRS-19	1985							0	0	0	0	0	0	0	0						
		ACRS-19	1986								0	0	0	0	0	0	0						
		MACRS-31.5	1987									0	0	0	0	0	0						
		MACRS-31.5	1988										0	0	0	0	0						
		MACRS-31.5	1989											0	0	0	0						
		MACRS-31.5	1990												0	0	0						
		MACRS-31.5	1991													0	0						
		MACRS-31.5	1992														0						

Projected Regular Tax Depr. on Historical Capex

Subtotal: Projected Regular Tax Depreciation for No Change in Basis Assets-->

| | | | | | | 0 | 0 | 0 | 0 | 0 | 0 | 0 | 0 | 0 | 0 | 0 | 0 | 0 | 0 | 0 | 0 | 0 | 0 |

Projected Regular Tax Depr. on Acq. Assets/New Capex

Projected Regular Tax Depreciation for Acquired Assets with New Basis-->

		MACRS-31.5	1993	18,000															548	572	572	572	572	572
		MACRS-31.5	1993		2,700														46	86	86	86	86	86
		MACRS-31.5	1994		2,900															50	92	92	92	92
		MACRS-31.5	1995		2,750																47	87	87	87
		MACRS-31.5	1996		3,000																	52	95	95
		MACRS-31.5	1997		3,000																		52	95
		MACRS-31.5	1998		3,250																			56

Subtotal: Projected Regular Tax Depreciation for New Capital Expenditures-->

| | | | | | | 0 | 0 | 0 | 0 | 0 | 0 | 0 | 0 | 0 | 0 | 0 | 0 | 46 | 136 | 225 | 317 | 412 | 512 |

| SUBTOTALS: | | | | 18,000 | | 0 | 0 | 0 | 0 | 0 | 0 | 0 | 0 | 0 | 0 | 0 | 0 | 594 | 707 | 797 | 888 | 983 | 1,083 |

EXHIBIT 22.55
05/20/92
03:26 PM

DEPRECIATION CALCULATIONS:
Page D-14
FILE: DEPR_REALA

REAL ESTATE

AMTI TAX:

AMTI Depreciation

Projected AMTI Depr. on Historical Capex

Description	Book Tax Life Category	Year	Acquired Assets	Capital Expend.	1981	1982	1983	1984	1985	1986	1987	1988	1989	1990	1991	1992	Sub-totals 1981-1992	1993	1994	1995	1996	1997	1998
	ACRS-15	1981		0		0	0	0	0	0	0	0	0	0	0	0	0	—	—	—	—	—	—
	ACRS-15	1982		0		0	0	0	0	0	0	0	0	0	0	0	0	—	—	—	—	—	—
	ACRS-15	1983		0		0	0	0	0	0	0	0	0	0	0	0	0	—	—	—	—	—	—
	ACRS-18	1984		0		0	0	0	0	0	0	0	0	0	0	0	0	—	—	—	—	—	—
	ACRS-19	1985		0		0	0	0	0	0	0	0	0	0	0	0	0	—	—	—	—	—	—
	ACRS-19	1986		0			0	0	0	0	0	0	0	0	0	0	0	—	—	—	—	—	—
	MACRS-31.5	1987		0			0	0	0	0	0	0	0	0	0	0	0	—	—	—	—	—	—
	MACRS-31.5	1988		0				0	0	0	0	0	0	0	0	0	0	—	—	—	—	—	—
	MACRS-31.5	1989		0					0	0	0	0	0	0	0	0	0	—	—	—	—	—	—
	MACRS-31.5	1990		0						0	0	0	0	0	0	0	0	—	—	—	—	—	—
	MACRS-31.5	1991		0							0	0	0	0	0	0	0	—	—	—	—	—	—
	MACRS-31.5	1992		0								0	0	0	0	0	0	—	—	—	—	—	—

Subtotal: Projected AMTI Depreciation for No Change in Basis Assets ---> 0

Projected AMTI Depreciation for Acquired Assets with New Basis --->

Description	Category	Year	Acquired Assets	Capital Expend.	Sub-totals 1981-1992	1993	1994	1995	1996	1997	1998
	MACRS-31.5	1993	18,000		0	430	450	450	450	450	450
	MACRS-31.5	1993		2,700		34	68	68	68	68	68
	MACRS-31.5	1994		2,900			36	72	72	72	72
	MACRS-31.5	1995		2,750				34	69	69	69
	MACRS-31.5	1996		3,000					38	75	75
	MACRS-31.5	1997		3,000						37	75
	MACRS-31.5	1998		3,250							41

Subtotal: Projected AMTI Depreciation for New Capital Expenditures --->
| 0 | 34 | 104 | 174 | 246 | 321 | 399 |

Projected AMTI Depr. on Acq. Assets/New Capex
| 0 | 464 | 554 | 624 | 696 | 771 | 849 |

SUBTOTALS:

ACE TAX:

ACE Depreciation

Projected ACE Depr. on Historical Capex

Description	Book Tax Life Category	Year	Acquired Assets	Capital Expend.	1981	1982	1983	1984	1985	1986	1987	1988	1989	1990	1991	1992	Sub-totals 1981-1992	1993	1994	1995	1996	1997	1998
	ACRS-15	1981		0		0	0	0	0	0	0	0	0	0	0	0	0	—	—	—	—	—	—
	ACRS-15	1982		0		0	0	0	0	0	0	0	0	0	0	0	0	—	—	—	—	—	—
	ACRS-15	1983		0		0	0	0	0	0	0	0	0	0	0	0	0	—	—	—	—	—	—
	ACRS-18	1984		0		0	0	0	0	0	0	0	0	0	0	0	0	—	—	—	—	—	—
	ACRS-19	1985		0		0	0	0	0	0	0	0	0	0	0	0	0	—	—	—	—	—	—
	ACRS-19	1986		0			0	0	0	0	0	0	0	0	0	0	0	—	—	—	—	—	—
	MACRS-31.5	1987		0			0	0	0	0	0	0	0	0	0	0	0	—	—	—	—	—	—
	MACRS-31.5	1988		0				0	0	0	0	0	0	0	0	0	0	—	—	—	—	—	—
	MACRS-31.5	1989		0					0	0	0	0	0	0	0	0	0	—	—	—	—	—	—
	MACRS-31.5	1990		0						0	0	0	0	0	0	0	0	—	—	—	—	—	—
	MACRS-31.5	1991		0							0	0	0	0	0	0	0	—	—	—	—	—	—
	MACRS-31.5	1992		0								0	0	0	0	0	0	—	—	—	—	—	—

Subtotal: Projected ACE Depreciation for No Change in Basis Assets ---> 0

Projected ACE Depreciation for Acquired Assets with New Basis --->

Description	Category	Year	Acquired Assets	Capital Expend.	Sub-totals 1981-1992	1993	1994	1995	1996	1997	1998
	MACRS-31.5	1993	18,000		0	430	450	450	450	450	450
	MACRS-31.5	1993		2,700		34	68	68	68	68	68
	MACRS-31.5	1994		2,900			36	72	72	72	72
	MACRS-31.5	1995		2,750				34	69	69	69
	MACRS-31.5	1996		3,000					38	75	75
	MACRS-31.5	1997		3,000						37	75
	MACRS-31.5	1998		3,250							41

Subtotal: Projected ACE Depreciation for New Capital Expenditures --->
| 0 | 34 | 104 | 174 | 246 | 321 | 399 |

Projected ACE Depr. on Acq. Assets/New Capex
| 0 | 464 | 554 | 624 | 696 | 771 | 849 |

SUBTOTALS:

Chapter 23

Leveraged Buyout Models

23.0 INTRODUCTION

Chapter 23 describes acquisition models that can be used for completing an initial *Leveraged Buyout Analysis (Initial LBO Model)* when information is limited, and a later stage LBO Analysis (*Final LBO Model*) after due diligence has been completed. Chapters 15 and 17 describe the theory behind these models.

An *Initial LBO Model* is prepared when the acquirer decides, on a preliminary basis, that the target company fits the acquirer's acquisition interests. This acquirer is usually an LBO firm but can be a strategic buyer looking to perform an LBO Analysis.

In most instances, an Initial LBO Model is prepared at the point when the only access the acquirer has to information about the target is a selling memorandum. A *Final LBO Model* is prepared after the acquirer has completed extensive due diligence of the target company. This model incorporates knowledge obtained during due diligence, as well as current assumptions about financing terms available to the acquirer for this particular acquisition.

In many instances, a *Monthly LBO Model* is prepared in conjunction with the Final LBO Model. This model examines the projected cash flow characteristics of the company in the first 12 months after the transaction would be consummated. This model is similar to the Final LBO Model in most respects.

23.1   AN EXAMPLE

The example that will be used in this chapter is the same used in the previous chapter and originally introduced in Chapter 10. We will assume that Harrison Corporation has prepared an LBO Analysis to understand the maximum purchase price that an aggressive LBO firm could pay. In completing the LBO Analysis Harrison has raised the purchase price to the maximum point where financing is believed to be available. This point was determined through trial and error. Typically, the maximum price that an LBO firm can pay is limited by interest coverage ratios mandated by the lenders and the rates of return that various capital providers require.

23.2   THE INITIAL LBO MODEL

The Initial LBO Model consists of the schedules listed below.

- Executive Summary (Exhibit 23–1).
- Financing, Tax, Transaction Costs and Acquisition Method Assumptions (Exhibit 23–2).
- Economic and Operating Assumptions (Exhibit 23–3).
- Income Statements (Exhibit 23–4).
- Statements of Net Assets (Exhibit 23–5).
- Statements of Changes in Financial Position (Exhibit 23–6).
- Ownership Breakdown and Calculation of Gross Residual Values (Exhibit 23–7).
- Net Residual Value Calculations—Assuming Sale (Exhibits 23–8 and 23–9).
- After-Tax Investment Return Calculations (Exhibit 23–10).
- Selected Financial Ratios (Exhibit 23–11).
- Summary Amortization Schedule (Exhibit 23–12).
- Summary Debt Amortization and Interest Expense Schedule (Exhibit 23–13).
- Debt Amortization Schedules (Exhibit 23–14 and 23–15).
- Debt Amortization and Preferred Stock Redemption Schedules (Exhibit 23–16).
- Financial Statement Tax Provision (Exhibit 23–17).

23.21   Executive Summary

The Executive Summary displays many of the key assumptions used in the LBO Analysis and the results of the analysis. The information in the Executive Summary is broken down into 10 sections, as Exhibit 23–1 indicates.

- *Uses of Funds:* The Uses of Funds section depicts the purchase price for the target operation and the additional cash (if any) that the acquirer believes is required to run the business. The acquisition cost includes the cost to acquire: (1) common stock, (2) any common stock options, and (3) preferred stock and related transaction expenses. The acquisition cost also includes the value of liabilities (excluding trade payables, accrued expenses and any deferred taxes) assumed by the acquirer.

  The cost to acquire Mareight Corporation is approximately $104 million, including roughly $4.2 million in transaction expenses.

- *Sources of Funds:* The Sources of Funds section includes assumptions regarding how the acquirer intends to finance the transaction. Sources of funds could include, but are not limited to, bank financing (revolver and term loans), sale/leaseback, mortgage, subordinated debt (senior, junior, discount and *payment-in-kind* [PIK]), increasing rate notes, preferred stock (straight and PIK), common equity, and the assumption of liabilities. The Sources of Funds section also displays the interest rates the acquirer expects to pay on the various financing instruments.

  Harrison has assumed that an aggressive LBO firm could obtain the bulk of the financing required for a $100 million transaction from one or more banks. This bank financing would consist of approximately $20.7 million in a revolving credit facility and $41 million in senior term debt. The remaining debt financing ($24 million) would be raised through a private placement of subordinated debt with warrants attached for approximately 20 percent of the common equity of Mareight.

- *Goodwill Calculation:* This section discloses the amount of goodwill that is created as a result of the transaction at the assumed purchase price. Note that, in this example, the entire amount of any excess paid over the existing book value of the target is allocated to goodwill. In an Initial LBO Model this is the proper assumption.

- *Transaction Costs:* This section displays the estimated transaction costs in absolute dollars and as a percent of the value of the transaction. Detailed transaction cost assumptions are input in a later schedule. In a highly leveraged transaction, it is not unusual to have total transaction costs (including all fees and expenses) approach 5 percent of the acquisition cost of the target.

In the Mareight transaction, total transaction costs are estimated to be 4.4 percent of the total cost.

- *Amortization Periods:* This section displays the amortization periods chosen for selected assets.

- *Miscellaneous:* This section contains a number of critical assumptions for the LBO Analysis, including the fiscal year that the acquirer will use, the years of the historical and projected financial results, and the accounting method to be used.

- *Purchase and Exit Multiples:* This section contains calculations of the purchase price as a multiple of sales, EBITDA, EBITA, EBIT, net cash flow (defined as EBITDA less cash taxes less capital expenditures), and net income for various periods.

  Generally, LBO firms and financing institutions base their investment decisions on a Base Case model that assumes that the exit multiple is approximately the same as the acquisition multiple. However, in the case of Mareight Corporation, Harrison made a very aggressive assumption that an LBO firm would be willing to invest assuming a significantly improved exit multiple over the acquisition multiple. This assumption has the effect of increasing the price that an LBO firm is willing to pay for Mareight.

- *Internal Rate of Return:* The Executive Summary contains an IRR Analysis under a sale assumption for key providers of capital. Generally, buyout firms assume that they will be selling their investment at the end of the forecast period. Therefore, no continuing value assumption calculations are included.

  The IRR analysis indicates that the senior subordinated debt holders can expect a rate of return in the low 20s. Management and the sponsoring LBO firm can expect rates of return on their equity investment of approximately 50 percent and 40 percent respectively.

  As discussed in Chapter 16, buyout firms do not consider NPV Analysis relevant. This is also true for the other capital providers to an LBO.

- *Equity Ownership Percentages:* This section outlines the breakdown of ownership interests in common equity, both when the transaction is initially completed and when the investment is liquidated.

- *Key Interest Coverages, Debt Paydown, Leverage and Revolver Information:* This section is critical in analyzing a leveraged investment in the target company. The interest coverage ratios and debt paydown calculations are important for determining the likelihood that financing will be available on the terms assumed in the model. For example, senior bank lenders may only provide funding if there is at least a 3 to 1 EBITDA to senior interest expense ratio in the first two years, and adequate cash flow to achieve over 50 percent debt paydown in five years. In the case of Mareight Corporation, the senior cash flow coverage ratios are adequate, but the net cash flow to cash interest expense ratio would be considered tight by most lenders. In addition, the total debt paydown over five years at 22.9 percent is inadequate for the vast majority of lenders.

It is typical that the financing structure of an LBO is refined as due diligence progresses and the level of confidence in the assumptions incorporated into the LBO model rises.

23.22 Financing, Tax, Transaction Costs and Acquisition Method Assumptions

This schedule displays (1) relevant assumptions for the various debt and equity instruments, including amortization period in years, any grace period before repayments must be made, and other miscellaneous assumptions, (2) tax assumptions used in the model, (3) transaction cost assumptions, and (4) a listing of the two categories of alternative acquisition methods that can be used to effect a transaction.

Tax assumptions for the Initial DCF Model include federal, state and local ordinary income and capital gains tax rates.

Transaction costs include investment banking fees, various financing fees, accounting, legal, appraisal, printing and miscellaneous expenses. These expenses are broken out so that a detailed estimate can be made. Generally, these expenses are not deductible for tax purposes. They are only deductible to the extent that they relate to financing the transaction, in which case they must be capitalized and amortized over the life of the financing.

The Acquisition Method Assumption section merely recites the alternative structures to choose from in deciding how to complete a transaction. The acquisition method assumption only applies in the Final LBO Model. A simplifying assumption is made in the Initial Model that book and tax depreciation are equal.

If the seller has clearly indicated the acquisition method to use and comprehensive capital expenditure and depreciation information is available, the acquirer should consider using the Final LBO Model, even at an early stage.

23.23 Economic and Operating Assumptions

See paragraph 22.33 for a description of Exhibit 23–3.

23.24 Income Statements

See paragraph 22.34 for a description of Exhibit 23–4.

23.25 Statements of Net Assets

See paragraph 22.35 for a description of Exhibit 23–5.

23.26 Statements of Changes in Financial Position

See paragraph 22.36 for a description of Exhibit 23–6.

23.27 Ownership Breakdown and Calculation of Gross Residual Values

The Ownership Breakdown schedule indicates how the common equity is distributed among the various capital providers, both initially and at the termination of the investment. The percentage ownership figures used at termination reflect the successful execution of the projections in the LBO model. These percentages are used in the gross residual value calculations.

23.28 Net Residual Value Calculations—Assuming Sale

The Net Residual Value—Assuming Sale schedule depicts the calculation of residual values under the three different residual value methods—EBITDA Multiple Method, EBITA Multiple Method and the P/E Multiple Method. All residual value calculations are performed assuming the target will be sold.

Gross and net residual calculations are performed for all instruments that either purchased common equity alongside the equity sponsor at the beginning of the transaction or received warrants to purchase common equity in conjunction with loaning funds to the sponsor to complete the transaction.

23.29   After-Tax Return Calculations

This schedule displays the IRR calculations for each of the three different Residual Value Methods including the five different residual value assumptions under each method. All calculations are made assuming the target is sold at the end of the forecast period.

23.30   Selected Financial Ratios

Exhibit 23–11 provides a more complete financial ratio analysis than the Executive Summary.

23.31   Summary Amortization Schedule

The Summary Amortization schedule displays the amortization for all transaction expenses, as well as goodwill, intangible assets and leased property under capital leases. The schedule also contains a summary of amortization expenses by tax category (deductible versus nondeductible).

23.32   Summary Debt Amortization and Interest Expense Schedules

Exhibit 23–13 summarizes the interest expense for the outstanding debt instruments, the mandatory summarized debt repayment schedule and optional debt repayments that are anticipated.

23.33   Debt Amortization and Preferred Stock Redemption Schedules

Exhibits 23–14 through 23–16 contain the debt amortization and interest expense calculations for all debt instrument alternatives included in the model.

Exhibit 23–16 contains the preferred stock redemption and dividend calculations for all preferred stock instrument alternatives included in the model.

23.34   Financial Statement Tax Provision

See paragraph 22.41 for a description of Exhibit 23–17.

MARRIGHT CORPORATION
LBO Analysis
Executive Summary

Exhibit 11.1
05/22/92
04:46 PM

Uses of Funds

	Amount	Percent
Common Shares Outstanding	1,000	
Options Outstanding	$0.00	
Average Exercise Price	$50,412.00	
Purchase Price per Share		
% of Shares Purchased	100.00%	
Purchase Common Equity	$50,412	60.6%
Purchase Preferred Stock	0	0.0%
Existing Liabilities to be refinanced	49,390	47.0%
Transaction Expenses	1,237	4.1%
Obligations under Capitalized Leases	0	0.0%
Pre-Payment Penalty	0	0.0%
Tax on Sale of Asset (Tax Basis)	0	0.0%
Additional Working Capital Cash	0	0.0%
Total Uses	**$164,237**	**100.0%**

Goodwill Calculation

Total Equity Purchase Price		$50,412
Adjustment to Book Value		
Existing Shareholders' Equity	$33,564	
Plus: Deferred Income Taxes	0	
Less: Existing Goodwill	0	
Less: Existing Organizational Costs	0	
Less: Value Allocated to PP&E	0	
Less: Value Allocated to Intangibles	0	
Net Book Value		33,564
Total Goodwill Created		**$17,048**

Transaction Costs

	Years
Total Transaction Costs	$4,237
% of Total Consideration	4.6%

Amortization Periods

	Years
Goodwill Amortization	40
Intangible Asset Amortization	5
Amortization of Leased Property under Capital Leases	25

Miscellaneous

	Years Ended December 31,
Fiscal Year	1989
Initial Fiscal Year	1993
Estimated Financial Statements Beginning	

	Purchase Accting (2)
Accounting Method ('Purchase' or 'Recap')	New Tax Basis(3)
Acquis. Method ('New' or 'No Change in')	
Initial 'Stub' Period Length	12 months
% of Annual Sales Occurring in Stub Period	100.0%
'Initial' or 'Final' model	Initial

Sources of Funds

	Amount	Percent	Rate	Spread Over LIBOR
Bank Revolver	$50,746	19.8%	9.00%	1.5000
Sale/Leaseback Financing	0	0.0%	11.00%	3.5000
Senior Term Loan A	41,000	39.1%	9.00%	2.0000
Senior Term Loan B	0	0.0%	13.50%	4.000
Senior Term Loan C	0	0.0%	14.00%	4.500
Mortgage Debt	0	0.0%	12.00%	4.500
Senior Subordinated Debt A	24,000	23.0%	13.33%	4.250
Senior Subordinated Debt B	0	0.0%	13.50%	1.000
Junior Subordinated Debt	0	0.0%	10.50%	3.000
Discount Subordinated Debt	0	0.0%	13.00%	3.500
Increasing Rate Note	0	0.0%	13.00%	1.500
PIK Preferred	0	0.0%	14.00%	4.000
Preferred Stock	0	0.0%		
Sr Sub'holder Common Equity	1,042	1.0%		
Management Common Equity	14,593	14.0%		
Sponsor Common Equity				
Other L.T. Liabs Assumed	2,856	2.7%		
Capitalized Lease Oblig.				
Excess Cash				
Total Sources	**$164,237**	**100.0%**		

Purchase and Exit Multiples (EBITDA Method Sidenote)

	1991	1992	1993	Terminal
Sales	0.73	0.6	0.5	0.7
EBITDA		6.2	5.5	13.7
EBITA		6.5	6.1	13.7
EBIT	7.0	7.7	7.2	14.1
Net Cash Flow (1)	4.6	7.5	7.3	13.9
Net Income		39.1	34.1	34.9

Key Interest Coverage, Debt Paydown, Interest and Revolver Information

	Clearing Bal. Sheet	Opening Bal. Sheet
Years Ended December 31,		
EBITDA/Total Interest Expense		
EBIT/Total Interest Expense		
Net CF/Total Interest Expense (1)		
EBITDA/Senior Interest Expense		
EBIT/Senior Interest Expense		
Net CF/Senior Interest Expense (1)		
EBITDA/Cash Interest Expense		
EBIT/Cash Interest Expense		
Net CF/Cash Interest Expense (1)		
Total Debt Outstanding	$0	$50,746
Cumulative Reduction		
All debt repaid in year	NA	
Total Sr. Debt Outstanding	$0	$41,000
Cumulative Reduction		
Sr. Debt repaid in year	NA	
Total Debt/Total Capital.		
Total Debt/Equity		
Total Senior Debt/Total Cap.		
Total Senior Debt/Equity		
Revolver Capacity (4)	$23,561	$19,292
Revolver Availability	$0,400	$7,321
Revolver Availability Percentage	100.0%	16.40%

Internal Rates of Return – Assumed Sale of Investment

EBITDA Multiple Method

	8.0	8.5	9.0	9.5	10.0
Terminal EBITDA Multiple					
Sponsor Common Equity	16.0%	37.7%	39.2%		42.1%
Management Common Equity	31.2%	55.5%			38.0%
Senior Subordinated Debt A	22.2%	21.2%	22.2%		34.6%

EBITA Multiple Method

	12.0	13.0	14.0	15.0	16.0
Terminal EBITA Multiple					
Sponsor Common Equity	25.7%	37.8%	39.2%	41.7%	43.5%
Management Common Equity	31.2%	54.2%	55.7%	58.5%	40.5%
Senior Subordinated Debt A	21.9%	22.3%	23.0%	24.3%	35.6%

P/E Multiple Method

	18.0	19.0	20.0	21.0	22.0
Terminal P/E Multiple					
Sponsor Common Equity	39.0%	39.8%	31.7%	32.8%	33.9%
Management Common Equity	44.2%	46.6%	47.1%	48.8%	49.6%
Senior Subordinated Debt A	19.8%	20.2%	20.6%	20.9%	21.2%

Equity Ownership Percentages

	1993	1994	1995	1996	1997	1998	Initial	Terminal
Sponsor Common Equity							77.1%	70.0%
Management Common Equity							2.3%	16.0%
Senior Subordinated Debt A							16.4%	20.0%
Junior Subordinated Debt							0.0%	0.0%
Public Shareholders							0.0%	0.0%
Total Equity Ownership							**100.0%**	**100.0%**

Equity Returns

	1993	1994	1995	1996	1997	1998
Sponsor Common Equity	2.36	2.85	3.55	3.85	4.43	4.66
Management Common Equity	1.46	1.76	1.97	2.21	2.43	2.37
Senior Subordinated Debt A	1.43	1.63	1.75	1.89	2.13	2.64
Junior Subordinated Debt	2.85	3.35	3.57	3.67	4.43	3.31
Public Shareholders	2.24	2.66	3.05	3.26	3.56	7.33

FOOTNOTES:

(1) Net Cash Flow equals EBITDA less cash taxes less capital Expenditures

(2) Do not use this model for a transaction involving Pooling of Interests Accounting.

(3) Choice of method not applicable in Initial model.

(4) 50% of inventory plus 85% of receivables plus 100% of cash.

MARRIOTT CORPORATION
LBO Analysis

Exhibit 11.1

05/21/92
04:47 PM

Financing, Tax, Transaction Cost and Acquisition Method Assumptions

Financing Assumptions

Revolver
Opening Balance	$20,746
Interest Rate	9.000%
Spread over Prime	1.500%

Senior Term Loan A
Opening Balance	$41,000
Interest Rate	9.500%
Spread over Prime	2.000%
Amortization (years)	7
Grace Period (years)	0

Senior Term Loan B
Opening Balance	$0
Interest Rate	13.000%
Spread over Prime	4.000%
Amortization (years)	8
Grace Period (years)	0

Senior Term Loan C
Opening Balance	$0
Interest Rate	14.000%
Spread over Prime	4.500%
Amortization (years)	8
Grace Period (years)	0

Sale/Leaseback
Opening Balance	$0
Interest Rate	11.000%
Spread over Prime	3.500%
Sale Price of Asset	$0
Gross Bk Value of Asset	$0
Acc Depr. of Asset	$0
Book Gain(Loss) on Sale	$0
Economic Life of Asset	0
Tax Basis of Asset	$0
AMT Basis of Asset	$0

Mortgage Debt
Opening Balance	$0
Interest Rate	12.000%
Spread over Prime	4.500%
Amortization (years)	15

Preferred Stock
Opening Balance	$0
Interest Rate	12.000%
Cash Dividend	4.500%
Spread over Prime	

PIK Preferred Stock
Opening Balance	$0
Dividend Rate	9.000%
Spread over Prime	1.500%

Senior Sub Debt
Opening Balance	$24,000
Interest Rate	12.125%
Spread over Prime	4.625%
Term (years)	

Senior Sub Debt
Opening Balance	$0
Interest Rate	9.500%
Spread over Prime	2.000%
Term (years)	

Discount Jr Sub Debt
Opening Balance	$0
YTM	10.500%
Spread over Prime	3.000%
Face Value	$0
Proceeds	0.000%
Coupon	
Term (years)	10

Junior Sub Debt
Opening Balance	$0
Interest Rate	13.000%
Spread over Prime	5.500%
Buy yr of Taro	
Buy yr of current coupon	1
Zero interest rate	13.000%
Current Coupon Rate	13.000%

Increasing Rate Note
Opening Balance	$0
Initial Interest Rate	13.000%
Spread over Prime	5.500%
Incremental Increase	0.500%
Prim	
Freq Interval (months)	3
Max Incr Period (months)	12
Redemption - End of Year	5

Common Stock
Minimum Cash Balance Req'd	$0
Interest on Cash Balances	7.000%
Shares Authorized	0
Shares Outstanding	1,400
Book Value of Equity	$25,564
Book Value per Share	$33,546.00

Tax Assumptions

Federal Tax Rate	34.000%
State and Local Tax Rate	6.000%
Capital Gains Tax Rate	28.000%
Alternative Minimum Tax Rate	20.000%
Long-Term Federal Tax-Exempt Bond Rate	6.7%
Built-in Gains (Losses) Qualifier	13.375%
Book Income Adjustment Rate (Post-1989)	75.000%
AMT NOL Use Limitation	90.000%
Acquired Book NOL	$0
Acquired Tax NOL	$0
Acquired AMT NOL	$0
Acquired MTC Credit	$0

Transaction Cost Assumptions

Advisory & Underwriting Fees
Transaction Fees	$1,657
Senior Term Loans A, B & C	$20
Increasing Rate Note	$0
Subordinated Debt	$60
Preferred Equity	$0
Accounting/Legal & Printing/Miscellaneous	$1,000
Total Fees and Expenses	**$4,337**

Amortization of Transaction Costs
Transaction	5	years
% related to financing	10%	
Accounting & Legal	1	year
% related to financing	10%	
Bank Fees	7	year
Increasing Rate Note Fee	5	year
Subordinated Debt Fees	10	year
Prepayment Penalty	7	year

Acquisition Methods

Method Used: New Tax Basis Acquisition Method

No Change in Tax Basis Acquisition Methods
1) Asset Acquisition
   A) Asset Acquisition
   B) Forward Merger
   C) Forward Subsidiary Merger
2) 338 Transaction
3) 338 (h)(10) Transaction

New Tax Basis Acquisition Methods
1) Stock Acquisition
   A) Stock Acquisition
   B) Reverse Merger
   C) Reverse Subsidiary Merger
2) Type A Reorganization
   A) Type A Forward Merger
   B) Type A Statutory Consolidation
   C) Type A Forward Subsidiary Merger
   D) Type A Reverse Subsidiary Merger
3) Type B Reorganization
   A) Type B Stock Exchange
   B) Type B Subsidiary Stock Exchange
4) Type C Reorganization
   A) Type C Stock for Assets Exchange
   B) Type C Subsidiary Stock for Assets Exchange

MAREIGHT CORPORATION
LBO Analysis
Economic and Operating Assumptions

Economic Assumptions

Year	Historical				Average 1989-92	Projected						Average 1993-98
	1989	1990	1991	1992		1993	1994	1995	1996	1997	1998	
GNP Growth Rate	3.5%	1.7%	0.0%	1.0%	1.5%	2.0%	2.5%	3.0%	3.0%	3.0%	3.0%	2.8%
Inflation Rate	4.6%	4.7%	5.5%	3.9%	4.7%	3.0%	3.0%	3.0%	3.0%	3.0%	3.0%	3.0%
Prime Interest Rate	9.6%	10.3%	9.5%	8.0%	9.3%	7.5%	7.5%	7.5%	7.5%	7.5%	7.5%	7.5%
Long-Term Treasury Bond Interest Rate	9.1%	8.4%	8.6%	7.9%	8.5%	6.8%	6.8%	6.8%	6.8%	6.8%	6.8%	6.8%

Sales and Margin Assumptions

Years Ended December 31,	Historical				Average 1989-92	Projected						Average 1993-98
	1989	1990	1991	1992		1993	1994	1995	1996	1997	1998	
Total Sales	$107,417	$113,656	$122,940	$133,302		$143,300	$154,047	$165,601	$178,021	$191,372	$205,725	
Growth Rate		5.8%	8.2%	8.4%	7.5%	7.5%	7.5%	7.5%	7.5%	7.5%	7.5%	7.5%
Gross Margin %	35.1%	34.5%	34.2%	34.7%	34.6%	34.5%	34.5%	34.5%	34.5%	34.5%	34.5%	34.5%
SG&A %	19.0%	19.0%	19.0%	19.0%	19.0%	19.0%	19.0%	19.0%	19.0%	19.0%	19.0%	19.0%
EBITDA Margin %	16.1%	15.5%	15.2%	15.7%	15.6%	15.5%	15.5%	15.5%	15.5%	15.5%	15.5%	15.5%

Capital Expenditure, Book and Tax Depreciation and Deferred Tax Assumptions

Years Ended December 31,	Historical				Average 1989-92	Projected						Average 1993-98
	1989	1990	1991	1992		1993	1994	1995	1996	1997	1998	
Net Sales	$107,417	$113,656	$122,940	$133,302		$143,300	$154,047	$165,601	$178,021	$191,372	$205,725	
Cost of Goods Sold	$69,714	$74,445	$80,895	$87,046		$93,861	$100,901	$108,468	$116,604	$125,349	$134,750	
Selling, General & Admin Expense	$20,409	$21,595	$23,359	$25,327		$27,227	$29,269	$31,464	$33,824	$36,361	$39,088	
Book and Tax Depreciation	$5,435	$6,297	$6,777	$7,022		$7,595	$8,164	$8,777	$9,435	$10,143	$10,903	
Book and Tax Depreciation as a % of Sales	5.1%	5.5%	5.5%	5.3%	5.3%	5.3%	5.3%	5.3%	5.3%	5.3%	5.3%	5.3%
Deferred Taxes	$0	$0	$0	$0		$526	$668	$731	$841	$1,036	$1,048	
Deferred Taxes as a % of Tax Provision						25.3%	25.0%	22.7%	21.9%	23.0%	19.8%	22.9%
Capital Expenditures	$5,658	$7,402	$6,285	$6,022		$7,738	$8,318	$8,942	$9,613	$10,334	$11,109	
Capital Expenditures as a % of Sales	5.3%	6.5%	5.1%	4.5%	5.4%	5.4%	5.4%	5.4%	5.4%	5.4%	5.4%	5.4%

Net Working Capital Assumptions

	1989	1990	1991	1992		1993	1994	1995	1996	1997	1998	Average 1993-98
Net Working Capital	$27,940	$27,243	$27,961	$31,515		$32,959	$35,431	$38,088	$40,945	$44,016	$47,317	
Net Working Capital as a % of Sales	26.0%	24.0%	22.7%	23.6%	24.1%	23.0%	23.0%	23.0%	23.0%	23.0%	23.0%	23.0%

MAREIGHT CORPORATION
LBO Analysis
Income Statements

Exhibit 23.4

05/22/92
04:47 PM

Years Ended December 31,	Historical				Average 1989-92	Projected						Average 1993-98
	1989	1990	1991	1992		1993	1994	1995	1996	1997	1998	
Net Sales	$107,417	$113,656	$122,940	$133,302		$143,300	$154,047	$165,601	$178,021	$191,372	$205,725	
Sales Growth %		5.8%	8.2%	8.4%	7.5%	7.5%	7.5%	7.5%	7.5%	7.5%	7.5%	7.5%
Cost of Goods Sold	$69,714	$74,445	$80,895	$87,046		93,861	$100,901	$108,468	$116,604	$125,349	$134,750	
Gross Profit	37,703	39,211	42,045	46,256		49,438	53,146	57,132	61,417	66,023	70,975	
Gross Margin %	35.1%	34.5%	34.2%	34.7%	34.6%	34.5%	34.5%	34.5%	34.5%	34.5%	34.5%	34.5%
Selling, General & Admin. Expenses	$20,409	$21,595	$23,359	$25,327		27,227	$29,269	$31,464	$33,824	$36,361	$39,088	
ESOP Contribution	0	0	0	0		0	0	0	0	0	0	
EBITDA	17,294	17,616	18,686	20,929		22,211	23,877	25,668	27,593	29,663	31,887	
EBITDA Margin %	16.1%	15.5%	15.2%	15.7%	15.6%	15.5%	15.5%	15.5%	15.5%	15.5%	15.5%	15.5%
Depreciation	5,435	6,297	6,777	7,022		7,595	8,164	8,777	9,435	10,143	10,903	
Amortization of Goodwill	0	0	0	0		426	426	426	426	426	426	
Amortization of Transaction Costs	0	0	0	0		1,505	505	505	505	505	213	
Amortization of Intangibles	0	0	0	0		0	0	0	0	0	0	
Total Depreciation and Amort.	5,435	6,297	6,777	7,022		9,526	9,095	9,708	10,366	11,074	11,543	
EBIT	11,859	11,319	11,909	13,907		12,686	14,782	15,960	17,227	18,589	20,345	
EBIT Margin %	11.0%	10.0%	9.7%	10.4%	10.3%	8.9%	9.6%	9.6%	9.7%	9.7%	9.9%	9.6%
Interest Income						0	0	0	0	0	0	
Interest Expense						8,672	8,390	8,119	7,779	7,358	6,841	
Net Interest Expense						8,672	8,390	8,119	7,779	7,358	6,841	
Other Expenses (Income)						0	0	0	0	0	0	
Loss (Gain) on Sale-Leaseback Asset						0	0	0	0	0	0	
Earnings Before Taxes						4,014	6,392	7,841	9,448	11,231	13,504	
Provision for Taxes												
Current						1,552	2,009	2,496	2,996	3,478	4,240	
Deferred						526	668	731	841	1,036	1,048	
Total Tax Provision						2,078	2,677	3,227	3,837	4,514	5,288	
Net Income Before Extraordinary Item &						1,936	3,715	4,615	5,611	6,717	8,216	
Minority Interest						0	0	0	0	0	0	
Minority Interest						0	0	0	0	0	0	
Extraordinary Item (After-Tax)						1,936	3,715	4,615	5,611	6,717	8,216	
Preferred Dividend - Stock						0	0	0	0	0	0	
Preferred Dividend - Cash						0	0	0	0	0	0	
Net Income to Common						$1,936	$3,715	$4,615	$5,611	$6,717	$8,216	

Page 5   FILE: SHT_F

MAREIGHT CORPORATION
LBO Analysis
Statements of Net Assets

Exhibit 23.5
05/22/92
04:47 PM

Years Ended December 31,	Historical 1989	1990	1991	1992	Closing Date Bal. Sheet	Adjustments DEBITS	Adjustments CREDITS	Beginning Bal. Sheet	Projected 1993	1994	1995	1996	1997	1998
Cash and Cash Equivalents	$3,313	$3,288	$1,111	$2,856	$2,856	($2,856)	$0	$0	$0	$0	$0	$0	$0	$0
Net Working Capital	27,940	27,243	27,961	31,515	31,515	0	0	31,515	32,959	35,431	38,088	40,945	44,016	47,317
Gross Property, Plant & Equipment	43,378	45,001	45,965	44,965	44,965	0	0	44,965	52,703	61,021	69,963	79,576	89,910	101,019
Less: Accumulated Depreciation	0	0	0	0	0	0	0	0	(7,595)	(15,759)	(24,536)	(33,971)	(44,114)	(55,017)
Net Property, Plant & Equipment	43,378	45,001	45,965	44,965	44,965	0	0	44,965	45,108	45,262	45,427	45,605	45,796	46,002
Leased Property Under Capital Leases														
Goodwill	0	0	0	0	0	17,048	0	17,048	16,622	16,196	15,769	15,343	14,917	14,491
Other Intangibles	0	0	0	0	0	0	0	0	0	0	0	0	0	0
Other Assets	3,141	3,289	2,704	3,616	3,616	0	0	3,616	3,616	3,616	3,616	3,616	3,616	3,616
Organizational Costs	0	0	0	0	0	4,237	0	4,237	2,733	2,228	1,723	1,219	714	501
Net Assets	$77,772	$78,821	$77,741	$82,952	$82,952	$18,429	$0	$101,381	$101,037	$102,732	$104,624	$106,728	$109,059	$111,926
Financed By:														
Current Portion of Long Term Debt	$0	$0	$0	$0	$0	$0	$5,857	$5,857	$5,857	$5,857	$5,857	$5,857	$5,857	$5,857
Long-Term Debt														
Revolver	0	0	0	0	0	0	0	0	0	0	0	0	0	0
Existing	0	0	0	0	0	0	20,746	20,746	23,797	26,966	29,369	30,878	31,313	30,773
Sale-Leaseback Obligation	0	0	0	0	0	0	0	0	0	0	0	0	0	0
Senior Term Loan A	0	0	0	0	0	0	41,000	35,143	29,286	23,429	17,571	11,714	5,857	0
Senior Term Loan B	0	0	0	0	0	5,857	0	0	0	0	0	0	0	0
Senior Term Loan C	0	0	0	0	0	0	0	0	0	0	0	0	0	0
Mortgage Debt	0	0	0	0	0	0	0	0	0	0	0	0	0	0
Senior Subordinated Debt A	0	0	0	0	0	0	24,000	24,000	24,000	24,000	24,000	24,000	24,000	24,000
Senior Subordinated Debt B	0	0	0	0	0	0	0	0	0	0	0	0	0	0
Junior Subordinated Debt	0	0	0	0	0	0	0	0	0	0	0	0	0	0
Discount Subordinated Debt	0	0	0	0	0	0	0	0	0	0	0	0	0	0
Increasing Rate Note	0	0	0	0	0	0	0	0	0	0	0	0	0	0
Total Long-Term Debt	0	0	0	0	0	5,857	85,746	79,889	77,083	74,394	70,941	66,592	61,170	54,773
Other Long-Term Liabilities	48,777	50,241	46,772	49,388	49,388	49,388	0	0	0	0	0	0	0	0
Unearned Profit on Capitalized Leases	0	0	0	0	0	0	0	0	0	0	0	0	0	0
Deferred Income Taxes	0	0	0	0	0	0	0	0	526	1,194	1,925	2,766	3,802	4,850
Minority Interest	0	0	0	0	0	0	0	0	0	0	0	0	0	0
PIK Preferred	0	0	0	0	0	0	0	0	0	0	0	0	0	0
Preferred Stock	0	0	0	0	0	0	0	0	0	0	0	0	0	0
Common Stock	1,000	1,000	1,000	1,000	1,000	1,000	15,635	15,635	15,635	15,635	15,635	15,635	15,635	15,635
Retained Earnings	27,995	27,580	29,969	32,564	32,564	32,564	0	0	1,936	5,651	10,266	15,877	22,595	30,810
ESOP Contra Account	0	0	0	0	0	0	0	0	0	0	0	0	0	0
Common Shareholders' Equity	28,995	28,580	30,969	33,564	33,564	33,564	15,635	15,635	17,571	21,286	25,901	31,512	38,230	46,446
Total Liabilities & Equity	$93,510	$95,439	$94,901	$97,181	$97,181	$107,238	$107,238	$101,381	$101,037	$102,732	$104,624	$106,728	$109,059	$111,926

MAREIGHT CORPORATION
LBO Analysis
Statements of Changes in Financial Position

Exhibit 23.6

05/22/92
04:47 PM

Years Ended December 31,	1993	1994	1995	1996	1997	1998
Sources of Cash						
Net Income to Common	$1,936	$3,715	$4,615	$5,611	$6,717	$8,216
Book Depreciation	7,595	8,164	8,777	9,435	10,143	10,903
Amortization of Intangibles	0	0	0	0	0	0
Deferred Tax	526	668	731	841	1,036	1,048
Amortization of Gain on Sale/Leaseback Asset						
Amort. of Leased Prop. under Capitalized Leases	0	0	0	0	0	0
Amortization of Goodwill & Fees	1,931	931	931	931	931	639
Accretion of Discount						
PIK Preferred Dividend	0	0	0	0	0	0
Total Sources	$11,988	$13,478	$15,053	$16,818	$18,827	$20,807
Uses of Cash						
Increase (Decrease) in Working Capital	$1,444	$2,472	$2,657	$2,857	$3,071	$3,301
Capital Expenditures	7,738	8,318	8,942	9,613	10,334	11,109
Debt Amortization						
Revolver	(3,051)	(3,169)	(2,403)	(1,508)	(435)	539
Sale-Leaseback Obligation	0	0	0	0	0	0
Senior Term Loan A	5,857	5,857	5,857	5,857	5,857	5,857
Senior Term Loan B	0	0	0	0	0	0
Senior Term Loan C	0	0	0	0	0	0
Mortgage Debt	0	0	0	0	0	0
Senior Subordinated Debt A	0	0	0	0	0	0
Senior Subordinated Debt B	0	0	0	0	0	0
Junior Subordinated Debt	0	0	0	0	0	0
Discount Subordinated Debt	0	0	0	0	0	0
Increasing Rate Note	0	0	0	0	0	0
Total Debt Amortization	2,806	2,688	3,454	4,349	5,422	6,396
Redemption of PIK Preferred	0	0	0	0	0	0
Redemption of Preferred Stock	0	0	0	0	0	0
Total Uses	$11,988	$13,478	$15,053	$16,818	$18,827	$20,807
Net Cash Flow	$0	$0	$0	$0	$0	$0

MAREIGHT CORPORATION
LBO Analysis
Ownership Breakdown and Calculation of Gross Residual Values

Exhibit 23.7
05/22/92
04:47 PM

Ownership Breakdown

Investor	Initial				Terminal	
	Value Rec (000s)	Shrs Received	% Shares	Ownership	Common Shares	Ownership
Sponsor Common Equity	$14,593	933		77.5%	933	70.0%
Management Common Equity	1,042	67		2.5%	133	10.0%
Sr. Subordinated A	0	0		20.0%	267	20.0%
Jr. Subordinated	0	0		0.0%	0	0.0%
Public Shareholders	NA	0		0.0%	0	0.0%
Equity	$15,635	1,000		100.0%	1,333	100.0%

Gross Residual Value Calculations – EBITA Multiple Method

EBDIAT Multiple	12.0	13.0	14.0	15.0	16.0
1998 EBITA	$20,984	$20,984	$20,984	$20,984	$20,984
Gross Residual Value (Sale Price)	251,808	272,792	293,776	314,760	335,743
Less:					
Total Debt	54,773	54,773	54,773	54,773	54,773
Preferred Stock	0	0	0	0	0
Plus:					
Cash & Equivalents	0	0	0	0	0
Warrants/Options Proceeds	0	0	0	0	0
Gross Residual Value of Common Equity	$197,034	$218,018	$239,002	$259,986	$280,970
Gross Value of Common Equity					
Sponsor Common Equity	137,924	152,613	167,301	181,990	196,679
Management Common Equity	19,703	21,802	23,900	25,999	28,097
Senior Subordinated Debt A	39,407	43,604	47,800	51,997	56,194
Junior Subordinated Debt	0	0	0	0	0
Gross Residual Value of Common Equity	$197,034	$218,018	$239,002	$259,986	$280,970

Gross Residual Value Calculations – EBITDA Multiple Method

EBITDA Multiple	8.0	8.5	9.0	9.5	10.0
1998 EBITDA	$31,887	$31,887	$31,887	$31,887	$31,887
Gross Residual Value (Sale Price)	255,099	271,043	286,987	302,930	318,874
Less:					
Total Debt	54,773	54,773	54,773	54,773	54,773
Preferred Stock	0	0	0	0	0
Plus:					
Cash & Equivalents	0	0	0	0	0
Warrants/Options Proceeds	0	0	0	0	0
Gross Residual Value of Common Equity	$200,326	$216,270	$232,213	$248,157	$264,101
Gross Value of Common Equity					
Sponsor Common Equity	140,228	151,389	162,549	173,710	184,870
Management Common Equity	20,033	21,627	23,221	24,816	26,410
Senior Subordinated Debt A	40,065	43,254	46,443	49,631	52,820
Junior Subordinated Debt	0	0	0	0	0
Gross Residual Value of Common Equity	$200,326	$216,270	$232,213	$248,157	$264,101

Gross Residual Value Calculations – P/E Multiple Method

P/E Multiple	18.0	19.0	20.0	21.0	22.0
1998 Net Income	$8,216	$8,216	$8,216	$8,216	$8,216
Gross Residual Value (Sale Price)	147,885	156,101	164,317	172,533	180,749
Less:					
Preferred Stock	0	0	0	0	0
Plus:					
Cash & Equivalents	0	0	0	0	0
Warrants/Options Proceeds	0	0	0	0	0
Gross Residual Value of Common Equity	$147,885	$156,101	$164,317	$172,533	$180,749
Gross Value of Common Equity					
Sponsor Common Equity	103,520	109,271	115,022	120,773	126,524
Management Common Equity	14,789	15,610	16,432	17,253	18,075
Senior Subordinated Debt A	29,577	31,220	32,863	34,507	36,150
Junior Subordinated Debt	0	0	0	0	0
Gross Residual Value of Common Equity	$147,885	$156,101	$164,317	$172,533	$180,749

Exhibit 23.8
05/22/92
04:47 PM

Page 8   FILE: SHT_I2

MAREIGHT CORPORATION
LBO Analysis
Net Residual Value Calculations - Assuming Sale

Net Residual Value Calculations - EBITA Multiple Method

EBITA Multiple	12.0	13.0	14.0	15.0	16.0
Sponsor Common Equity					
Gross Residual Value	$137,924	$152,613	$167,301	$181,990	$196,679
Tax Basis	14,593	14,593	14,593	14,593	14,593
Gain (Loss) on Sale	123,331	138,020	152,708	167,397	182,086
Capital Gains Tax Rate	38.0%	38.0%	38.0%	38.0%	38.0%
Tax on Sale	46,866	52,447	58,029	63,611	69,193
Gross Residual Value	137,924	152,613	167,301	181,990	196,679
Taxes on Sale	46,866	52,447	58,029	63,611	69,193
Net Residual Value	$91,058	$100,165	$109,272	$118,379	$127,486
Management Common Equity					
Gross Residual Value	$19,703	$21,802	$23,900	$25,999	$28,097
Tax Basis	1,042	1,042	1,042	1,042	1,042
Gain (Loss) on Sale	18,661	20,760	22,858	24,957	27,055
Capital Gains Tax Rate	38.0%	38.0%	38.0%	38.0%	38.0%
Tax on Sale	7,091	7,889	8,686	9,484	10,281
Gross Residual Value	19,703	21,802	23,900	25,999	28,097
Taxes on Sale	7,091	7,889	8,686	9,484	10,281
Net Residual Value	$12,612	$13,913	$15,214	$16,515	$17,816
Senior Subordinated Debt A					
Gross Residual Value	$39,407	$43,604	$47,800	$51,997	$56,194
Tax Basis	0	0	0	0	0
Gain (Loss) on Sale	39,407	43,604	47,800	51,997	56,194
Capital Gains Tax Rate	38.0%	38.0%	38.0%	38.0%	38.0%
Tax on Sale	14,975	16,569	18,164	19,759	21,354
Gross Residual Value	39,407	43,604	47,800	51,997	56,194
Taxes on Sale	14,975	16,569	18,164	19,759	21,354
Net Residual Value	$24,432	$27,034	$29,636	$32,238	$34,840
Junior Subordinated Debt					
Gross Residual Value	$0	$0	$0	$0	$0
Tax Basis	0	0	0	0	0
Gain (Loss) on Sale	0	0	0	0	0
Capital Gains Tax Rate	38.0%	38.0%	38.0%	38.0%	38.0%
Tax on Sale	0	0	0	0	0
Gross Residual Value	0	0	0	0	0
Taxes on Sale	0	0	0	0	0
Net Residual Value	$0	$0	$0	$0	$0

Net Residual Value Calculations - EBITDA Multiple Method

EBITDA Multiple	8.0	8.5	9.0	9.5	10.0
Sponsor Common Equity					
Gross Residual Value	$140,228	$151,389	$162,549	$173,710	$184,870
Tax Basis	14,593	14,593	14,593	14,593	14,593
Gain (Loss) on Sale	125,635	136,795	147,956	159,117	170,277
Capital Gains Tax Rate	38.0%	38.0%	38.0%	38.0%	38.0%
Tax on Sale	47,741	51,982	56,223	60,464	64,705
Gross Residual Value	140,228	151,389	162,549	173,710	184,870
Taxes on Sale	47,741	51,982	56,223	60,464	64,705
Net Residual Value	$92,487	$99,406	$106,326	$113,246	$120,165
Management Common Equity					
Gross Residual Value	$20,033	$21,627	$23,221	$24,816	$26,410
Tax Basis	1,042	1,042	1,042	1,042	1,042
Gain (Loss) on Sale	18,991	20,585	22,179	23,774	25,368
Capital Gains Tax Rate	38.0%	38.0%	38.0%	38.0%	38.0%
Tax on Sale	7,216	7,822	8,428	9,034	9,640
Gross Residual Value	20,033	21,627	23,221	24,816	26,410
Taxes on Sale	7,216	7,822	8,428	9,034	9,640
Net Residual Value	$12,816	$13,805	$14,793	$15,782	$16,770
Senior Subordinated Debt A					
Gross Residual Value	$40,065	$43,254	$46,443	$49,631	$52,820
Tax Basis	0	0	0	0	0
Gain (Loss) on Sale	40,065	43,254	46,443	49,631	52,820
Capital Gains Tax Rate	38.0%	38.0%	38.0%	38.0%	38.0%
Tax on Sale	15,225	16,436	17,648	18,860	20,072
Gross Residual Value	40,065	43,254	46,443	49,631	52,820
Taxes on Sale	15,225	16,436	17,648	18,860	20,072
Net Residual Value	$24,840	$26,817	$28,794	$30,771	$32,748
Junior Subordinated Debt					
Gross Residual Value	$0	$0	$0	$0	$0
Tax Basis	0	0	0	0	0
Gain (Loss) on Sale	0	0	0	0	0
Capital Gains Tax Rate	38.0%	38.0%	38.0%	38.0%	38.0%
Tax on Sale	0	0	0	0	0
Gross Residual Value	0	0	0	0	0
Taxes on Sale	0	0	0	0	0
Net Residual Value	$0	$0	$0	$0	$0

MARFRIGHT CORPORATION Exhibit 23.9
LBO Analysis
Net Residual Value Calculations – P/E Multiple Method   05/22/92
Net Residual Value Calculations – Assuming Sale   04:47 PM

Net Residual Value Calculations – P/E Multiple Method					
P/E Multiple	18.0	19.0	20.0	21.0	22.0
Sponsor Common Equity					
Gross Residual Value	$103,520	$109,271	$115,022	$120,773	$126,524
Tax Basis	14,593	14,593	14,593	14,593	14,593
Gain (Loss) on Sale	88,927	94,678	100,429	106,180	111,931
Capital Gains Tax Rate	38.0%	38.0%	38.0%	38.0%	38.0%
Tax on Sale	33,792	35,978	38,163	40,348	42,534
Gross Residual Value	103,520	109,271	115,022	120,773	126,524
Taxes on Sale	33,792	35,978	38,163	40,348	42,534
Net Residual Value	$69,728	$73,293	$76,859	$80,425	$83,990
Management Common Equity					
Gross Residual Value	$14,789	$15,610	$16,432	$17,253	$18,075
Tax Basis	1,042	1,042	1,042	1,042	1,042
Gain (Loss) on Sale	13,747	14,568	15,390	16,211	17,033
Capital Gains Tax Rate	38.0%	38.0%	38.0%	38.0%	38.0%
Tax on Sale	5,224	5,536	5,848	6,160	6,472
Gross Residual Value	14,789	15,610	16,432	17,253	18,075
Taxes on Sale	5,224	5,536	5,848	6,160	6,472
Net Residual Value	$9,565	$10,074	$10,584	$11,093	$11,602
Senior Subordinated Debt A					
Gross Residual Value	$29,577	$31,220	$32,863	$34,507	$36,150
Tax Basis	0	0	0	0	0
Gain (Loss) on Sale	29,577	31,220	32,863	34,507	36,150
Capital Gains Tax Rate	38.0%	38.0%	38.0%	38.0%	38.0%
Tax on Sale	11,239	11,864	12,488	13,113	13,737
Gross Residual Value	29,577	31,220	32,863	34,507	36,150
Taxes on Sale	11,239	11,864	12,488	13,113	13,737
Net Residual Value	$18,338	$19,357	$20,375	$21,394	$22,413
Junior Subordinated Debt					
Gross Residual Value	$0	$0	$0	$0	$0
Tax Basis	0	0	0	0	0
Gain (Loss) on Sale	0	0	0	0	0
Capital Gains Tax Rate	38.0%	38.0%	38.0%	38.0%	38.0%
Tax on Sale	0	0	0	0	0
Gross Residual Value	0	0	0	0	0
Taxes on Sale	0	0	0	0	0
Net Residual Value	$0	$0	$0	$0	$0

Exhibit 23-10
05/22/92
05:17 PM

MAREIGHT CORPORATION
LBO Analysis
After-Tax Investment Returns Calculations

IRR Calculations - EBITDA Method

Sponsor Common Equity	Investment	1993	1994	1995	1996	1997	1998	IRR
Cash Flows - 12.0x EBITDA Multiple	($14,593)	0	0	0	0	0	91,058	35.7%
Cash Flows - 13.0x EBITDA Multiple	(14,593)	0	0	0	0	0	100,165	37.9%
Cash Flows - 14.0x EBITDA Multiple	(14,593)	0	0	0	0	0	109,272	39.9%
Cash Flows - 15.0x EBITDA Multiple	(14,593)	0	0	0	0	0	118,379	41.7%
Cash Flows - 16.0x EBITDA Multiple	(14,593)	0	0	0	0	0	127,486	43.5%
Management Common Equity								
Cash Flows - 12.0x EBITDA Multiple	($1,042)	0	0	0	0	0	12,612	51.5%
Cash Flows - 13.0x EBITDA Multiple	(1,042)	0	0	0	0	0	13,913	54.0%
Cash Flows - 14.0x EBITDA Multiple	(1,042)	0	0	0	0	0	15,214	56.3%
Cash Flows - 15.0x EBITDA Multiple	(1,042)	0	0	0	0	0	16,515	58.5%
Cash Flows - 16.0x EBITDA Multiple	(1,042)	0	0	0	0	0	17,816	60.5%
Senior Subordinated Debt A								
Interest Payments		$2,910	$2,910	$2,910	$2,910	$2,910	$2,910	
Principal Repayments								
Cash Flows - 12.0x EBITDA Multiple	($24,000)	2,910	2,910	2,910	2,910	2,910	51,342	21.9%
Cash Flows - 13.0x EBITDA Multiple	(24,000)	2,910	2,910	2,910	2,910	2,910	53,944	22.7%
Cash Flows - 14.0x EBITDA Multiple	(24,000)	2,910	2,910	2,910	2,910	2,910	56,546	23.5%
Cash Flows - 15.0x EBITDA Multiple	(24,000)	2,910	2,910	2,910	2,910	2,910	59,148	24.3%
Cash Flows - 16.0x EBITDA Multiple	(24,000)	2,910	2,910	2,910	2,910	2,910	61,750	25.0%
Junior Subordinated Debt								
Cash Interest Payments	$0	$0	$0	$0	$0	$0	$0	
Principal Repayments								
Cash Flows - 12.0x EBITDA Multiple	$0	0	0	0	0	0	0	N/A
Cash Flows - 13.0x EBITDA Multiple	0	0	0	0	0	0	0	N/A
Cash Flows - 14.0x EBITDA Multiple	0	0	0	0	0	0	0	N/A
Cash Flows - 15.0x EBITDA Multiple	0	0	0	0	0	0	0	N/A
Cash Flows - 16.0x EBITDA Multiple	0	0	0	0	0	0	0	N/A

IRR Calculations - P/E Method

Sponsor Common Equity	Investment	1993	1994	1995	1996	1997	1998	IRR
Cash Flows - 18.0x P/E Multiple	($14,593)	0	0	0	0	0	69,728	29.8%
Cash Flows - 19.0x P/E Multiple	(14,593)	0	0	0	0	0	73,293	30.9%
Cash Flows - 20.0x P/E Multiple	(14,593)	0	0	0	0	0	76,859	31.9%
Cash Flows - 21.0x P/E Multiple	(14,593)	0	0	0	0	0	80,425	32.9%
Cash Flows - 22.0x P/E Multiple	(14,593)	0	0	0	0	0	83,990	33.9%
Management Common Equity								
Cash Flows - 18.0x P/E Multiple	($1,042)	0	0	0	0	0	9,565	44.7%
Cash Flows - 19.0x P/E Multiple	(1,042)	0	0	0	0	0	10,074	46.0%
Cash Flows - 20.0x P/E Multiple	(1,042)	0	0	0	0	0	10,584	47.2%
Cash Flows - 21.0x P/E Multiple	(1,042)	0	0	0	0	0	11,093	48.3%
Cash Flows - 22.0x P/E Multiple	(1,042)	0	0	0	0	0	11,602	49.4%
Senior Subordinated Debt A								
Interest Payments		$2,910	$2,910	$2,910	$2,910	$2,910	$2,910	
Principal Repayments								
Cash Flows - 18.0x P/E Multiple	($24,000)	2,910	2,910	2,910	2,910	2,910	45,248	19.8%
Cash Flows - 19.0x P/E Multiple	(24,000)	2,910	2,910	2,910	2,910	2,910	46,267	20.2%
Cash Flows - 20.0x P/E Multiple	(24,000)	2,910	2,910	2,910	2,910	2,910	47,285	20.6%
Cash Flows - 21.0x P/E Multiple	(24,000)	2,910	2,910	2,910	2,910	2,910	48,304	20.9%
Cash Flows - 22.0x P/E Multiple	(24,000)	2,910	2,910	2,910	2,910	2,910	49,323	21.2%
Junior Subordinated Debt								
Cash Interest Payments	$0	$0	$0	$0	$0	$0	$0	
Principal Repayments								
Cash Flows - 18.0x P/E Multiple	$0	0	0	0	0	0	0	N/A
Cash Flows - 19.0x P/E Multiple	0	0	0	0	0	0	0	N/A
Cash Flows - 20.0x P/E Multiple	0	0	0	0	0	0	0	N/A
Cash Flows - 21.0x P/E Multiple	0	0	0	0	0	0	0	N/A
Cash Flows - 22.0x P/E Multiple	0	0	0	0	0	0	0	N/A

IRR Calculations - EBITDA Method

Sponsor Common Equity	Investment	1993	1994	1995	1996	1997	1998	IRR
Cash Flows - 8.0x EBITDA Multiple	($14,593)	0	0	0	0	0	92,487	36.0%
Cash Flows - 8.5x EBITDA Multiple	(14,593)	0	0	0	0	0	99,406	37.7%
Cash Flows - 9.0x EBITDA Multiple	(14,593)	0	0	0	0	0	106,326	39.2%
Cash Flows - 9.5x EBITDA Multiple	(14,593)	0	0	0	0	0	113,246	40.7%
Cash Flows - 10.0x EBITDA Multiple	(14,593)	0	0	0	0	0	120,165	42.1%
Management Common Equity								
Cash Flows - 8.0x EBITDA Multiple	($1,042)	0	0	0	0	0	12,816	51.9%
Cash Flows - 8.5x EBITDA Multiple	(1,042)	0	0	0	0	0	13,805	53.8%
Cash Flows - 9.0x EBITDA Multiple	(1,042)	0	0	0	0	0	14,793	55.6%
Cash Flows - 9.5x EBITDA Multiple	(1,042)	0	0	0	0	0	15,782	57.3%
Cash Flows - 10.0x EBITDA Multiple	(1,042)	0	0	0	0	0	16,770	58.9%
Senior Subordinated Debt A								
Interest Payments		$2,910	$2,910	$2,910	$2,910	$2,910	$2,910	
Principal Repayments								
Cash Flows - 8.0x EBITDA Multiple	($24,000)	2,910	2,910	2,910	2,910	2,910	51,750	22.0%
Cash Flows - 8.5x EBITDA Multiple	(24,000)	2,910	2,910	2,910	2,910	2,910	53,727	22.7%
Cash Flows - 9.0x EBITDA Multiple	(24,000)	2,910	2,910	2,910	2,910	2,910	55,704	23.3%
Cash Flows - 9.5x EBITDA Multiple	(24,000)	2,910	2,910	2,910	2,910	2,910	57,681	23.8%
Cash Flows - 10.0x EBITDA Multiple	(24,000)	2,910	2,910	2,910	2,910	2,910	59,658	24.4%
Junior Subordinated Debt								
Cash Interest Payments	$0	$0	$0	$0	$0	$0	$0	
Principal Repayments								
Cash Flows - 8.0x EBITDA Multiple	($24,000)	0	0	0	0	0	0	N/A
Cash Flows - 8.5x EBITDA Multiple	(24,000)	0	0	0	0	0	0	N/A
Cash Flows - 9.0x EBITDA Multiple	(24,000)	0	0	0	0	0	0	N/A
Cash Flows - 9.5x EBITDA Multiple	(24,000)	0	0	0	0	0	0	N/A
Cash Flows - 10.0x EBITDA Multiple	(24,000)	0	0	0	0	0	0	N/A

MARRIOTT CORPORATION
LBO Analysis
Selected Financial Ratios

Years Ended December 31,	Historical 1989	1990	1991	1992	Beginning Bal. Sheet	1993	1994	Projected 1995	1996	1997	1998
Percent of Total Capitalization											
Sr. Term, Mtg., Revolver & Sale-Lsbk Debt	0.0%	0.0%	0.0%	0.0%	60.9%	58.6%	55.4%	51.4%	46.6%	40.9%	34.2%
Senior and Junior Subordinated Debt	0.0%	0.0%	0.0%	0.0%	23.7%	23.9%	23.6%	23.4%	23.1%	22.8%	22.4%
Total Long Term Debt	0.0%	0.0%	0.0%	0.0%	84.6%	82.5%	79.0%	74.8%	69.7%	63.7%	56.6%
Preferred Equity	0.0%	0.0%	0.0%	0.0%	0.0%	0.0%	0.0%	0.0%	0.0%	0.0%	0.0%
Common Equity	100.0%	100.0%	100.0%	100.0%	15.4%	17.5%	21.0%	25.2%	30.3%	36.3%	43.4%
Net Income as a % of Total Assets	0.0%	0.0%	0.0%	0.0%	0.0%	1.7%	3.1%	3.7%	4.4%	5.1%	6.1%
Net Income as a % of Common Equity	0.0%	0.0%	0.0%	0.0%	0.0%	11.0%	17.5%	17.8%	17.8%	17.6%	17.7%
EBITDA::	$17,294	$17,616	$18,686	$20,929		$22,211	$23,877	$25,668	$27,593	$29,663	$31,887
EBIT::	$11,859	$11,319	$11,909	$13,907		$12,686	$14,782	$15,960	$17,227	$18,589	$20,345
Net Cash Flow::	$17,294	$17,616	$18,686	$20,929		$12,922	$13,551	$14,230	$14,984	$15,851	$27,648
Total Interest Coverage:											
EBITDA/Interest Expense						2.56	2.85	3.16	3.55	4.03	4.66
EBIT/Interest Expense						1.46	1.76	1.97	2.21	2.53	2.97
Net Cash Flow/Interest Expense (1)						1.49	1.62	1.75	1.93	2.15	4.04
Senior Interest Coverage (2):											
EBITDA/Senior Interest Expense						3.85	4.36	4.93	5.67	6.67	8.11
EBIT/Senior Interest Expense						2.20	2.70	3.06	3.54	4.18	5.18
Net Cash Flow/Sen. Interest Expense (1)						2.24	2.47	2.73	3.08	3.56	7.03
Subordinated Interest Coverage:											
EBITDA-Sen. Interest Exp/Sub Int Expense						5.65	6.32	7.03	7.81	8.66	9.61
EBIT-Senior Interest Exp/Sub Int Expense						2.38	3.20	3.69	4.25	4.86	5.64
Net CF-Sen. Int Exp/Sub Int Expense (1)						2.46	2.77	3.10	3.48	3.92	8.15
Fixed Charge Coverage:											
EBITDA/Interest Exp. + Preferred Dividend						2.56	2.85	3.16	3.55	4.03	4.66
EBIT/Interest Exp. + Preferred Dividend						1.46	1.76	1.97	2.21	2.53	2.97
Net CF/Interest Exp. + Pref. Dividend (1)						1.49	1.62	1.75	1.93	2.15	4.04
Cash Interest Coverage											
EBITDA/Cash Interest Expense						2.56	2.85	3.16	3.55	4.03	4.66
EBIT/Cash Interest Expense						1.46	1.76	1.97	2.21	2.53	2.97
Net Cash Flow/Cash Interest Expense (1)						1.49	1.62	1.75	1.93	2.15	4.04
Debt Service Coverage											
Net CF/Reqd Principal Pmt + Interest Exp											

(1) Net Cash Flow = EBITDA - Cash Taxes - Capital Expenditures
(2) Senior Interest is computed on revolver, mortgage, sale-leaseback and senior term loans A, B and C.

MAREIGHT CORPORATION
LBO Analysis
Summary Amortization Schedule

Exhibit 23.12

05/22/92
04:47 PM

Years Ended December 31,

Transaction Fees	Years	Opening Bal. Sheet	1993	1994	1995	1996	1997	1998
Beginning Balance			$4,237	$2,733	$2,228	$1,723	$1,219	$714
Amortization:								
Transaction	5	$1,457	291	291	291	291	291	0
Bank Loans	7	820	117	117	117	117	117	117
Increasing Rate Note	5	0	0	0	0	0	0	0
Subordinated Debt	10	960	96	96	96	96	96	96
Preferred Equity	5	0	0	0	0	0	0	0
Accounting & Legal	1	1,000	1,000	0	0	0	0	0
Pre-Payment Penalty	7	0	0	0	0	0	0	0
Ending Balance		$4,237	$2,733	$2,228	$1,723	$1,219	$714	$501

NOTE: Transaction costs not directly related to the financing are not deductible.

Goodwill	Initial	1993	1994	1995	1996	1997	1998
Beginning Balance	$17,048	$17,048	$16,622	$16,196	$15,769	$15,343	$14,917
Amortization 40 Years		426	426	426	426	426	426
Ending Goodwill	$17,048	$16,622	$16,196	$15,769	$15,343	$14,917	$14,491

Intangible Assets	Initial	1993	1994	1995	1996	1997	1998
Beginning Balance		$0	$0	$0	$0	$0	$0
Plus: Additions		0	0	0	0	0	0
Amortization 5 Years		0	0	0	0	0	0
Ending Intangible Assets	$0	$0	$0	$0	$0	$0	$0

Leased Property Under Capital Leases	Initial	1993	1994	1995	1996	1997	1998
Beginning Balance		$0	$0	$0	$0	$0	$0
Plus: Additions		0	0	0	0	0	0
Amortization 25 Years		0	0	0	0	0	0
Ending Intangible Assets	$0	$0	$0	$0	$0	$0	$0

	1993	1994	1995	1996	1997	1998
Deductible Amortization	$471	$271	$271	$271	$271	$213
Non-Deductible Amortization	1,459	659	659	659	659	426
Total Amortization	$1,931	$931	$931	$931	$931	$639

Exhibit 23.13

MAREIGHT CORPORATION
LBO Analysis
Summary Debt Amortization and Interest Expense Schedule

05/22/92
04:47 PM

Interest Expense

	1993	1994	1995	1996	1997	1998
Cash Interest Expense						
Revolver	$1,867	$2,142	$2,427	$2,643	$2,779	$2,818
Senior Term Loan A	3,895	3,339	2,782	2,226	1,669	1,113
Senior Term Loan B	0	0	0	0	0	0
Senior Term Loan C	0	0	0	0	0	0
Mortgage Debt	0	0	0	0	0	0
Sale-Leaseback Financing	0	0	0	0	0	0
Senior Subordinated Debt A	2,910	2,910	2,910	2,910	2,910	2,910
Senior Subordinated Debt B	0	0	0	0	0	0
Junior Subordinated Debt	0	0	0	0	0	0
Discount Jr Subordinated Debt	0	0	0	0	0	0
Increasing Rate Note	0	0	0	0	0	0
Total Cash Interest Expense	$8,672	$8,390	$8,119	$7,779	$7,358	$6,841
Non-Cash Interest Expense						
Junior Subordinated Debt	$0	$0	$0	$0	$0	$0
Discount Jr Subordinated Debt	0	0	0	0	0	0
Total Non-Cash Interest Expense	$0	$0	$0	$0	$0	$0
Total Interest Expense	$8,672	$8,390	$8,119	$7,779	$7,358	$6,841
Long-Term Debt Amortization						
Required	$5,857	$5,857	$5,857	$5,857	$5,857	$5,857
Optional	0	0	0	0	0	539
Total Long-Term Debt Amortization	$5,857	$5,857	$5,857	$5,857	$5,857	$6,396
Long-Term Debt Outstanding						
Current Portion	$5,857	$5,857	$5,857	$5,857	$5,857	$5,857
Non-Current Portion	77,083	74,394	70,941	66,592	61,170	54,773
Total Long-Term Debt Outstanding	$82,940	$80,252	$76,798	$72,449	$67,027	$60,631
Accretion on Discount Jr Subordinated Debt	$0	$0	$0	$0	$0	$0

HAREIGHT CORPORATION
LBO Analysis
Debt Amortization Schedules

Exhibit 23.14

05/22/92
04:47 PM

Senior Term Loan A

	Opening Balance	1993	1994	1995	1996	1997	1998	1999	2000	2001	2002
Beginning Balance		$41,000	$35,143	$29,286	$23,429	$17,571	$11,714	$5,857	$0	$0	$0
Amortization 7 years		5,857	5,857	5,857	5,857	5,857	5,857	5,857	0	0	0
Grace Period 0 year											
Ending Balance - Total	$41,000	$35,143	$29,286	$23,429	$17,571	$11,714	$5,857	$0	$0	$0	$0
Less: Current Portion	5,857	5,857	5,857	5,857	5,857	5,857	5,857	0	0	0	0
Ending Balance - LTD	$35,143	$29,286	$23,429	$17,571	$11,714	$5,857	$0	$0	$0	$0	$0
Interest Exp. 9.500%		$3,895	$3,339	$2,782	$2,226	$1,669	$1,113	$556	$0	$0	$0

Senior Term Loan B

	Opening Balance	1993	1994	1995	1996	1997	1998	1999	2000	2001	2002
Beginning Balance		$0	$0	$0	$0	$0	$0	$0	$0	$0	$0
Amortization 6 years		0	0	0	0	0	0	0	0	0	0
Grace Period 0 year											
Ending Balance - Total	$0	$0	$0	$0	$0	$0	$0	$0	$0	$0	$0
Less: Current Portion	0	0	0	0	0	0	0	0	0	0	0
Ending Balance - LTD	$0	$0	$0	$0	$0	$0	$0	$0	$0	$0	$0
Interest Exp. 13.500%		$0	$0	$0	$0	$0	$0	$0	$0	$0	$0

Senior Term Loan C

	Opening Balance	1993	1994	1995	1996	1997	1998	1999	2000	2001	2002
Beginning Balance		$0	$0	$0	$0	$0	$0	$0	$0	$0	$0
Amortization 6 years		0	0	0	0	0	0	0	0	0	0
Grace Period 0 year											
Ending Balance - Total	$0	$0	$0	$0	$0	$0	$0	$0	$0	$0	$0
Less: Current Portion	0	0	0	0	0	0	0	0	0	0	0
Ending Balance - LTD	$0	$0	$0	$0	$0	$0	$0	$0	$0	$0	$0
Interest Exp. 14.000%		$0	$0	$0	$0	$0	$0	$0	$0	$0	$0

Senior Subordinated Debt A

	Opening Balance	1993	1994	1995	1996	1997	1998	1999	2000	2001	2002
Beginning Balance		$24,000	$24,000	$24,000	$24,000	$24,000	$24,000	$24,000	$24,000	$0	$0
Amortization 8 years		0	0	0	0	0	0	0	24,000	0	0
Ending Balance - Total	$24,000	$24,000	$24,000	$24,000	$24,000	$24,000	$24,000	$24,000	$0	$0	$0
Less: Current Portion	$24,000	$24,000	$24,000	$24,000	$24,000	$24,000	$24,000	24,000	0	0	0
Ending Balance - LTD	$24,000	$24,000	$24,000	$24,000	$24,000	$24,000	$24,000	$0	$0	$0	$0
Interest Exp. 12.125%		$2,910	$2,910	$2,910	$2,910	$2,910	$2,910	$2,910	$2,910	$0	$0

Senior Subordinated Debt B

	Opening Balance	1993	1994	1995	1996	1997	1998	1999	2000	2001	2002
Beginning Balance		$0	$0	$0	$0	$0	$0	$0	$0	$0	$0
Amortization 5 years		0	0	0	0	0	0	0	0	0	0
Ending Balance - Total	$0	$0	$0	$0	$0	$0	$0	$0	$0	$0	$0
Less: Current Portion	0	0	0	0	0	0	0	0	0	0	0
Ending Balance - LTD	$0	$0	$0	$0	$0	$0	$0	$0	$0	$0	$0
Interest Exp. 12.375%		$0	$0	$0	$0	$0	$0	$0	$0	$0	$0

Page 14   FILE: SKT_M2   Exhibit 33.14

MARRIOTT CORPORATION
LBO Analysis
Debt Amortization Schedule (cont'd)

05/22/92
04:47 PM

	Opening Balance	1993	1994	1995	1996	1997	1998	1999	2000	2001	2002
Increasing Rate Note											
Beginning Balance	0	0	0	0	0	0	0	0	0	0	0
Redemption		0	0	0	0	0	0	0	0	0	0
Ending Balance	$0	$0	$0	$0	$0	$0	$0	$0	$0	$0	$0
Less: Current Portion	0	0	0	0	0	0	0	0	0	0	0
Ending Balance - LTD	$0	$0	$0	$0	$0	$0	$0	$0	$0	$0	$0
Average Interest Rate		13.00%	13.75%	14.75%	15.75%	16.75%	0.00%	0.00%	0.00%	0.00%	0.00%
Interest Expense		$0	$0	$0	$0	$0	$0	$0	$0	$0	$0

Initial Interest Rate	13.000%	
Incremental Increase	0.500%	Freq Interval (months)
Rate Cap	19.000%	Mo Incr Period (months)
		Redemption - End of Year

	Opening Balance	1993	1994	1995	1996	1997	1998	1999	2000	2001	2002
Revolver											
Beginning Balance		$20,744	$23,797	$26,966	$29,360	$30,878	$31,313	$30,773	$30,773	$30,773	$30,773
New Borrowings		3,053	3,169	2,393	1,506	435	539	0	0	0	0
Reduction of Debt		0	0	0	0	0	0	0	0	0	0
Ending Balance	$20,744	$20,744	$23,797	$26,966	$29,360	$30,878	$31,313	$30,773	$30,773	$30,773	$30,773
Interest Exp. 9.000%		$1,867	$2,143	$2,427	$2,643	$2,775	$2,818	$2,770	$2,770	$2,770	$2,770

	Opening Balance	1993	1994	1995	1996	1997	1998	1999	2000	2001	2002
Junior Subordinated Debt											
Beginning Balance		0	0	0	0	0	0	0	0	0	0
Amortization		0	0	0	0	0	0	0	0	0	0
Accretion		0	0	0	0	0	0	0	0	0	0
Ending Balance	$0	$0	$0	$0	$0	$0	$0	$0	$0	$0	$0
Less: Current Portion	0	0	0	0	0	0	0	0	0	0	0
Ending Balance - LTD	$0	$0	$0	$0	$0	$0	$0	$0	$0	$0	$0

Cash Interest		
Non-Cash Interest		
Beginning year of Zero	1	
Beginning Yr of Curr. Coupon	3	
Zero Interest Rate	13.000%	
Current Coupon Rate	13.000%	

	Opening Balance	1993	1994	1995	1996	1997	1998	1999	2000	2001	2002
Sale-Leaseback Financing											
Beginning Balance		0	0	0	0	0	0	0	0	0	0
Amortization		0	0	0	0	0	0	0	0	0	0
Ending Balance	$0	$0	$0	$0	$0	$0	$0	$0	$0	$0	$0
Less: Current Portion	0	0	0	0	0	0	0	0	0	0	0
Ending Balance - LTD	$0	$0	$0	$0	$0	$0	$0	$0	$0	$0	$0

Interest Exp. 11.000%		$0
Tax Rate(?)		0
Sale Price of Asset		0
Gross Bk Value of Asset		0
Acc Deprec of Asset		0
Book Gain (Loss) on Sale		0
Economic Life of Asset (yrs)		0
Tax Basis of Asset		0
AMT Basis of Asset		0

MARRIGHT CORPORATION
LBO Analysis
Debt Amortization and Preferred Stock Redemption Schedules

Discount Jr Subordinated Debt

	Opening Balance	1993	1994	1995	1996	1997	1998	1999	2000	2001	2002
Beginning Balance		$0	$0	$0	$0	$0	$0	$0	$0	$0	$0
Amortization		0	0	0	0	0	0	0	0	0	0
OID Accretion		0	0	0	0	0	0	0	0	0	0
Ending Balance	$0	$0	$0	$0	$0	$0	$0	$0	$0	$0	$0
Less: Current Portion	0	0	0	0	0	0	0	0	0	0	0
Ending Balance - LTD	$0	$0	$0	$0	$0	$0	$0	$0	$0	$0	$0
Cash Interest		$0	$0	$0	$0	$0	$0	$0	$0	$0	$0
Non-Cash Interest		$0	$0	$0	$0	$0	$0	$0	$0	$0	$0

Face Value $0
Proceeds $0
YTM   10.500%
Coupon   0.000%
Term (years)   10

NOTE: If using stub period function, OID Accretion formulas must be modified.

Mortgage Debt

		1993	1994	1995	1996	1997	1998	1999	2000	2001	2002
Beginning Balance		$0	$0	$0	$0	$0	$0	$0	$0	$0	$0
Amortization (15 years)		0	0	0	0	0	0	0	0	0	0
Ending Balance		$0	$0	$0	$0	$0	$0	$0	$0	$0	$0
Less: Current Portion		0	0	0	0	0	0	0	0	0	0
Ending Balance - LTD		$0	$0	$0	$0	$0	$0	$0	$0	$0	$0
Interest Exp. (12.000%)		$0	$0	$0	$0	$0	$0	$0	$0	$0	$0

Preferred stock

	Opening Balance	1993	1994	1995	1996	1997	1998	1999	2000	2001	2002
Beginning Balance		$0	$0	$0	$0	$0	$0	$0	$0	$0	$0
Stock Dividend (Redemption)		0	0	0	0	0	0	0	0	0	0
Ending Balance	$0	$0	$0	$0	$0	$0	$0	$0	$0	$0	$0
Cash Dividend (12.000%)		$0	$0	$0	$0	$0	$0	$0	$0	$0	$0

PIK Preferred

	Opening Balance	1993	1994	1995	1996	1997	1998	1999	2000	2001	2002
Beginning Balance		$0	$0	$0	$0	$0	$0	$0	$0	$0	$0
Stock Dividend (Redemption)		0	0	0	0	0	0	0	0	0	0
Ending Balance	$0	$0	$0	$0	$0	$0	$0	$0	$0	$0	$0
Stock Dividend (9.000%)		$0	$0	$0	$0	$0	$0	$0	$0	$0	$0

MAREIGHT CORPORATION
LBO Analysis
Financial Statement Tax Provision

Exhibit 17

05/22/92
04:47 PM

Years Ended December 31,	1993	1994	1995	1996	1997	1998
Earnings Before Taxes	$4,014	$6,392	$7,841	$9,448	$11,231	$13,504
Permanent Differences						
Goodwill Amortization	426	426	426	426	426	426
Other Non-Deductible Amortization	1,033	233	233	233	233	0
Total Permanent Differences	1,459	659	659	659	659	426
Taxable Income Before NOL	5,473	7,051	8,501	10,108	11,890	13,930
NOL						
Available	0	0	0	0	0	0
Current	0	0	0	0	0	0
Utilized	0	0	0	0	0	0
Taxable Income After NOL	5,473	7,051	8,501	10,108	11,890	13,930
State Taxes 6.00%	328	423	510	606	713	836
Taxable Income After NOL and State Taxes	5,145	6,628	7,991	9,501	11,177	13,094
Federal Tax 34.00%	1,749	2,254	2,717	3,230	3,800	4,452
Credits	0	0	0	0	0	0
Net Federal Taxes	1,749	2,254	2,717	3,230	3,800	4,452
State Taxes	328	423	510	606	713	836
Foreign Taxes	0	0	0	0	0	0
Total Book Tax Provision	$2,078	$2,677	$3,227	$3,837	$4,514	$5,288
Effective Tax Rate	51.8%	41.9%	41.2%	40.6%	40.2%	39.2%

23.4 THE FINAL LBO MODEL

The distinctions between the Initial LBO and Final LBO models are the same as the distinctions between the Initial DCF and Final DCF models. See paragraph 22.5.

The Final LBO Model consists of the schedules listed below. All schedules have been described above or in paragraph 22.6. The figures appearing in the Final LBO Model relate to the example in Chapter 10.

- Executive Summary (Exhibit 23–18).
- Financing, Tax, Transaction Costs and Acquisition Method Assumptions (Exhibit 23–19).
- Economic and Operating Assumptions (Exhibit 23–20).
- Capital Expenditure Assumptions (Exhibit 23–21).
- Book and Tax Depreciation Rate Assumptions (Exhibits 23–22 to 23–24).
- Income Statements (Exhibit 23–25).
- Balance Sheets (Exhibit 23–26).
- Statements of Changes in Financial Position (Exhibit 23–27).
- Ownership Breakdown and Calculation of Gross Residual Values (Exhibit 23–28).
- Net Residual Value Calculations—Assuming Sale (Exhibits 23–29 and 23–30).
- After-Tax Investment Return Calculations (Exhibit 23–31).
- Selected Financial Ratios (Exhibit 23–32).
- Summary Amortization Schedule (Exhibit 23–33).
- Summary Debt Amortization and Interest Expense Schedule (Exhibit 23–34).
- Debt Amortization Schedules (Exhibits 23–35 and 23–36).
- Debt Amortization and Preferred Stock Redemption Schedules (Exhibit 23–37).
- Financial Statement Tax Provision (Exhibit 23–38).
- Current and Deferred Taxes (Exhibit 23–39).
- Alternative Minimum Tax (Exhibit 23–40).
- Comparison of Calculated and Actual Values of Net Property, Plant and Equipment (Exhibit 23–41).
- Historical Capital Expenditures (Exhibit 23–42).
- Summary Historical Book Depreciation Schedule (Exhibit 23–43).
- Summary Projected Book Depreciation Schedule (Exhibit 23–44).

- Summary Regular Tax Depreciation Schedule (Exhibit 23–45).
- Summary AMT Depreciation Schedule (Exhibit 23–46).
- Summary ACE Depreciation Schedule (Exhibit 23–47).
- Historical and Projected Book, Regular Tax, AMTI and ACE Depreciation—3-Year (Exhibits 23–48 and 23–49).
- Historical and Projected Book, Regular Tax, AMTI and ACE Depreciation—5-Year (Exhibits 23–50 and 23–51).
- Historical and Projected Book, Regular Tax, AMTI and ACE Depreciation—7-Year (Exhibits 23–52 and 23–53).
- Historical and Projected Book, Regular Tax, AMTI and ACE Depreciation—10-Year (Exhibits 23–54 and 23–55).
- Historical and Projected Book, Regular Tax, AMTI and ACE Depreciation—15-Year (Exhibits 23–56 and 23–57).
- Historical and Projected Book, Regular Tax, AMTI and ACE Depreciation—20-Year (Exhibits 23–58 and 23–59).
- Historical and Projected Book, Regular Tax, AMTI and ACE Depreciation—Real Estate (Exhibits 23–60 and 23–61).

23.41   Executive Summary

Although there are a significant number of additional assumptions in the Final LBO Model the format for the Executive Summary remains the same.

23.42   Financing, Tax, Transaction Costs and Acquisition Method Assumptions

There are no changes from the Initial LBO Model.

23.43   Economic and Operating Assumptions

See paragraph 22.53 for a description of Exhibit 23–20.

23.44   Capital Expenditure Assumptions

The Final LBO Model is designed to deal with both acquisition methods (New Cost Basis and No Change in Basis acquisition methods). If the acquisition method to be modeled is a New Cost Basis acquisition method, the Final LBO Model allows the acquirer to allocate value among all the acquired depreciable assets and computes the proper book and tax depreciation amounts. Alternatively, if the acquisition is structured as a No Change in Basis acquisition, the Final LBO Model permits the acquirer to input depreciation expense estimates for existing assets, by asset category. All capital expenditures expected postclosing are input by asset category under both methods.

Exhibit 23–21 is the schedule for inputting recent historical and projected capital expenditures by asset category. Also, the book life of each asset category can be defined on this schedule.

Exhibits 23–22, 23–23 and 23–24 contain book and tax depreciation rate assumptions for all asset categories. The rates appearing on these schedules should be adjusted, as required, to reflect the actual class lives of asset categories of the target company.

Chapter 6 describes the importance of depreciation as a deduction. To properly calculate depreciation deductions in an acquisition, a substantial number of support schedules are required. Depreciation calculations for book, regular tax, Alternative Minimum Tax and Adjusted Current Earnings purposes for all asset categories are calculated in Exhibits 23–48 through 23–61. The calculations on these pages are summarized in Exhibits 23–44 through 23–47.

The various depreciation related schedules work together in the manner described in paragraph 22.54.

23.45   Current and Deferred Taxes

This schedule calculates the breakdown of the current tax provision between current taxes payable and deferred taxes. It accomplishes this by adjusting book earnings before taxes for both permanent and timing differences between book and taxable income. The resulting sum, reduced by any tax loss carryforward, is then subjected to federal and state income taxes. The Alternative Minimum Tax, discussed in the following paragraph, is compared to the regular tax liability and the target's net federal tax liability is calculated. The target's MTC Credit is also calculated.

The target's deferred tax amount is equal to the difference between the company's book tax provision and its current tax liability.

23.46   Alternative Minimum Tax

The Alternative Minimum Tax rules are discussed at length in paragraph B.10. This schedule puts the AMT rules into effect in the model. Note that the largest AMT adjustments tend to be the AMT depreciation adjustment and the ACE income adjustment.

Page 1   FILE: SHT_A

MARRIOTT CORPORATION
LBO Analysis
Executive Summary

EXHIBIT 11.14
05/22/92
05:29 PM

Uses of Funds

	Amount	Percent
Common Shares Outstanding	1,000	
Options Outstanding	0	
Average Exercise Price	$0.00	
Purchase Price per Share	$56,612.00	
# of Shares Purchased	100.00%	
Purchase Common Equity	$50,612	48.6%
Purchase Preferred Stock	0	0.0%
Existing Liabilities to be refinanced	49,388	47.4%
Transaction Expenses	4,237	4.1%
Obligations under Capitalized Leases	0	0.0%
Pre-Payment Penalty	0	0.0%
Tax on Sale of Asset (Tax Basis)	0	0.0%
Additional Working Capital Cash	0	0.0%
Total Uses	$104,237	100.0%

Goodwill Calculation

Total Equity Purchase Price		$50,612
Adjustments to Book Value		
Plus: Existing Shareholders' Equity	$33,564	
Plus: Deferred Income Taxes	0	
Less: Existing Goodwill	0	
Less: Existing Organizational Costs	0	
Less: Value Allocated to PP&E	0	
Less: Value Allocated to Intangibles	0	
Net Book Value		33,564
Total Goodwill Created		$17,048

Sources of Funds

	Amount	Percent	Bank Rate	Spread Over Base Rate: Loan
Bank Revolver	$20,746	19.9%	9.00%	1.50%
Sale/Leaseback Financing	0	0.0%	11.00%	3.50%
Senior Term Loan A	41,000	39.3%	13.00%	2.00%
Senior Term Loan B	0	0.0%	13.50%	4.00%
Senior Term Loan C	0	0.0%	14.00%	6.00%
Mortgage Debt	0	0.0%	12.00%	4.00%
Senior Subordinated Debt A	24,000	23.0%	12.13%	4.25%
Senior Subordinated Debt B	0	0.0%	12.37%	6.00%
Junior Subordinated Debt	0	0.0%	12.75%	3.50%
Increasing Rate Note	0	0.0%	10.50%	3.00%
PIK Preferred	0	0.0%	9.00%	1.50%
Preferred Stock	0	0.0%	12.00%	4.00%
Sr Subholders Common Equity	0	0.0%		
Management Common Equity	1,642	1.6%		
Sponsor Common Equity	14,593	14.0%		
Capitalized Lease Oblig.	0	0.0%		
Excess Cash	2,656	2.7%		
Total Sources	$104,237	100.0%		

Transaction Costs

	Years
Total Transaction Costs	$4,237
% of Total Consideration	4.1%

Amortization Periods

	Years
Goodwill Amortization	40
Intangibles Amortization	5
Amortization of Leased Property under Capital Leases	25

Miscellaneous

	Years Ended December 31
Fiscal Year	
First Historical Year	1989
Estimated Financial Statements Beginning	1993

Accounting Method ('Purchase' or 'Recap')   Purchase Acctg (2)
Amount of Basis Step Up or No Change in ...   New Tax Basis(3)
Initial 'Stub' Period Length   100.0%
% of Annual Sales Occurring in Stub Period   Final
'Initial' or 'Final' model

FOOTNOTES:
(1) Net Cash Flow equals EBITDA less Cash Taxes less Capital Expenditures
(2) Do not use this model for a transaction involving Pooling
(3) Choice of method not applicable in Initial model.
(4) 50% of inventory plus 80% of receivables plus 100% of cash.

Purchase and Exit Multiple (EBITDA Method Midpoint)

	1993	1994	Terminal
Sales	0.73	4.69	
EBITDA	4.7	4.5	4.5
EBITA	7.3	6.3	11.4
EBIT	7.0	5.3	11.7
Net Income	4.6	4.3	13.8
Net Cash Flow (1)		21.5	15.7

Key Interest Coverage, Debt Paydown, Leverage and Revolver Information

Years Ended December 31.	1993	1994	...	1996	1997	1998
EBITDA/Total Interest Expense				3.47	3.68	4.37
EBIT/Total Interest Expense				2.64	2.88	3.54
Net CF/Total Interest Expense (1)				1.71	1.85	3.56
EBITDA/Senior Interest Expense				5.44	6.25	7.36
EBIT/Senior Interest Expense				4.14	4.88	5.97
Net CF/Senior Interest Expense (1)				2.79	3.39	5.99
EBITDA/Cash Interest Expense				3.47	3.88	4.37
EBIT/Cash Interest Expense				2.64	2.88	3.54
Net CF/Cash Interest Expense (1)				1.71	1.85	3.56

Total Debt Outstanding				$73,743	$72,132	$47,501
Cumulative Reduction				11.7%	13.9%	24.0%
Total Sr. Debt Outstanding				$17,571	$11,734	$5,657
Cumulative Reduction				57.1%	71.4%	26.7%
Sr. Debt repaid in year						

Total Debt/Total Capital				46.4%	59.1%	52.8%
Total Debt/Equity				184.2%	144.6%	112.2%
Total Senior Debt/Total Cap.				4.3%	39.3%	24.2%
Total Senior Debt/Equity				135.0%	96.5%	72.5%
Revolver Capacity (4)				$28,582	$39,933	$43,933
Revolver Availability				$41,651	$81,493	$91,333
Revolver Availability Percentage				73.3%	72.4%	73.6%

Internal Rates of Return - Assumes Sale of Investment

EBITDA Multiple Method
	0.0	8.5	9.5	10.0
Terminal EBITDA Multiple				
Sponsor Common Equity	35.3%	37.0%	38.5%	40.1%
Management Common Equity	51.0%	53.0%	54.4%	56.3%
Senior Subordinated Debt A	21.7%	22.4%	23.0%	23.4%

EBITA Multiple Method
	12.0	13.0	14.0	16.0
Sponsor Common Equity	40.0%	42.3%	44.3%	46.2%
Management Common Equity	56.3%	59.0%	61.4%	64.6%
Senior Subordinated Debt A	23.6%	24.5%	25.4%	26.2%

P/E Multiple Method
	18.0	20.0	22.0	24.0
Sponsor Common Equity	34.9%	36.9%	37.1%	39.0%
Management Common Equity	50.4%	51.9%	53.3%	54.4%
Senior Subordinated Debt A	21.6%	22.0%	22.4%	23.3%

Equity Ownership Percentages

	Initial	Terminal
Sponsor Common Equity	77.5%	78.0%
Management Common Equity	22.5%	2.5%
Junior Subordinated Debt	0.0%	0.0%
Public Shareholders	0.0%	0.0%
Total Equity Ownership	100.0%	100.0%

Page 2   FILE: SHT_D

MARRIOTT CORPORATION
LBO Analysis
Financing, Tax, Transaction Cost and Acquisition Method Assumptions

Exhibit 22.13   05/23/92
05:39 PM

Financing Assumptions

Revolver
Opening Balance	$20,746
Interest Rate	9.000%
Spread over Prime	1.500%

Senior Term Loan A
Opening Balance	$41,000
Interest Rate	9.500%
Spread over Prime	2.000%
Amortization (years)	7
Grace Period (years)	0

Senior Term Loan B
Opening Balance	$0
Interest Rate	13.500%
Spread over Prime	6.000%
Amortization (years)	6
Grace Period (years)	0

Senior Term Loan C
Opening Balance	$0
Interest Rate	14.000%
Spread over Prime	6.500%
Amortization (years)	6
Grace Period (years)	0

Sale/Leaseback
Opening Balance	$0
Interest Rate	11.000%
Spread over Prime	3.500%
Sale Price of Asset	$0
Gross Bk Value of Asset	$0
Acc Deprec of Asset	$0
Book Gain(Loss) on Sale	$0
Economic Life of Asset	$0
Tax Basis of Asset	$0
AMT Basis of Asset	$0

Mortgage Debt
Opening Balance	$0
Interest Rate	12.000%
Spread over Prime	4.500%
Amortization (years)	15

Preferred Stock
Opening Balance	$0
Cash Dividend	12.000%
Book Value of Equity	4.500%

LYX Preferred Stock
Opening Balance	$0
Dividend Rate	9.000%
Spread over Prime	1.500%

Senior Sub Debt A
Opening Balance	$24,000
Interest Rate	12.125%
Spread over Prime	4.125%

Senior Sub Debt B
Opening Balance	$0
Interest Rate	12.375%
Spread over Prime	4.875%

Discount Jr Sub Debt
Opening Balance	$0
YTM	10.500%
Spread over Prime	3.000%
Face Value	$0
Proceeds	0.000%
Coupon	10
Term (years)	
Beg yr of current coupon	3
Zero interest rate	13.000%
Current Coupon Rate	13.000%

Junior Sub Debt
Opening Balance	$0
Interest Rate	13.000%
Spread over Prime	5.500%
Beg yr of zero	1

Increasing Rate Note
Opening Balance	$0
Initial Interest Rate	13.000%
Spread over Prime	5.500%
Incremental Increase	0.500%
Freq Interval (months)	6
Mo Incr Period (months)	12
Redemption - End of Year	5

Common Stock
Minimum Cash Balance Req'd	$0
Interest on Cash Balances	7.000%
Shares Authorized	1,000
Shares Outstanding	1,000
Book Value of Equity	$33,564
Book Value per Share	$33,564.00

Tax Assumptions

Federal Tax Rate	34.000%
State and Local Tax Rate	6.000%
Capital Gains Tax Rate	34.000%
Alternative Minimum Tax Rate	20.000%
Long-Term Federal Tax-Exempt Bond Rate	8.75%
Built-In Gains (Losses) Qualifier	25.00%
Book Income Adjustment Rate (Post-1989)	75.00%
AMT NOL Use Limitation	90.00%
Acquired Book NOL	$0
Acquired Tax NOL	$0
Acquired AMT NOL	$0
Acquired NTC Credit	$0

Transaction Cost Assumptions

Advisory & Underwriting Fees
Transaction Fee	$1,457	1.50%
Senior Term Loans A, B & C	$20	2.00%
Senior Term Loan Note	0	0.00%
Increasing Rate Note	960	4.00%
Subordinated Debt		5.00%
Preferred Equity		
Accounting/Legal & Printing/Miscellaneous	1,000	4.36%
Total Fees and Expenses	**$4,237**	

Amortization of Transaction Costs
Transaction	5	years
% related to financing	20%	
Accounting & Legal	1	year
% related to financing	20%	
Bank Fees	7	year
Increasing Rate Note Fee	7	year
Subordinated Debt Fees	10	year
Prepayment penalty	7	year

Acquisition Methods

Method Used: New Basis Acquisition Method

No Change in Tax Basis Acquisition Methods
1) Asset Acquisition
   A) Stock Acquisition
   B) Reverse Merger
   C) Forward Subsidiary Merger
2) 338 Transaction
3) 338(h)(10) Transaction

New Tax Basis Acquisition Methods
1) Stock Acquisition
   A) Asset Acquisition
   B) Forward Merger
   C) Forward Subsidiary Merger
2) Type A Reorganization
   A) Type A Forward Merger
   B) Type A Statutory Consolidation
   C) Type A Forward Subsidiary Merger
   D) Type A Reverse Subsidiary Merger
3) Type B Reorganization
   A) Type B Stock Exchange
   B) Type B Subsidiary Stock Exchange
4) Type C Reorganization
   A) Type C Stock for Assets Exchange
   B) Type C Subsidiary Stock for Assets Exchange

MAREIGHT CORPORATION
LBO Analysis
Economic and Operating Assumptions

Exhibit 23.20
05/22/92
05:29 PM

Economic Assumptions

Year	Historical				Average 1989-92	Projected						Average 1993-98
	1989	1990	1991	1992		1993	1994	1995	1996	1997	1998	
GNP Growth Rate	3.5%	1.7%	0.0%	1.0%	1.5%	2.0%	2.5%	3.0%	3.0%	3.0%	3.0%	2.8%
Inflation Rate	4.6%	4.7%	5.5%	3.9%	4.7%	3.0%	3.0%	3.0%	3.0%	3.0%	3.0%	3.0%
Prime Interest Rate	9.6%	10.3%	9.5%	8.0%	9.3%	7.5%	7.5%	7.5%	7.5%	7.5%	7.5%	7.5%
Long-Term Treasury Bond Interest Rate	9.1%	8.4%	8.6%	7.9%	8.5%	6.8%	6.8%	6.8%	6.8%	6.8%	6.8%	6.8%

Sales and Margin Assumptions
Years Ended December 31,

	1989	Historical			Average 1989-92	Projected						Average 1993-98
		1990	1991	1992		1993	1994	1995	1996	1997	1998	
Total Sales	$107,417	$113,656	$122,940	$133,302		$143,300	$154,047	$165,601	$178,021	$191,372	$205,725	
Growth Rate		5.8%	8.2%	8.4%	7.5%	7.5%	7.5%	7.5%	7.5%	7.5%	7.5%	7.5%
Gross Margin %	35.1%	34.5%	34.2%	34.7%	34.6%	34.5%	34.5%	34.5%	34.5%	34.5%	34.5%	34.5%
SG&A %	19.0%	19.0%	19.0%	19.0%	19.0%	19.0%	19.0%	19.0%	19.0%	19.0%	19.0%	19.0%
EBITDA Margin %	16.1%	15.5%	15.2%	15.7%	15.6%	15.5%	15.5%	15.5%	15.5%	15.5%	15.5%	15.5%

Calculation of Components of Net Working Capital

	1989	Historical			Average 1989-92	1993	1994	1995	1996	1997	1998	Average 1993-98
		1990	1991	1992								
Accounts Receivable	$14,123	$15,083	$13,677	$14,732		$15,704	$16,882	$18,148	$19,509	$20,972	$22,545	
Days Sales Outstanding (365 days/yr)	48.0	48.4	40.6	40.3	40.5	40.0	40.0	40.0	40.0	40.0	40.0	40.0
Inventory	$24,344	$23,357	$27,075	$25,903		$28,443	$30,576	$32,869	$35,334	$37,984	$40,833	
Inventory Turnover	2.9	3.2	3.0	3.4	3.2	3.3	3.3	3.3	3.3	3.3	3.3	3.3
Other Current Assets	$5,211	$5,421	$4,369	$5,109		$5,015	$5,392	$5,796	$6,231	$6,698	$7,200	
% of Sales	4.9%	4.8%	3.6%	3.8%	3.7%	3.5%	3.5%	3.5%	3.5%	3.5%	3.5%	3.5%
Accounts Payable	$9,973	$9,555	$8,993	$7,475		$9,952	$10,699	$11,501	$12,364	$13,291	$14,288	
Days Payables Outstanding (365 days/yr)	40.4	36.3	31.5	24.3	27.9	30.0	30.0	30.0	30.0	30.0	30.0	30.0
Accrued Liabilities	$4,939	$5,627	$5,133	$5,421		$5,933	$6,378	$6,857	$7,371	$7,924	$8,518	
% of COGS and SG&A	5.5%	5.9%	4.9%	4.8%	4.9%	4.9%	4.9%	4.9%	4.9%	4.9%	4.9%	4.9%
Current Taxes Payable	$826	$1,436	$3,034	$1,333		$550	$477	$584	$873	$1,028	$1,200	
% of Current Taxes Payable	0.0%	0.0%	0.0%	0.0%	0.0%	20.0%	20.0%	20.0%	20.0%	20.0%	20.0%	20.0%
Net Working Capital	$27,940	$27,243	$27,961	$31,515		$32,726	$35,295	$37,871	$40,467	$43,412	$46,572	
% of Sales	26.0%	24.0%	22.7%	23.6%	23.2%	22.8%	22.9%	22.9%	22.7%	22.7%	22.6%	22.6%
Increase (Decrease)		($697)	$718	$3,554		$1,211	$2,569	$2,576	$2,595	$2,946	$3,160	

Exhibit 23.21
05/22/92
05:29 PM

MAREIGHT CORPORATION
LBO Analysis
Capital Expenditure Assumptions

Capital Expenditures and Acquired Property, Plant and Equipment by Category

Accounting Category	Book Class Life	Tax Life Category	Historical 1989	1990	1991	1992	Average 1988-91	Acquired PP&E	Estimate 1993	1994	Projected 1995	1996	1997	1998
Land	NA	Land	$0	$0	$0	$0	$0	$9,700	$0	$0	$0	$0	$0	$0
Autos	5	3-Year (1)	0	0	0	0	0	3,500	650	675	700	725	750	775
Prod Eqp	8	5-Year (2)	0	0	0	0	0	9,000	2,000	1,800	2,100	2,500	2,250	2,400
Prod Eqp	12	7-Year (3)	0	0	0	0	0	10,265	2,388	2,943	3,392	3,388	4,334	4,684
Barges	15	10-Year (4)	0	0	0	0	0	0	0	0	0	0	0	0
Waste Facility	20	15-Year (5)	0	0	0	0	0	0	0	0	0	0	0	0
Sewers	30	20-Year (6)	0	0	0	0	0	0	0	0	0	0	0	0
Real Estate	30	Real Est. (7)	0	0	0	0	0	12,500	2,700	2,900	2,750	3,000	3,000	3,250
Total Capital Expenditures			$0	$0	$0	$0	$0	$44,965	$7,738	$8,318	$8,942	$9,613	$10,334	$11,109

Property, Plant and Equipment Acquired: $44,965 (8)

(1) Includes autos.
(2) Includes trucks, computers, office equipment.
(3) Includes office furniture.
(4) Includes vessels, single purpose agricultural facilities.
(5) Includes telephone distribution facilities.
(6) Includes municipal sewers.
(7) Includes non-residential real property; does not include land.
(8) Must allocate acquired gross property, plant and equipment to various asset categories.

MARRIOTT CORPORATION
ABO Analysis
Book and Tax Depreciation Rate Assumptions

Exhibit 11-13
05/23/91
05:29 PM

Autos — Tax Category: 3-Year (Book Class Life 5)

		Acq'd Assets	Regular Tax			
Year	Book Depr. %	Book Depr. %	ACRS Depr. %	MACRS % (1)	AMTI % (2)	ACE Depr. % (3)
1	10.00%	20.00%	25.00%	33.33%	21.43%	14.29%
2	20.00%	20.00%	38.00%	44.45%	33.47%	28.57%
3	20.00%	20.00%	37.00%	14.81%	23.45%	28.57%
4	20.00%	20.00%		7.41%	21.65%	28.57%
5	20.00%	20.00%				
6	10.00%					

(1) MACRS Depreciation Percentages - Half-Year Convention
(2) 150% Declining Balance with Switch to Straight Line - Assumes 3.5-yr class life and half-year convention.
(3) Straight Line Depreciation - Assumes 3.5-year class life and half-year convention.

Prod Exp — Tax Category: 5-Year (Book Class Life 8)

		Acq'd Assets	Regular Tax			
Year	Book Depr. %	Book Depr. %	ACRS Depr. %	MACRS % (1)	AMTI % (2)	ACE Depr. % (3)
1	6.25%	12.50%	15.00%	20.00%	7.49%	5.26%
2	12.50%	12.50%	22.00%	32.00%	14.56%	10.53%
3	12.50%	12.50%	21.00%	19.20%	12.25%	10.53%
4	12.50%	12.50%	21.00%	11.52%	10.40%	10.53%
5	12.50%	12.50%	21.00%	11.52%	8.97%	10.53%
6	12.50%	12.50%		5.76%	9.17%	10.53%
7	12.50%	12.50%			9.17%	10.53%
8	12.50%	12.50%			9.17%	10.53%
9	12.50%				9.16%	10.53%
10	6.25%					

(1) MACRS Depreciation Percentages - Half-Year Convention
(2) 150% Declining Balance with Switch to Straight Line - Assumes 9.5-year class life and half-year convention.
(3) Straight Line Depreciation - Assumes 9.5-year class life and half-year convention.

Prod Exp — Tax Category: 7-Year (Book Class Life 12)

		Acq'd Assets	Regular Tax			
Year	Book Depr. %	Book Depr. %	ACRS Depr. %	MACRS % (1)	AMTI % (2)	ACE Depr. % (3)
1	4.17%	8.33%	Not Applic.	14.29%	6.25%	4.17%
2	8.33%	8.33%		24.49%	11.72%	8.33%
3	8.33%	8.33%		17.49%	10.26%	8.33%
4	8.33%	8.33%		12.49%	8.97%	8.33%
5	8.33%	8.33%		8.93%	7.85%	8.33%
6	8.33%	8.33%		8.92%	7.33%	8.33%
7	8.33%	8.33%		8.93%	7.33%	8.33%
8	8.33%	8.33%		4.46%	7.33%	8.33%
9	8.33%	8.33%			7.33%	8.33%
10	8.33%	8.33%			7.33%	8.33%
11	8.33%	8.33%			7.33%	8.33%
12	8.33%	8.33%			7.33%	8.33%
13	4.17%				3.66%	4.17%

(1) MACRS Depreciation Percentages - Half-Year Convention
(2) 150% Declining Balance with Switch to Straight Line - Assumes 13-yr class life and half-year convention.
(3) Straight Line Depreciation - Assumes 13-year class life and half-year convention.

Barges — Tax Category: 10-Year (Book Class Life 15)

		Acq'd Assets	Regular Tax			
Year	Book Depr. %	Book Depr. %	ACRS Depr. %	MACRS % (1)	AMTI % (2)	ACE Depr. % (3)
1	3.33%	6.67%		10.00%	4.39%	2.44%
2	6.67%	6.67%		18.00%	8.20%	5.71%
3	6.67%	6.67%		14.40%	7.50%	5.71%
4	6.67%	6.67%		11.52%	6.68%	5.71%
5	6.67%	6.67%		9.22%	6.37%	5.71%
6	6.67%	6.67%		7.37%	5.74%	5.71%
7	6.67%	6.67%		6.55%	5.74%	5.71%
8	6.67%	6.67%		6.55%	5.74%	5.71%
9	6.67%			6.56%	5.74%	5.71%
10	6.67%			6.55%	5.00%	5.71%
11	6.67%			3.28%	5.00%	5.71%
12	6.67%				5.00%	5.71%
13	6.67%				5.00%	5.71%
14	6.67%				5.00%	5.71%
15	3.33%				5.00%	5.71%
16					5.00%	5.71%
17						
18						

(1) MACRS Depreciation Percentages - Half-Year Convention
(2) 150% Declining Balance with Switch to Straight Line - Assumes 17.5-yr class life and half-year convention.
(3) Straight Line Depreciation - Assumes 17.5-year class life and half-year convention.

— Tax Category: 15-Year (Book Class Life 20)

		Acq'd Assets	Regular Tax			
Year	Book Depr. %	Book Depr. %	ACRS Depr. %	MACRS % (1)	AMTI % (2)	ACE Depr. % (3)
1	2.50%	5.00%		5.00%	3.57%	1.97%
2	5.00%	5.00%		10.00%	6.88%	4.74%
3	5.00%	5.00%		9.50%	6.34%	4.74%
4	5.00%	5.00%		8.55%	5.95%	4.74%
5	5.00%	5.00%		7.70%	5.39%	4.74%
6	5.00%	5.00%		6.93%	5.15%	4.74%
7	5.00%	5.00%		6.23%	4.75%	4.74%
8	5.00%	5.00%		5.90%	4.75%	4.74%
9	5.00%	5.00%		5.91%	4.75%	4.74%
10	5.00%	5.00%		5.91%	4.74%	4.74%
11	5.00%	5.00%		5.90%	4.75%	4.74%
12	5.00%	5.00%		5.91%	4.74%	4.74%
13	5.00%	5.00%		5.90%	4.75%	4.74%
14	5.00%	5.00%		5.91%	4.74%	4.74%
15	5.00%	5.00%		5.90%	4.75%	4.74%
16	5.00%	5.00%		2.95%	4.74%	4.74%
17	5.00%				4.75%	4.74%
18	5.00%				4.74%	4.74%
19	5.00%				4.75%	4.74%
20	5.00%				4.74%	4.74%
21	2.50%				2.51%	2.39%

(1) MACRS Depreciation Percentages - Half-Year Convention
(2) 150% Declining Balance with Switch to Straight Line - Assumes 21-yr class life and half-year convention.
(3) Straight Line Depreciation - Assumes 21-year class life and half-year convention.

NOTE: Review IRS Publication 534 on Depreciation to determine if class life assumptions are correct. Change from half-year convention to mid-quarter convention if more than 40% of property is placed in service during the last 3 months of the year.

FILE: SHT_AB2

MAREIGHT CORPORATION
LBO Analysis
Book and Tax Depreciation Rate Assumptions (continued)

Exhibit 23.23
05/22/92
05:29 PM

Accounting Description	Book Class Life	Tax Category	Year	Book Depr. %	Acq'd Assets Book Depr. %	Regular Tax		AMTI Depr. % (2)	ACE Depr. % (3)
						ACRS Depr. %	MACRS Depr. % (1)		
Sewers	30	20-Year	1	1.67%	3.33%	Not Applic.	3.750%	2.113%	1.408%
			2	3.33%	3.33%		7.219%	4.136%	2.817%
			3	3.33%	3.33%		6.677%	3.961%	2.817%
			4	3.33%	3.33%		6.177%	3.794%	2.817%
			5	3.33%	3.33%		5.713%	3.634%	2.817%
			6	3.33%	3.33%		5.285%	3.480%	2.817%
			7	3.33%	3.33%		4.888%	3.333%	2.817%
			8	3.33%	3.33%		4.522%	3.192%	2.817%
			9	3.33%	3.33%		4.462%	3.057%	2.817%
			10	3.33%	3.33%		4.461%	2.928%	2.817%
			11	3.33%	3.33%		4.462%	2.804%	2.817%
			12	3.33%	3.33%		4.461%	2.686%	2.817%
			13	3.33%	3.33%		4.462%	2.572%	2.817%
			14	3.33%	3.33%		4.461%	2.535%	2.817%
			15	3.33%	3.33%		4.462%	2.535%	2.817%
			16	3.33%	3.33%		4.461%	2.535%	2.817%
			17	3.33%	3.33%		4.462%	2.535%	2.817%
			18	3.33%	3.33%		4.461%	2.535%	2.817%
			19	3.33%	3.33%		4.462%	2.535%	2.817%
			20	3.33%	3.33%		4.461%	2.535%	2.817%
			21	3.33%	3.33%		2.231%	2.535%	2.817%
			22	3.33%	3.33%			2.535%	2.817%
			23	3.33%	3.33%			2.535%	2.817%
			24	3.33%	3.33%			2.535%	2.817%
			25	3.33%	3.33%			2.535%	2.817%
			26	3.33%	3.33%			2.536%	2.817%
			27	3.33%	3.33%			2.535%	2.817%
			28	3.33%	3.33%			2.535%	2.817%
			29	3.33%	3.33%			2.535%	2.817%
			30	3.33%	3.33%			2.535%	2.817%
			31	1.67%				2.536%	2.817%
			32					2.535%	2.817%
			33					2.536%	2.817%
			34					2.535%	2.817%
			35					2.536%	2.817%
			36					2.535%	2.817%

(1) MACRS Depreciation Percentages - Half-Year Convention
(2) 150% Declining Balance with switch to straight Line - Assumes 35.5-yr class life and half-year convention.
(3) Straight Line Depreciation - Assumes 35.5-year class life and half-year convention

NOTES: Review IRS Publication 534 on Depreciation to determine if class life assumptions are correct. Change from half-year convention to mid-quarter convention if more than 40% of property is placed in service during the last 3 months of the year.

MARRIOTT CORPORATION
LBO Analysis
Book and Tax Depreciation Rate Assumptions (continued)

Regular Tax

Exhibit 22.24
05/23/92
05:29 PM

				Actual Applicable Dates				Acquired Assets			New Capital Expenditures		
				1/1/81-3/15/84	3/15/84-5/8/85	5/8/85-12/31/86							
				Assumed Applicable Years									
				1991-93	1994	1985-86							
Accounting Descrip- tion	Book Class Life	Tax Category	Year	Acq'd Assets Book Depr. %	15-Yr ACRS Depr. %(1)	18-Yr ACRS Depr. %(1)	19-Yr ACRS Depr. %(1)	MACRS Depr. %(2)	AMT Depr. %(3)	ACE Depr. %(3)	MACRS Depr. %(2)(4)	AMT Depr. %(5)	ACE Depr. %(5)
Real Estat.	30	15-Year	1	1.67%	12.00%	10.00%	8.80%	3.042%	2.39%	2.39%	1.720%	1.25%	1.25%
		18-Year	2	3.33%	10.00%	9.00%	8.40%	3.175%	2.50%	2.50%	3.175%	2.50%	2.50%
		19-Year	3	3.33%	9.00%	8.00%	7.60%	3.175%	2.50%	2.50%	3.175%	2.50%	2.50%
		ACRS	4	3.33%	8.00%	7.00%	6.90%	3.175%	2.50%	2.50%	3.175%	2.50%	2.50%
		5	3.33%	7.00%	6.00%	6.30%	3.175%	2.50%	2.50%	3.175%	2.50%	2.50%
		31.5-Year MACRS	6	3.33%	6.00%	6.00%	5.70%	3.175%	2.50%	2.50%	3.175%	2.50%	2.50%
		7	3.33%	6.00%	5.00%	5.20%	3.174%	2.50%	2.50%	3.174%	2.50%	2.50%
		8	3.33%	6.00%	5.00%	4.70%	3.175%	2.50%	2.50%	3.175%	2.50%	2.50%
		9	3.33%	6.00%	5.00%	4.20%	3.174%	2.50%	2.50%	3.174%	2.50%	2.50%
		10	3.33%	5.00%	5.00%	4.20%	3.175%	2.50%	2.50%	3.175%	2.50%	2.50%
		11	3.33%	5.00%	5.00%	4.20%	3.174%	2.50%	2.50%	3.174%	2.50%	2.50%
		12	3.33%	5.00%	5.00%	4.20%	3.175%	2.50%	2.50%	3.175%	2.50%	2.50%
		13	3.33%	5.00%	4.00%	4.20%	3.174%	2.50%	2.50%	3.174%	2.50%	2.50%
		14	3.33%	5.00%	4.00%	4.20%	3.175%	2.50%	2.50%	3.175%	2.50%	2.50%
		15	3.33%	5.00%	4.00%	4.20%	3.174%	2.50%	2.50%	3.174%	2.50%	2.50%
		16	3.33%		4.00%	4.20%	3.175%	2.50%	2.50%	3.175%	2.50%	2.50%
		17	3.33%		4.00%	4.20%	3.174%	2.50%	2.50%	3.174%	2.50%	2.50%
		18	3.33%		4.00%	4.20%	3.175%	2.50%	2.50%	3.175%	2.50%	2.50%
		19	3.33%			0.20%	3.174%	2.50%	2.50%	3.174%	2.50%	2.50%
		20	3.33%				3.175%	2.50%	2.50%	3.175%	2.50%	2.50%
		21	3.33%				3.174%	2.50%	2.50%	3.174%	2.50%	2.50%
		22	3.33%				3.175%	2.50%	2.50%	3.175%	2.50%	2.50%
		23	3.33%				3.174%	2.50%	2.50%	3.174%	2.50%	2.50%
		24	3.33%				3.175%	2.50%	2.50%	3.175%	2.50%	2.50%
		25	3.33%				3.174%	2.50%	2.50%	3.174%	2.50%	2.50%
		26	3.33%				3.175%	2.50%	2.50%	3.175%	2.50%	2.50%
		27	3.33%				3.174%	2.50%	2.50%	3.174%	2.50%	2.50%
		28	3.33%				3.175%	2.50%	2.50%	3.175%	2.50%	2.50%
		29	3.33%				3.174%	2.50%	2.50%	3.174%	2.50%	2.50%
		30	3.33%				3.175%	2.50%	2.50%	3.175%	2.50%	2.50%
		31	1.67%				3.174%	2.50%	2.50%	2.174%	2.50%	2.50%
		32					1.720%	2.50%	2.50%	0.030%	2.50%	2.50%
		33						2.50%	2.50%		2.50%	2.50%
		34						2.50%	2.50%		2.50%	2.50%
		35						2.50%	2.50%		2.50%	2.50%
		36						2.50%	2.50%		2.50%	2.50%
		37						2.50%	2.50%		2.50%	2.50%
		38						2.50%	2.50%		2.50%	2.50%
		39						2.50%	2.50%		2.50%	2.50%
		40						2.50%	2.50%		2.50%	2.50%
		41						1.25%	1.25%		1.25%	1.25%

(1) ACRS Depreciation Percentages - Assumes property placed in service in the first month of the year.
(2) MACRS Depreciation Percentages - Assumes property placed in service in middle of first month of the year.
(3) Straight Line Depreciation - Assumes 40-year class life and property placed in service in middle of first month of the year.
(4) MACRS Depreciation Percentages - Assumes property placed in service in middle of 6th month of the year.
(5) Straight Line Depreciation - Assumes 40-year class life and half-year convention.

NOTES: Review IRS Publication 534 on Depreciation to determine if class life assumptions are correct. Change from half-year convention to mid-quarter convention if more than 40% of property is placed in service during the last 3 months of the year.

MAREIGHT CORPORATION
LBO Analysis
Income Statements

Exhibit 23.25
05/22/92
05:29 PM

Years Ended December 31,	Historical				Average 1989-92	Projected						Average 1993-98
	1989	1990	1991	1992		1993	1994	1995	1996	1997	1998	
Net Sales	$107,417	$113,656	$122,940	$133,302		$143,300	$154,047	$165,601	$178,021	$191,372	$205,725	
Sales Growth %		*5.8%*	*8.2%*	*8.4%*	*7.5%*	*7.5%*	*7.5%*	*7.5%*	*7.5%*	*7.5%*	*7.5%*	*7.5%*
Cost of Goods Sold	$69,714	$74,445	$80,895	$87,046		$93,861	$100,901	$108,468	$116,604	$125,349	$134,750	
Gross Profit	37,703	39,211	42,045	46,256		49,438	53,146	57,132	61,417	66,023	70,975	
Gross Margin %	*35.1%*	*34.5%*	*34.2%*	*34.7%*	*34.6%*	*34.5%*	*34.5%*	*34.5%*	*34.5%*	*34.5%*	*34.5%*	*34.5%*
Selling, General & Admin. Expenses	$20,409	$21,595	$23,359	$25,327		$27,227	$29,269	$31,464	$33,824	$36,361	$39,088	
ESOP Contribution	0	0	0	0		0	0	0	0	0	0	
EBITDA	17,294	17,616	18,686	20,929		22,211	23,877	25,668	27,593	29,663	31,887	
EBITDA Margin %	*16.1%*	*15.5%*	*15.2%*	*15.7%*	*15.6%*	*15.5%*	*15.5%*	*15.5%*	*15.5%*	*15.5%*	*15.5%*	*15.5%*
Depreciation	5,435	6,297	6,777	7,022		3,432	4,117	4,856	5,665	6,531	6,689	
Amortization of Goodwill	0	0	0	0		426	426	426	426	426	426	
Amortization of Transaction Costs	0	0	0	0		1,505	505	505	505	505	213	
Amortization of Intangibles	0	0	0	0		0	0	0	0	0	0	
Total Depreciation and Amort.	5,435	6,297	6,777	7,022		5,362	5,048	5,787	6,596	7,462	7,328	
EBIT	11,859	11,319	11,909	13,907		16,849	18,829	19,881	20,998	22,201	24,559	
EBIT Margin %	*11.0%*	*10.0%*	*9.7%*	*10.4%*	*10.3%*	*11.8%*	*12.2%*	*12.0%*	*11.8%*	*11.6%*	*11.9%*	*11.9%*
Interest Income						0	0	0	0	0	0	
Interest Expense						8,672	8,477	8,257	7,960	7,655	7,302	
Net Interest Expense						8,672	8,477	8,257	7,960	7,655	7,302	
Other Expenses (Income)						0	0	0	0	0	0	
Loss (Gain) on Sale-Leaseback Asset						0	0	0	0	0	0	
Earnings Before Taxes						8,177	10,352	11,624	13,038	14,546	17,257	
Provision for Taxes												
Current						2,752	2,384	2,919	4,363	5,138	6,002	
Deferred						906	1,796	1,744	837	634	710	
Total Tax Provision						3,658	4,180	4,663	5,200	5,772	6,713	
Net Income Before Extraordinary Item &						4,519	6,172	6,961	7,839	8,774	10,544	
Minority Interest						0	0	0	0	0	0	
Minority Interest						0	0	0	0	0	0	
Extraordinary Item (After-Tax)						0	0	0	0	0	0	
						4,519	6,172	6,961	7,839	8,774	10,544	
Preferred Dividend - stock						0	0	0	0	0	0	
Preferred Dividend - Cash						0	0	0	0	0	0	
Net Income to Common						$4,519	$6,172	$6,961	$7,839	$8,774	$10,544	

Exhibit 23.26
05/22/92
06:31 PM

MAREIGHT CORPORATION
LBO Analysis
Balance Sheets

Years Ended December 31,	Historical 1989	Historical 1990	Historical 1991	Historical 1992	Closing Date Bal. Sheet	Adjustments DEBITS	CREDITS	Beginning Bal. Sheet	1993	1994	1995	1996	1997	1998
Current Assets														
Cash & Cash Equivalents	$3,313	$3,288	$1,111	$2,856	$2,856	($2,856)	$0	$0	$0	$0	$0	$0	$0	$0
Accounts Receivable (Net)	14,123	15,083	13,677	14,732	14,732	0	0	$14,732	15,704	16,882	18,148	19,509	20,972	22,545
Inventory	24,344	23,357	27,075	25,903	25,903	0	0	$25,903	28,443	30,576	32,869	35,334	37,984	40,833
Other Current Assets	5,211	5,421	4,369	5,109	5,109	0	0	$5,109	5,015	5,392	5,796	6,231	6,698	7,200
Total Current Assets	46,991	47,149	46,232	48,600	48,600	(2,856)	0	45,744	49,162	52,850	56,813	61,074	65,655	70,579
Gross Property, Plant & Equipment	43,378	45,001	45,965	44,965	44,965	0	0	$44,965	52,703	61,021	69,963	79,576	89,910	101,019
Less: Accumulated Depreciation								$0	(3,432)	(7,549)	(12,405)	(18,070)	(24,601)	(31,290)
Net Property, Plant & Equipment	43,378	45,001	45,965	44,965	44,965	0	0	44,965	49,271	53,472	57,558	61,506	65,309	69,729
Leased Property Under Capital Leases	0	0	0	0	0	0	0	0	0	0	0	0	0	0
Goodwill	0	0	0	0	0	17,048	0	17,048	16,622	16,196	15,769	15,343	14,917	14,491
Other Intangible Assets	0	0	0	0	0	0	0	0	0	0	0	0	0	0
Other Assets	3,141	3,289	2,704	3,616	3,616	0	0	3,616	3,616	3,616	3,616	3,616	3,616	3,616
Organizational Costs						4,237	0	4,237	2,733	2,228	1,723	1,219	714	501
Total Assets	$93,510	$95,439	$94,901	$97,181	$97,181	$18,429	$0	$115,610	$121,404	$128,362	$135,480	$142,759	$150,211	$158,916
Current Liabilities														
Current Portion of LT Debt	$0	$0	$0	$0	$0	$0	$5,857	$5,857	$5,857	$5,857	$5,857	$5,857	$5,857	$5,857
Accounts Payable	9,973	9,555	8,993	7,475	7,475	0	0	7,475	9,952	10,699	11,501	12,364	13,291	14,288
Accrued Liabilities	4,939	5,627	5,133	5,421	5,421	0	0	5,421	5,933	6,378	6,857	7,371	7,924	8,518
Current Taxes Payable	826	1,436	3,034	1,333	1,333	0	0	1,333	550	477	584	873	1,028	1,200
Total Current Liabilities	15,738	16,618	17,160	14,229	14,229	0	5,857	20,086	22,293	23,411	24,799	26,465	28,100	29,864
Long-Term Debt														
Revolver														
Existing	0	0	0	0	0	0	20,746	20,746	24,765	28,494	31,376	34,171	36,438	37,981
Sale-Leaseback Obligation	0	0	0	0	0	0	0	0	0	0	0	0	0	0
Senior Term Loan A	0	0	0	0	0	5,857	41,000	35,143	29,286	23,429	17,571	11,714	5,857	0
Senior Term Loan B	0	0	0	0	0	0	0	0	0	0	0	0	0	0
Senior Term Loan C	0	0	0	0	0	0	0	0	0	0	0	0	0	0
Mortgage Debt	0	0	0	0	0	0	0	0	0	0	0	0	0	0
Senior Subordinated Debt A	0	0	0	0	0	0	24,000	24,000	24,000	24,000	24,000	24,000	24,000	24,000
Senior Subordinated Debt B	0	0	0	0	0	0	0	0	0	0	0	0	0	0
Junior Subordinated Debt	0	0	0	0	0	0	0	0	0	0	0	0	0	0
Discount Sub Debt	0	0	0	0	0	0	0	0	0	0	0	0	0	0
Increasing Rate Note	0	0	0	0	0	0	0	0	0	0	0	0	0	0
Total Long-Term Debt	48,777	50,241	46,772	49,388	49,388	5,857	85,746	79,889	78,051	75,922	72,948	69,886	66,295	61,981
Other Long-Term Liabilities	0	0	0	0	49,388	49,388		0	0	0	0	0	0	0
Obligations under Capitalized Leases	0	0	0	0	0	0	0	0	906	2,702	4,445	5,282	5,916	6,627
Deferred Income Taxes	0	0	0	0	0	0	0	0	0	0	0	0	0	0
Minority Interest	0	0	0	0	0	0	0	0	0	0	0	0	0	0
PIK Preferred	0	0	0	0	0	0	0	0	0	0	0	0	0	0
Preferred Stock	0	0	0	0	0	0	0	0	0	0	0	0	0	0
Common Stock	1,000	1,000	1,000	1,000	1,000	1,000	15,635	15,635	15,635	15,635	15,635	15,635	15,635	15,635
Retained Earnings	27,995	27,580	29,969	32,564	32,564	32,564	0	0	4,519	10,691	17,653	25,491	34,265	44,810
ESOP Contra Account	0	0	0	0	0	0	0	0	0	0	0	0	0	0
Common Shareholders' Equity	28,995	28,580	30,969	33,564	33,564	33,564	15,635	15,635	20,154	26,326	33,288	41,126	49,901	60,445
Total Liabilities & Equity	$93,510	$95,439	$94,901	$97,181	$97,181	$107,238	$107,238	$115,610	$121,404	$128,362	$135,480	$142,759	$150,211	$158,916

MAREIGHT CORPORATION
LBO Analysis
Statements of Changes in Financial Position

Exhibit 23.27

05/22/92
05:29 PM

Years Ended December 31,	1993	1994	1995	1996	1997	1998
Sources of Cash						
Net Income to Common	$4,519	$6,172	$6,961	$7,839	$8,774	$10,544
Book Depreciation	3,432	4,117	4,856	5,665	6,531	6,689
Amortization of Intangibles	0	0	0	0	0	0
Deferred Tax	906	1,796	1,744	837	634	710
Amortization of Gain on Sale/Leaseback Asset						
Amort. of Leased Prop. under Capitalized Leases	0	0	0	0	0	0
Amortization of Goodwill & Fees	1,931	931	931	931	931	639
Accretion of Discount						
PIK Preferred Dividend	0	0	0	0	0	0
Total Sources	$10,787	$13,016	$14,492	$15,271	$16,870	$18,583
Uses of Cash						
Increase (Decrease) in Working Capital	$1,211	$2,569	$2,576	$2,595	$2,946	$3,160
Capital Expenditures	7,738	8,318	8,942	9,613	10,334	11,109
Debt Amortization						
Revolver	(4,019)	(3,729)	(2,883)	(2,795)	(2,266)	(1,543)
Sale-Leaseback Obligation	0	0	0	0	0	0
Senior Term Loan A	5,857	5,857	5,857	5,857	5,857	5,857
Senior Term Loan B	0	0	0	0	0	0
Senior Term Loan C	0	0	0	0	0	0
Mortgage Debt	0	0	0	0	0	0
Senior Subordinated Debt A	0	0	0	0	0	0
Senior Subordinated Debt B	0	0	0	0	0	0
Junior Subordinated Debt	0	0	0	0	0	0
Discount Subordinated Debt	0	0	0	0	0	0
Increasing Rate Note	0	0	0	0	0	0
Total Debt Amortization	1,838	2,128	2,974	3,062	3,591	4,314
Redemption of PIK Preferred	0	0	0	0	0	0
Redemption of Preferred Stock	0	0	0	0	0	0
Total Uses	$10,787	$13,016	$14,492	$15,271	$16,870	$18,583
Net Cash Flow	$0	$0	$0	$0	$0	$0

MAREIGHT CORPORATION
LBO Analysis
Ownership Breakdown and Calculation of Gross Residual Values

Exhibit 23.28
05/22/92
05:29 PM

Ownership Breakdown

Investor	Initial Value Rec (000s)	Initial Shrs Received	Initial % shares	Initial Ownership	Terminal Common Shares	Terminal Ownership
Sponsor Common Equity	$14,593	933	77.5%		933	70.0%
Management Common Equity	1,042	67	2.5%		133	10.0%
Sr. subordinated A	0	0	20.0%		267	20.0%
Jr. subordinated	0	0	0.0%		0	0.0%
Public Shareholders	NA	0	0.0%		0	0.0%
Equity	$15,635	1,000	100.0%		1,333	100.0%

Gross Residual Value Calculations – EBITDA Multiple Method

EBITDA Multiple	8.0	8.5	9.0	9.5	10.0
1998 EBITDA	$31,887	$31,887	$31,887	$31,887	$31,887
Gross Residual Value (Sale Price)	255,099	271,043	286,987	302,930	318,874
Less:					
Total Debt	61,981	61,981	61,981	61,981	61,981
Preferred Stock	0	0	0	0	0
Plus:					
Cash & Equivalents	0	0	0	0	0
Warrants/options Proceeds	0	0	0	0	0
Gross Residual Value of Common Equity	$193,119	$209,062	$225,006	$240,950	$256,893
Gross Value of Common Equity					
Sponsor Common Equity	135,183	146,344	157,504	168,665	179,825
Management Common Equity	19,312	20,906	22,501	24,095	25,689
Senior Subordinated Debt A	38,624	41,812	45,001	48,190	51,379
Junior Subordinated Debt	0	0	0	0	0
Gross Residual Value of Common Equity	$193,119	$209,062	$225,006	$240,950	$256,893

Gross Residual Value Calculations – P/E Multiple Method

P/E Multiple	18.0	19.0	20.0	21.0	22.0
1998 Net Income	$10,544	$10,544	$10,544	$10,544	$10,544
Gross Residual Value (Sale Price)	189,799	200,344	210,888	221,432	231,977
Less:					
Preferred stock	0	0	0	0	0
Plus:					
Cash & Equivalents	0	0	0	0	0
Warrants/options Proceeds	0	0	0	0	0
Gross Residual Value of Common Equity	$189,799	$200,344	$210,888	$221,432	$231,977
Gross Value of Common Equity					
Sponsor Common Equity	132,859	140,240	147,622	155,003	162,384
Management Common Equity	18,980	20,034	21,089	22,143	23,198
Senior subordinated Debt A	37,960	40,069	42,178	44,286	46,395
Junior subordinated Debt	0	0	0	0	0
Gross Residual Value of Common Equity	$189,799	$200,344	$210,888	$221,432	$231,977

Gross Residual Value Calculations – EBITA Multiple Method

EBDIAT Multiple	12.0	13.0	14.0	15.0	16.0
1998 EBITA	$25,198	$25,198	$25,198	$25,198	$25,198
Gross Residual Value (Sale Price)	302,382	327,580	352,779	377,977	403,176
Less:					
Total Debt	61,981	61,981	61,981	61,981	61,981
Preferred stock	0	0	0	0	0
Plus:					
Cash & Equivalents	0	0	0	0	0
Warrants/options Proceeds	0	0	0	0	0
Gross Residual Value of Common Equity	$240,401	$265,600	$290,798	$315,997	$341,195
Gross Value of Common Equity					
Sponsor Common Equity	168,281	185,920	203,559	221,198	238,837
Management Common Equity	24,040	26,560	29,080	31,600	34,120
Senior Subordinated Debt A	48,080	53,120	58,160	63,199	68,239
Junior Subordinated Debt	0	0	0	0	0
Gross Residual Value of Common Equity	$240,401	$265,600	$290,798	$315,997	$341,195

MAREIGHT CORPORATION
LBO Analysis
Net Residual Value Calculations - Assuming Sale

Exhibit 23.29
05/22/92
05:29 PM

Page 12   FILE: SHT_I2

Net Residual Value Calculations - EBITA Multiple Method

	EBITA Multiple				
	12.0	13.0	14.0	15.0	16.0
Sponsor Common Equity					
Gross Residual Value	$168,281	$185,920	$203,559	$221,198	$238,837
Tax Basis	14,593	14,593	14,593	14,593	14,593
Gain (Loss) on Sale	153,688	171,327	188,965	206,604	224,243
Capital Gains Tax Rate	38.0%	38.0%	38.0%	38.0%	38.0%
Tax on Sale	58,401	65,104	71,807	78,510	85,212
Gross Residual Value	168,281	185,920	203,559	221,198	238,837
Taxes on Sale	58,401	65,104	71,807	78,510	85,212
Net Residual Value	$109,880	$120,816	$131,752	$142,688	$153,624
Management Common Equity					
Gross Residual Value	$24,040	$26,560	$29,080	$31,600	$34,120
Tax Basis	1,042	1,042	1,042	1,042	1,042
Gain (Loss) on Sale	22,998	25,518	28,038	30,558	33,078
Capital Gains Tax Rate	38.0%	38.0%	38.0%	38.0%	38.0%
Tax on Sale	8,739	9,697	10,654	11,612	12,569
Gross Residual Value	24,040	26,560	29,080	31,600	34,120
Taxes on Sale	8,739	9,697	10,654	11,612	12,569
Net Residual Value	$15,301	$16,863	$18,425	$19,988	$21,550
Senior Subordinated Debt A					
Gross Residual Value	$48,080	$53,120	$58,160	$63,199	$68,239
Tax Basis	0	0	0	0	0
Gain (Loss) on Sale	48,080	53,120	58,160	63,199	68,239
Capital Gains Tax Rate	38.0%	38.0%	38.0%	38.0%	38.0%
Tax on Sale	18,270	20,186	22,101	24,016	25,931
Gross Residual Value	48,080	53,120	58,160	63,199	68,239
Taxes on Sale	18,270	20,186	22,101	24,016	25,931
Net Residual Value	$29,810	$32,934	$36,059	$39,184	$42,308
Junior Subordinated Debt					
Gross Residual Value	$0	$0	$0	$0	$0
Tax Basis	0	0	0	0	0
Gain (Loss) on Sale	0	0	0	0	0
Capital Gains Tax Rate	38.0%	38.0%	38.0%	38.0%	38.0%
Tax on Sale	0	0	0	0	0
Gross Residual Value	0	0	0	0	0
Taxes on Sale	0	0	0	0	0
Net Residual Value	$0	$0	$0	$0	$0

Net Residual Value Calculations - EBITDA Multiple Method

	EBITDA Multiple				
	8.0	8.5	9.0	9.5	10.0
Sponsor Common Equity					
Gross Residual Value	$135,183	$146,344	$157,504	$168,665	$179,825
Tax Basis	14,593	14,593	14,593	14,593	14,593
Gain (Loss) on Sale	120,590	131,750	142,911	154,072	165,232
Capital Gains Tax Rate	38.0%	38.0%	38.0%	38.0%	38.0%
Tax on Sale	45,824	50,065	54,306	58,547	62,788
Gross Residual Value	135,183	146,344	157,504	168,665	179,825
Taxes on Sale	45,824	50,065	54,306	58,547	62,788
Net Residual Value	$89,359	$96,278	$103,198	$110,118	$117,037
Management Common Equity					
Gross Residual Value	$19,312	$20,906	$22,501	$24,095	$25,689
Tax Basis	1,042	1,042	1,042	1,042	1,042
Gain (Loss) on Sale	18,270	19,864	21,459	23,053	24,647
Capital Gains Tax Rate	38.0%	38.0%	38.0%	38.0%	38.0%
Tax on Sale	6,943	7,548	8,154	8,760	9,366
Gross Residual Value	19,312	20,906	22,501	24,095	25,689
Taxes on Sale	6,943	7,548	8,154	8,760	9,366
Net Residual Value	$12,369	$13,358	$14,346	$15,335	$16,323
Senior Subordinated Debt A					
Gross Residual Value	$38,624	$41,812	$45,001	$48,190	$51,379
Tax Basis	0	0	0	0	0
Gain (Loss) on Sale	38,624	41,812	45,001	48,190	51,379
Capital Gains Tax Rate	38.0%	38.0%	38.0%	38.0%	38.0%
Tax on Sale	14,677	15,889	17,100	18,312	19,524
Gross Residual Value	38,624	41,812	45,001	48,190	51,379
Taxes on Sale	14,677	15,889	17,100	18,312	19,524
Net Residual Value	$23,947	$25,924	$27,901	$29,878	$31,855
Junior Subordinated Debt					
Gross Residual Value	$0	$0	$0	$0	$0
Tax Basis	0	0	0	0	0
Gain (Loss) on Sale	0	0	0	0	0
Capital Gains Tax Rate	38.0%	38.0%	38.0%	38.0%	38.0%
Tax on Sale	0	0	0	0	0
Gross Residual Value	0	0	0	0	0
Taxes on Sale	0	0	0	0	0
Net Residual Value	$0	$0	$0	$0	$0

MARRIOTT CORPORATION
LBO Analysis
Net Residual Value Calculations - P/E Multiple Method

Exhibit 23.30
05/22/92
05:29 PM

Net Residual Value Calculations - Assuming Sale

P/E Multiple	18.0	19.0	20.0	21.0	22.0
Sponsor Common Equity					
Gross Residual Value	$132,859	$140,240	$147,622	$155,003	$162,384
Tax Basis	14,593	14,593	14,593	14,593	14,593
Gain (Loss) on Sale	118,266	125,647	133,028	140,409	147,791
Capital Gains Tax Rate	38.0%	38.0%	38.0%	38.0%	38.0%
Tax on Sale	44,941	47,746	50,551	53,356	56,160
Gross Residual Value	132,859	140,240	147,622	155,003	162,384
Taxes on Sale	44,941	47,746	50,551	53,356	56,160
Net Residual Value	$87,918	$92,495	$97,071	$101,647	$106,223
Management Common Equity					
Gross Residual Value	$18,980	$20,034	$21,089	$22,143	$23,198
Tax Basis	1,042	1,042	1,042	1,042	1,042
Gain (Loss) on Sale	17,938	18,992	20,047	21,101	22,156
Capital Gains Tax Rate	38.0%	38.0%	38.0%	38.0%	38.0%
Tax on Sale	6,816	7,217	7,618	8,018	8,419
Gross Residual Value	18,980	20,034	21,089	22,143	23,198
Taxes on Sale	6,816	7,217	7,618	8,018	8,419
Net Residual Value	$12,164	$12,817	$13,471	$14,125	$14,779
Senior Subordinated Debt A					
Gross Residual Value	$37,960	$40,069	$42,178	$44,286	$46,395
Tax Basis	0	0	0	0	0
Gain (Loss) on Sale	37,960	40,069	42,178	44,286	46,395
Capital Gains Tax Rate	38.0%	38.0%	38.0%	38.0%	38.0%
Tax on Sale	14,425	15,226	16,027	16,829	17,630
Gross Residual Value	37,960	40,069	42,178	44,286	46,395
Taxes on Sale	14,425	15,226	16,027	16,829	17,630
Net Residual Value	$23,535	$24,843	$26,150	$27,458	$28,765
Junior Subordinated Debt					
Gross Residual Value	$0	$0	$0	$0	$0
Tax Basis	0	0	0	0	0
Gain (Loss) on Sale	0	0	0	0	0
Capital Gains Tax Rate	38.0%	38.0%	38.0%	38.0%	38.0%
Tax on Sale	0	0	0	0	0
Gross Residual Value	0	0	0	0	0
Taxes on Sale	0	0	0	0	0
Net Residual Value	$0	$0	$0	$0	$0

Exhibit 23.31
05/22/92
05:29 PM

MAREIGHT CORPORATION
LBO Analysis
After-Tax Investment Returns Calculations

IRR Calculations – EBITA Method

IRR Calculations – EBITA Method

Sponsor Common Equity	Investment	1993	1994	1995	1996	1997	1998	IRR
Cash Flows – 12.0x EBITA Multiple	($14,593)	0	0	0	0	0	89,359	35.3%
Cash Flows – 13.0x EBITA Multiple	(14,593)	0	0	0	0	0	96,278	37.0%
Cash Flows – 14.0x EBITA Multiple	(14,593)	0	0	0	0	0	103,198	38.5%
Cash Flows – 15.0x EBITA Multiple	(14,593)	0	0	0	0	0	110,118	40.1%
Cash Flows – 16.0x EBITA Multiple	(14,593)	0	0	0	0	0	117,037	41.5%
Management Common Equity								
Cash Flows – 12.0x EBITA Multiple	($1,042)	0	0	0	0	0	12,369	51.0%
Cash Flows – 13.0x EBITA Multiple	(1,042)	0	0	0	0	0	13,358	53.0%
Cash Flows – 14.0x EBITA Multiple	(1,042)	0	0	0	0	0	14,346	54.8%
Cash Flows – 15.0x EBITA Multiple	(1,042)	0	0	0	0	0	15,335	56.5%
Cash Flows – 16.0x EBITA Multiple	(1,042)	0	0	0	0	0	16,323	58.2%
Senior Subordinated Debt A								
Interest Payments		$2,910	$2,910	$2,910	$2,910	$2,910	$2,910	
Principal Repayments		0	2,910	2,910	2,910	2,910	24,000	
Cash Flows – 8.0x EBITDA Multiple	($24,000)	2,910	2,910	2,910	2,910	2,910	50,857	21.7%
Cash Flows – 8.5x EBITDA Multiple	($24,000)	2,910	2,910	2,910	2,910	2,910	52,834	22.4%
Cash Flows – 9.0x EBITDA Multiple	($24,000)	2,910	2,910	2,910	2,910	2,910	54,811	23.0%
Cash Flows – 9.5x EBITDA Multiple	($24,000)	2,910	2,910	2,910	2,910	2,910	56,788	23.6%
Cash Flows – 10.0x EBITDA Multiple	($24,000)	2,910	2,910	2,910	2,910	2,910	58,765	24.2%
Junior Subordinated Debt								
Cash Interest Payments		$0	$0	$0	$0	$0	$0	
Principal Repayments	$0	0	0	0	0	0	0	
Cash Flows – 8.0x EBITDA Multiple		0	0	0	0	0	0	N/A
Cash Flows – 8.5x EBITDA Multiple		0	0	0	0	0	0	N/A
Cash Flows – 9.0x EBITDA Multiple		0	0	0	0	0	0	N/A
Cash Flows – 9.5x EBITDA MUltiple		0	0	0	0	0	0	N/A
Cash Flows – 10.0x EBITDA MUltiple		0	0	0	0	0	0	N/A

IRR Calculations – EBITA Method

Sponsor Common Equity	Investment	1993	1994	1995	1996	1997	1998	IRR
Cash Flows – 12.0x EBITA Multiple	($14,593)	0	0	0	0	0	109,880	40.0%
Cash Flows – 13.0x EBITA Multiple	(14,593)	0	0	0	0	0	120,816	42.2%
Cash Flows – 14.0x EBITA Multiple	(14,593)	0	0	0	0	0	131,752	44.3%
Cash Flows – 15.0x EBITA Multiple	(14,593)	0	0	0	0	0	142,688	46.2%
Cash Flows – 16.0x EBITA Multiple	(14,593)	0	0	0	0	0	153,624	48.0%
Management Common Equity								
Cash Flows – 12.0x EBITA Multiple	($1,042)	0	0	0	0	0	15,301	56.5%
Cash Flows – 13.0x EBITA Multiple	(1,042)	0	0	0	0	0	16,863	59.0%
Cash Flows – 14.0x EBITA Multiple	(1,042)	0	0	0	0	0	18,425	61.4%
Cash Flows – 15.0x EBITA Multiple	(1,042)	0	0	0	0	0	19,988	63.6%
Cash Flows – 16.0x EBITA Multiple	(1,042)	0	0	0	0	0	21,550	65.7%
Senior Subordinated Debt A								
Interest Payments		$2,910	$2,910	$2,910	$2,910	$2,910	$2,910	
Principal Repayments		0	2,910	2,910	2,910	2,910	24,000	
Cash Flows – 12.0x EBITA Multiple	($24,000)	2,910	2,910	2,910	2,910	2,910	56,720	23.6%
Cash Flows – 13.0x EBITA Multiple	(24,000)	2,910	2,910	2,910	2,910	2,910	59,844	24.5%
Cash Flows – 14.0x EBITA Multiple	(24,000)	2,910	2,910	2,910	2,910	2,910	62,969	25.3%
Cash Flows – 15.0x EBITA Multiple	(24,000)	2,910	2,910	2,910	2,910	2,910	66,094	26.2%
Cash Flows – 16.0x EBITA Multiple	(24,000)	2,910	2,910	2,910	2,910	2,910	69,218	27.0%
Junior Subordinated Debt								
Cash Interest Payments		$0	$0	$0	$0	$0	$0	
Principal Repayments	$0	0	0	0	0	0	0	
Cash Flows – 12.0x EBITA Multiple		0	0	0	0	0	0	N/A
Cash Flows – 13.0x EBITA Multiple		0	0	0	0	0	0	N/A
Cash Flows – 14.0x EBITA Multiple		0	0	0	0	0	0	N/A
Cash Flows – 15.0x EBITA Multiple		0	0	0	0	0	0	N/A
Cash Flows – 16.0x EBITA Multiple		0	0	0	0	0	0	N/A

IRR Calculations – P/E Method

Sponsor Common Equity	Investment	1993	1994	1995	1996	1997	1998	IRR
Cash Flows – 18.0x P/E Multiple	($14,593)	0	0	0	0	0	87,918	34.9%
Cash Flows – 19.0x P/E Multiple	(14,593)	0	0	0	0	0	92,495	36.0%
Cash Flows – 20.0x P/E Multiple	(14,593)	0	0	0	0	0	97,071	37.1%
Cash Flows – 21.0x P/E Multiple	(14,593)	0	0	0	0	0	101,647	38.2%
Cash Flows – 22.0x P/E Multiple	(14,593)	0	0	0	0	0	106,223	39.2%
Management Common Equity								
Cash Flows – 18.0x P/E Multiple	($1,042)	0	0	0	0	0	12,164	50.6%
Cash Flows – 19.0x P/E Multiple	(1,042)	0	0	0	0	0	12,817	51.9%
Cash Flows – 20.0x P/E Multiple	(1,042)	0	0	0	0	0	13,471	53.2%
Cash Flows – 21.0x P/E Multiple	(1,042)	0	0	0	0	0	14,125	54.4%
Cash Flows – 22.0x P/E Multiple	(1,042)	0	0	0	0	0	14,779	55.6%
Senior Subordinated Debt A								
Interest Payments		$2,910	$2,910	$2,910	$2,910	$2,910	$2,910	
Principal Repayments		0	2,910	2,910	2,910	2,910	24,000	
Cash Flows – 18.0x P/E Multiple	($24,000)	2,910	2,910	2,910	2,910	2,910	50,445	21.6%
Cash Flows – 19.0x P/E Multiple	(24,000)	2,910	2,910	2,910	2,910	2,910	51,753	22.0%
Cash Flows – 20.0x P/E Multiple	(24,000)	2,910	2,910	2,910	2,910	2,910	53,060	22.4%
Cash Flows – 21.0x P/E Multiple	(24,000)	2,910	2,910	2,910	2,910	2,910	54,368	22.8%
Cash Flows – 22.0x P/E Multiple	(24,000)	2,910	2,910	2,910	2,910	2,910	55,675	23.2%
Junior Subordinated Debt								
Cash Interest Payments		$0	$0	$0	$0	$0	$0	
Principal Repayments	$0	0	0	0	0	0	0	
Cash Flows – 18.0x P/E Multiple		0	0	0	0	0	0	N/A
Cash Flows – 19.0x P/E Multiple		0	0	0	0	0	0	N/A
Cash Flows – 20.0x P/E Multiple		0	0	0	0	0	0	N/A
Cash Flows – 21.0x P/E Multiple		0	0	0	0	0	0	N/A
Cash Flows – 22.0x P/E Multiple		0	0	0	0	0	0	N/A

Exhibit 23.32

05/22/92
05:29 PM

MAREIGHT CORPORATION
LBO Analysis
Selected Financial Ratios

Years Ended December 31,	Historical				Beginning Bal. sheet	Projected					
	1989	1990	1991	1992		1993	1994	1995	1996	1997	1998
Percent of Total Capitalization											
Sr. Term, Mtg., Revolver & Sale-Lsbk Debt	0.0%	0.0%	0.0%	0.0%	60.9%	57.6%	53.4%	48.9%	44.3%	39.5%	34.2%
Senior and Junior subordinated Debt	0.0%	0.0%	0.0%	0.0%	23.7%	23.1%	22.2%	21.4%	20.5%	19.7%	18.7%
Total Long Term Debt	0.0%	0.0%	0.0%	0.0%	84.6%	80.6%	75.6%	70.3%	64.8%	59.1%	52.9%
Preferred Equity	0.0%	0.0%	0.0%	0.0%	0.0%	0.0%	0.0%	0.0%	0.0%	0.0%	0.0%
Common Equity	100.0%	100.0%	100.0%	100.0%	15.4%	19.4%	24.4%	29.7%	35.2%	40.9%	47.1%
Net Income as a % of Total Assets	0.0%	0.0%	0.0%	0.0%	0.0%	3.7%	4.8%	5.1%	5.5%	5.8%	6.6%
Net Income as a % of Common Equity	0.0%	0.0%	0.0%	0.0%	0.0%	22.4%	23.4%	20.9%	19.1%	17.6%	17.4%
EBITDA::	$17,294	$17,616	$18,686	$20,929		$22,211	$23,877	$25,668	$27,593	$29,663	$31,887
EBIT::	$11,859	$11,319	$11,909	$13,907		$16,849	$18,829	$19,881	$20,998	$22,201	$24,559
Net Cash Flow::	$17,294	$17,616	$18,686	$20,929		$11,721	$13,175	$13,807	$13,617	$14,191	$25,885
Total Interest Coverage:											
EBITDA/Interest Expense						2.56	2.82	3.11	3.47	3.88	4.37
EBIT/Interest Expense						1.94	2.22	2.41	2.64	2.90	3.36
Net Cash Flow/Interest Expense (1)						1.35	1.55	1.67	1.71	1.85	3.54
Senior Interest Coverage (2):											
EBITDA/Senior Interest Expense						3.85	4.29	4.80	5.46	6.25	7.26
EBIT/Senior Interest Expense						2.92	3.38	3.72	4.16	4.68	5.59
Net Cash Flow/Sen. Interest Expense (1)						2.03	2.37	2.58	2.70	2.99	5.89
Subordinated Interest Coverage:											
EBITDA-Sen. Interest Exp/Sub Int Expense						5.65	6.29	6.98	7.75	8.56	9.45
EBIT-Senior Interest Exp/Sub Int Expense						3.81	4.56	4.99	5.48	6.00	6.93
Net CF-Sen. Int Exp/Sub Int Expense (1)						2.05	2.61	2.91	2.94	3.25	7.39
Fixed Charge Coverage:											
EBITDA/Interest Exp. + Preferred Dividend						2.56	2.82	3.11	3.47	3.88	4.37
EBIT/Interest Exp. + Preferred Dividend						1.94	2.22	2.41	2.64	2.90	3.36
Net CF/Interest Exp. + Pref. Dividend (1)						1.35	1.55	1.67	1.71	1.85	3.54
Cash Interest Coverage											
EBITDA/Cash Interest Expense						2.56	2.82	3.11	3.47	3.88	4.37
EBIT/Cash Interest Expense						1.94	2.22	2.41	2.64	2.90	3.36
Net Cash Flow/Cash Interest Expense (1)						1.35	1.55	1.67	1.71	1.85	3.54
Debt Service Coverage											
Net CF/Reqd Principal Pmt + Interest Exp											

(1) Net Cash Flow = EBITDA - Cash Taxes - Capital Expenditures
(2) Senior Interest is computed on revolver, mortgage, sale-leaseback and senior term loans A, B and C.

MAREIGHT CORPORATION
LBO Analysis
Summary Amortization Schedule

Exhibit 23.33

05/22/92
05:29 PM

Years Ended December 31, Transaction Fees		Opening Bal. Sheet	1993	1994	1995	1996	1997	1998
Beginning Balance			$4,237	$2,733	$2,228	$1,723	$1,219	$714
Amortization:	Years							
Transaction	5	$1,457	291	291	291	291	291	291
Bank Loans	7	820	117	117	117	117	117	117
Increasing Rate Note	5	0	0	0	0	0	0	0
Subordinated Debt	10	960	96	96	96	96	96	96
Preferred Equity	5	0	0	0	0	0	0	0
Accounting & Legal	1	1,000	1,000	0	0	0	0	0
Pre-Payment Penalty	7	0	0	0	0	0	0	0
Ending Balance		$4,237	$2,733	$2,228	$1,723	$1,219	$714	$501

NOTE: Transaction costs not directly related to the financing are not deductible.

Goodwill		Initial	1993	1994	1995	1996	1997	1998
Beginning Balance			$17,048	$16,622	$16,196	$15,769	$15,343	$14,917
Amortization	40 Years		426	426	426	426	426	426
Ending Goodwill		$17,048	$16,622	$16,196	$15,769	$15,343	$14,917	$14,491

Intangible Assets		Initial	1993	1994	1995	1996	1997	1998
Beginning Balance			$0	$0	$0	$0	$0	$0
Plus: Additions			0	0	0	0	0	0
Amortization	5 Years		0	0	0	0	0	0
Ending Intangible Assets		$0	$0	$0	$0	$0	$0	$0

Leased Property Under Capital Leases		Initial	1993	1994	1995	1996	1997	1998
Beginning Balance			$0	$0	$0	$0	$0	$0
Plus: Additions			0	0	0	0	0	0
Amortization	25 Years		0	0	0	0	0	0
Ending Intangible Assets		$0	$0	$0	$0	$0	$0	$0

	1993	1994	1995	1996	1997	1998
Deductible Amortization	$471	$271	$271	$271	$271	$213
Non-Deductible Amortization	1,459	659	659	659	659	426
Total Amortization	$1,931	$931	$931	$931	$931	$639

MAREIGHT CORPORATION
LBO Analysis
Summary Debt Amortization and Interest Expense Schedule

Exhibit 23.34

05/22/92
05:29 PM

Interest Expense	1993	1994	1995	1996	1997	1998
Cash Interest Expense						
Revolver	$1,867	$2,229	$2,564	$2,824	$3,075	$3,279
Senior Term Loan A	3,895	3,339	2,782	2,226	1,669	1,113
Senior Term Loan B	0	0	0	0	0	0
Senior Term Loan C	0	0	0	0	0	0
Mortgage Debt	0	0	0	0	0	0
Sale-Leaseback Financing	0	0	0	0	0	0
Senior Subordinated Debt A	2,910	2,910	2,910	2,910	2,910	2,910
Senior Subordinated Debt B	0	0	0	0	0	0
Junior Subordinated Debt	0	0	0	0	0	0
Discount Jr Subordinated Debt	0	0	0	0	0	0
Increasing Rate Note	0	0	0	0	0	0
Total Cash Interest Expense	$8,672	$8,477	$8,257	$7,960	$7,655	$7,302
Non-Cash Interest Expense						
Junior Subordinated Debt	$0	$0	$0	$0	$0	$0
Discount Jr Subordinated Debt	0	0	0	0	0	0
Total Non-Cash Interest Expense	$0	$0	$0	$0	$0	$0
Total Interest Expense	$8,672	$8,477	$8,257	$7,960	$7,655	$7,302
Long-Term Debt Amortization						
Required	$5,857	$5,857	$5,857	$5,857	$5,857	$5,857
Optional	0	0	0	0	0	0
Total Long-Term Debt Amortization	$5,857	$5,857	$5,857	$5,857	$5,857	$5,857
Long-Term Debt Outstanding						
Current Portion	$5,857	$5,857	$5,857	$5,857	$5,857	$5,857
Non-Current Portion	78,051	75,922	72,948	69,886	66,295	61,981
Total Long-Term Debt Outstanding	$83,908	$81,780	$78,805	$75,743	$72,152	$67,838
Accretion on Discount Jr Subordinated Debt	$0	$0	$0	$0	$0	$0

MAREIGHT CORPORATION
LBO Analysis
Debt Amortization Schedules

Exhibit 23.35
05/22/92
05:29 PM

Senior Term Loan A

	Opening Balance	1993	1994	1995	1996	1997	1998	1999	2000	2001	2002
Beginning Balance		$41,000	$35,143	$29,286	$23,429	$17,571	$11,714	$5,857			
Amortization 7 years		5,857	5,857	5,857	5,857	5,857	5,857	5,857			
Grace Period 0 year											
Ending Balance - Total	$41,000	$35,143	$29,286	$23,429	$17,571	$11,714	$5,857	$0	$0	$0	$0
Less: Current Portion	5,857	5,857	5,857	5,857	5,857	5,857	5,857	0	0	0	0
Ending Balance - LTD	$35,143	$29,286	$23,429	$17,571	$11,714	$5,857	$0	$0	$0	$0	$0
Interest Exp. 9.500%		$3,895	$3,339	$2,782	$2,226	$1,669	$1,113	$556	$0	$0	$0

Senior Term Loan B

	Opening Balance	1993	1994	1995	1996	1997	1998	1999	2000	2001	2002
Beginning Balance		0	0	0	0	0	0	0	0	0	0
Amortization 6 years		0	0	0	0	0	0	0	0	0	0
Grace Period 0 year											
Ending Balance - Total	$0	$0	$0	$0	$0	$0	$0	$0	$0	$0	$0
Less: Current Portion	0	0	0	0	0	0	0	0	0	0	0
Ending Balance - LTD	$0	$0	$0	$0	$0	$0	$0	$0	$0	$0	$0
Interest Exp. 13.500%		$0	$0	$0	$0	$0	$0	$0	$0	$0	$0

Senior Term Loan C

	Opening Balance	1993	1994	1995	1996	1997	1998	1999	2000	2001	2002
Beginning Balance		0	0	0	0	0	0	0	0	0	0
Amortization 6 years	$0	0	0	0	0	0	0	0	0	0	0
Grace Period 0 year	0										
Ending Balance - Total	$0	$0	$0	$0	$0	$0	$0	$0	$0	$0	$0
Less: Current Portion		0	0	0	0	0	0	0	0	0	0
Ending Balance - LTD	$0	$0	$0	$0	$0	$0	$0	$0	$0	$0	$0
Interest Exp. 14.000%		$0	$0	$0	$0	$0	$0	$0	$0	$0	$0

Senior Subordinated Debt A

	Opening Balance	1993	1994	1995	1996	1997	1998	1999	2000	2001	2002
Beginning Balance		$24,000	$24,000	$24,000	$24,000	$24,000	$24,000	$24,000	$24,000	$0	$0
Amortization 8 years	$24,000	0	0	0	0	0	0	0	0	0	0
Ending Balance - Total	$24,000	$24,000	$24,000	$24,000	$24,000	$24,000	$24,000	$24,000	$24,000	$0	$0
Less: Current Portion		$24,000	$24,000	$24,000	$24,000	$24,000	$24,000	24,000	24,000	0	0
Ending Balance - LTD	$24,000	$2,910	$2,910	$2,910	$2,910	$2,910	$2,910	$0	$0	$0	$0
Interest Exp. 12.125%		$2,910	$2,910	$2,910	$2,910	$2,910	$2,910	$2,910	$2,910	$0	$0

Senior Subordinated Debt B

	Opening Balance	1993	1994	1995	1996	1997	1998	1999	2000	2001	2002
Beginning Balance		0	0	0	0	0	0	0	0	0	0
Amortization 5 years	$0	0	0	0	0	0	0	0	0	0	0
Ending Balance - Total	$0	$0	$0	$0	$0	$0	$0	$0	$0	$0	$0
Less: Current Portion	$0	0	0	0	0	0	0	0	0	0	0
Ending Balance - LTD	$0	$0	$0	$0	$0	$0	$0	$0	$0	$0	$0
Interest Exp. 12.375%		$0	$0	$0	$0	$0	$0	$0	$0	$0	$0

MARRIOTT CORPORATION
LBO Analysis
Debt Amortization Schedule (cont'd)

	Opening Balance	1993	1994	1995	1996	1997	1998	1999	2000	2001	2002
Increasing Rate Note											
Beginning Balance	$0	$0	$0	$0	$0	$0	$0	$0	$0	$0	$0
Redemption	0	0	0	0	0	0	0	0	0	0	0
Ending Balance	$0	$0	$0	$0	$0	$0	$0	$0	$0	$0	$0
Less: Current Portion		0	0	0	0	0	0	0	0	0	0
Ending Balance - LTD	$0	$0	$0	$0	$0	$0	$0	$0	$0	$0	$0
Average Interest Rate		13.00%	13.75%	14.75%	13.75%	14.75%	0.00%	0.00%	0.00%	0.00%	0.00%
Interest Expense		$0	$0	$0	$0	$0	$0	$0	$0	$0	$0

Initial Interest Rate 13.00%
Incremental Increase 0.50%   Freq Interval (months)   6
Rate Cap   19.00%   No Incr Period (months) 12
                          Redemption - End of Year 5

Revolver											
Beginning Balance		$20,746	$24,745	$28,456	$31,276	$34,171	$36,418	$37,981	$37,981	$37,981	$37,981
New Borrowings		4,019	3,730	2,840	2,795	2,246	1,563	0	0	0	0
Reduction of Debt		0	0	0	0	0	0	0	0	0	0
Ending Balance	$20,746	$24,745	$28,456	$31,276	$34,171	$36,418	$37,981	$37,981	$37,981	$37,981	$37,981
Interest Exp.	9.00%	$1,867	$2,225	$2,564	$2,824	$3,075	$3,279	$3,418	$3,418	$3,418	$3,418

Junior Subordinated Debt											
Beginning Balance	$0	$0	$0	$0	$0	$0	$0	$0	$0	$0	$0
Amortization		0	0	0	0	0	0	0	0	0	0
Accretion		0	0	0	0	0	0	0	0	0	0
Ending Balance	$0	$0	$0	$0	$0	$0	$0	$0	$0	$0	$0
Less: Current Portion		0	0	0	0	0	0	0	0	0	0
Ending Balance - LTD		$0	$0	$0	$0	$0	$0	$0	$0	$0	$0

Cash Interest   0
Non-Cash Interest   0
Beginning year of Zero   1
Beginning Yr of Curr. Coupon 3
Zero Interest Rate   13.00%
Current Coupon Rate   13.00%

Sale-Leaseback Financing											
Beginning Balance	$0	$0	$0	$0	$0	$0	$0	$0	$0	$0	$0
Amortization		0	0	0	0	0	0	0	0	0	0
Ending Balance	$0	$0	$0	$0	$0	$0	$0	$0	$0	$0	$0
Less: Current Portion		0	0	0	0	0	0	0	0	0	0
Ending Balance - LTD	$0	$0	$0	$0	$0	$0	$0	$0	$0	$0	$0

Interest Exp.   11.00%
Term (years)   0
Gross Price of Asset $0
Book Value of Asset $0
Accum Depr of Asset $0
Book Gain (loss) on Sale 0
Economic Life of Asset (Yrs) 0
Tax Basis of Asset $0
Amt Basis of Asset $0

Page 20   FILE: SHT_N3

HAREIGHT CORPORATION
LBO Analysis
Debt Amortization and Preferred Stock Redemption schedules

Exhibit 23.37

05/22/92
05:29 PM

Discount Jr subordinated Debt	Opening Balance	1993	1994	1995	1996	1997	1998	1999	2000	2001	2002
Beginning Balance		$0	$0	$0	$0	$0	$0	$0	$0	$0	$0
Amortization		0	0	0	0	0	0	0	0	0	0
OID Accretion		0	0	0	0	0	0	0	0	0	0
Ending Balance	$0	$0	$0	$0	$0	$0	$0	$0	$0	$0	$0
Less: Current Portion	0	0	0	0	0	0	0	0	0	0	0
Ending Balance - LTD	$0	$0	$0	$0	$0	$0	$0	$0	$0	$0	$0
Cash Interest		$0	$0	$0	$0	$0	$0	$0	$0	$0	$0
Non-Cash Interest		$0	$0	$0	$0	$0	$0	$0	$0	$0	$0

Face Value $0
Proceeds $0
YTM   10.500%
Coupon   0.000%
Term (years)   10

NOTE: If using stub period function, OID Accretion formulas must be modified.

Mortgage Debt		1993	1994	1995	1996	1997	1998	1999	2000	2001	2002
Beginning Balance		$0	$0	$0	$0	$0	$0	$0	$0	$0	$0
Amortization	15 years	0	0	0	0	0	0	0	0	0	0
Ending Balance	$0	$0	$0	$0	$0	$0	$0	$0	$0	$0	$0
Less: Current Portion	0	0	0	0	0	0	0	0	0	0	0
Ending Balance - LTD	$0	$0	$0	$0	$0	$0	$0	$0	$0	$0	$0
Interest Exp. 12.000%		$0	$0	$0	$0	$0	$0	$0	$0	$0	$0

Preferred Stock	Opening Balance	1993	1994	1995	1996	1997	1998	1999	2000	2001	2002
Beginning Balance		$0	$0	$0	$0	$0	$0	$0	$0	$0	$0
Stock Dividend (Redemption)		0	0	0	0	0	0	0	0	0	0
Ending Balance	$0	$0	$0	$0	$0	$0	$0	$0	$0	$0	$0
Cash Dividend 12.000%		$0	$0	$0	$0	$0	$0	$0	$0	$0	$0

PIK Preferred	Opening Balance	1993	1994	1995	1996	1997	1998	1999	2000	2001	2002
Beginning Balance		$0	$0	$0	$0	$0	$0	$0	$0	$0	$0
Stock Dividend (Redemption)		0	0	0	0	0	0	0	0	0	0
Ending Balance	$0	$0	$0	$0	$0	$0	$0	$0	$0	$0	$0
Stock Dividend 9.000%		$0	$0	$0	$0	$0	$0	$0	$0	$0	$0

MAREIGHT CORPORATION
LBO Analysis
Financial Statement Tax Provision

Years Ended December 31,	1993	1994	1995	1996	1997	1998
Earnings Before Taxes	$8,177	$10,352	$11,624	$13,038	$14,546	$17,257
Permanent Differences						
Goodwill Amortization	426	426	426	426	426	426
Other Non-Deductible Amortization	1,033	233	233	233	233	0
Total Permanent Differences	1,459	659	659	659	659	426
Taxable Income Before NOL	9,636	11,011	12,284	13,697	15,206	17,683
NOL						
Available	0	0	0	0	0	0
Current	0	0	0	0	0	0
Utilized	0	0	0	0	0	0
Taxable Income After NOL	9,636	11,011	12,284	13,697	15,206	17,683
State Taxes 6.00%	578	661	737	822	912	1,061
Taxable Income After NOL and State Taxes	9,058	10,351	11,547	12,876	14,293	16,622
Federal Tax 34.00%	3,080	3,519	3,926	4,378	4,860	5,652
Credits	0	0	0	0	0	0
Net Federal Taxes	3,080	3,519	3,926	4,378	4,860	5,652
State Taxes	578	661	737	822	912	1,061
Foreign Taxes	0	0	0	0	0	0
Total Book Tax Provision	$3,658	$4,180	$4,663	$5,200	$5,772	$6,713
Effective Tax Rate	44.7%	40.4%	40.1%	39.9%	39.7%	38.9%

MAREIGHT CORPORATION
LBO Analysis
Current and Deferred Taxes

| | | | | --------- Projected --------- | | |
Years Ended December 31,	1993	1994	1995	1996	1997	1998
Earnings Before Taxes	$8,177	$10,352	$11,624	$13,038	$14,546	$17,257
Permanent Differences						
Goodwill Amortization	426	426	426	426	426	426
Other Non-Deductible Amortization	1,033	233	233	233	233	0
Total Permanent Differences	1,459	659	659	659	659	426
Timing Differences						
Depreciation - Regular Tax/Book Diff.	2,386	5,884	3,440	2,204	1,671	1,872
Other	0	0	0	0	0	0
Total Timing Differences	2,386	5,884	3,440	2,204	1,671	1,872
Regular Taxable Income Before NOL	7,250	5,127	8,844	11,494	13,534	15,811
NOL						
Available	0	0	0	0	0	0
Current	0	0	0	0	0	0
Utilized	0	0	0	0	0	0
Regular Taxable Income After NOL	7,250	5,127	8,844	11,494	13,534	15,811
State Taxes	435	308	531	690	812	949
Regular Taxable Income After NOL and State	6,815	4,819	8,313	10,804	12,722	14,863
Federal Tax	2,317	1,639	2,826	3,673	4,326	5,053
Tentative Minimum Tax	2,078	2,077	2,321	2,588	3,104	3,462
Indicated Alternative Minimum Tax	0	438	0	0	0	0
MTC Credit						
Available	0	0	438	0	0	0
Current	0	438	0	0	0	0
Utilized	0	0	438	0	0	0
Net Federal Taxes	2,317	2,077	2,388	3,673	4,326	5,053
State Taxes	435	308	531	690	812	949
Foreign Taxes	0	0	0	0	0	0
Total Current Taxes	2,752	2,384	2,919	4,363	5,138	6,002
Total Book Tax Provision	3,658	4,180	4,663	5,200	5,772	6,713
Deferred Taxes	$906	$1,796	$1,744	$837	$634	$710

MAREIGHT CORPORATION
LBO Analysis
Alternative Minimum Tax

Exhibit 23.40

05/22/92
05:29 PM

Years Ended December 31,	1993	1994	1995	1996	1997	1998
Regular Taxable Income	$7,250	$5,127	$8,844	$11,494	$13,534	$15,811
State Taxes	435	308	531	690	812	949
Regular Taxable Income After State Taxes	6,815	4,819	8,313	10,804	12,722	14,863
AMT Adjustments						
Depreciation - AMTI/Regular Tax Diff.	2,937	4,635	2,872	1,932	2,590	2,286
Long-Term Contracts post 2/28/86	0	0	0	0	0	0
Installment Sales of Certain Property	0	0	0	0	0	0
Total AMT Adjustments	2,937	4,635	2,872	1,932	2,590	2,286
Regular Tax NOL Deduction	0	0	0	0	0	0
AMT Corporate Tax Preference Items						
Depletion	0	0	0	0	0	0
Intangible Drilling Costs	0	0	0	0	0	0
Accelerated Depreciation of Real Property Placed into Service Before 1987	0	0	0	0	0	0
Total Tax Preferences	0	0	0	0	0	0
Pre-Adjustment AMT Income	9,752	9,454	11,185	12,736	15,312	17,149
ACE Income Adjustment						
Pre-Adjustment AMT Income	9,752	9,454	11,185	12,736	15,312	17,149
Depreciation - ACE/AMTI Difference	849	1,238	560	271	277	214
Other	0	0	0	0	0	0
ACE Income	10,602	10,692	11,745	13,008	15,589	17,363
Less: Pre-Adjustment AMT Income	(9,752)	(9,454)	(11,185)	(12,736)	(15,312)	(17,149)
Subtotal	849	1,238	560	271	277	214
	x 75.0%	x 75.0%	x 75.0%	x 75.0%	x 75.0%	x 75.0%
ACE Adjustment	637	929	420	203	208	160
AMT Income Before NOL	10,389	10,383	11,605	12,940	15,520	17,310
AMT NOL Deduction (90% limitation)						
Available	0	0	0	0	0	0
Current	0	0	0	0	0	0
Utilized	0	0	0	0	0	0
AMT Income	10,389	10,383	11,605	12,940	15,520	17,310
Tentative Minimum Tax	2,078	2,077	2,321	2,588	3,104	3,462
AMT Credits	0	0	0	0	0	0
Regular Tax Liability	2,317	1,639	2,826	3,673	4,326	5,053
Alternative Minimum Tax	$0	$438	$0	$0	$0	$0

MAREIGHT CORPORATION

LBO Analysis

Comparison of Calculated and Actual Values of
Net Property, Plant and Equipment

Exhibit 23.41

05/22/92
05:29 PM

Calculated Value of Net Property, Plant and Equipment

Book Description	Book Life	Tax Category	1981-1992 Capital Expenditures	1981-1992 Accumulated Depreciation	Net Property, Plant and Equipment
Land	NA	Land	$0	-	$0
Autos	5	3-Year	0	0	0
Prod Eqp	8	5-Year	0	0	0
Prod Eqp	12	7-Year	0	0	0
Barges	15	10-Year	0	0	0
Waste Facility	20	15-Year	0	0	0
Sewers	30	20-Year	0	0	0
Real Estate	30	Real Estate (1)	0	0	0
		Total Calculated Value			$0

Comparison of Calculated and Actual Values

	Net Property, Plant and Equipment
Calculated Value	$0
Actual Value	44,965
Difference	($44,965)
Percent of Actual Value	-100.00%

(1) Real Estate excludes all land.
Note: If the calculated and actual property, plant and equipment book value numbers are roughly the same then it is appropriate to
use the calculated tax depreciation figures in the projections. However, the best alternative is to get tax depreciation forecasts

MAREIGHT CORPORATION
LBO Analysis
Historical Capital Expenditures
1981 - 1988

Exhibit 23.42

05/22/92
05:29 PM

Book Description	Book Life	Tax Category	1981	1982	1983	1984	1985	1986	1987	1988
Land	NA	Land	$0	$0	$0	$0	$0	$0	$0	$0
Autos	5	3-Year	0	0	0	0	0	0	0	0
Prod Eqp	8	5-Year	0	0	0	0	0	0	0	0
Prod Eqp	12	7-Year							0	0
Barges	15	10-Year	0	0	0	0	0	0	0	0
Waste Facility	20	15-Year							0	0
Sewers	30	20-Year							0	0
Real Estate	30	Real Estate (1)	0	0	0	0	0	0	0	0
Total Capital Expenditures			$0	$0	$0	$0	$0	$0	$0	$0

(1) Excluding land.

MAREIGHT CORPORATION
LBO Analysis
Summary Historical Book Depreciation Schedule
For Purposes of Calculating Current Net Property, Plant and Equipment

Exhibit 23.43
05/22/92
05:29 PM

Book Description	Book Life	Tax Category	1981	1982	1983	1984	1985	1986	1987	1988	1989	1990	1991	1992	1981-1992 Total
Autos	5	3-Year	$0	$0	$0	$0	$0	$0	$0	$0	$0	$0	$0	$0	$0
Prod Eqp	8	5-Year	0	0	0	0	0	0	0	0	0	0	0	0	0
Prod Eqp	12	7-Year	0	0	0	0	0	0	0	0	0	0	0	0	0
Barges	15	10-Year	0	0	0	0	0	0	0	0	0	0	0	0	0
Waste Facility	20	15-Year	0	0	0	0	0	0	0	0	0	0	0	0	0
Sewers	30	20-Year	0	0	0	0	0	0	0	0	0	0	0	0	0
Real Estate	30	Real Estate (1)	0	0	0	0	0	0	0	0	0	0	0	0	0
Total Depreciation			$0	$0	$0	$0	$0	$0	$0	$0	$0	$0	$0	$0	$0

(1) Excluding land.

MAREIGHT CORPORATION
LBO Analysis
Summary Projected Book Depreciation schedule

Exhibit 23.44

05/22/92
05:29 PM

Book Description	Book Life	Acquired Assets	1993	1994	1995	1996	1997	1998
Autos	5	3-Year	$700	$700	$700	$700	$700	$0
Prod Eqp	8	5-Year	1,125	1,125	1,125	1,125	1,125	1,125
Prod Eqp	12	7-Year	855	855	855	855	855	855
Barges	15	10-Year	0	0	0	0	0	0
Waste Facility	20	15-Year	0	0	0	0	0	0
Sewers	30	20-Year	0	0	0	0	0	0
Real Estate	30	Real Estate (1)	417	417	417	417	417	417
		New Capital Expenditures						
Autos	5	3-Year	$65	$198	$335	$478	$625	$713
Prod Eqp	8	5-Year	125	363	606	894	1,191	1,481
Prod Eqp	12	7-Year	100	322	586	868	1,190	1,566
Barges	15	10-Year	0	0	0	0	0	0
Waste Facility	20	15-Year	0	0	0	0	0	0
Sewers	30	20-Year	0	0	0	0	0	0
Real Estate	30	Real Estate (1)	45	138	233	328	428	533
			$3,432	$4,117	$4,856	$5,665	$6,531	$6,689

Exhibit 23.45
05/22/92
05:29 PM

MAREIGHT CORPORATION
LBO Analysis
Summary Regular Tax Depreciation Schedule

Book Description	Book Life	Carryover Basis Assets	1981	1982	1983	1984	1985	1986	1987	1988	1989	1990	1991	1992	1981-1992 Total	1993	1994	1995	1996	1997	1998
Autos	5	3-Year	$0	$0	$0	$0	$0	$0	$0	$0	$0	$0	$0	$0	$0	$0	$0	$0	$0	$0	$0
Prod Eqp	8	5-Year	0	0	0	0	0	0	0	0	0	0	0	0	0	0	0	0	0	0	0
Prod Eqp	12	7-Year	0	0	0	0	0	0	0	0	0	0	0	0	0	0	0	0	0	0	0
Barges	15	10-Year	0	0	0	0	0	0	0	0	0	0	0	0	0	0	0	0	0	0	0
Waste Facility	20	15-Year	0	0	0	0	0	0	0	0	0	0	0	0	0	0	0	0	0	0	0
Severs	30	20-Year	0	0	0	0	0	0	0	0	0	0	0	0	0	0	0	0	0	0	0
Real Estate	30	Real Estate	0	0	0	0	0	0	0	0	0	0	0	0	0	0	0	0	0	0	0
		Acquired Assets																			
Autos	5	3-Year														$1,167	$1,556	$518	$259		
Prod Eqp	8	5-Year														1,800	2,880	1,728	1,037	1,037	518
Prod Eqp	12	7-Year														1,467	2,514	1,795	1,282	917	916
Barges	15	10-Year														0	0	0	0	0	0
Waste Facility	20	15-Year														0	0	0	0	0	0
Severs	30	20-Year														0	0	0	0	0	0
Real Estate	30	Real Estate														380	397	397	397	397	397
		New Capital Expenditures																			
Autos	5	3-Year														$217	$514	$630	$701	$726	$751
Prod Eqp	8	5-Year														400	1,000	1,380	1,748	2,091	2,244
Prod Eqp	12	7-Year														341	1,005	1,623	2,128	2,623	3,223
Barges	15	10-Year														0	0	0	0	0	0
Waste Facility	20	15-Year														0	0	0	0	0	0
Severs	30	20-Year														0	0	0	0	0	0
Real Estate	30	Real Estate														46	136	225	317	412	512
			$0	$0	$0	$0	$0	$0	$0	$0	$0	$0	$0	$0	$0	$5,818	$10,001	$8,296	$7,869	$8,202	$8,561

Note: If possible, obtain projected regular tax depreciation figures from target company and input on this schedule.

MAREIGHT CORPORATION
LBO Analysis
Summary Alternative Minimum Tax Depreciation Schedule

Exhibit 23.46
05/22/92
05:29 PM

Book Description	Book Life	Carryover Basis Assets	1981	1982	1983	1984	1985	1986	1987	1988	1989	1990	1991	1992	1981-1992 Total	1993	1994	1995	1996	1997	1998
Autos	5	3-Year	$0	$0	$0	$0	$0	$0	$0	$0	$0	$0	$0	$0	$0	$0	$0	$0	$0	$0	$0
Prod Eqp	8	5-Year	0	0	0	0	0	0	0	0	0	0	0	0	0	0	0	0	0	0	0
Prod Eqp	12	7-Year	0	0	0	0	0	0	0	0	0	0	0	0	0	0	0	0	0	0	0
Barges	15	10-Year	0	0	0	0	0	0	0	0	0	0	0	0	0	0	0	0	0	0	0
Waste Facility	20	15-Year	0	0	0	0	0	0	0	0	0	0	0	0	0	0	0	0	0	0	0
Sewers	30	20-Year	0	0	0	0	0	0	0	0	0	0	0	0	0	0	0	0	0	0	0
Real Estate	30	Real Estate	0	0	0	0	0	0	0	0	0	0	0	0	0	0	0	0	0	0	0
		Acquired Assets																			
Autos	5	3-Year														$750	$1,178	$786	$786		
Prod Eqp	8	5-Year														710	1,309	1,103	928	825	825
Prod Eqp	12	7-Year														642	1,203	1,052	921	806	752
Barges	15	10-Year														0	0	0	0	0	0
Waste Facility	20	15-Year														0	0	0	0	0	0
Sewers	30	20-Year														0	0	0	0	0	0
Real Estate	30	Real Estate														299	313	313	313	313	313
		New Capital Expenditures																			
Autos	5	3-Year														$139	$364	$523	$689	$714	$739
Prod Eqp	8	5-Year														158	433	672	929	1,167	1,388
Prod Eqp	12	7-Year														149	464	802	1,125	1,467	1,858
Barges	15	10-Year														0	0	0	0	0	0
Waste Facility	20	15-Year														0	0	0	0	0	0
Sewers	30	20-Year														0	0	0	0	0	0
Real Estate	30	Real Estate														34	104	174	246	321	399
			$0	$0	$0	$0	$0	$0	$0	$0	$0	$0	$0	$0	$0	$2,881	$5,366	$5,425	$5,936	$5,613	$6,274

Note: If possible, obtain projected alternative minimum tax depreciation figures from target company and input on this schedule.

MAREIGHT CORPORATION
LBO Analysis
Summary ACE Depreciation Schedule

Exhibit 23.47
05/22/92
05:29 PM

Book Description	Book Life	Carryover Basis Assets	1981	1982	1983	1984	1985	1986	1987	1988	1989	1990	1991	1992	1981-1992 Total	1993	1994	1995	1996	1997	1998
Autos	5	3-Year	$0	$0	$0	$0	$0	$0	$0	$0	$0	$0	$0	$0	$0	$0	$0	$0	$0	$0	$0
Prod Eqp	8	5-Year	0	0	0	0	0	0	0	0	0	0	0	0	0	0	0	0	0	0	0
Prod Eqp	12	7-Year	0	0	0	0	0	0	0	0	0	0	0	0	0	0	0	0	0	0	0
Barges	15	10-Year	0	0	0	0	0	0	0	0	0	0	0	0	0	0	0	0	0	0	0
Waste Facility	20	15-Year	0	0	0	0	0	0	0	0	0	0	0	0	0	0	0	0	0	0	0
Sewers	30	20-Year	0	0	0	0	0	0	0	0	0	0	0	0	0	0	0	0	0	0	0
Real Estate	30	Real Estate	0	0	0	0	0	0	0	0	0	0	0	0	0	0	0	0	0	0	0
Acquired Assets																					
Autos	5	3-Year														$500	$1,000	$1,000	$1,000		
Prod Eqp	8	5-Year														473	948	948	948	947	948
Prod Eqp	12	7-Year														428	855	855	855	855	855
Barges	15	10-Year														0	0	0	0	0	0
Waste Facility	20	15-Year														0	0	0	0	0	0
Sewers	30	20-Year														0	0	0	0	0	0
Real Estate	30	Real Estate														299	313	313	313	313	313
New Capital Expenditures																					
Autos	5	3-Year														$93	$282	$479	$682	$707	$732
Prod Eqp	8	5-Year														105	305	511	753	1,003	1,248
Prod Eqp	12	7-Year														100	322	586	868	1,190	1,566
Barges	15	10-Year														0	0	0	0	0	0
Waste Facility	20	15-Year														0	0	0	0	0	0
Sewers	30	20-Year														0	0	0	0	0	0
Real Estate	30	Real Estate														34	104	174	246	321	399
			$0	$0	$0	$0	$0	$0	$0	$0	$0	$0	$0	$0	$0	$2,031	$4,128	$4,865	$5,665	$5,336	$6,060

Note: If possible, obtain projected ACE tax depreciation figures from target company and input on this schedule.

Exhibit 23.48
05/22/92
05:29 PM

DEPRECIATION CALCULATIONS:
Page D-1   FILE: DEPR_3

Acct. Desc.	Book Life	Tax Category	3-YEAR PROPERTY
Autos	5		

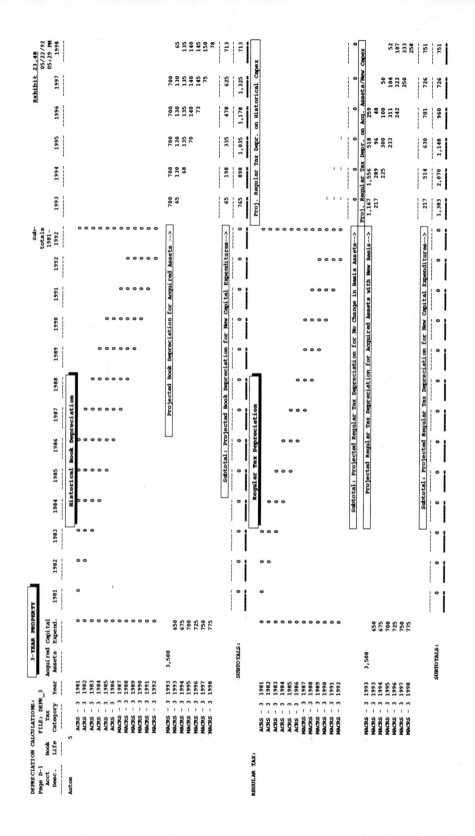

Historical Book Depreciation

Tax Category	Year	Acquired Assets	Capital Expend.	1981	1982	1983	1984	1985	1986	1987	1988	1989	1990	1991	1992	sub-totals 1981-1992	1993	1994	1995	1996	1997	1998
ACRS - 3	1981		0	0												0						
ACRS - 3	1982		0		0	0										0						
ACRS - 3	1983		0			0	0	0								0						
ACRS - 3	1984		0				0	0	0							0						
ACRS - 3	1985		0					0	0	0						0						
ACRS - 3	1986		0						0	0	0					0						
MACRS - 3	1987		0							0	0	0				0						
MACRS - 3	1988		0								0	0	0			0						
MACRS - 3	1989		0									0	0	0		0						
MACRS - 3	1990		0										0	0	0	0						
MACRS - 3	1991		0											0	0	0						
MACRS - 3	1992		0												0	0						
MACRS - 3	1993	3,500	650														700	700	700	700	700	65
MACRS - 3	1993		675														65	130	130	130	130	135
MACRS - 3	1994		700															68	135	135	135	140
MACRS - 3	1995		725																70	140	140	145
MACRS - 3	1996		750																	73	145	150
MACRS - 3	1997		775																		75	78
MACRS - 3	1998																					

Projected Book Depreciation for Acquired Assets -->

| SUBTOTALS: | | 3,500 | | 0 | 0 | 0 | 0 | 0 | 0 | 0 | 0 | 0 | 0 | 0 | 0 | 65 | 198 | 335 | 478 | 625 | 713 |

Subtotal: Projected Book Depreciation for New Capital Expenditures -->

| | | | | 0 | 0 | 0 | 0 | 0 | 0 | 0 | 0 | 0 | 0 | 0 | 0 | 765 | 898 | 1,035 | 1,178 | 1,325 | 713 |

Regular Tax Depreciation

REGULAR TAX:

Tax Category	Year	Acquired Assets	Capital Expend.	1981	1982	1983	1984	1985	1986	1987	1988	1989	1990	1991	1992	sub-totals 1981-1992	1993	1994	1995	1996	1997	1998
ACRS - 3	1981		0	0												0						
ACRS - 3	1982		0		0	0										0						
ACRS - 3	1983		0			0	0	0								0						
ACRS - 3	1984		0				0	0	0							0						
ACRS - 3	1985		0					0	0	0						0						
ACRS - 3	1986		0						0	0	0					0						
MACRS - 3	1987		0							0	0	0				0						
MACRS - 3	1988		0								0	0	0			0						
MACRS - 3	1989		0									0	0	0		0						
MACRS - 3	1990		0										0	0	0	0						
MACRS - 3	1991		0											0	0	0						
MACRS - 3	1992		0												0	0						

Proj. Regular Tax Depr. on Historical Capex

Subtotal: Projected Regular Tax Depreciation for No Change in Basis Assets -->

| | | | | 0 | 0 | 0 | 0 | 0 | 0 | 0 | 0 | 0 | 0 | 0 | 0 | 0 | 0 | 0 | 0 | 0 | 0 |

Proj. Regular Tax Depr. on Acq. Assets/New Capex

Projected Regular Tax Depreciation for Acquired Assets with New Basis -->

MACRS - 3	1993	3,500	650														1,167	1,556	518	259		
MACRS - 3	1993		675														217	289	96	48	50	52
MACRS - 3	1994		700															225	300	100	104	107
MACRS - 3	1995		725																233	311	322	333
MACRS - 3	1996		750																	242	250	258
MACRS - 3	1997		775																			
MACRS - 3	1998																					

Subtotal: Projected Regular Tax Depreciation for New Capital Expenditures -->

| SUBTOTALS: | | 3,500 | | 0 | 0 | 0 | 0 | 0 | 0 | 0 | 0 | 0 | 0 | 0 | 0 | 217 | 514 | 630 | 701 | 726 | 751 |
| | | | | 0 | 0 | 0 | 0 | 0 | 0 | 0 | 0 | 0 | 0 | 0 | 0 | 1,383 | 2,070 | 1,148 | 960 | 726 | 751 |

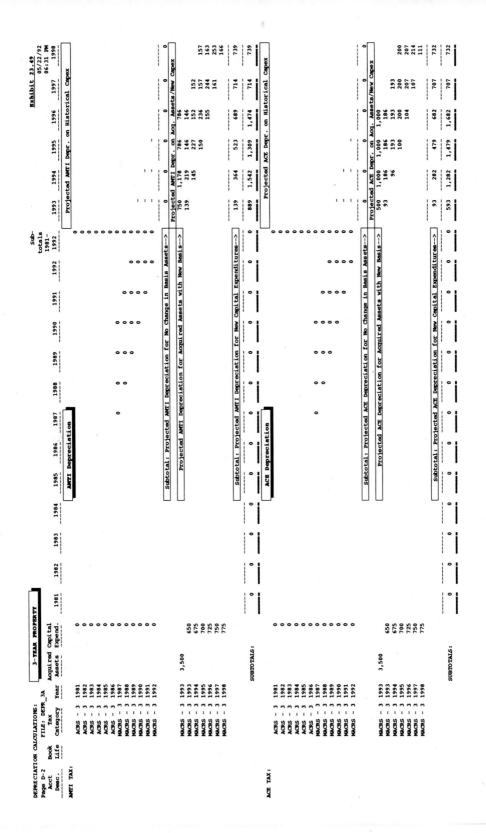

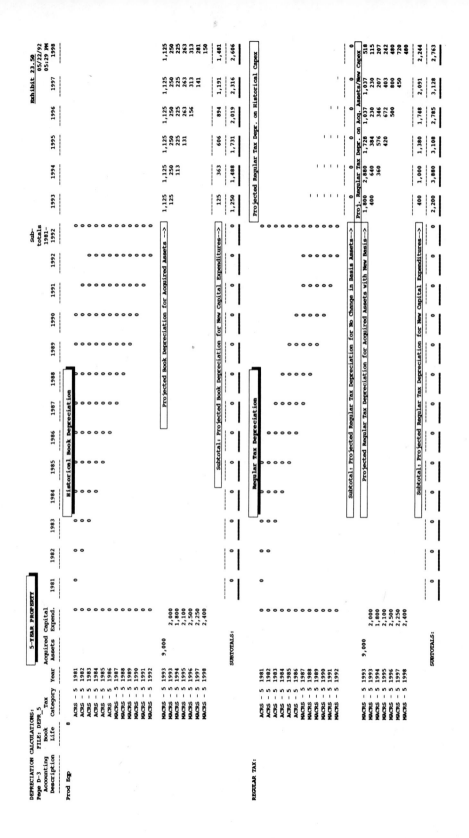

Exhibit 23.50
05/22/92
05:29 PM
1997   1998

DEPRECIATION CALCULATIONS:
Page D-3
FILE: DEPR_5

5-YEAR PROPERTY

Accounting Description	Book Life	Tax Category	Year	Acquired Assets	Capital Expend.	1981	1982	1983	1984	1985	1986	1987	1988	1989	1990	1991	1992	sub-totals 1981-1992	1993	1994	1995	1996	1997	1998
Prod Exp	8																							

Historical Book Depreciation

Tax Category	Year	Acquired Assets	Capital Expend.	1981	1982	1983	1984	1985	1986	1987	1988	1989	1990	1991	1992	1993	1994	1995	1996	1997	1998
ACRS - 5	1981		0	0	0	0	0	0	0													
ACRS - 5	1982		0		0	0	0	0	0	0												
ACRS - 5	1983		0			0	0	0	0	0	0											
ACRS - 5	1984		0				0	0	0	0	0	0										
ACRS - 5	1985		0					0	0	0	0	0	0									
ACRS - 5	1986		0						0	0	0	0	0	0								
MACRS - 5	1987		0							0	0	0	0	0	0							
MACRS - 5	1988		0								0	0	0	0	0	0						
MACRS - 5	1989		0									0	0	0	0	0	0					
MACRS - 5	1990		0										0	0	0	0	0	0				
MACRS - 5	1991		0											0	0	0	0	0	0			
MACRS - 5	1992		0												0	0	0	0	0	0		

Projected Book Depreciation for Acquired Assets -->

Tax Category	Year	Acquired Assets	Capital Expend.	1993	1994	1995	1996	1997	1998
MACRS - 5	1993	9,000		1,125	1,125	1,125	1,125	1,125	1,125
MACRS - 5	1993		2,000	125	250	250	250	250	250
MACRS - 5	1994		1,800		113	225	225	225	225
MACRS - 5	1995		2,100			131	263	263	263
MACRS - 5	1996		2,500				156	313	313
MACRS - 5	1997		2,250					141	281
MACRS - 5	1998		2,400						150

Subtotal: Projected Book Depreciation for New Capital Expenditures -->

	1993	1994	1995	1996	1997	1998
	125	363	606	894	1,191	1,481
SUBTOTALS:	1,250	1,488	1,731	2,019	2,316	2,606

REGULAR TAX:

Regular Tax Depreciation — Projected Regular Tax Depr. on Historical Capex

Tax Category	Year	Acquired Assets	Capital Expend.	1981	1982	1983	1984	1985	1986	1987	1988	1989	1990	1991	1992
ACRS - 5	1981		0	0	0	0	0	0	0						
ACRS - 5	1982		0		0	0	0	0	0	0					
ACRS - 5	1983		0			0	0	0	0	0	0				
ACRS - 5	1984		0				0	0	0	0	0	0			
ACRS - 5	1985		0					0	0	0	0	0	0		
ACRS - 5	1986		0						0	0	0	0	0	0	
MACRS - 5	1987		0							0	0	0	0	0	0
MACRS - 5	1988		0								0	0	0	0	0
MACRS - 5	1989		0									0	0	0	0
MACRS - 5	1990		0										0	0	0
MACRS - 5	1991		0											0	0
MACRS - 5	1992		0												0

Subtotal: Projected Regular Tax Depreciation for No Change in Basis Assets -->

Projected Regular Tax Depreciation for Acquired Assets with New Basis -->

Tax Category	Year	Acquired Assets	Capital Expend.	Proj. Regular Tax Depr. on Acq. Assets / New Basis					
				1993	1994	1995	1996	1997	1998
MACRS - 5	1993	9,000		1,800	2,880	1,728	1,037	1,037	518
MACRS - 5	1993		2,000	400	640	384	230	230	115
MACRS - 5	1994		1,800		360	576	346	207	207
MACRS - 5	1995		2,100			420	672	403	242
MACRS - 5	1996		2,500				500	800	480
MACRS - 5	1997		2,250					450	720
MACRS - 5	1998		2,400						480

Subtotal: Projected Regular Tax Depreciation for New Capital Expenditures -->

	1993	1994	1995	1996	1997	1998
	400	1,000	1,380	1,748	2,091	2,244
SUBTOTALS:	2,200	3,880	3,108	2,785	3,128	2,763

DEPRECIATION CALCULATIONS:
Page D-4
FILE: DEPR.5A

5-YEAR PROPERTY

Exhibit 23.51
05/22/92
05:29 PM

Column layout: Accounting Description | Book Life | Tax Category | Year | Acquired Assets | Capital Expend. | 1981 | 1982 | 1983 | 1984 | 1985 | 1986 | 1987 | 1988 | 1989 | 1990 | 1991 | 1992 | sub-totals 1981–1992 | 1993 | 1994 | 1995 | 1996 | 1997 | 1998

AMTI TAX:

AMTI Depreciation

Tax Category	Year	Acquired Assets	Capital Expend.	Depreciation 1981–1998
ACRS – 5	1981	0	0	0
ACRS – 5	1982	0	0	0
ACRS – 5	1983	0	0	0
ACRS – 5	1984	0	0	0
ACRS – 5	1985	0	0	0
ACRS – 5	1986	0	0	0
ACRS – 5	1987	0	0	0
MACRS – 5	1988	0	0	0
MACRS – 5	1989	0	0	0
MACRS – 5	1990	0	0	0
MACRS – 5	1991	0	0	0
MACRS – 5	1992	0	0	0
				Subtotal: 0

Projected AMTI Depr. on Historical Capex

Projected AMTI Depr. on No Change in Basis Assets-->

Year	1993	1994	1995	1996	1997	1998
No Change in Basis Assets	710	1,309	1,103	928	825	825

Projected AMTI Depr. on Acq. Assets/New Capex: 0 | 0 | 0 | 0 | 0 | 0

Subtotal: Projected AMTI Depreciation for No change in Basis Assets-->

1993	1994	1995	1996	1997	1998
868	1,741	1,775	1,857	1,993	2,213

Projected AMTI Depreciation for Acquired Assets with New Basis-->

Tax Category	Year	Acquired Assets	Capital Expend.	1993	1994	1995	1996	1997	1998
MACRS – 5	1993	9,000	2,000	158	291	245	206	183	183
MACRS – 5	1994		1,800		142	262	221	186	165
MACRS – 5	1995		2,100			166	305	257	217
MACRS – 5	1996		2,500				197	364	306
MACRS – 5	1997		2,250					178	327
MACRS – 5	1998		2,400						189

SUBTOTALS: 9,000

Subtotal: Projected AMTI Depreciation for New Capital Expenditures-->

1993	1994	1995	1996	1997	1998
158	433	672	929	1,167	1,388

ACE TAX:

ACE Depreciation

Tax Category	Year	Acquired Assets	Capital Expend.	Depreciation 1981–1998
ACRS – 5	1981	0	0	0
ACRS – 5	1982	0	0	0
ACRS – 5	1983	0	0	0
ACRS – 5	1984	0	0	0
ACRS – 5	1985	0	0	0
ACRS – 5	1986	0	0	0
ACRS – 5	1987	0	0	0
MACRS – 5	1988	0	0	0
MACRS – 5	1989	0	0	0
MACRS – 5	1990	0	0	0
MACRS – 5	1991	0	0	0
MACRS – 5	1992	0	0	0
				Subtotal: 0

Projected ACE Depr. on Historical Capex

Projected ACE Depr. on Acq. Assets/New Capex: 0 | 0 | 0 | 0 | 0 | 0

Year	1993	1994	1995	1996	1997	1998
No Change in Basis Assets	473	948	948	948	947	948

Subtotal: Projected ACE Depreciation for No change in Basis Assets-->

1993	1994	1995	1996	1997	1998
579	1,253	1,458	1,700	1,949	2,195

Projected ACE Depreciation for Acquired Assets with New Basis-->

Tax Category	Year	Acquired Assets	Capital Expend.	1993	1994	1995	1996	1997	1998
MACRS – 5	1993	9,000	2,000	105	211	211	211	210	211
MACRS – 5	1994		1,800		95	190	190	190	189
MACRS – 5	1995		2,100			110	221	221	221
MACRS – 5	1996		2,500				132	263	263
MACRS – 5	1997		2,250					118	237
MACRS – 5	1998		2,400						126

SUBTOTALS: 9,000

Subtotal: Projected ACE Depreciation for New Capital Expenditures-->

1993	1994	1995	1996	1997	1998
105	305	511	753	1,003	1,248

Exhibit 23.52
05/22/92
05:29 PM

DEPRECIATION CALCULATIONS:
Page D-5   FILE: DEPR_7

7-YEAR PROPERTY

Accounting Description	Book Life	Tax Category	Year	Acquired Assets	Capital Expend.	1981	1982	1983	1984	1985	1986	1987	1988	1989	1990	1991	1992	sub-totals 1981-1992	1993	1994	1995	1996	1997	1998
Prod Exp	12																							

Historical Book Depreciation

		MACRS - 7	1987		0							0	0	0	0	0	0	0						
		MACRS - 7	1988		0								0	0	0	0	0	0						
		MACRS - 7	1989		0									0	0	0	0	0						
		MACRS - 7	1990		0										0	0	0	0						
		MACRS - 7	1991		0											0	0	0						
		MACRS - 7	1992		0												0	0						

Projected Book Depreciation for Acquired Assets -->

		MACRS - 7	1993	10,265															855	855	855	855	855	855
		MACRS - 7	1993		2,388														100	199	199	199	199	199
		MACRS - 7	1994		2,943															123	245	245	245	245
		MACRS - 7	1995		3,392																141	283	283	283
		MACRS - 7	1996		3,388																	141	282	282
		MACRS - 7	1997		4,334																		181	361
		MACRS - 7	1998		4,684																			195

Subtotal: Projected Book Depreciation for New Capital Expenditures -->

| | | | | | | | | | | | | | | | | | | | 100 | 322 | 586 | 868 | 1,190 | 1,566 |
| SUBTOTALS: | | | | | | 0 | 0 | 0 | 0 | 0 | 0 | 0 | 0 | 0 | 0 | 0 | 0 | 0 | 955 | 1,177 | 1,441 | 1,724 | 2,045 | 2,421 |

REGULAR TAX:

Regular Tax Depreciation

		MACRS - 7	1987		0							0	0	0	0	0	0	0						
		MACRS - 7	1988		0								0	0	0	0	0	0						
		MACRS - 7	1989		0									0	0	0	0	0						
		MACRS - 7	1990		0										0	0	0	0						
		MACRS - 7	1991		0											0	0	0						
		MACRS - 7	1992		0												0	0						

Subtotal: Projected Regular Tax Depreciation for No Change in Basis Assets -->

Projected Regular Tax Depr. on Historical Capex

| | | | | | | | | | | | | | | | | | | | 0 | 0 | 0 | 0 | 0 | 0 |

Projected Regular Tax Depreciation for Acquired Assets with New Basis -->

Proj Regular Tax Depr. on Acq. Assets/New Capex

		MACRS - 7	1993	10,265															1,467	2,514	1,795	1,282	917	916
		MACRS - 7	1993		2,388														341	585	418	298	213	213
		MACRS - 7	1994		2,943															421	721	515	368	263
		MACRS - 7	1995		3,392																485	831	593	424
		MACRS - 7	1996		3,388																	484	830	593
		MACRS - 7	1997		4,334																		619	1,061
		MACRS - 7	1998		4,684																			669

Subtotal: Projected Regular Tax Depreciation for New Capital Expenditures -->

| | | | | | | | | | | | | | | | | | | | 341 | 1,005 | 1,623 | 2,128 | 2,623 | 3,223 |
| SUBTOTALS: | | | | | | 0 | 0 | 0 | 0 | 0 | 0 | 0 | 0 | 0 | 0 | 0 | 0 | 0 | 1,808 | 3,519 | 3,418 | 3,410 | 3,540 | 4,138 |

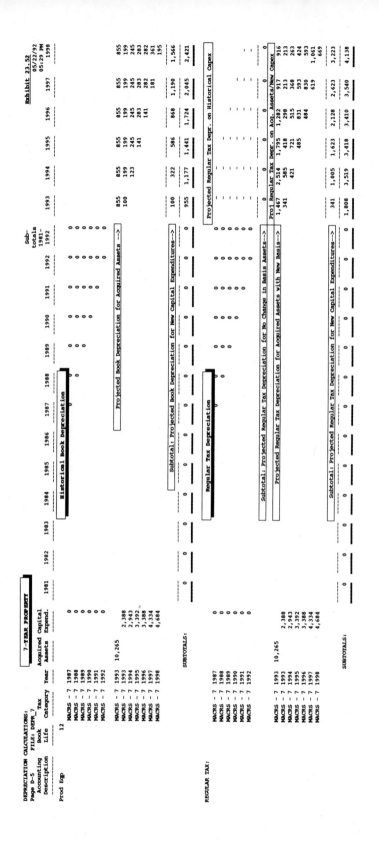

Exhibit 23.53
05/22/92
05:29 PM

DEPRECIATION CALCULATIONS:
Page D-6   FILE: DEPR_7A

7-YEAR PROPERTY

AMTI TAX:

AMTI Depreciation

Projected AMTI Depr. on Historical Capex

Accounting Description	Book Life	Tax Category	Year	Acquired Assets	Capital Expend.	1981	1982	1983	1984	1985	1986	1987	1988	1989	1990	1991	1992	Subtotals 1981-1992	1993	1994	1995	1996	1997	1998
	MACRS	- 7	1987	0										0	0	0	0		—	—	—	—	—	—
	MACRS	- 7	1988	0									0	0	0	0	0		—	—	—	—	—	—
	MACRS	- 7	1989	0								0	0	0	0	0	0		—	—	—	—	—	—
	MACRS	- 7	1990	0									0	0	0	0	0		—	—	—	—	—	—
	MACRS	- 7	1991	0										0	0	0	0		—	—	—	—	—	—
	MACRS	- 7	1992	0											0	0	0		—	—	—	—	—	—

Subtotal: Projected AMTI Depreciation for No Change in Basis Assets--> 0 ... 0

Projected AMTI Depreciation for Acquired Assets with New Basis-->

Projected AMTI Depr. on Acq. Assets/New Capex

Accounting Description	Book Life	Tax Category	Year	Acquired Assets	Capital Expend.	1993	1994	1995	1996	1997	1998
	MACRS	- 7	1993	10,265		642	1,203	1,052	921	806	752
	MACRS	- 7	1993			149	280	245	214	187	175
	MACRS	- 7	1994		2,388		184	345	398	264	231
	MACRS	- 7	1995		2,943			212	348	348	304
	MACRS	- 7	1996		3,392				212	397	347
	MACRS	- 7	1997		3,388					271	508
	MACRS	- 7	1998		4,334						293
					4,684						

Subtotal: Projected AMTI Depreciation for New Capital Expenditures--> 149 / 464 / 802 / 1,125 / 1,467 / 1,858

SUBTOTALS: 791 / 1,667 / 1,854 / 2,046 / 2,273 / 2,611

ACE TAX:

ACE Depreciation

Projected ACE Depr. on Historical Capex

Accounting Description	Book Life	Tax Category	Year	Acquired Assets	Capital Expend.	1981–1992	1993	1994	1995	1996	1997	1998
	MACRS	- 7	1987	0		0	—	—	—	—	—	—
	MACRS	- 7	1988	0		0	—	—	—	—	—	—
	MACRS	- 7	1989	0		0	—	—	—	—	—	—
	MACRS	- 7	1990	0		0	—	—	—	—	—	—
	MACRS	- 7	1991	0		0	—	—	—	—	—	—
	MACRS	- 7	1992	0		0	—	—	—	—	—	—

Subtotal: Projected ACE Depreciation for No Change in Basis Assets--> 0 ... 0

Projected ACE Depreciation for Acquired Assets with New Basis-->

Projected ACE Depr. on Acq. Assets/New Capex

Accounting Description	Book Life	Tax Category	Year	Acquired Assets	Capital Expend.	1993	1994	1995	1996	1997	1998
	MACRS	- 7	1993	10,265		428	855	855	855	855	855
	MACRS	- 7	1993			100	199	199	199	199	199
	MACRS	- 7	1994		2,388		123	245	245	245	245
	MACRS	- 7	1995		2,943			141	283	283	283
	MACRS	- 7	1996		3,392				141	282	282
	MACRS	- 7	1997		3,388					181	361
	MACRS	- 7	1998		4,334						195
					4,684						

Subtotal: Projected ACE Depreciation for New Capital Expenditures--> 100 / 322 / 586 / 868 / 1,190 / 1,566

SUBTOTALS: 527 / 1,177 / 1,441 / 1,724 / 2,045 / 2,421

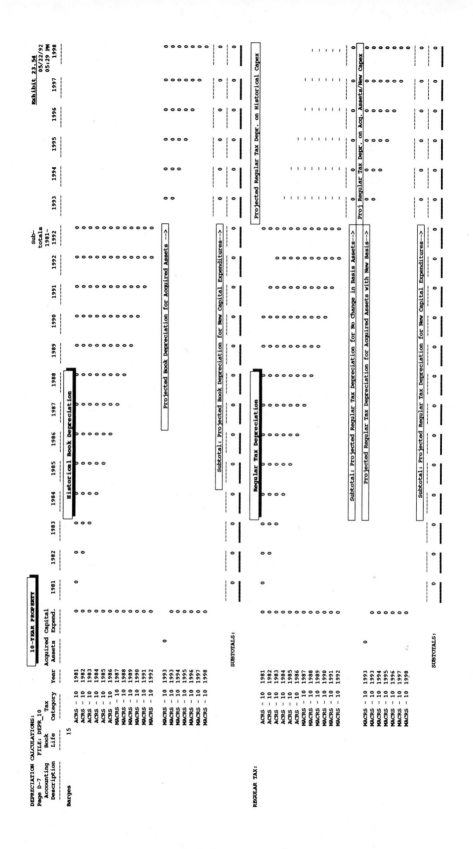

Exhibit 23.54
05/22/92
05:29 PM

Exhibit 22.55
05/22/92
05:29 PM

DEPRECIATION CALCULATIONS:
Page D-8
FILE: DEPR_10A

10-YEAR PROPERTY

Accounting Description	Book Tax Life	Tax Category	Year	Acquired Assets	Capital Expend.	1981	1982	1983	1984	1985	1986	1987	1988	1989	1990	1991	1992	Sub-totals 1981-1992	1993	1994	1995	1996	1997	1998

AMTI TAX:

AMTI Depreciation

Projected AMTI Depr. on Historical Capex

	ACRS – 10	1981	0															—	—	—	—	—	—
	ACRS – 10	1982	0															—	—	—	—	—	—
	ACRS – 10	1983	0															—	—	—	—	—	—
	ACRS – 10	1984	0															—	—	—	—	—	—
	ACRS – 10	1985	0						0									—	—	—	—	—	—
	ACRS – 10	1986	0							0								—	—	—	—	—	—
	MACRS – 10	1987	0								0	0						—	—	—	—	—	—
	MACRS – 10	1988	0									0	0	0				—	—	—	—	—	—
	MACRS – 10	1989	0										0	0	0			—	—	—	—	—	—
	MACRS – 10	1990	0											0	0	0		—	—	—	—	—	—
	MACRS – 10	1991	0												0	0	0	—	—	—	—	—	—
	MACRS – 10	1992	0													0	0	—	—	—	—	—	—

Subtotal: Projected AMTI Depreciation for No Change in Basis Assets ---> 0 0 0 0 0 0 0 0 0 0 0 0 0 0 0 0 0 0 0

Projected AMTI Depr. on Acq. Assets/New Capex

	MACRS – 10	1993	0															0	0	0	0	0	0
	MACRS – 10	1993																0	0	0	0	0	0
	MACRS – 10	1994	0															0	0	0	0	0	0
	MACRS – 10	1995	0															0	0	0	0	0
	MACRS – 10	1996	0															0	0	0	0
	MACRS – 10	1997	0															0	0	0
	MACRS – 10	1998	0															0	0

Subtotal: Projected AMTI Depreciation for New Capital Expenditures ---> 0 0 0 0 0 0 0 0 0 0 0 0 0 0 0 0 0 0 0

SUBTOTALS: 0   0   0   0   0   0   0   0   0   0   0   0   0   0   0   0   0   0   0

ACE TAX:

ACE Depreciation

Projected ACE Depr. on Historical Capex

	ACRS – 10	1981	0															—	—	—	—	—	—
	ACRS – 10	1982	0															—	—	—	—	—	—
	ACRS – 10	1983	0															—	—	—	—	—	—
	ACRS – 10	1984	0															—	—	—	—	—	—
	ACRS – 10	1985	0						0									—	—	—	—	—	—
	ACRS – 10	1986	0							0								—	—	—	—	—	—
	MACRS – 10	1987	0								0	0						—	—	—	—	—	—
	MACRS – 10	1988	0									0	0	0				—	—	—	—	—	—
	MACRS – 10	1989	0										0	0	0			—	—	—	—	—	—
	MACRS – 10	1990	0											0	0	0		—	—	—	—	—	—
	MACRS – 10	1991	0												0	0	0	—	—	—	—	—	—
	MACRS – 10	1992	0													0	0	—	—	—	—	—	—

Subtotal: Projected ACE Depreciation for No Change in Basis Assets ---> 0 0 0 0 0 0 0 0 0 0 0 0 0 0 0 0 0 0 0

Projected ACE Depr. on Acq. Assets/New Capex

	MACRS – 10	1993	0															0	0	0	0	0	0
	MACRS – 10	1993																0	0	0	0	0	0
	MACRS – 10	1994	0															0	0	0	0	0	0
	MACRS – 10	1995	0															0	0	0	0	0
	MACRS – 10	1996	0															0	0	0	0
	MACRS – 10	1997	0															0	0	0
	MACRS – 10	1998	0															0	0

Subtotal: Projected ACE Depreciation for New Capital Expenditures ---> 0 0 0 0 0 0 0 0 0 0 0 0 0 0 0 0 0 0 0

SUBTOTALS: 0   0   0   0   0   0   0   0   0   0   0   0   0   0   0   0   0   0   0

Exhibit 23.56
05/22/92
05:29 PM

DEPRECIATION CALCULATIONS:
Page D-9   FILE: DEPR_15

15-YEAR PROPERTY

Description	Accounting Life	Book Category	Tax	Year	Acquired Assets	Capital Expend.	1981	1982	1983	1984	1985	1986	1987	1988	1989	1990	1991	1992	sub-totals 1981-1992	1993	1994	1995	1996	1997	1998
Waste Facility	20																								

Historical Book Depreciation

	ACRS - 15	1981																
	ACRS - 15	1982																
	ACRS - 15	1983																
	ACRS - 15	1984																
	ACRS - 15	1985																
	ACRS - 15	1986																
	MACRS - 15	1987	0							0						0	0	0	0	0
	MACRS - 15	1988	0								0					0	0	0	0	0
	MACRS - 15	1989	0									0	0			0	0	0	0	0
	MACRS - 15	1990	0										0	0		0	0	0	0	0
	MACRS - 15	1991	0											0	0	0	0	0	0	0
	MACRS - 15	1992	0												0	0	0	0	0	0

Projected Book Depreciation for Acquired Assets —>

	MACRS - 15	1993	0														0					
	MACRS - 15	1993															0					
	MACRS - 15	1994															0					
	MACRS - 15	1995															0					
	MACRS - 15	1996															0					
	MACRS - 15	1997															0					
	MACRS - 15	1998															0					

SUBTOTALS: 0 0 0 0 0 0 0 0 0 0 0 0 0 0 0 0 0 0 0

Subtotal: Projected Book Depreciation for New Capital Expenditures—>

REGULAR TAX:

Regular Tax Depreciation

	ACRS - 15	1981																
	ACRS - 15	1982																
	ACRS - 15	1983																
	ACRS - 15	1984																
	ACRS - 15	1985																
	ACRS - 15	1986																
	MACRS - 15	1987								0					0	0	0	0	0
	MACRS - 15	1988									0				0	0	0	0	0
	MACRS - 15	1989									0	0			0	0	0	0	0
	MACRS - 15	1990										0	0		0	0	0	0	0
	MACRS - 15	1991											0	0	0	0	0	0	0
	MACRS - 15	1992												0	0	0	0	0	0

Subtotal: Projected Regular Tax Depreciation for No Change in Basis Assets—>

Proj Regular Tax Depr. on Acq. Assets/New Capex

Projected Regular Tax Depreciation for Acquired Assets with New Basis —>

	MACRS - 15	1993	0													0	0	0	0	0	0
	MACRS - 15	1993														0	0	0	0	0	0
	MACRS - 15	1994														0	0	0	0	0	0
	MACRS - 15	1995														0	0	0	0	0	0
	MACRS - 15	1996														0	0	0	0	0	0
	MACRS - 15	1997														0	0	0	0	0	0
	MACRS - 15	1998														0	0	0	0	0	0

Subtotal: Projected Regular Tax Depreciation for New Capital Expenditures—>

SUBTOTALS: 0 0 0 0 0 0 0 0 0 0 0 0 0 0 0 0 0 0 0

Projected Regular Tax Depr. on Historical Capex

Exhibit 23.57
05/22/92
05:29 PM

DEPRECIATION CALCULATIONS:
Page D-10   FILE: DEPR_15A

15-YEAR PROPERTY

Accounting Description	Book Life	Tax Category	Year	Acquired Assets	Capital Expend.	1981	1982	1983	1984	1985	1986	1987	1988	1989	1990	1991	1992	sub-totals 1981-1992	1993	1994	1995	1996	1997	1998

AMTI TAX:

Projected AMTI Depr. on Historical Capex

		ACRS - 15	1981															0	-	-	-	-	-	-
		ACRS - 15	1982															0	-	-	-	-	-	-
		ACRS - 15	1983															0	-	-	-	-	-	-
		ACRS - 15	1984															0	-	-	-	-	-	-
		ACRS - 15	1985															0	-	-	-	-	-	-
		ACRS - 15	1986															0	-	-	-	-	-	-
		MACRS - 15	1987	0							0	0	0	0	0	0	0	-	-	-	-	-	-
		MACRS - 15	1988	0								0	0	0	0	0	0	-	-	-	-	-	-
		MACRS - 15	1989	0									0	0	0	0	0	-	-	-	-	-	-
		MACRS - 15	1990	0										0	0	0	0	-	-	-	-	-	-
		MACRS - 15	1991	0											0	0	0	-	-	-	-	-	-
		MACRS - 15	1992	0												0	0	-	-	-	-	-	-

Subtotal: Projected AMTI Depreciation for No Change in Basis Assets-->   0   0   0   0   0   0   0   0   0   0   0   0   0

Projected AMTI Depreciation for Acquired Assets with New Basis-->

		MACRS - 15	1993	0													0	0	0	0	0	0	0
		MACRS - 15	1993	0													0	0	0	0	0	0	0
		MACRS - 15	1994	0													0	0	0	0	0	0	0
		MACRS - 15	1995	0													0	0	0	0	0	0	0
		MACRS - 15	1996	0													0	0	0	0	0	0	0
		MACRS - 15	1997	0													0	0	0	0	0	0	0
		MACRS - 15	1998	0													0	0	0	0	0	0	0

Subtotal: Projected AMTI Depreciation for New Capital Expenditures-->   0   0   0   0   0   0   0   0   0   0   0   0   0

SUBTOTALS: 0   0   0   0   0   0   0   0   0   0   0   0   0

ACE TAX:

ACE Depreciation

Projected ACE Depr. on Historical Capex

		ACRS - 15	1981															0	-	-	-	-	-	-
		ACRS - 15	1982															0	-	-	-	-	-	-
		ACRS - 15	1983															0	-	-	-	-	-	-
		ACRS - 15	1984															0	-	-	-	-	-	-
		ACRS - 15	1985															0	-	-	-	-	-	-
		ACRS - 15	1986															0	-	-	-	-	-	-
		MACRS - 15	1987	0							0	0	0	0	0	0	0	-	-	-	-	-	-
		MACRS - 15	1988	0								0	0	0	0	0	0	-	-	-	-	-	-
		MACRS - 15	1989	0									0	0	0	0	0	-	-	-	-	-	-
		MACRS - 15	1990	0										0	0	0	0	-	-	-	-	-	-
		MACRS - 15	1991	0											0	0	0	-	-	-	-	-	-
		MACRS - 15	1992	0												0	0	-	-	-	-	-	-

Subtotal: Projected ACE Depreciation for No Change in Basis Assets-->   0   0   0   0   0   0   0   0   0   0   0   0   0

Projected ACE Depr. on Acq. Assets/New Capex

		MACRS - 15	1993	0													0	0	0	0	0	0	0
		MACRS - 15	1993	0													0	0	0	0	0	0	0
		MACRS - 15	1994	0													0	0	0	0	0	0	0
		MACRS - 15	1995	0													0	0	0	0	0	0	0
		MACRS - 15	1996	0													0	0	0	0	0	0	0
		MACRS - 15	1997	0													0	0	0	0	0	0	0
		MACRS - 15	1998	0													0	0	0	0	0	0	0

Subtotal: Projected ACE Depreciation for New Capital Expenditures-->   0   0   0   0   0   0   0   0   0   0   0   0   0

SUBTOTALS: 0   0   0   0   0   0   0   0   0   0   0   0   0

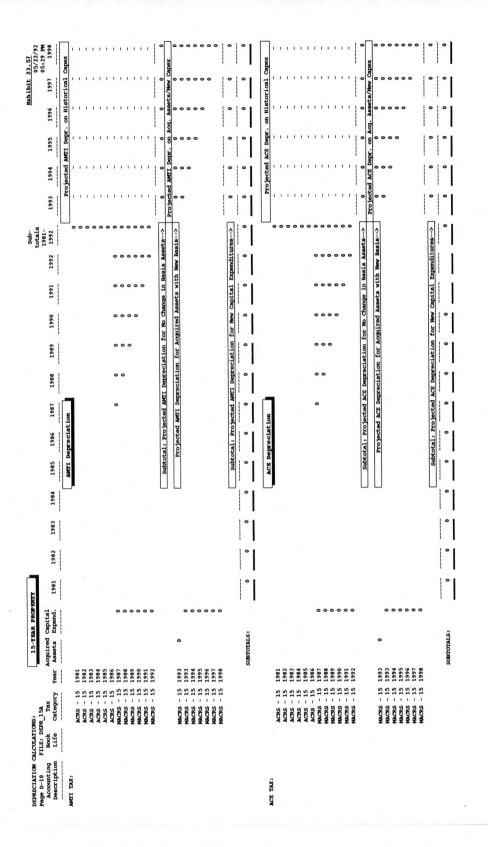

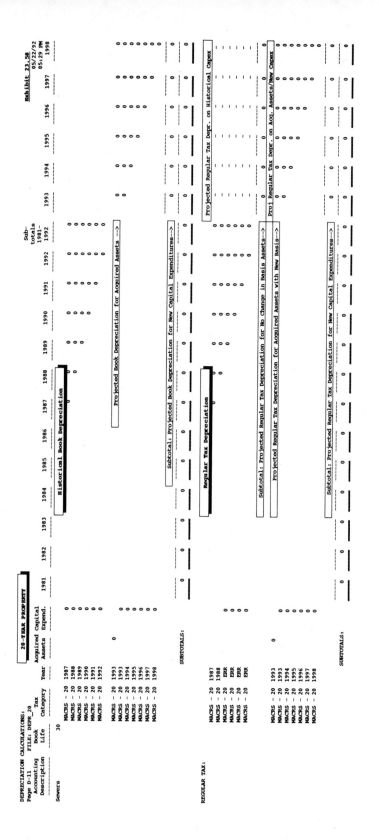

DEPRECIATION CALCULATIONS:
Page D-11   FILE: DEPR_20

Exhibit 23.58
05/22/92
05:29 PM

20-YEAR PROPERTY

Accounting Book   Tax
Description Life   Category   Year

Sewers
        30

Historical Book Depreciation

Projected Book Depreciation for Acquired Assets -->

Projected Book Depreciation for New Capital Expenditures-->

Subtotal: Projected Book Depreciation for New Capital Expenditures-->

REGULAR TAX:

Regular Tax Depreciation

Projected Regular Tax Depr. on Historical Capex

Subtotal: Projected Regular Tax Depreciation for No Change in Basis Assets-->

Projected Regular Tax Depr. on Acq. Assets/New Capex

Projected Regular Tax Depreciation for Acquired Assets with New Basis-->

Subtotal: Projected Regular Tax Depreciation for New Capital Expenditures-->

Acquired Capital
Assets   Expend.

SUBTOTALS:

SUBTOTALS:

MACRS - 20 1987
MACRS - 20 1988
MACRS - 20 1989
MACRS - 20 1990
MACRS - 20 1991
MACRS - 20 1992

MACRS - 20 1993
MACRS - 20 1993
MACRS - 20 1994
MACRS - 20 1995
MACRS - 20 1996
MACRS - 20 1997
MACRS - 20 1998

MACRS - 20 1987
MACRS - 20 1988
MACRS - 20 ERR
MACRS - 20 ERR
MACRS - 20 ERR

MACRS - 20 1993
MACRS - 20 1993
MACRS - 20 1994
MACRS - 20 1995
MACRS - 20 1996
MACRS - 20 1997
MACRS - 20 1998

Subtotals
1981-
1981 1982 1983 1984 1985 1986 1987 1988 1989 1990 1991 1992 1993 1994 1995 1996 1997 1998

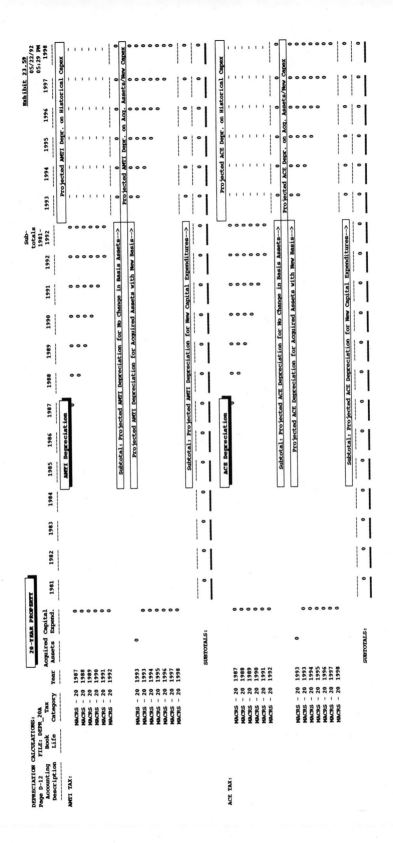

Exhibit 23.60
05/22/92
05:29 PM

DEPRECIATION CALCULATIONS:
Page D-13   FILE: DEPR_REAL

REAL ESTATE

REGULAR TAX:

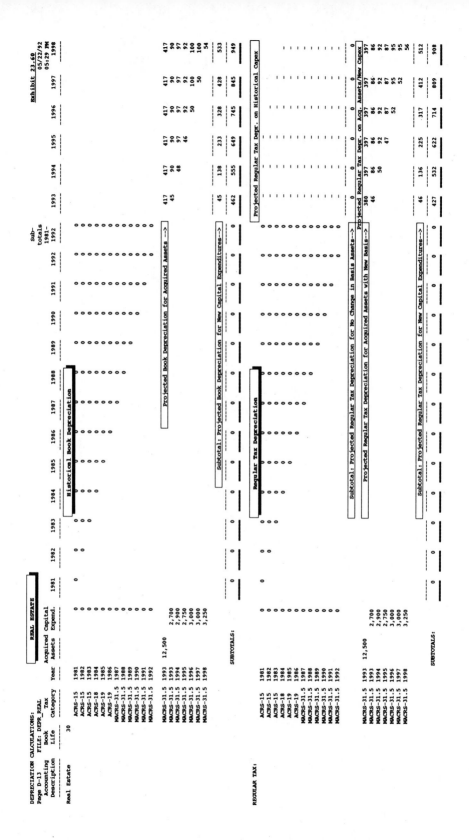

Description	Accounting Life	Book Tax Category	Year	Acquired Assets	Capital Expend.	1981	1982	1983	1984	1985	1986	1987	1988	1989	1990	1991	1992	sub-totals 1981-1992	1993	1994	1995	1996	1997	1998
Real Estate	30																							

Historical Book Depreciation

		ACRS-15	1981	12,500		0	0	0	0	0	0	0	0	0	0	0	0	0	417	417	417	417	417	417
		ACRS-15	1982				0	0	0	0	0	0	0	0	0	0	0	0	45	90	90	90	90	90
		ACRS-15	1983					0	0	0	0	0	0	0	0	0	0	0		48	97	97	97	97
		ACRS-18	1984						0	0	0	0	0	0	0	0	0	0			46	92	92	92
		ACRS-19	1985							0	0	0	0	0	0	0	0	0				50	100	100
		ACRS-19	1986								0	0	0	0	0	0	0	0					50	100
		MACRS-31.5	1987									0	0	0	0	0	0	0						54
		MACRS-31.5	1988										0	0	0	0	0	0						
		MACRS-31.5	1989											0	0	0	0	0						
		MACRS-31.5	1990												0	0	0	0						
		MACRS-31.5	1991													0	0	0						
		MACRS-31.5	1992														0	0						

Projected Book Depreciation for Acquired Assets -->

		MACRS-31.5	1993		2,700														45	138	233	328	428	533
		MACRS-31.5	1994		2,900																			
		MACRS-31.5	1995		2,750																			
		MACRS-31.5	1996		3,000																			
		MACRS-31.5	1997		3,000																			
		MACRS-31.5	1998		3,250																			

Subtotal: Projected Book Depreciation for New Capital Expenditures-->

SUBTOTALS: 0 0 0 0 0 0 0 0 0 0 0 0 0 462 555 649 745 845 949

Regular Tax Depreciation

		ACRS-15	1981	12,500		0	0	0	0	0	0	0	0	0	0	0	0	0						
		ACRS-15	1982				0	0	0	0	0	0	0	0	0	0	0	0						
		ACRS-15	1983					0	0	0	0	0	0	0	0	0	0	0						
		ACRS-18	1984						0	0	0	0	0	0	0	0	0	0						
		ACRS-19	1985							0	0	0	0	0	0	0	0	0						
		ACRS-19	1986								0	0	0	0	0	0	0						
		MACRS-31.5	1987									0	0	0	0	0	0						
		MACRS-31.5	1988										0	0	0	0	0						
		MACRS-31.5	1989											0	0	0	0						
		MACRS-31.5	1990												0	0	0						
		MACRS-31.5	1991													0	0						
		MACRS-31.5	1992														0						

Subtotal: Projected Regular Tax Depreciation for No Change in Basis Assets-->

Projected Regular Tax Depreciation for Acquired Assets with New Basis-->

Projected Regular Tax Depr. on Acq. Assets with New Basis --> 0 0 0 0 0 0 380 397 397 397 397 397

Projected Regular Tax Depr. on Historical Capex

		MACRS-31.5	1993		2,700														46	86	86	86	86	86
		MACRS-31.5	1994		2,900															50	92	92	92	92
		MACRS-31.5	1995		2,750																47	87	87	87
		MACRS-31.5	1996		3,000																	52	95	95
		MACRS-31.5	1997		3,000																		52	95
		MACRS-31.5	1998		3,250																			56

Subtotal: Projected Regular Tax Depreciation for New Capital Expenditures-->

SUBTOTALS: 0 0 0 0 0 0 0 0 0 0 0 0 0 427 532 622 714 809 908

DEPRECIATION CALCULATIONS:
Page D-14   FILE: DEPR_REALA

REAL ESTATE

Exhibit 23.61
05/22/92
05:29 PM

AMTI TAX:

AMTI Depreciation

Description / Accounting Book Life	Tax Category	Year	Acquired Assets	Capital Expend.	1981	1982	1983	1984	1985	1986	1987	1988	1989	1990	1991	1992	Sub-totals 1981-1992	1993	1994	1995	1996	1997	1998
	ACRS-15	1981	0								0	0	0	0	0	0	0						
	ACRS-15	1982	0								0	0	0	0	0	0	0						
	ACRS-15	1983	0								0	0	0	0	0	0	0						
	ACRS-18	1984	0								0	0	0	0	0	0	0						
	ACRS-19	1985	0								0	0	0	0	0	0	0						
	ACRS-19	1986	0								0	0	0	0	0	0	0						
	MACRS-31.5	1987	0									0	0	0	0	0	0						
	MACRS-31.5	1988	0										0	0	0	0	0						
	MACRS-31.5	1989	0											0	0	0	0						
	MACRS-31.5	1990	0												0	0	0						
	MACRS-31.5	1991	0													0	0						
	MACRS-31.5	1992	0														0						
Subtotal: Projected AMTI Depreciation for No Change in Basis Assets-->					0	0	0	0	0	0	0	0	0	0	0	0	0	0	0	0	0	0	0

Projected AMTI Depr. on Historical Capex

Projected AMTI Depreciation for Acquired Assets with New Basis

Description / Accounting Book Life	Tax Category	Year	Acquired Assets	Capital Expend.	1993	1994	1995	1996	1997	1998
	MACRS-31.5	1993	12,500		299	313	313	313	313	313
	MACRS-31.5	1993		2,700	34	68	68	68	68	68
	MACRS-31.5	1994		2,900		36	73	73	73	73
	MACRS-31.5	1995		2,750			34	69	69	69
	MACRS-31.5	1996		3,000				38	75	75
	MACRS-31.5	1997		3,000					38	75
	MACRS-31.5	1998		3,250						41
Subtotal: Projected AMTI Depreciation for New Capital Expenditures-->					34	104	174	246	321	399
SUBTOTALS:			12,500		333	416	487	559	634	712

ACE TAX:

ACE Depreciation

Description / Accounting Book Life	Tax Category	Year	Acquired Assets	Capital Expend.	1981	1982	1983	1984	1985	1986	1987	1988	1989	1990	1991	1992	Sub-totals 1981-1992	1993	1994	1995	1996	1997	1998
	ACRS-15	1981	0								0	0	0	0	0	0	0						
	ACRS-15	1982	0								0	0	0	0	0	0	0						
	ACRS-15	1983	0								0	0	0	0	0	0	0						
	ACRS-18	1984	0								0	0	0	0	0	0	0						
	ACRS-19	1985	0								0	0	0	0	0	0	0						
	ACRS-19	1986	0								0	0	0	0	0	0	0						
	MACRS-31.5	1987	0									0	0	0	0	0	0						
	MACRS-31.5	1988	0										0	0	0	0	0						
	MACRS-31.5	1989	0											0	0	0	0						
	MACRS-31.5	1990	0												0	0	0						
	MACRS-31.5	1991	0													0	0						
	MACRS-31.5	1992	0														0						
Subtotal: Projected ACE Depreciation for No Change in Basis Assets-->					0	0	0	0	0	0	0	0	0	0	0	0	0	0	0	0	0	0	0

Projected ACE Depr. on Historical Capex

Projected ACE Depreciation for Acquired Assets with New Basis

Description / Accounting Book Life	Tax Category	Year	Acquired Assets	Capital Expend.	1993	1994	1995	1996	1997	1998
	MACRS-31.5	1993	12,500		299	313	313	313	313	313
	MACRS-31.5	1993		2,700	34	68	68	68	68	68
	MACRS-31.5	1994		2,900		36	73	73	73	73
	MACRS-31.5	1995		2,750			34	69	69	69
	MACRS-31.5	1996		3,000				38	75	75
	MACRS-31.5	1997		3,000					38	75
	MACRS-31.5	1998		3,250						41
Subtotal: Projected ACE Depreciation for New Capital Expenditures-->					34	104	174	246	321	399
SUBTOTALS:			12,500		333	416	487	559	634	712

Section Five

Conclusion

Section Five described both initial and final DCF and LBO models. The initial DCF or LBO models are utilized early in the process, while the final models are prepared after a greater understanding of the target and the transaction is obtained. The final models include all the tax considerations identified in Section Two.

Section Six

Investment Returns and Risk

Section Six

Introduction

Chapter 24 brings together the valuation results for all the techniques described in Sections Four and Five. These results include both the estimates of a target's value in the marketplace and the value of the target to an individual acquirer.

The valuation analysis pertaining to an individual acquirer includes a matrix of net present values and internal rates of return.

The topic of risk is also covered in Chapter 24. Risk analysis techniques discussed include Scenario and Sensitivity Analysis and an analysis of the impact of the acquisition on the acquiring company's liquidity and expected financial performance.

Chapter 24

Summary Valuation and Risk Analysis

24.0 INTRODUCTION

This chapter brings together the results of all the valuation techniques described in Section Four. It also outlines an effective presentation format for DCF Analysis that describes the potential investment returns that are expected by the acquiring entity over the range of likely purchase prices. This analysis should enable the acquiring entity to make a reasoned decision about whether to proceed with a particular acquisition opportunity.

Another topic dealt with in this chapter is risk analysis. Two useful techniques for analyzing risk in a transaction are Scenario Analysis and Sensitivity Analysis.

The final topic covered in this chapter is the need to analyze the impact of the acquisition on the acquiring company's current and projected financials.

24.1 MARKET VALUE ANALYSIS SUMMARY

Exhibit 24–1 depicts an example of a set of value ranges that the valuation techniques described in Section Four produced for the target company described in Chapter 10. The shaded part of each bar represents the value range.

EXHIBIT 24–1
Mareight Corp. Summary Market Value Analysis

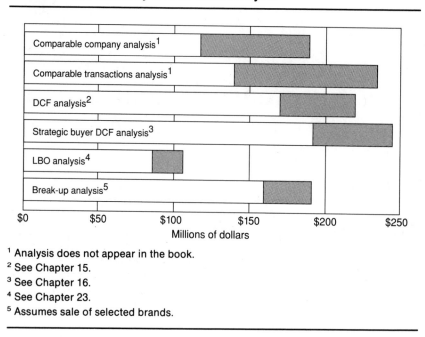

¹ Analysis does not appear in the book.
² See Chapter 15.
³ See Chapter 16.
⁴ See Chapter 23.
⁵ Assumes sale of selected brands.

24.2   VALUATION SUMMARY FOR AN ACQUIRER

As discussed in Chapter 15, the best estimate one can give top management of the returns associated with a proposed acquisition is either a range of IRRs or NPVs that the acquirer can expect given a spectrum of likely purchase prices. A matrix and corresponding graphs of IRRs and NPVs for Harrison's proposed acquisition of Mareight analyzed in the Final DCF Model in Chapter 22 appear in Exhibits 24–2, 24–3 and 24–4. The NPVs in these exhibits are based on the median discount rate for the EBDIAT Multiple Method of calculating residual value.

The NPV increases as the price increases in Exhibits 24–2 and 24–4 because of the assumption that depreciable asset values are higher at higher prices. See paragraph 10.3 for asset values assumed. The increase in asset values creates a larger tax shield that increases the target's projected cash flow. If appraisals are available the value of assets would be much more uniform across the purchase price range being considered. See paragraphs 7.11b and C.11 for a discussion of the proper book and tax methods for allocating value among assets.

EXHIBIT 24–2
IRRs and NPVs for Mareight Corp. Acquisition
(Most Likely Case—EBDIAT Multiple Method Assumption)

	Purchase Price (in Millions of Dollars)				
	$100	*$130*	*$160*	*$190*	*$220*
IRRs[1]	26%	21%	16%	13%	10%
NPVs[1] [2]	$188	$192	$196	$200	$204

[1] Continuing value assumption.
[2] Assumes 12 percent discount rate.

EXHIBIT 24–3
Mareight Corp. IRR Analysis (Most Likely Case)

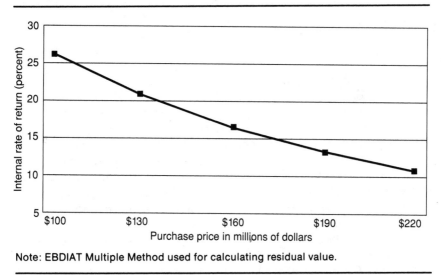

Note: EBDIAT Multiple Method used for calculating residual value.

EXHIBIT 24–4
Mareight Corp. NPV Analysis (Most Likely Case)

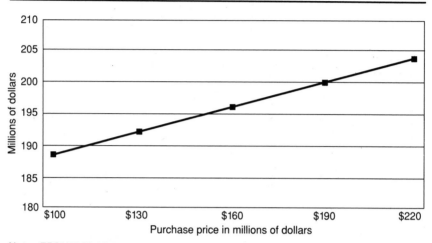

Note: EBDIAT Multiple Method used for calculating residual value and 12 percent discount rate assumed.

24.3 RISK ANALYSIS

The optimum approach for analyzing risk in a transaction is to conduct a Monte Carlo simulation of the projected results of the company. This technique involves defining probability factors for different outcomes for all the variables that affect the target's cash flow (e.g., prices of products sold, volumes, costs, working capital, etc.), and running a model that generates a distribution of expected returns. This technique is never used in practice because it is impractical to define all the required interrelationships for all variables over the length of the forecast period.

In practice, two complementary risk analysis approaches are used— Scenario Analysis and Sensitivity Analysis. *Scenario Analysis* involves developing a comprehensive set of alternate operating scenarios for the target and evaluating the NPVs and IRRs under these scenarios. *Sensitivity Analysis* involves determining the impact a change in an individual variable will have on the projected investment returns and net present value.

24.31   Scenario Analysis

Typically, the alternate set of operating scenarios are called Best Case, Worst Case and Most Likely Case operating scenarios. What is an operating scenario? It is a comprehensive set of assumptions concerning all variables that affect cash flow.

Scenario Analysis does not attempt to define the probability of occurrence of any individual variable or operating scenario. The probability of the operating scenario is subjectively determined by the decision maker.

24.31a   Analyzing Synergies

Companies are often faced with potential acquisition candidates in the same or closely related fields. In such cases incremental cost savings or revenues (hereafter, *synergies*) are generally expected. As a rule, acquiring companies do not want to pay for the value associated with the synergy to be realized. Unfortunately, many times the company to be acquired has sought out the acquiring company precisely because of the value of the incremental revenues or cost savings that will result from a combination of the two companies. In these instances, it is unlikely that the acquiring company will be able to consummate a purchase at a price that does not include some value for the synergies.

If synergies are expected, the acquiring company needs to prepare a set of operating scenarios that incorporate them (see Chapter 16). These scenarios would be in addition to an operating scenario that did not include the expected synergies.

24.31b   Presenting the Results

A matrix of IRRs and NPVs and corresponding graphs under Best Case, Worst Case and Most Likely Case scenarios both with and without synergies for Mareight Corporation appear in Exhibits 24–5, 24–6 and 24–7. This analysis was prepared by Harrison based on its estimates for General's expected synergies (see Chapters 15 and 16).

EXHIBIT 24–5
IRRs and NPVs for Mareight Corp. Acquisition under All Scenarios

	Purchase Price (in Millions of Dollars)				
	$100	*$130*	*$160*	*$190*	*$220*
Internal Rates of Return					
Including Synergies					
Best Case	35%	28%	23%	19%	16%
Most Likely Case	30	23	18	15	12
Worst Case	26	19	15	11	8
Excluding Synergies					
Best Case	32%	26%	21%	17%	14%
Most Likely Case	27	21	16	12	9
Worst Case	22	16	12	8	6
Net Present Values					
Including Synergies					
Best Case	$270	$270	$270	$270	$270
Most Likely Case	216	216	216	216	216
Worst Case	181	181	181	181	181
Excluding Synergies					
Best Case	$246	$246	$246	$246	$246
Most Likely Case	194	194	194	194	194
Worst Case	159	159	159	159	159

EXHIBIT 24–6
Mareight Corp. IRR Analysis (All Scenarios)

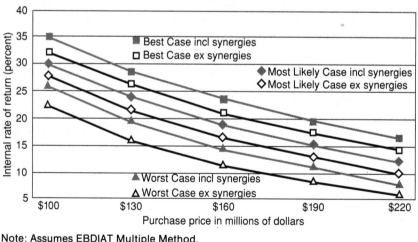

Note: Assumes EBDIAT Multiple Method.

EXHIBIT 24–7
Mareight Corp. NPV Analysis (All Scenarios)

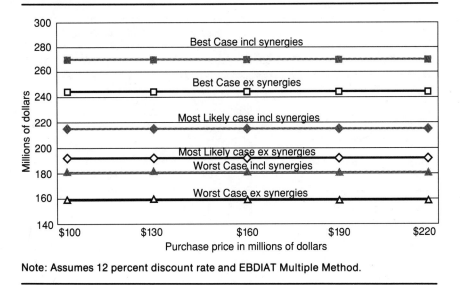

Note: Assumes 12 percent discount rate and EBDIAT Multiple Method.

24.32   Sensitivity Analysis

Sensitivity Analysis indicates the impact that a change in an individual variable will have on an acquisition's NPV or IRR. Sensitivity analysis does not provide any guidance as to the probability of any value for a variable occurring.

   Example 24A   Harrison was concerned about Mareight's gross margin. As a result, Harrison performed sensitivity analysis on this variable over the range of likely purchase prices. Harrison analyzed a 2 percent difference both higher and lower from the most likely gross margin percentage. The outcome of this analysis is illustrated in the matrix in Exhibit 24–8 and the graphs appearing in Exhibits 24–9 and 24–10.

EXHIBIT 24–8
Mareight Corporation Sensitivity Analysis—Gross Margin
(Excluding Synergies)

	Purchase Price (in Millions of Dollars)				
	$100	*$130*	*$160*	*$190*	*$220*
Internal Rates of Return					
+2%	30%	23%	19%	15%	12%
Most Likely Case	27%	21%	16%	12%	9%
−2%	23%	17%	13%	10%	7%
Net Present Values					
+2%	$219	$219	$219	$219	$219
Most Likely Case	194	194	194	194	194
−2%	168	168	168	168	168

EXHIBIT 24–9
Mareight Corp. IRR Sensitivity Analysis (2% Change in Gross Margin)

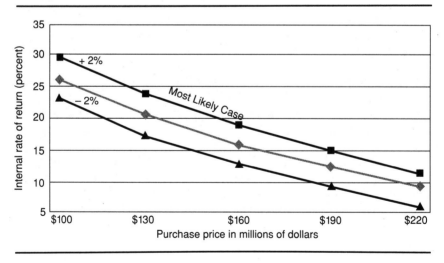

EXHIBIT 24–10
Mareight NPV Sensitivity Analysis (2% Change in Gross Margin)

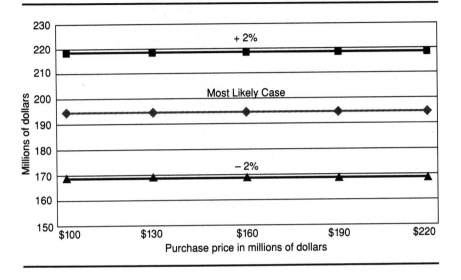

24.4   IMPACT ON THE ACQUIRING COMPANY

The final step required to assess an acquisition is to analyze its impact on the acquiring company's (1) projected cash flows, (2) earnings and earnings per share, particularly whether there will be any dilution to existing shareholders, (3) liquidity, and (4) overall capital structure. The analysis is performed by consolidating the target company's acquisition model with the acquiring company's forecast financial statements. It is important to determine the effect of the acquisition on the overall capital structure if it is possible that the acquisition will change the credit rating of the company. This analysis is performed only if the target company is material in relation to the acquiring company.

Two acquisitions that had disastrous results because of management's failure to adequately analyze the impact of the acquisition on the acquiring company's liquidity and overall financial strength were Wickes Cos.'s acquisition of Gamble-Skogmo and Baldwin United Corp.'s purchase of Mortgage Guaranty Insurance Corp. Both companies were forced into Chapter 11 as a result of these acquisitions.

24.5 COMMONSENSE TEST

A final approach that is helpful in reviewing whether to bid on a particular target company is to assume (1) that you had acquired the company, (2) that it was a financial disaster, and (3) that you are now looking back on your acquisition decision to determine what should have tipped you off that this was not going to be an attractive company. This exercise usually helps bring to the fore the "commonsense" risks that should be avoided. For example, acquiring a commodity business with razor thin margins in a leveraged acquisition usually violates commonsense. Unless the purchase price is very attractive relative to long-term M&A pricing and the financing package is extremely flexible, the acquirer has a high probability of failure. A downturn in margins will occur, and when it does, the investor's equity investment will become worthless.

Chapter 25

Concluding Note

25.0 INTRODUCTION

The use of the analytical techniques advocated in this book should improve the likelihood of consummating an acquisition at a price that will result in an acceptable rate of return on invested funds. However, a solid analytical approach to analyzing acquisitions is only one ingredient in successfully targeting and consummating transactions. This chapter will touch on some of the other key ingredients, including determining the seller's motivation in a transaction and the importance of due diligence and timing. The chapter closes with a list of other sources of valuable investment advice.

25.1 KNOW THE SELLER'S MOTIVES

In many acquisition situations, understanding the seller's motivations is the key to structuring a winning proposal. Sellers' motivations are diverse, ranging from maximizing cash proceeds to maintaining an active presence in the business for the owners or their offspring.

25.2 IMPORTANCE OF DUE DILIGENCE

The best acquisition analysis in the world is worthless if it does not reflect the true state of affairs and prospects at the target company. The only way to determine the true prospects for a target company is to spend a significant amount of time questioning and probing current managers and reviewing internal documents. Due diligence done well requires a skeptical approach to the company's recent reported results. Why? It is typical that a seller will "dress up the bride" for the sale. Generally, this means that the seller will defer expenditures that benefit the company long-term but that negatively impact current earnings (e.g., research and development expenditures). In addition, the seller will take other short-term actions that will prop up the current earnings of the company, such as accelerating revenues or delaying current maintenance expenditures.

25.3 TIMING IS EVERYTHING

The key to running a successful business is usually knowing when to invest in a particular technology or product. This is equally true for investing in an acquisition.

25.4 OTHER SOURCES OF INVESTMENT ADVICE

A great number of books offer tips on how to invest. Only a few of these are truly worthwhile. Four that the author believes provide valuable insights include: Michael Porter's *Competitive Strategy: Techniques for Analyzing Industries and Competitors*; Robert Buzzell's and Bradley Gale's *The PIMS (Profit Impact of Market Strategy) Principles: Linking Strategy to Performance*; Peter Lynch's *One Up on Wall Street*; and John Train's *The New Money Masters*.

Section Six

Conclusion

Chapter 24 brings together the results of all the valuation techniques described in Sections Four and Five. It described the results of the market valuation analysis as well as the valuation analysis for an individual acquirer. The results for an individual acquirer were depicted in a matrix of NPVs and IRRs from the DCF model.

Chapter 24 also discussed the risk issue in transactions. Risk analysis techniques discussed included Scenario and Sensitivity Analysis and analyzing the impact of the acquisition on the acquiring company.

Appendixes

Appendix A

DCF Techniques

A.0 INTRODUCTION

Throughout the book, calculations are performed that require an in-depth understanding of Discounted Cash Flow (DCF) methods. These include the Net Present Value (NPV) and Internal Rate of Return (IRR) methods of evaluating investment proposals.

An acquisition is similar to any other capital expenditure proposal. It requires an outlay of funds with a defined present cash value with the hope of receiving a greater cash flow stream in the future. The major factor differentiating the analysis of an acquisition from other capital budgeting problems is its complexity—hundreds of assumptions are required to put together a realistic financial model of the expected cash stream. Nevertheless, the DCF methods that are used to analyze simple projects are equally applicable to acquisitions.

A.1 DCF THEORY

The theory underlying the use of DCF methods is that a dollar received immediately is preferable to a dollar received at some future date. Why is this so? Because the dollar received today can be put to work and will be worth more than a dollar in the future.

> ***Example AA***   *ABC Corporation sells a product for $1,000. The buyer says that he would like to pay the $1,000 in one year. ABC Corporation can earn 5 percent simple interest by putting any excess cash in the bank. Marketing consid-*

erations aside, ABC Corporation would want the $1,000 now rather than later because if it gets the $1,000 now and invests it in the bank, it will have $1,050 at the end of the year.

If a dollar today is worth more than a dollar at some future date, how does a person know when some future amount greater than a dollar is equal in value to a dollar today? To find this point, it is necessary to understand compounding and discounting. Virtually everyone has had experience with compound interest.

Example AB   *ABC Corporation puts $1,000 in a bank account earning 5 percent annually. At the end of three years ABC Corporation has $1,158 calculated as follows:*

Year	Initial Amount	Interest Rate	Period End Amount	Interest Received
1	$1,000	5%	$1,050	$50
2	1,050	5	1,103	53
3	1,103	5	1,158	55

The reason the interest received in Years 2 and 3 exceeds 5 percent of the initial $1,000 is that ABC Corporation is receiving interest on previously received interest.

Rather than set out the calculations necessary to find the compound value of $1, a table is provided in Exhibit A–1 that indicates the amount that $1 will grow to over different time periods using various compound interest rates.

Example AC   *ABC Corporation puts $1,500 in the bank expecting to earn 15 percent compounded annually for five years. How much will ABC Corporation receive at the end of five years? If we look at Exhibit A–1, we see that the factor for five periods at 15 percent is 2.0114. Therefore, ABC Corporation will receive $3,017 in five years ($1,500 × 2.0114).*

Example AD   *Same facts as Example AC except that ABC's money will be compounded semiannually. If this is the case, we look to the factor for 10 periods at 7.5 percent, which is 2.0610. Given this assumption, ABC Corporation will receive $3,091 in five years ($1,500 × 2.0610).*

EXHIBIT A–1
Compound Value of $1

Period	Interest Rate					
	5.0%	7.5%	10.0%	12.5%	15.0%	17.5%
1	1.0500	1.0750	1.1000	1.1250	1.1500	1.1750
2	1.1025	1.1556	1.2100	1.2656	1.3225	1.3806
3	1.1576	1.2423	1.3310	1.4238	1.5209	1.6222
4	1.2155	1.3355	1.4641	1.6018	1.7490	1.9061
5	1.2763	1.4356	1.6105	1.8020	2.0114	2.2397
6	1.3401	1.5433	1.7716	2.0273	2.3131	2.6316
7	1.4071	1.6590	1.9487	2.2807	2.6600	3.0922
8	1.4775	1.7835	2.1436	2.5658	3.0590	3.6333
9	1.5513	1.9172	2.3579	2.8865	3.5179	4.2691
10	1.6289	2.0610	2.5937	3.2473	4.0456	5.0162

Discounting is the reverse of compounding. In discounting, one is trying to determine the value today of a dollar received at some point in the future.

Example AE   *ABC Corporation owns a noninterest-bearing note for $5,000 due in three years. If we assume ABC will discount the note at 10 percent, what is the note worth today? Exhibit A–1 indicates that $1 will grow to $1.3310 if it compounds for three years at 10 percent. Thus the following relationship holds:*

$$\frac{1}{1.3310} = \frac{X}{\$5,000}$$

Solving for X, we find that the present value of $5,000 is $3,757.

Rather than continually solving for X, one can use Exhibit A–2, which provides the factors for the present value of $1. These factors were arrived at using the reciprocals of compound factors. For example, the reciprocal for 1/1.3310 is .7513. This factor, multiplied by $5,000, yields the $3,757 answer to Example AE.

Example AF   *ABC Corporation will receive $10,000 in five years and wants to determine its present value using a 12.5 percent discount factor. The discount factor for five periods at 12.5 percent is .5549. Therefore, the present value of the sum to be received is $5,549 ($10,000 × .5549).*

EXHIBIT A–2
Present Value of $1

Period	\ Interest Rate\ 5.0%	7.5%	10.0%	12.5%	15.0%	17.5%
1	0.9524	0.9302	0.9091	0.8889	0.8696	0.8511
2	0.9070	0.8653	0.8264	0.7901	0.7561	0.7243
3	0.8638	0.8050	0.7513	0.7023	0.6575	0.6164
4	0.8227	0.7488	0.6830	0.6243	0.5718	0.5246
5	0.7835	0.6966	0.6209	0.5549	0.4972	0.4465
6	0.7462	0.6480	0.5645	0.4933	0.4323	0.3800
7	0.7107	0.6028	0.5132	0.4385	0.3759	0.3234
8	0.6768	0.5607	0.4665	0.3897	0.3269	0.2752
9	0.6446	0.5216	0.4241	0.3464	0.2843	0.2342
10	0.6139	0.4852	0.3855	0.3079	0.2472	0.1994

Example AG ABC Corporation expects to receive cash at the end of each of the next four years. The cash flows are as indicated below. Using a 17.5 percent discount factor, what is the present value of these cash flows?

Period	Cash Flow	17.5% Discount Factor	Present Value
1	$700	0.8511	$596
2	1,225	0.7243	887
3	1,943	0.6164	1,198
4	420	0.5246	220
	$4,288		$2,901

A.2 NET PRESENT VALUE METHOD

NPV Analysis involves discounting the net cash flows expected from a project at a single discount rate. The initial cost of the project is a negative cash flow at time period 0. The investment rule to apply with NPV Analysis is that a project should be undertaken if the NPV is a positive number, whereas if it is a negative, the project should be dropped.

Example AH XYZ Corporation is considering the acquisition of ABC Corporation for $10 million. XYZ expects net cash flows from the acquisition as *stated below. The discount rate XYZ has decided to apply is 15 percent. Should XYZ buy ABC?*

Period	Net Cash Flow	15.0% Discount Factor	Net Present Value
0	($10,000)	1.0000	($10,000)
1	$1,000	0.8696	870
2	$3,833	0.7561	2,898
3	$3,800	0.6575	2,499
4	$6,400	0.5718	3,659
5	$673	0.4972	334
	$5,706		NPV $260

Answer: Yes, XYZ should buy ABC Corporation because the project has a positive NPV.

A.3   INTERNAL RATE OF RETURN METHOD

IRR Analysis calculates the rate of return that equates the present value of the expected net cash flows of the project with the cost of the project. The investment rule to follow if IRR Analysis is used is to undertake a project if its IRR exceeds a "hurdle rate of return" set by management. This rate is typically the project's WACC.

Example AI   *Same facts as Example AH, except that management's cutoff rate of return for this investment is 13 percent. What is the acquisition's internal rate of return and should XYZ purchase ABC?*

Period	Net Cash Flow	16.0% Discount Factor	Net Present Value
0	($10,000)	1.0000	($10,000)
1	1,000	0.8621	862
2	3,833	0.7432	2,849
3	3,800	0.6407	2,434
4	6,400	0.5523	3,535
5	673	0.4761	320
	$5,706		NPV $0

Answer: The calculations indicate that if the net cash flows are discounted at 16 percent, the NPV of the project is $0. Therefore, XYZ should buy ABC Corporation because the project has an IRR (16 percent) that exceeds the cutoff return set by management (13 percent).

A.4 WHICH METHOD IS PREFERABLE?

Under normal circumstances the two methods will give the same results. However, it is important to note that the two methods are based on different reinvestment assumptions. NPV Analysis assumes that all proceeds can be reinvested at the discount rate used. The IRR method assumes that all proceeds can be reinvested at the IRR. In most cases, the NPV assumption is the better assumption.

An analyst should be aware that there can be practical problems with IRR Analysis. In certain circumstances, it can produce several internal rates of return for a project. In a typical project, there is one cash outflow in the first period followed by cash receipts in periods thereafter. In these situations only one IRR can exist. However, if there are cash outflows in more than one period, multiple IRRs can be generated. In such cases NPV Analysis should be used to analyze the project.

Despite the shortcomings of the IRR method, it is used extensively in the book, reflecting its use in practice. Why is this so? IRR Analysis is preferred by many over NPV Analysis because it results in a return figure that executives easily relate to.

Appendix B

Basic U.S. Tax Rules

B.0   INTRODUCTION

This appendix describes selected U.S. tax rules that affect transactions and valuation. Concepts discussed include the present tax rate structure, taxation of capital gains and losses at both the shareholder and corporate levels, depreciation rules, recapture provisions and net operating losses.

B.1   FEDERAL INCOME TAX RATES FOR CORPORATIONS

The ordinary corporate income tax rate is 34 percent for taxable income above $335,000. Corporations with taxable income less than $335,000 receive the benefit of a graduated rate structure as detailed below.

Taxable Income	Tax Rate
$ 0–$50,000	15%
50,000–75,000	25
75,000–100,000	34
100,000–335,000	39
335,000+	34

B.2   COMBINED EFFECTIVE FEDERAL, STATE AND CITY CORPORATE TAX RATE

The assumption used throughout this book is that the combined effective federal, state and city corporate income tax rate to use in analyzing transactions is 38 percent (see Exhibit B–1). This rate assumes a combined state and city tax rate of approximately 6 percent, which, when tax effected for federal income tax purposes and added to the 34 percent federal income tax rate, yields a tax rate of approximately 38 percent. The combined state and city tax rate of 6 percent is used for illustration purposes. It is important in analyzing any transaction to incorporate appropriate state and city tax rates. For example, if a prospective acquisition candidate generates all of its taxable income within New York City, the appropriate combined state and city tax rate would be approximately 20 percent.

EXHIBIT B–1
Combined Effective Federal, State and City Corporate Income Tax Rate

Earnings before taxes (EBT)	$1,000,000	
State and city income tax rate	6%	
State and city income tax liability		$60,000
Earning before federal income taxes	940,000	
Federal income tax rate	34%	
Federal income tax liability		319,600
Total state and federal liability		$379,600
Total liability as a % of EBT		38%

B.3   FEDERAL INCOME TAX RATES FOR INDIVIDUALS

Nominally, there are three tax brackets—15, 28 and 31 percent. However, the actual top tax rate is above the stated 31 percent because of (a) a limitation of itemized deductions and (b) the phaseout of the personal and dependency exemptions. The top tax rate is approximately 34 percent for a family of four that earns more than $150,000 in adjusted gross income.

The itemized deduction limitation acts to disallow $300 of itemized deductions for every $10,000 of adjusted gross income above $100,000. This equates to a 1 percent tax increase.

The personal and dependency exemptions are phased out gradually for single taxpayers who have adjusted gross incomes between $100,000 and $225,000, and for couples with adjusted gross incomes between $150,000 and $275,000. This provision has the effect of a 0.5 percent tax increase in the marginal tax rate for each exemption claimed.

B.4   COMBINED EFFECTIVE FEDERAL, STATE AND CITY PERSONAL TAX RATE

The assumption used throughout this book is that the total effective personal income tax rate is 38 percent. This rate assumes a combined state and city tax rate of approximately 6 percent, which, when tax effected for federal income tax purposes, yields a total personal income tax rate of approximately 38 percent (see Exhibit B–2). The combined state and city tax rate of 6 percent is used for illustration purposes. Appropriate state and city tax rates should be used in each acquisition analysis.

All states except Alaska, Florida, Nevada, South Dakota, Texas, Washington and Wyoming impose some kind of personal income tax. In addition, a number of cities (e.g., New York) also impose an income tax.

EXHIBIT B–2
Combined Effective Federal, State and City Personal Income Tax Rate

Earnings before taxes (EBT)	$1,000,000	
State and city income tax rate	6%	
State and city income tax liability		$60,000
Earning before federal income taxes	940,000	
Federal income tax rate	34%	
Federal income tax liability		319,600
Total state and federal liability		379,600
Total liability as a % of EBT		38%

B.5   DIVIDENDS RECEIVED DEDUCTION

A corporation may deduct from gross income (1) 70 percent of the dividends received from a domestic corporation in which it owns less than 20 percent of the stock; (2) 80 percent of the dividends received from a domestic corporation in which it owns between 20 percent and 80 percent of the stock, and (3) 100 percent of the qualifying dividends received from a corporation that is a member of its affiliated group (distributing corporation owned 80 percent or more).

B.6 COMBINED EFFECTIVE FEDERAL, STATE AND CITY CAPITAL GAINS TAX

Gain on the sale or exchange of a capital asset that has been held for the required holding period is taxed at ordinary income tax rates for corporations and varying rates for individuals. The maximum federal capital gains tax rate for individuals is 28 percent.

The assumption used throughout this book is that the effective capital gains tax rate is 38 percent for corporations and 32 percent for individuals. The individual capital gains tax rate assumes a combined state and city tax rate of approximately 6 percent, which, when tax effected for federal income tax purposes and added to the 28 percent maximum federal capital gains tax rate for individuals, yields a tax rate of 32 percent. The combined state and city tax rate of 6 percent is used for illustration purposes. Appropriate tax rates should be used in each analysis (see Exhibit B–3).

EXHIBIT B–3
Combined Effective Federal, State and City Personal Capital Gains Tax Rate

Capital gains	$1,000,000	
State and city income tax rate	6%	
State and city income tax liability		$60,000
Capital gains before federal income taxes	940,000	
Federal "maximum" capital gains tax rate	28%	
Federal capital gains tax liability		263,200
Total federal, state and city capital gains tax liability		323,200
Total liability as a % of capital gains		32%

The subparagraphs below describe the federal income tax rules regarding capital gains and losses. Applicable state and city laws vary widely and must be reviewed for each transaction.

B.61 Required Holding Period

The required holding period for long-term capital gain or loss treatment is "more than one year." If the required holding period requirement is not met, the gain or loss is short-term.

B.62 Capital Assets Defined

A capital asset is defined as property (whether or not connected with a trade or business) held by the taxpayer, which does not include (1) inventory, (2) accounts receivable, (3) depreciable business property, (4) real property used in a trade or business, and (5) some miscellaneous other assets.

B.63 Section 1231 Assets

The definition of capital assets specifically excludes real property and depreciable property used in a business. This exclusion drastically curtails the opportunity to sell all the assets of a business and be taxed on any gain as if the sale involved capital assets. However, IRC Section 1231 alleviates the problem for the taxpayer. Under Section 1231, gains and losses on property used in a trade or business (which includes real property, depreciable business property and certain other items) are netted together. If the gains exceed the losses, both the gains and losses shall be considered as arising from the sale or exchange of a long-term capital asset. However, if the losses exceed the gains, the net loss will be offset against ordinary taxable income. The net effect of this provision is that the individual taxpayer gets the best of both worlds; he is taxed at capital gains rates if there are gains, yet he gets an ordinary loss deduction if there are losses.

Example BA ABC Corporation sells all of its assets. All assets have been held for the required holding period. These assets include certain Section 1231 assets listed below. Depreciation recapture is disregarded in this example.

	Tax Basis	Fair Market Value per Contract	Recognized Gains
Land	$50,000	$60,000	$10,000
Building	140,000	200,000	60,000
Machinery	200,000	250,000	50,000
Net recognized gain			$120,000

Since there is a net gain on Section 1231 items, the taxpayer will treat all gains and losses as if they arose from the sale of a capital asset that had been held for the required holding period.

The benefit afforded by Section 1231 cannot be manipulated through the judicious timing of transactions to produce gains or losses in selected years. Net Section 1231 gain will be treated as ordinary income to the extent that the sum of the net Section 1231 gains and losses for the previous five years is a loss.

B.64 Interplay of Section 1231 with Depreciation Recapture Provisions

The Section 1231 gain on the sale or exchange of real property and depreciable property used in a trade or business is computed by deducting the depreciation recaptured under Section 1245 and 1250 from the total gain. Depreciation recapture is discussed in paragraph B.9.

Example BB   *ABC Corporation sells all of its assets. All assets have been held for the required holding period. These assets include certain Section 1231 assets listed below. Depreciation recapture under Section 1250 relating to the building amounts to $20,000 and depreciation recapture under Section 1245 relating to the machinery amounts to $30,000.*

	Tax Basis	Fair Market Value	Recognized Gains	Depreciation Recapture	Section 1231 Gain
Land	$50,000	$60,000	$10,000		$10,000
Building	140,000	200,000	60,000	$20,000	40,000
Machinery	200,000	250,000	50,000	30,000	20,000
			$120,000	$50,000	$70,000

ABC Corporation will treat the $70,000 gain as if it arose from the sale of a capital asset and will have $50,000 ordinary income under the recapture provisions.

B.65   Federal Tax on Capital Gains and Losses

The first step in determining the tax on the sale of capital assets is to net (a) all long-term capital gains with long-term capital losses and (b) all short-term capital gains with all short-term capital losses. Having done this, the long-term gains or losses are then netted with the short-term gains or losses as shown in Exhibit B–4.

The taxation of the alternatives varies depending on whether the taxpayer is an individual or a corporation. (Note: In the discussion below, the terms net long/short-term gains/losses refer to the column "Alternative Results.")

B.65a   Individuals

All capital gains of individuals are taxed as ordinary income at the rates described above, subject to a maximum federal capital gains tax rate of 28 percent. Generally, this means that in the case of alternatives 1, 2 and 3, all gains are included with a taxpayer's other income and taxed at the regular individual rates. When capital losses exceed capital gains, as in alternatives 4, 5 and 6, the overall losses that may be deducted against ordinary income are limited to $3,000 per year.

Individuals may carry over a net capital loss for an unlimited number of years until the capital loss is used up. Any capital loss carried over retains its characterization as long-term or short-term.

B.65b   Corporations

All capital gains of corporations are taxed as ordinary income at the rates described above. This means that in the case of alternatives 1, 2 and 3, all gains are included with a taxpayer's other income and taxed at the regular rates. When capital losses exceed capital gains, as in alternatives 4, 5 and 6, the corporation may not offset these losses against ordinary income to any extent. The corporation may only carry back the capital loss to each of the three preceding taxable years or carry it forward to any of the five successive years and offset any capital gains in those years. All losses carried backward or forward are treated as short-term losses. If the capital losses are not used in either the carryback or carryforward years, they are lost as deductions.

EXHIBIT B–4
Federal Tax on Capital Gains and Losses

Alternative	Net Long-Term Gain or Loss Alternatives	+	Net Short-Term Gain or Loss Alternatives	=	Alternative Results
1	Any net long-term gain	+	Any net short-term gain	=	Net long-term gain + net short-term gain
2	Larger net long-term gain	+	Smaller net short-term loss	=	Net long-term gain
3	Smaller net long-term loss	+	Larger net short-term gain	=	Net short-term gain
4	Smaller net long-term gain	+	Larger net short-term loss	=	Net short-term loss
5	Any net long-term loss	+	Any net short-term loss	=	Net long-term loss + net short-term loss
6	Larger net long-term loss	+	Smaller net short-term gain	=	Net long-term loss

B.7   DEPRECIATION RULES

Generally, depreciation of assets for U.S. federal income tax purposes is governed by five sets of rules. Which set of rules is appropriate for a particular asset depends on when the asset was placed in service. Exhibit B–5 lists the governing rules and time periods. It should be noted that state income tax rules regarding depreciation can differ substantially from these federal rules.

EXHIBIT B–5
Summary of Federal Income Tax Depreciation Rules

Applicable Rules	Assets Placed in Service
Modified Accelerated Cost Recovery System (MACRS)	1987 and thereafter
Alternative Depreciation System (ADS)	1987 and thereafter
Accelerated Cost Recovery System (ACRS)	1981–1986
Class Life ADR System (CLADR)	1971–1980
Class Life System (CLS)	Prior to 1971

Property is depreciable if it (1) is used in business or held for the production of income, (2) has a determinable life longer than one year, and (3) is something that wears out, decays, becomes obsolete or loses value from natural causes.

Depreciable property may be either tangible or intangible. *Tangible property* is property that can be seen or touched. Generally, all tangible property is depreciable. *Intangible property* is property such as goodwill, a copyright or a franchise. Intangible property can be depreciated only if one can determine its useful life. Examples of depreciable intangible property include patents, copyrights, agreements not to compete, customer lists, subscription lists, franchises, and designs. All depreciable intangible property can only be depreciated using the straight-line method. Examples of nondepreciable intangible property include goodwill, trademarks and trade names.

Depreciable property may be real or personal. *Real property* is land and generally anything that is erected on, growing on, or attached to land. Land is never depreciable. *Personal property* is property that is not real property.

B.71   Modified Accelerated Cost Recovery System

The *Modified Accelerated Cost Recovery System (MACRS)* requires the cost of eligible property be recovered over specified periods using statutory recovery methods. The classification that an asset falls into determines which recovery period and method to use. MACRS applies to all tangible property placed in service after December 31, 1987.

A taxpayer may irrevocably elect to use the *Alternative Depreciation System (ADS)* which provides for straight-line depreciation over the regular recovery period for an asset, or *Alternative MACRS*, instead of MACRS. Taxpayers must use Alternative MACRS, which provides for reduced MACRS deductions, for tangible property used outside the U.S., tax-exempt use property and miscellaneous other assets. An election to use ADS or Alternative MACRS can be made on a class by class basis for all property placed in service in a given year.

B.71a   MACRS Property Classes
Each item of property depreciated under MACRS is assigned to one of eight property classes. The class to which property is assigned is determined by its class life. Class lives for most assets are listed in a table in IRS Publication 534. The eight property classes are:

- *3-year property:* Property with a class life of four years or less. It includes over-the-road tractors and special tools such as jigs, dies, molds, and patterns used in selected industries.
- *5-year property:* Property with a class life of 4 to 10 years. It includes office machinery, computers, cars and trucks, and property used in connection with research and experimentation.
- *7-year property:* Property with a class life of 10 to 16 years. It includes office furniture and fixtures.
- *10-year property:* Property with a class life of 16 to 20 years. It includes vessels, barges and tugs, and any single purpose agricultural structure.

- *15-year property:* Property with a class life of 20 to 25 years. It includes roads, shrubbery, municipal wastewater treatment plants and telecommunications facilities.
- *20-year property:* Property with a class life of 25 years or more, other than Section 1250 real property with a class life of 27.5 years or more. It includes municipal sewers and farm buildings.
- *27.5-year residential real property:* Includes any structure where 80 percent or more of the gross rental income is rental income from dwelling units. It also includes manufactured homes that are residential rental property and elevators and escalators.
- *31.5-year nonresidential real property:* Includes any Section 1250 real property that is not residential real property and has a class life of more than 27.5 years. It includes elevators and escalators.

B.71b   Amount of Depreciation Deduction

The amount of the depreciation deduction for any year is determined by multiplying the tax basis of the asset by the applicable percentage in Exhibits B–6, B–7 or B–8.

A number of averaging conventions are used in MACRS. A *mid-month convention* applies to 27.5-year residential real property and 31.5-year nonresidential real property. This convention assumes that property is placed in service, or disposed of, in the middle of the month. A *half-year convention* applies to all other property classes. This convention assumes that property is placed in service in the middle of the year. However, the half-year convention cannot be used if more than 40 percent of the property placed in service for the year is put in service during the last three months of the year. If this is the case, a *mid-quarter convention* must be used. This convention assumes that all property placed in service during a quarter is placed in service at the midpoint of the quarter.

EXHIBIT B–6
MACRS Depreciation Rates by Year by Class of Property*

Recovery Year	Class of Property					
	3-Year	5-Year	7-Year	10-Year	15-Year	20-Year
1	33.33%	20.00%	14.29%	10.00%	5.00%	3.75%
2	44.45	32.00	24.49	18.00	9.50	7.22
3	14.81	19.20	17.49	14.40	8.55	6.68
4	7.41	11.52	12.49	11.52	7.70	6.18
5		11.52	8.93	9.22	6.93	5.71
6		5.76	8.92	7.37	6.23	5.29
7			8.93	6.55	5.90	4.89
8			4.46	6.55	5.90	4.52
9				6.56	5.91	4.46
10				6.55	5.90	4.46
11				3.28	5.91	4.46
12					5.90	4.46
13					5.91	4.46
14					5.90	4.46
15					5.91	4.46
16					2.95	4.46
17						4.46
18						4.46
19						4.46
20						4.46
21						2.23

* Depreciation rates based on half-year convention.

EXHIBIT B–7
MACRS Depreciation Rates by Year for 27.5-Year Residential Property*

Recovery Year	Month of Year that Asset is Placed in Service				
	1	3	6	9	12
1	3.485%	2.879%	1.970%	1.061%	0.152%
2	3.636	3.636	3.636	3.636	3.636
3	3.636	3.636	3.636	3.636	3.636
4	3.636	3.636	3.636	3.636	3.636
5	3.636	3.636	3.636	3.636	3.636
6	3.636	3.636	3.636	3.636	3.636
7	3.636	3.636	3.636	3.636	3.636
8	3.636	3.636	3.636	3.636	3.636
9	3.636	3.636	3.636	3.636	3.636
10	3.637	3.637	3.637	3.636	3.636
11	3.636	3.636	3.636	3.637	3.637
12	3.637	3.637	3.637	3.636	3.636
13	3.636	3.636	3.636	3.637	3.637
14	3.637	3.637	3.637	3.636	3.636
15	3.636	3.636	3.636	3.637	3.637
16	3.637	3.637	3.637	3.636	3.636
17	3.636	3.636	3.636	3.637	3.637
18	3.637	3.637	3.637	3.636	3.636
19	3.636	3.636	3.636	3.637	3.637
20	3.637	3.637	3.637	3.636	3.636
21	3.636	3.636	3.636	3.637	3.637
22	3.637	3.637	3.637	3.636	3.636
23	3.636	3.636	3.636	3.637	3.637
24	3.637	3.637	3.637	3.636	3.636
25	3.636	3.636	3.636	3.637	3.637
26	3.637	3.637	3.637	3.636	3.636
27	3.636	3.636	3.636	3.637	3.637
28	1.970	2.576	3.485	3.636	3.636
29				0.758	1.667

* Depreciation rates based on mid-month convention.

EXHIBIT B–8
MACRS Depreciation Rates by Year for 31.5-Year
Nonresidential Property*

Recovery Year	Month of Year that Asset is Placed in Service				
	1	3	6	9	12
1	3.042%	2.513%	1.720%	0.926%	0.132%
2	3.175	3.175	3.175	3.175	3.175
3	3.175	3.175	3.175	3.175	3.175
4	3.175	3.175	3.175	3.175	3.175
5	3.175	3.175	3.175	3.175	3.175
6	3.175	3.175	3.175	3.175	3.175
7	3.175	3.175	3.175	3.175	3.175
8	3.175	3.175	3.174	3.175	3.175
9	3.174	3.174	3.175	3.174	3.175
10	3.175	3.175	3.174	3.175	3.174
11	3.174	3.174	3.175	3.174	3.175
12	3.175	3.175	3.174	3.175	3.174
13	3.174	3.174	3.175	3.174	3.175
14	3.175	3.175	3.174	3.175	3.174
15	3.174	3.174	3.175	3.174	3.175
16	3.175	3.175	3.174	3.175	3.174
17	3.174	3.174	3.175	3.174	3.175
18	3.175	3.175	3.174	3.175	3.174
19	3.174	3.174	3.175	3.174	3.175
20	3.175	3.175	3.174	3.175	3.174
21	3.174	3.174	3.175	3.174	3.175
22	3.175	3.175	3.174	3.175	3.174
23	3.174	3.174	3.175	3.174	3.175
24	3.175	3.175	3.174	3.175	3.174
25	3.174	3.174	3.175	3.174	3.175
26	3.175	3.175	3.174	3.175	3.174
27	3.174	3.174	3.175	3.174	3.175
28	3.175	3.175	3.174	3.175	3.174
29	3.174	3.174	3.175	3.174	3.175
30	3.175	3.175	3.174	3.175	3.174
31	3.174	3.174	3.175	3.174	3.175
32	1.720	2.249	3.042	3.175	3.174
33				0.661	1.455

* Depreciation rates based on mid-month convention.

B.72   Alternative Depreciation System

The *Alternative Depreciation System (ADS)* is an alternate depreciation system that a taxpayer can elect on a property-by-property basis, at the time an asset is placed in service. It provides for depreciation rates and recovery periods that are slower and longer than MACRS. ADS uses the straight-line method of depreciation. Personal property is depreciated using this method over the applicable class life of the property. Real property is depreciated over a 40-year recovery period. See Exhibits B–9 and B–10.

EXHIBIT B–9
ADS Depreciation Rates by Year for Personal Property

| Recovery Year | Applicable Class Life | | | | | |
	3-Year	5-Year	7-Year	10-Year	15-Year	20-Year
1	16.67%	10.00%	7.14%	5.00%	3.33%	2.50%
2	33.33	20.00	14.29	10.00	6.67	5.00
3	33.33	20.00	14.29	10.00	6.67	5.00
4	16.67	20.00	14.29	10.00	6.67	5.00
5		20.00	14.29	10.00	6.67	5.00
6		10.00	14.29	10.00	6.67	5.00
7			14.29	10.00	6.67	5.00
8			7.14	10.00	6.67	5.00
9				10.00	6.67	5.00
10				10.00	6.67	5.00
11				5.00	6.67	5.00
12					6.67	5.00
13					6.67	5.00
14					6.67	5.00
15					6.67	5.00
16					3.33	5.00
17						5.00
18						5.00
19						5.00
20						5.00
21						2.50

Notes: See IRS Publication 534 for depreciation rates for other class lives; assumes half-year convention.

EXHIBIT B–10
ADS Depreciation Rates by Year for Real Property

Month in the First Recovery Year the Property Is Placed in Service	If the Recovery Year Is:		
	Year 1	Years 2 to 40	Year 41
1	2.396%	2.500%	0.104%
2	2.188	2.500	0.312
3	1.979	2.500	0.521
4	1.771	2.500	0.729
5	1.563	2.500	0.937
6	1.354	2.500	1.146
7	1.146	2.500	1.354
8	0.938	2.500	1.562
9	0.729	2.500	1.771
10	0.521	2.500	1.979
11	0.313	2.500	2.187
12	0.104	2.500	2.396

B.73   Accelerated Cost Recovery System

ACRS was enacted in 1981 and represented a significant departure from prior depreciation systems. ACRS applies to all recovery property that was placed in service between 1981 and 1986. *Recovery property* is defined as tangible property of a character subject to the allowance for depreciation that is used in a trade or business, or is held for the production of income. Practically speaking, this definition covers most assets with the major exceptions being intangible assets, land, and assets subject to depletion allowances.

B.73a   Classes of Recovery Property

Each item of recovery property is assigned to one of seven classes.

- *3-year property:* Personal property and other tangible property (not including a building or its structural components) used as an integral part of manufacturing, production, extraction or the furnishing of utility-like services that has a present class life of four years or less or is used in connection with research and experimentation. This class of property includes automobiles, trucks and certain other assets.

- *5-year property:* All personal property and other tangible property (not including a building or its structural components) used as an integral part of manufacturing, production, extraction or the furnishing of utility-like services that are not included in the 3-year class. This class includes most machinery and equipment and single purpose agricultural and storage structures.

- *10-year property:* This class includes certain public utility property, real property with a present class life of 12.5 years or less, theme and amusement park structures, railroad tank cars, and miscellaneous other items.

- *15-year public utility property:* This class includes all public utility property other than real property, 3-year property, and public utility property included in the 10-year property class. It includes electric, gas, water, and telephone utility plants.

- *15-year real property:* This class includes all real property not included in another class (e.g., buildings, components, and improvements) that was placed in service prior to March 15, 1984. After that date it only includes low income housing realty.

- *18-year real property:* This class includes all real property not included in another class (e.g., buildings, components, and improvements) that was placed in service after March 15, 1984, and before May 9, 1985.

- *19-year real property:* This class includes all real property not included in another class (e.g., buildings, components, and improvements) that was placed in service after May 8, 1985, and before 1987.

B.73b   Amount of Depreciation Deduction

The amount of the depreciation deduction for any year is determined by multiplying the tax basis of the asset by the applicable percentage in Exhibit B–11.

B.73c   Straight-Line Election

A taxpayer could have elected to recover costs by using a straight-line method over the regular recovery period or a longer period. The election generally would have applied to all property in a class. However, for 15-year real property the straight-line election could have been made on a property by property basis.

EXHIBIT B–11
ACRS Depreciation Rates by Year by Class of Property

Recovery Year	Class of Property						
	3-Year	5-Year	10-Year	15-Year Real Property*	15-Year Public Utility	18-Year*	19-Year*
1	25%	15%	8%	12%	5%	10%	8.8%
2	38	22	14	10	10	9	8.4
3	37	21	12	9	9	8	7.6
4		21	10	8	8	7	6.9
5		21	10	7	7	6	6.3
6			10	6	7	6	5.7
7			9	6	6	5	5.2
8			9	6	6	5	4.7
9			9	6	6	5	4.2
10			9	5	6	5	4.2
11				5	6	5	4.2
12				5	6	5	4.2
13				5	6	4	4.2
14				5	6	4	4.2
15				5	6	4	4.2
16						4	4.2
17						4	4.2
18						4	4.2
19							4.2
20							0.2

* Assumes property placed in service January 1.

B.74   Class Life Asset Depreciation Range System

The *Class Life Asset Depreciation Range (CLADR)* System is used for all tangible personal property placed in service after 1970 but before 1981. Under this system, if salvage value is 10 percent or less of original cost, an election could be made to ignore salvage value in calculating depreciation.

B.74a   Classifying Assets
The CLADR System provides for separate classes for most types of assets. Each class has a stated useful life and possibly a range of useful lives that are used in calculating depreciation deductions for assets in that class. When a class has a range of useful lives, a taxpayer can select any useful life within the range.

B.74b   Permissible Methods

The specifically authorized depreciation methods included (a) straight-line, (b) sum-of-the-years' digits, or (c) any acceptable double-declining balance method. However, any reasonable method of computing depreciation is permissible, as long as it is consistently applied.

- *Straight-Line Method:* Depreciation is calculated by reducing the basis by the salvage value and dividing the remainder by the useful life.

  Example BC   *Tangible personal property costs $5,000, has a five-year useful life and $100 salvage value, which is ignored since it is under 10 percent of cost. Annual depreciation under the straight-line method would be ($5,000/5) = $1,000.*

- *Sum-of-the-years'-digits method:* To calculate depreciation under this method, the years of an asset's useful life must first be totaled (hereafter called sum-of-the-years'-digits). The deduction is figured by multiplying the asset's basis (less salvage value if it exceeds 10 percent of cost) by a fraction; the numerator is the remaining useful life at the beginning of the year, and the denominator is the sum-of-the-years'-digits. This method could only be used for new tangible assets with a useful life of three years or more.

  Example BD   *Assume the same facts as Example BC except that the sum-of-the-years'-digits method is used.*

		Depreciation Deduction
1st year	$5,000 × 5/15	$1,667
2nd year	$5,000 × 4/15	1,333
3rd year	$5,000 × 3/15	1,000
4th year	$5,000 × 2/15	667
5th year	$5,000 × 1/15	333
		$5,000

- *Declining-balance method:* Depreciation is calculated by multiplying the asset's tax basis, reduced by all previously deducted depreciation, by the appropriate declining-balance rate. The declining-balance rates are all expressed as a percentage of straight-line rates. The maximum declining-balance rates that could be used are:

Type of Property	Maximum Declining-Balance Rate
New tangible personal property	200%
Used tangible personal property	150
Real property	150

Example BE   *Same facts as Example BD except that the 200 percent declining-balance method is used. The annual straight-line depreciation rate would be 20 percent; therefore the 200 percent declining-balance method rate is 40 percent.*

Year	Remaining Basis	Declining-Balance Rate	Depreciation Allowed
1	$5,000	40%	$2,000
2	3,000	40	1,200
3	1,800	40	720
4	1,080	40	432
5	648	40	259
	Total		$4,611

This method does not completely depreciate the asset over its useful life. Therefore, to maximize depreciation deductions, companies change method to straight-line depreciation at the point where the straight-line method yields a larger deduction than the declining-balance method.

B.75   Class Life System

An elective *Class Life System (CLS)* was provided for calculating depreciation deductions in 1971 and later years on assets placed in service before 1971. Generally, this system operated in the same manner as the CLADR System except that under CLS there were no ranges within each class of assets. Therefore, an asset falling within a particular class was depreciated based on a singular useful life, technically known as the asset guideline period, for that class.

B.8   DEPRECIATION RECAPTURE

The federal income tax depreciation recapture provisions were enacted to tax as ordinary income, rather than capital gains, all or a portion of the gain on the sale of certain property. State income tax depreciation recapture rules can differ substantially from the federal income tax rules.

Property subject to depreciation recapture is either Section 1245 or Section 1250 property.

B.81   Section 1245 Property

Section 1245 Property is either personal property or other tangible property (not including a building or its structural components) used as an integral part of (a) manufacturing, (b) production, (c) extraction, or (d) the furnishing of transportation, communications, electrical energy, gas, water or sewage disposal services. Other tangible property includes research facilities, bulk storage facilities associated with (a)–(d) above, and miscellaneous other property.

Gain on the sale of Section 1245 property is taxed as ordinary income to the extent of all depreciation and amortization deductions claimed.

B.82 Section 1250 Property

Section 1250 Property is all depreciable real property that is not subject to the Section 1245 recapture provision.

All gain on the sale of Section 1250 property is taxed as ordinary income to the extent of the excess of the post-1969 depreciation allowances over the depreciation that would have been available if the straight-line method had been used. All depreciation on Section 1250 property disposed of within one year of being placed in service will be recaptured. In addition, for corporations, the amount treated as ordinary income is increased by 20 percent of the additional amount that would be treated as ordinary income if the property were subject to the Section 1245 recapture rules.

B.9 GENERAL BUSINESS AND INVESTMENT TAX CREDITS

The General Business Credit is the sum of five components: (1) Investment Tax Credit—includes investment, business energy and rehabilitation tax credits; (2) Targeted Jobs Tax Credit; (3) Alcohol Fuels Credit; (4) Increased Research Credit; (5) Low-Income Housing Credit. The General Business Credit in any year cannot exceed net income tax minus the greater of: (a) the tentative minimum tax, or (b) 25 percent of the net regular tax liability above $25,000.

B.10 ALTERNATIVE MINIMUM TAX

Congress enacted the *Alternative Minimum Tax (AMT)* so that no taxpayer with substantial economic income could avoid significant tax liability. The AMT is an independent tax system, separate from the system used to compute a taxpayer's regular tax liability. However, the AMT is not an alternative to the regular tax. Taxpayers pay their regular tax, and if they have an AMT liability, this amount is added to the regular tax.

B.101 Calculation of AMT

AMT equals the excess, if any, of the *Tentative Minimum Tax (TMT)* over the regular tax. The TMT is 20 percent (24 percent in the case of an individual) of the taxpayer's *Alternative Minimum Taxable Income (AMTI)* over an exemption amount, reduced by the *AMT Foreign Tax Credit (AMT FTC)*. AMTI is equal to the taxpayer's taxable income adjusted for various items, including AMT depreciation, the *Adjusted Current Earnings Income (ACE Income)* adjustment, the *AMT Net Operating Loss (AMT NOL)* adjustment and certain other adjustments and tax preference items. Once the AMT liability has been calculated, the taxpayer can calculate the *Minimum Tax Credit (MTC)* that can be used to offset future regular tax liability. A corporate taxpayer's AMT is calculated as set forth in Exhibit B–12.

EXHIBIT B–12
Calculation of Corporate Alternative Minimum Tax

Regular taxable income			$XXX
AMT depreciation adjustment			+
Other AMT adjustments (other than ACE and AMT NOL)			+
Regular tax NOL deduction			+
AMT corporate tax preferences			+
Preadjustment AMTI			$XXX
ACE Income adjustment			
Preadjustment AMTI	$XXX		
Depreciation adjustment	+		
Intangible drilling costs	+		
Other	+		
ACE		$XXX	
Less: Preadjustment AMTI		–	
Subtotal		$XXX	
ACE adjustment multiplier—75%		75%	
ACE adjustment			+/– $XXX
Subtotal			$XXX
AMT NOL (90% limitation)			–
AMTI			$XXX
AMT exemption			–
Subtotal			$XXX
Precredit TMT (20% corporate rate × subtotal)			$XXX
AMT FTC (subject to 90% limitation)			–
Postcredit TMT			$XXX
Regular tax			–
AMT			$XXX

B.102 AMT Adjustments and Preference Items

- *AMT depreciation adjustment:* AMT adjustments such as depreciation can either increase or decrease AMT income. Generally, AMT depreciation is less than regular tax depreciation. However, it can exceed regular tax depreciation over time. In this circumstance, the AMT depreciation adjustment is negative.

  The AMT depreciation rules require slower depreciation of personal and real property than the regular tax depreciation system, MACRS. AMT depreciation is usually the same as ADS depreciation. However, personal property is depreciated using the 150 percent declining-balance method with a switch to straight-line depreciation when that system produces a larger deduction. The recovery period for personal property under AMT depreciation is the applicable asset class life while the recovery period for real property is 40 years. The mid-month, mid-quarter and mid-year conventions that apply for regular tax purposes also apply for AMT purposes.

  The AMT depreciation rates for personal property, assuming the mid-year convention, appear in Exhibit B–13. The AMT depreciation rates for real property, assuming a mid-month convention, appear in Exhibit B–10.

- *Other AMT Adjustments (Other than ACE and AMT NOL):* These include adjustments for mining exploration and development costs, long-term contracts, certain installment sales, basis adjustments on the disposition of certain property and miscellaneous other items.

EXHIBIT B–13
AMT Depreciation Rates by Year for Personal Property

Recovery Year	Applicable Class Life					
	3-Year	5-Year	7-Year	10-Year	15-Year	20-Year
1	25.00%	15.00%	10.71%	7.50%	5.00%	3.750%
2	37.50	25.50	19.13	13.88	9.50	7.219
3	25.00	17.85	15.03	11.79	8.55	6.677
4	12.50	16.66	12.25	10.02	7.70	6.177
5		16.66	12.25	8.74	6.93	5.713
6		8.33	12.25	8.74	6.23	5.285
7			12.25	8.74	5.90	4.888
8			6.13	8.74	5.91	4.522
9				8.74	5.90	4.462
10				8.74	5.91	4.461
11				4.37	5.90	4.462
12					5.91	4.461
13					5.90	4.462
14					5.91	4.461
15					5.90	4.462
16					2.95	4.461
17						4.462
18						4.461
19						4.462
20						4.461
21						2.231

Notes: See IRS Publication 534 for depreciation rates for other class lives; assumes half-year convention.

- *Regular Tax NOL Deduction:* The regular tax NOL deduction must be added back to taxable income for AMT purposes.
- *AMT Corporate Tax Preferences:* These include depletion, intangible drilling costs, reserves for losses on bad debts of financial institutions and miscellaneous other items.
- *ACE Income Adjustment:* Generally, the ACE Income Adjustment will result in the largest adjustment to taxable income. This adjustment is the successor to the book income adjustment, enacted by Congress in 1986. The book income adjustment's purpose was to tax corporations that reported book income for financial reporting purposes but little, if any, regular taxable income. The ACE income adjustment is based on tax concepts, whereas its predecessor was primarily based on financial accounting concepts of book income. ACE represents a third tax system that is independent from the regular and AMT tax systems.

    The ACE adjustment is calculated by starting with AMTI and making certain adjustments. These include another depreciation adjustment, certain adjustments related to earnings and profits, adjustments for intangible drilling costs, LIFO inventory and installment sales. For the majority of manufacturing companies, the most important adjustment is the depreciation adjustment.

    ACE depreciation, for property placed in service after 1989, is relatively straightforward. The ADS System is utilized. ADS, as previously described, requires the application of the straight-line method and the applicable convention to the adjusted basis of an asset. See Exhibits B–9 and B–10. The rules are more complicated for assets placed in service before 1990.

    Once the ACE adjustment has been calculated, a corporate

taxpayer must increase or decrease AMTI by 75 percent of the difference between ACE and preadjustment AMTI. However, the ACE adjustment cannot decrease preadjustment AMTI in any year by more than the amount that it increased AMTI in prior years.

Consolidated groups must calculate their ACE and preadjustment AMTI on a consolidated basis instead of on a separate-company basis.

- *AMT NOL:* Since the AMT is a separate tax system, it requires the calculation of a separate NOL. Generally, the AMT NOL is calculated in the same manner as the regular NOL. However, it takes into account the AMT adjustments and preferences.

A taxpayer cannot reduce its AMT income by more than 90 percent using an NOL. An AMT NOL can be carried back 3 years and forward 15 years—the same as the regular NOL.

B.103   AMT Exemption Amount

Corporate taxpayers enjoy a $40,000 exemption, which reduces AMTI. However, this exemption is phased out as AMTI increases from $150,000 to $310,000. We ignore the exemption amount in this book.

B.104   AMT Foreign Tax Credit

Taxpayers are permitted to use their AMT FTC to reduce their AMTI. The calculation of the AMT FTC is extremely complex and beyond the scope of this book.

B.105 Minimum Tax Credit

The MTC rules are designed to prevent a taxpayer from being taxed twice on the same income. It permits a taxpayer to recover AMT paid that merely reflected deferral of tax liability (e.g., accelerated depreciation).

The MTC is equal to the amount of AMT paid in a given year, plus AMT paid in prior years. It can be used to offset regular tax liability, but only to the point where the taxpayer's regular tax after reduction for MTC equals the tentative minimum tax. MTCs can be carried forward indefinitely. However, carryback is not permitted.

B.11 ESTIMATED TAX PAYMENTS

Generally, a corporation must pay 90 percent of its estimated tax quarterly. The four payments are due on the 15th day of the 4th, 6th, 9th and 12th months of the corporation's tax year. In addition, the remaining 10 percent of the corporation's tax is due by the 15th day of the third month after the end of the corporation's fiscal year. An alternate seasonal method of computing tax payments is available in certain instances.

Corporations must constantly recalculate their payments, given that estimates of tax liability change during the year. The recalculation is made by subtracting the payments made to date from the estimated tax liability for the year and dividing the resulting sum by the number of quarterly payments remaining to be made.

A corporation must pay a penalty tax if it underpays its estimated tax liability by more than 10 percent. The penalty tax is based on the prime rate and is adjusted semiannually. One of the exceptions is that no penalty tax will be imposed if payments made equal the tax paid for the preceding year. However, this exception is not available for corporations with taxable income of at least $1 million in any one of the three preceding years.

B.12 NET OPERATING LOSSES

A *Net Operating Loss (NOL)* is the excess of allowable deductions over gross income. As a general rule, an NOL may be carried back three years and deducted against prior income. A corporation with an NOL (an "NOL corporation") may elect to forgo this carryback period. An NOL may also be carried forward 15 years and deducted against future years' income.

Companies that have NOLs are potentially attractive acquisition targets, even if the NOL corporation does not have a viable business, because the target's NOLs might be used to offset another operation's taxable income. Current tax law does not restrict the use of an NOL where the equity ownership of the NOL corporation does not change by more that 50 percent over a three-year period. Thus, it is attractive for acquirers seeking NOLs to purchase a minority equity stake in an NOL company over a three-year period.

If ownership of a loss corporation does change significantly, the tax rules require that there be an annual limitation on the use of the NOL. This limitation is equal to the product of the value of the loss corporation's equity at the time of the ownership change multiplied by the federal long-term tax-exempt rate, a published rate.

The NOL tax rules do not place any limitations on the ability of a loss corporation to purchase a profitable business and offset its NOL against the income from the acquired business.

B.121 Ownership Change

An ownership change occurs if, as a result of an "owner shift involving a 5 percent shareholder" or an "equity structure shift," the percentage of stock (based on value) owned by one or more 5 percent shareholders increases by more than 50 percentage points over the lowest percentage of stock owned by such shareholders at any time during a three-year testing period. It should be noted that an "equity structure shift" will invariably involve an "owner shift involving a 5 percent shareholder."

A *5 percent shareholder* is one who owns at least 5 percent of the stock of the corporation. All less-than-5 percent shareholders are aggregated and treated generally as one 5 percent shareholder. Stock sales by less-than-5 percent shareholders do not generally give rise to an ownership change.

Examples of ownership changes include:

- A purchase or sale of loss corporation stock by someone who either before or after the transaction is a 5 percent shareholder.
- An issuance of stock by the loss corporation that affects the percentage of stock ownership of one or more 5 percent shareholders.
- A redemption of loss corporation stock that affects the percentage of stock ownership of one or more 5 percent shareholders.
- A loss corporation merges into a profitable corporation and the loss corporation's shareholders receive less than 50 percent of the entity's stock.

- A publicly held corporation with no shareholders owning 5 percent of the company sells more than 50 percent of the company in a secondary stock offering.

In determining whether an ownership change has occurred, the constructive ownership rules are applied, albeit with several exceptions. The most noteworthy exception provides that stock owned by a corporation is attributed to all of its shareholders in proportion to their interests in the corporation. Also, transfers resulting from gifts, death, divorce or separation are disregarded in determining whether an ownership change has occurred.

Stock, for purposes of calculating an ownership change, includes all common or preferred stock except stock that would not be treated as such under the consolidated return rules (e.g., nonvoting, nonconvertible, nonparticipating preferred stock).

The testing period is generally the three-year period ending on the day of any owner shift or any equity structure shift. In the case of multiple ownership changes over a period of time, the testing period applicable to the second ownership change does not begin before the day after the first ownership change.

Example BF   *On September 30, 1989, ABC Corporation is owned equally by five shareholders: A, B, C, D and E. On that date Z purchases A's and B's stock. On December 1, 1989, E purchases C's stock in an unrelated transaction. There is an ownership change on December 1, 1989, because on that date there has been a total increase of 60 percentage points in ownership. Z's percentage interest exceeds his lowest interest in ABC Corporation during the preceding three years by 40 percent and E's percentage interest exceeds by 20 percent his lowest interest in ABC Corporation during the testing period.*

B.122   Effect of Ownership Change

Upon an ownership change, two provisions limit the loss corporation's NOL carryforwards. First, if a continuity of business test is not satisfied, all carryforwards will be disallowed. Second, if the continuity of business requirement is satisfied, an absorption limitation will limit the rate at which the NOL may be used.

B.123   Continuity of Business Test

This test requires that the acquiring corporation either (1) continue the acquired corporation's historic business, or (2) use, in any business, a significant portion of the acquired corporation's business assets. A firm's *historic business* is the business most recently conducted by the acquired corporation. Furthermore, if the acquired corporation has more than one line of business, the acquiring corporation will satisfy the test if it continues a significant line of business. According to IRS regulations, the acquiring corporation can satisfy the continuity test if it continues one of three approximately equal lines of business that were previously conducted by the acquired corporation. Continuity of business must be maintained for at least two years following an ownership change to prevent an NOL from being disallowed.

B.124   Annual Limitation on Carryforwards (Section 382 Limitation)

A corporation that is entitled to a loss carryover after an ownership change is the *new loss corporation*. This definition covers both corporate successors to the loss corporation in a merger or other combination and to the loss corporation itself in a stock acquisition. The *old loss corporation* is the loss corporation prior to the ownership change.

If an ownership change occurs and the business enterprise requirement is met, the new loss corporation's ability to use a "prechange loss" is limited on an annual basis to the product of the value of the stock of the old loss corporation immediately before the ownership change and the *long-term tax-exempt rate*. This amount is known as the *Section 382 Limitation*.

A *prechange loss* includes (1) for the taxable year in which an ownership change occurs, the portion of the loss corporation's NOL that is allocable (determined on a daily pro rata basis, without regard to recognized built-in gains or losses,) to the period in such year before the change date; (2) NOL carryforwards from taxable years prior to the ownership change year; and (3) certain recognized built-in losses and deductions.

If a company has income that can be offset by both a prechange loss and an NOL that is not subject to any limitation, taxable income is first offset by the prechange loss.

B.125   Value of the Loss Corporation

Generally, the value of the loss corporation is the fair market value of the corporation's stock immediately before the ownership change. If a redemption occurs in connection with the ownership change—either before or after the change—the value of the loss corporation is determined after taking the redemption into account. Warrants, options, contracts to acquire stock, convertible debt and similar interests are treated as stock for purposes of determining the value of the loss corporation.

In situations where a parent company has solvent loss subsidiaries, they should be liquidated into the parent company before the parent is acquired, in an effort to increase the NOL limitation by taking into account the parent company's assets.

Generally, the value of the loss corporation must be reduced by all capital contributions made during the two years preceding an ownership change. Furthermore, if a corporation has nonbusiness assets that comprise one-third or more of the corporation's total asset value, then the value of the loss corporation must be reduced by the net excess value of nonbusiness assets. The *net excess value of the nonbusiness assets* is defined as the value of the nonbusiness assets reduced by the indebtedness attributable to such assets.

B.126 Built-In Losses

The rules governing built-in losses were designed to prevent an acquirer from circumventing the NOL rules by purchasing a company with unrealized losses in some or all of its assets and realizing these "built-in" losses after the acquisition is completed.

The limitation on the use of built-in losses does not come into effect unless the corporation has a Net Unrealized Built-in Loss. A *Net Unrealized Built-in Loss* is defined as the amount by which the fair market value of the loss corporation's assets immediately before the ownership change is less than the aggregate adjusted bases of the corporation's assets at that time. Under a de minimis requirement, the Net Unrealized Built-in Loss rules are not applied if the amount of the Net Unrealized Built-in Losses do not exceed 25 percent of the value of the corporation's assets immediately before the ownership change. Cash and marketable securities are generally ignored in making this calculation.

Example BG   ABC Corporation owns two assets: asset X, with a basis of $150 and a value of $0 (a built-in loss asset), and asset Y, with a basis of $0 and a value of $50 (a built-in gain asset). ABC Corporation has a Net Unrealized Built-in Loss of $100 (the excess of the aggregate bases of $150 over the aggregate value of $50).

If a corporation has a Net Unrealized Built-in Loss, any loss that it recognizes on the disposition of any asset during the five-year period following the ownership change is treated as a loss from a prechange period. This rule applies unless the corporation establishes (1) the asset was not held at the time of the ownership change date, or (2) the loss exceeds the amount of the unrealized loss on the asset that was "built-in" on the ownership change date.

B.127   Built-In Gains

The rules governing built-in gains were designed to preserve for an acquirer the full benefit of prechange losses in offsetting gains on the sale of assets where the corporation had a Net Unrealized Built-in Gain as of the ownership change date. A *Net Unrealized Built-in Gain* is defined as the amount by which the value of a corporation's assets exceeds the aggregate basis of such assets immediately before the ownership change.

The rule governing built-in gains does not come into play unless the amount of the Net Unrealized Built-in Gain exceeds 25 percent of the value of the loss corporation's assets.

If the corporation has a Net Unrealized Built-in Gain, the amount of its available loss carryover in any year is increased by the amount of any recognized built-in gains on dispositions of assets during the five-year period following the ownership change. This rule does not apply unless the corporation establishes (1) it owned the asset in question before the ownership change, and (2) the recognized gain on the asset does not exceed the gain on the asset that was built-in on the ownership change date.

B.128   Valuation Requirements

It is important that the loss corporation have its assets valued by a third party as of the ownership change date because the burden of proof is on the loss corporation to support valuations of assets that are disposed of within five years where there are built-in gains or losses.

B.129   Bankruptcy Rules

Generally, NOLs are not limited after bankruptcy if the corporation's shareholders and "qualified" creditors obtain at least 50 percent of the bankrupt's stock as ordered by the court. A qualified creditor is one who held a claim for at least 18 months before the bankruptcy filing or acquired the claim in the ordinary course of business. It should be noted that this rule does not apply in informal "workout" situations.

Net operating losses are reduced in these circumstances by the interest deducted by the loss corporation during the period beginning with the first day of the third tax year before the change year and ending on the date such change occurs.

If a second ownership change takes place within two years of bankruptcy, all NOLs arising before the first ownership change will be eliminated.

B.1210 Consolidated Return Regulations

The regulations provide that when an acquired corporation becomes a member of an affiliated group, the acquired corporation's preacquisition NOL carryforward is subject to the *Separate Return Limitation Year (SRLY)* rules. SRLY rules allow a consolidated group to deduct the preconsolidation losses of the acquired company only against the acquired corporation's postconsolidation income. Furthermore, these rules provide that "built-in" losses may be deducted only against the acquired corporation's postacquisition income.

The *Consolidated Return Change of Ownership (CRCO)* rules require that NOL carryforwards of the consolidated group that arise before a change of ownership may be used only against taxable income of the preacquisition members of the group.

B.13 LIMITATIONS ON CARRYFORWARDS

The limitations on the use of unused business credits and capital loss carryforwards are similar to the limitations on the use of NOLs. If there is an ownership change, any preacquisition capital loss used in a postacquisition year will reduce the Section 382 limitation for that year. Furthermore, unused credits can be used in a postacquisition year only to the extent that the company's Section 382 limitation has not been used up following application of the company's capital loss, NOL and foreign tax credit carryforwards.

B.14 STATE AND LOCAL TAXES

State and local taxes are an important consideration in most acquisition transactions. However, many acquirers assume that if they have worked out the federal tax problems in a deal, the state and local tax issues will take care of themselves. Nothing could be further from the truth. There are a number of problems to focus on:

- Differences between federal and state definitions of taxable income. For example, a number of states do not allow MACRS depreciation.
- The effect that the transaction will have on state apportionment factors. Will the deal result in higher apportionment factors to high tax rate states?
- The extent to which anticipated internal restructurings after a transaction will give rise to state and local tax liabilities (income taxes, sales and use taxes, and property taxes).
- The effect that the acquisition's structure and financing will have on state and local taxable income. For example, if all acquisition debt is kept at a holding company level in a single state, this may materially affect the company's total state and local tax liabilities.
- The effect of the transaction on a corporation's unemployment experience rating. This rating will affect how much the acquiring corporation must pay into the state unemployment fund. This consideration is particularly important in transactions where significant layoffs will occur as part of the deal.
- The effect of the transaction on property tax assessments.

Appendix C

Accounting for an Acquisition

C.0 INTRODUCTION

The accounting treatment for an acquisition should not affect the decision to acquire a target or the purchase price decision. Nevertheless, acquisition accounting is an important consideration in any transaction because the decision maker needs to understand:

1. The impact on the acquiring company's earnings and earnings per share.
2. The effect of the transaction on the balance sheet of the acquiring company.
3. The target's projected separate division or company results.

The impact on the acquiring company's earnings is a very important consideration for the decision maker because the executive's future compensation is often tied to the performance of the total company. The third consideration is important to the executive who will be responsible for bringing in the results. The acquiring company's financing sources will have a substantial interest in all these items as well.

Three accounting methods are prescribed by the accounting profession for acquisitions: the Purchase Method of Accounting, the Pooling of Interests Method and the Insider LBO Method. The purpose of this chapter is to describe these mutually exclusive methods. It should be noted that the asset and liability values recorded for accounting purposes under the alternative methods typically differ from the values recorded for tax purposes. Furthermore, the decision on which method to apply is made without reference to the legal form of the transaction or the tax nature of the contemplated transaction.

C.1   PURCHASE METHOD OF ACCOUNTING

The *Purchase Method of Accounting* requires that the assets and liabilities of the target company be recorded on the books of the acquiring company at their fair market values as of the acquisition date. The reported income of the acquiring company includes the operations of the target company after the date of acquisition based on these recorded values. The Purchase Method is based on the theory that the accounting should follow the economic substance of a bargained transaction.

The two principal questions in Purchase Accounting are: (1) How do we determine the fair value of specific assets and liabilities? (2) Having determined the assets' and liabilities' fair value, how do we allocate the purchase price among the acquired assets and liabilities?

C.11   Valuing Specific Assets and Liabilities

In valuing specific assets and liabilities, the tax basis of the asset or liability is not a factor in determining their fair value, but it does impact the values recorded for accounting purposes. The following techniques are applied in valuing specific items for accounting purposes:

- *Cash:* valued dollar for dollar.
- *Marketable securities:* valued at current net realizable values.
- *Receivables:* valued by discounting, at appropriate current interest rates, the amounts to be received less any necessary bad debt or collection costs.
- *Inventories: Finished goods* and *work in process* inventories are valued at estimated selling prices less the sum of (a) costs to complete, (b) costs of disposal, and (c) a reasonable profit allowance for the completing and selling effort. The concept of a "reasonable profit allowance" is very subjective. Many companies take advantage of this to, in effect, buy earnings. *Raw Material* inventories are valued at current replacement cost.
- *Plant and equipment:* For that portion of plant and equipment to be used by the acquiring company, a value should be recorded equal to the current replacement costs for similar capacity, unless the expected use by the acquirer indicates a lower value. In most instances, this means that an appraised value is used. Current

replacement cost may be determined from either the used asset market or the new asset market, less an estimated amount for depreciation. Plant and equipment that is to be sold should be valued at net realizable value.

- *Intangible assets:* that can be identified (e.g., contracts, patents, customer lists, favorable leases, etc.) should be valued at their appraised values.
- *Other assets:* including land, natural resources, and nonmarketable securities should be valued at appraised values.
- *Goodwill:* is valued as indicated in paragraph C.22.
- *Liabilities:* All liabilities (except income taxes) are to be valued by discounting the amounts to be paid at appropriate current interest rates.

C.12   Accounting for Income Taxes

The following basic principles are applied in accounting for income taxes. These principles are described in a Financial Accounting Standards Board (FASB) 109, Accounting for Income Taxes, which was recently issued.

- A current tax liability or asset is recognized for estimated taxes payable or refundable on tax returns for the current year.
- A deferred tax liability or asset is recognized for the estimated future tax effects attributable to temporary differences and carryforwards using the enacted marginal tax rate. Temporary differences are defined below. *Carryforwards* are deductions or credits that cannot be used in the current year tax return but that may be carried forward to reduce taxable income or taxes payable in future years. Future realization of any deferred tax assets, including carryforwards, depends on the existence of sufficient taxable income of the appropriate character (e.g., ordinary income or capital gain) within an applicable time frame. In the U.S. federal tax jurisdiction, the *marginal tax rate* is the regular tax rate.
- Current and deferred tax liabilities and assets are based on provisions of the enacted tax law; the effects of future changes in tax laws or rates are not anticipated.
- Deferred tax assets are reduced by a *valuation allowance* if, based on the weight of available evidence, it is "more likely than not" that all or a portion of these assets will not be realized. The valuation allowance should reduce the deferred tax assets to an amount that is more likely than not to be realized. "More likely than not" means a level of likelihood that is at least slightly more than 50

percent. This standard requires the recognition of deferred tax assets that are expected to be realized and prohibits recognition where realization is not expected. The standard dictates that forming a conclusion that a valuation allowance is unnecessary when there are cumulative losses in recent years should be extremely difficult.

- Discounting deferred tax assets or liabilities is prohibited.

C.12a Temporary Differences Defined

In a transaction accounted for by the Purchase Method, there are generally differences between the assigned values and the tax bases of the assets and liabilities of the target company. These differences will result in taxable income or deductible amounts in future periods when the reported amounts of the assets and liabilities are recovered and settled, respectively. These differences are called *temporary differences* for accounting purposes. Temporary differences that will result in taxable amounts in future years are *taxable temporary differences* and temporary differences that will result in deductible amounts in future years are referred to as *deductible temporary differences*.

C.12b Accounting for Temporary Differences

Accounting rules now require that an asset or liability should be recognized for the deferred tax consequences associated with temporary differences with only a few exceptions. The major exceptions are that a deferred tax liability or asset should not be recognized for temporary differences associated with (1) goodwill for which amortization is not tax deductible, (2) unallocated negative goodwill, (3) leveraged leases, and (4) certain miscellaneous other items.

It should be noted that a deferred tax liability or asset is recognized for temporary differences associated with the amortization of goodwill in tax jurisdictions where the amortization of goodwill is a proper tax deduction.

C.12c Realization of Tax Assets After the Transaction

If a deferred tax asset is not recognized for the acquired entity's deductible temporary differences or carryforwards at the time of acquisition, any tax benefits for those items recognized later in the financial statements shall be applied first, to reduce to zero any goodwill related to the acquisition; second, to reduce to zero other noncurrent intangible assets related to the acquisition; and third, to reduce income tax expense.

C.12d   Classification of Deferred Taxes

Deferred taxes must be classified into current and noncurrent amounts based on the classification of the related asset or liability for financial reporting. A deferred tax liability or asset that is not related to a particular asset or liability (e.g., carryforwards) must be classified according to the expected reversal date of the temporary difference.

C.12e   Taxable vs. Nontaxable Acquisitions

There is no distinction between taxable and nontaxable acquisitions accounted for using the Purchase Method. In both cases accounting rules require the recognition of deferred tax liabilities and assets (with valuation allowances if required) for the deferred tax consequences of differences between the assigned values and the tax bases of the assets and liabilities. In a nontaxable transaction, such differences will almost always exist and in taxable transactions they may exist.

C.13   General Allocation Rules

The general rules to follow in allocating the purchase price among assets acquired and liabilities assumed are:

1. Assign value to all tangible and identifiable intangible assets based on their fair market values.
2. Assign values to all liabilities assumed based on the present value of those liabilities.
3. If necessary, assign a value to goodwill equal to the difference between the purchase price and the net fair market value of the assets acquired and liabilities assumed.
4. Establish a deferred tax liability or asset for differences between assigned values and the tax bases of assets and liabilities except for (a) the portion of goodwill for which amortization is not deductible (i.e., goodwill amortization in the U.S.), (b) unallocated negative goodwill and (c) miscellaneous other circumstances.
5. If necessary, reduce the values assigned to noncurrent assets by a proportionate share of the difference between the purchase price and the net fair market value of the assets purchased and liabilities assumed. In unusual circumstances where the noncurrent assets have been reduced to zero value and a bargain purchase still remains, then record a deferred credit on the balance sheet. This deferred credit is "negative goodwill."

Example CA ABC Corporation sells all of its assets and liabilities to XYZ Corporation in an Asset Acquisition for $1,700. What values would XYZ Corporation record for accounting purposes?

	Asset and Liability Values on ABC's Books	Assumed Fair Market Values	Values Recorded on XYZ's Books
Accounts receivable	$100	$100	$100
Inventories	300	900	900
Property, plant & equipment	700	1,100	1,100
Accounts payable & accrued expenses	(400)	(400)	(400)
	$700	$1,700	$1,700

When the purchase price exceeds the net fair market value of the assets purchased and liabilities assumed, goodwill is recorded for accounting purposes. *Goodwill* is defined as the excess of the cost of the acquired enterprise over the sum of the amounts assigned to identifiable assets acquired less liabilities assumed. Generally, goodwill arises because of an expectancy of earnings in excess of a normal return on the assets employed in the business. The expectancy of excess returns can come from any number of factors, including location, trade secrets, brand names, reputation, or management skill. Any goodwill recorded must be amortized over its useful life, which cannot exceed 40 years. However, the SEC occasionally requires amortization over a much shorter period. Generally, straight-line amortization is used, although another method may be employed if it is more appropriate.

Example CB Same facts as Example CA except that XYZ Corporation pays $2,000.

	Asset and Liability Values on ABC's Books	Assumed Fair Market Values	Values Recorded on XYZ's Books
Accounts receivable	$100	$100	$100
Inventories	300	900	900
Property, plant & equipment	700	1,100	1,100
Goodwill			300*
Accounts payable & accrued expenses	(400)	(400)	(400)
	$700	$1,700	$2,000

* Purchase price less net fair market values of assets purchased and liabilities assumed ($2,000 − $1,700 = $300).

In cases where there is a *Bargain Purchase* (the purchase price is less than the net fair market value of the assets purchased and liabilities assumed), the values assigned to noncurrent assets (excluding long-term investments) are reduced by the difference between the purchase price and the net fair market value of the assets purchased and liabilities assumed.

Example CC   *Same facts as Example CA except that XYZ Corporation pays $1,500.*

	Asset and Liability Values on ABC's Books	Assumed Fair Market Values	Values Recorded on XYZ's Books	Tax Basis Recorded on XYZ's Books
Accounts receivable	$100	$100	$100	$100
Inventories	300	900	900	810
Property, plant & equipment	700	1,100	900[1]	990
Accounts payable & accrued expenses	(400)	(400)	(400)	(400)
Deferred taxes			0[2]	
	$700	$1,700	$1,500	$1,500

[1] Fair market value of property, plant and equipment less the difference between the net fair market value of the assets purchased and liabilities assumed and the purchase price ($1,100 − ($1,700 − $1,500) = $900).

[2] Deferred tax account is zero due to offsetting debits and credits of $34.2 ($90 difference between book and tax values for both inventory and PP&E × 38% tax rate).

In the situations where the noncurrent assets have been reduced to zero value and a bargain purchase still remains, a deferred credit for the excess of the value of identifiable assets over the cost of the target company should be recorded. This deferred credit is referred to as *negative goodwill*. This deferred credit appears on the balance sheet between long-term debt and stockholders' equity and is amortized into income.

Example CD   *Same facts as Example CA except that XYZ Corporation pays $500.*

	Liability Values on ABC's Books	Asset and Assumed Fair Market Values	Values Recorded on XYZ's Books	Tax Basis Recorded on XYZ's Books
Accounts receivable	$100	$100	$100	$100
Inventories	300	900	900	360
Property, plant & equipment	700	1,100	0	440
Accounts payable & accrued expenses	(400)	(400)	(400)	(400)
Deferred taxes			(38)[1]	
Negative goodwill			(62)[2]	
	$700	$1,700	$500	$500

[1] Deferred taxes are calculated as follows: Inventory ($900 assigned value less − $360 tax basis = $540 × 38% tax rate = $205.2 deferred tax credit). Property, plant and equipment ($0 assigned value − $440 tax basis = $440 × 38% tax rate = $167.2 deferred tax debit).

[2] Amount of bargain purchase after reducing net noncurrent assets (property, plant and equipment) to $0 and recording deferred taxes.

In the four preceding examples we have made two important assumptions: (1) that the cost of the acquisition was known and (2) the fair market values of all assets and liabilities were known. The first assumption is valid if the acquiring company paid cash. But what if other consideration is used to effect the transaction? How is the cost of the acquisition determined in that situation for accounting purposes? The basic rule in such cases is that cost is determined either by the fair value of the consideration given or by the fair value of the property acquired, whichever is more clearly evident.

C.14   Push Down Accounting

Push Down Accounting is the establishment of a new cost basis for the acquired entity's assets and liabilities in the acquired entity's financial statements, based on the amount paid for the acquired entity's securities.

The SEC staff adopted a policy in 1983, published in SEC Staff Accounting Bulletin No. 54, of requiring Push Down Accounting in acquisition transactions that result in an entity becoming substantially wholly owned. Generally, the existence of a significant minority interest or publicly held securities in the acquired entity will eliminate the SEC requirement to apply Push Down Accounting.

Push Down Accounting has not been adopted by the FASB. In addition, it has not been subjected to formal rule-making procedures by the SEC. Hence, it is only applicable for companies that are required to file financial statements with the SEC. However, most national accounting firms encourage its application.

C.15   Allocating Value in "Bust-up" Deals

The *Bust-up* deal is one in which the acquirer purchases a company with more than one line of business and immediately after seeks to sell off business lines. The buyer's objective in executing this strategy is to minimize the purchase price for the business that he ultimately wants to keep. A variation on this theme is a *Total Bust-up*, where the buyer purchases the company and thereafter puts the entire company on the market, albeit in chunks that he believes will be most attractive to potential buyers of the company's various lines.

Accounting standards generally dictate that the businesses that will be sold in a Bust-up deal should not be consolidated with the acquirer's business. The businesses to be sold should be valued at their estimated fair market values and treated as a single line item in the financial statements "net assets held for disposition." In arriving at their fair market values, the cash flows expected while they are held for sale should be taken into account. If it is expected that it will take some time to execute the sales, the estimated proceeds should be discounted.

The deferred tax account should reflect the expected tax liability associated with the divestitures.

C.16   Allocation Period

Typically the fair market values of all the assets and liabilities have not been estimated by the closing date of an acquisition. Accounting rules permit a period of up to one year to identify and quantify the assets acquired and liabilities assumed in an acquisition.

C.17 Preacquisition Contingencies

Occasionally, the target company will have an asset or liability that is hard to value. The most obvious example involves potential legal judgments either for or against the target.

Example CE In 1989 Shamrock Holdings was bidding for Polaroid Corporation. Polaroid had a lower court judgment against Eastman Kodak that was under appeal. The potential outcome of this appeal was uncertain. If Polaroid won the suit on appeal it would reap a windfall that was material to the financial condition of Polaroid. If Shamrock had acquired Polaroid it would have faced the problem of valuing this preacquisition contingency.

The proper accounting for this type of acquired asset or liability is to include it in the allocation of the purchase price if during the allocation period there is adequate information with which to value it. If no such information exists until after the allocation period, the effects of a preacquisition contingency will be included in income in the accounting period in which such effects become known if it is a loss or when realized if the contingency results in a gain.

C.18 Differences between Book and Tax Allocations

The technique for allocating the purchase price for tax purposes for a New Cost Basis Acquisition Method is described in paragraph 7.11a. This technique differs from the approach described above for allocating value to assets and liability accounts using the Purchase Method of Accounting. An obvious result is that the allocations for book and tax purposes do not agree.

The book and tax differences can often be substantial where a New Cost Basis Acquisition Method is used to effect the transaction and the transaction is accounted for using the Purchase Method of Accounting. However, these differences usually pale next to the book and tax differences that result when a No Change in Basis Acquisition Method is used and the deal is accounted for using the Purchase Method. It should be noted that this is the most frequently encountered transaction in today's environment (e.g., Stock Acquisition accounted for using the Purchase Method).

C.19   Financial Statement Disclosure

If the Purchase Method of Accounting is used to record an acquisition, the notes to the financial statements of the acquiring company must describe the target, the date it was acquired, the cost of the acquisition including the types of consideration exchanged, the amount of any goodwill resulting from the transaction, and any contingent payments, options, or commitments associated with the acquisition. Furthermore, the acquiring company must disclose the following results of operations on a pro forma basis: (1) operating results for the current period, assuming the acquisition took place at the beginning of the period; and (2) if comparative financial statements are presented, operating results for the immediately preceding period, assuming the transaction had been effected at the beginning of the period. Pro forma presentation of the results of operations of any other periods is not permitted. The pro forma information disclosed must include revenue, income before extraordinary items, net income and earnings per share.

C.2   INSIDER LBO METHOD OF ACCOUNTING

The *Insider LBO Method of Accounting* requires that NEWCO's investment in OLDCO be accounted for using part fair value and part predecessor basis. It is prescribed in Emerging Issue Task Force Issue No. 88–16: Basis in Leveraged Buyout Transactions (EITF 88–16). The Insider LBO Method of Accounting is only applicable where there has been a change of control in the target company (OLDCO) and shareholders of OLDCO continue to hold a voting equity interest in the holding company (NEWCO), as part of NEWCO's control group, which has been formed for purposes of acquiring OLDCO in a leveraged buyout (LBO).

    If a change of control has occurred, the carrying amount of NEWCO's investment in OLDCO is generally determined as follows: (1) the lesser of the continuing shareholders' residual interest in either OLDCO or NEWCO is carried over at the continuing shareholders' predecessor basis, and (2) the remainder of NEWCO's investment in OLDCO is valued at fair value.

    Numerous complex rules set forth in EITF 88–16 must be examined to determine whether a change of control has occurred, the makeup of NEWCO's control group, the calculation of continuing shareholders' residual interests in both OLDCO and NEWCO, and numerous other technicalities surrounding the application of this accounting approach.

EITF 88–16 should be studied thoroughly if the contemplated transaction is an LBO with existing shareholders of the target becoming shareholders in NEWCO. In addition EITF 90–12, Allocating Basis to Individual Assets and Liabilities for Transactions within the Scope of Issue No. 88–16 should also be reviewed.

C.3   POOLING OF INTERESTS METHOD OF ACCOUNTING

The *Pooling of Interests Method of Accounting* is based on the assumption that certain transactions are merely arrangements between stockholder groups to exchange equity securities. It results in the financials of each of the parties to the transaction being combined, as if they were never separate. The only accounting adjustment to record in these situations is a change in the ownership interests of the stockholders. This is effected by eliminating the capital stock of the target company and recording the new stock issued by the acquiring company to the target company's shareholders. Otherwise, the acquiring company and the target company merely combine assets and liabilities at their historical book values on the acquisition date.

Generally, transactions accounted for using the Pooling of Interests Method are nontaxable transactions. However, they can, in certain instances, be taxable transactions.

C.31   Criteria for Pooling

Twelve specific criteria must be met for a transaction to qualify for Pooling of Interests treatment. If any of the criteria are not met, the transaction must be accounted for using the Purchase Method. The criteria are classified into three categories: (a) attributes of the combining companies, (b) manner of combining the interests, and (c) absence of planned transactions.

C.31a   *Attributes of the Combining Companies*

1. *Autonomy:* Each of the combining companies must be autonomous and must not have been a division or subsidiary of another corporation for two years prior to the initiation of the plan of combination. Generally, a new enterprise meets this requirement unless it is a successor to part or all of an entity that does not meet the requirement. A division or subsidiary can be exempted from this requirement if it was divested as a result of a judicial or governmental order.

2. *Independence:* The combining entities must be independent of the other combining entities. This means that a combining entity can hold no more than 10 percent of the outstanding voting common stock of another combining entity.

C.31b   Manner of Combining the Interests

1. *Single transaction:* The combination must be accomplished within one year according to a specific plan or by a single transaction. A plan of combination is initiated on the earlier of (a) the date that the major terms of a plan, including the exchange ratio, are announced publicly or otherwise formally communicated to the shareholders of one of the combining companies or (b) the date that shareholders of a combining company are notified in writing of an exchange offer. A delay beyond one year in completing the transaction generally precludes pooling treatment, unless the delay is caused by a governmental authority or litigation.

2. *Exchange of shares:* The surviving corporation must issue only common stock with rights identical to those of the majority of its outstanding voting common stock, in exchange for substantially all of the voting common stock of the other combining entities at the date the plan of combination is consummated. A class of stock that has voting control is the majority class for purposes of this requirement. Furthermore, "substantially all of the voting common stock" means 90 percent or more. The "substantially all" requirement enables the issuing company to acquire 10 percent or less for cash or other consideration.

Generally, debt or equity securities that are essentially the same as voting common (e.g., convertible debt, stock options or warrants) must be exchanged for only voting common stock.

A transaction may still be accounted for as a pooling of interests, where a combining company does not have a controlling class of common stock because of the existence of one or more classes of voting preferred stock, if the issuing company exchanges its common stock for substantially all of the voting common and preferred stock of the combining company.

If the issuing company does not have a controlling class of common stock because of the existence of one or more classes of preferred stock, then pooling of interests treatment is precluded unless the issuing company issues common stock in exchange for sufficient shares of its outstanding voting preferred stock such that its common stock obtains voting control prior to the date of combination.

3. *No change in equity interests:* None of the combining entities may change the equity interest of the voting common stock through exchanges, retirements, issuances, or distributions in contemplation of effecting the combination. This requirement applies to the two-year period before the plan of combination is initiated and between the initiation and consummation dates.

4. *Treasury stock transactions:* Any of the combining entities may reacquire shares of voting common stock, but only if the purpose is unrelated to the business combination. Shares purchased during the two years preceding the transaction are presumed tainted and will preclude pooling treatment. Furthermore, after the plan of combination is initiated, only a normal number of shares may be so reacquired.

5. *Ratio of shareholder interest:* Each individual common shareholder who exchanges stock must receive a voting common stock interest exactly in proportion to its relative voting common stock interest before the transaction. This requirement precludes the payment of a premium to a control group of shareholders.

6. *Voting rights:* The voting rights of the stockholders of any of the combined entities cannot be deprived or restricted as part of the plan of combination.

7. *Contingent consideration:* The combination must be resolved at the date the plan of combination is consummated. There can be no provision for the issuance of additional consideration based on earnings or market values after the date of consummation. However, there may be contingency agreements relating to conditions that exist or are pending on the closing date. For example, the exchange ratio could be adjusted to take into account the closing date final balance sheet, which will not be known on the closing date. Also, an agreement regarding the outcome of a pending lawsuit would not jeopardize pooling treatment.

C.31c   Absence of Planned Transactions

1. *Reacquisition of common stock:* The combined entity cannot agree, directly or indirectly, to retire or reacquire any or part of the common stock issued to effect the combination. Moreover, there cannot be a requirement on the part of former shareholders of the combining corporation to sell or not sell the voting common stock that they receive in the transaction. The SEC requires that no "affiliate" (a control group holding 10 percent or more of the outstanding common stock of either the issuer or the combining company or any officer or director) sell his stock until such time as financial results covering at least 30 days of postmerger combined operations have been published.

2. *Arrangements for benefit of certain shareholders:* The combined enterprise cannot enter into other financial arrangements for the benefit of the former stockholders of a combining enterprise, such as a guaranty of loans secured by stock issued in the combination, that, in effect, negates the exchange of equity securities.

3. *Asset dispositions:* The combined enterprise cannot intend or plan to dispose of a significant part of the assets of the combining enterprises within two years after the combination, other than disposals in the ordinary course of business of the formerly separate enterprises and to eliminate duplicate facilities or excess capacity. Generally, "significant" has been defined to mean operations that are more than 10 percent of operating profits, sales or assets.

The prior or planned disposition of a significant part of the combined company will not preclude pooling treatment if the disposition is required by a government agency or the courts.

A spinoff of part of the combined entity to the shareholders after the transaction will not necessarily preclude pooling treatment. Furthermore, it is possible to sell a minority interest in a subsidiary of the combined entity to raise financing.

C.32   Accounting for Income Taxes

If a transaction that will be accounted for using the Pooling of Interests Method is nontaxable, no changes are required in the tax accounts. However, if such a transaction is taxable, the change in the tax basis of the net assets acquired will result in temporary differences. The deferred tax consequences of these temporary differences are recognized and measured. Recognizable tax benefits attributable to an increase in tax basis are allocated to contributed capital as of the acquisition date. Tax benefits attributable to the increase in tax basis that become recognizable for accounting purposes after the combination date are reported as a reduction of income tax expense.

C.33   Financial Statement Disclosure

Any company that applies the Pooling of Interests Method of accounting to a combination must report results of operations for the period in which the combination occurs as though the enterprises had been combined as of the beginning of the period. Furthermore, balance sheets and other financial information of the separate enterprises, as of the beginning of the period, must be presented as though the companies had been combined at that date. Any financial statements and financial information of the separate enterprises presented for prior years must also be restated on a combined basis to furnish comparative information. All restated financial statements and financial summaries must indicate clearly that financial data is on a combined basis.

The notes to the financial statements of a combined enterprise must disclose a description of the combined entities, detailed information (including, for example, revenue, extraordinary items, and net income) of the results of operations of the previously separate companies for the period before the combination that are included in current combined net income and miscellaneous other information.

Appendix D

The Sale Process

D.0 INTRODUCTION

The purpose of this appendix is to describe the overall process generally used to sell a business.

D.1 THE SALE PROCESS

The sale process can be characterized as having five separate phases:

- *Organization:* In this phase the owners, management and/or the board of directors (1) put together a project team, including an investment banker, an attorney, accountants and internal management personnel; (2) educate the team about the business to be sold; (3) establish goals with respect to the sale; (4) identify a list of prospective purchasers; and (5) decide on a sale strategy.
- *Preparation of descriptive memorandum:* In this phase, the project team works closely to prepare an offering memorandum that describes the business as it is presently being conducted, as well as its potential for expansion.
- *Approaching potential buyers:* In this phase, potential buyers are approached and asked if they would be interested in acquiring the business. If they express interest, a confidentiality agreement is forwarded for their signature, prior to distributing the descriptive selling memorandum.
- *Due diligence phase:* In this phase, buyers are permitted access to

the management and facilities of the business. Typically, management of the business makes a presentation describing the business, and significant additional data concerning the company is made available to prospective buyers.

- *Negotiating definitive agreement and closing:* In this phase, a buyer or buyers are selected for detailed negotiations regarding a purchase agreement. These negotiations lead to the signing of the definitive purchase agreement. The closing of the sale takes place soon thereafter.

Each of these phases will be discussed in detail below.

D.11   Organization

Once the decision to sell has been made, the owner/management must select a team of internal people and external advisors to work on the project. The principal outside advisor is a competent investment banker.

There are several reasons to hire an investment banker. One is to access the contacts and market knowledge that an investment bank has. Another is that the investment banker should be able to significantly reduce the amount of disruption caused to the business and permit management to continue to focus most if its time on running the business rather than running the sale process. Third, an intermediary provides major advantages during negotiations. The investment bank can insulate its client from the misunderstandings and ill will that often occur, and put forth proposals and ideas in negotiations that do not necessarily have to be accepted by the client. Finally, an investment bank can usually complete the transaction very quickly.

A competent attorney, either from inside the company or outside counsel, should also be added to the team early in the process.

One of the first items for the team to plan is how communications with employees and customers are to be handled. The decisions regarding such communications should coincide with the desire for confidentiality in the sale process.

The initial tasks for the investment bankers are to familiarize themselves with the business and prepare a valuation analysis. This analysis should include the tax aspects of the anticipated transaction, so that the after-tax proceeds can be forecast. This valuation analysis serves as a basis for establishing realistic expectations in the sale, including expectations regarding the type of acceptable consideration. If an owner has unrealistic expectations in a sale, this is the point at which they should be confronted. Otherwise, the owner/management runs the risk of putting the organization through a tremendous strain for nothing. An unsuccessful sale can also potentially create an image in the marketplace that the business is "damaged goods that couldn't be sold." Such an image could depress the value of the business in a future sale.

The valuation discussion should also serve as a forum for the owners of the business to outline any other objectives they have in the sale (e.g., putting their employees in a good corporate home, making sure that the business's employees are retained, or making sure that management gets a piece of the equity in the company).

If conjunction with the valuation analysis, the client and his investment banker will compile a list of buyers (the "List") for the business. This list will include all the parties known to be interested in businesses similar to the one to be sold. The banker will make sure to include on this list the organizations that have contacted the company in the past about the business to be sold and the competitors and other companies that management believes may have an interest in acquiring the business. Generally, the resulting list will have four categories of buyers: domestic strategic buyers, foreign strategic buyers, LBO firms including current management and conglomerate buyers. It is typical for the List to be categorized according to some subjective measure of probability of interest (e.g., "A" list buyers versus "B" list buyers).

Once the List and the valuation analysis have been completed, the investment bank will recommend a selling strategy based on the objectives for the transaction. This strategy deals with whom to contact, when and how to contact them and the process for moving forward with them in the event they are interested in acquiring the business.

Owners, managements, and boards of directors decide to sell businesses for a wide variety of reasons, including strategic considerations, a cash flow crisis, lack of family members to continue the business and many others. The reason for the sale is important because in certain instances it will directly impact the decision about the process that will be used to sell the business. For example, if the decision to sell is made because of a looming cash flow crisis, the company may not have the time to conduct a Two-Stage Auction Process. It may be limited to a quick sale to the most likely strategic buyer.

There are numerous sale strategies that an investment banker and his client might devise. However, broadly defined they tend to fall into four types:

1. *Public Auction:* In this approach, a public announcement is made indicating that the company is "exploring alternatives" with respect to the business. This announcement is often made at the point when the company has just completed the descriptive selling memorandum. The purpose of the announcement is to alert the entire business community that the company is considering the sale of the business and that any interested parties should step forward and contact the company right away. One of the business reasons for making such an announcement, aside from the possible legal requirements, is that the number of prospective interested acquirers is quite broad, and a public announcement is determined to be the best way to adequately address the full range of potential acquirers. Generally, this type of approach will elicit numerous interested parties, assuming that the business is not in distress. A major negative associated with making a public announcement is that it tends to increase the amount of disruption caused to the business.

A *Two-Stage Auction Process* will probably be used to maximize value in a Public Auction. In a Two-Stage Auction the investment banker contacts a number of prospective buyers at about the same time as the public announcement, and distributes descriptive selling memorandums to qualified buyers, who sign confidentiality agreements. A sample confidentiality letter appears in Exhibit D–1. The descriptive selling memorandums will be accompanied by a cover letter indicating that indications of interest (*Indications*) are due on a certain date. A sample of such a cover letter appears in Exhibit D–2. Once Indications are received, the company, in consultation with its investment banker, will narrow down the list of prospective buyers that will be permitted to continue. The companies allowed to continue to the second round will be given access to management, a tour of the business's facilities, and access to a data room of information about the business. Second round participants will also be given a draft purchase agreement, which they will be asked to review and mark up for any proposed changes that they would require. The second round will culminate on a certain date, when bidders will be required to put forward fully financed offers. Once these offers have been submitted, one or more bidders will be selected to negotiate final definitive purchase agreements. The purpose of selecting more than one bidder at this juncture is to maintain the competitive spirit of the process while the final agreement is being negotiated. Once the final agreement is signed, a closing typically would occur shortly after the expiration of the applicable Hart-Scott-Rodino and other applicable government-related waiting periods (see Appendix F).

During the 1980s the Two-Stage Auction Process was used for the majority of sales handled by Wall Street investment banks. Although the 1990s are proving to be a much harsher environment to close transactions in, it is reasonable to expect that the Two-Stage Auction Process will still be used in a majority of sales handled by Wall Street firms. However, this

EXHIBIT D–1
Sample Confidentiality Agreement

Date

Dear Sirs:

In connection with your consideration of a possible transaction with ABC Company (the "Company") pursuant to which you would acquire its Widget division ("Widget"), you have requested financial and other information concerning the business and affairs of Widget. As a condition to the Company furnishing to you and your directors, officers, employees, agents, advisors and potential financing sources (collectively "representatives") financial and other information that has not heretofore been made generally available on a nonconfidential basis, you agree to treat such information furnished to you by or on behalf of the Company or its representatives, and all analyses, compilations, studies and other material prepared by you or your representatives containing or based, in whole or in part, on any such information furnished by or on behalf of the Company or any of its representatives (collectively, the "evaluation material"), as follows:

(1) You recognize and acknowledge the competitive value and confidential nature of the evaluation material and the damage that could result to the Company if information contained therein is disclosed to any third party.

(2) You agree that the evaluation material will be used solely for the purpose of evaluating the transaction described above. You also agree that you will not disclose any of the evaluation material to any third party without the prior written consent of the Company; provided, however, that any such information may be disclosed to your representatives who need to know such information for the purpose of evaluating the transaction described above and who agree to keep such information confidential and to be bound by this agreement to the same extent as if they were parties thereto.

(3) In the event that you or your representatives are requested in any proceeding to disclose any evaluation material, you will give the Company prompt notice of such request so that the Company may seek an appropriate protective order. If, in the absence of a protective order, you or your representatives are nonetheless compelled to disclose such evaluation material, you or your representatives, as the case may be, may disclose such information in such proceeding without liability hereunder; provided, however, that you give the Company written notice of the information to be disclosed as far in advance of its disclosure as is

practicable and, upon the Company's request and at its expense, use your best efforts to obtain assurances that confidential treatment will be accorded to such information.

(4) Without the prior written consent of the Company, you and your representatives will not disclose to any person either the fact that discussions or negotiations are taking place concerning a possible transaction with the Company or any of the terms, conditions or other facts with respect to any such possible transaction including the status thereof; provided, that you may make such disclosure if you have received the written opinion of your outside counsel that such disclosure must be made by you in order that you not commit a violation of law.

(5) All inquiries, requests for information and other communications with the Company shall be made through Mr. Joseph H. Marren at Wall Street Investment Bank.

(6) In the event that the transaction contemplated by this agreement is not consummated, neither you nor your representatives shall, without the prior written consent of the Company, use any of the evaluation material for any purpose. Upon the Company's request, you will promptly redeliver to the Company all copies of all evaluation material furnished to you or your representatives by or on behalf of the Company and will destroy all analyses, compilations, studies and other material based in whole or in part on such material prepared by you or your representatives.

(7) You and your representatives shall have no obligation hereunder with respect to any information in the evaluation materials to the extent that such information (a) has been made public other than by acts of you or your representatives in violation of this agreement or (b) becomes available to you on a nonconfidential basis from a source that is entitled to disclose it on a nonconfidential basis.

(8) You hereby acknowledge that although the Company has endeavored to include in the evaluation material information known to it that it believes to be relevant to your evaluation, you understand that neither the Company nor any of its representatives makes any representation or warranty as to the accuracy or completeness thereof and you agree that neither the Company nor any of its representatives shall have any liability with respect to the evaluation material or any use thereof.

(9) You agree that money damages would not be a sufficient remedy for any breach of this agreement by you or your representatives, and that, in addition to all other remedies, the Company shall be entitled to specific performance and injunctive or other equitable relief as a remedy for any such breach, and you further agree to waive, and to use your best efforts to cause your representatives to waive, any such requirement for the securing or posting of any bond in connection with such remedy. You agree to be responsible for any breach of this agreement by any of your representatives.

(10) No failure or delay by the Company or any of its representatives in exercising any right, power or privilege under this agreement shall operate as a waiver thereof nor shall any single or partial exercise thereof preclude any other or further exercise of any right, power or privilege hereunder.

(11) In case any provision of this agreement shall be invalid, illegal or unenforceable, the validity, legality and enforceability of the remaining provisions of the agreement shall not in any way be affected or impaired thereby.

(12) This agreement shall be governed by and construed in accordance with the laws of the State of New York.

Please acknowledge your agreement to the foregoing by countersigning this letter in the place provided below and returning it to Wall Street Investment Bank.

Very truly yours,

Joseph H. Marren

Executed and Agreed
This _____ day of _____ 1992.
Company: _____
By: _____
Title: _____

---

process should not be used if the business to be sold is particularly complex or the financial structure of the transaction is very unusual.

2. *Controlled Auction:* In a Controlled Auction, the number of prospective acquirers that are contacted is limited to some extent and no public announcement is made concerning the availability of the business. Generally, the Two-Stage Auction Process is used to narrow down the number of prospective buyers.

One of the realities that many managements fail to adequately anticipate is the fact that the business is being sold generally becomes common knowledge in its industry, even if the Controlled Auction involves a limited number of prospective buyers and they all sign appropriate Confidentiality Agreements. This event must be planned for.

3. *Targeted Sale:* In a Targeted Sale, a very limited number of strategic buyers are approached concerning their interest in acquiring the business. No public announcement is made concerning its availability.

A Targeted Sale strategy is chosen when it is believed that the list of prospective buyers that could pay an acceptable price is quite small. If the

EXHIBIT D–2
Sample Two-Stage Auction Process Cover Letter

Date

Dear Sirs:

ABC Company (the "Company") has retained Wall Street Investment Bank ("Wall Street") as its financial advisor to explore alternatives regarding the possible sale of its Widget division ("Widget"). Wall Street is the Company's exclusive financial agent in connection with the sale of Widget.

The offering procedure will be conducted in two phases: Phase I: the Information Review Phase and Phase II: the Due Diligence Phase. As part of Phase I we have enclosed a Confidential Offering Memorandum describing the business and affairs of Widget. The enclosed Confidential Offering Memorandum, collectively with any additional information that will be made available to you, will be referred to as the "Evaluation Material." All such Evaluation Material is protected by the Confidentiality Agreement which you previously executed.

If, after reviewing this information, you wish to continue in the review process, such interest should be communicated in writing to Wall Street no later than X date, one month from today. Wall Street will promptly notify those potential purchasers who are selected to participate in Phase II of the review process shortly thereafter. Selection will be based on the following criteria:

(1) receipt of a satisfactory written expression of interest, including consideration to be received by the Company;

(2) receipt of a list outlining the principal due diligence items that you will need answered before submitting a definitive proposal; and

(3) satisfactory demonstration of the potential purchaser's ability to complete a transaction based upon financial, business and other factors.

During Phase II, the selected groups will be given access to management, facilities and other information to complete their review. In anticipation of your evaluation process, the Company will establish a Data Room at Wall Street's offices, which will contain substantially all of the information needed for potential purchasers to complete their due diligence investigation. Wall Street will be responsible for scheduling the use of the Data Room.

During Phase II, we will distribute an Acquisition Agreement to qualified purchasers for their review and comment. Wall Street will keep all potential purchasers informed as to the timing of Phases I and II on an equal basis. The Company reserves the right to amend or terminate these offering procedures at any time and in any respect.

All potential purchasers should direct all data and other requests to Wall Street. Potential purchasers are not to call the Company directly.

Sincerely

Joseph H. Marren

Targeted Sale strategy is chosen, it is unlikely that a Two-Stage Auction Process will be used. It is more likely that a Single-Stage Process will be utilized.

A Targeted Sale strategy is also the process of choice for sales of unattractive businesses, businesses that are exceedingly complex, businesses that must be sold with unusual financial structures, or businesses that must be sold quickly.

In a Single-Stage Process each party contacted that expresses an interest will be given a descriptive memorandum upon signing a confidentiality agreement. Once a party has reviewed the descriptive memorandum, it will be given access to management, the facilities and a data room if it indicates that it could reach a valuation range that is acceptable. An alternate process that is often used is to let all targeted buyers who are interested proceed to the due diligence phase without indicating where they are on valuation. The goal of this approach is to get prospective buyers more interested in the business before requiring them to indicate their valuation thinking.

The process in a Targeted Sale is often more open-ended than either the Public Auction or the Controlled Auction. While many times the Targeted Sale works like the second round of a Two-Stage Auction, there are also instances where there is no definitive time frame for submission of bids. This reflects the thin nature of the interest for the business.

4. *Negotiated Sale:* In certain limited circumstances, there is only one buyer for a particular property. This typically occurs in situations where the business to be sold is physically adjacent to the prospective buyer's operations, fits perfectly into a prospective buyer's portfolio of products, or is jointly owned with the prospective buyer and contract rights give the prospective buyer the right to buy the interest he does not own. In these circumstances, a Negotiated Sale strategy is often chosen.

When a business is to be sold in a Negotiated Sale, there are generally no strict procedures laid down. Rather, negotiations begin and proceed at a fairly leisurely pace, reflecting the seller's desire not to appear overanxious to sell and the buyer's desire not to appear overanxious to buy. If it is at all practical, the seller should attempt to bring in a competitive bidder to move the process along more quickly. In addition, it is highly likely that such a move would improve the offer price from the likely buyer.

Once the strategy for selling the business has been agreed upon, the company and its investment banker can finalize the *Time and Responsibilities Schedule (T&R)*. This document lays out the time frame for completing the sale, the individual tasks that must be performed to reach a successful conclusion and who is responsible for completing each task. A typical T&R appears in Exhibit D–3. However, a deal can be completed in a shorter time frame than this schedule suggests. Generally, sales take between three and nine months from the date the process is started.

EXHIBIT D–3
Sample Time & Responsibilities Schedule

	Responsibility	Weeks
Organization		
Initial T&R prepared	C, IB	1
Complete valuation analysis	IB	1–2
Develop list of prospective buyers	C, IB	1–2
Prepare confidentiality agreement	C, A	1–2
Agree on sale strategy	C, IB	3–4
Preparation of Descriptive Memorandum		
Initial draft	IB	2–3
Review and revise draft	C, IB	3–4
Approve final draft	C	4
Approaching Potential Buyers		
Initial contact	IB	4
Send confidentiality letter	IB	4–5
Obtain signed confidentiality letters	IB	5–7
Distribute descriptive memorandum	IB	6–7
Obtain indications of interest	IB	11
Due Diligence		
Prepare initial draft purchase agreement	C, A	5–8
Review initial draft purchase agreement	C, A, IB	8–9
Finalize draft purchase agreement	C, A, IB	10
Schedule meetings & plant tours	IB	11–12
Meetings & plant tours	C, IB	12–14
Final bids due	IB	15
Negotiate Definitive Agreement and Close		
Evaluate final bids	C, A, IB	15–16
Select final bidder(s)	C, IB	16
Negotiate and execute definitive agreement	C, A, IB	16–17
Prepare governmental filings	C, A, IB	17–18
Closing		21–25

Note: C = Client; IB = Investment Banker; A = Attorney.

D.12   Preparation of Descriptive Memorandum

During the preparation of descriptive memorandum phase of the sale process, the investment banker conducts an extensive investigation of the business. The investment banker's investigation is designed to provide an understanding of the business and the industry it operates in. This includes the current set of dynamics affecting the industry, the competitive positions of the various players in the industry, the strengths and weaknesses of the business to be sold, the outlooks for both the industry and the business and the quality of the management team running the business.

Based upon his review of the business, the investment banker will prepare a first draft of the descriptive selling memorandum. This draft will typically be refined over a series of meetings and result in a document that fully describes the present operations of the business. More importantly, the document should describe in some detail all the significant opportunities for expanding the business from its present scope. Such opportunities include the ability to produce other products with existing facilities or market additional products through present channels of distribution.

One of the important decisions to be made about the descriptive memorandum is how complete it should be. Should it be merely a "teaser" that only gives a broad overview of the business, or should it be a comprehensive memorandum that addresses all the major issues/opportunities facing the business? The answer generally depends on the expected audience for the document—how knowledgeable they are about the company and its industry. It also depends on how much confidential information the selling company thinks should be released in an initial memorandum that is widely distributed.

A Table of Contents of a typical selling memorandum prepared by a Wall Street investment bank appears in Exhibit D–4.

EXHIBIT D–4
Typical Descriptive Selling Memorandum

Table of Contents

Page

D.13   Approaching Potential Buyers

During this phase potential buyers are contacted regarding their interest in reviewing the descriptive selling memorandum. Generally, the investment banker will call an appropriate official at each potential buyer's organization. Depending on the circumstances, this may be the chief executive officer, the president/general manager of one of the subsidiaries, the corporate development officer, another corporate officer or its investment banker.

However, if the number of potential buyers is limited, the seller and/or its investment banker may personally visit with these buyers to present the opportunity face-to-face. Such an approach is designed to elicit a quicker, more direct response from the potentially interested parties than a mere phone call. The personal touch tends to give the prospective buyer a greater feeling that he can negotiate a transaction rather than just participate in a standard Two-Stage Auction Process.

Assuming a prospective buyer exhibits interest in proceeding, a confidentiality letter is forwarded to the buyer immediately. Once this is signed, the process continues.

D.14 Due Diligence

During the due diligence phase, prospective buyers are permitted access to management, the facilities and a data room. Typically, management of the business makes a presentation to all prospective buyers that outlines the business and its prospects in more detail than appears in the descriptive offering memorandum. In a Two-Stage Auction, the amount of due diligence that a prospective buyer is permitted is limited. In other circumstances, the amount of due diligence can be quite extensive.

During the due diligence phase, prospective buyers are often given a draft of the purchase agreement that the seller is willing to sign concerning the sale of the business. The buyers review and mark up this draft with proposed changes as part of their due diligence effort.

One of the investment banker's primary responsibilities during this phase is to supervise the collection and dissemination of due diligence data. This reduces the burden on management and the disruption to the business.

D.15 Negotiating Definitive Agreement and Closing

Once the due diligence phase has been completed, final bids are requested for the business. Once the final bids are received, the seller, in consultation with its investment banker, will generally select one or more parties with which to negotiate a final purchase agreement, assuming there is some amount of negotiation necessary. These negotiations will focus on firming up the representations and warranties that the parties will agree to. Such negotiations often have an impact on the final price.

After negotiating the definitive purchase agreement, all applicable government filings will be made, and a closing will take place after government clearances are obtained.

Appendix E

Federal Securities and State Laws

E.0 INTRODUCTION

Appendix E provides a brief overview of the federal securities laws as well as the state laws associated with corporate governance that impact the ability to consummate a transaction or its timing. This overview focuses on

1. The various methods of acquiring a public company.
2. The impact of using "securities" as part of the consideration in an acquisition.
3. The issue of when negotiations regarding a potential transaction must be disclosed publicly.
4. The additional disclosure required when the anticipated transaction involves existing shareholders or management participating in the buying group (a *"Going-Private Transaction"*).

E.1 METHODS OF ACQUIRING A PUBLIC COMPANY

Generally, there are only three ways to acquire a publicly owned company. These include acquiring substantially all of the company's assets, effecting a merger or consolidation with the target, or acquiring the target's stock through a tender offer. (See Chapter 6.) Important legal variations of these alternatives are depicted in Exhibit E–1 and described in detail below. An additional way to obtain control of a publicly owned company that does not appear in Exhibit E–1 and will not be dealt with in this appendix is a proxy contest.

EXHIBIT E–1
Methods of Acquiring a Public Company

		Variations
	Acquisition of Assets	Asset Acquisition
Legal	Merger or Consolidation	Single-Step Merger or Consolidation Two-Step Tender Offer
Methods	Stock Acquisition	Single-Step Tender Offer Two-Step Tender Offer Market Sweep

E.11   Acquisition of Assets

Generally, if a public company is selling all or substantially all of its assets, applicable state laws require that its board of directors adopt and approve the sale agreement, then submit the transaction to its shareholders, who must vote to approve the transaction.

Federal securities laws require that the selling company's shareholders be furnished with (a) a *proxy statement*, if proxies or consents are being solicited with respect to the shareholders meeting; or (b) an *information statement*, if no proxies or consents will be solicited but a shareholders meeting will be held. The proxy statement must be prepared in accordance with requirements of *Regulation 14A* of the *Securities Exchange Act of 1934 (the "Exchange Act")*, and the information statement must conform with the requirements of *Regulation 14C* of the Exchange Act.

It takes a significant amount of time for a deal to close when proxy materials or an information statement must be sent to shareholders. Proxy materials, once prepared, can take four to six weeks to clear the SEC. In addition, the length of time between mailing the proxy statement and the shareholders meeting is determined by applicable state law and the selling company's charter and bylaws. The minimum length of time between the mailing of the information statement and the shareholders meeting is 20 days, according to the Exchange Act.

E.12   Merger or Consolidation

Almost all acquisitions of public companies involve a merger—either alone or as a second step to a tender offer. Why? The beauty of a merger, from an acquisition perspective, is that it permits an acquirer to obtain

100 percent ownership without 100 percent voluntary participation by the target company's shareholders.

The mechanics of mergers and consolidations are governed by applicable state laws. In most instances, the board of directors of each company that is merging or consolidating must adopt and approve the agreement and plan of merger or consolidation, then submit the plan to the shareholders of the respective companies for their approval. However, if the acquiring company already owns a specified percentage of the stock of the target company (generally 90 percent), most states have laws that permit a *Short-Form Merger* that does not require a vote of either the stockholders or the board of the target. Assuming a shareholder vote is required, which shareholders are permitted to vote on the transaction and the percentage of votes necessary to approve a merger is governed by applicable state law.

An acquirer can often sidestep the need to obtain the approval of its shareholders through a *Forward* or *Reverse Subsidiary Merger* (see paragraphs 7.11a and 7.21a for a description of these acquisition methods). In these transactions, the target merges into a subsidiary of the acquirer or the subsidiary of the acquirer merges into the target. The use of a subsidiary that is incorporated in the same state as the target can often expedite the merger and reduce complexity.

The federal securities law requirements for a merger or consolidation are the same as for an Asset Acquisition. Shareholders of the companies to be merged or consolidated must be furnished with (a) a proxy statement, if proxies or consents are being solicited with respect to the shareholders meeting; or (b) an information statement, if no proxies or consents will be solicited but a shareholders meeting will be held. The proxy statement must be prepared in accordance with requirements of Regulation 14A of the Exchange Act and the information statement must conform with the requirements of Regulation 14C of the Exchange Act.

In a *Single-Step Merger* or *Consolidation*, the acquiring company and the target generally merge or consolidate without any prior stock or asset transactions between them. However, in a *Two-Step Tender Offer*, the merger or consolidation is preceded by a Tender Offer in which the acquiring company acquires a controlling interest in the target company. Typically, the controlling interest acquired is enough to approve the "second step" under applicable state law—the merger of the target and the acquiring company. In many cases, the controlling interest acquired in the Tender Offer is sufficient for the acquirer to effect a Short-Form Merger.

Most states provide dissenting shareholders to a merger *appraisal rights*, which is the right to receive cash equal to the court's appraised value of their shares. These rights typically do not hold up a transaction.

E.13   Stock Acquisition

A controlling interest in the target company can also be acquired through a tender offer or a specific type of open market purchase program (hereafter a *"Market Sweep"*). However, prior to launching a tender offer an acquirer can accumulate a significant stake in the target through either open market purchases or negotiated block purchases.

The *Williams Act*, a 1968 amendment to the Exchange Act, is the federal securities law that governs tender offers. The Williams Act was designed to protect shareholders of target companies by imposing disclosure and reporting requirements, as well as providing investors sufficient time to assess this information and make an informed decision with regard to tendering their securities.

Although the Williams Act governs tender offers, it does not define what a "tender offer" is! Therefore, it has been left to the courts to define the term. A *Tender Offer* has been defined as "a general, publicized bid by an individual or group to buy shares of a publicly owned company, the shares of which are traded on a national securities exchange, at a price substantially above the current market price."

On the day that a tender offer commences, the bidder must file a *Tender Offer Statement on Schedule 14D–1* with the SEC, and deliver it to the target company. The Schedule 14D–1 must include: who the bidder is, the source of the bidder's funding, the purpose of the transaction, disclosure about any negotiations with the target company to date, the consideration being offered, and financial information about the bidder and the target company.

The Exchange Act requires that the target company must inform its shareholders of its position with respect to the tender offer within 10 business days of the offer being made. The form filed with the SEC is *Schedule 14D–9*. Prior to informing its shareholders of its position the target can send its shareholders a *Stop-Look-and-Listen* letter, which asks shareholders to hold off making a decision on the offer until they have heard the company's position.

A tender offer must remain open for at least 20 business days. If the purchase price is either increased or decreased or the percentage of securities to be bought is changed, the tender offer must remain open for at least 10 days. Once a tender offer has been announced, a bidder may not purchase shares except through the tender offer. If the number of shares tendered exceeds the amount sought, then shares are purchased on a pro rata basis. Tendering shareholders may withdraw shares tendered up until the time they are actually purchased.

Although it is theoretically possible to have a One-Step Tender Offer succeed in achieving a 100 percent ownership position for the acquirer, this does not happen in the real world. The typical procedure to achieve this result is through a Two-Step Tender Offer. In a Two-Step Tender Offer the tender offer gives the acquirer enough of a majority of the stock of the target to assure that the second step can be accomplished. The second step is a merger.

Open-market purchases or purchases from a limited number of sophisticated investors are not tender offers. A *Market Sweep* is a technique whereby a bidder that has launched a tender offer terminates the tender and proceeds to purchase a significant amount of stock from a limited number of sophisticated investors. After a tender offer is announced, the amount of target company stock held by sophisticated investors (*arbitrageurs*) increases significantly. This increases the likelihood that the acquiring company can accumulate a significant amount of stock outside of a tender offer in a Market Sweep.

E.13a   13D Filings for 5 Percent Owners of Equity Securities

It is typical for bidders to acquire some amount of target company stock before they launch a tender offer. The Exchange Act requires that within 10 days of acquiring beneficial ownership of 5 percent of any class of an equity security, a bidder must file a *Schedule 13D* with the SEC and the target company. The information contained on the filing includes the name of the acquirer, the source of funds, and most importantly, the purpose of the investment. A 13D filing must be amended promptly whenever there is a material change in the information reported. The 13D disclosure is designed to make public the existence of an ownership position that could affect the market value of the security.

E.13b   Target Company's Charter and Bylaws

A target company's charter and bylaws have a significant effect on the ability of an acquirer to purchase the company through a tender offer or merger. Charter amendments must be approved by the company's shareholders. However, the board of directors may amend the company's bylaws without shareholder approval, assuming the bylaws authorize such action. A variety of *"shark repellent"* amendments are often made to a company's charter and bylaws, making it more difficult for a hostile acquirer to obtain control. Examples of shark repellent amendments appear below:

- *Supermajority voting provisions* require 66 2/3 or 80 percent of the target's shareholders votes before a merger can be effected.

- *Classified (staggered) board provisions* generally provide that no more than one third of the board members can be elected at the annual shareholders' meeting.
- *Fair price provisions* require supermajority approval for a merger unless the price paid to minority shareholders equals or exceeds either the highest price paid or percentage premium paid by the acquirer in acquiring the target's shares before the merger. These provisions are designed to defend against two-tier offers.
- *Provisions requiring supermajority to amend bylaws* require a super-majority vote of shareholders (66 2/3 or 80 percent) to amend the company's bylaws.
- *Provisions limiting the calling of special shareholder meetings* require that a special meeting may be called only by the president or a majority of the company's directors.
- *Provisions limiting shareholder action by consent* generally require a shareholder meeting to take action unless written consents are received from all shareholders.
- *Provisions limiting the size of the board* require that the board size cannot be increased or decreased beyond a particular number of directors.
- *Provisions limiting the ability to remove directors* require that a director cannot be removed except for cause.
- *Increases in authorized common stock* permit the board of directors to grant stock lockups to preferred bidders and issue stock with disparate voting rights without having to obtain shareholder approval.
- *Authorization for blank check preferred stock* permit the board of directors to grant supervoting preferred stock without having to obtain shareholder approval.
- *Antigreenmail provisions* require shareholder approval for the repurchase of shares from a limited number of shareholders at a premium price.
- *Authorization to consider noneconomic factors* permits the board to consider the impact of a transaction on its employees, customers, suppliers and the communities the company's facilities are located in.
- *Provision to give notice* requires shareholders to provide written notice in advance of business they want to raise at a shareholders meeting.
- *Provisions requiring formal consent procedure* require that a share-

holder who wants the corporation to act by consent must notify the board of directors and request that a record date be set for determining shareholders eligible to sign consents.

- *Provisions limiting shareholders' power to fill board vacancies* require that vacancies be filled only by a majority or a supermajority of directors voting.

E.13c   Poison Pills

The term *poison pill* refers to a type of defensive technique against hostile takeovers usually adopted by a target company's board of directors as an amendment to the company's bylaws. A poison pill is actually a *shareholder rights plan*. Shareholder rights plans are designed (1) to make it very difficult and expensive for a hostile acquirer to complete a two-tiered transaction, a front-end loaded transaction, or a transaction to purchase a significant minority interest that probably would be a controlling interest; and (2) to encourage a party interested in acquiring the company to negotiate with the board of directors.

Generally, shareholder rights plans present a hostile acquirer with the possibility that the company's existing shareholders will be able to dilute the acquirer's equity interest by exercising rights to purchase, at a substantial discount, either additional equity in the target or stock of the acquirer. A wide variety of shareholder rights plans have been developed. The most popular include:

1. *Flip-over Plans.* In this type of plan rights or warrants with a relatively long-term life (10 years) are distributed as a dividend to shareholders. These rights are neither detachable nor exercisable until a triggering event occurs. Until the triggering event, or a short period thereafter, the rights are redeemable at the board's discretion. This redemption feature permits the board to negotiate with the acquirer. Typical triggering events would include a tender offer for the company's stock or the acquisition of a certain percentage of the company's stock.

Flip-over rights are targeted at the second-step transaction after a triggering event has occurred. The Flip-over rights initially permit a shareholder to purchase common or preferred stock of the issuer at a price based on the long-term value of the company's stock over the life of the right. The exercise price is typically a multiple (generally three times) of the current market value of the company's stock at the date of issuance. However, the right also permits the holder to purchase, under certain circumstances, stock having a market value twice the exercise price of a right. For example, upon the consummation of a second-step transaction the holder of a right is entitled to purchase stock of the surviving entity at 50 percent of market value. The fact that the holder can purchase the surviving company's stock is why the right is said to "flip-over."

2. *Flip-in Plans.* These rights plans are similar to Flip-over Plans. However, they permit rights holders to purchase target company stock at a substantial discount (half price), once a triggering event has occurred, such as a hostile acquirer accumulating more than 20 percent of the target company's stock. A variation of a Flip-in Plan is an *Adverse Person Flip-in Plan*, which provides that the board of the target company can reduce the flip-in threshold percentage (e.g., from 20 percent to 10 percent) if a majority of the outside directors determine that a substantial acquirer of the company's stock is an Adverse Person, who is seeking greenmail or other short-term financial gain.

3. Back-end Plans. These entitle a holder of a right, which has been distributed to shareholders as a dividend, to put to the issuer a share of common stock in exchange for cash, preferred stock or debt having a market value substantially in excess of the current market value of the common stock, if a triggering event occurs. A typical triggering event would be that an acquirer exceeds a certain level of ownership.

E.13d   State Takeover Statutes

A large number of states have enacted *Second Generation State Takeover Statutes* designed to circumvent the constitutional flaws in earlier takeover statutes. These statutes, as well as other similar statutes, must be considered in acquisitions of publicly held companies.

For example, there is a second generation *Control Share Statute* that has withstood Supreme Court scrutiny. The Indiana statute, which was the subject of a Supreme Court's opinion, provides that shares acquired in a Control Share Acquisition lose their voting rights unless voting rights are granted to such shares by an affirmative vote of a majority of each class of stock, excluding shares owned by the acquiring person or officers or inside directors. A *Control Share Acquisition* occurs whenever a person purchases shares in a corporation that would bring his voting power above certain limits (e.g., 20 percent).

E.13e   Directors' Responsibilities

Generally, directors of target companies are protected from liability by the Business Judgment Rule. In addition, the Business Judgment Rule protects the boards' decisions from attack.

The *Business Judgment Rule* is a judicial presumption that "the directors of the corporation acted on an informed basis, in good faith and in the honest belief that the action was taken in the best interests of the company" *Aronson v. Lewis* 473 A.2nd 805, 812 (Del. 1984). The presumption protects directors unless it can be proven that the directors violated either their duty of care or their duty of loyalty.

The *duty of care* requires directors to make an informed decision. They must avail themselves of all material information reasonably accessible to them before making a decision. The *duty of loyalty* requires directors to act in the best interests of the corporation. A director cannot act in bad faith or look to have the corporation enter into a transaction in which the director has a personal interest.

E.13f Insider Trading

It is important for prospective acquirers to understand the insider trading laws because, once an acquirer becomes a beneficial owner of more than 10 percent of the equity securities of the target company, the acquirer becomes an insider. *Section 16(b) of the Exchange Act* prohibits short-swing profits (profits by trading the company's securities within a six-month period) by insiders. All such profits must be paid to the company. There are limited exemptions to this short-swing rule, including the involuntary sale of stock in a merger.

E.13g Margin Rules

The Federal Reserve has margin rules which prohibit secured lending unless the market value of the "margin stock" securing the loan exceeds 50 percent of the loan. *Margin stock* includes most publicly traded stocks. These margin rules can often affect highly leveraged tender offers and stock purchase programs.

E.2 EFFECT OF USING SECURITIES AS CONSIDERATION IN TRANSACTIONS

Generally, if securities are used as part of the consideration given in either a tender offer or merger, or the acquisition will be financed through the issuance of securities, the acquirer must file a registration statement complying with the *Securities Act of 1933 (Securities Act)*. The term *securities* includes notes, stock, bonds, debentures, evidences of indebtedness, voting trust certificates, puts, calls, options, warrants, rights to acquire any of the foregoing and other interests.

The registration statement filed with the SEC must be declared effective before any offer to sell securities (for acquisition purposes, "offer to sell securities" means issue securities as consideration in a transaction) can be made. A typical case where securities are offered as consideration is an *Exchange Offer*.

There are exceptions to this registration requirement, which are defined in Regulation D under the Securities Act. The principal exception involves a *private placement* of securities.

In addition to complying with federal securities laws, state *Blue Sky* securities laws must be complied with. These laws require the registration of securities with the state prior to the sale of securities in the state.

Finally, the *New York Stock Exchange (NYSE)* and *American Stock Exchange (ASE)* require that shareholder approval be obtained in certain circumstances—if the consideration given by the acquiring company could result in an increase in its common stock outstanding above a specified percentage (18.5 percent for the NYSE and 20 percent for the ASE).

E.3   GOING-PRIVATE TRANSACTIONS

Going-private transactions are governed by *Rule 13e–3 of the Exchange Act*, which is designed to protect shareholders against the conflicts of interest that exist in going-private transactions, as well as from the information advantages that insiders have in these transactions. The rule protects shareholders by requiring a significant amount of additional disclosure.

Going-private transactions include: (a) a tender offer by the issuer for its own securities; (b) the purchase by the issuer of its own securities; (c) the solicitation of either proxies or consents in connection with a merger, consolidation or sale of substantially all the assets of the company; where the transaction will result in the issuer either having less than 300 shareholders or being delisted.

In a going-private transaction, the issuer must file a 13e–3 form, which discloses the terms of the transaction as well as the process by which those terms were arrived at, including alternatives considered and the factors upon which the required assessment of fairness by the company is based.

E.4   DISCLOSURE OF NEGOTIATIONS

The Supreme Court in *Basic Incorporated, et al. v. Levinson, et al.* set forth the test as to whether or not preliminary merger or acquisition negotiations are material under Rule 10b–5 of the Exchange Act. The Supreme

Court indicated that whether negotiations are material depends on the facts and circumstances of the particular case. The Court expressly rejected a "bright line" test that negotiations do not become material until an agreement in principle as to price and structure have been reached. In addition, the Court indicated that a company that has a "no comment" policy with respect to rumors or market activity is not misleading under Rule 10b–5, unless there are special circumstances that impose a duty to disclose.

Appendix F

Antitrust Laws

F.0 INTRODUCTION

Appendix F provides an overview of the antitrust laws as they are applied to mergers and acquisitions. The federal antitrust laws are an important consideration in most acquisitions because they require premerger notification of the transaction to the *Department of Justice (DOJ)* and the *Federal Trade Commission (FTC), collectively the "Agencies."* In addition, once the filing is made, the parties must wait a specified period before consummating the transaction, during which time these institutions may take action to stop the transaction.

Other antitrust related laws, or actions, that affect transactions include state antitrust statutes, regulatory statutes that affect mergers and acquisitions in certain industries, and finally, third-party lawsuits.

F.1 FEDERAL ANTITRUST LAWS AFFECTING M&A

Three principal federal laws affect mergers and acquisitions: (1) Section 7 of the Clayton Act, (2) Sections 1, 2, and 3 of the Sherman Act, and (3) Section 5(a)(6) of the Federal Trade Commission Act. The most important of these is Section 7 of the Clayton Act.

F.2   SECTION 7 OF THE CLAYTON ACT

Section 7 of the Clayton Act (Clayton Act) was originally enacted in 1914, modified in 1950 by the *Celler-Kefauver* amendment, and amended again in 1980. The Clayton Act prohibits mergers and acquisitions that are likely to result in a substantial lessening of competition.

F.21   Hart-Scott-Rodino

The *Hart-Scott-Rodino Antitrust Improvements Act (Hart-Scott)* was enacted in 1976, Title II of which became *Section 7A of the Clayton Act.* Hart-Scott requires that parties contemplating a significant acquisition provide advance notification and extensive market and financial data to both the DOJ and the FTC, in order that they may undertake an analysis to determine if the proposed transaction will significantly lessen competition.

Information must be provided to both the DOJ and the FTC because they have concurrent jurisdiction to enforce the Clayton Act. The FTC and DOJ coordinate their activities closely. Each has built up expertise in different industries and generally divide filings accordingly.

F.21a   Transactions Covered by Hart-Scott

Hart-Scott only applies if both *size-of-person* and *size-of-transaction* tests are satisfied. The size-of-person test may be satisfied in three ways:

1. If the acquiring person has annual net sales or total assets of $100 million or more and the acquired person is engaged in manufacturing and has annual net sales or total assets of $10 million or more.
2. If the acquiring person has annual net sales or total assets of $100 million or more and the acquired person is not engaged in manufacturing but has total assets of $10 million or more.
3. If the acquiring person has annual net sales or total assets of $10 million or more and the acquired person has annual net sales of $100 million or more.

The size-of-transaction test is satisfied whenever, as a result of the transaction, the acquiring person holds voting securities or assets of the acquired person valued in excess of $15 million. In addition, the size-of-transaction test is satisfied if, as a result of the transaction, the acquiring person obtains control (buys more than 50 percent of the voting securities) of an acquired person with annual net sales or total assets of $25 million or more.

F.21b Required Filing and Initial Waiting Period

If the tests outlined above are met, the parties to the transaction must file a *Premerger Notification and Report Form (Premerger Form)*. The Premerger Form is designed to enable the enforcement authorities to review the legality of the proposed transaction.

One of the most important aspects of Hart-Scott is the effect that it has on the timing of a transaction. Hart-Scott requires an initial waiting period of 30 calendar days (only 15 days in the case of a cash tender offer) after the Premerger Form is filed before the transaction can be consummated. However, early termination of this initial waiting period may be granted by the government when it is convinced that the transaction poses no competitive problems.

F.21c Request for Additional Information

The DOJ or the FTC may request additional information or documents from one or both of the parties to the transaction. These requests for information can be quite challenging to fulfill. However, the most significant aspect of this *second request* is that it prolongs the time for consummating a transaction. Once a second request has been issued, the transaction cannot be consummated until 20 days (10 days in the case of a cash tender offer) after all parties to the transaction have complied with it.

F.21d Negotiating a Settlement

If the DOJ or FTC believes that the transaction presents problems under the antitrust laws, they have the power to bring suit to block the transaction. However, in many instances, the DOJ or FTC will block a transaction because a part of the transaction has anticompetitive effects. A frequent solution in such cases involves the government and the parties to the transaction entering into a consent decree to dispose of certain businesses that give rise to the antitrust concerns.

F.22 Merger Guidelines

The DOJ originally issued *Merger Guidelines (Guidelines)* in 1968 and revised them in 1982 and 1984. These Guidelines defined a *horizontal merger* as a merger between firms in the same product and geographic market. *Nonhorizontal mergers* are mergers between firms that do not operate in the same market. In April 1992, the DOJ and FTC jointly issued *Horizontal Merger Guidelines*. These Guidelines state the enforcement policy of the Agencies concerning horizontal mergers and acquisitions subject to the Clayton Act, Section 1 of the Sherman Act, or Section 5 of the FTC

Act. They describe the analytical framework and specific standards generally used to analyze transactions.

The theme of the Guidelines is that mergers should not be permitted to create or enhance "market power" or to facilitate its exercise. *Market power* is defined as the ability to profitably maintain prices above competitive levels for a significant period of time.

The Guidelines indicate that the Agencies will go through the following process in an effort to answer the ultimate question: whether the horizontal merger is likely to create or enhance market power or to facilitate its exercise.

1. Assess whether the merger would significantly increase concentration and result in a concentrated market.
2. Assess whether the merger, in light of market concentration and other factors that characterize the market, raises concerns about potential adverse competitive effects.
3. Assess whether entry would be timely, likely and sufficient either to deter or counteract the competitive effects of concern.
4. Assess any efficiency gains that reasonably cannot be achieved by the parties through other means.
5. Assess whether, but for the merger, either party to the transaction would be likely to fail, causing its assets to exit the market.

In the case of a nonhorizontal merger, the Agencies will review the transaction to see whether it has any anticompetitive effects. A nonhorizontal merger could have anticompetitive effects if it removes a significant potential entrant from the marketplace, creates significant barriers to entry in a market or facilitates collusion.

F.22a Market Definition

A merger is unlikely to create or enhance market power or facilitate its exercise unless it significantly increases concentration and results in a concentrated market. Accordingly, for each product or service (product) of each firm, a market must be defined.

The Guidelines define a *market* as a group of products and a geographic area such that a hypothetical firm that is the only present and future seller of those products in that area would possess market power—the power profitably to restrict output and raise prices. A firm that is the only present seller of those products, in that area, would not be able to exercise market power if its attempt to impose a small but significant and nontransitory price increase would cause buyers to switch to other products or to products in other areas or would induce other firms to begin selling the particular products. Firms that sell products to which consumers would switch and that would begin selling the particular products would prevent the exercise of market power and should be included in the market.

The Guidelines translate these principles of market power into a market-definition standard that has become known as the *5 percent test*. Markets are delineated by postulating a "small but significant and non-transitory" price increase (generally, an increase of 5 percent for one year) for each product of each merging firm at the firm's location and examining the likely responses of buyers and market participants. If these competitive responses would cause the price increase to be un-profitable, then the area and group of products are expanded to include additional products and areas until the price increase would be profitable to impose. At that point—when it would be profitable for a hypothetical firm that was the only seller of the products in that area to impose a "small but significant and nontransitory" increase in price—the group of products and the area are considered to be a market.

Market participants include firms selling the market's products in the market's geographic area, including vertically integrated competitors. Uncommitted entrants that do not produce or sell the relevant product in the market but would enter the market quickly in response to a small but significant and nontransitory price increase are also market participants. Entry must be likely to occur within one year and without the expenditure of significant sunk costs. Sunk costs are the costs uniquely incurred to supply the relevant product and geographic area.

In defining the relevant market using the process described above, several other points are important.

- The 5 percent test is a flexible standard. If circumstances warrant, the Agencies may postulate a larger or smaller price increase.
- The relevant "price" is whatever is considered to be the price of the product at the stage of the industry being examined (e.g., retail price in the retailing industry).
- The Agencies will consider additional relevant product markets consisting of a particular use or uses by groups of buyers of the product.

F.22b   Market Concentration and the
Herfindahl-Hirschman Index

The Agencies use the Herfindahl-Hirschman Index (HHI) to analyze market concentration. Market concentration is a function of the number of firms in a market and their respective market shares. The HHI is calculated by summing the squares of the individual market shares of all the firms included in the market as previously defined. In determining market shares, the Agencies prefer to use dollar sales or shipments if branded or relatively differentiated products are involved and physical capacity, reserves, or dollar production if relatively homogeneous, undifferentiated products are involved. Examples of HHI calculations for different fictitious markets appear in Exhibit F–1.

EXHIBIT F–1

Sample HHI Calculations for Various Market Structures

Competitor	Market A		Market B		Market C	
	Market Share	Market Share Squared	Market Share	Market Share Squared	Market Share	Market Share Squared
A	100%	10,000	50%	2,500	33%	1,111
B			50	2,500	33	1,111
C					33	1,111
HHI		10,000		5,000		3,333

Competitor	Market D		Market E		Market F	
	Market Share	Market Share Squared	Market Share	Market Share Squared	Market Share	Market Share Squared
A	25%	625	20%	400	17%	278
B	25	625	20	400	17	278
C	25	625	20	400	17	278
D	25	625	20	400	17	278
E			20	400	17	278
F					17	278
HHI		2,500		2,000		1,667

Competitor	Market G		Market H		Market I	
	Market Share	Market Share Squared	Market Share	Market Share Squared	Market Share	Market Share Squared
A	14%	204	13%	156	11%	123
B	14	204	13	156	11	123
C	14	204	13	156	11	123
D	14	204	13	156	11	123
E	14	204	13	156	11	123
F	14	204	13	156	11	123
G	14	204	13	156	11	123
H			13	156	11	123
I					11	123
HHI		1,429		1,250		1,111

EXHIBIT F–1 (Continued)

Competitor	Market J Market Share	Market J Market Share Squared	Market K Market Share	Market K Market Share Squared	Market L Market Share	Market L Market Share Squared
A	10%	100	35%	1,225	25%	625
B	10	100	21	441	15	225
C	10	100	14	196	12	144
D	10	100	8	64	9	81
E	10	100	7	49	6	36
F	10	100	5	25	6	36
G	10	100	5	25	5	25
H	10	100	5	25	5	25
I	10	100			4	16
J	10	100			4	16
K					3	9
L					3	9
M					2	4
N					1	1
HHI		1,000		2,050		1,252

The Agencies have divided the spectrum of market concentration, as measured by the HHI, into three categories:

- *Unconcentrated (HHI less than 1,000):* The Agencies will not challenge mergers with a postmerger HHI of less than 1,000, except in extraordinary circumstances.

- *Moderately Concentrated (HHI between 1,000 and 1,800):* The Agencies are unlikely to challenge the merger if it results in an increase in the HHI of less than 100. However, the Agencies are likely to challenge mergers that produce an increase in the HHI greater than 100, unless the Agencies conclude on the basis of the postmerger HHI, the increase in the HHI, and the presence of other factors described below that the merger is not likely to substantially lessen competition.

   An empirical study by the DOJ indicates that the HHI thresholds at 1,000 and 1,800 correspond roughly to four-firm concentration ratios of 50 percent and 70 percent, respectively.

- *Concentrated (HHI greater than 1,800):* The Agencies are unlikely to challenge the merger if the increase in the HHI is less than 50. The

Agencies are likely to challenge transactions that result in an increase in the HHI greater than 50, unless they conclude on the basis of the postmerger HHI, the increase in the HHI, and the presence of other factors described below that the merger is not likely to lessen competition. Only in extraordinary circumstances will the Agencies not challenge a merger where there is a 100 point or more increase in the HHI and the postmerger HHI exceeds 1,800.

The Agencies will consider several qualitative factors that may affect the significance of the concentration and market share data. For example, the Agencies may conclude that a given firm's historical market share overstates its future competitive significance if that firm does not have access to a new technology that is important for long-term viability in the market. Another consideration is the degree of difference between the products and locations in the market and substitutes outside the market.

The Agencies will consider a variety of other factors, especially where the decision to challenge a merger is a close call. These include the homogeneity of the relevant product, the availability of pricing information, the history of anticompetitive conduct in the industry, the ability of fringe players to increase output and the market performance.

F.22c   Entry Analysis
A merger is not likely to create or enhance market power or to facilitate its exercise if entry into the market is so easy that market participants could not profitably maintain a price increase above premerger levels. Entry is easy if it is timely, likely and sufficient in its magnitude, character and scope to deter or counteract the competitive effects of concern.

F.22d   Nonhorizontal Mergers
The 1992 Horizontal Merger Guidelines do not include a discussion of nonhorizontal mergers. Specific guidance on such mergers is contained in the 1984 Guidelines, read in the context of the 1992 revisions to the treatment of horizontal mergers. The number of enforcement actions brought against these types of transactions is fairly limited. However, the DOJ may challenge a nonhorizontal merger in the following situations: (1) if it eliminates a significant potential entrant to the market that is having a positive competitive effect on the market, (2) if it is a vertical merger between a supplier and a customer that creates competitively objectionable barriers to entry in either the upstream or the downstream markets, (3) if it is a vertical merger between a supplier and a retailer that

facilitates collusion in the upstream market, (4) if it is a vertical merger in which an upstream supplier acquires a particularly disruptive buyer, and (5) if a monopoly utility acquires a supplier of its fixed or variable inputs.

F.22e Efficiencies—An Important Factor

The Agencies will consider the efficiencies that will be brought about by either a horizontal or nonhorizontal merger as an important factor. The efficiencies the Agencies will recognize include economies of scale, better integration of production facilities, plant specialization, lower transportation costs, and the like. The greater the competitive risk associated with the merger, the greater the level of efficiencies to be proven.

F.22f The Failing Firm Defense

The Agencies are unlikely to challenge an anticompetitive merger when the failing firm is unable to meet its financial obligations in the near future, it probably would not be able to be successfully reorganized under the Bankruptcy Act, and it has made a good faith effort to obtain offers to buy the company from other parties and absent the transaction, the assets of the failing firm would exit the relevant market.

In the case of "failing divisions," the proponents of the merger must establish that the division would be liquidated if it is not sold and that the seller has made a good faith effort to obtain offers for the company from other parties.

F.3 SECTIONS 1, 2 AND 3 OF THE SHERMAN ACT

Ordinarily, when the DOJ or FTC challenge a merger, both Section 7 and the Sherman Act are invoked. Sections 1, 2 and 3 of the Sherman Act are both civil and criminal statutes.

A brief description of the three sections appears below:

- *Section 1:* "Every contract, combination in the form of trust or otherwise, or conspiracy, in restraint of trade or commerce among the several States, or with foreign nations is declared to be illegal. . . ."
- *Section 2:* "Every person who shall monopolize, or attempt to monopolize, or combine or conspire with any other person or persons, to monopolize any part of the trade or commerce among the several States, or with foreign nations, shall be deemed guilty of a felony. . . ."

- *Section 3:* basically the same as Section 1, except that it applies to territories and the District of Columbia.

F.4   SECTION 5(a)(6) OF THE FTC ACT

Section 5(a)(6) of the Federal Trade Commission Act permits the FTC to prevent "unfair methods of competition in commerce and unfair or deceptive acts or practices in commerce." A merger may be an unfair method of competition or unfair act or practice.

F.5   ANTITRUST REGULATION IN CERTAIN INDUSTRIES

Certain industries are regulated by federal agencies. These include, for example, the aviation industry, which is governed by the Civil Aeronautics Board; the banking industry, which is governed by the Federal Reserve Board; and the transportation industry, which is governed by the Interstate Commerce Commission.

Generally, in regulated industries, a federal agency must approve any merger. In addition, in these industries there is often legislation that grants immunity from the antitrust laws. However, even in cases where legislation immunizing a regulated industry from the federal antitrust laws does not exist, a merger transaction that is approved by a federal agency as being in the public interest will generally not have any additional antitrust hurdles to clear. The applicable agency generally must have reviewed the competitive aspects of the merger in determining whether it was in the public interest.

F.6   STATE ANTITRUST LAWS

All states have antitrust laws or unfair trade practice laws that can affect transactions.

F.7   PRIVATE ACTIONS

A private party can bring suit to enjoin a merger, assuming that party can show that it will be injured by the merger. Generally, the parties that could be harmed by a merger include consumers (unlikely to organize a lawsuit), competitors (the Supreme Court in *Cargill v. Monfort of Colorado* significantly reduced the situations where a competitor has the right to bring suit), customers, suppliers or the target company, in the case of a hostile bid.

Private parties are entitled to treble damages, assuming they can prove that they have been injured by the anticompetitive nature of a transaction. However, private parties normally sue to enjoin a transaction from occurring in the first place. To succeed in such an action, the party must have a strong case showing that it would succeed at trial.

Appendix G

The Supervisory Definition of Highly Leveraged Transactions

G.0 INTRODUCTION

The Office of the Comptroller of the Currency, the Federal Deposit Insurance Corporation (FDIC), and the Board of Governors of the Federal Reserve System (collectively the "Agencies") jointly adopted a common definition of *Highly Leveraged Transactions (HLTs)* on October 30, 1989. In February 1990 and February 1991 the Agencies issued guidance to examiners regarding this definition. In July 1991 the Agencies, in response to questions and comments regarding the designation, reporting and delisting of HLTs, sought public comment on all aspects of the HLT definition and criteria, as well as comments on specific issues raised by questions the Agencies had received. After reviewing the status of the definition, the Agencies decided to phase out the use of the definition and to discontinue regulatory reporting by banking organizations after June 30, 1992.

The Agencies decided to phase out use of the HLT definition because the Agencies determined that it had accomplished its original purposes. The HLT definition had (1) encouraged financial institutions to focus attention on the need for internal controls and review mechanisms to monitor this type of financing transaction and (2) highlighted the need to structure HLT credits in a prudent manner consistent with the risks involved.

G.1   SUMMARY OF DEFINITION

A bank or bank holding company is considered to be involved in a highly leveraged transaction when credit is extended to or investment is made in a business where the financing transaction involves the buyout, acquisition, or recapitalization of an existing business and one of the following criteria is met:

(a) The transaction results in a liabilities-to-assets leverage ratio higher than 75 percent; or

(b) The transaction at least doubles the subject company's liabilities and results in a liabilities-to-assets leverage ratio higher than 50 percent; or

(c) The transaction is designated an HLT by a syndication agent or a federal bank regulator.

Appendix H

Exon-Florio

H.0   INTRODUCTION

The proposed purchase in 1988 of an 80 percent share of Fairchild Semi-conductor Corporation by Fujitsu, Ltd. raised Congressional concern that legislation did not exist to prevent takeovers of U.S. firms by foreign companies that raise national security considerations. As a result, Congress amended Section 721 of the Defense Production Act of 1950 effective August 1988, to authorize the president or his designee to investigate and stop certain transactions which could result in foreign control of an entity engaged in U.S. commerce for reasons of national security. In addition, the president is authorized to direct the attorney general to seek divestment relief in the district court. The amendment is known as *The Exon-Florio Amendment (Exon-Florio)*. Exon-Florio was permanently reauthorized by legislation signed by President Bush in August 1991.

H.1   FILING AND WAITING PERIOD

The Treasury Department issued final regulations implementing Exon-Florio in November 1991. These regulations indicate that a formal Exon-Florio notification may be filed with the *Committee on Foreign Investment in the United States (CFIUS)* whenever a foreign person could control a U.S. company that provides products or key technologies essential to the U.S. defense industrial base.

Once the written notification is filed, any investigation by CFIUS must begin within 30 days. The investigation must be completed within

45 days of its initiation. Finally, the president must announce his decision whether or not to take action within 15 days of the completion of the investigation. Thus, the total process can take up to 90 days.

If notification is not given, a transaction covered by Exon-Florio will remain indefinitely subject to divestment. However, such divestment is possible only if the purpose for the divestment is based on circumstances existing at the time the transaction was consummated.

H.2   DEFINITION OF NATIONAL SECURITY

The regulations do not contain a clear definition of "national security." However, the regulations do indicate that notice is not required when the entire output of the company being acquired consists of products or services that clearly have no relation to national security (e.g., toy, food, hotel, restaurant and legal services companies). The lack of definition of national security will be of help to U.S. companies that are the targets of foreign companies in hostile tender offers. It is likely that the target will attempt to invoke Exon-Florio to at least delay a foreign company's offer.

H.3   ENFORCEMENT

The only order to date blocking the sale of a company has been the ban of the sale of Mamco Manufacturing Corporation to China National Aero-Technology Import & Export Corporation (CATIC), a company controlled by the Chinese government. Mamco is a small Seattle machine shop with sales of approximately $20 million. This order was given early in 1990.

Notes

CHAPTER 4

1. Motion of Plaintiff for Preliminary Injunction Denied, Pennzoil Company v. Getty Oil Company, Gordon P. Getty, Trustee of the Sarah C. Getty Trust, The J. Paul Getty Museum, a California charitable trust, and Texaco Inc., a Delaware corporation, In the Court of Chancery of the State of Delaware in and for New Castle County, February 6, 1984. pp. 31–33.
2. Brief of Amicus Curiae of the Attorney General of the State of New York, Texaco Inc. vs. Pennzoil Company, In the Court of Appeals for the First Supreme Judicial District of Texas. pp. 2–3.
3. Anthony J. P. Farris, Letter to J. Donald Bowen, Esq., Helm Plethcher & Hogan, December 28, 1984.

CHAPTER 6

1. See Boris I. Bittker and James S. Eustice, *Federal Income Taxation of Corporations and Shareholders*, 5th ed. (Boston, Mass.: Warren, Gorham & Lamont, 1987), par 14.03, 14.11 and 14.51 for a more detailed discussion of these doctrines.

Bibliography

Accounting Principles Board Opinion No. 16, "Accounting for Business Combinations." New York: American Institute of Certified Public Accountants, 1970.

Accounting Principles Board Opinion No. 17, "Accounting for Intangibles." New York: American Institute of Certified Public Accountants, 1970.

Affidavit of Hugh Jones. Pennzoil Company v. Texaco Inc., District Court of Harris County.

Altman, Edward I. *The High Yield Debt Market*. Homewood, Ill.: Dow Jones-Irwin, 1990.

Altman, Edward I., and Scott A. Nammacher. *Investing in Junk Bonds*. New York: John Wiley & Sons, Inc., 1987.

Baird, Patrick & Co., Inc. "The Pennzoil-Texaco Litigation." *Institutional Report*, September 1987.

Bartlett, Marshall P. "The Joint Election Under Section 388(h)(10)." *Tax Lawyer* 42, no. 2.

Benjamin, Harvey L.; Barry A. Bryer; and John P. McLoughlin. *Leveraged Acquisitions and Buyouts 1990*. New York: Practicing Law Institute, 1990.

Benjamin, Harvey L., and Michael B. Goldberg. *Leveraged Acquisitions and Buyouts 1989*. New York: Practicing Law Institute, 1989.

Bittker, Boris I., and James S. Eustice. *Federal Income Taxation of Corporations and Shareholders*. 5th ed. Boston, Mass.: Warren, Gorham & Lamont, 1986.

Block, Dennis, and Harvey L. Pitt. *Hostile Battles for Corporate Control 1989*. New York: Practicing Law Institute, 1989.

Brealey, Richard A., and Stewart C. Myers. *Principles of Corporate Finance.* 4th ed. New York: McGraw-Hill, Inc., 1991.

Brief of Amicus Curiae of the Attorney General of the State of New York. Texaco Inc. vs. Pennzoil Company, In the Court of Appeals for the First Supreme Judicial District of Texas.

Brief of Amicus Curiae. The Business Council of New York State, Inc. Texaco Inc. vs. Pennzoil Company. In the Court of Appeals for the First Supreme Judicial District of Texas, July 11, 1986.

Buzzell, Robert D., and Bradley T. Gale. *The PIMS Principles: Linking Strategy to Performance.* New York: The Free Press, 1987.

Clark, John J. *Business Merger and Acquisition Strategies.* Engelwood Cliffs, N.J.: Prentice-Hall, Inc., 1985.

Copeland, Tom; Tim Koller; and Jack Murrin. *Valuation: Measuring and Managing the Value of Companies.* New York: John Wiley & Sons, Inc., 1990.

Cottle, Sidney; Roger F. Murray; and Frank E. Block. *Graham and Dodd's Security Analysis.* 5th ed. New York: McGraw-Hill, Inc., 1988.

Deming, John R., and Bret W. Wise. "ESOP Accounting: Past, Present and Future." *CPA Journal,* June 1990.

Eustice, James S. *Federal Income Taxation of Corporations and Shareholders 1991 Cumulative Supplement No. 3.* Boston, Mass.: Warren, Gorham & Lamont, 1991.

Feinberg, Paul C. "Adjusted Current Earnings—The Future Is Now." *The Journal of Corporate Taxation.* Summer 1991.

Ferrara, Ralph C.; Meredith M. Brown; and John H. Hall. *Takeovers: Attack and Survival.* Boston, Mass.: Butterworth Legal Publishers, 1987.

Financial Accounting Standard No. 109, "Accounting for Income Taxes." Norwalk, Conn.: Financial Accounting Standards Board, 1992.

Fox, B. *Corporate Acquisitions and Mergers.* New York: Matthew Bender & Co., Inc., 1991.

Freeman, Louis S. *Tax Strategies for Corporate Acquisitions, Dispositions, Financings, Joint Ventures, Reorganizations and Restructurings 1990.* New York: Practicing Law Institute, 1990.

Fridson, Martin S. *High Yield Bonds.* Chicago: Probus Publishing Company, 1989.

Frisch, Robert A. *ESOPs and LBOs.* Rockville Centre, N.Y.: Farnsworth Publishing Co., 1985.

Gorman, Jerry. "LBO Accounting: Consensus at Last." *Journal of Accountancy,* August 1989, pp. 68–78.

————. "LBO Accounting: Unveiling the Mystery of Carryover Basis." *Journal of Accountancy*, October 1988, pp. 76–80.

Graham, Benjamin. *The Intelligent Investor*. 4th ed. New York: Harper & Row, 1973.

Hann, Charles R., and Phyllis Savage. *11th Annual Institute for Corporate Counsel: Acquisitions and Divestitures*. New York: Practicing Law Institute, 1988.

Herz, John W., and Charles H. Ballar, eds. *Business Acquisitions*. 2nd ed. New York: Practicing Law Institute, 1981.

Internal Revenue Service. *Publication 534: Depreciation*. Washington, D.C.: Internal Revenue Service, 1991.

Interpretations of APB Opinion Nos. 16 and 17. 7th ed. Chicago: Arthur Andersen & Co., 1988.

Kalish, Gerald. *ESOPs*. Chicago: Probus Publishing Company, 1989.

Karlinsky, Stewart S. "The Final AMT ACE Regulations." *The Tax Advisor*, June 1991, pp. 347–56.

Katz, Melvin, and Ronald M. Loeb. *Acquisitions and Mergers 1988*. New York: Practicing Law Institute, 1988.

————. *Acquisitions and Mergers in a Changing Environment*. New York: Practicing Law Institute, 1990.

Key, Stephen L., ed. *The Ernst & Young Management Guide to Mergers and Acquisitions*. New York: John Wiley & Sons, Inc., 1989.

Laverty, Brian L., and Dennis J. Gaffney. "Multiple AMT Asset Bases." *The Tax Advisor*, January 1992.

Lederman, Lawrence. *Corporate Restructurings 1990*. New York: Practicing Law Institute, 1990.

Lederman, Lawrence, and Martin Nussbaum. *Corporate Deleveragings and Restructurings*. New York: Practicing Law Institute, 1991.

Lynch, Peter. *One Up on Wall Street*. New York: Simon and Schuster, 1989.

Maloney, David M., and Michael G. Brandt. "Taxable and Nontaxable Acquisitive Techniques: A Case of the Basics Not Being Basic." *The Journal of Corporate Taxation*, Autumn 1987.

Motion of Plaintiff for Preliminary Injunction Denied. Pennzoil Company v. Getty Oil Company, Gordon P. Getty, Trustee of the Sarah C. Getty Trust, The J. Paul Getty Museum, a California charitable trust, and Texaco Inc., a Delaware corporation. In the Court of Chancery of the State of Delaware in and for New Castle County, February 6, 1984.

1991 All States Tax Handbook. Englewood Cliffs, N.J.: Maxwell Macmillan, 1991.

1991 U.S. Master Tax Guide. Chicago: Commerce Clearing House, 1991.

Pennzoil Co. v. Texaco Inc., #85–1798. United States Supreme Court.

Pennzoil Company. *Pennzoil vs. Texaco: A Brief History.* Houston: The Company, 1988.

Petzinger, Thomas, Jr. *Oil & Honor: The Texaco–Pennzoil Wars.* New York: The Berkley Publishing Group, 1988.

Porter, Michael E. *Competitive Strategy: Techniques for Analyzing Industries and Competitors.* New York: The Free Press, 1980.

Rappaport, Alfred. *Creating Shareholder Value.* New York: The Free Press, 1986.

Reed, Stanley Foster and Lane and Edson P. C. *The Art of M&A.* Homewood, Ill.: Dow Jones-Irwin, 1989.

Reply brief of appellant Texaco Inc. Texaco vs. Pennzoil Company. In the Court of Appeals for the First Supreme Judicial District of Texas, July 24, 1986.

Rock, Milton, and Robert H. Milton. *Corporate Restructuring.* New York: McGraw-Hill, Inc., 1990.

Rook, Lance W. *Tax Planning for the Alternative Minimum Tax.* New York: Matthew Bender & Co., Inc., 1991.

Shecter, Howard L. *Acquiring or Selling the Privately Held Company 1991.* New York: Practicing Law Institute, 1991.

Smith, Charles R. *ESOPs 1990.* New York: Practicing Law Institute, 1990.

Texaco Inc. Memorandum in Support of Its Motion for Judgment and Motion for Judgment Notwithstanding the Verdict. Pennzoil Company v. Texaco Inc. District Court of Harris County, Texas, December 4, 1985.

Weil, Peter H. *Troubled Leveraged Buyouts 1990.* New York: Practicing Law Institute, 1990.

Whalley, Judy, and Christian S. White. *The Antitrust Division and the FTC Speak on Current Developments in Federal Antitrust Enforcement and Consumer Protection.* New York: Practicing Law Institute, 1991.

Willens, Robert. *Taxation of Corporate Capital Transactions.* New York: John Wiley & Sons, Inc., 1984.

———. "Use of Leveraged Recaps: Formal Structural Differences Yield Uncertain Tax Results." *Journal of Taxation of Investments,* Winter 1988.

Willens, Robert, and Ahron H. Haspel. *Taxation of Corporate Capital Transactions 1990 Cumulative Supplement No. 1.* New York: John Wiley & Sons, Inc., 1990.

Index